HIDDEN HISTORY

Drugs, Geography, and Human Addiction

Terry David Church

Kendall Hunt
publishing company

Cover images © Shutterstock.com

www.kendallhunt.com
Send all inquiries to:
4050 Westmark Drive
Dubuque, IA 52004-1840

Dedication

This textbook is dedicated to my students; thank you for being amazing!

Contents

Table of Contents

AcknowledGments

This textbook would not be possible without the support of some very special people at the USC Alfred E. Mann School of Pharmacy and Pharmaceutical Sciences, namely my Dean, Vassilios Papadopoulos; my Chair, Eunjoo Pacifici; and my mentors, Daryl Davies and Frances Richmond. Each of whom have encouraged me to teach, research, write, and grow as an academic. I owe a special thanks to my office neighbor, colleague, and friend, Nancy Pire-Smerkanich. To the students who took my RXRS-201: The History and Geography of Drugs in the Fall of 2021, thank you for helping me decide on the title of this book! To my colleagues and friends in the USC Institute for Addiction Science, Jessica Barrington-Trimis, Jennifer Lewis, Adam Leventhal, Ricky Bluthenthal, and Victoria Williams thank you for your support and inspiring me. To the administrative staff in the School of Pharmacy and Pharmaceutical Sciences' Department of Regulatory and Quality Sciences—Deborah Schroyer, Julie Lee, and Erin Chow—thank you for being amazing. To the academic staff of the Pharmacy Undergraduate Programs—Randa Issa and Whitney Tang—thank you for being amazing cheerleaders! To my amazing editorial staff at Kendall Hunt—Michele Bahr—thank you for being patient and guiding me through the publication process. To my friends at Stone and Compass who make my Maymester travel abroad course in the Balkans a success—Rob, Andy, and Borko—thank you for teaching me about folk medicine and introducing me to Bulgaria.

This book would not have been possible without the support of my family. My father, Leo Church, taught me to dream and my mother, Judith Church, encouraged me to live those dreams. Additionally, I could not have completed this project without the support and good-hearted harassment from my five older siblings—Denise, Debbie, Tina, Tim, and Tammy. The support from my siblings, their wonderful families, and my amazing nieces and nephews has been outstanding—thank you all! To my three brothers-in-law, five nieces, eight nephews, seven great-nieces, and five great-nephews— wow, there are a lot of us—thank you for always encouraging me to "get 'er done," even if at times you were not exactly sure what I was getting done!

The heart of this textbook is dedicated to my caring and understanding partner, Daryl Stephen Evans. You thought the research and writing of one dissertation was enough, and here I did it all over again in writing this textbook… You have encouraged and inspired me all along the way. Thank you!

Finally, to my students, past, present, and future—thank you for allowing me to have the best job in the world! Teaching and mentoring you is the greatest honor I have ever been bestowed. Thank you for always inspiring me and making life interesting!

Author Bio

Dr. Terry David Church is currently an assistant professor in regulatory and quality sciences at the University of Southern California (USC), School of Pharmacy. He is an assistant director of Pharmacy Undergraduate Programs and teaches in the Pharmacy Undergraduate Program. Prof. Church's academic focus is on application of pharmaceutical regulations, patterns of addiction, disaster management, and education and training. His areas of interest and expertise include history and geography of drugs; biorepository regulation and ethics; drug addiction and regulation of controlled substances; regulatory practices for continuity and disaster planning; and policies and ethics for academic research.

Dr. Church received his doctor of science and master of science degrees in regulatory sciences from the University of Southern California. He earned a master of arts degree in cultural anthropology from Temple University. His doctoral thesis evaluated regulatory practices for continuity and disaster planning for biobanks in the United States. **Dr. Church** is a faculty fellow of the USC Center for Excellence in Teaching and an assistant director of the Education and Training Consortium of the Institute for Addiction Sciences. He serves as a co-director of the STAR-BRAVO science educational program in partnership with BRAVO Medical Magnet High School of Los Angeles and USC.

After receiving his master's degree from Temple, **Dr. Church** worked at the University of Pennsylvania's Office of Human Research as the operations director for research. He initially worked to help implement human subjects research protections and monitor all clinical trial activity ongoing and planned. He then took a position at USC Norris Comprehensive Cancer Center as a program manager. He was responsible for all research, clinical, and community activities for women's cancers, translational cancer research, and adolescent and young adult cancers. For well over 10 years, **Dr. Church** managed the operation and development of investigator initiated trials.

In his spare time, **Dr. Church** is a cyclist, amateur painter, and part-time crafter. He has completed his second AIDS/LifeCycle® bike ride, riding from San Francisco to Los Angeles. This 545-mile bike ride helps raise awareness and funding for HIV education, treatment, and prevention.

Introduction

This textbook is not a comprehensive treatise on drugs from every epoch nor from every geographic location. The reasons for this are page length and the limits of our historical and archaeological records. This is not a comprehensive compendium that attempts to chronicle the deeds of every single person or of every historical event. This text will touch on events and the people who lived through them in relation to key moments in shared pharmacologic history. This textbook is, at the heart of it, the story of the human need for medicinal and longing for hedonic drugs. It will trace the contours of history, geography, and human civilization as we have encountered, compounded, distilled, and engineered a wide variety of substances. This textbook will challenge our perception of the past and will hopefully give us a better perspective of our present. Some terminology in this book can have dual meaning and it can be synonymous. For example, euphoria and high, narcotic and psychoactive, or psychedelic and hallucinogen. When the meaning of the word needs to be precise, the accurate term or intended meaning will be stated. This book is "science-lite," however, there will be parts where we will need to rely on neuroscience, biology, anatomy, and pharmacology to provide context and make sense of the drugs encountered. Much of our collective history related to drugs has been hidden and not discussed. It was often easier to omit or cover up substance use and addiction than it was to confront it head on. It is hoped that by highlighting the variety of human production, consumption, and indulgence, we can illuminate our complex relationship with substances.

The past offers an extraordinarily rich and vivid database from which we can learn about how our ancestors lived and the central role drugs has played throughout societies[1]. The question you may have been asking is why are history and geography discussed in relation to drugs? They seem like two vastly different areas of interest. *History* refers to the study of past events, more precisely, the study of the past events of humans. *Geography* encapsulates the study of the lands, features, phenomenon, places, and the relationships between humans and the environments they inhabit. Additionally, geography refers to the unique and complex political and economic conditions imposed upon environments by humans[2]. History and geography are intrinsically tied together. Many historical events become anchored by geographic features. Every historical event that has occurred or will occur has done so at or in a geographical location. Many of our major historical events have been titled after their associated geographical locations, such as the Treaty of Nanjing, the Battle of Gettysburg, and the Battle of Thermopylae. History permits us to review temporal changes across geographic events and between

1

past and present situations. We have cataloged the changing interactions between human societies and their environments over time. There have been expansions and reductions of past empires, limits and boundaries of ancient civilizations, routes of prior human migrations, studies of battles and wars, fad and failure of past medical treatments, and a wide assortment of historical events and sensations related to the human experience and drugs.

To set the stage, we will need some foundational terminology. ***Drug*** represents any substance that when inhaled, injected, smoked, consumed, absorbed topically through the skin, or dissolved under the tongue causes a physiological change in the body[3]. Drugs can be divided into licit and illicit categories. ***Licit*** in Latin translates to "within the law" and represents legally allowed or permitted drugs. Examples of licit drugs include alcohol, caffeine, and nicotine—even though these are highly addictive, they are sold legally for consumption. ***Illicit*** in Latin translates to "not within the law" and represents drugs that are forbidden by laws, rules, or customs. Drugs are classified as illicit because they are seen as posing a threat to individual or public health. Examples of illicit drugs include heroin, cocaine, and methamphetamine. In pharmacology, drugs have a slightly different meaning. ***Pharmacologic drugs*** are chemical substances of known structure, other than a nutrient of an essential dietary ingredient, which, when administered to a living organism, produce a biological effect. ***Pharmacological effect*** can be understood as the physiological, psychological, and/or biochemical changes produced by a drug in therapeutic concentration. It is important to know that drugs often do not have a single pharmacological effect. Drugs produce several pharmacological effects and can express differently across individuals and populations. ***Pharmaceutical drug***, also referred to as ***medicine*** or ***medication***, represents a chemical substance used to treat, cure, prevent, or diagnose a disease or to promote wellbeing. In the modern world, we divide pharmaceutical drugs into two categories, which are prescription drug and over-the-counter (OTC) drug. ***Prescription drug*** is a pharmaceutical drug that legally requires a medical prescription to be dispensed. ***Over-the-counter drug (OTC)*** is a pharmaceutical drug that can be obtained without prescription. ***Recreational drug*** represents any substance with pharmacological effects that is taken voluntarily for personal pleasure or satisfaction rather than for medicinal purposes, and these can include both licit and illicit drugs. ***Street drug*** is a fancy way of indicating any illicit drugs that can be found on the "street" or obtained illegally through the black market. Street drugs tend to be taken for nonmedical reasons and typically are used for their mind-altering, mood-enhancing, stimulating, or sedating effects.

Human history extends back over millennia; however, as can be seen in Figure 1.1, our time with alcohol and synthetic drugs has been relatively short. In the short time of written history, ~5,000 years, we have developed a rich cultural and medicinal history. Mesopotamian culture believed that illness was a punishment sent by the gods for violation of the moral code[4]. Ancient Egyptians believed that the body was a system of channels for air, tears, blood, urine, sperm, and feces. Ancient Greek medicine intertwined the spiritual with the physical in an amalgamation of theory and practice, which were continuously expanding through new ideologies and trials. Ancient Roman medicine was heavily influenced by earlier medical practices but added unique contributions in surgery and pharmacology. Ancient Chinese medicine combined herbal medicines and various mind and body practices to treat or prevent health. Ayurvedic medicine of the Indus Valley relied on the universal interconnectedness, the body's constitution, and life forces to provide a comprehensive treatment in ancient India. Islamic medicine through the ancient Arabian, Persian, and Ottoman peoples preserved, systematized, and developed the medical knowledge of classical antiquity.

Figure 1.1   Timeline of Human History

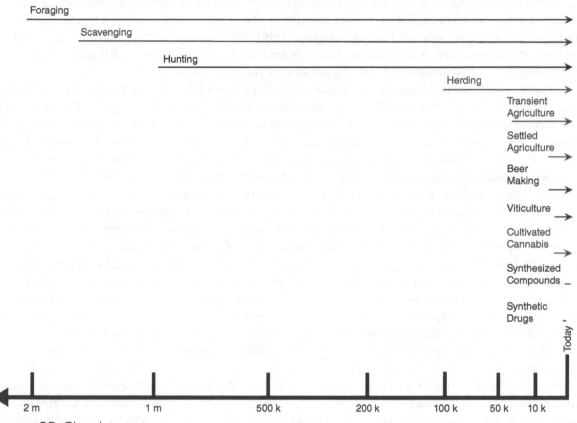

Source: T.D. Church

There are ancient drugs used worldwide today like beer, wine, and cannabis, which had their origins early in human history. The world's first winery was found in present day Armenia, dating back ~6,100 years. The earlies evidence of beer dates to ~7,000 years ago. Many of our ancient societies were fond of alcohol, often it was safer to drink beer or wine than it was to consume the water. Ancient Mesopotamians had beer and wine. Ancient Egyptians and Greeks had beer and wine, with the Egyptians preferring beer and the Greeks favoring wine. Ancient Romans indulged in wine. The first recorded use of cannabis is ~2700 BCE and was a medicine used by Emperor Yándi (sometimes identified as Shen Nung) in China. Recreational cannabis use was recorded ~3000 BCE in China but it is believed to be a practice that is much older[5]. Many burial sites in China, India, and Syria contained cannabis and date back to between 15000 and 10000 BCE. Consumption and smoking of cannabis were common in the ancient world and varied in terms of societal acceptance.

The Sumerians first recorded opium cultivation ~3400 BCE, but it has been used by many of the ancient cultures[6]. The primary utility of opium was not too dissimilar to today's use as medicine. There exists evidence of opium being used recreationally by the Chinese and the Romans. The opium plant (Papaver somniferum) was used in ancient civilizations (4000–1000 BCE) for a variety of medicinal purposes and in religious ceremonies. The native range of opium poppy is probably the Eastern Mediterranean, but extensive cultivation and introduction of the species throughout Europe since ancient times have helped to obscure its origins. The opium poppy requires a temperate climate and typically blooms between June and August. The flower consists of four white, mauve, red, or orange petals, sometimes with dark markings around the base of the flower. All parts of the plant exude white latex when wounded with the latex being the harvestable opium.

Marcus Aurelius Antoninus Augustus (121–180 CE) has been labeled as one of the greatest Roman Emperors of all time[7]. He was a known philosopher and held opium in high regard. Marcus Aurelius was grounded in the Stoic tradition of philosophy, which would have been extremely complementary to his drug of choice[8]. Opium as a recreational substance was only available to the upper echelons of Roman society. Roman physicians and surgeons on the battlefield used opium for general sedation but not in great quantities. Laudanum, the wonder elixir, rose from the Renaissance to dominate opioid addiction until the mid-1800s CE[9]. Smoking opium became problematic in the eighteenth and nineteenth centuries CE, first in China and then spread with the Chinese migrant workers to Europe and the Americas. When opium is smoked, the high from the drug is experienced much faster and is much more addictive. The real problems with opium would begin in the nineteenth century CE with the invention of the hypodermic syringe and the synthesis of morphine followed by heroin. Even before chemists understood the structure of morphine, an even more addictive derivative of opium, heroin, was created. Treating morphine with acetic anhydride produced diacetylmorphine or more commonly referred to as diamorphine. Bayer gave diamorphine the brand name Heroin[10]. No one was prepared for the addictiveness of this new drug and ~150 years later we are still dealing with the social problems of this once lauded miracle cure.

For a substantial portion of human history, *folk medicine* or the treatment of disease or injury based on traditions that utilized indigenous plants as remedies dominated our medical knowledge. By the time humans had begun building and living in cities, it was possible to find *apothecaries*. The apothecary was the first pharmacists and were responsible for formulating and dispensing *materia medica* (sometimes poisons too) to physicians, surgeons, and patients. Materia medica is Latin for "healing materials" and is often used in pharmacy to describe plant-based medicines. *Alchemists* helped to advance many of the chemical sciences in the search for the quintessential and base elements that made up all things. Alchemists helped in the discovery of distillation, which gave humankind more potent alcohols. Medicine plodded along for centuries with minor changes until the early part of the nineteenth century CE where we began to extract the pure compounds from plants giving us new synthetic chemicals such as morphine and cocaine. By the late nineteenth century CE, there were increasingly fewer natural products being used in medicine and many more synthetic substances[11]. Several dye and chemical companies would reconfigure their facilities and began research labs geared toward the discovery of medical chemicals. Some of those companies included Bayer and Hoffman-LaRoche. The modern pharmaceutical industry in the United States began during 1818–1822 CE when less than a dozen chemical manufacturers constructed factories in Philadelphia. From the efforts of these fledgling companies, our modern pharmaceutical industry took root. Our modern medical technology has progressed to a level where we can keep bodies alive even if the brain is dead. In the last 200 years, there have been breakthrough drugs that have allowed us to cure and manage disease in unprecedented ways. There have also been drugs that are deadly and, in their wake, follows addiction and death.

Addiction is a very complex disease. The term addiction is derived from the Latin verb *addicere*, which refers to the process of binding or tying things together. In a way addiction ties the addicted to a substance or behavior. Today we use addiction to broadly refer to a chronic adherence or attachment to drugs. In 1964 CE, the World Health Organization (WHO) defined addiction as "a state of periodic or chronic intoxication detrimental to the individual and society, which is characterized by an overwhelming desire to continue taking the drug and to obtain it by any means"[12]. The WHO definition of addiction served as the standard for several decades. More recently, the National Institute on Drug Abuse (NIDA) has defined addiction as:

> ". . . a chronic, relapsing brain disease that is characterized by compulsive drug-seeking and use, despite harmful consequences. It is considered a brain disease because drugs change the brain - they change its structure and how it works. These brain changes can be long lasting and can lead to the harmful behaviors seen in people who abuse drugs"[13].

To simplify our working definition of ***addiction***, it is the compulsive using of drugs in spite of the terrible consequences. Addiction does have some commonalities as it does require the user to have developed a dependency to the substance, either psychological or physical. ***Psychological dependence*** is the mental inability to stop using the drug or drugs. ***Physical dependence*** is the body's need to constantly have the drug or drugs. Figure 1.2 highlights the multifactorial addiction pathway in more detail. There are some key features that characterize addictive behavior: (1) inability to control behavior; (2) increase in tolerance levels; (3) difficulty in maintaining relationships; (4) symptoms of withdrawal (depression, irritability) when behavior is interrupted; and (5) continuation of behavior despite negative consequences.

Figure 1.2 Addiction Pathway

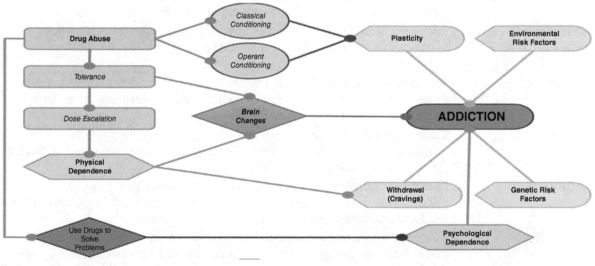

Source: T.D. Church

The human brain is the most complex organ in the body, and it plays a very crucial role in the addiction process. The brain is roughly 3 pounds in mass of gray and white matter and is responsible for all human activity—driving a car, enjoying a meal, breathing, creating an artistic masterpiece, playing

Borderlands 3 on PS4, performing music, and enjoying everyday activities. The brain governs basic functions, enables interpretation and response to stimuli, and shapes our behavior. Basically, your brain is who you are—everything you think and feel, everything you know and will come to know, and who are.

The brain works through a complex set of neurons that communicate via neurotransmitters[14]. *Neurons* are extremely specialized cells responsible for processing and transmitting cellular signals via electronical and chemical signaling. The average human has billions of neurons in their brain. Each neuron functions like a switch. When the switch is "on," it allows information to pass along it, and when the switch is "off," it halts information. When a neuron receives a signal from other neurons connected to it, the neuron will "fire" and transmit its own signal to the surrounding neurons. *Neurotransmitters* are chemical messengers that carry, amplify, and equalize signals between neurons and other cells in the body. *Synapse* is the gap between neurons and represents the space that neurotransmitters are released into for signaling. *Transporters* are there to recycle neurotransmitters by returning them to the neuron they were released from, which effectively limits or stops the signal between the neurons. Table 1.1 represents eight of the most prominent neurotransmitters and their general uses in the brain, and the neurotransmitters denoted with an asterisk (*) play a role in addiction and addictive behavior.

Table 1.1 Top 8 Neurotransmitters Associated with Addiction

Neurotransmitter	Function
Adrenaline	**Fight or flight neurotransmitter**; released in stressful or exciting situations; increases heart rate and blood flow, leading to a physical boost of energy and heightened awareness/alertness.
Noradrenaline	**Focus/concentration neurotransmitter**; affects attention and response actions in the brain; contracts blood vessels, increases blood flow.
Dopamine*	**Pleasure neurotransmitter**; feelings of pleasure and motivation; responsible for repeat behavior that promotes or releases dopamine; implications for addictive behavior.
Serotonin*	**Mood neurotransmitter**; promotes wellbeing and happiness; helps to regulate sleep and digestive system regulation; exercise and exposure to light help promote serotonin.
GABA	**Calming neurotransmitter**; calms the CNS; elevated levels of GABA improve focus and low levels of GABA cause anxiety; used in motor control and vision.
Acetylcholine	**Learning neurotransmitter**; involved in thinking, learning, and memory acquisition; responsible for activating muscle action in the body; associated with attention and awareness.
Glutamate	**Memory neurotransmitter**; most prevalent brain neurotransmitter; involved in learning and memory; responsible for the development and creation of nerve contacts.
Endorphin*	**Euphoria neurotransmitter**; released during exercise, excitement, and sex; produces wellbeing and euphoria; reducing pain; implications for addictive behavior.

Source: T.D. Church

Drugs interfere with the way neurons in the brain send, receive, and process signals through the use of neurotransmitters. Cannabis and opium can activate neurons because their chemical structures mimic the body's natural neurotransmitters. This allows the drugs to attach onto and active the neurons. While similar, these drugs are unable to activate the neurons in the same way, leading to abnormal messages being sent along the neuronal network. Methamphetamine or cocaine causes the neurons to release abnormally large amounts of natural neurotransmitters or prevent recycling of brain chemicals by interfering with transporters. These drugs amplify or disrupt the normal communication between neurons within the brain.

Figure 1.3 Diagram of the Brain

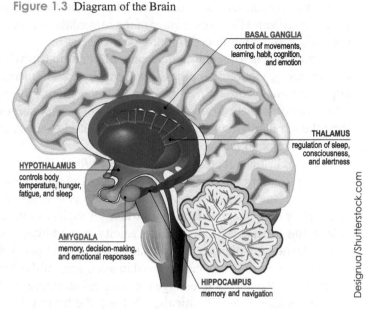

There are many parts of the brain that are important for addiction, but three of the best-known parts are the basal ganglia, amygdala, and prefrontal cortex (Figure 1.3). *Basal ganglia* has an important role to play in positive motivation, which includes the pleasurable effects of healthy activities such as eating, socializing, and sex[15]. The basal ganglia is involved in the formation of habits and routines. These structures form a key area of what is sometimes referred to as the brain's "reward circuit." Exogenous drugs tend to over-activate this area of the brain, producing the euphoric feelings of the drug high. Repeated exposure to the drug causes the circuitry of the basal ganglia to adapt to the presence of the drug, which diminishes the drugs sensitivity and makes it hard to feel pleasure from anything besides the drug.

Amygdala has a crucial role to play in the stressful feelings of anxiety, irritability, and unease, which are often present during withdrawal as the drug high fades[15]. These feelings act as motivation for the user to seek out the drug to feel better and stave off those unpleasant feelings. The amygdala becomes increasingly sensitive with increased use. Overtime, a drug addict will use their substance of choice to get temporary relief from the discomfort of withdrawal, rather than to get high. It functions to keep them in a state of balance between drug euphoria and the pain of withdrawal.

Prefrontal cortex governs our executive functions, and it is responsible for our ability to think, plan, solve problems, make decisions, and exert self-control over our impulses (Figure 1.4). The prefrontal cortex is the last part of the brain to mature, which happens ~25 years of age[15]. The late maturation makes teens and young adults the most vulnerable for damage or permanent changes in the

Figure 1.4 Prefrontal Cortex

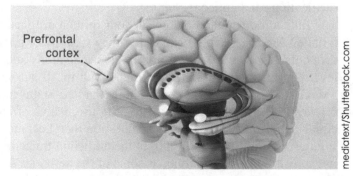

prefrontal cortex. Drugs change the balance between prefrontal cortex and the reward center of the basal ganglia and the stress center of the amygdala to make a person with an addiction seek out drugs compulsively with reduced impulse control.

Euphoria is a mental and emotional condition in which a person experiences intense feelings of wellbeing, elation, happiness, excitement, contentment, and joy[16]. Drugs produce pleasure or euphoria, what is often times referred to as the "high," through surges of chemical signaling of endorphins and other neurotransmitters. Some drugs cause surges of these neurotransmitters much greater than the smaller bursts naturally produced with healthy rewards like eating, exercise, music, creative pursuits, or social interaction.

Neuroplasticity, better known as *brain plasticity*, refers to the brain's ability to change and adapt as a result of experience[17]. Brains possess the remarkable capacity to reorganize pathways, create new connections, and, in some cases, create new neurons. Brain plasticity does come with limitations: (1) it can vary by age; (2) it involves a variety of processes; (3) environment plays an essential role in the process; and (4) brain plasticity is not always good or beneficial. There are two types of brain plasticity, which are functional and structural plasticity. *Functional plasticity* is the ability of the brain to move functions from a damaged area of the brain to other undamaged areas. *Structural plasticity* is the ability to change the physical structure of the brain as a result of learning.

Drugs alter brain chemicals, affecting the brain's decision-making processes, stress regulation, memory, and emotions. The brain of someone who misuses drugs adjusts by producing fewer neurotransmitters or by reducing the number of receptors that can receive signals. The person's ability to experience pleasure from naturally rewarding activities becomes reduced. This explains why individuals who misuse drugs eventually feel "flat," without motivation, lifeless, and/or depressed. People who have used drugs for an extended period of time often report that they are unable to enjoy things that they previously found pleasurable. As the brain changes due to drug use, the person needs to continue taking drugs to experience normal levels of reward and pleasure. This cycle causes the individual to need to take larger amounts of the drug to produce the high a process called tolerance.

Some may say drug tolerance is a crucial factor in developing addiction. *Drug tolerance* is a reduced reaction to a drug following repeated use. This results in the body needing an increased dose of the drug to achieve the same level of high. The increased dose may amplify the drug's effect, but it will most likely accelerate tolerance. Increases in tolerance further reduce the drug's effect and requires an increased dose to achieve or maintain the high. It is a vicious cycle. While it is true that drug tolerance follows drug use, it does not necessarily indicate a sign of drug dependence or addiction. There are many prescription drugs that we can become tolerant to overtime like blood pressure medications and anticoagulants.

Take a moment and picture in your mind a drug user. Who is that individual? Are they male or female? Are they young or old? Are they wealthy or poor? Are they college students or high school dropouts? *Drug users* are found in all occupations and professions, at all income and social class levels, in all racial and ethnic groups, and in all age groups. In 2020, an estimated 12% of individuals 12-years-of-age and over in the United States have used an illicit drug recently (in the past 30 days)[18]. No one is immune to drug use, which often leads to drug dependence. Drug use is an equal-opportunity affliction. The question then becomes when does a drug user become an addict? Figures 1.5 and 1.6 help highlight the addiction trajectory. It can be difficult to pinpoint when drug use transitions into addiction, as some of the activities society considers to be indicative of addiction also represent normal and prescribed patterns of drug administration (Figure 1.5). Instead, control over drug use and the need to pursue the drug are usually what we consider as being problematic. Drug use that increases in frequency over time to the point of continuous administration of drug throughout the day would point toward addiction (Figure 1.6).

Figure 1.5   What Is Needed for Addiction?

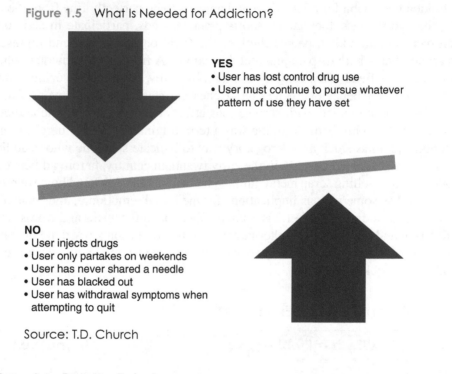

YES
• User has lost control drug use
• User must continue to pursue whatever pattern of use they have set

NO
• User injects drugs
• User only partakes on weekends
• User has never shared a needle
• User has blacked out
• User has withdrawal symptoms when attempting to quit

Source: T.D. Church

Figure 1.6   Drug Use Trajectory

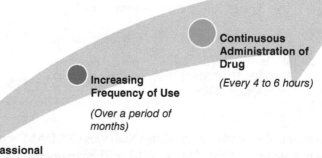

Continusous Administration of Drug
(Every 4 to 6 hours)

Increasing Frequency of Use
(Over a period of months)

Occassional Experimentation

Source: T.D. Church

When it comes to addiction, there are cases where the addiction is not apparent because the addict has learned how to interact socially and mask their drug use. These types of addicts are referred to as *functioning addict* or *high-functioning addict*. A functioning addict is an individual who is able to hide their drug use and are able to fulfill most social obligations. A high-functioning addict has hidden their habit for a long time and appears to be perfectly fine from the outside—they go to work, they go to class, they attend sports practice, study, participate in activities, and so on. Often when picturing an addict, people think of the *fiend* or *junkie*. A fiend represents a cultural ideal of an addict that is both disparaging and demeaning. A fiend is an individual who is extremely addicted to a drug. A fiend often cannot function physically, emotionally, or mentally without the drug. Fiends can develop behaviors such as lying, cheating, stealing, missing work, financial instability, and legal issues that escalate with very serious effects that may destroy the addict's life as well as everyone associated with them. A junkie was a term originally given to heroin users in the early twentieth century and has stuck as a derogatory way to indicate someone who is addicted to drugs. The name junkie was adapted because in the early twentieth century, heroin addicts supported their habit by collecting and selling scrap metal, junk. What we call an addict and how we refer to someone with an addiction has some serious implications for the social, emotional, and mental well-being of the individual who is addicted. Table 1.2 is a small collection of the terms and words typically used to describe addiction and provides some alternatives, and this builds on work done in communications, health policy, sociology, and anthropology to help alleviate the stigmatization drug users feel and can limit their ability to seek help[19].

Table 1.2 Addiction Dialogue Examples

AVOID	Why It Is Problematic	Alternatives
Addict, Abuser, Junkie	Defining the person by their illness	Person in active addiction, person with SUD
Abuse	Negates the fact that addictive disorders are a medical condition; blames the illness solely on the individual	Misuse, harmful use, risky use
Clean, Dirty	Associated with illness symptoms and filth	Negative, positive, substance-free
Habit or Drug Habit	Implies that resolution of the SUD is a matter of willpower	SUD, OUD, AUD

In 2020, the National Center for Drug Abuse Statistics (NCDAS) generated statistics on drug use, a reported 9.2% of people in the United States (21.7 million people) aged 12 or older needed substance treatment in the past year[20]. Only 2.5 million received treatment, which left 19.2 million people without treatment. In 2016, the RAND Corporation reported that drug users in the United States spent $100 billion annually buying cocaine, heroin, cannabis, and methamphetamines[21]. Among publicly funded drug treatment centers, the most common reasons for admission into treatment can be found in Figure 1.7. One of the more interesting percentages from Figure 1.7 is poly-addiction. ***Poly-addiction*** is being addicted to multiple substances at the same time. In addition to poly-drug use, it is important to keep in mind that substance addiction and mental health issues often occur together[22]. This is referred to as ***co-occurring disorders***. Mental health issues and addiction exist hand-in-hand as the result of a coping strategy of an individual. They are using the tools available to them to cope with trauma or pain, often substance use is the only tool in their toolkit. When considering treatment for co-occurring disorders, it is important to remember that the underlying cause of distress and coping must be addressed to be successful with the addiction treatment.

Figure 1.7   Drug Treatments by Drug of Addiction

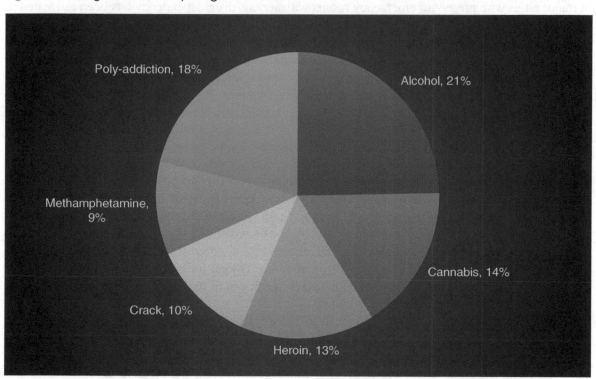

Source: T.D. Church

Demographic patterns of drug addiction point to individuals between 18 and 25 years of age representing those who are most likely to use illicit drugs. Caucasians/Whites represent the largest racial/ethnic group among drug consumers at ~19%, followed by American Indians/Alaska Natives at ~16%. Individuals of mixed race represented ~15%, African Americans/Blacks were ~12%, and Hispanic/Latinx constituted ~10%[20]. Males overall are more likely than females to be current illicit drug users. Pregnant women are less likely to use drugs than similar age women who are not pregnant. Individuals who do not complete high school tend to use illicit drugs more frequently. Unemployment increases the tendency to use more illicit drugs by ~20% over individuals who are gainfully employed. The Arrestee Drug Abuse Monitoring (ADAM) report, which presents data obtained at the time of arrest, found that ~40% of all arrestees tested positive for the presence of multiple drugs[23]. The Department of Justice (DOJ) in 2020 reported that 42% of state prisoners and 36% of federal prisoners reported they had committed their offenses while under the influence of drugs[24].

The economics of drug use provides some interesting statistics to consider[25]. The estimated cost of drug use to U.S. society from lost productivity, health care costs, and so on is ~$6,120 per second. The typical narcotic habit is estimated to be around $150 per day. The annual cost of daily use of OxyContin or Vicodin has been estimated to be ~$30,000. Methamphetamine addiction will cost the dependent user ~$75,000 per year. Heroin addicts tend to steal three to five times the actual cost of their drugs to be able to maintain their habit that has an annual cost of ~$160,000. Prostitutes in major cities who present to emergency rooms with serious drug dependency has been estimated to be three out of four.

Why do people become attracted to drugs? Addicted individuals are dependent upon particular sets of experience. Any behavior that stimulates an individual can become addictive. Some may use them for therapeutic reasons, to relieve pain and some symptoms of illness. Spiritual reasons, to enhance religious experiences or as part of their religious rites. Social reasons, to fit in with peers, as a rite of passage, or a part of cultural norms and expectations. Relaxation reasons, to relax after a tension filled day of work or school. Pleasure reasons, to experience or heighten good feelings. Stress reasons, to relieve stress, tension, or anxiety. Avoidance reasons, to avoid, forget, or postpone one's worries and concerns. These constitute a few of the reasons why people may become attracted to drugs. It could be for any of the above reasons alone or in consort that bring people to drug use.

Drug use does tend to cause major simultaneous changes to occur in the user. The social and psychological rewards from the effects of the drug "high" result in the illusion of temporary satisfaction and postponement of social pressures and anxieties leading to a superficial belief that problems and/or concerns are nonproblematic. Pharmacologically, the nonmedical use of most drugs alters body chemistry largely by interfering with or affecting homeostatic functioning. Drugs enhance, slow down, speed up, or distort the reception and transmission of reality. Some drugs may satisfy an inborn or genetically programed need or desire.

There are four factors that are known to influence drug use, and they exist across biological, cultural, social, and environmental factors[26]. *Biological factors* recognize that substance abuse and addiction involve biological and genetic factors. The pharmacology of drug use focuses on how the ingredients of drugs affect the body and the nervous system. *Cultural factors* consider how societal views, determined by custom and tradition, affect our initial approach and potential use of a drug. *Social factors* look at the specific reasons why a drug is taken (e.g., curing an illness, self-medicating, trying to escape from reality, peer pressure, family upbringing, and membership into drug abusing subcultures). *Environmental factors* affect the amount of drug use determined by our physical surroundings (music concerts, bars, nightclubs, or fraternity parties).

Sometimes, drug use begins as drug misuse. There are six examples of drug misuse, which may seem harmless but could be the first nascent steps toward full-blown addiction. These are not presented in any order of severity or increasing risk. The first example of drug misuse is taking a larger dose than what has been prescribed. Another example is the use of OTC or psychoactive drugs in excess without medical supervision or consultation. A third example is mixing drugs with alcohol or other types of drugs. Using old medicines to self-treat new symptoms of an illness is a fourth example. A fifth example of drug misuse is the discontinuation of prescribed drugs at will and/or against physician's directions. And, the sixth example, administering prescribed drugs to a family member without medical consultation and/or supervision. Each of these examples of misuse pushes the boundaries between use and addiction.

The study of drugs might cause us to rethink the history we have been taught. One of the goals of this book is to help paint a picture of our ancestors as they were, not as an idealized and romanticized history that presents the past as some grand aspirations of civilizations clad in marble and gleaming edifices. This book hopes to challenge the conventional imagination of history. Just as women, people of color, and members of the LGBTQI+ communities, whose stories have been largely absent from history, so has drug use and addiction. This is perhaps part of the Victorian belief that if we do not discuss it, it will eventually go away. If we do not acknowledge addiction, it did not happen. Addiction and drug use have often been hidden from our view. Hidden and not often discussed, with a very distinct feeling of covering up or concealing the truth. Hidden and not often discussed because it is incongruent with current beliefs and social mores related to alcohol and substances.

Throughout history, addiction and the misuse of drugs have been conceptualized as a bad habit, failures of healthy choices, failures of morality, symptoms of other problems, a chronic disease, a series of poor decisions, and/or the result of peer pressure. This book seeks to traces the contours of these ideas from the dawn of our civilizations to our modern time. This book is laid out thematically to move us from our oldest history forward. Every attempt to keep the timeline moving forward in a linear fashion has been made; however, there may be instances where our timelines overlap and converge. This book is laid out in 15 chapters. Our earliest prehistory can be found in Chapter 02, where we will discuss the paleolithic and neolithic periods. Chapters 03, 04, and 05 represent the classical age and focus on Ancient Egypt, Greece, and Rome. Chapters 06, 07, 08, and 09 cover trade, discovery, colonization, and empire building by focusing on the Silk Road, Maritime Empires, the New World, and the Opium Wars. Chapter 10 is all about poisons and how we have used them historically, politically, and socially to build and destroy dynasties. Chapter 11 looks at the nineteenth century by first examining quackery and then discussing the scientific advances that have created modern pharmacies. Chapter 12 focuses our attention on music and media in the twentieth century by looking at the 1960s–2000s and the relationship between drugs and commercialization. Chapter 13 gives us a look into the regulations, ethics, and legal aspects of drug control in the modern era. Chapter 14 broadly investigates modern forms of poisons that exist in chemical, biological, and atomic forms of war and terror. Finally, Chapter 15 brings us back to the concept of addiction and provides some concluding thoughts and pathways forward with regards to our current state of drug use. This journey we are about to embark upon hopes to shed light on facets of human history that have often been hidden from view.

REFERENCES

1. Crocq, M.-A. (2022). Historical and cultural aspects of man's relationship with addictive drugs. *Dialogues in Clinical Neuroscience*, **9**(4), 355–361.
2. Baker, A. R. (2003) *Geography and history: Bridging the divide.* Cambridge, UK: Cambridge University Press. p. 279.

3. Seifert, R. (2019) *Basic knowledge of pharmacology*. Cham, Switzerland: Springer. p. 492.

4. Zucconi, L. M. (2019) *Ancient medicine: From Mesopotamia to Rome*. Grand Rapids, MI: Wm. B. Eerdmans Publishing Co. p. 400.

5. Sample, I. (2019). Earliest known signs of cannabis smoking unearthed in China. *The Guardian*: New York, NY.

6. Booth, M. (2013) *Opium: A history*. New York, NY: St. Martin's Griffin.

7. Africa, T. W. (1961). The opium addiction of Marcus Aurelius. *Journal of the History of Ideas*, **22**(1): 97–102.

8. Retief, F. P. (2007). *Marcus Aurelius: Was he an opium addict? Acta Classica*, **2007**(sup-2): 132–137.

9. Jay, M. (2010). *High society: The central role of mind-altering drugs in history, science, and culture*. New York, NY: Simon & Schuster. p. 192.

10. Berger, K. (2021). Chemist creates Aspirin and Heroin: German chemist Felix Hoffmann worked on the substances at Bayer during a 2-week period in 1897. *Pharmacy Times*, **87**(2): 86.

11. Jones, A. W. (2011). Early drug discovery and the rise of pharmaceutical chemistry. *Drug Testing and Analysis*, **3**(6): 337–344.

12. WHO. (1964) *WHO Expert Committee on Addiction-Producing Drugs [Meeting Held in Geneva from 25 to 30 November 1963]: Thirteenth Report*. Geneva, Switzerland: World Health Organization.

13. NIDA. (2020). *Drug Misuse and Addiction*. https://nida.nih.gov/publications/drugs-brains-behavior-science-addiction/drug-misuse-addiction [cited 23 October 2022].

14. Jasanoff, A. (2018). *The biological mind: How brain, body, and environment collaborate to make us who we are*. New York, NY: Basic Books. p. 304.

15. DK. (2020). *How the brain works: The facts visually explained*. New York, NY: Penguin Random House. p. 244.

16. Bühler, K.-E. (2005). Euphoria, ecstacy, inebriation, abuse, dependence, and addiction: A conceptual analysis. *Medicine, Health Care and Philosophy*, 8(1): 79–87.

17. Li, G., Forero, M. G., Wentzell, J. S., Durmus, I., Wolf, R., Anthoney, N. C., Parker, M., Jiang, R.., Hasenauer, J., Strausfeld, N. James., Heisenberg, M., & Hidalgo, A. (2020). A toll-receptor map underlies structural brain plasticity. *Elife*9(e52743): 1–32. Available at: https://doi.org/10.7554/eLife.52743.

18. SAMHSA. (2022). 2020 *National Survey on Drug Use and Health*. Substance Abuse and Mental Health Services Administration: https://www.samhsa.gov/data/report/2020-nsduh-detailed-tables.

19. Room, R., Hellman, M., & Stenius, K. (2015). Addiction: The dance between concept and terms. *The International Journal of Alcohol and Drug Research*, **4**(1): 27–35.

20. NCDAS. (2020). *Drug Abuse Statistics*. National Center for Drug Abuse Statistics: https://dugabusestatistics.org.

21. Midgette, G., Davenport, S., Caulkins, J. P., & Kilmer, B. (2019). What America's users spend on illegal drugs, 2006–2016. *RAND Corporation*: Santa Monica, CA. p. 95.

22. Sussman, S., Leventhal, A., Bluthenthal, R. N., Freimuth, M., Forster, M., & Ames, S. L. (2011). A framework for the specificity of addictions. *International Journal of Environmental Research and Public Health*, **8**(8): 3399–3415.

23. Hunt, D. & Rhodes, W. (2011). *Arrestee Drug Abuse Monitoring Program II in the United States, 2010*. Inter-university Consortium for Political and Social Research [distributor]: University of Michigan.

24. United States Department of Justice. Office of Justice Programs. Bureau of Justice Statistics. (2022). *Annual Survey of Jails, 2020*. Inter-university Consortium for Political and Social Research [distributor]: University of Michigan.

25. Moeller, K. & Sandberg, S. (2019). Putting a price on drugs: An economic sociological study of price formation in illegal drug markets. *Criminology*, **57**(2): 289–313.

26. Lende, D. H. (2005). Wanting and drug use: A biocultural approach to the analysis of addiction. *Ethos*, **33**(1): 100–124.

Chapter 2

Remote antiquity

Our earliest history is the most difficult for us to fully understand, due in large part to the lack of written record. This leaves us with many unanswered questions about our early ancestors. Thankfully, more and more information is being amassed, thanks to the efforts of skilled archaeologists, anthropologists, and historians every day. This information strengthens and challenges our understanding of our ancestors. It is an exciting time to be a scholar, as novel information about our collective past is being revealed across so many academic disciplines associated with human history.

The two human epochs that make up our remote antiquity are the Paleolithic and the Neolithic. The Paleolithic occurred between 2.6 million BCE and 10,000 BCE and was dominated by stone tools and weapons. There was some art, very few settlements, and no written history. The Neolithic began around 10,200 BCE and lasted until 3,000 BCE. The Neolithic witnessed the rise of improved stone tools, exceptionally crafted obsidian blades, and more art. The Neolithic age is when farming and animal husbandry appear in conjunction with more permanent settlements and proto-writing systems. There was a rapid advancement in these periods that saw the formation of civilizations, development of new subsistence strategies, and implements for war. There have been many ages of humankind between the Paleolithic and our current Anthropocene (1945 CE–Present). Our contemporary age consists mostly of rapid technological advancements, and our Anthropocene is an epoch where human activities have begun to have a significant and negative global impact on Earth's geology and ecosystems. The Neolithic was the start of an ever-expanding technology boom, where human societies began massive building efforts and the transformation of vast tracks of land for agriculture, horticulture, and aquaculture.

Figure 2.1   Lascaux Cave Paleolithic Painting

2.1 Paleolithic Era

Paleolithic translates to "old stone age" and was characterized by the use of simple stone tools. It is the longest era in human history, spanning from 2.6 million BCE to 10,000 BCE. This was a time when more than one of our hominin relatives roamed the planet side by side. The now-extinct species of Neanderthal (~100,000–35,000 years ago) and Cro-Magnon (~40,000 years ago) are two examples[1]. Stone tools were the first cultural artifacts that archaeologists and historians utilized to reconstruct human life during the Paleolithic. While the Paleolithic is characterized by the use of knapped stone tools, wood and bone were most definitely used. Indeed, there were other organic commodities adapted for tools and clothing most likely fashioned from leather or vegetable fibers. However, time has ensured that the organic-based artifacts were not preserved to any great degree, but the stone tools have been plentiful. In addition, several cave paintings have been discovered depicting scenes of fruit and vegetable gathering and hunting of large game carried out in small groups, and daily life of our early ancestors.

The Paleolithic is divided into three distinct parts, including the Lower Paleolithic, Middle Paleolithic, and Upper Paleolithic. The Lower Paleolithic represents the first part of human history and spans from ~2.6 million BCE to ~250,000 BCE. Humans during this period were highly nomadic and tended to utilize caves and natural outcroppings for protection from the elements and predators. The major technological contribution was the discovery and use of fire[2]. The Middle Paleolithic represents the second stage, spanning from ~250,000 BCE to ~30,000 BCE. The continuous interspecies mating and evolution of humans had reached the Neanderthal phase, which is best characterized by their sophisticated intelligence and improved weapons and tools used for more efficient hunting and gathering. The Upper Paleolithic marked the third stage, occurring from ~30,000 BCE to ~10,000 BCE. This period witnessed an explosion of artistic development as seen in cave paintings, clay statues, bone carvings, and fine ornamental beads. During this period of interspecies mating and evolution, humans reached the Cro-Magnon phase, who were more expressive in their arts and ability to communicate.

Paleolithic peoples were limited by their hunting and gathering capabilities, which kept them predominately nomadic, following the herds and seasonal vegetation for sustenance. It is believed that they were primarily polygamous and, on rare occasions, practiced monogamy. Skeletal remains show sexual dimorphism was more pronounced in the Lower Paleolithic hominins, such as Homo Erectus, than in modern humans, who have become less polygamous than other primates. This suggests that Lower Paleolithic hominins took multiple mates throughout their lives because species that have the most pronounced sexual dimorphism tend to have multiple partners. Their religion was possibly *apotropaic* and would have involved some form of *sympathetic magic.*

Socially, Paleolithic hominins would have been organized in **Bands**. Bands are a human social organization consisting of a relatively small number of people (typically between 30 and 50 individuals). The bands formed a fluid, egalitarian community where members cooperated in activities such as food gathering, security, ritual, and care for children and elders. Bands would have been composed of several families. There is evidence that bands would sometimes join into larger **macrobands** for activities such as acquiring mates and celebrations or when resources were abundant.

Paleolithic humans were highly adaptable due to the necessities of their environment. The climate, which was temperate at the beginning of the Paleolithic, began to get very cold ~100,000 BCE. Thick ice sheets dominated the lands of the Northern Hemisphere and ocean levels dropped. Early people had to adapt to survive in this cooler and harsher environment. Paleolithic populations were spread out, and it has been estimated that the overall population at its height was less than 1 million people in the world[3]. Based on paleoarchaeological samples, average adult height would have been around 5′7″ (~1.7 meters) for males and 5′3″ (~1.6 meters) for females. Median life span was 35 years old for males and 30 years old for females. Infant mortality was high and has been estimated to be between 20% and 30%. Short height, young age at mortality, and high infant mortality were due to a combination of stresses revolving around nomadism, climate, and warfare for resources.

Figure 2.2 Paleolithic Stone Tools

ThomasLENNE/Shutterstock.com

The Paleolithic coincides with the first evidence of tool construction. Tools would have been made of wood, bone, and stone. There would have been immense cultural value ascribed to these tools, and they represent one of the first specialized professions developed by mankind. The types of tools found most frequently include simple pebble tools, chopping tools, and point tools. *Simple pebble tools* were deliberately selected as materials for knapping other stones into specific tools. *Chopping tools* were born out of an advanced pebble tradition and featured a manufactured sharp flaked edge. *Point tools* were a refinement to prior stone tool production and introduced changes to knapping techniques to produce more cutting edges across the surface of the stone. The most advanced form of point tool was the *projectile points,* which would have been tied with sinew or plant fibers and bound with resin to a spear, arrow, or atlatl shaft predominately employed for hunting and fishing.

Figure 2.3 Venus of Willendorf

Paleolithic peoples would have had a *naturalistic* culture, meaning they were remarkably close to nature. They lived based on the food that could be found or hunted and were solely dependent upon nature to stay alive. They hunted for meat and gathered food, firewood, materials for tools, clothes, and shelters. Unparalleled by any other society that followed them, Paleolithic peoples had an abundance of leisure time. They also had a very low population density due in part to lower body fat, infanticide, intense endurance exercise (following the game and evading predators), early weaning of infants, and nomadic lifestyle.

Dan Shachar/Shutterstock.com

Formalized religion most likely began in the Paleolithic age. It would have progressed from rituals to traditions to religion[4]. *Rituals* are sequences of activities involving gestures, words, and objects performed in a sequestered or sacred place, and often performed according to a set sequence of events. Rituals have been common features of all known human societies. *Traditions* represent beliefs or behaviors passed down within a group or society with symbolic meaning or special significance with origins in the past. Traditions refer to beliefs or customs that are prehistoric, with lost or arcane origins, and often thought to exist from time immemorial. *Religion* can be thought of as a set of formalized spiritual beliefs. Religion is composed of behavior patterns where ritual, tradition, and spirituality are combined. Religion carries within it the origin stories of the people and provides rules by which its members should live and conduct themselves. Through religion, our first laws and code of ethics would have become formalized.

Figure 2.4 Burial Goods and Human Fossils

Xolodan/Shutterstock.com

Religious behavior is an amalgamation of ritual, spirituality, mythology, and magical thinking. We know that Paleolithic peoples had some type of religious belief, due to the number of *intentional burials* uncovered in Europe, Asia, and the Middle East. Intentional burials contain arranged bodies, usually in a comfortable resting position and contain grave goods, flowers, and gifts. Intentional burials show a concern for the dead and a transcendence beyond daily life.

Based on comparative studies with contemporary hunter and gatherer groups, we believe Paleolithic peoples held one of three religious belief systems consisting of animism, totemism, or apotropaic magic[5]. *Animism* is the belief that objects, places, or creatures (real or imagined) all possess a distinct spiritual essence. Animism perceives everything known and unknown—animals, plants, rocks, rivers, weather systems, human handiwork, and even some words as being animated or capable of becoming animated. Through this animation, it is believed that supernatural power could be observed and potentially harnessed. *Totemism* refers to a spiritual kinship between a human or group of humans and a particular animal or natural object like a tree, a rock, or an environmental formation. The totem animal or plant is believed to be an ancestor, guardian, or spiritual benefactor of the individuals who believe in them. The natural object or animal takes on a spiritual significance and often is adopted as an emblem or sigil of an individual or clan. *Apotropaic* is not necessarily a religion on its own but represents a form of powerful magic. Apotropaic refers to protective magic intended to turn away harm or evil influences. Apotropaic observances were practiced out of vague superstition or tradition and consisted of things like good luck charms, gestures (crossed fingers for luck), and offerings of food to spirits for their assistance in warding off the evil eye.

One of the more puzzling, if not mystifying, sets of artifacts from the Paleolithic era are megaliths. *Megaliths* are giant stone slabs, some weighing as much as a compact car, that were used to construct a structure or monument, either alone or together with other stones. It has been estimated that there are ~35,000 megaliths in Europe alone and are dispersed broadly from the Mediterranean Sea to Sweden. They have been found in Africa, the Middle East, North America, and Asia. Megaliths are structures made of exceptionally large and heavy stones without the use of mortar or concrete. They cantilever and balance delicately upon one another, defying gravity and natural forces. Speculation over what they were used for continues to be debated, some believe them to be tombs, while others see them as earthworks, terraces, celestial observatories, religious centers, military outposts, or trade locations. These structures would have taken many hours to construct and would have been extremely labor intensive.

Figure 2.5   El Pozuelo Megalith Huelva, Andalucia, Spain

agsaz/Shutterstock.com

Why would Paleolithic peoples expend the energy to build such structures or put themselves at potential risk of death or injury during construction? These megaliths were obviously of great cultural value if prehistoric peoples were willing to risk so much to construct them.

Paleolithic peoples placed a lot of cultural value on plants, as seen in the types of plants left within burials, caringly painted on rock walls, and purposefully inurned among some of the megalith structures. *Paleoethnobotany* is the study of remains of plants cultivated or used by people in ancient times, which have survived in the archaeological context. Paleoethnobotany is based on the recovery and identification of plant remains and the ecological and cultural information available from their modern counterparts. Some of the major themes of paleoethnobotanical research include the use of wild plants, origins of agriculture and domestication, and co-evolution of human–plant interactions. Oat straw, goldenrod, and marshmallow root were some of the earliest medicines we know our ancestors were using based on plant materials found in burials and observation of modern hunter/gatherer people (Figure 2.6).

Medical substances have been used throughout human history. These substances can be foods, herbs, medicines, drugs, or represent a combination of these utilities. Humans have been drawn to them to improve social interactions; facilitate mating and sex; heighten cognitive performance; facilitate recovery and coping with stress; self-medication for negative emotions, psychological distress, and other mental health problems and symptoms; therapeutic utility; sensory curiosity—expansion of experimental horizons; and euphoria or hedoina—pleasure seeking. In terms of drug effect, Table 2.1 will be useful for understanding the pharmacologic class of drugs most frequently represented in plant materials from Paleolithic sites.

Although modern medicine has provided new routes for the administration of drugs, our ancient ancestors were confined to four routes for drug delivery. Drug routes during the Paleolithic and Neolithic would have been delivered via external application, fumigation, orally, or rectally. *External application* would have been the direct application of medicines to the skin and would have consisted of things such as raw meat, oils, and honey. *Fumigation* would have been the delivery of drugs via smoke and would have been done through active inhalation or passive inhalation. *Active inhalation* would have been done by directly smoking a given substance. *Passive inhalation* refers to the inhaling of secondhand smoke or being exposed to fumes. *Oral* is the administration of drugs by way of the mouth wherein the drugs are ingested as raw drug parts or in a mixture. *Rectal* is the administration by way of the rectum and would consist of suppositories or enemas.

Figure 2.6   Earliest Medicines

Oatstraw
(antispasmodic, diuretic, and stimulant)

Goldenrod
(anti-inflammatory)

Codonopsis Root
(immune system booster)

Blue Vervain
(antipyretic and antidepressant)

Coltsfoot
(antitussive)

Skullcap
(sleep aid and antianxiety)

Wild Cherry Bark
(antitussive and antipyretic)

Marshmallow Root
(anti-inflammatory and urinary tract inflammation)

Schisandra Berry
(stimulant and anti-inflammatory)

Honeysuckle Flower
(digestive disorders, antibacterial and antimicrobial)

Angelica Root
(carminative)

Horehound
(expectorant, anthelmintic)

Slippery Elm Bark
(diuretic)

Astragalus Root
(helps reduce diabetes)

Cramp Bark
(anti-inflammatory)

Source: T.D. Church

In terms of early medicines, it is believed that Paleolithic peoples practiced an early form of *herbalism*. Herbalism refers to the study of botany and the use of plants intended for medical purposes or for supplementing missing nutritional components in the diet. Plants have been the basis for medical treatments throughout all human history. Today, this type of medicine would fall under the categories of "traditional medicine" or "alternative medicine." Herbal medicines also include fungal and bee products, minerals, shells, and some animal parts among the repertoire of curative elements. *Folk medicine* consists of the healing practices and understanding of body physiology, and

Table 2.1 Pharmacological Drug Classes

Analgesic
• Relieves pain, produces mild euphoric feeling
Anodyne
• Relieves pain, less potent than an analgesic
Antibacterial
• Kills and prevents the growth of bacteria
Anthelmintic
• Kills and expells worms from the small and large intestines
Antimicrobial
• Kills and prevents the growth of microbes and bacteria
Antipyretic
• Reduces fever
Antitussive
• Relieves cough
Astringent
• Prevents bleeding and secretion from wounds, causes tissues to constrict
Carminative
• Facilitates burping and removal of gas from the stomach
Cathartic
• Induces vomiting, potent and highly powerful purgative
Demulcent
• Sooths and relieves skin irritation
Diuretic
• Increases the amount of urine and the frequency with which one needs to urinate
Expectorant
• Aids in the expelling of phlem and other bronchial secretions from the lungs
Hypotensive
• Aids in reducing blood pressure

Source: T.D. Church

health promotion and maintenance known to some within a culture, transmitted informally as general knowledge, and practiced or applied by anyone who had prior experience. Folk medicine falls into the same categories of "traditional medicine" or "alternative medicine," and occasionally is referred to as "indigenous medicine," "complementary medicine," or "natural medicine" in modern parlance. Folk medicines and herbalism were the earliest forms of medical and pharmacological practices in human societies. Folk medicines formed the foundation of modern medicine and pharmacology.

Paleolithic societies focused locally on the flora and fauna of the area in which they were inhabiting. Due to their nomadic lifestyle, these people encountered broader diversity in plants than modern humans in most cases. Many of these plants were localized to specific areas and would only be accessible during migrations. It is believed that women and the elderly, who have represented the primary gatherers, cared for the health of their families. Plant materials were an important source of cures for diseases throughout history. The fund of knowledge related to these plants would have been passed down orally from mother to daughter, through the generations. Learning the edible from the poisonous, the therapeutic from the virulent, and the useful from the innate must have been a very harrowing undertaking. To be sure, many individuals either died or had bad experiences being the first to try a new fruit, berry, or leaf from a previously unknown plant. The bad experiences probably manifested as bad hallucinogenic experiences, diarrhea, sweating, vomiting, and/or extreme nausea. Without these pioneering individuals and their penchant for trial and error, the edible versus poisonous plants would not have become known.

Figure 2.7 Mayan Shaman

Ammit Jack/Shutterstock.com

Three unique fields of study have emerged to help make sense of the potential medicines our earliest ancestors may have used. The fields of ethnomedicine, ethnobotanical medicine, and ethnopharmacology draw from a diverse set of academic disciplines, including anthropology, archaeology, biology, medicine, and pharmacology. Each of these fields of study focus on the traditional medicines used by specific groups of people. These fields seek to understand the cultural, medical, and pharmacological dimensions of human medicines used in the historical past, and through direct observation by applying what hunter and gatherer groups use today, it is possible to deduce the medicines used historically. *Traditional medicine* refers to any form of indigenous healthcare system with ancient roots, distinct cultural bonds, trained healers, and a theoretical construct. *Ethnomedicine* is the comparison of traditional medicines based on bioactive compounds in plants and animals and practiced by various ethnic groups. Ethnomedicine includes ways of reconstructing past medical practices by examining the archaeological record in tandem with existing traditional societies. *Ethnobotanical medicine* is the study of the uses of plants in medicine by specific ethnic or sociocultural groups. A subset is *ethnopharmacology,* which combines anthropology and pharmacy to study traditional medicines based on bioactive compounds in plants and animals.

We know that some plants held importance and significance for our ancestors. We know this by looking at the dispersal and migratory patterns of plants globally. If we rewound the clock to the earliest human ancestors, ~2.3 million years ago, we would have found ourselves in the Cradle of Humankind. Today, Sterkfontein Caves in South Africa are a UNESCO World Heritage Site where the oldest remains of our ancestors were discovered. South Africa is unique in terms of its diverse flora and fauna. It represents one of the richest temperate zones globally, with an estimated ~25,000 specific and intraspecific taxa from ~370 plant families[6]. Some have estimated that ~15% of the Earth's vascular plant flora can be found in South Africa, representing less than 2.5% of the Earth's total surface area. Being one of the richest centers of plant biodiversity makes South Africa equally rich in traditional medicines. There is an excellent historic record that highlights ~5,700 different plant taxa (out of the 25,000) in the archaeological record. Even more astounding, ~3,000 of these are recognized medically in the present day. Our earliest ancestors made use of biodiversity and carried with them the plants they revered and used.

Figure 2.8   Jewelweed flower and seed pod

Arctic Flamingo/Shutterstock.com

During the Ice Age, migrations of megafauna and plants were accompanied by early humans who traversed the Bering Strait Land Bridge[7]. If left to their own devices, plants have five methods of seed dispersal, including gravity, mechanical, animal, water, and air. Each of these is fairly self-explanatory. Seeds drop from plants naturally due to gravity. A good example of mechanical dispersal, for those who have lived in North America, is the jewelweed seed pods (Figure 2.8). These pods explode upon touch and eject their seeds into the environment. Animal dispersal, we will discuss further below. Water can carry seeds far from their originator, as can wind. The animal form of dispersal involves the seeds of plants animals have eaten being deposited post-digestion in another location. We can see these migratory patterns of animals who consume plants via grasses and trees moving in vast swaths seemingly alongside the herds that consume them. The other method of seed dispersal relies on humans. We tend to be a bit more deliberate, transplanting fruits, vegetables, herbs, medicinal, and recreational plants we enjoy or find useful from location to location.

Some examples of human plant dispersal can be seen across medicinal, spiritual, and communal plants. An example of medicinal plant dispersal can be seen in the dodder, a non-flowering plant long used by people in Mongolia to relieve asthma; the stems of the plant are boiled to produce a steam that is inhaled by the asthma patient. Goldthread, the flowering cousin of dodder, was used by Native Americans in a hot bath treatment for tuberculosis. Goldthread would typically be harvested while the plant was flowering to get the full effect. Native peoples in Asia and America still utilize the dodder as an **emetic**, to induce vomiting, by brewing the stems and then drinking the compounded liquid. The whole plant can be eaten for use as a contraceptive.

Examples of plants with a spiritual property that were dispersed by our Paleolithic ancestors are cannabis and harmal. The wider world of today is certainly no stranger to cannabis, with thousands of cannabis legalization debates taking place within the United States and across the globe. Cannabis is sometimes referred to as "weed," an apt designation due to its ability to be grown in a variety of climates. It might be a surprise to discover that a 2,700-year-old grave in Western China exhibited the earliest known evidence of the drug being used as a psychoactive substance from ancient times. A little under 780 grams (~1.7 pounds) of cannabis was found in a shaman's grave alongside braziers

Figure 2.9 Goldthread (L) and Dodder (R)

Figure 2.10 Harmal (L) and Cannabis (R)

and snuffing trays, which may have been used to consume the drug. Long before finding its way into the shaman's grave, cannabis would have been used by our ancestors for a variety of things—food, fun, and even clothing. Harmal, commonly used by West Indian, Iranian, and Andean cultures, is native to the Mediterranean. Although not directly related to cannabis, harmal has been used in traditional medicine for its anti-depression properties. It has recently been discovered woven into the hair of mummified people in North Chile. The remains are believed to be from 800 CE to 1200 CE far earlier than trade would have happened between Western Conquistadors and Native Incans.

The final group of plants is considered to be highly communal and required investment and coordinated effort to bear the fruits—no pun intended—of labor. Grapes are used to make wine, and hops are used to make beer. We find these plants in the archaeological record dating back to ~20,000 years. Grapes are an intensive investment, as grape vines typically take seven years to reach maturation and bear fruit. This would require annual tending, meaning the vines would need to be checked upon periodically to ensure they were pest-free and growing. This could have coincided with seasonal migrations following game but represent an early form of domestication. Hops are a less-intensive investment and take between three and four months to bear fruit. But it does take a coordinated effort for both plants to reach maturation and a communal effort to prepare the fruit for fermentation.

Figure 2.11   Hops (L) and Grapes (R)

Ancestral early hominids were most likely making wines, beers, meads, and mixed fermented beverages[8]. Wild fruits, chewed roots and grains, honey, and all manner of herbs and spices gathered from their local environments would have been employed in the fermentation process. Wide-scale brewing and fermenting did not begin until much later in human history, but there is evidence to support our earliest ancestors gathering grapes and hops for microscale fermenting. Fermented beverages would have been seasonal in our earliest history. There would have been an immense communal effort to collect and produce the microscale fermented beverages. Medicinal properties that were definitely ascribed to these beverages much later in history would have had their beginnings during the Paleolithic. Patrick McGovern, Scientific Director of the Biomolecular Archaeology Project for Cuisine, Fermented Beverages, and Health at the University of Pennsylvania, stated that "making fruit into alcohol ushed in humankind's first biotechnology based on empirical observation"[9]. He further indicated, "it is quite possible that much of what we consider uniquely human—music, dance, theater, religious storytelling and worship, language, and a thought process that would eventually become science—were stimulated by the creation and consumption of alcoholic beverages during the Paleolithic period"[10]. Midas Touch, Ancient Brew, represents a unique collaboration with Dogfish Head Brewery in which McGovern was able to chemically identify the chemical composition of a fermented beverage thousands of years old and from less than a milliliter of material.

Fermented fruits and beverages have been a part of the traditional repertoire of healing practices for thousands of years. ***Traditional healers***, sometimes functioned as spiritual leaders, were individuals who served the health needs of the people in their group. One of the earliest traditional healer professions that is still with us today is that of a doula. ***Doulas*** are birth companions and post-birth supporters who assist pregnant women before, during, and after childbirth. Traditional healers often held sacred roles presiding over the affairs of life and death in their groups, and took on the role of ceremonial and ritual leaders. A good example of this can be seen in the group of healers known as shamans. A ***shaman*** was regarded as having access to and influence in the world of benevolent and malevolent spirits. They typically entered the spirit world under the influence of a psychoactive substance-induced trance. These individuals would have practiced a variety of mystical arts and divination side by side with healing. They would have passed their traditions on through oral history and apprenticeship where their knowledge moved from one generation to the next. In many early societies, women performed the role of traditional healers and shamans.

Shamans have historically fulfilled multiple roles within a group, often being thought of as priests, magicians, soothsayers, legal authorities, adjudicators, lore keepers, medical professionals, and even political advisors. *Soothsayers* are individuals who claimed to have the ability to predict the future through magic, intuition, or other rational means. Soothsaying entailed the ability to foretell events and foresee the future or potential outcomes the future held. Shamans would have had a vast knowledge related to medicinal, poisonous, and psychoactive plants. Shamanic imagery and artwork suggest that humans have been using mind-altering substances for thousands of years. Shamans

Figure 2.12   Head Spices of the Paleolithic

__Myrrh__ - functions like opium; targets mu- and delta-opioid receptors in the brain

__Frankincense__ - functions like Valium; containing dehydroabietic acid that targets the GABA receptors in the brain

__Saffron__ - contains a GABA antagonist as well as safrole that is a component used to manufacture MDMA

__Cinnamon__ - contains both safrole and eugenol; both components are used to manufacture MDMA

__Agarwood__ - is a sedative and analgesic

__Spikenard__ - boosts serotonin, dopamine, and GABA acting like a memory enhancer

__Pomegranate__ - serotonin, melatonin, and tryptamines causing general relaxation

Source: T.D. Church

would have been responsible for organizing worship and sacrifices. It is believed that in accordance with their closeness to the environment and nature, shamans were attuned to and understood celestial movements, and developed the first lunar calendars. Skilled shamans were able to track the solstice and could predict when herds would return or when specific plants would be in bloom. Shamans are believed to have helped in the creation of written language, art, and ceremony. However, shamans by custom or choice did not record their knowledge in written or artistic form. Instead, shamans relied on oral tradition. Shamans were there to help interpret the divine and utilize their skills to protect people from all manner of harm and ills.

A unique and historically divine sacrament of many religions has been the use of incense in the practice of holy events and ceremonies. Often quoted in religious texts as "head spices," there have been seven forms of incense used historically and, in the present, as religious offerings. These head spices are also capable of tweaking the human brain. Before being utilized as incense and quoted in the major religious texts, these head spices were most likely used by shamans and holy people in pre-history. Burial goods from sites dating back ~12,000–10,000 years contain one or more of these seven incenses. Figure 2.12 shows an image of the incenses, their common name, and the effect these incenses can have on the human brain. There are examples from ancient burials of Neanderthals where these incenses, either as sap, bark, root, flower, or fruit, have been inurned.

2.2 Neolithic Era

The *Neolithic*, or "new stone age," began ~10,200 BCE until ~3,000 BCE. This was a period marked by profound cultural, technological, and geological changes. The Last Glacial Maximum (LGM) had receded, the climate was gradually warming, and ushered in a profound climate event, the Younger Dryas. The Younger Dryas is often linked to the Neolithic Revolution, in particular to the adoption of agriculture in the Levant. *Levant* is an approximate historical geographical area referring to a large portion of land in the Eastern Mediterranean, encompassing present-day Syria, Lebanon, Jordan, Israel, Palestine, Turkey, parts of Greece, and Northern Egypt. The cold and dry climate caused by the Younger Dryas lowered the overall carrying capacity of the Levant for hunting and gathering. The climatic deterioration caused by the Younger Dryas has been theorized to have initiated cereal cultivation as the primary subsistence strategy.

Figure 2.13 Gobekli Tepe Early Civilization

Mehmet Cetin/Shutterstock.com

At the start of the Neolithic, people lived in small tribes composed of multiple bands or lineages. Settlements transitioned from seasonally inhabited to permanently settled and the first cities began to appear. Pottery and written languages started to be more readily available and more prolific in the archaeological record. The Neolithic's most impactful change was in subsistence patterns. Farming had been limited to a narrow range of plants, both wild and domesticated. There was a dramatic increase in the abundance of einkorn wheat, millet, and spelt in the archaeological record as these staple crops were domesticated and spread widely throughout the Levant. Animal domestication occurred around the same time and included dogs, sheep, goats, cattle, and pigs. The domestication of large animals, ~8,000 BCE, resulted in a dramatic increase in social inequality in most of the areas where it occurred. Possession of livestock allowed for competition between households, and, as some historians have postulated, resulted in inherited inequalities of wealth[11]. Economically speaking, families and households were still largely independent with the household being viewed as the center of life and livelihood.

The Neolithic represents the beginnings of complex societies. *Complex societies* in anthropology and archaeology refer to a social formation described as a formative (sometimes developed) state. The key hallmarks of complex society are defined by division of labor, increased trade, proliferation of customs and laws, and exponential increases in population size. *Division of labor* allows for members of society to become specialized in particular activities and crafts. *Trade* relates to goods and services being exchanged for food, goods, or services. *Customs and laws* allow for daily life to be regulated, behaviors are controlled, and punishment and reward are standardized. *Population size* indicates that the larger the population, the more complex and specialized the people become. To become a complex society, there need to be enough surplus food sources to support a social (read as non-food producing) group of individuals. Complex societies promoted the formation and maintenance of hierarchy. *Hierarchy* implies a ruling elite, supported by bureaucrats, administrative buildings and elite residences, and clothing and adornments to signify different social stations or responsibilities.

The environmental pressures coupled with rapid population expansion led to crises, which forced Neolithic peoples to adopt new strategies to survive, including the domestication of animals, cultivation of crops, and participation in complex societies. Complex societies enabled specialization in labor, technological advances, government, and religion. There were dramatic changes in subsistence strategies and the social structures to support those changes. The pressures of becoming sedentary and living in larger groups led to the rise of alcohol and other pharmacologically active consumables such as cannabis and opium. The new social paradigm was related to production of goods and led to what anthropologists have defined as social competition. *Social competition* is a model for understanding hierarchical structures. It is a model focused on a *wealth* rather than a *dearth* of resources, which enabled people to engage in high-risk production activities such as cultivation and domestication[12].

The dramatic and abrupt shift in subsistence strategies has been termed the Neolithic Revolution. It was a complete reworking of sociopolitical and cultural systems to rise to the challenges of population explosions and dwindling resources. Changes in the subsistence methods required greater social cohesion and control to maintain. *Subsistence strategies* simply mean methods used to support life. There are five main strategies. *Foraging* represents the process of gathering food from uncultivated plants or undomesticated animals and is central to the hunter–gatherer lifestyle seen in the Paleolithic. *Pastoralism* is the domestication of animals as a food source. Pastoralism does not depend on the ability to grow crops as the domestic animals could be "free range," allowing the herds to graze and eat in their natural habitats. *Horticulture* concerns the intentional cultivation of plants for personal use. The intent of horticulture is not to grow an abundance of food, but to grow enough to sustain life within the group. Horticulture involves crop rotation and focusing on multiple types of plant food sources. ***Aquaculture*** is the deliberate farming of crustaceans, mollusks, aquatic plants, algae, and other aquatic organisms usually in controlled aquatic environments. Aquaculture employs man-made "closed" systems where the breeding, rearing, and harvesting can take place in a variety of water systems from ponds and rivers to lakes and oceans. Aquaculture is one of the most resource-efficient ways to produce protein. ***Agriculture*** is large-scale production of food for larger population. Agriculture is the practice of farming and includes cultivation of the soil for crops and rearing of animals for food and other products. Agriculture tends to focus on the growing of cereal grains and legumes and rearing of a few types of animals.

Agriculture not only represented a massive change in how we lived, but it was an enormous gamble with the stakes being life or death. The Paleolithic was focused on hunter–gatherer strategies to survive and represented an ***immediate return*** on nutritional investment. The Paleolithic valued consumption over accumulation of food and was much more egalitarian. Food was shared with all present on the day it was acquired, where everyone had their fill. The Neolithic transitioned to agriculture and as a result was provided a ***delayed return*** on nutritional investment. The work of cultivation was invested over extended periods of time before a sufficient yield was produced for harvesting and consumption. This delay between labor investment and consumption required a hierarchical structure to manage the burden. The hierarchy would have had the authority to distribute work, control yields, and partition out vital assets. Delayed return presents an elevated risk in the long delay of time between agricultural effort and nutritional payoff. Unanticipated problems such as droughts, pests, and even theft would alter yields from season to season. Agriculture was a delayed-return investment, whose potential nutritional payoff needed to be discounted because unanticipated problems and unforeseen events had the ability to dramatically reduce the future availability of food. Future discounting introduced stress, strife, corruption, exploitation, and fear in the people of the Neolithic. Well, among the lower tiers of the Neolithic hierarchy, at least.

Figure 2.14   Future Discounting of Subsistence Benefits and Deficits

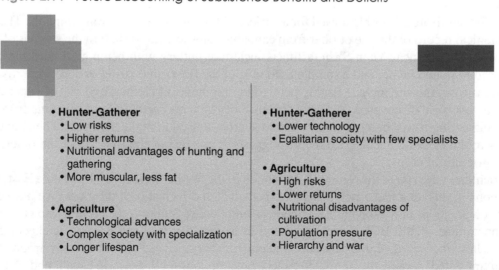

• **Hunter-Gatherer**
  • Low risks
  • Higher returns
  • Nutritional advantages of hunting and gathering
  • More muscular, less fat

• **Agriculture**
  • Technological advances
  • Complex society with specialization
  • Longer lifespan

• **Hunter-Gatherer**
  • Lower technology
  • Egalitarian society with few specialists

• **Agriculture**
  • High risks
  • Lower returns
  • Nutritional disadvantages of cultivation
  • Population pressure
  • Hierarchy and war

Source: T.D. Church

The perpetuation of agriculture and cultivation was, in part, motivated by the sociocultural forces of competitive feasting, which granted political power and allowed for the pursuit of the self-interests of the elite. Psychoactive substances and grand feasts were used to reduce the problems embedded in the future-discounting related to the delayed-returns inherent in agriculture. *Feasts* were important social and political events for our ancient ancestors[13]. The agency of fermented beverages (wine and beer) would have been harnessed as arenas for inculcating ideologies, creating the sense of group cohesion, and reinforcing social differentiation. The competition of feasting by the elites introduced new and exotic foods and spices as well as ushered in innovative technologies. These innovative technologies and foods were a way to impress guests you invited to feast. Feasts required the production and storage of enormous quantities of food and drink that would be gluttonously consumed over the course of a day or multiple days. Many of the domesticated food stuffs were costly status symbols, which helped usher in the end of egalitarianism via grand feasting of lower nutritional quality foods. The pepper is a notable example; it has little nutritional value, but as a spice, it had the ability to alter and complement the food being served. Successful organizers of feasts were able to obtain sociopolitical power and, as a result, improved their reproductive success. In fact, the tradition of a marriage banquet is a lasting homage to Neolithic feasting customs. Funeral banquets represent another, albeit, a more somber example of the power of feasting[14].

Neolithic funerals across Asia and the Middle East were dope—literally! Mourners burned plants with high levels of tetrahydrocannabinol (THC) as part of these mortuary rituals. Cannabis would have been burnt in large braziers—the Godzillas of incense burners—effectively getting an entire crowd of people to inhale cannabis smoke. While studying these gargantuan incense burners found at ancient burial sites, researchers used gas chromatography-mass spectrometry. They were able to isolate and identify cannabinoid compounds in the preserved braziers[15]. These astonishing results from their tests indicated that the chemical signature was a potent level of THC. The sample was much stronger than was typical for wild plants, which indicates that the samples were from actively cultivated cannabis. Moreover, from cannabis that had been artificially selected for its psychoactive potency.

The first cultivated fiber plant used for a variety of human handicrafts was cannabis. The earliest archaeological record of the use of fiber from cannabis dates to 12,000 BCE in the steppes of present-day China. At a site near Yuan-Shan, artifacts including pottery with hemp cord markings, a stone beater used to pound hemp, and a spindle used to spin the fibers into string or cord were discovered. Other items from the site include fishing nets, rope, fragments of clothes, and bits of paper all made from cannabis were discovered. We have evidence of cannabis seeds in food middens from around the site, indicating it was being stored as a food source or used to make hemp oil. The abundance of cannabis in the early archaeological record suggests it was one of the first, if not the oldest, known human agricultural crops.

Agriculture gave rise to the Neolithic Revolution in the Fertile Crescent of the Middle East. The first civilizations in this area had a rich history of medicinal and recreational drug use. We have evidence from the civilizations of Mesopotamia, Phoenicia, and Pontus. Sumer is the earliest known civilization of Mesopotamia, ~4,500 BCE, which is located in present-day Iraq and Kuwait. Archaeologists and historians have recovered ~2,000 cuneiform tablets from the ruins of Sumer, with only around 600 having been translated. Among the translated tablets, prescriptions for drugs have been found. A few of the tablets could be considered to be medical "treatises" and have commentary on diseases such as fevers,

Figure 2.15 Cuneiform Payment in Beer

Source: Trustees of the British Museum

worms and flukes, venereal diseases, and skin lesions. One amazing find was a tablet with the world's first description of an early aspirin. The tablet has detailed instructions on how to render willow bark as a tea, which would be drunk to alleviate the symptoms of fever, pain, and inflammation. The inner bark of willow contains trace amounts of salicylic acid, a natural precursor for our modern manufactured aspirin that contains acetylsalicylic acid. In the city of Sumer, residents enjoyed many benefits of urban life. We have vivid accounts of people exchanging goods for commodities, gambling and playing board games, and daily life portrayed in detail within cuneiform clay tablets. *Cuneiform* is a logographic form of writing distinguished by its wedge-shaped markings, made by pressing a blunt reed (*stylus*) into a soft clay tablet. *Logographic* is a writing system where a symbol or sign is used to represent an entire word or concept. One of the more interesting cuneiform tablets recently translated is an early "pay stub" wherein 5,000 years ago, one lucky worker was paid for their labor in beer. This type of receipt for work is incredibly common and has been documented in several Mesopotamian tablets.

Babylon was the most famous city from ancient Mesopotamia whose majestic ruins are in present-day Iraq, a little under 60 miles (96 kilometers) southwest of Baghdad. The city is thought to have been established ~4,000 BCE. Babylon was the jewel of ancient Mesopotamian society and boasted many social and technical innovations. The city was renowned for its massive city walls and ornate buildings. It had a reputation as a place of scholars and held cultural and educational prestige among the ancient cities of the Levant. It has been referred to by some as the cradle of civilization. Within Babylon, we find the earliest known record of an apothecary, or ancient pharmacy, a place where drugs and poisons were prepared and sold. Healers of this time often filled the roles of priests, pharmacists, and physicians all in one. There have been found and translated ~450 cuneiform tablets related to health, drugs, or medicine from the city of Babylon. These tablets contain the prescription and directions for compounding over 400 unique drugs. The first evidence of brothels as a formal establishment was located in Babylon and in places where patrons could purchase all

Figure 2.16 Ishtar gates of Babylon, Iraq

manner of sex, fetish, wine, and opium. There is evidence that cannabis would have been burnt in large incense braziers, making the experience even more exotic for those who entered the brothel.

Tapputi-Belatekallim was a Babylonian noblewoman and skilled perfumer who committed some of her technical skills in making palm perfume "fit for a king" onto a Babylonian cuneiform tablet dating back to over 3,000 BCE[16]. On the surface, perfume may not seem like a very scientific endeavor, but making good perfumes is a highly technical process and involves knowledge of both chemistry and botany. Perfumes and other fragrant substances were held in very high esteem in many ancient societies. In Babylon, ***perfume*** had four crucial uses—(1) used as a cosmetic, (2) used in performing religious and political rituals, (3) used for its magical properties, and (4) used as medicine. In addition to perfume, ancient Babylonians used ***essential oils*** to treat infections and ailments, which were prepared by perfumers who functioned as a kind of early pharmacists.

Figure 2.17 Muricidae Sea Snail

Phuong D. Nguyen/Shutterstock.com

Phoenicia was an ancient civilization located along the coast of the Mediterranean Sea in the area of present-day Syria, Lebanon, and Israel. The Phoenician ancient capital city of Tyre was founded around 3,000 BCE. The Phoenicians were expert seafaring people and are credited as being the first international traders. They were highly skilled in shipbuilding, glassmaking, the production of dyes, and had an impressive level of skill in the manufacture of luxury and common goods. ***Tyrian*** was their most famous dye, obtained from the harvesting of the mucus gland of predatory sea snails from the Muricidae family of marine mollusks. Tyrian is a purple dye manufactured and used in the robes of royalty by many civilizations. The color is often referred to as royal purple or blue. The word Phoenicia is derived from the Greek, *phoinikes*, meaning "purple people" because the production of Tyrian dye would stain the skin of the workers. The Phoenicians are credited with the creation of the Western Alphabet. Our word phonics, which refers to a method of teaching people to read by correlating sounds with letters or groups of letters in an alphabetic writing system, is derived from the name Phoenicia and pays homage to their introduction of the alphabet. Among all of their many accomplishments, the Phoenicians perfected dentistry in the ancient world. They were known to have made false teeth out of ivory, and these false teeth were anchored to existing teeth by thin gold wire. There are a number of skeletal remains sporting this incredible feat of dental work[17]. It is even more astounding if you consider there were no pain relievers, sedatives, or antibiotics for this type of procedure. They had opium and wine that would have been used to dull the pain, but the individual would have been fully awake when their new dentures were implanted and wired in.

Pontus was a region of land on the southern shore of the Black Sea, which has a unique set of natural resources with powerful characteristics known to both promote and deplete health. There is an overabundance of venomous snakes and insects, and a higher-than-normal volume of poisonous and deadly plants. The curious lands of Pontus were home to the mysterious *Agari*, Scythian shamans who were part of nomadic tribes that claimed the steppes surrounding the Black Sea as home. The Agari were experts in antidotes and poisons of all types, and their skills were highly sought after by ancient kings and queens. The Agari were skilled in the use of *viperids*, venom harvested from vipers in the Caucasus Mountains, which they used in tiny amounts to staunch/slow uncontrollable hemorrhage associated with arrow and/or spear wounds[18].

The Pontus region of the Black Sea teems with poisonous flora and fauna. *Pontic honey*, or mad honey, is a wild honey from the Pontus region[19]. Pontic honey is distilled by bees from the nectar of rhododendrons and oleander, two flowering plants that contain deadly neurotoxins for most mammals. *Pontic ducks* have a steady diet of hellebore, belladonna, and other baneful plants, rendering the flesh and blood of the duck poisonous. *Pontic beavers* were highly valued, especially the males. The testicles of the Pontic beavers were valued for treating fever, boosting immunity, improving sexual vigor, and as an aphrodisiac perfume[20]. *Castoreum*, the beaver musk gland of the Pontic beavers, contains high concentrations of salicylic acid (active ingredient in aspirin), which was a result of the copious amount of willow bark consumed by the beavers. Castoreum was used medically to treat anxiety, insomnia, menstrual cramps, and other conditions. Castoreum extract was used as fragrance and perfume, sometimes added to soaps, and used for cleaning the skin.

Figure 2.18   Tattoos on the lower back of Ötzi

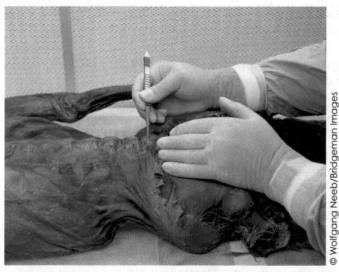

© Wolfgang Neeb/Bridgeman Images

Bridgeman image—Credit line forthcoming from PERMS.

Deep in the Tyrolean Ötztal Alps, on the Italy–Austria border, a revolutionary archaeological discovery was made by a German tourist, Helmut Simon, on September 19, 1991. Ötzi, also called the Iceman or the Tyrolean Iceman, was discovered. Ötzi is a wet mummy, meaning that his tissue, bones, and organs are well preserved, thanks to the glacier ice he was found in. He underwent an extremely rare process of preservation where the humidity was preserved in his cells, unlike the intentional desiccation processes of most embalming or dehydration techniques for preparation of the dead. Ötzi's entire body achieved a state of elasticity and, although it became shrunken, his body remained in the same condition as it was the day he died. This high level of preservation has been giving us valuable insights into his state of health when he was alive. Ötzi is around 5,300 years old. Based on functional osteology studies of his femur, Ötzi's age has been placed between 42 and 45 at the time of death. He was a little over 5′2″ and had a shoe size equivalent to today's 8.5. He weighed ~110 pounds (~50 kilograms) and had very little subcutaneous fat. He had a cut, wiry, sporty figure.

Ötzi was so well preserved that we have been able to clearly see and map 61 tattoos across the surface of his skin[21]. These tattoos were made by fine incisions into the skin, which then had pulverized charcoal rubbed into the wound. In closer inspection of the tattoos, researchers have made some startling discoveries. The locations of Ötzi's tattoos follow acupuncture lines used in traditional Chinese medicine as therapies today. The charcoal and placement of the tattoos are believed to have soothed the pain of arthritis. His tattoos most likely served a very real therapeutic purpose and gave Ötzi some respite from the aches and pains of arthritis.

Additionally, researchers were able to recover Ötzi's clothing and travel kit. He was adorned with a leather belt, loincloth, goat-skin leggings, bear-skin cap, outer cape, leather shoes, and a backpack. Ötzi carried an array of stone arrowheads, arrow shafts, a flint knife, a flint scraper, and a yew wood bow. Ötzi carried a small satchel, in which tree fungus was found[22]. Under closer investigation, it was determined to be an anthelmintic, which he was using to treat his active intestinal hookworm infestation. There were also hop hornbeam flowers in the satchel, which he would have used for the anti-inflammatory and analgesic qualities, most likely to help alleviate pain from his arthritis.

2.3 Neolithic Revolution

There were several unique social and cultural revolutions occurring in the stone age that would alter human history in profound ways. Two of the most prominent were the transition to agriculture and the curation of a vast number of plants as drugs. Drugs would have initially been ingested as part of the food and drink of our ancestors. The effects of these drugs on mood could have been conflated with nutritional benefits. Today, the distinction between drugs and food is drawn along the lines of nutritional value. Foods do affect brain chemistry, and different foods alter it in different ways. Think about how you feel after eating a piece of chocolate or sipping on some coffee or tea. Our brain chemistry can be altered to create cravings for a particular food; in the same way, our brain chemistry can be altered to create cravings for a particular drug, alcohol, or tobacco.

Adult humans today regularly consume psychoactive substances derived from plants domesticated during the Neolithic, including alcohol, caffeine, chocolate, tobacco, and sugars. *Psychoactive substances* influence thought or emotion through biochemical action upon the central nervous system. When exogenously consumed, they are referred to as "drugs." Ancient users may not have perceived "drugs" in the same way that we do today. Ancient consumers most likely saw them as desirable, good-tasting, and good-feeling foods. In addition, ancient people most likely had great respect for the traders or merchants who dealt with psychoactive substances. "Habitual users of psychoactive substances tend to develop a psychological or physical dependency on them, and, in turn on the trader or merchant who provides them"[23].

Psychoactive substances have been found to play a faciliatory role in colonization of conquered lands. They were used to entice people into labor arrangements. They were used as a reward for labor and cultivation outputs. The balance between mood and motivation is a critical component in mass cultivation, and if applied appropriately, psychoactive substances help attain that balance[24]. Psychoactive substances have been widely used in many cultures, and historically, they have been major trade goods. They were typically the most highly valued goods, often gaining religious and social significance.

The historical record is rich with evidence related to psychoactive substances. Cultivation and domestication of these substances served many psychosocial roles in early civilizations. Archaeologic records show that the psychoactive substances in Table 2.2 were cultivated in copious quantities and have been found in Neolithic sites throughout Europe and Asia. Early trade networks between

Table 2.2   Geographic Region and Psychoactive Substance Production

Location	Psychoactive Substance Production
West and East Asia	Alcohol and cannabis
South America	Alcohol, coca, tobacco, and cacao
Europe	Opium and the crop complex from West and East Asia
Africa	Kola

Source: T.D. Church

Asia, Europe, and Africa would have been instrumental in moving psychoactive substances and cultivation techniques across cultures and among civilizations.

Psychoactive substances have the capacity to reduce the subjective stressors of living in groups. These substances tend to make the social constraints of living in close quarters with others bearable, and the individual feels independent while remaining within society. Some have argued that the temporary benefits from periodic use of psychoactive substances include feeling part of a social group, enjoyment, creativity, relief of pain and anxiety, relaxation, control over waking and sleep cycles, and improved concentration and memory. Psychoactive substance use during the Neolithic was not a problem shared by a minority of people, as it is today. Use of these substances was important, and a routine shaper of behavior for the majority of Neolithic and post-Neolithic humans. These substances promoted pro-social behavior and conformity to social constraints, and reduced stress from communal-living, work, and social status. These substances would have been cultivated to promote tolerance of larger, more impersonal social structures, and the behaviors required of individuals living in communal settlements. In terms of future-discounting, psychoactive substances would provide substitutive rewards in the present, which facilitated commitments to work for uncertain future rewards, and they would have been used to elicit appropriate responses during work.

Psychotropic, or psychoactive, chemical substances change brain function and result in alterations in perception, mood, consciousness, cognition, and/or behavior. Psychotropic substances are best known for the changes they bring to consciousness. This use of this class of drug can be traced to human prehistory and beyond. Some researchers have postulated, "the urge to alter one's consciousness is as primary as the drive to satiate thirst, hunger, or sexual desire"[25]. It appears our species' penchant for substances that alter one's state of mind is universal across time, culture, and history.

Psychoactive substances are classified into one of four classes. *Euphoric* substances produce an experience or effect of pleasure or excitement and intense feelings of well-being and happiness. *Stimulant* activates the central nervous system, and produces feelings of alertness and stimulation of the mind. *Sedative* produces calmative, sleep-inducing, and anxiety-reducing sensations with occasional perceptual changes akin to the feeling of lucid dreaming. And the final classification, *hallucinogens* are substances that produce distinct alterations in perception, sensation of space and time, and fluctuations in emotional states.

The use of psychoactive substances has often preceded agriculture and the domestication of plants. In contemporary hunter/gatherer societies, the use of psychoactive substances is widespread, which leads many scholars to believe it would have been similar in Paleolithic societies. These substances would have been used for ritual purposes, such as shamanic trances and vision quests.

Our ancestors most likely cultivated and artificially selected psychoactive substances based on the drugs' effect of being either perception-altering or mood-altering. Table 2.3 lists the main differences between the two effects of psychoactive substances.

Table 2.3 Interactions from Psychoactive Substances

Element	Perception-Altering	Mood-Altering
Anatomy	Stimulates central nervous system	Stimulates brain reward pathway
Effect	Substances cause departure from ordinary reality • Distortions in perception • Alterations in thought • Variations in mood	Highly prized substances due to effects • Amicability • Reduction of stress • Feelings of liberation
Utility	Creates a dreamlike state	Creates a stress-free state
Experience	Shaman or guide to the spirit world required to make the experience good	Shaman or guide to the spirit world not required; self-medication can bring about good experiences

Perception-altering drugs fall into one of three classifications, hallucinogens, entactogens, or entheogens. The perception-altering *hallucinogens* are further divided into psychedelics, dissociatives, and deliriants. *Psychedelics* manifest hidden but real aspects of the mind. A modern example of a psychedelic would be LSD. *Dissociatives* produce feelings of detachment from one's body and produce analgesia, amnesia, and, in rare instances, catalepsy. Ketamine is an example of a dissociative drug. *Deliriants* induce a state of delirium, characterized by extreme confusion and inability to control one's actions. PCP is an example of a deliriant drug. *Entactogens* represent drugs that promote feelings of emotional closeness, with psilocybin mushrooms being a good example of this drug class. *Entheogens* tend to promote mystical experiences. Many entheogens are euphoriant drugs that produce feelings of well-being, and this class of drug tends to have a high affinity for serotonin receptors. Two good examples of entheogens are peyote and ayahuasca.

Mood-altering drugs fall into one of five classifications, namely, stimulants, classical hallucinogens, hypnotics, analgesics, and aphrodisiacs. *Stimulants* produce a euphoric effect and result in increased activity throughout the body. Stimulants give the user a sensation of heightened energy levels and enhanced focus. The most common stimulants today are caffeine and cocaine. *Classical hallucinogens* cause individuals to hallucinate and induce perceptual and cognitive distortions. Classical hallucinogens are similar to psychedelics with our modern example being LSD. *Hypnotics*, or soporifics, tend to induce the feeling of inebriation and are often utilized to induce, extend, or improve the quality of sleep. Hypnotics are related to sedatives; however, sedative drugs serve to calm or relieve anxiety while hypnotic drugs are to induce sleep or anesthesia. Lunesta or Ambien would be examples of modern prescription drugs in the hypnotic class. *Analgesics* are strong pain relievers that could also produce euphoric effects. Opium is the classic example of an analgesic. *Aphrodisiac* represents the class of love drugs and are sought after for their ability to increase one's libido and stimulate sexual desire. Aphrodisiacs can cause psychological effects that increase sexual pleasure experienced with some hallucinogenic drugs, or they can cause physiological effects that alter one's hormone levels or increase blood flow to certain body parts. An aphrodisiac with a long history of use is red ginseng; however, results are not universal. Like many aphrodisiacs, the consistent proof of red ginseng's ability to return on the claim of improved sexual performance eludes scientific inquiry.

2.4 Pharmacosocial Transitions in the Stone Age

The transition from the Paleolithic to the Neolithic witnessed a pharmacological shift in the varieties and amounts of psychoactive substances being consumed. The shamanic perception-altering substances gave way to self-medicated mood-altering substances. These changes impacted the ways these substances were produced. The Neolithic saw increases in the quantity and frequency of consumption as well as increases in the range of individuals using these substances. The production of psychoactive substances represented an additional labor burden. These substances have no nutritional value and would have required subsistence surpluses of food with nutritional value to fuel the labor necessary for their cultivation. It is a zero-sum game in terms of caloric expenditure to farm psychoactive substances.

Perhaps the biggest transition between Paleolithic and Neolithic was the adaptation to social living. There are emotional and psychological elements that needed to be balanced as individuals attempted to make sense of new access patterns to food, increasing security, dominance of a hierarchical system, limited access to mates, and success in competitive interactions. There were many incalculable repercussions to overcome as well. Increasing numbers of people were being sustained by cultivation and animal domestication, creating a self-perpetuating reliance on agriculture. The self-sufficient paradigms of the Paleolithic were replaced by the interdependent and complex paradigms of the Neolithic. With the shift in food acquisition, there was specialization of labor, compartmentalization by class, and the emergence of economic inequality. Power and control of goods become a hereditary right. The Neolithic witnessed the start of written history and the recording of human interactions within new socio-political economies. The political economy focused on accumulation of wealth, hereditary servitude, taxation on labor and production, control through laws and customs, and war for expansion and access to added resources. Religion became more formalized and helped to reinforce the hierarchical system. Humans were in effect civilized through ritual and custom and placated by psychoactive substances to reduce the stress of civilization.

REFERENCES AND FURTHER READINGS

1. Harrold, F. B. (2020). Paleolithic archaeology, ancient behavior, and the transition to modern Homo. In G. Bräuer & F. H. Smith (Eds.), *Continuity or replacement* (pp. 219–230). CRC Press.
2. Goldberg, P., Miller, C. E., & Mentzer, S. M. (2017). Recognizing fire in the Paleolithic archaeological record. *Current Anthropology, 58*(S16), S175–S190.
3. Bergström, A., & Tyler-Smith, C. (2017). Paleolithic networking. *Science, 358*(6363), 586–587.
4. Turner, V. (1977). *The ritual process.* Cornell University Press.
5. Solomon, A. (2019). Bones, pigments, art and symbols: Archaeological evidence for the origins of religion. In J. R. Feierman & L. Oviedo (Eds), *The evolution of religion, religiosity and theology* (pp. 256–270). Routledge.

6. Hardy, K. (2018). Plant use in the Lower and Middle Palaeolithic: Food, medicine and raw materials. *Quaternary Science Reviews, 191,* 393–405.

7. Wooller, M. J., Saulnier-Talbot, E., Potter, B. A., Belmecheri, S., Bigelow, N., Choy, K., Cwynar, L. C., Davies, K., Graham, R. W., Kurek, J., Langdon, P., Medeiros, A., Rawcliffe, R., Wang, Y. & Williams, J. W. (2018). A new terrestrial Palaeoenvironmental record from the Bering Land Bridge and context for human dispersal. *Royal Society Open Science, 5*(6), 180145–180156.

8. McGovern, P. E. (2009). *Uncorking the past* (p. 348). University of California Press.

9. McGovern, P. E. (2013). *Ancient wine* (p. 392), Princeton University Press.

10. McGovern, P. E. (2017). *Ancient brews: Rediscovered and re-created* (p. 336). W. W. Norton & Company.

11. Kohler, T. A., Smith, M. E., Bogaard, A., Feinman, G. M., Peterson, C. E., Betzenhauser, A., Pailes, M., Stone, E. C., Prentiss, A. M., Dennehy, T. J., Ellyson, L. J., Nicholas, L. M., Faulseit, R. K., Styring, A., Whitlam, J., Fochesato, M., Foor, T. A., & Bowles, S. (2017). Greater post-Neolithic wealth disparities in Eurasia than in North America and Mesoamerica. *Nature, 551*(7682), 619–622.

12. Wadley, G., & Hayden, B. Pharmacological influences on the Neolithic transition. *Journal of Ethnobiology, 35*(3), 566–584.

13. Halstead, P. (2004). Farming and feasting in the Neolithic of Greece: The ecological context of fighting with food. *Documenta Praehistorica, 31,* 151–161.

14. Goring-Morris, N., & Horwitz, L. K. (2007). Funerals and feasts during the Pre-Pottery Neolithic B of the Near East. *Antiquity, 81*(314), 902–919.

15. Sample, I. (2019). Earliest known signs of cannabis smoking unearthed in China. *The Guardian.*

16. Raign, K. R. (2021). The art of ancient Mesopotamian technical manuals and letters: The origins of instructional writing. *Technical Communication Quarterly, 31*(1), 1–18.

17. Vukovic, A. A., Bajsman, A., Zukić, S., & Šečić, S. (2009). Cosmetic dentistry in ancient time – short review. *Bulletin of the International Association for Paleodontology, 3*(2), 9–13.

18. Calvete, J. J. (2013). Snake venomics: From the inventory of toxins to biology. *Toxicon, 75,* 44–62.

19. Tatli, O. (2017). The Black Sea's poison; Mad honey. *Journal of Analytical Research in Clinical Medicine, 5*(1), 1–3.

20. Devecka, M. (2013). The traffic in glands. *The Journal of Roman Studies, 103,* 88–95.

21. Deter-Wolf, A., Robitaille, B., Krutak, L., & Galliot, S. (2016). The world's oldest tattoos. *Journal of Archaeological Science: Reports, 5,* 19–24.

22. Dorfer, L., Moser, M., Bahr, F., Spindler, K., Egarter-Vigl, E., Giullén, S., Dohr, G., & Kenner, T. (1999). A medical report from the stone age? *The Lancet, 354*(9183), 1023–1025.

23. Jankowiak, W., & Bradburd, D. (2016). Using drug foods to capture and enhance labor performance: A cross-cultural perspective. In E. D. Whitaker (Ed.), *Health psychology* (pp. 491–494). Routledge.

24. Jankowiak, W. R., & Bradburd, D. (2003). *Drugs, labor, and colonial expansion.* University of Arizona Press.

25. Wadley, G. (2016). How psychoactive drugs shape human culture: A multi-disciplinary perspective. *Brain Research Bulletin, 126*(Pt. 1), 138–151.

Ancient Egypt: Magic and Medicine

I n Western History, classical civilizations are represented traditionally by the cultures of the ancient Mediterranean, in particular the cultures of the Greek and Roman worlds. Scholars focus on the study of literatures, classical languages, art, philosophy, political thought, and histories from the perspective of people living in those civilizations and their impact for later periods. Egypt, due to its long history, is at times referred to as an Ancient Civilization, or as being a civilization of Antiquity. The cultural legacies of Egyptian, Hellenic, and Roman periods had a profound influence on Egyptian history and have imprinted upon the laws, customs, and cultures of modern civilizations[1]. Scientific advancements in architecture, mathematics, and engineering enabled the building of grand monuments and cities. Knowledge of medicinal plants grew and expanded through trade and conquest to build a thriving system of medical arts. As these societies developed, their use of these plants grew and their ability to use some of them with great precision increased. This botanical knowledge did not focus solely on those plants used in healing. There was growing interest in the use of plants for recreationally related activities and there was increasing interest in the creation and refinement of poisons. Minerals and plant products were being employed in a burgeoning cosmetics industry, including a wide range of hair care products and make-up for both sexes. The inventiveness and imagination of these civilizations seemed boundless. Yet as they achieved new levels of knowledge, they would often gain additional levels of depravity. In many cases, they were the architects of their own demise and were often ushering in the collapse of their societies to the raucous sounds of jubilation.

3.1 Ancient Egypt

Ancient Egypt, for the purposes of this book, will be divided into two crucial periods—Dynastic Egypt (~3,100–332 BCE) and Ptolemaic Egypt (~332–32 BCE). Dynastic Egypt, also referred to as Pharaonic Egypt, represents the time when the lands of *Kemet* were mostly unified under a single ruler. Kemet, "black land" in ancient Egyptian, is what they called their land. It occupied a thin stretch of cultivatable land stretching from the Nile delta south along the banks of the great river. The name refers to the rich, dark soil that was deposited in annual floods along the length of the Nile River. This exceptionally fertile soil allowed the Egyptians to cultivate a wide variety of agricultural goods and provided sustenance to the settlements that began to emerge along the Nile River.

Ptolemaic Egypt was a legacy of Alexander III the Great of Macedon. It was a period of Hellenistic and Egyptian synchronism, which saw marked changes being incorporated into Egyptian society and culture. This was an era ruled by an external Macedonian Greek royal dynasty. This was a dynasty that never truly became Egyptian and was a 300-year period dominated by the Ptolemy family. The Ptolemies coexisted as both Egyptian pharaohs and Greek monarchs. For most of the dynasty, the rulers remained completely Greek, both in their language and traditions. Egypt underwent many changes during this period and would witness fundamental changes in art, architecture, religion, and society. Incorporation into the Roman Empire under Gaius Julius Caesar Octavianus (Augustus) would end Ptolemaic control of Egypt and would usher in over 1000 years of foreign rule over the land of Pharaoh.

Figure 3.1 Map of Ancient Egypt

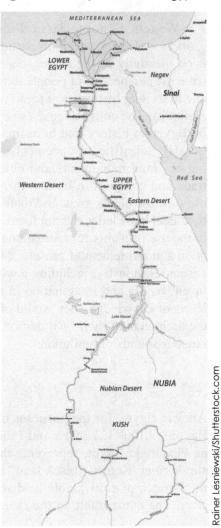

Rainer Lesniewski/Shutterstock.com

3.1.1 Dynastic Egypt

"Concerning Egypt itself I shall extend my remarks to a great length, because there is no country that possesses so many wonders, nor any that has such a number of works which defy description. Not only is the climate different from that of the rest of the world, and the river unlike any other rivers, but the people also, in most of their manners and customs, exactly the reverse the common practice of mankind." Herodotus, *The Histories*[2].

Herodotus, sometimes referred to as the "father of history," described Egypt as being mysterious and a land where everything was vastly different to the rest of the known world at the time. For almost 30 centuries—from its unification in ~3100 BCE to its conquest by Alexander the Great in 332 BCE— Egypt was the preeminent civilization in the Mediterranean world (Figure 3.1). Dynastic Egypt is typically divided into pharaonic dynasties. In ancient Egypt, dynasties were represented by a series of rulers sharing a common origin or lineage. These dynasties are traditionally divided into 32 dynasties, which are commonly grouped by modern Egyptologists into "kingdoms" and "intermediate periods" (Table 3.1). The intermediate periods were often turbulent and comprised periods of foreign invasion and/or civil war.

Table 3.1 Periods of Ancient Egypt

Period Name	BCE
Early Dynastic Period	3100–2686
Old Kingdom	2687–2181
First Intermediate Period	2181–2040
Middle Kingdom	2130–1649
Second Intermediate Period	1725–1550
New Kingdom	1550–1077
Third Intermediate Period	1069–656
Late Period	664–332
Ptolemaic Age	332–30

Source: T. D. Church (table design); Bary J. Kemp (data)[3]

Dynastic Egypt is where many of the classical elements of ancient Egyptian culture were developed, expanded upon, and refined. These elements consisted of language; religion; art, literature, and music; and architecture. The written language of the ancient Egyptians consisted of everyday (or business) writing, *hieratic*, and ceremonial (or sacred) writing, *hieroglyphic*. The religion consisted of ***anthropomorphic*** deities from a pantheon of ~125 documented gods and goddesses. Anthropomorphic refers to a human form combined with non-human qualities. In ancient Egypt, this produced gods and goddesses with the body of a human and the head of an animal as the predominate anthropomorphic form (e.g., Figure 3.2). The ancient Egyptian religion was founded upon the concepts of ***order and chaos*** as the central philosophy. Order and chaos were believed to be in a destructive struggle vying with each other for supremacy. Order was represented by all things good, moral, and attentive to the upholding of justice. Chaos was emboldened by all things bad, immoral, and representative of anarchy. Egypt was renowned in the ancient world for several things. However, it was the numerous and lavish festivals and religious carnivals that were both wonderous and debaucherous. These festivals and carnivals were remarked upon by historians like Herodotus; deplored by satirists like Pliny the Elder; and enamored by geographers like Strabo[2, 4, 5].

The art, literature, and music of ancient Egypt followed rigid codes of meaning, and among the artistic representations and literary works followed an extremely strict

Figure 3.2 Ancient Egyptian Gods, Thoth (L) and Horus (R) baptizing pharaoh with immortality

hemro/Shutterstock.com

set of visual rules (Figure 3.3). The musical ensembles consisted of harps, flutes, and drums. In addition, there were two distinct instruments, the *ney* and the *oud* [3]. The *ney* is an exceptionally long flute, and the *oud* is a pear-shaped stringed instrument both of which produce very unique sounds. The very first graphic novel was produced in ancient Egypt, the highly stylized and religious compendium, the *Book of the Dead*. Other art works include sculpture; murals on the walls of temples, tombs, and buildings; and exquisitely crafted jewelry.

A vast amount of art and architecture in ancient Egypt represents the deeply rooted beliefs in life after death and adoration of their gods[6]. Stone and mud brick dominated Egyptian construction methods, due to the lack of woodlands. Stone was preferred for many of the royal buildings and temples. The architecture that remains displays some of the most impressive and exquisite works known to art history. Walls and columns were often covered in artistic scenes and adorned with hieroglyphics (Figure 3.4). The precision and skill demonstrated in their construction of monumental structures is a testament to the craftsmanship and cultural organization of the ancient Egyptians.

When asked to think of Egypt, most people will picture either the pyramids, sphinx, obelisk, or a similar grand stone monument. These iconic buildings capture our modern imagination equally as they did for the ancient Egyptians (see Figure 3.5). Royal building was demanding work and as recent discoveries in the Giza necropolis have shown, workers were well compensated. *Necropolis* is a large, elaborate series of tomb related monuments, the word translates from the Greek meaning "city of the dead." The Giza necropolis contains the pyramids, sphinx, smaller tombs, mastabas, funerary buildings, shrines, temples, granaries,

Figure 3.3 Ancient Egyptian Musicians from the tomb of Benia

Svetla Ilieva/Shutterstock.com

Figure 3.4 Egyptian Architecture, Hypostyle Hall at the Temple of Karnak

Bist/Shutterstock.com

Figure 3.5 Giza Necropolis

AlexAnton/Shutterstock.com

breweries, and housing for the workers. The myth that royal buildings and mega construction were undertaken solely with slave labor has been countered with evidence obtained from the Giza necropolis that clearly shows the remains of a purpose-built village for the thousands of workers[7]. There are ancient name stamps and seals that provide bureaucratic evidence of logistics on a grand scale, which was required to feed and house the workers. Discarded animal bones in the trash dumps of the necropolis show that the workers were getting the best cuts of meat. The skeletons of some workers found near the necropolis show healed bones, indicating the availability of skilled medical care. Enormous quantities of beer and bread were made in bakeries and breweries within the necropolis. ancient texts indicated a staple diet of bread and beer as being distributed as rations to those working in royal labor projects. Within these texts we find the word **per shana**, roughly translated to "house of the commissariat," indicating a vast food production complex with bakeries, breweries, and granaries for the workers. The beer jars that have been found within the necropolis are all a standard size, and this has allowed archaeologists to calculate payments. From these calculations it is believed that working in the Giza necropolis, the beer ration a worker was allotted was 4–5 liters of beer per day.

Imhotep, whose name translates to "the one who comes in peace," lived during the Old Kingdom, ca. 2667–2648 BCE. He was of high importance within the royal court of Pharaoh Djoser and among many of his titles held the role of chancellor. He was a polymath and has been credited with being the architect of the step pyramid, high priest of Ra at Heliopolis, poet, judge, engineer, magician, scribe, astronomer, astrologer, and physician. He was the first physician in the historical record to have utilized plants for medicine. He has been credited with the diagnosis and medical treatment of over 200 medical issues. Represented within those medical issues were included—15 diseases of the abdomen, 11 of the bladder, 10 of the rectum, 29 of the eyes, and 18 of the skin, hair, nails, and tongue[8]. Today, we consider Imhotep to be the "father of modern medicine." In addition, Imhotep was believed to be a powerful magician. In ancient Egypt, medicine and magic were inseparable and to be a good healer, one had to be a skilled magician.

Magic can be best understood as an action taken to bring about an effect through the use of supernatural forces. For the ancient Egyptians, words and images were intricately linked to magic. Hieroglyphics were words and images. The word or the name of something could conjure up an image. Names of beings, both mortal and divine, were used to gain power over another or to help ward off illness or curses. The *cartouche* which is used to denote the name of pharaohs or deities was a magical act of encircling hierographic characters, done to keep away evil spirits, and used to tie and protect whatever was encircled (Figure 3.6). *Hieroglyph* translates to "sacred writing" and is a form of *logographic* writing[9].

Figure 3.6 Cartouches in the temple of Hatshepsut

D-VISIONS/Shutterstock.com

Logographic refers to a script that uses pictographs to represent words, concepts, and phonemes. ***Hieroglyphic script*** consists of an arrangement of pictures and symbols, some of which had independent meanings, while others were used in combinations (Figure 3.7). Hieroglyphics took quite some time to decode and translate into French, English, or German, which were the predominate languages of the early Egyptologists. Part of the problem was the lack of formal conventions of writing in a consistent and set direction. Hieroglyphics could be written left to right, right to left, top to bottom, or bottom to top. The direction of the text, as we have come to discover, was

Figure 3.7   Hieroglyphic Script In this example, the hieroglyphs would be read from top to bottom, left to right.

Piotr Velixar/Shutterstock.com

indicated by the direction the hieroglyphics were facing, in particular characters that resemble animals or humans. To complicate matters further, hieroglyphic script is devoid of vowels, punctuation, or even spacing between words. The ancient Egyptians believed the hieroglyphic script to be an immensely powerful source of magic. The ancient scribes would occasionally render some "dangerous" hieroglyphs powerless by including cut marks into the characters, for example, cobras would often appear cut in half or thirds. In this way, the ancient scribes were rendering the glyphs powerless, should the hieroglyphics become enchanted and if magically commanded into being the cobra would not be able to harm anyone.

Spells and incantations using both the spoken and written word were used in ritual and everyday life among the ancient Egyptians. ***Spells*** are made up of words, spoken or unspoken, which were considered by the user to invoke a desired magical effect. Spells, at times synonymous with charms, were written on or infused into an object. ***Incantations*** are the use of spells or verbal charms and are spoken to engage a ritual of magic. Incantations can be either written or recited and function as a magical formula of words designed to produce particular effects. Often when examining mummies or burial goods, Egyptologists will find spells or incantations written on small papyri scrolls that would have been worn about the neck as a form of protection for the wearer. The performance of spells, incantations, and other rituals requiring the use of religious and magical paraphernalia, none of them could work without the aid of words[10].

The magical traditions of ancient Egypt were intricately connected to the spoken and written word. The primary rationale behind magic and curses were (and remain today) aimed at punishing or changing behavior, warding off disaster, and controlling the actions of other people[10]. ***Curses***, sometimes referred to as a jinx, hex, or dark spell, can be verbalized, written, or cast through elaborate rituals. The goal of a curse is to see harm or misfortune befall the recipient of the curse. In the ancient Egyptian tradition, curses were powerful phenomenon and would often involve the summoning of the wrath of the gods or the presence of evil forces[11]. Curses were enhanced by invoking a supernatural type of adversary. For example, one could invoke a spirit or the body of a dead person. A well-constructed curse could entice an ancestor who was angry or insulted at having been slighted or ignored to unleash their vengeance upon the mortals who did not honor them. Curses were thought to be a major cause of illnesses and injuries. Egyptologists have found evidence in letters written to the dead, imploring them to cease their curses on the living[12]. Curses, insect infestation, snake bites, and scorpion stings were all common and frequent occurrences in the lives of the ancient Egyptians—all of which could be treated by magicians, physicians, or priests.

There were several magical implements that could be deployed for protection by the ancient Egyptians, consisting of cippi, stela, and amulets. *Cippi* (singular cippus) are small votive statues or shrines, typically found in homes and were believed to confer protection to the members of the household. The cippi provided protection from attack by certain animals, protection against curses, or to confer health and prosperity. *Stela* (plural stelae) are vertical tablets made of slabs of stone or wood and were created in a variety of shapes. Stela usually bear inscriptions, reliefs, or paintings and were used as ritual and commemorative monuments. Stela were most often found in temples or important public places. *Amulets* were personal ornaments inscribed with a magical incantation or symbol to aid the wearer in achieving a goal or protecting them from disease or misfortune[13]. The sheer volume and types of amulets found in the archaeological record have caused Egyptologists to sort them into one of two general categories either as homopoeic or phylactic. *Homopoeic* amulets bear the likeness of living creatures or specific parts of the living creatures that the wearer wanted to assimilate. The image of a crocodile might be considered to protect the wearer from harm when they were near or in the water, for example. A more modern example is the *cornicello*, the horn-shaped charm made of gold, silver, or other material and worn for luck, virility, and strength. Figure 3.8 are homopoeic amulets, called *ushabti*, found in royal tombs and were representations of servants, craftspeople, and artists inscribed with magical spells that the Pharaoh could enact to bring these servants to life and serve in them in their afterlife. *Phylactic* amulets had the power to protect the wearer against disease and would ward away evils causing illness, injury, or harm. Phylactic amulets are defined as being either apotropaic or theomorphic. *Apotropaic* amulets had the power to avert evil influences; to push away the effects of the evil eye. An apotropaic amulet would often be fashioned in the shape of an animal one wished to avoid, like a hippo or cobra. *Theomorphic* amulets took the form or representative symbol of a deity and would be worn to gain the favor or protection from a specific god or goddess. A modern version of a theomorphic amulet would be the wearing of a patron saint's medallion. Many of the statues and amulets would have had an inscription either written in hieroglyphics or hieratic to boost their magical potency.

Figure 3.8 Egyptian Ushabti, a Form of Amulet

One of the more amazing magical texts, which ancient Egyptians used for nearly 1,500 years, was the *Book of the Dead*. Although, that name is a misrepresentation of what the text truly is. It is not a book per se, more of a collection of hymns, magical spells, and instructions for the dead to follow as they "came forth by day" or "emerged forth into the light"[9, 14]. It was, in essence, a collection of resurrection tomes and enchantments. The texts and images of the *Book of the Dead* were

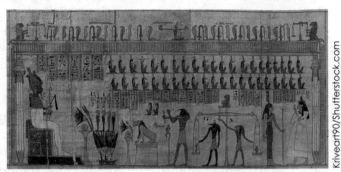

Figure 3.9 Book of the Dead, Amneti, Thoth; Anubis, and Horus Weighing of the Heart

Krivearf90/Shutterstock.com

magical and religious. The text functioned as a bonified walk-through guide that prepared the books owner for all the traps, evils, and misguiding features the soul would encounter as it navigated the underworld. The *Book of the Dead* equipped its owner with the mystical names of the entities they would encounter in the afterlife, giving them power over many of the obstacles they would encounter (Figure 3.9).

The Egyptian afterlife was very much envisioned to be a continuation of one's life on earth. After one had passed through various difficulties and trials, their soul would be judged in the Hall of Truth. Anubis, the jackal headed god of the underworld, would weigh the deceased's soul against a feather[12]. If their soul was lighter than the feather, they would progress to a paradise which was a perfect reflection of their life on Earth. If the soul was heavier than the feather, their soul would face an eternal death as they were devoured by Ammit, the chimeric demon who had the head of a crocodile, the torso of a leopard, and the hindquarters of a hippopotamus[3]. After the successful judgement of the soul, the soul would pass through the Hall of Truth, cross over Lily Lake to rest in the Field of Reeds where one would find all that one had lost in life and could enjoy it for eternity. In order to reach that paradise, however, one needed to know where to go, how to address certain gods, who to offer beer or other drugs to, what to say at certain times, and how to conduct oneself in the land of the dead. While living, Egyptians would spend as much money as they could afford and pay scribes to compose a personalized *Book of the Dead* just for their journey. Many of these scrolls were pro forma and scribes simply had to write in the name and some general details related to the individual. The more one paid, though, the more personalized and ornate their scroll would become.

Religion in ancient Egypt was unique it combined beliefs and practices from medicine, magic, science, psychiatry, spiritualism, mythology, and herbology. At the heart of the religion was Ma'at or the belief in finding harmony in all things and formed the Egyptian concept of cosmic order and balance. The philosophy of ma'at allowed for individuals to rationalize the life events occurring around them and was the cornerstone of their cultural and ethical value systems. The keepers of the balance were the priests and scribes, who could read and write in the language of the gods. A scribe was a position of high importance as they were the ones who could write in both the language of the sacred, hieroglyphics; and the language of commerce, hieratic [9, 15]. The training to become a scribe was exceptionally long and arduous, with children being sent to the temples to learn from an early age and continuing until they became master scribes and/or priests ~12 years after joining. Priests and scribes were the caretakes of the temple complexes. They performed the rituals and observances and they cared for the deities that resided within the temples. In addition, they performed the duties of doctors, healers, astrologers, scientists, psychologists, and dream interpreters for the people.

Egyptian priests were responsible for the healing of the people, and the protection of their mortal souls. They accomplished their tasks through magic and medicine. Through their roles as scribes these priest-healers began documenting diseases, medicines, and treatments. From their work we were given two particularly important aspects that remain used in modern medicine—etiology and diagnosis. *Etiology*, or aetiology, is the study of how a disease or condition is cause; including the various sets of causes or the manner of causation that led from a simple insult to the body to a full-blown disease. The Egyptians had a variety of medicines and cures for both humans and animals, all of which was carefully curated into papyrus scrolls. The earliest account of a medical texts originates from ancient Egypt and two of the most famous papyri are discussed below. *Diagnosis* is the art and science of identifying a disease from its signs and symptoms. ancient Egyptians developed the first documented diagnostic system. Their system consisted of a three-tier mechanism for diagnosis: (1) listen to the patient's complaint, and verify the complaint with your own hands and eyes; (2) reach a diagnosis by employing experience and consulting the medical scrolls; and (3) provide a treatment course, monitor the outcome, and adjust treatment as needed[8, 16]. The ancient Egyptians were tied very closely to religion, and it should come as no surprise that their cures often were performed with spells and magical elements intended to ward off evil spirits and alleviate illness. Often the priest-healers would incorporate the use of *deity interventions*, which encompassed incantations or enhancements to invoke or praise a deity and enlist the power of the gods to aid in healing the ill. There was both a reverence and importance given to names, often just the speaking of the name of a god was enough to harness their power or an aspect of their nature. If the name of a god, a spirit, an ancestor, or dangerous animal was known it was possible for the speaker to gain power over it. In a way, this functioned through the principle of *similia similibus* (like is cured by like). For example, if you had been stung by a scorpion, the priest-healer would draw the hieroglyphic sign for scorpion above the wound, invoke the goddess Serqet (scorpion goddess of protection), and make a small incision to draw the venom out of the injured[17].

Much of the medical knowledge of ancient Egypt was codified in papyri scrolls, only a few of these medical papyri are intact and survive to date. In total there are ~12 complete texts housed in museums and private collections. Two of the most famous and well-studied papyri are the Edwin Smith Papyrus and the Ebers Papyrus. The Edwin Smith papyrus is the oldest surviving surgical document from antiquity and dates to ~1600 BCE[18]. It consists of 48 case histories, and they are arranged according to bodily organ, much like a modern anatomy book. The presented cases are typical and do not represent individual case reviews, which shows a prominent level of study into the diseases covered. This text detailed a very objective examination process which included visual and olfactory clues, palpation of the injured area, and taking of the pulses. After this examination and consultation with the papyrus for similar cases, the physician judges the patient's changes of survival and makes one of three diagnoses: (1) an aliment I can treat; (2) an aliment I can contend with; or (3) an aliment I cannot treat[16]. Among the treatments describe in the papyrus were closing of wounds with sutures (wounds of the lip, throat, and shoulder); proper bandaging; use of splints; prevention and curing of infection with honey; and stopping bleeding with raw meat[19].

The papyrus Ebers is perhaps the most famous plant medicine encyclopedia from the ancient world dating to ~1550 BCE and presenting 700 magical formulas and folk remedies[20, 21]. This papyrus detailed afflictions ranging from crocodile bites to toenail pai. It provided methods to rid the house of pests like flies, rats, and scorpions. It has one of the most accurate descriptions of the circulatory system until more modern times, noting the existence of blood vessels throughout the body and theorized that the heart's function was central to blood supply throughout the body. The Ebers papyrus contained magical spells designed to protect from supernatural intervention in the diagnosis, treatment, and preparation of herbal remedies. The papyrus covered subjects such as dementia, depression, diagnosis of pregnancy, gynecological matters, contraception, dentistry, treatment of burns, removal of tumors, and bone-setting[22].

Among the medical papyri, the dispensing of medicines was carefully stipulated. There are explicit instructions for providing exact dosage. They detailed the manner in which the medicine was to be taken. For internal medications, the instructions listed whether to take with food or wine, and for external applications it detailed how the medicine was to be applied. There was great sophistication shown by several the remedies of the ancient Egyptians. There were some puzzling and counterintuitive beliefs especially relating to poisons. Chief among these beliefs was the reliance upon and use of *hormesis*[17]. Hormesis is a consistent and low-dose delivery of toxins, which was believed to active a protective mechanism. The idea was an individual could build up tolerance to poisons if they were exposed to tiny amounts daily. The minute doses of poisonous substances could be analogous to the concept of a modern-day vaccine. Sadly, it did not always work the way it was intended and death from poisoning in the royal courts was often carried out by one's own hand not some stealthy and hidden assassin. Hormesis was most popular among the royal court and seems to vary in popularity from dynasty to dynasty. Most often it would involve delivery of the drugs within the palace or temple.

Egyptian temple complexes had similar layouts and design elements, with the standard temple design following a tripartite plan. The layout consisted of an outer courtyard, a hypostyle (large columned) hall, and the sanctuary[6]. These elements could be multiplied and could be enclosed by additional rooms, but the base design was consistent. A common addition was an enormous entry gate flanked by two larger pylons that framed the entrance to the courtyard, which gave visitors a grandiose approach as they arrived at the temple complex. Temples were symmetric and were laid out following a single line of approach. Most were constructed facing the Nile with the formal structures running from east to west. Most temples needed their own estate to be successful, where they could grow fruits and vegetables to feed the priests and harvest papyrus to make paper for the scribes. Temples were almost always surrounded by other support facilities. *Sanatoria* was a specialized support building and was the equivalent of a medical (or magical) clinic with some attributes of a modern hospital. The sick and injured would come to seek healing from the gods. People would seek the wisdom of the priests and scholars of the temple for family members who were too sick to make the trip to the temple[23]. *Incubation Chamber* were sleep temples, or better thought of as dream temples, and they functioned as spiritual hospital wards. These dream temples were used for healing a variety of ailments both physically and spiritually affecting the patient. Treatment involved putting the patient into a trance-like-state and encouraging them to sharing the events of their dreams, which priests would interpret to determine the best course of treatment. Meditation, fasting, baths, and sacrifices made to the patron deity or other spirits would have been part of the ritual. *Mammisi* translates to "birth house" and was a structure with considerable religious significance. It was as the name implies associated with births, including the mysterious birth of the gods and celebration of their births.

Celebration and reverence were the main themes to many of the religious ceremonies of the ancient Egyptians. There was no distinction at Egyptian religious festivals between those acts considered *holy* and those which our modern sensibility would label *profane[15]*. One's whole life was open for exploration during Egyptian festivals, including sexual activity; drunkenness; prayer; and blessings for one's sex life, for one's health; and offerings made in gratitude thanksgiving, and supplications. Families would attend the festivals together from teenagers, young couples, and those hoping to find a mate. Elder members of the community, the wealthy, the poor, the ruling class, and the slaves were all part of the religious life of the community. Egyptian religion and the daily lives of the people were complexly interwoven into the tapestry of life with each other.

The beauty of daily life was often shown in detail in tomb murals. In 1964 in Saqqara, Egypt a tomb was discovered and has since baffled Egyptologists who at first believed they had found a tomb of twin brothers (Figure 3.10). The two men, Niankhkhnum and Khnumhotep, were depicted in murals showing the two men holding hands, embracing intimately, and touching noses (ancient Egyptian equivalent to making out)[24]. Inscriptions revealed that both men held the title of Royal Manicurists and Chief or Palace Manicurists. The two men ingenuously had their names decoratively intertwined above the entrance to the inner chamber of the tomb as "Niankh-Khum-Hotep," literally translated to "joined in life and joined in peace (or death)"[25]. In the outer part of the tomb the two men are depicted as sitting, arm in arm, greeting offering-bearers and visitors to their burial place. In other scenes, they are walking together holding hands, touring, and inspecting their tomb. In the inner part is displayed a lavish banquet scene, where the two men are entertained by dancers, and musicians; drinking beer; partaking of what appears to be cannabis from an incense brazier; and being offered blue lotus. There are many scenes of the two embracing, not as family members would, but as lovers did.

Figure 3.10 Niankhkhnum and Khnumhotep Tomb Image

Source: https://www.worldhistory.org/image/14159/mastaba-of-niankhkhnum--khnumhotep/

Ancient Egyptians were not prudish about sex or sexuality. However, it was not socially acceptable to bear children out of wedlock. Throughout human history there have been attempts to control fertility. These attempts have always been depended on social factors and religious beliefs have played a large part in the acceptance or prohibition of contraception[26]. Ancient Egypt venerated fertility and saw birth as a natural and sacred act and in some periods, contraceptives were seen as criminal while in others they were venerated[27]. The first traces of condoms date back to ~1350 BCE. These early condoms were composed of colored linen soaked in olive oil and wrapped in intestinal membranes from sheep[28]. We are not certain on their rate of success, but it was definitely a unique innovation to the aged old problem of premarital sex. Additional contraceptive methods consisted of **birth control cones** and **spermicides**. Birth control cones were made from ground pomegranate, which was mixed with beeswax and shaped into a cone with the intent of vaginal insertion. This may have been moderately effective, as pomegranate contains natural estrogens. Modern birth control utilizes estrogen hormones to inhibit the hypothalamic-pituitary complex and it is believed that these birth control cones may have functioned in a similar manner[29]. Akin to the modern birth control pill, these ancient cones would have been most effective if they were utilized on a regular basis. Spermicides from ancient Egypt, on the other hand, probably did not work as intended. Physicians as early as ~1780 BCE would prescribe an ointment or cream made from crocodile or elephant excrements mixed with honey, dates, or other sticky fruits[30]. These most assuredly produced a myriad of unintended side effects and reactions.

Egyptian males between the ages of 12 and 14 faced their own unique sexual rite of passage. Ritual circumcision among ancient Egyptian males was seen as marking the movement into adulthood (Figure 3.11). There are reliefs depicting male circumcision in tombs around the necropolis of Saqqara dating from ~2400 BCE[31, 32]. This was a ritual practice carried out by priests on pre-adolescent and adolescent males, using a sharp stone and black henbane. **Black henbane**, Hyoscyamus niger, is a poisonous plant from the nightshade family. It is known to have psychoactive properties, which induces visual hallucinations and produces a sensation of flight or of floating. Henbane does have mild to moderate

Figure 3.11   Male Circumcision, Saqqara, Egypt

Source: T. D. Church personal photos 2017

anesthetic qualities and after ingestion is followed simultaneously by peripheral inhibition and stimulation of the central nervous system. Hallucinations, dilated pupils, and restlessness are known side effects from the plant. Low and average doses of henbane can produce inebriation and generalized numbing effects. High doses are lethal. Average doses are associated with some aphrodisiac effects, especially among males who experience priapism. Initial effects last for three to four hours, with aftereffects lasting for up to 72 hours. Black henbane was a medication often employed by physicians and priests of ancient Egypt for minor surgeries and in the care of wounded soldiers.

The dream flower, **blue lotus**, is a flower of immense beauty, intoxicating scent, and inebriating effect. Physically it is a small, round, blue flowering species of lotus that floats in the marshy delta and irrigation canals of Egypt (Figure 3.12). The flowers bloom between 9:30 am and 3:00 pm and reach their potency around the fourth day of their bloom. Blue lotus (Nelumbo nucifera) contains the psychoactive alkaloid aporphine, which is like a weaker version of MDMA[33]. The blue lotus is often depicted in Egyptian art being carved in stone, painted on tombs and temple walls, and named in several papyri. Frequently it is depicted in murals and frescos and is connected with "party scenes" of people dancing or making merry[6]. It had significant spiritual and magical qualities and was utilized in a few religious rites. The effects of blue lotus are varied and appear to be both sedative and stimulating. The sedative aspects are due to the natural anti-anxiety properties of aporphine and could be used for stress relief and insomnia. The stimulating effects induce euphoria, pleasant, warm physical changes and is felt in the upper body. When taken in significant dosage it appears to provide altered perception, cognition, mood, and consciousness.

Blue lotus was seen as the "party drug" of ancient Egypt. There are accounts of the aphrodisiac qualities of the flower, which led no doubt to its use in religiously charged carnal relations. So important was blue lotus that it is cited within the *Book of the Dead* in a few areas. Religiously, blue lotus would most likely have been used in the incubation chambers to induce prophetic dream states. The impact of the vividness of dreams and potential dream recall would have been valuable to the priests interpreting the dreams. Some of the accounts from ancient sources indicate that the dreamlike sensation produced by the plant while awake continued into sleep itself and most likely provided dreams that were more colorful and lifelike. Blue lotus was such a valuable plant to the ancient Egyptian that they developed several industries related to its preparation and use (Table 3.2).

Figure 3.12 Egyptian Blue Lotus

Little daisy/Shutterstock.com

3.1.2 Ptolemaic Egypt

Our story of Ptolemaic Egypt begins with Alexander the Great of Macedon. Alexander was perhaps the greatest military genus produced by the ancient world. He was the warrior-king Alexander III of Macedon (356–323 BCE), known to us today as Alexander the Great. He conquered lands that stretched from Greece to Egypt, through present-day Turkey, Iran, and Pakistan (Figure 3.13). Alexander combined his battlefield successes with a unique kingdom-building strategy. Alexander spent his 13-year reign working to unite East and West through military might and cultural exchange. His reputation grew so quickly that by the time of his death at age 32 he was seen by some as having godlike attributes. In 15 years of conquest, Alexander never lost a single battle. He founded nearly 70 cities across his vast empire, 20 carried the name Alexandria and 1 Bucephala (the name of his favorite war horse). Alexander was known to enjoy a good party. He used drinking and feasting as a

Table 3.2 Preparations of Blue Lotus

Cold Press Extraction

- The petals of the blue lotus were pressed using heavy weights and mixed with cold water; the oils float above the water and were separated out as essential oils

Essential Oils

- Highly aromatic and concentrated plant extracts that have not only the characteristic scent of the plant, but contain many of the properties used for medicinal or recreational applications

Perfumery

- Making of a perfume from the essential oils extracted from the blue lotus

Blue Lotus Resin

- Resin is a dense waxy-like substance made by compressing sticky flowers at the peak of their flowering cycle

Blue Lotus Wine

- Blue lotus flowers and buds steeped in wine to infuse the wine
- As the flowers tend to have a bitter taste, sweet wine or wine mixed with honey would have been used

Blue Lotus Tea

- Boiling water is poured over the sticky flowers and allowed to steep

Source: T. D. Church

way of building comradery among his men (Figure 3.14). In one account of his revelry we are told he once held a drinking contest with his soldiers and when all was said and done, Alexander was standing and 42 of his soldiers had died from alcohol poisoning[34].

Alexander had conquered Egypt in 332 BCE and established himself as Pharoah. He named his close friend and general, Ptolemy as Satrap of Egypt. *Satrap* was a title taken from the Persian Empire and was equivalent to a regional governor. Satraps often times held exceptional amounts of power and privilege, as they acted on the behalf of the king or emperor within their appointed area. In prior dynasties, Satraps would make claims to the throne when the king had died unexpectedly without appointment of an heir.

Figure 3.13 Map of Alexander's Empire

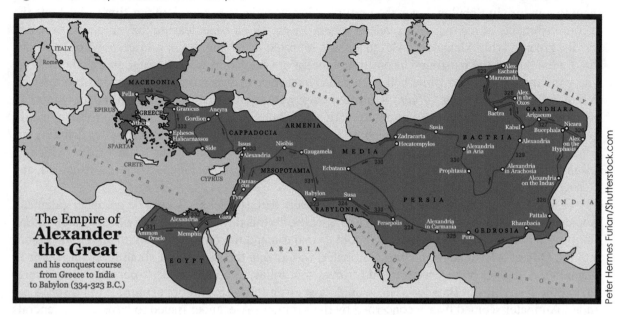

The Empire of
**Alexander
the Great**
and his conquest course
from Greece to India
to Babylon (334-323 B.C.)

Peter Hermes Furian/Shutterstock.com

Alexander had many wives, but according to contemporary writers his true loves were his horse and his best friend Hephaestion. Sadly, after a raucous night of drinking in Babylon, Hephaestion fell ill and died in 324 BCE. Plutarch commented that "Alexander's grief was uncontrollable . . . [35]" and added that he ordered many signs of mourning, notably that the manes and tails of all horses should be shorn, the demolition of the battlements of the neighboring cities, and the banning of flutes and every other kind of music during the period of mourning. These gestures did not go unnoticed by the cynic philosophers of Athens who commented publicly that

Figure 3.14 Alexander and Bucephalus, Sarcophagus, Istanbul, Turkey

Gokhan Dogan/Shutterstock.com

"Alexander was only defeated once, and that was by Hephaestion's thighs"[36].

The events surrounding Alexander's death are suspicious, to say the least. There are some peculiar details leading up to the days before his death that have been attributed by scholars both modern and contemporary to either a claim of murder or an allegation of infectious disease. For the first time since leaving Macedonia, Alexander's generals refused to follow him into conquest. In the spring of 326 BCE, his army refused to cross the Indus River[37]. The generals insisted that the men longed to be back in Macedonia with their families. After much debate, Alexander relented, and the army began the march back to Babylon. Alexander sent messengers to all his generals and satraps, calling them to join him in Babylon. Upon their return, Alexander decreed a week of feasting to celebrate the accomplishments of his men. Alexander's generals were all on edge, fearing they might be executed for disagreeing with Alexander. Alexander was reported as having drank a large bowl of unconstituted wine during the feasting. Unconstituted meant not diluted by adding water as was the custom. The wine most likely had white hellebore added as a spice as was customary in wine from this era. White hellebore (*Veratrum album*) was often employed as an herbal treatment to induce vomiting; but in small doses it functioned as an aromatic and would have added hints of spice to the wine. In the unconstituted wine, the white hellebore would have been very potent. Shortly after drinking his wine, Alexander was reported to have convulsed. He suffered an agonizing 10 days, after which he fell into a coma. Two days after entering the coma Alexander eventual died. No heir was named, and no successor appointed prior to Alexander's death.

To say that events surrounding Alexander's death were suspicious, would be an understatement. Ancient sources leave us with some conflicting clues. To this day scholars are divided with one camp claiming the death was due to either typhoid or malaria and the other camp adamant it was poisoning[38]. One of Alexander's generals, Antipater, was among the most vocal about returning home to Macedon. Antipater had even arranged for own son, Iollas, to be Alexander's personal wine-bearer during the festivities in Babylon. This would have given Iollas several opportunities to poison Alexander. Antipater seemed overly concerned by the summons Alexander issued to have all his generals meet in Babylon. This type of summons was not something Alexander had never done before. The gesture put many of Alexander's men on edge and a conspiracy to poison Alexander could have been orchestrated. Antipater may have tasked his son with the dangerous and deadly job of poisoning their King and comrade. Contemporary sources further indicate that Alexander had pain in his abdomen and would periodically cry out[39, 40]. These symptoms mimic someone who had been poisoned.

Other historians and scholars have claimed Alexander to have died from typhoid fever or malaria. The accounts we have of Alexander's death indicated some of his initial symptoms were chills, sweats, exhaustion, and a very high fever[41]. These symptoms are akin to the onset of many infectious diseases, including typhoid fever. Between the fifth and fourth day before his death, Alexander was reported to have gone mute. This could be a symptom of both typhoid fever and some poisons. We may never know the cause for Alexander's death for certain. What we do know is that in June 323 BCE Alexander died, and the world he had crafted would never be the same again.

Alexander's body did not begin to show signs of desiccation or decomposition until the 6th day after his death. After a lavish state funeral, Alexander's body was reportedly placed into a coffin filled with honey to preserve his body for the trip back to Macedonia[37]. As the funerary caravan set out, it was allegedly interdicted by Ptolemy I and Alexander's body was stolen away to Egypt. By securing Alexander's body, Ptolemy aimed to be seen as the one true heir of Alexander's empire. Without an heir to his vast empire, Alexander's legacy was quickly shattered into smaller territories held by his appointed satraps and generals, the ***diadochi***[42]. Diadochi translates to "the inheritors" or a better translation might be the "successors." The diadochi of Alexander were once friends and family members bound together through blood and triumph. But these brothers-in-arms would become bitter rivals who fought for control of Alexander's crumbling empire after his death in 323 BCE. As the dust settled, there appeared 8 contenders, the true diadochi who carved up and fought armed disputes with one another to fulfill their own visions of what Alexander's legacy should be. The diadochi are listed in Table 3.3.

Table 3.3 Diadoachi of Alexander's Empire

Antigonus*	Satrap of Lycia and Phrygia

• Commander of the allied Greek infantry of Alexander's army

Antipater	Satrap of Macedonia and Greece

• 320 BCE he became regent of Alexander's Empire, but died in 319 BCE
• Named one of the officers in his army as successor, instead of his own son Cassander

Cassander*	Satrap of Macedonia and Greece

• A son of Antipater

Craterus	Guardian of the Royal Family

• Infantry and Naval Commander of Alexander
• Ordered to command the veterans as they returned home to Macedonia

Lysimachus	Satrap of Thrace and Dacia

• Thessalian officer and General in Alexander's Army

Perdiccas*	Regent of the Empire; Guardian of the Royal Family

• General of the Macedonian Phalanx (heavy infantry) and commander of the calvary

Ptolemy*	Satrap of Egypt

• One of Alexander's most trusted generals, confidants, and friend

Seleucis*	Satrap of Asia Minor, Syria, and Mesopotamia

• General of Alexander's Hoplite Infantry

Source: T. D. Church

After many years of brutal battle, three of the 8 diadochi were dead and the lands of Alexander's Empire were once again redistributed and carved up. The once grand empire of Alexander had been relegated to 5 smaller, fractioned kingdoms that would be prone to fighting with one another for hundreds of years following Alexander's death. The remaining five individuals are denoted in Table 3.3 with an asterisk (*) after their name. Among the five, there were three of Alexander's somatophylakes, elite and appointed bodyguards personally selected from Macedonian nobility. The remaining somatophylakes were Lysimachus, Perdiccas, and Ptolemy.

After Alexander's death, Ptolemy took the name Soter (Greek for "savior") and became the sovereign ruler of Egypt from 323 to 283 BCE[43]. Ptolemy I: Soter began a Hellenistic dynasty which would rule Egypt for a little over three centuries. He made the sleepy little port city of Alexandria his capital and began a series of grand constructions to create one of the ancient world's most magnificent cities. Ptolemy assimilated some aspects of Egyptian culture into court but maintained many of his native Greek and Macedonian traditions. He assumed the title of Pharoah in 305 BCE in a ceremony full of pomp and extravagance[44]. The title of Pharaoh seems to be a situational title in the court of Ptolemy I, being used among Egyptian audiences. He, predominantly, and much to the chagrin of his contemporary Greeks, used the title Basileus, Greek for "monarch," "king,", or "emperor." There exists some controversy related to Ptolemy's family lineage. Historically, there was a propaganda campaign made by Ptolemy to show his birthright to Alexander's kingdom. Some scholars believe Ptolemy to be an illegitimate son of Philip II of Macedon. If this is true, it would make Ptolemy a half-brother of Alexander and would have legitimatized his claim to Alexander's throne. The two had been intimate friends since childhood, with Ptolemy being only a few years older than Alexander.

Ptolemy would become the name taken by every male ruler of the dynasty. Ptolemaic queens, some of whom were the sisters of their husbands, took either the name of Cleopatra, Arsinoe, or Berenice (Figure 3.15). By far the most infamous Ptolemaic ruler of the line was Egypt's very last queen, Cleopatra VII Philopater, whom in modern times we refer to simply as Cleopatra (69–30 BCE). Cleopatra was a diplomat, naval commander, linguist, poet, perfumer, and medical author. Of all the prior 13 Ptolemaic rulers, she was the first to learn to read, write, and speak the Egyptian language. She is recorded as being fluent in over 9 languages[1]. Cassius Dio, in describing Cleopatra said, "for she was a woman of surpassing beauty, and at that time, when she was in the prime of her youth, she was most striking. She also possessed a most charming voice and a knowledge of how to make herself agreeable to everyone"[45]. Today, Cleopatra is best known for her role in two prominent Roman political battles. First, she was preeminent in the conflict between Gnaeus Pompeius Magnus (Pompey) and Gaius Julius Caesar (Caesar). After Caesar's death, she was central to the civil war between Gaius Julius Caesar Octavianus (Augustus) and Marcus Antonius (Marc

Figure 3.15   Cleopatra, Egyptian Museum, Cairo

Source: T. D. Church, image taken 15 March 2012; Cairo, Egypt

Antony). Her romanticized, thanks in large part to Shakespeare, suicide by cobra bite presents a noble end to an enigmatic ruler but is perhaps one of the tallest tales ever told, as we will discuss a little later. Cleopatra's death, however, did mark the end of Ptolemaic rule in Egypt and heralded the conquest by Rome. The historical record related to Cleopatra is biased as many of the Roman commentators viewed her as the downfall of two noble roman houses and as a result her treatment has not been the best nor most accurate portrayal of her life.

There are only fragments of the medical and cosmetic writings of Cleopatra's, *Gynaeiciarum Libri[46]*. What remains contains remedies for hair disease, baldness, and dandruff. In another text, which scholars cannot say for certain was written by Cleopatra titled *Cosmetics*, we have instructions for dying and curling hair for a variety of festivals and ceremonial occasions[47]. She proposed a standard list of weights and measurements to be used for pharmacological purposes in an attempt to standardize treatments. A recipe for perfumed soap created by Cleopatra is still in use today by perfume makers in Cairo[48]. There are exaggerated claims of existing instructions for an aphrodisiac perfume with the intent of heightening and intensifying sexual encounters, which has been attributed to Cleopatra but never verified.

The art and science of scent was very important in ancient Egyptian culture, and they valued perfumes and cosmetics highly. By the time of Cleopatra, Egypt had many centuries of perfecting and honing their skills in aromatherapy. ***Aromatherapy*** is the practice of using the natural oils extracted from the roots, stems, bark, leaves, and/or flowers of plants to produce scented oils. These oils would be used to enhance psychological, emotional, and physical well-being. It is not clear who initially developed the techniques to extract the essence of flowers, both Mesopotamia and Egypt excelled in the science of aromatherapy and perfume making[49]. Among the Egyptians, body care and beauty started with cleanliness. Unpleasant smells were a sign of poor health and an impure spirit, whereas pleasant smells revealed the presence of the divine and sacred. Men and women of all classes in ancient Egypt, applied oils to their bodies daily as a mechanism of skin hydration and protection from the hot and arid conditions[3]. Egyptians of all classes were known to bath daily and used perfumes and aromatic oils to improve their scents.

Under the Ptolemies, learning flourished and formed what scholars have named the ***Graeco-Egyptian Syncretism***. This syncretism was a blending of Greek and Egyptian cultures that brought about a renaissance of architecture and art. The Temple of Hathor in Dendera represents the culmination of the arts and the merging of the two cultures (Figure 3.16). The syncretism extended to medicine and pharmacy as well. During the Ptolemaic dynasty, the Greek and Egyptian pharmacopeias were cross-referenced and merged. It is estimated that the Greeks had ~201 unique drugs, while the Egyptians had ~141. Medical knowledge of the Egyptians

Figure 3.16 Temple of Hathor, Dendera

Abrilla/Shutterstock.com

with their intimate knowledge of anatomy and physiology were transferred to Greece. Through trade with foreign nations, the Egyptians were able to incorporate new herbs and plants into their medical practice. While earlier ancient Egyptian remedies consisted of a limited number of cultivated herbs and plants; the Ptolemies pushed the limits of the plant-based knowledge to exceptional heights. Together their combined drug knowledge grew and was applied to new ailments and conditions in unique and unprecedented ways[33]. There was an increase in specialized medical devices, including refined surgical equipment. New specialist professions within medicine flourished, two of the most prominent being dentistry and gynecology. Dentistry became a prominent fixture in the court of Ptolemaic rulers[16]. Gynecology and prenatal care became standard throughout the kingdom, and access was free to women throughout the lands of Egypt.

The Ptolemies developed an amazing new festival to be held every 4 years, the ***Ptolemaieia***. Among the Greeks the Ptolemaieia equaled the Olympic games in size and stature and for the Egyptians it helped to reinforce the power and prestige of the Ptolemaic Royal Dynasty. No expense was spared, and it was expected that everyone would participate in the revelry. The Ptolemaieia included Bacchanalian feasts with copious amounts of drinking, gambling, sex, and all other forms of debauchery[15]. There were parades featuring highly detailed and imaginatively constructed floats, depicting scenes from Greek and Egyptian mythologies.

Alexandria, the jewel of the Ptolemaic dynasty, became a great center of science, medicine, and learning. It housed the Great Library of Alexandria and was to become legendary for the vast wealth of knowledge it reportedly stored and the wisdom it generated. The library was begun by Alexander the Great, who wanted a repository for all the knowledge of Egypt. This project was continued by the Ptolemies, who transformed Alexandria into the leading cultural center of the Mediterranean. It is estimated that at its height the library contained ~400,000 scrolls. Some have commented on the drive of the Ptolemies to collect and curate all the books of all of the peoples of the world likening it to a familial addiction without satiation[50]. In acquiring this vast repository of knowledge, the Ptolemies purchased some of the scrolls, had others gifted, and instituted a policy of having every ship that came into the harbor searched for writings. They would confiscate the writing, take it to the Great Library where scribes would copy the writings verbatim, and then the copy would be returned to the ship of origin.

The tone of the scientific and medical knowledge produced a nascent research paradigm that would influence scientific theory for generations. This paradigm featured a very progressive and open-minded line of inquiry that would become known as the ***empirical method***. The empirical method was a philosophy, which held at its core that everything was open to questioning and investigation. Statements like "it was the will of the gods" were no longer rationale to explain why a phenomenon occurred. Reason and observation became standard tools of inquiry. An empirical school of medicine was founded in 330 BCE in Alexandria that attracted many of the ancient world's best physicians and medical scholars[51]. This medical school became instrumental in the transmission of Greek and Egyptian medicine and after the Roman conquest of Egypt would continue by transmitting Greek, Egyptian, and Roman medicine.

Greek, and eventually Roman, physicians came to Egypt to learn about anatomy and physiology. The practice of dissection was forbidden in Greece and frowned up by the Romans. Egyptian knowledge of human anatomy and physiology was derived from the centuries old practice of embalming the dead through mumification[3]. As they prepared a body for mumification, it gave the Egyptians opportunity to study the structures and organs of the body. ***Mummification*** in Egypt was a process that took 70 days to treat, clean, and expertly wrap the body for burial. The first step of mummification was to remove all internal parts that might decay or putrefy rapidly. The brain, which the Egyptians did not consider to be of importance, was removed by carefully inserting special hooked instruments through the nostrils to pull out the bits. All internal organs, save the heart, would be removed through a small incision made on the left side of the abdomen. The organs would be washed and then dipped into natron before being placed into separate canopic jars (Figure 3.17). The embalmers removed all moisture from the body by covering it with natron and keeping it covered by the salt for 50–60 days. Finally, the body would be washed and anointed with essential oils prior to being wrapped with strips of linen soaked in resin. Great care was taken to preserve the body for the afterlife.

From our modern perspective, we might be inclined to think of the Egyptian pharmacopoeia as being weak. The majority of their treatment was aimed at expressed symptoms, and they employed magic and invocation of deities to assist in the curing of disease. But their medical practices were far more sophisticated than we originally believed. Close attention was given to diet and exercise. In fact, many Egyptians practiced "Het Heru" or **Kemetic Yoga**, with some of the earliest

Figure 3.17 Tutankhamun's Canopic Jars, Cairo Museum

ever recorded yoga poses and postures recorded in hieroglyphs on temple walls. Another daily practice for young men and young women focused around **Tahtib,** an Egyptian martial art with a focus on the use of a stick as the primary weapon of choice[52]. In addition to diet and exercise, the Egyptians drew their drugs from a wide array of animal, mineral, and vegetable substances.

Ptolemaic medicine incorporated a standardized method for **vehicle** and **dosage** of all medicines, which made it easy for physicians in different parts of the kingdom to make and prescribe the exact same medications[17]. **Vehicle** refers to a carrier or some inert liquid medium, often used as a solvent (or diluent) that allowed for a medicinally active agent to be formulated and/or administered. Common vehicles from Ptolemaic medicine included water, honey, milk, oil, wine, and beer. It was not uncommon for two or more vehicles to be utilized, depending upon the medication being administered. **Dosage**, or the specific amount of weight of a medicine to be taken at a given time, was done by volume in the Ptolemaic period. Today, we utilize weight as the base measure for our medicines. Volume did vary to some degree and depending upon the author or classification scheme of the time the measurements might not be consistent. There are some volume notations that we are not sure of due to our inability to full appreciate the translations.

There were a number of drugs drawn from animal sources[51]. Honey was one of the most widely used drugs in the ancient world and was used for its antibacterial and antifungal properties. Milk was often used as a drug vehicle and came from cows and goats. Excrement from cats, donkeys, birds, lizards, crocodiles, flies, and people had a large range of uses, mostly external applications—which does not make it sound any better. Blood from a wide range of animals both hot (fresh) and cold (not so fresh) were utilized. Urine was used as a vehicle for external application of medications and frequently employed in enemas. Placenta was used for cosmetic purposes as it prevented the greying of hair. Meat would be applied to bruises and external wounds, a practice utilized by boxers in modern times. Liver from several animals was used and held the most utility from a pharmacological perspective. Liver contains ~85% of the body's store of B12 and A vitamins and is an effective way to replenish these vitamins. Testicles, brains, and hearts of varied species were also used to make medicines.

The Egyptians held special reverence for the venom obtained from a blistering beetle (Figure 3.18), because of its aphrodisiac qualities. Colloquially, we refer to this venom as *Spanish fly*. Depending upon the dose consumed, however, symptoms could vary widely. At low doses, the consumer would feel irritation and pain in their bladder and urethra. Moderate doses caused *priapism*, an erection that lasts longer than 4 hours without sexual stimulation. High doses cause abdominal pain, vomiting, diarrhea, and shock with death occurring in rare cases due to renal or multi-organ failure. It was the moderate dose of this "love drug" from the "love bug" that the venom was widely, albeit ineffectually, used as an aphrodisiac.

Figure 3.18 Blistering Beetle, the Egyptian "Love Bug"

kurt_G/Shutterstock.com

Egyptians had a particular fondness for a wide variety of minerals and stones[22]. They used many of them for cosmetic applications and medication. The most popular mineral was *natron*, a very strongly osmotic mineral. Natron is a natural soda ash salt and held the ability to draw out fluid and reduce swelling in living tissue and could dry out a corpse in preparation for embalming. Common salt was often mixed into warm water and utilized as a mild emetic to induce vomiting. Malachite was pulverized and ground into a powder and mixed with oils to create green eye paint. It had antibacterial properties and unknowingly was used to treat ophthalmic conditions like pink eye. Lapis lazuli was also used as eye paint and to treat ophthalmic conditions. Lapis was a very precious commodity, which raised the expectation of a cure when it was utilized. We know today that lapis is insoluble in human body fluids and as a result held no real therapeutic potential. Pyrolusite, or manganese oxide, was used to create a very lustrous and iridescent deep grey eye paint, and potentially was beneficial in treating ocular degeneration.

Ancient Egyptians excelled in the art and science of cosmetics, especially cosmetics applied to the eye. *Kohl*, an ancient eye cosmetic, was made by crushing and combining stibnite, lead, and oil[53]. The mixture was used as eyeliner to contour and / or darken the eyelids in a manner similar to modern mascara or harquus. *Harquus* or tishraat can be made from henna, but more frequently are permanent tattoos worn by Berber women in North Africa, predominately in Morocco, Algeria, Tunisia, and Egypt. Harquus is represented by a series of geometric and spiral shaped patterns drawn onto the face, neck, back of hands, and tops of feet. Kohl was applied with a small stick or reed, tracing lines around the upper and lower lids. These lines were at times extended into intricate shapes around the face. Kohl was worn by men and women of all ages in ancient Egypt and the practice was adopted by the Ptolemies as well. Kohl, as we were to discover recently, was more than simple cosmetics as it functioned as an ancient form of sun protection. Modern athletes who play sports outdoors often apply a black strip of beeswax, paraffin, and carbon under their eyes to reduce any glare from the sun.

The use of plants and herbs throughout ancient Egyptian history was extensive. Today, we have only fully appreciated a fraction of the plants and herbs the Egyptians used[33]. Part of our issue is the difficulty recognizing the plants being discussed and then assessing their therapeutic potential. Sometimes the disease being discussed in the hieroglyphics has no equivalent English translation. In three thousand years from now, an archaeologist might find reference to a strange flowering plant referred to only as a snapdragon (Figure 3.19). They would be able to translate "snap" and "dragon," but what plant might that be if there are no other references available? How many of us use the formal taxa of Antirrhinum majus when we talk about or write about snap-dragons? This is the exact problem we face with attempting to understand some ancient

Figure 3.19   Antirrhinum majus, Snapdragon

Fabrizio Guarisco/Shutterstock.com

Egyptian descriptions of plants, herbs, and even diseases. It is vital to know which part of the plant was being utilized, when it was harvested, and how it was prepared. Even if we know the species, the pharmacological properties and effects may not be known or fully explained. ***Narcotics***, while not always mentioned for their pain-relieving properties, were often used for religious and recreational purposes, including *Papaver somniferum* (Poppy), *Cannabis sativa* (Sativa), *Mandragora officinalis* (Mandrake), and *Nymphaea crulea* (Blue lily).

Alexandria, akin to most port cities in the ancient world, had areas frequented by the sellers of both euphoric and poisonous drugs[15]. These drugs would have been sold through third party distribution. An eclectic group of individuals would have frequented these areas of the city in search of drugs. Physicians in search of potential remedies, motley crowds in search of pleasure, and nefarious individuals pursuing for a deadly poison. Drugs would have been available in a variety of forms, raw plants, ointments, perfume, and/or spices. The Egyptian drug trade under Ptolemaic rule was very lucrative and the trade networks were extensive extending Egyptian contact with the Far East, Arabia, Northern Africa, Greece, Spain, and Italy. ***Apothecae***, literal translation of "storeroom" in Greek, was the place where imported and exported drug products were stored. The person responsible for distributing the drugs, ***apothecaries***, "store man" in Greek, would provide lists each day of the products they had for sale based on their inventory.

Ptolemaic Egypt ended with the reign of Cleopatra. Upon conquering Marcus Antonius (Antony) in the Battle of Actium and routing Cleopatra's army in the Battle of Alexandria, Gaius Julius Caesar Octavianus (Augustus) was keen on taking Cleopatra with him back to Rome as the centerpiece of his Triumph. ***Roman triumph*** was a civil ceremony and religious rite held as a way to publicly celebrate and consecrate the military success of a great general[54]. These events were typically granted to commanders who had led Roman forces to victory in the service of the Senate and People of Rome. It was as Rome's chief citizen that the commander triumphed on the behest of the people of Rome, for the honor of the Senate, and the glory of the gods. Triumphs were lavish and ornate displays composed of a celebration of the victor, a grand promenade and victory procession, and a public recitation of achievement. There would be feasting along with a few days of public games held to honor the commander and his gallant efforts. The victory procession was a spectacle to be witnessed as the victor paraded all of the exotic spoils of war, beasts native to the region conquered, floats reenacting key moments of the conquest, and it would culminate at the Temple of Jupiter Optimus Maximus where the captured leaders of the enemy would be ritually killed to the delight of the Roman onlookers[55]. Cleopatra, though, would not be Rome's Triumph as she died in her palace in Alexandria while in the custody of Augustus.

The death of Cleopatra is still very much shrouded in mystery and has become a romanticized tale of despair and pure honor. Cleopatra and two of her handmaidens, Iras and Charmion, were found dead in the morning of 12 August 30 BCE by Augustus. Cleopatra had been sequestered to her chambers in the royal palace under Roman guard while awaiting transport to Rome (Figure 3.20). Somehow, though, Cleopatra had somehow managed to take her own life and disgrace Augustus' attempts to make her the jewel of his grand Triumph. Classically we have been told that Cleopatra died through envenomation (snake bite), but as the evidence will show it was most likely empoisonation (poisoning)[56].

Figure 3.20　Bust of Cleopatra VII Philopater; Berlin, Germany

Envenomation is the process where venom is delivered through fang or stinger of a venomous animal. In Egypt there are a few poisonous snakes, but the two most likely candidates would be the Egyptian cobra and the Egyptian viper. Their venom is extremely hemotoxic and causes subcutaneous hemorrhage where the bite occurs. The individual who has been bitten faces a very brutal death resulting from intestinal hemorrhage, decreased blood pressure, and blood clotting. The venom of the cobra will reach the heart within 2–4 hours, while the venom of the viper takes between 6 and 12 hours[57]. To kill all three—Cleopatra, Iras, and Charmion—the snakes would have needed to be huge with an average length of 3–4 m (9.8–13 ft) and weight of 6 kg (13 lbs)[57]. Snakes of this size would have been difficult to hide in basket of figs, as we are told occurred in romantic retellings of Cleopatra's death. The other problem is only 22–30% of snakebite victims die after cobra or viper envenomation. The odds that a snake large enough and that had potent enough venom could kill three adults is a bit far-fetched. Surely the men standing guard outside of the Queen's bedchambers would have heard screams, moans of agony, and thrashing about as the three women writhed in agony.

Empoisonation is the process by which poison is administered either by oneself or others. We can discount Cleopatra being poisoned by any of her Roman enemies, as they definitely wanted to see her taken to Rome for Triumph. In the same vein, we can discount her being poisoned by Egyptians. Cleopatra had removed any rival to her authority from the royal court and by all accounts from contemporary scholars the people of Egypt loved her deeply. We need to bear in mind that Cleopatra would have had a deep understanding of poisons[56]. She herself was a skilled perfumer and herbalist. She possessed a personal apothecary full of potions, poisons, and potential antidotes. Cleopatra would have been able to make a poison to end her own life. From the accounts of ancient sources, neither Cleopatra nor her handmaidens showed any signs of swelling or bruising from a snake bite. Nor reports of screams or struggling were recorded in the accounts from the guards standing watch over the Queen's apartment.

The Ptolemies ushered in many great advances for Egypt in the development of science, medicine, and art. The Ptolemies exported Egyptian physicians and drugs to far away kingdoms, greatly expanding the prestige of Egyptian doctors. Sadly, the Ptolemies were the cause of Egypt's downfall and the subjugation to the Roman Empire. After Cleopatra's death the culture of Egypt would be fundamentally changed as successive waves of foreign influences dominated the land of the Pharoah's from Roman to Christian to Islam. The vast and wonderous knowledge of the ancient scholars once housed in the Great Library of Alexandria was lost to the sands of time as the library dwindled in importance and religious zealotism saw the desecration of the great works it housed. Egypt would forever be exploited, lost to mythology, and rediscovered in the Age of Enlightenment. During the 1800–1900s an exploitative set of military campaigns, armchair archaeologists, and travelers took so many cultural and historical treasures from Egypt leading to what scholars call the Rape of the Nile. Sadly, to this day we do not fully understand nor appreciate the intricacies of the grand and mighty culture of the ancient Egyptians.

REFERENCES

1. Plutarch, L. M. (1914 [48 CE]). In L. C. Library (Ed.), *Plutarch's Lives: The Lives of the Noble Grecians and Romans* (p. 802). W. Heinemann.
2. Herodotus. (1996 [440 BCE]). *The histories* (p. 771). Penguin Classics.
3. Kemp, B. J. (2018). *Ancient Egypt: Anatomy of a civilization* (3rd ed., p. 414). Routledge.
4. Strabo. (1917 [17 CE]). In Loeb Classical Library, H. L. Jones & J. R. S. Sterrett (Eds.), *Geographica, I: Libri I, II* (Vol. 1, p. 575). Harvard University Press.
5. Pliny, G. S. (1967 [45 CE]). In H. Rackham (Ed.), *Natural history in ten volumes: Volume I. Praefatio, Libri I, II* (Vol. I, p. 378). Harvard University Press.
6. Riggs, C. (2014). *Ancient Egyptian art and architecture: A very short introduction* (p. 132). Oxford University Press.
7. David, A. R. (2002). *The pyramid builders of ancient Egypt: A modern investigation of pharaoh's workforce* (p. 298). Routledge.
8. Ritner, R. K. (2000). Innovations and adaptations in ancient Egyptian medicine. *Journal of Near Eastern Studies, 59*(2), 107–117.
9. Ellis, N. (2020). *Hieroglyphic words of power: Symbols for magic, divination, and dreamwork.* Simon and Schuster.
10. Zinn, K. (2013). Magic, Pharaonic Egypt. In R. S. Bagnall, et al. (Eds.), *The encyclopedia of Ancient History* (p. 7768). Wiley-Blackwell.
11. Régen, I. (2013). Curses, Egypt. In R. S. Bagnall, et al. (Eds.), *The encyclopedia of Ancient History* (p. 7768). Blackwell Publishing Ltd.
12. Nyord, R. (2020). Experiencing the dead in ancient Egyptian healing texts. In U. Steinert (Ed.), *Systems of classification in premodern medical cultures: Sickness, health, and local epistemologies* (pp. 84–106). Routledge.
13. Hamid, A., & Sami, D. (2016). Some Remarkable Amulets in Ancient Egyptian Art. *Journal of Association of Arab Universities for Tourism and Hospitality, 13*(4), 11–21.

14. Budge, E. A. W. (1967). *The Book of the Dead: The Papyrus of Ani in the British Museum*. Dover Publications.

15. León, V. (2009). *Working IX to V: Orgy Planners, Funeral Clowns, and Other Prized Professions of the Ancient World* (p. 336). Walkerand Company.

16. Eltaieb, F. A. (2019). Ancient Egyptian Healers. *Evidence-Based Nursing Research*, *1*(1), 1–3.

17. Sanchez, G., & Harer, W. B. (2019). Toxicology in Ancient Egypt. In P. Wexler (Ed.), *Toxicology in antiquity* (2nd ed., pp. 73–82). Academic Press.

18. Meltzer, E. S., & Sanchez, G. M. (2014). *The Edwin Smith Papyrus: Updated translation of the trauma treatise and modern medical commentaries* (p. 400). Lockwood Press.

19. Qamar, W., & Rehman, M. U. (2020). In M. U. Rehman & S. Majid (Eds.), *Brief history and traditional uses of honey*, in *therapeutic applications of honey and its phytochemicals* (pp. 1–10). Springer

20. Ghalioungui, P. (1987). *The Ebers Papyrus: A new English translation, commentaries and glossaries*. Academy of Scientific Research and Technology.

21. Yaniv, Z. (2014). In Z. Yaniv and N. Dudai (Eds.), *Introduction: Medicinal Plants in Ancient traditions*, in *medicinal and aromatic plants of the Middle-East* (pp. 1–7). Springer.

22. Nunn, J. F. (2002). *Ancient Egyptian medicine* (p. 240). University of Oklahoma Press.

23. Abouelata, M. (2018). Travel to the Healing Centers in the Egyptian Temples: the Prototype of the Modern Medical Tourism. *Egyptian Journal of Archaeological and Restoration Studies*, *8*(2), 121–132.

24. Reeder, G. (2000). Same-sex desire, conjugal constructs, and the tomb of Niankhkhnum and Khnumhotep. *World Archaeology*, *32*(2), 193–208.

25. Evans, L., & Woods, A. (2016). Further evidence that Niankhkhnum and Khnumhotep were twins. *The Journal of Egyptian Archaeology*, *102*(1), 55–72.

26. Quarini, C. A. (2005). History of contraception. *Women's Health Medicine*, *2*(5), 28–30.

27. El-Meliegy, A. (2008). La sessualità nell'Antico Egitto | Sexuality in ancient Egypt. *Medicina Sessuale e Riproduttiva [Italian Journal of Sexual and Reproductive Medicine]*, *15*(2), 116–118.

28. Youssef, H. (1993). The history of the condom. *Journal of the Royal Society of Medicine*, *86*(4), 226–228.

29. Smith, L. (2011). The Kahun gynaecological papyrus: Ancient Egyptian medicine. *BMJ Sexual & Reproductive Health*, *37*(1), 54–55.

30. Christopher, E. (2006). Religious aspects of contraception. *Reviews in Gynaecological and Perinatal Practice*, *6*(3–4), 192–198.

31. Kaicher, D. C., & Swan, K. G. (2010). A cut above: Circumcision as an ancient status symbol. *Urology*, *76*(1), 18–20.

32. Dunsmuir, W., & Gordon, E. (1999). The history of circumcision. *BJU International*, *83*(s 1), 1–12.

33. Abdelhady, M. E.-M. (2020). The habituation of the ancient Egyptians and the methods of treatment. *International Journal of Tourism and Hospitality Management*, *3*(1), 73–102.

34. Liappas, J., et al. (2003). Alexander the Great's relationship with alcohol. *Addiction*, *98*(5), 561–567.

35. Plutarch, L. M. (1936 [100 CE]). In P. Theelen (Ed.), *De Fortuna Seu Virtute Alexandri [On the Fortune or the Virtue of Alexander]* (pp. 382–487). Loeb Classical Library.

36. Aelian. (1997 [486 CE]). In C. Eliano, et al. (Eds.), *Varia Historia [Historical miscellany]*. Harvard University Press.

37. Frasin, I. (2019). Greeks, Barbarians and Alexander the Great: The Formula for an Empire. *The Athens Journal of History*, *5*(3), 209–224.

38. Mayor, A. (2019). In P. Wexler (Ed.), *Alexander the Great: A questionable death*, in *toxicology in antiquity* (2nd ed., pp. 151–159). Academic Press.

39. Tóth, I. (2007). Apologia Alexandrou (Arrian: Anabasis 1. 7–9). *Acta Antiqua*, *47*(4), 397–410.

40. Siculus, D. (1868 [60 BCE]). In L. A. Dindorf (Ed.), *Bibliotheca historica* (p. 639). Ghent University.

41. Gamble, N., & Bloedow, E. (2017). A medical-historical examination of the death of Alexander the Great. *Journal of Ancient History and Archaeology*, *4*(3), 18–29.

42. Bennett, B., & Roberts, M. (2013). *The Wars of Alexander's Successors, 323–281 BC* (Vol. 1, p. 236). Pen & Sword Books.

43. Mittelman, R. J. (2020). Macedonian, Greek, or Egyptian? Navigating the royal additive identities of Ptolemy I Soter and Ptolemy II Philadelphus. In A. W. Irvin (Ed.), *Community and identity at the edges of the classical world* (pp. 119–137). John Wiley & Sons, Inc.

44. Roisman, J. (1984). Ptolemy and his rivals in his history of Alexander. *The Classical Quarterly*, *34*(2), 373–385.

45. Dio, C. (1914 [180 CE]). Dio's Roman history. In E. Cary and H. B. Foster (Eds.), *The Loeb classical library* (Vol. VII, p. 480). William Heinemann.

46. Ebers, G. M. (1894). *Kleopatra: Historischer roman* (Vol. 26, p. 572). Deutsche Verlags-Anstalt.

47. Frangié-Joly, D. (2016). Perfumes, aromatics, and purple dye: Phoenician Trade and production in the Greco-Roman period. *Journal of Eastern Mediterranean Archaeology & Heritage Studies*, *4*(1), 36–56.

48. Burgdorf, W. H., & Hoenig, L. J. (2015). Cleopatra, queen of dermatology. *JAMA Dermatology*, *151*(2), 236–236.

49. Hancock, J. F. (2021). *Spices, scents and silk: Catalysts of World Trade* (p. 338). CAB International.

50. Thomas, J. J. (2021). The Ptolemy Painting? Alexander's "right-hand man" and the origins of the Alexander Mosaic. *Journal of Roman Archaeology*, *34*(2), 1–16.

51. Lang, P. (2013). Medicine and society in Ptolemaic Egypt. In *Studies in ancient medicine* (Vol. 41, p. 309). Brill.

52. Dervenis, K., & Lykiardopoulos, N. (2007). *The martial arts of ancient Greece: Modern fighting techniques from the Age of Alexander*. Simon and Schuster.

53. Mahmood, Z. A., Azhar, I., & Ahmed, S. W. (2019). In P. Wexler (Ed.), *Kohl use in antiquity: Effects on the eye*, in *toxicology in antiquity* (2nd ed., pp. 93–103). Academic Press.

54. Pearson, S. (2021). Triumphal Splendor. In S. Pearson, et al. (Eds.), *The triumph and trade of Egyptian objects in Rome: Collecting art in the ancient Mediterranean* (p. 302). De Gruyter.

55. Flower, H. (2020). Augustus, Tiberius, and the End of the Roman Triumph. *Classical Antiquity, 39*(1), 1–28.

56. Tsoucalas, G., & Sgantzos, M. (2019). The death of Cleopatra: Suicide by snakebite or poisoned by her enemies? In P. Wexler (Ed.), *Toxicology in antiquity* (2nd ed., pp. 83–92). Academic Press.

57. María, R. A. (2021). Toxicology and snakes in ptolemaic Egyptian dynasty: The suicide of Cleopatra. *Toxicology Reports, 8*, 676–695.

Ancient Greece: Science and Art of Medicine

G reece in classical history was in prominence from 1100 BCE to 332 BCE. We will discuss Greek history from two distinct periods of time: Homeric Greece 1100 BCE to 511 BCE and Classical Greece 510 BCE to 332 BCE. Homeric Greece sets the foundations for many of the social and political ideologies that have influenced future societies. There was not a unified Greece as we think of nations today during the Homeric Age; instead, there were a tapestry of city-states united by a common language and shared cultural beliefs. Most of the city-states were ruled via oligarchy, where a ruling council of nobles were responsible for administration and law and a king served as religious official and/or commander of the army. The council of nobles was responsible for advising and assisting the king and functioned to prevent him from tyrannical rule. A few of the city-states had abolished the monarchy and replaced it with a representative democracy, where again the nobles of the city were responsible for the administration of daily activities. Sparta was an anomaly in the way women were seen as near equal citizens. Sparta was the only city-state that allowed women to inherit, manage, and own land with many of the Spartan women becoming exceptionally wealthy. There was a fair amount of war among the city-states as they vied for control of the fertile valleys that punctuate the Grecian landscape. Classical Greece or the Hellenistic Age witnessed one of the deadliest civil wars to ravage the Greeks, and the resulting Peloponnesian War saw several political hegemonies extending the city-states into nation-states. *Hegemony* is a form of control of one state over others using political, economic, or military means. Thebes was one of the city-states that rebelled against the Spartan hegemony by deploying the Sacred Band of Thebes, an army that consisted of 150 pairs of male lovers. The Sacred Band of Thebes was an elite force who remained invincible between 378 BCE and 338 BCE. The Sacred Band fell together as one unified corps, who according to Plutarch, were deeply mourned by Philip II of Macedon—the father of Alexander the Great—their opponent at the Battle of Chaeronea[1]. The close of Classical Greece witnessed the defeat of Athens and Sparta by Alexander the Great, who then unified the Hellenic peoples and ushered in a period of Pan-Hellenic expansion. Throughout this rich and dramatic history was the development of a very modern looking medical system. Through warfare, the ancient Greeks were able to hone a variety of biological and chemical weapons of war. Poisoning was a real concern among the nobility and learned elite. More secretive and exclusive were the mysteries and cults who used psychoactive substances to initiate new members and have a shared religious epiphany.

4.1   Homeric Greece

The Homeric Age witnessed many technological changes and advances among
the Greek City-States. There was a highly
sophisticated knowledge of metallurgy,
as bronze tools and weapons became
widespread. Bronze requires a degree
of specialization as it requires the forger
to smelt copper with tin and arsenic or
nickel in specific quantities to get a useful
metal[2]. The additive metals and minerals
in the smelting process produces a range
of alloys, producing different useful properties such as strength, durability, ductil-
ity, or machinability. The ancient Greeks
boasted one of the highest literacy rates of
the ancient world at the time, and signifi-

Figure 4.1   Greek Pottery, Heroes in Battle

Silviu Hisom/Shutterstock.com

cant importance was placed on writing and formal education. The ancient Greeks were master ship
builders, unrivaled at astral navigation, and ingenious in creating some of the world's continuously
used artificial harbors. During the Homeric Age, advanced forms of pottery were made possible
through the development of the potter's wheel. In addition, methods for firing pottery became better
controlled and could be done with higher temperatures. New and unique glazes added to the unique-
ness of Greek pottery (Figure 4.1). Sculpture became amazingly lifelike, and the materials expanded
to the use of marble. City streets were paved and formed in right angles, which helped with transportation, movement, and general navigation of compact urban centers.

The *polis*, or city, was the center of life and culture for the *poleis*, the people. *Metropolis* or
"mother city" was used by the Greeks to denote the sponsoring city-state of a colony; however, today,
we use the term metropolis to denote a large industrial, economic, or cultural center of urban life[3].
The polis typically consisted of a fortified central city used to control the surrounding lands. Most
Greek cities incorporated some standard design features including an agora, an acropolis, and access
to a dedicated harbor. The *agora* was a central public space, and it functions as the nexus of athletic,
artistic, spiritual, political, mercantile, and philosophical lives of the people. The *acropolis* was any
citadel, fortified keep, or building complex built on the highest point within the walls of the city. The
most famous acropolis can be found in Athens and is home to several ancient buildings and temples
including the Erechtheion and the Parthenon both of which are Temples to Athena.

The Greeks were not shy when it came to enacting and conducting wars. Yet through the application of two key philosophies, hubris and xenia, the Greeks proved to be among the most hospitable
to travelers and journeymen. *Hubris* is related to displays of extreme pride or extreme arrogance,
similar to our modern concept of chutzpah. The ancient Greeks were not focused too intently on
self-image, instead they were hyper-attuned to the ways words and actions were used to embarrass,
shame, or overly aggrandize others. An individual who was placed in a demeaning situation was
equally as wrong as outright self-humiliation or self-depredation. The story of Odysseus and the

Cyclops in Homer's Odyssey is a good example of hubris and the effects of tempting the fates or the gods[4]. Spoiler alert, the cyclops loses his eye and his breakfast at the same time as Odysseus had tricked the cyclops. Sadly, drunk on the success of the successful escape of his crew, Odysseus taunted the cyclops and blatantly mocked Poseidon, the cyclops's father, which brough hubris down onto the ship and subsequent journey home of Odysseus.

Xenia represents one of the most sacred and traditional Greek philosophies and centers around the concept of hospitality. Xenia embodies the generosity and graciousness one shows upon encountering a stranger, who may appear in any condition and who are far from home. It represents the height of geniality and requires one to host the stranger as a guest in their home. This philosophy created an incredibly unique relationship between host and guest. At the heart of the philosophy of xenia were three basic rules of conduct: (1) respect from the host to the guest; (2) respect from the guest toward their host; and (3) a useful parting gift from the host to their guest, typically something the guest may need as they continued their travels[5]. These basic rules of xenia are detailed further in Figure 4.2.

Figure 4.2   Components of Xenia

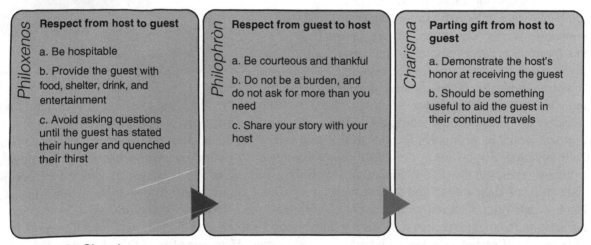

Source: T.D. Church

There is a classic fable regarding Xenia and Zeus, respectively the gods of lightning and thunder (additionally known as Zeus Xenios, the god of foreigners and hospitality). The classic fable has several variations, depending upon the author, but the theme of the fable is consistent and acts as a warning to always be hospitable, because guests can often be more than they appear[5]. The fable takes us to the ancient region of Tyana, which is situated in modern-day Cappadocia, Turkey. Zeus, wh enjoyed shapeshifting usually with the intent of seduction, had disguised himself as a poor tra He decided to test the hospitality of Tyana and sought shelter from the homes of the people in After a few of the wealthy people of the city closed the door in his face and raising the ire walked out of the city and past the grand city walls. He noticed a very modest home give his request for shelter one more attempt before casting judgement upon the w

Baucis and Philemon were an elderly couple who were extremely poor, with a meager amount of stew and only a few drops of wine. However, upon hearing the request for shelter from Zeus, they generously offered the "stranger" shelter, the best seat at their small table, the first serving of their stew, and the last of their wine. As the night progressed, Baucis realized that despite refilling the cup of their stranger many times throughout the night, the wine amphora never went empty. Upon leaving—in some of the fables—Baucis offers Zeus their only blanket to keep the traveling stranger warm at night. Zeus razed the city of Tyana and again depending upon the version of the fable either turned the modest home into a temple or palace where Baucis and Philemon lived out their remaining days in luxury. This fable was told to remind Greeks to always be hospitable, to always follow the tenants of Xenia, because you never know who may appear at your door requesting your help.

Among the aristocratic and noble men of ancient Greece, no other event was as important as the *symposia*. Symposia were lavish banquets hosted by men for their peers (Figure 4.3). The word symposia translated from the Greek means "to drink together." Women, except for those hired as entertainment, were expressly forbidden from attending. Wives, daughters, sisters, and aunts were either cloistered to distant parts of the home or sent away for the evening. Symposia typically began around 4 p.m.

Figure 4.3 Paestum, Tomb of the Diver, Symposia

Simone Crespiatico/Shutterstock.com

and continued for many hours, often into the early hours of the following morning. Extravagant and excessive amounts of food, inordinate volumes of wine, an assortment of sexual pleasures, and entertainment would be prominent features of the symposia. W. J. Slater described symposia as "places for the ostentatious display not just of gilded ceilings or inlaid floors, Ionian couches, exotic entertainment, or luxury vases, but also of the cultural quality of host and guests"[6]. These events allowed the nobility to peacock their wealth and fortune under the guise of philosophical discourse, or artistic display. These events often featured wine constituted with water and frequently contained psychoactive plant extracts. As the night progressed, it was not uncommon for those attending the symposia to engage in a wide variety of sexual activities with both men and women. *Hetaerae* were highly skilled and broadly trained courtesans who provided sex, music, poetry, and conversation were often employed and invited. *Pornai*, on the other hand, would not typically be invited to symposia. Pornai were prostitutes who were either slaves or lower-class women, who typically plied sexual services without any of the refinement or sophistication of the hetaerae[7].

Medicine took shape in Bronze Age Greece; however, the concept of medicine from this period is often confusing to modern scholars. *Pharmakon* is a Greek word that can mean "drug" or imply a "remedy" and/or a "poison" depending upon the context of its use. It is a splendid example of the concept of a vox media, or middle voice, wherein the word construct and use was negative or positive all dependent upon context. Pharmakon could refer to something of medicinal utility (positive) or something poisonous, venomous, or toxic (negative). Occasionally, pharmakon appears in texts with a modifier that makes the interpretation clearer and easier to decipher, but this practice is far from the norm. Two of the most common modifiers are *evergetikos*—benefiting one's health—and *epivlavis*—harming one's health. If pharmakon was not confusing enough as is, the word could be associated with herbs and cooking. Pepper and marjoram were used for both their healing properties and their aroma or taste to season foods.

The ancient Greek physicians were the first to mix pharmaceutical plants with an excipient. ***Pharmaceutical plants*** represent plants utilized for pharmaceutical preparations. In our earliest history, these plants would have been harvested from the available wild stock. In Bronze Age Greece, these plants were being cultivated, usually alongside other food crops and many of the pharmaceutical plants, and became herbs and seasonings utilized in food preparation. ***Excipients*** are additive materials to medicine that have no pharmaceutical action and are there to aid in the intake or absorption of the active drug. Excipients usually serve one of two purposes: (1) they aid in the digestion of herbal drugs, and (2) they help ensure the quality of the drug being produced by distributing the active compounds within the preparation. The ancient Greeks utilized common grasses that were finely chopped and ground as their most common excipient. These common grasses held no additional effects, nor did they enhance any deleterious effects on the pharmaceutical plants within the various remedies.

The ancient Greeks were the first to recognize that ***alkaloids*** gave potency or other affects to plant medicines[8]. Alkaloids represent any class of nitrogenous organic compounds that produce physiological effects on humans. They tend not to dissolve completely in water. Scholars who study Bronze Age Greece have determined that the Greeks had understood that only organic solvents worked to release the active effect of the alkaloids. Alkaloids have been shown to have pronounced actions on humans and today include drugs (morphine) and poisons (strychnine).

The ancient Greeks believed it possible for some individuals to have an insane, uncontrollable desire to consume poisonous or intoxicating substances. They named this tendency ***toxicomania***, and it was typically used to describe individuals who overindulged in drinking wine[9]. To the Greeks, the social and individual danger of drugs was centered around an over consumption of wine. All other drugs were not viewed as being problematic or of concern. Wine, on the other hand, was a necessary evil, as it had the power to enlighten individuals or carry them to the precipice of depravity. The Greeks were familiar with and used opium, cannabis (likely), nepenthes (pitcher plant), wine, and, in exceedingly rarer instances, beer for both medical and recreational uses. The ancient Greeks when they considered toxicomania, they believed that only alcohol—wine in particular—was the source of many of the world's woes. These calamities were often associated with Dionysus, the god of wine, vegetation, pleasure, festivity, madness, and wild lust or frenzy. A play by Euripides titled *The Bacchae* puts the depravity of Dionysus on full display and in very real detail as Dionysus used his powers to trick women into murdering and mutilating their son, lover, and king[10]. Dionysus allowed for horrendous acts to unfold all because he felt slighted by the king and sought retribution.

The Greeks have the first documented focus into sports medicine, and are often credited with their inventiveness in the creation and use of ***performance-enhancing drugs***[8]. Performance-enhancing drugs are taken for a few reasons, namely, (1) to assist in completing a mental activity or complex task; (2) to provide additional endurance in sports; or (3) to confer an advantage (on the field of battle, for sports, in the bedroom, or even in the competition of chasing grades). The ancient Greeks used performance-enhancing drugs consisting of herbal concoctions, wine potions, hallucinogens, and animal parts (most popular being hearts and testicles)[11]. Soldiers and athletes were among the group who were most likely to consume performance-enhancing substances. These groups of individuals were known to ingest raw animal testicles prior to battle or competition. It was believed that consuming raw testicles was a sign of masculinity and would confer great strength and vitality upon the consumer[12].

Both war and sport often were accompanied by pain, and pain management became a central concern to the ancient Greek physicians. They continued to experiment with a variety of materials to help alleviate pain. *Dwale* was believed to be an indispensable compound to control pain during and after surgical interventions[8]. Dwale composition varied from one physician to another, but most contained a similar set of ingredients. These ingredients included the bile of a boar, fresh lettuce, red wine vinegar, bryony root, hemlock, opium, and henbane. The ingredients would have been brewed together wine or water for a few hours before being divided into tinctures. This concoction worked, often too well, and could led to the patient suffering a fatal overdose. The reasons for the overdoses were tied to fundamental flaws in how the ancient Greeks understood the mechanics of anesthesia and pain therapy in ancient Greece. Not only was there a poor methodology of administration of the drugs, there were also a lack of dosing controls[9]. The ancient Greeks did not fully appreciate how to attenuate the therapeutic benefits to the interventions their patients needed. Often the mixture carried more hemlock than opium or double the hemlock and henbane. As can be surmised, it was a very inexact and highly dangerous concoction to make and could deadly to consume. If surgeons needed to perform surgery, their best option for success was to be as quick and precise as possible. This meant that surgical interventions were less complex and tended to keep surgery as a therapeutic treatment to a minimum.

While dwale was a very delicate medication to manufacture and use, the Greeks had other more effective methods for resolving localized pain. The *Olympic victor's dark ointment (OVDO)* was an opium-enriched patch, applied to the surface of the skin of athletes who were suffering from pain due to the rigors of sport[13]. Through experimental archaeology and history, scholars from Copenhagen University went about recreating OVDO and determined the patch consisted of several ingredients— antimony, cadmium, saffron, frankincense, myrrh, acacia, gummi, opium, pompholyx, aloe, and, to bind it all together, a raw egg. The mixture has the consistency of a dark greenish brown honey, and when applied as a covering for a localized area, it dried rapidly. The dried OVDO did retain some elastic properties and like modern kinesiology black sports tape, helped to reduce swelling. The OVDO had the added benefit of soothing inflammation and pain as it promoted healing. This fragrant topical paste acted both systemically to lower pain thresholds while having local effects to reduce inflammatory mechanisms. The measurements of the transdermal transfer of morphine conducted by the team from Copenhagen University found a transfer comparable to 25% of modern transdermal patches[13]. OVDO when compounded had the texture of a thick plaster, which functioned to cool the skin and soothe the muscles below as it dried. The cooling coupled with the pain-relieving effects helped to reduce inflammation and bruising. There are ancient accounts of it being utilized for lacerations around the eye, reducing the severity of black eyes among wrestlers and Olympic competitors (Figure 4.4)[12].

Figure 4.4 Ancient Greek Wrestler's

Storm Is Me/Shutterstock. com

Olympians and athletes in ancient Greece followed a very standard routine.

Before competing, the athletes would take off all their clothes and cover themselves in olive oil[12]. All sport in ancient Greece was done in the buff, whether running or grappling with another man, the sport was practiced entirely naked[11]. At the end of training or competition, the athletes would be covered in dirt, dried olive oil, sweat, and any number of environmental particulates. The athletes would stand and allow *gloios* collectors to use specialized bronze instruments (Figure 4.5) to scrape the sweat, dead skin cells, oil, and dirt off their bodies. The resulting sludge was called gloios, and it was sold as a medi-

Figure 4.5   Greek Gloios Collector (Roman Strigil)

Zhuravlev Andrey/Shutterstock.com

cine. The more well known the athlete, the higher the price one could fetch from their gloios. People would use the gloios for several purposes—some would rub it on their skin to look younger, others believed it calmed aches and pains in the bones, could make one virile and amorous, and restored strength.

Opium was still the most favored drug used for pain and pleasure in ancient Greece. Opium use began in prehistoric times and was carried by traders and merchants from civilization to civilization. Many ancient cultures held the opium poppy in exceedingly high esteem, and it became associated with specific gods. Our modern word morphine derives its name from Morpheus, the Greek god of dreams. In fact, the ancient Greeks associated the poppy with many members of Morpheus' family—his grandmother, Nyx, the goddess of the night; his father, Hypnos, the god of sleep; and his uncle, Thanatos, god of death[8]. The ancient Greeks in the Bronze Age had refined and perfected the process of making teas prepared from opium poppies for a variety of ailments. Until recently, we had believed that smoking opium was not practiced in Europe until the late fifteenth century; however, recent archaeological evidence has uncovered ancient pipes containing opium residue in Greece dating to ~1200 BCE[14]. There are also a number of vases from this same period, which detail the harvesting of poppies by incising the poppy seed capsule to gather the opium latex for smoking[8]. In a way, the Greeks pioneered the techne of opium consumption. Techne is an ancient Greek word with a very dynamic meaning. It is the root word for the word "technology," but it was used to describe a craft or skill within a craft. Its use is similar to the Chinese concept of tao or the Japanese philosophy of do. Techne refers to both art and the artform. There could be a techne of wrestling, a techne of hoplites, and even a techne of opium smoking.

While opium could be utilized to alleviate one from earthly pain and suffering, the ancient Greeks believed in a far more powerful drug. An elixir used by the gods that, if consumed by a mortal, would grant them divine immortality. *Ambrosia*, which translates to "immortality," was the food—sometimes drink—of the Greek pantheon[15]. It was a mythical substance that was depicted as bestowing longevity and health upon whoever consumed it, be they gods or mortals. It was believed to have the power to change the old and frail into the young and vigorous. Ambrosia was closely related to another form of sustenance of the gods, *nectar* (a compound word from nek—"death," and tar—"surmounting"). ***Ichor*** was a substance that represented an ethereal fluid, believed by the Greeks to be the blood of the gods and immortals. If a mortal happened to drink ichor, they would become imbued with the qualities of the immortal who provided the ichor. If it were Aphrodite, the mortal would have power over love and the heart. If it were Aries, the mortal would become the god of war and carnage. If it were Athena, the mortal would be bestowed with wisdom, handicraft, and warfare. Ichor was used in Medieval and Renaissance medical texts to describe a watery discharge from a wound or ulcer, often described as having a very unpleasant or nauseating smell. Ambrosia, nectar, and ichor feature prominently in Greek mythology and classical writing as a way for mortal men to become divine.

There were individuals who could help the ancient Greeks understand the will or direction of the divine and were priests and priestesses who were devoted to serving at the temple or shire of a particular god or goddess. One of the most revered was the Pythian Oracle of Delphi, who served at the Temple of Apollo (Figure 4.6). The name Pythia relates to the heroic story in which Apollo defeated the monstrous serpent Python. Pythos was the former name of Delphi, and to the ancient Greeks was considered to be the site of the center of the Earth. In early times, the Temple was dedicated to Gaia, the primordial goddess of the

Figure 4.6 Temple of Apollo, Oracle of Delphi

Lefteris Papaulakis/Shutterstock.com

Earth. Around the eighth century BCE, the shire was dedicated to Apollo. The name Pythia remained as an epithet used to refer to the high priestess and oracle at the temple. Among the ancient Greeks, the oracle's powers were highly revered and were never doubted[16]. If there were inconsistencies between the prophecies and actual events, the failure was placed on the individual not being able to correctly interpret the prophecy. The failure never resided in the oracle or her skill at divination. Many of the prophesies were often worded very ambiguously and were highly cryptic, see Figure 4.7 as an example. In some ancient accounts, the Pythia sat on a three-legged stool over a crack in the stone floor (or wall—it is not consistent among sources), and she would inhale vapors as they emanated from the crack. These brain-altering vapors would provide the visions of the future from divine sources. Classical authors including Herodotus[17], Ovid[18], Plato[19], and Plutarch[1] describe this interaction, with a minority of them indicating the vapor pushed the Pythia into a frenzied state, where her speech required decoding by temple priests. During archaeological studies conducted at the site, ***Pythian gases***, a mixture of methane, ethylene, and benzene, were detected. There was, in addition, the residue of some now forgotten herbal incense[20]. Together it is believed this concoction when inhaled would have allowed the priestess to enter a trance and hallucinate. These hallucinations were decoded as prophecies, and for a time could move nations to war, inspire kings, and provide hope to those in need. For fourteen centuries, the Oracle of Delphi helped determine the course of Greek history through prophesy. Sadly, Christians in the fourth century CE abolished prophecy and equated it with witchcraft. The Temple was closed, and the wonder of the oracle became shrouded in mythology and legend.

Figure 4.7   A Prophecy Given by the Oracle to King Xerxes of Persia Prior to the Battle of Thermopylae

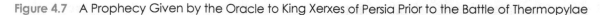

When reading, keep in mind that a comma denotes a pause in speech. As you read each version of the following sentence, mentally pause where the comma has been placed and consider how to interpret the meaning of what you have read.

YOU WILL GO YOU WILL RETURN NEVER IN WAR WILL YOU PERISH	YOU WILL GO YOU WILL RETURN, NEVER IN WAR WILL YOU PERISH	YOU WILL GO YOU WILL RETURN NEVER, IN WAR WILL YOU PERISH

Source: T.D. Church

The Homeric Age was one of wonder and superstition. It provided the world with the first concept of addiction in the form of toxicomania, which was equated to the overconsumption and reliance upon wine. Drugs had both magical and practical uses during this time. The collective utility of many of these substances is—by our modern conception—questionable at best. However, these drugs and how they were developed, collected, and utilized formed the basic foundation of modern medicine.

4.2 Classical Greece

The period between 510 BCE and 323 BCE represents the Classical Age of Greece. It is a period of momentous change and advancement in terms of technical, social, and cultural developments. These changes and advancements would go on to influence Western development in many profound ways. Among the technological achievements were the discovery and mastery of iron work. The ancient Greeks have been credited with the invention of the gear, screw, rotary mills, screw press, and tumbler locks. These were made possible by advancements in mathematics with the development of geometry, calculus, and advanced mathematics with an understanding of prime numbers. Engineering brought a unique understanding of hydrology, enabling the creation of the water clock, water organ, canal locks, showers, plumbing, and steam operated machines (though the latter were only utilized for spectacle, i.e., the magical opening of the doors at the Temple of Zeus). Navigation was improved through accurate cartography, use of the astrolabe, and proper surveying of both land and sea. Transportation was improved by the creation of lighthouses and the adoption of the three-masted ship (sometimes referred to as a mizzen). The Classical Age of Greece was an era born out of war and conflict—first between the Greeks and the Persians, then between the Athenians and the Spartans—but its legacy is one of unprecedented political and cultural achievement (Figure 4.8).

Figure 4.8   Map of Greece during the Peloponnesian War, Athenian League vs Spartan League

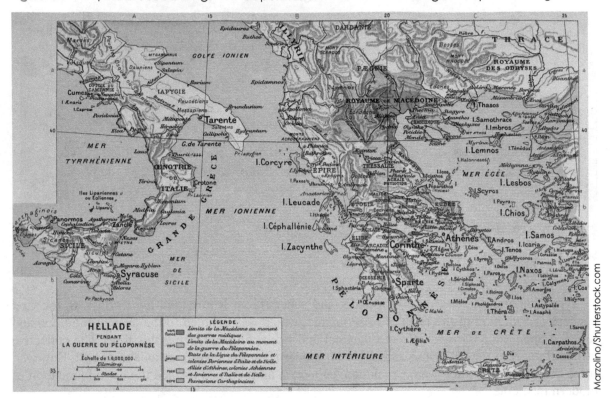

The ancient Greek world was turned upside down between 431 BCE and 401 BCE, which were dominated by the Peloponnesian Wars. There were two periods of intense fighting between which a brief period of uneasy peace existed for a little under six years[21]. When the dust settled, the ancient Greek world had been reshaped. Athens, the city-state renowned for art, philosophy, democracy, and diplomacy became subjugated. Sparta, the city-state known for military rule and brutality, became established as the leading power. The economic costs of war were felt throughout Greece and poverty became widespread. The social costs of war were equally as devastating, and Greece entered a series of civil wars that would become a common occurrence for the remainder of Greek history, persisting into the twentieth century. The Peloponnesian Wars ended after a series of prolonged battles, starvation, civil unrest, and widespread disease. Athens was besieged and ultimately forced to surrender to Sparta in 401 BCE. The surrender stripped Athens of its grand city walls, its imposing naval fleet, and desolation of all overseas colonies. Corinth and Thebes, city-states that were part of the Spartan League, demanded that Athens be razed, and all her women enslaved with all the men being executed. Sparta refused these terms, and after enduring additional pressure from Corinth and Thebes, stated "Sparta will have the same friends and enemies as Athens"[22].

In the aftermath of the Peloponnesian Wars, there was a return to the gods especially in terms of healing. Not all Greeks went to physicians when ill, many sought divine intervention. Many would go to the *Asclepieia*—spaces within the Temples of Asclepios, reserved for those poor in health, where they could bathe, sleep, and meditate. Those who went to an Asclepeia were expected to leave offerings to Asclepios, typically a cock or goat upon leaving the temple. To those left destitute after the Peloponnesian Wars, this was a lofty price, but such was the cost for good health. Ancient Greek physicians began seeking out natural explanations as to why someone got ill, recovered, or died. They began cataloging all the symptoms and outcomes, slowly building a comprehensive diagnostic and therapeutic system. Many of the drugs used were derived from either plants or animals.

Anesthesia was still troublesome, and the Greeks did not possess a reliable drug for pain or surgery. As a result, they looked for other ways of controlling both pain and consciousness, should the need arise for surgical intervention. The Greeks of the Classical Age were among the first civilizations to comprehend that local pressure applied proximally to a site of trauma or surgical site rendered real effects in the control of localized pain. By applying pressure on both the blood vessels and nerve endings (what we call pressure points), the ancient Greeks found that pain could be numbed or temporarily reduced. Two key areas written about and frequently used were the brachial plexus and carotid arteries. Pressure to the brachial plexus could provide at least suboptimal anesthetic and analgesic conditions that allowed for minor surgery to be performed on the hands. Bilateral local pressure to the carotid arteries would render patients' unconscious as long as pressure was maintained, which was an effective method to provide temporary sedation[23]. After removal of pressure, the patient regained consciousness quickly with their pain returning equally as fast. The problem with pressure to the carotid arteries was that it could result in irreversible fatal problems if pressure is held too long. Applying pressure to the carotid arteries mimics the effect of high blood pressure even when it did not exist. Consequently, the brain would send out a signal to lower blood pressure, which resulted in dilation of blood vessels. This dilation assured that not enough blood reached the brain, which caused temporary paralysis. If pressure was applied long enough, the paralysis would turn into coma followed by brain death from lack of oxygen to the brain. A skilled practitioner, however, was able to use these two pressure points and many more to profound effect. In turn, surgical techniques rapidly expanded as physicians gained more experience. Still the best approach was to get in and get out of the surgical site as quickly as possible.

Priests often were employed in the art of healing, and if no physical ailment could be determined, they would turn to the supernatural. A concoction used by priests, and sometimes warriors, is referred to as *kykeon*,[1] which roughly translates to "stirred" or "mixed," helped them to reach an altered state of consciousness. It was a beverage with a wide variety of preparations. Some kykeon were made of water, barley, and herbs[24]. Others were made of wine and aged grated cheese. Still others contained psychoactive compounds such as psylocibin, nepenthes, or similar plant within the brew. It is the latter form of kykeon that was preferred by priests and warriors. It was said that the kykeon could induce a trance or dream-like state but also had the ability to bring frenzied energy. With the dream-like version, priests would have patients enter an *incubatio*. Similar to what the Egyptians did, the incubatio was a healing and deeply sacred drug-induced dream that would allow the priests to diagnose and properly cure their sick patient. Priests who consumed the kykeon were said to be able to enter the

---

[1] For a very candid look at how to make Kykeon, I recommend checking out Max Miller's Tasting History episode on YouTube: https://youtu.be/XtkAU4juIZU.

dream realm and cure the ill from a variety of supernatural ailments while dreaming. Warriors on the other hand would consume kykeon before battle and would allow the psychoactive brew to give them increased energy. Kykeon brought priests closer to the divine and made warriors fierce.

The ancient Greeks were well versed in the use of drugs that cured as well as those that could be harnessed for death. Spartans were known to use ergot to poison the water wells of their enemies. Athenians were documented poisoning the water supply of besieged towns with hellebore. Archers from nearly every city-state were known to tip their arrows with snake venom, human blood, and even feces to

Figure 4.9 Ergot on Rye

Manfred Ruckszio/Shutterstock.com

cause wounds to become infected. Not only were these methods brutal, but they were tactics used to psychologically unnerve those who experienced their application. Ergot was the worst poison of the bunch [9, 24]. ***Ergot*** is a parasitic fungus that can be found growing on rye and if ingested—accidentally or otherwise—leads to a condition called ***ergotism*** (Figure 4.9). Ergotism refers to the way the poison expresses in the human body, and it can take one of two gruesome forms, depending upon the individual and the amount of poison ingested (Figure 4.10).

Poison and the threat of being poisoned was something that the wealthy and nobility of Classical Greece feared; many of them became obsessed with the potential of falling victim to poisoning. It was not uncommon for wealthy individuals to use slaves as food and wine testers, who had the sole responsibility of being the first to eat and/or drink anything offered to their patron[25]. This innate fear of poisons led many to seek out a ***theriaka***, antidote to a single and often specific poison, or a ***panacea***, antidote to all poisons. These antidotes contained a variety of drugs and poisons such as hemlock, aconite, and opium[26]. Each one was different with varying levels of potency and toxicity depending upon the priest or physician who compounded the antidote. Many of the aristocracy of ancient Greece believed that by metronomically dosing small amounts of poison daily, they would develop or build up an immunity to the poison. Metronomic dosing, borrowing the term from modern chemotherapy, relies on a low and continuous dose typically administered daily[27]. The idea was that via a daily regimen of poison, the individual would gain immunity to said poison. Unfortunately, there were a wide variety of poisons and thus would have required small doses of several poisons administered at once, which most likely led to many unintentional poisonings among the Greek aristocracy.

When considering poisons, there are three varieties of poisons that are categorized based on their effect[9]. As a poisoner, it is important to know which category of poisons you are employing. The first category are slow acting poisons that are applied over time, these tend to affect the brain. The second category are slow acting poisons, which affects the body via one or more organ systems at a time. Finally, the third category are rapid acting poisons. The rapid acting poisons are used with the

Figure 4.10   Ergot Poisoning Symptomology

Ergotism Symptomology	
Dependent upon the individual and amount of ergot ingested	
Convulsive Symptoms	**Dangerous Symptoms**
• This form of ergotism is usually associated with a mild exposure to erogt, and the poison expresses as painful seizures and muscle spasms.	• This form of ergotism is associated with an extended or large exposure to ergot, and is a result of the vasoconstriction induced by the ergot fungus.
• Other symptoms: diarrhea, paresthesia (feeling of "pins and needless"), and itching.	• It affects fingers and toes, leading to desquamation (peeling of the skin), weak peripheral pulses, loss of peripheral sensation, edema, and the death and loss of affected tissues.
• Mental effects including mania or psychosis, headaches, nausea, and vomiting.	• Limbs resembled charcoal and looked as though they were burnt by fire. Most limbs would autoamputate with minor pain or blood loss.
• People who survive exhibit dementia or delirium that does not resolve.	• In some cases, it leads to sepsis and shock due to infection.

Source: T.D. Church

intent to bring about death as quickly as possible. Depending upon the circumstance, the poisoner may want to choose a slower acting poison, this would allow for plausible deniability. If people who attend your dinner parties frequently die quickly and, in your home, a lot of attention will be focused on your activities as the host. Conversely, if people die a few days or weeks after attending one of your parties, it becomes more difficult to isolate the who, what, where, and why of the poisoning.

A discussion of poison would be amiss if it omitted Socrates when discussing the Classical Age of the Greeks. The story of his poisoning represents a classic tragedy. Socrates was a well-respected Athenian philosopher, though he never penned any of his ideas to paper nor generated any known texts (Figure 4.11). All accounts of Socrates come to us from his pupils Plato, Xenophon, Aristophanes, Euclid, and Plato's student Aristotle. Socrates death makes him an enigmatic figure in Greek history. At the end of the Peloponnesian Wars, Socrates was accused of impiety a heinous and profoundly serious crime among the ancient Athenians. *Impiety* can best be described as the desecration and mockery of the divine, typically it was used to identify mockery of divine objects such as shrines, temples, and statues. This was a very politically charged time in Athens, and many believed Socrates who spoke out against democracy was engaging a form of impiety toward democracy. His accusers painted Socrates actions as sedition and treason against Athens. In a trail that lasted one day, Socrates was found guilty by a jury of one hundred Athenian male citizens on three counts: (1) worshipping false gods; (2) failure to follow the state religion; and (3) corrupting youth through his practices and inflammatory teachings. As was the custom in Athens, Socrates was asked to propose his own penalty for his transgressions. He could have requested to become ostracized and live out his remaining days in exile. However, he did not believe his crimes warranted such a drastic measure, instead as recounted by Plato, Socrates proposed that Athens provide him with free housing and free daily meals for the services he provided the city[28]. Other sources say that he proposed paying a fine of the meager silver he had in his possession[29]. The jury rejected his proposed punishment and instead ordered the death of Socrates by poison in 399 BCE. Hemlock has been referred to as the "walking death" or the "walker's death," because after administering hemlock the individual poisoned would be instructed to walk around until their legs went numb, this was most likely done to ensure a correct dosage had been administered and being appropriately metabolized. A slow creeping numbness would spread from the feet up the body until it reaches the diaphragm. Hemlock contains toxic alkaloids that affect nerve impulse transmission in muscles, eventually delivering death through respiratory failure[29]. An antidote has never been discovered for hemlock and it

Figure 4.11 Socrates

Stefanos Kyriazis/Shutterstock.com

remains one of the deadliest poisons known to humans. In defiance to his charges of worshipping false gods and failure to follow state religion, Socrates last words to Plato were ". . . we owe a rooster to Asclepius. Please, make this offering to him and do not forget the debt"[28].

Religion in ancient Greece was filled with beliefs, rituals, and mythology emanating from both public religion and cult practices. The ancient Greeks had mystery cults designed to produce an ecstatic religious experience (Figure 4.12). *Mysteries* were secret rites and required initiation into a cult to gain access to the knowledge or revelations of the cult. Mystery cults were closed organizations, whose practices were only known to the initiated, and their secrecy was guarded by the initiated. *Cult* stems from the same root as "cultivate" in Latin, which provides some context to understand how the ancients worshiped[30]. Ancient Greek religion was less predicated on faith or belief than it was on concrete participatory events including but not limited to prayer, sacrifice, votive offerings, competitions, processions, construction of monuments, and festivals. Similar to how we water and weed a garden, religion of the past required participation in order to encourage growth. The pantheon of ancient Greece was full of gods who were favorable toward mortals, some who were neutral, and some who were openly opposed and hostile. All of these had to be cultivated following age-old rituals and customs. Cults were sometimes shrouded in privacy and secrecy, other times they were practiced in the open. Cults were an ingenious adaptation of much older shamanistic rites and functioned to serve as a bridge between nature and civilization. Many of the cults had rites and rituals that were performed in nature, in the woods, and away from cities. Among the most famous mystery cults were the Cult of Dionysius, Cult of Isis, Cult of Mithra, Cult of Attis, Cult of Pan, and Cult of Aphrodite.

Among the better known of the mystery cults was the Eleusinian Mysteries. This mystery cult held initiations every year in Eleusis and was focused on the cult of Demeter and Persephone. The timing of the initiation ceremony coincided with the spring equinox, marking the flourishing of nature. The mythology surrounding Demeter and Persephone was used to explain the annual transition of nature through the seasons[31]. Demeter was the goddess of agriculture and fertility and responsible for bringing a bountiful crop to the people. Persephone, the beloved daughter of Demeter and the goddess of spring and nature, was tasked with painting the flowers of the world and bringing them to life. Hades, one of the brothers of Demeter and the god of the underworld, saw Persephone's magnificent beauty, and before Persephone could finish her task, she was taken by Hades to his kingdom (Figure 4.13). Persephone knew to not

Figure 4.12   Eleusinian Mystery Cult Vase

Andronos Haris/Shutterstock.com

Figure 4.13   Kidnapping of Persephone

Opachevsky Irina/Shutterstock.com

partake in any consumption of food or drink in the underworld as it would condemn her to life in the underworld. After a few days, Hades bid Persephone to join him in his chariot to tour his underworld kingdom. Through some trickery, Hades convinced Persephone to eat a pomegranate that sealed her fate. Meanwhile, Demeter was distraught and began searching the world for her daughter, neglecting her duties. As she did so, fields went fallow, fruits withered and died on the vine, draughts and famine began to rise, and the abundance of nature was not being afforded to the mortals. Zeus intervened and granted Persephone six months in the mortal realm and six months in the underworld every year. This is how the ancient Greeks made sense of the change in the seasons. When Persephone was in the realm of Hades, Demeter was mournful (fall and winter), and when Persephone was in the realm of mortals, Demeter was joyful (spring and summer).

With regards to the Eleusinian Mysteries, the full details of the rites, ceremonies, and beliefs were closely guarded and not preserved through written word. What we know comes to us from archaeological evidence and contemporary commentaries[32]. The Eleusinian Mysteries involved visions of Persephone, Demeter, and Hades in the conjuring of lifecycles, seasons, and the afterlife. We know that entheogenic drugs were a consistent feature of the rites, ceremonies, and experiences of many of the mysteries. For nearly 2,000 years, initiates would come to Eleusis in the spring and consume entheogenic laced wine, dance, sing, and fornicate in nature[33]. Mysteries, as the word insinuates, were ancient cults shrouded in ritual secrecy and initiations. Many of these initiation rituals involved the consumption of wine laced with an entheogen. *Entheogens* represent any substance ingested to catalyze or generate an altered state of consciousness, which provides deep spiritual significance to the consumer. Entheogen is a more precise term than psychoactive or hallucinogenic when discussing these types of substances because the experience is tied to and relevant to a deeply spiritual experience or event. *Psychoactive* is a bit of a catch-all term these days and is most frequently employed to describe any substance "affecting the mind." *Hallucinogens* refer to substances that alter perception, mood, and reality for the consumer. Entheogens have been shown in studies to provide high-voltage, slow-wave, synchronous brain activity, with highly expressed activity occurring between the emotional and behavioral areas of the brain[34].

Entheogens are rarely abused as substances, and as many scholars believe, mundane recreational use of entheogens in the ancient world was nonexistent[35]. Entheogen preparation was extremely secret and only a few individuals possessed the knowledge related to the plant sources and specifics of harvesting/extracting and preparation. Many people today have heard of ayahuasca but very few know how to find the plants, harvest the necessary parts, and brew them into the concoction consumed by modern psychonauts. In addition, problems are likely to occur when entheogens are taken outside of a ritual context and without the supervision and support of an experienced facilitator. Individuals who attempt to prepare the complex mixture of plants can result in an inferior preparation at best or a gravely toxic combination at the worst. There are concerns when self-administering entheogens that could result in an overdose with severe psychological and physiological symptoms. As a result, these substances are rarely abused.

Entheogens are known to cause unpleasant and often undesirable physiological side effects. The psychospiritual and therapeutic benefits attributed to the entheogenic experiences tend to outweigh the benign and transitory toxicities experienced. Nausea, cramps, vomiting, profuse sweating, and diarrhea represent minor inconveniences when considering the profundity of experiences in what can best be described as divine communion[36]. An experienced guide—shaman or priest—who can anticipate these bad experiences and help the initiate through them is crucial for the success of the entheogenic experience. The *ordeal* of the initiates comprised the physiological and psychological discomforts that arise while participating in the ecstatic experience of the entheogens[34, 37]. The ordeal introduces a sense of humility and gives the initiate fundamental understanding, additional meaning, broader perspective, and deeper emotional impact with their experiences. Mild to moderate symptomatic difficulties would not have been considered "bad," instead they would have been seen as part of the sacred and spiritual journey in becoming fully initiated into a mystery cult.

Shifting gears from entheogenic mystery cults our focus will return to practical medicine. In 460 BCE, Hippocrates Asclepiades was born on the island of Cos near the city of Halicarnassus (Figure 4.14). Asclepiades translates to "descendant of Asclepius" and scholars are not certain if this name was a family name indicating descent from Asclepius or if it was ascribed due to his work as a physician. Today, most people refer to him simply as Hippocrates. We often refer to him as the father of modern medicine, due in large part to the ***Hippocratic Corpus***. The Hip-

Figure 4.14 Hippocrates Asclepiades of Cos

pocratic Corpus is a collection of 70 written works and represents the oldest surviving complete medical text from antiquity[38]. Hippocrates believed in that diet and exercise were in and of themselves cures for many of the ailments people faced. Reluctantly, if individuals were unable to follow his prescription of better diet and more exercise, Hippocrates would provide medicine. He recognized that physical manipulation was necessary to cure some physical troubles, like setting a dislocated hip. In all instances, Hippocrates believed in moderation and observation. What lives on of Hippocrates legacy in modern medicine is his commitment to the treatment of disease.

The Hippocratic Oath, one of the best-known sections within the Hippocratic Corpus, represents one of the earliest forms of medical ethics. Originally, the oath required new physicians to swear by the right of several healing gods and goddesses to uphold ethical standards related to the craft of medicine. While the oath has been traditionally attributed to Hippocrates, most modern scholars contend that Hippocrates did not write the oath himself[39-41]. The oldest text dates to ~275 CE, which is over 600 years after Hippocrates lived. The text does outline good practices that physicians should follow and the key tenet "primum non nocere" (Latin: First, do no harm) has been a cornerstone of medical ethics for over 1,800 years.

One legacy of Hippocrates that took a long time for medicine to shake off was a reliance on the four humors in medical diagnosis. The four humors were believed to originate in the liver and were important in understanding harmony in bodily processes. This harmony when out of balance required a strict regimen of diet, activity, and exercise, all designed to eliminate the imbalanced humor from the body[8, 38]. The humors each had an element, which was associated with a season, specific qualities, and a cause (Table 4.1). For centuries, this format of diagnosis was dominant in medicine. It was believed that good health was a result of a harmonious balance and continuous interworking of the humors. The humors were not seen as simple descriptions of physical substances. They were believed to affect the mind, thoughts, emotions, and overall well-being of individuals in varied and profound ways.

Table 4.1 Hippocratic Humors and Associations

Humor	Cause	Qualities	Elemental Cause	Season
Melancholic	Black Bile	Cold and Dry	Too Much Earth	Autumn
Sanguine	Blood	Hot and Moist	Too Much Air	Spring
Phlegmatic	Phlegm	Cold and Moist	Too Much Water	Winter
Choleric	Yellow Bile	Hot and Dry	Too Much Fire	Summer

Overall well-being was a central focus of ancient Greek medicine with aspects of general health, diet, fitness, psychology, and spirituality being seen as important to promoting and preserving heath. To maintain health, changes of habits and environments were often advised, which included bathing, perspiration, walking, massage, and diet. Hippocrates was instrumental for his writing about the benefits of hydrotherapy for helping to balance many of the elements of the human condition and promote healing[42]. Thermal hot springs, due to the supernatural power attributed to the warm waters and their vapors, were often sacred spaces where temples dedicated to healing first arose in ancient Greece. The early physicians in Greece wrote about the beneficial properties of sulfur hot springs, especially for healing the skin and for alleviating muscular and joint pains associated with arthritis[43]. Hippocrates spent many pages in a few of his writings to talk about thermal water, wherein he described the different chemical features and the effects of hot and cold water on the human body[44]. Bathing as therapy became a natural component of healing practices in ancient Greece and gave rise to three distinct forms of medicinal baths—*balneotherapy*, *loutrotherapy*, and *fangotherapy*[43]. Balneotherapy is the practice of being immersed in mineral water or mineral-rich mud. This type of bathing could involve hot or cold water and featured either relaxed or stimulated (through moving water) bathing. Mineral baths were preferred for the ill and could have included silica, sulfur, selenium, and radium depending upon the composition of the natural hot spring mineral deposits. Loutrotherapy required a hot bath wherein different concentrations of medicinal herbs and minerals would be added and required the bather to soak their whole body. The idea here was that the active components of the medicated concentration would exert their effects through skin absorption and vapor inhalation. Fangotherapy was a body treatment in which mineral-rich thermal mud, clay, or peat was spread over the body and massaged into the skin. It was used with the belief that is purified, revitalized, and deep cleaned the body to help reduce or remove toxins. All three forms of bathing therapy have persisted and today are components that can be found in several luxury or upscale beauty spas. Today, we tend to think of these forms of bathing as a cosmetic ritual; however, to the Greeks, they were a cornerstone in the promotion of good health.

Ancient Greece profoundly influenced our modern world in many fundamental ways, including law, math, science, literature, philosophy, astronomy, arts, and medicine. There were many unique applications of drugs ranging from therapeutic to strategic to recreational uses. For the first time, there was discussion of addiction through the belief of alcohol as leading some individuals to an inexhaustible desire for consumption, which they labeled toxicomania. From the writings of philosophers and physicians who wrote about disease and recommended treatments, a foundation for modern medical practices has emerged. From these scientific philosophers, we were able to connect illnesses with lifestyle, diet, exercise, and the environment.

REFERENCES

1. Plutarch, L.M., *Plutarch's Lives: The Lives of the Noble Grecians and Romans.* 1914 [48 CE], London, UK: Loeb Classical Library. 802.
2. Middleton, G. D. (2020). In G. D. Middleton (Ed.), *Collapse and transformation: The Late Bronze Age to Early Iron Age in the Aegean* (p. 280). Havertown, PA: Oxbow Books.
3. Wilson, B. (2020). *Metropolis: A history of the city, humankind's greatest Invention* (p. 464). New York, NY: Doubleday.
4. Homer, (1919 [725 BCE]). In A. T. Murray (Ed.), *The Odyssey* (2nd ed., p. 465). Boston, MA: Harvard University Press.
5. Pitt-Rivers, J. (2012). The law of hospitality. *HAU: Journal of Ethnographic Theory*, **2**(1), 501–517.
6. Slater, W. J. (1991). *Dining in a classical context* (p. 217). Ann Arbor, MI: University of Michigan Press.
7. Chrystal, P. (2016). *In Bed with the Ancient Greeks* (p. 288). Gloucestershire, UK: Amberley Publishing Limited.
8. Tesseromatis, C. (2020). Drugs in greek mythology and medicine. *Journal of Medicinal Plants*, **8**(2), 38–43.
9. Touwaide, A. (2019). Harmful botanicals. In P. Wexler (Ed.), *Toxicology in antiquity* (2nd ed., pp. 387–399). Academic Press.
10. Euripides, (1986 [455 BCE]). In E. R. Dodds (Ed.), *Bacchae* (p. 253), Oxford University Press: Oxford.
11. Papagelopoulos, P. J., Mavrogenis, A. F., & Soucacos, P. N. (2004). Doping in ancient and modern Olympic Games. *Orthopedics*, **27**(12), 1226–1231.
12. Younger, J. G. (2021). Sport and spectacle in the Greek Bronze Age. In A. Furtell & T. F. Scanlon (Eds). *The Oxford handbook sport and spectacle in the ancient world* (pp. 47–61). Oxford University Press: Oxford, UK.

13. Harrison, A. P., Hansen, S. H. & Bartels, E. M. (2012). Transdermal opioid patches for pain treatment in ancient Greece. *Pain Practice*, **12**(8), 620–625.

14. Goodman, J., Sherratt, A. & Lovejoy, P. E. (2014). Consuming habits: Drugs in history and anthropology. In J. Goodman, A. Sherratt, P. E. Lovejoy (Eds.), *Global and historical perspectives on how cultures define drugs* (2 ed., p. 304). London: Routledge.

15. Baratz, A. (2015). The source of the Gods' immortality in archaic Greek literature. *Scripta Classica Israelica*, **34**, 151–164.

16. Scott, M. (2020). The Oracle at Delphi: Unknowability at the heart of the ancient Greek world. *Social Research: An International Quarterly*, **87**(1), 51–74.

17. Herodotus, (1996 [440 BCE]). *The histories* (p. 771). New York, NY: Penguin Classics.

18. Ovid, P. N. (1960 [8 CE]). In R. Humphries (Ed.). *Metamorphoses*. Bloomington, IN: Indiana University Press.

19. Plato, (1909 [385 BCE]). In R. G. Bury (Ed.). *The symposium* (2nd ed, p. 179). Ann Arbor, MI: Heffer.

20. de Boer, J. Z. (2019). The Oracle at Delphi: The pythia and the pneuma, intoxicating gas finds, and hypotheses, In P. Wexler (Ed.). *Toxicology in Antiquity: History of Toxicology and Environmental Health* (pp. 141–149). Elsevier: London, UK.

21. Thucydides, *History of the Peloponnesian War*. 1965 [404 BCE], Boston, MA: Harvard University Press. 459.

22. Xenophon, (1965 [404 BCE]). In H. G. Dakyns (Ed.). 2012 [362 BCE]. *Hellenica* (p. 196). London, UK: Independently Published.

23. Mavrogenis, A. F., Saranteas, T., Markatos, K., Kotsiou, A., & Tesseromatis, C. (2019). Pharmacies for pain and trauma in ancient Greece. *International Orthopaedics*, **43**(6), 1529–1536.

24. Carod-Artal, F. J. (2013). Psychoactive plants in ancient Greece. *Neurosciences and History*, **1**(1), 28–38.

25. Johnston, C. E. (2014). Beware of that cup!: The role of food-tasters in ancient society. In *Classical Studies* (p. 134.). University of Otago: Dunedin, New Zealand.

26. Touwaide, A. (2019). Nicander, Thêriaka, and Alexipharmaka: Venoms, poisons, and literature. In P. Wexler (Ed.) *Toxicology in antiquity* (pp. 105–115). Elsevier: London, UK.

27. Forte, V. A. & Garcia, A. A. (2014). Metronomic chemotherapy in gynecological cancers. In G. Bocci & G. Francia (Eds.). *Metronomic chemotherapy: Pharmacology and clinical applications* (pp. 203–216). Springer Nature: Berlin, Germany.

28. Plato, (2006 [339 BCE]). In J. J. Helm (Ed.). *Apology*. Wauconda, IL: Bolchazy-Carducci Publishers, Inc.

29. Arihan, O., S. K. Arihan, & Touwaide, A. (2019). The case against Socrates and his execution. In P. Wexler (Ed.). *Toxicology in antiquity* (2nd ed., pp. 117–129). Elsevier: London, UK.

30. Larson, J. (2007) *Ancient Greek cults: A guide*. New York, NY: Routledge.

31. Keller, M. L. (1988). The Eleusinian mysteries of Demeter and Persephone: Fertility, sexuality, and rebirth. *Journal of Feminist Studies in Religion*, **4**(1), 27–54.

32. Cosmopoulos, M. B. (2005). *Greek mysteries: The archaeology of ancient Greek secret cults* (p. 288). London, UK: Routledge.

33. Ustinova, Y. (2013). To live in joy and die with hope: Experiential aspects of Ancient Greek mystery rites. *Bulletin - Institute of Classical Studies*, **56**(2), 105–123.

34. Hoffman, M. A. (2019). Entheogens (psychedelic drugs) and the ancient mystery religions. In P. Wexler (Ed.). *Toxicology in antiquity* (pp. 353–362), Elsevier: London, UK.

35. Ruck, C. A. P. (2019). *Entheogens in ancient times: Wine and the rituals of Dionysus*. In P. Wexler (Ed.) *Toxicology in antiquity* (2nd ed., pp. 343–352). Academic Press.

36. Dannaway, F. R. (2010.) Strange fires, weird smokes, and psychoactive combustibles: Entheogens in ancient tradition. *Journal of Psychoactive Drugs*, **42**(4), 485–497.

37. Ustinova, Y. (2020). Alteration of consciousness in Ancient Greece: Divine mania. *History of Psychiatry*, **31**(3), 257–273.

38. Hippocrates (2014 [430 BCE]). In E. Craik (Ed.). *The 'Hippocratic' corpus: Content and context* (1st ed., p. 344). London, UK: Routledge.

39. Doyle, D. J. (2021). Exploring the Hippocratic oath: A critical look at medicine's oldest surviving guide to medical ethics. *Ethics in Biology, Engineering and Medicine: An International Journal*, **12**(1), 21–30.

40. Leven, K.-H. (2019). The invention of Hippocrates: Oath, letters and Hippocratic corpus. In U. Tröhler, S. Reiter-Theil, & E. Herych (Eds.). *Ethics codes in medicine* (pp. 3–23). Routledge: London, UK.

41. Tolsa, C. (2019) On the origins of the Hippocratic oath. *Greek, Roman, and Byzantine Studies*, **59**(4), 621–645.

42. Gianfaldoni, S., Tchernev, G., Wollina, U., Roccia, M. G., Fioranelli, M., Gianfaldoni, R., & Lotti, T. (2017). History of the baths and thermal medicine. *Open Access Macedonian Journal of Medical Sciences*, **5**(4), 566–568.

43. Tsitsis, N., Polkas, G., Daoutis, A., Prokopiou, E., & Kourkouta, L. (2013). Hydrotherapy in Ancient Greece. *Balkan Military Medical Review*, **16**(4), 462–466.

44. Hippocrates, (1881 [400 BCE]). *Airs, Waters, and Places* (p. 107). London, UK: Printed - not for sale - by Messrs. Wyman & Sons.

Ancient Rome: Surgery and Anesthesia

Chapter 5

A s told through legend, Rome was founded in 753 BCE by the twins Romulus and Remus (Figure 5.1), and the city grew from a small backwater town in central Italy into a vast empire. At the height of prominence, Rome encompassed the majority of continental Europe, England, much of western Asia, northern Africa, and the Islands of the Mediterranean. Roman influence extends to many civilizations today with a few of those influences found in language, the modern Western or Latin alphabet, the calendar, standard currency, plumbing, paved roads, public architecture, and the eventual emergence and spread of Christianity. Rome functioned as a monarchy for 300 years, a

Figure 5.1 Abandoned Twins, Romulus and Remus, Raised by a She-Wolf

freevideophotoagency/Shutterstock.com

republic for 450 years, and an empire for 450 years. Roman history extends for a period of nearly 1,200 years. Through golden ages of peace and prosperity to the decline and fall of the empire, Rome helped shape the history of human civilization. Roman influence will be explored via two distinct periods, the Republic of Rome (509 BCE to 27 BCE) and Imperial Rome (27 BCE to 476 CE). Rome was held together by political and military might, which was supported by a vast communications network unlike anything previously seen. This network extended knowledge and introduced many beneficial practices that dramatically improved the standard of living for many Roman citizens. This connectedness through roads and communication influenced the development of medicine, surgery, and public health. The Romans were highly resilient and adapted many practices of those they conquered, incorporating the elements they saw as beneficial to the well-being of the citizens. Medical and pharmaceutical knowledge and practice were quite advanced for the time. Surgery and medicine advanced to maintain the health of the Roman war machine—a healthy army was a healthy civilization. Sadly, when the Western Roman Empire fell in 476 CE, medical knowledge in Europe declined and no considerable progress was made again in Europe until the Renaissance.

5.1 Republic of Rome

Rome was built out of war and conquest and as a result Roman warfare was extraordinarily successful. The Roman army was a professional organization and was arguably among the most effective fighting forces in history[1, 2]. The Roman army did not win every battle, but it used every opportunity to learn from every engagement it undertook. Battles may have been lost, but when Rome set its sights on conquest, it rarely lost the war. Every encounter enhanced Rome's strategies and added to her vast tactical playbook. Even after defeat, the Romans would come back. Romans had one objective in all military engagements and would pursue that goal unremittingly. It was the drive for success that pushed Roman warfare forward. The Romans had an innovative and adaptable army, centralized command, expert engineers, roads with a constant line of supply, surgeons and physicians, and a network of loyal allies. Romans had adopted an inclusive approach to the peoples it conquered. Incorporation instead of annihilation worked to the benefit of Rome by strengthening and expanding the political and military reach of the Republic. The Roman army was the Republic's largest expenditure and as a result captured territory, resources, wealth, and slaves (the latter being necessary for frontier defense) made war and conquest a constant Roman preoccupation.

Senatus Populusque Quid Romanus (*SPQR*), meaning the Senate and People of Rome, became a prominent symbol of Rome during the Republican period of Rome and lasted into the Imperial period (Figure 5.2). The abbreviation SPQR could be found on buildings, military standards and banners, roads, coins, and public works. It represented the legal and political power of Rome as it highlighted the sovereignty and ultimate source of Rome's political power. The phrase indicated all power came from the people of Rome and highlighted the democratic nature or intent of the Roman Republic. The government of the Republic consisted of ~500 senators who served for life, many of whom were

Figure 5.2 SPQR on Pedestal of a Statue in Rome

Zoltan Tarlacz/Shutterstock.com

from the patrician class. The senate was led by two consuls, who were annually elected[3]. The consuls had veto power over the other's actions. Roman society was divided into two classes of individuals, patricians and plebians. *Patricians* represented the land-holding aristocracy, many of whom traced—or claimed to trace—their ancestry to the founding of Rome. *Plebians* were far mor numerous and represented the citizen-commoners. Ancient Romans had an extraordinarily strong tradition and morality that required men to participate in public service. A distinct system of *patronage* existed among the men in ancient Rome[4]. It was a formalized relationship between a *patronus* and their *cliens*. The patronus was the protector, provider, sponsor, and benefactor of their cliens. The patronus typically was wealthy, held power and prestige, and would enable their cliens through monetary assistance or political favors. The cliens became duty bound to assist, repay, and obey their patronus. The patronage system was a fundamental aspect of Roman life and has persisted—albeit it in a slightly altered format—until today. In a way it was the early blueprint of the mafia system.

At the heart of Roman life was *latifundia*[5]. Latifundia were extensive parcels of land, specifically privately owned land. Latifundium were estates of the patricians and they specialized in export of agricultural products—grains, olives, grapes, etc. The wealth of the patricians was measured by the amount of land they owned and the agricultural yield they produced. Whether that yield was sold at market for a profit or stored at home for sustenance, latifundia provided a means of survival, either in the form of sustenance or as currency and both could help influence social order. All levels of Roman society depended on the land for their survival as well as the preserver of their social status. The ability of Roman citizens to identify and acquire useful drugs from their environment was a direct result of a culture deeply tied to the harmonious relationship between people and their land.

Roman citizens benefited from the incorporation of new territories by virtue of goods, luxuries, and slaves. By 146 BCE Greece had become a province of Rome and by 27 BCE Rome controlled not only mainland Greece, but all the Greek-speaking lands and islands throughout the Mediterranean. As with all conquered lands, the Romans incorporated Greek concepts, ideas, and beliefs. The Romans used many ideas of the Greeks, but they did not simply copy them. A quote from Strabo, a Greek Geographer and Historian who lived during the transition from the Republic to the Empire, described this penchant of the Romans. "The Greeks are famous for their cities and in this they aimed at beauty. The Romans excelled in those things which the Greeks took little interest in such as the building of roads, aqueducts, and sewers"[6]. Any of the Greek ideas that were impractical were ignored. Rome focused on those ideas that lead to the direct improvement of the quality of life of the citizens.

Citizens in Rome had a fairly consistent supply of grain, which in turn was made into bread or *puls* a thick porridge often seasoned with herbs, cheese, or oil. Fruits and vegetables were likely available for the majority of citizens in regular abundance. The lower class did not consume as much meat as the upper class per capita. Breakfast, when eaten, was consumed early in the day, and was not always eaten. Lunch was typically a quick meal of bread and cheese or could be more elaborate with meat, fish, vegetables, and fruits. Dinner was the main meal of the day and would have at least two courses, more if the meal were at a wealthy home. Dinner fell into two categories in Roman homes, *convivum* and *festum[7]*. Convivum, meaning "living together," was your typical dinner or meal spent together as a family. In later years it would be relegated to meaning the "commoners' meal" or the "average person's meal." Festum, on the other hand, were lavish banquet feasts with the sole intention of impressing one's guests. Festive consumption of food and wine was an important social ritual in the Roman world. Wealthy and elite Romans threw extravagant parties featuring luxurious tableware. Festum were highly competitive events, as families attempted to exceed the parties of their friends and neighbors. They would have diverse, sometimes perverse, forms of entertainment that included poetry, music, dancers, acrobats, and orgies[8]. The food would be outrageous and sometimes feature illegal foods with some reported delicacies being brains of pheasants, stewed ostrich, roasted flamingo, dolphin meatballs, ragout of brains and bacon, stuffed dormice, and tongues of pigeons[9]. These foods would have had condiments like *garum*, a pungent and salty fermented fish sauce. The condiment was made by leaving fish meat, blood, and guts to ferment inside clay vessels under the Mediterranean sun. Copious amounts of *mulsum*, a honey infused sweet wine, would have been served. It was expected that guests would gorge themselves, rest for an hour or so, and continue eating. Vomiting was seen as a sign the meal was good as the vomiter needed to make room for more food. Among the wealthy, feasting usually began around 5 pm and would last for many hours. It was not unheard of for the feasts to end in orgies and all manner of polyamorous activities, but this was not a staple at every feast. In some ways, these feasts were near religious experiences for those enamored of food, sex, and gluttony.

Romans tended to be more spiritual than they were religious. Yes, they had gods and goddesses and many homes held an alter or small shrine for their household gods and venerated family elders. But they were more pragmatic with their religious beliefs, at least in the Republican period. Superstition, magic, and a belief in the supernatural were on the other hand quite prominent among the ancient Romans. This led to the use of amulets and lucky charms as being ubiquitous. The Romans used a variety of protective elements to confer safety, to improve health, to ward off the evil eye, to improve one's luck, to gain a lover, or to provide spiritual guidance and balance. Prominent among these protective elements were fascinum (Figure 5.3), tintinnabula, and bulla[10, 11]. *Bulla* were protective amulets that resembled a modern locket. Bulla were given to young boys, who would wear the bulla to improve their health or to ward off the evil eye. Bulla sometimes contained a *fascinum* or phallus shaped amulet, which was added around the age of 9 and worn until the boy married. Soldiers would continue to wear a fascinum (without the bulla) under their tunics for protection and luck while at war. Homes and intersection of roads would have fascinum carved into stone or wood to provide safety and protection to families and travelers, respectively. Some homes featured *tintinnabula* or winged fascinum adorned with tiny bells and functioned as windchimes to protect and grant good health and fortune to the home. Penises, flying or not, represented much more than sex or sexuality. To the ancient Romans a penis represented health, safety, luck, protection, fertility, and spiritual guidance.

Figure 5.3   Winged Fascinum, Pompeii, Italy; Via dell'Abbondanza

Mazerath/Shutterstock.com

Figure 5.4   Gladiators of Colosseum in Rome, Flavian Amphitheatre

David Gonzalez Rebollo/Shutterstock.com

A more well-known representation of Roman culture were the gladiatorial games (Figure 5.4). At first glance it may seem as though these battles were all about *sanguis et arena*, "blood and sand." A gory way to entertain people through the spectacle of battle and displays of blood. But these battles represented much more than the stark contrast of life and death. They served to help reinforce fundamental Roman values and beliefs. Values that included courage in the face of death, self-discipline, firmness of body and mind, endurance, noble pursuits, contempt of death, love of glory, the ability to rise from defeat, and the desire to win. Additionally, the games existed as a form of social control. They represented the absolute and unquestionable power of Rome. Gladiatorial battles were public displays where law and order took center stage and showed the consequences for those who disobeyed. Gladiators were mostly comprised of convicted criminals, captured enemies from war, enslaved peoples who had been purchased at auction, or acquired through the debts they owed. Gladiators could win back their freedom, but their freedom was contingent upon their winning of battles and the favor of the cheering crowds. Winning gladiators were often treated like modern day rock stars, many were even seen as sex symbols and objects of desire. Gladiators were sexually exploited by the aristocracy, who would order the gladiators to have sex with women and other slaves while they watched[8]. Gladiators were often used to satiate the carnal desires of the elite. Even the blood of gladiators was considered to embody sexual prowess and many old men would cover themselves in Gladiator blood before engaging coitus[12]. Gladiator blood was a highly sought-after commodity as it was believed that the blood could cure epilepsy, improve fertility, make skin youthful and radiant, and restore youth and vigor. *Munera* were specialized vendors, who after a gladiator was felled and his body removed from the arena would sell the still warm blood to the crowd[8]. By 400 CE, Gladiatorial battles were outlawed which led Romans to begin seeking out the blood of executed criminals to replace the cures once conferred through the blood of Gladiators.

Spectacles in Rome were events viewed and participated in by the public. These events needed to have an audience who were tacitly entertained in order to be considered successful. They needed to be extraordinary and often were extravagant in their waste of resources. Spectacles could occur in a variety of venues. Gladiatorial games and circus events, theatrical and musical performances, religious ceremonies, triumphal processions, and could even occur more privately at banquets and during funerals[13]. There have been archaeological discoveries in Rome and Ostia which depicts women who participated in Gladiatorial combat. *Gladiatrix*, a modern term, were female gladiators. To be certain, women in combat was something that would have been both a spectacle and a direct affront to Roman civility. This would have been infinitely worse if the woman was from an upper-class family or if she was of foreign nobility. Women in Roman society had extremely limited rights and exceedingly strict social roles. These warrior women would have turned the normal Roman social conventions on its head and put their foot on the throat of Roman social order. These women would have fought each other, wild animals, or even midgets to entertain audiences[14]. They would have most assuredly been viewed as a vulgar rarity in Roman society. An inscription found in Ostia, Italy, indicated that women engaged in fighting, the "*gladiators mulieres*" could be found here[15]. These women would have been exotic markers of exceptionally lavish if not gaudy spectacles for public entertainment.

Public entertainment and public works projects were major concerns of Roman senators. A happy public was an easy one to control. To this end, Rome built aqueducts to bring fresh water into cities, shopping areas, public buildings, temples, roads, sewers, cisterns, and baths. Personal hygiene was a major concern in the daily life of all Romans. Baths were associated with health and many of the public baths featured statues of Asclepius (god of healing) and his daughter Hygeia (goddess of good health). Public baths were used by rich and poor, men and women, the old and the young[16]. Every Roman settlement held at least one public bath. The average entrance fee was a quadrans (equivalent to 1/16th of a penny). This low price ensured that every Roman citizen could access and afford the baths. Sick people were encouraged to bathe, as the Romans believed bathing would help one regain good health. Unfortunately, it most likely only succeeded in spreading disease as these baths would have offered the perfect conditions for many bacteria and viruses to thrive. Roman bathhouse design changed throughout Roman history and feature both fashionable and practical elements. There were three core features that could reliably be found in a Roman bathhouse: the calderum (hot), frigidarum (cold), and tepidarium (warm/tepid)[17]. These features consisted of hot, cold, and warm pools of water. Bathers would progress through each pool before laying on a large heated stone or marble slab to help dry-off and relax upon.

Romans during the Republic period, like the Greeks and the Egyptians before them, helped to improve pharmacology and medicine. Rome was hyper focused on public health. Poor hygiene was viewed as a constant source of disease. Rome built aqueducts to bring fresh water into a city and sewers to take waste away. They believed in exercise and care for the body. In the early part of the Republic, there were very few professional doctors. Most doctors served in the military and would provide services to citizens upon retiring from active duty. Thus, the head of the household was often the de facto physician for the family. It was hoped that they had enough information about herbal cures and general medicine to be able to treat most illnesses in the home.

Medicine or *medicamenta* was a catch-all term in Latin that best described all crafts or skills associated with the body and its surroundings. Medicamenta in writing was used to describe five distinct things (Table 5.1)[18]. Equally as confusing were the words related to drugs and medications. *Venena* (plural, venenum) were substances or practices capable of altering anything they come into contact with, including the body, mind, or both[19]. Sometimes a value was given to the term venena to help make sense of the intended use. *Bonum* meaning good or in this context benign or inoffensive, when combined as venena bonum would refer to therapeutic drugs. *Malum* meaning bad or in this context baneful or harmful, when combined as venena malum would refer to poisons. The person who administered the venena was referred to as the *veneficium*. The person who prepared the

Table 5.1 Definition of Medicamenta

1. Cosmetic, paint, or wash
2. Artificial improvement (i.e., glass eye, wooden finger)
3. Drug or remedy to poison
4. Poison or toxin
5. Pigment for artisans

Source: T.D. Church

venena was the **venefici**. Within the Roman legal system, one needed to prove that the venena had lethal consequences or cause a serious decline in someone's health if litigating for a verdict of *summum supplicium* (death penalty) to be rendered to the venefici. Ambiguity in the word venena point to a very intriguing conceptualization the Romans held. In the Roman legal system and potentially in everyday life the difference between remedy and poison was not dependent upon the substance itself, but in the amount and intent of the dose.

Rome paid remarkably close attention to the health and fortitude of her soldiers. Without soldiers, the Republic would collapse. Basic health in the military had a focus on access to clean water, providing adequate food, and keeping fit. Soldiers were often on the move, with most legions marching between 15 and 20 miles (24 and 32 km) a day for five consecutive days. The soldiers would be given a day of respite and then would be back on their rigid marching schedule. After each day's march, the legion would setup a marching camp with light fortifications, usually wooden palisades, where they would stay overnight. Staying in one place too long would expose soldiers to attach as well as to the illnesses that existed in a particular area and thus, they were moved around frequently. Romans had developed the first documented field military hospitals[20]. These were constructed with freshwater intakes, drainage, and sewage systems. There were tents for surgery, tents for examination of patients, tents for preparation of medicines and medical tools, and tents dedicated to those who needed continuous medical care (think basic Critical Care Ward). Roman medical philosophy held that soldiers recovered quicker in a hygienic environment. Other unique Roman inventions were the first dedicated military medical corps. This corps was charged with providing aid to the soldiers both on and off the field of battle. The military corps had a rudimentary triage system to help identify move wounded soldiers out of the theatre of war and into the field hospital base on severity of wounds and likelihood of survival. The **tourniquet** was a battlefield invention of the military corps to stop blood loss and allow the wounded soldier to be transported to the field hospital. Romans documented the practice of boiling surgical instruments in water to disinfect them prior to surgery. The Romans had a sophisticated system for removal of cataracts with some highly precise instruments to assist with the procedure. In terms of medical devices, they were skilled at creating artificial limbs and digits using wood, metal, and plaster.

Doctors who treated the general population often times fulfilled multiple roles and functioned as physicians, pharmacists, surgeons, and beauticians. They were skilled at providing drugs, cosmetics, perfumes, and even styling the hair of their clients. Throughout Roman history, there were no substances that functioned *purely* as a cosmetic and *only* as a cosmetic[21]. They had even developed plant and animal extracts to dye hair, some examples are listed in Figure 5.5. Cosmetics in the age of

Figure 5.5 Roman Hair Dye from Plant Extracts

the Republic tended to be used by Roman women in the aristocracy. Cosmetics were used by some men and the lower classes of women to a lesser extent. Some of the cosmetics were quite dangerous and others were quite odd by modern standards. *Fair complexion* was seen as the height of beauty. It implied that the individual did not spend too much time outside under the sun, ergo the individual was not working class. Men from all classes were not expected to have fair complexions. Women with fair complexion implied health, fertility, and a promising marriage partner. To aid in making the complexion even fairer, women turned to white lead. *White lead* was made by steeping lead shavings in vinegar and leaving the concoction to evaporate[22, 23]. The resultant white powder was applied to the face as a powder or mixed with oil, beeswax, or animal fat to produce a paste. White lead has a cumulative effect on the body. It would corrode the surface of the skin, contributed to central nervous system damage, internal organ damage, and infertility. As the face corroded, the women would pack more white lead onto the face to cover the damage, which introduced even more lead into their bodies[22].

White lead powder provided a blank canvas, however in the right light it could make one look dead or lifeless with no natural color shining through. As any good cosmetologist or avid fan of Ru Paul's Drag Race can attest, it is important to build upon and contour one's face from a good base. Roman women added rouge to the lips and cheeks. The two most popular forms of rouge consisted of powders made from *red lead* (lead tetroxide) and *cinnabar* (red mercuric sulfide, see Figure 5.6) [23]. Red lead and cinnabar are brilliant read pigments and were used to heighten the color of the cheeks and lips to create a complexion compared to the subtle colors of nature. Both substances were known poisons by Roman physicians during the Republic. Inhaling the dust or powder from either red lead or cinnabar would have led to serious health hazards including, mental deterioration, high blood pressure, joint and muscle pain, memory and concentration problems, headache, abdominal pain, mood disorders, miscarriages, and hair loss. Truly, there is pain in the pursuit of beauty.

Figure 5.6   Cinnabar/Red Mercuric Sulfide

S_E/Shutterstock.com

Planned body hair removal was a common practice among Roman women and some men. They had a number of methods to assist in hair removal, including *depilatories*, *tweezing*, and *epilation*[24]. Depilatories are liquid or cream preparations that are used to remove unwanted hair from the body. Depilatory creams during the Republic would have included pitch, quick lime, donkey fat, she-goat gall, bat's blood, and even powdered viper skin according to some existing sources[22, 24]. Many of the depilatory creams included some very toxic ingredients, with arsenic being a frequently used additive[23]. Tweezing is a mechanical process of removing hair by using a device to pull the hairs out of the skin. Anyone who has ever tweezed a hair can report that the act is both painful and mildly irritating. It may be a transitory pain, but in the moment feels a little like the effects will last for eternity. Tweezers are essentially safe to use as a hair removal option as there are no chemicals involved but can cause minor infections or increase acne not properly cleaned prior to use. Epilation is the removal of hair by pulling it from the roots through sugaring or waxing. Waxing is a technique in which a warm sticky paste is made from bee's wax or honey applied to the skin. A strip of cloth is pressed onto the paste and after the paste has cooled it is pulled off quickly. This action removes the hair and elicits a scream (vocalized or not) from the most seasoned waxee. Traditionally, in ancient Rome, hair would have been removed in saunas where people would have been steam treated and the pores on their skin were opened. This would have helped to make the act of waxing a little less painful but did not remove the pain completely.

Culturally, we are led to believe that a true and virtuous Roman man took to shaving with a passion[25]. This is true during the time of the Republic, however beards became fashionable in the late Imperial period. Julius Gaius Caesar was reported to have had his beard plucked out by tweezers. While this sounds extremely painful it represents an improvement forward from vigorously rubbing a pumice stone all over the face to remove unwanted facial hair. Young Roman men celebrated their first shave with an elaborate party to welcome adulthood, called the *novacila*. Wherein the pumice stone would make an appearance again to rub any stubble off the face. This would be followed by a massage with oils and perfumes to help soften and soothe the irritated skin, some of the oils would have contained opium and mint. The Roman equivalent of a barbershop, the *tonsor*, served as a meeting place where news and gossip would be exchanged over a nice shave. The tonsor was usually located in the men's section of the bathhouse but were also portable as a tonsor could come to your home if needed. In general, the Roman view on manscaping saw that the richer one was, the less body hair they sported. Scruff, beards, and facial hair were considered to be uncivilized for men especially during the Republic[25]. Facial hair carried the connotation of being a slave or servant, and it most definitely indicated you were someone from the lower classes of society.

All classes of Roman society utilized wine as a regular vehicle for drugs as well as being a drug itself. Wine was often infused with different herbs, which would have functioned to provide a small degree of effect given the wine's ability to extract active compounds from the additive herbs. A brief list of common herbs used by the Romans can be found in Figure 5.7, with two or more being infused at any given time. The problem with this approach, however, was knowing if the right herbs were being infused for a particular illness. An example of this was the Roman penchant to use *Artemisia abrotanum* (lover's plant or lemon plant)[26]. It was a known antiseptic and functioned as a good mosquito repellant. Infused in tiny amounts into wine and it was believed to be an antidote for minor poisons. Too much Artemisia abrotanum in the wine and it would become highly poisonous. Roman antidotes to poison were often complex concoctions and difficult to reproduce with accuracy. Many of the antidotes were developed through trial and error. Rigorous experimentation related to poisons and antidotes was often conducted upon prisoners condemned to death[27]. These individuals would be offered their freedom if they consumed poison, followed by a potential candidate antidote, and observation of effect. Those who survived were granted their freedom and those who died—usually in a very painful and horrific way from the poison—were fulfilling their mandated court sentence.

Figure 5.7   Herbal Medicines from the Roman Republic

Source: T.D. Church

Among the herbal remedies the Romans utilized, there was one venerated as both a drug and symbol of honor. **Laurel** (bay leaf as it is known today) is lightly narcotic and the Romans associated the effects of laurel with trances and the work of oracles. Laurel was a symbol of the god Apollo and a symbol of triumph over adversity. Laurel wreaths were worn as symbols of victory, honor, and triumph. The classical version of the Roman crown used laurel leaves and would eventually become a symbol of the power of Roman emperors (Figure 5.8). Laurel garlands became architectural elements to adorn homes and public buildings as it was believed that the plant protected from disease, evil spells, and lightening. Laurel was important as a drug, but it was not employed for its medicinal quality rather for its supposed association with oracles[28].

One of the more unique recreational drugs used by the Romans came from a fish, the **sarpa salpa** (Figure 5.9). Sarpa salpa is a species of sea bream found in the warm waters of the Mediterranean. It just so happens that upon consumption of the head of this fish, users report vivid LSD-like hallucinations. The fish earned the moniker "Dream Fish" because of the nightmares often associated with the experience of consuming the fish's brain. The

Figure 5.8 Laurel Crown, Emperor Caligula

Kizel Cotiw-an/Shutterstock.com

Figure 5.9 Sarpa Salpa, the Dream Fish

Al Carrera/Shutterstock.com

brain of the fish produced a very potent form of **ichthyoallyeinotoxism**, a condition which causes hallucinogenic effects due to either the poisonous or toxic nature of a specific fish organ. It is best characterized as an extreme type of food poisoning. The ichthyoallyeinotoxism response to the sarpa salpa manifests with vivid auditory and visual hallucinations, delirium, disturbances in motor coordination, nausea, nightmares, vertigo, and central nervous system disorders. These symptoms can persist for as long as 36 hours and is dependent upon the age of the fish at consumption, the amount of fish brain consumed, and the age of the individual eating the fish.

The Roman Republic was an era of expansion and brought many exotic and new customs into Roman society. The Romans expanded and built upon many of the technologies of the lands they conquered to build a strong state. Conquered peoples were assimilated into the Roman way of life and their religious beliefs, languages, and cultural practices that were congruent with Roman belief were incorporated. The key to Roman success was their professional military, the engineers who built reliable roads and provided clean water, and the physicians who provided life-saving medicines and techniques. Sadly, the Republic was turned upside down by Julius Gaius Caesar and his adopted heir, Augustus. Augustus saw the end to one of Rome's most bloody civil wars and instituted the reign of the Emperor's. Under his rule, Rome was prosperous and entered into a brief period of peace. The actions of Augustus, however, would mark significant changes for Roman civilization and was the first fray in the cloak of Roman invincibility.

5.2 Imperial Rome

At the height of Imperial power, ca. 117 CE, Rome controlled the entire Mediterranean Sea and her boarders stretched from Britain in the Northwest to Egypt in the Southeast (Figure 5.10). Beginning in 27 BCE and lasting until 476 CE, Imperial Rome was ruled by ~70 emperors, with the first 12 emperors claiming blood relation to Julius Gaius Caesar. This did not stop all the remaining emperors from adding Caesar to their many titles and accolades. Imperial Rome was the center of a vast empire whose boarders expanded and contracted until the empire declined. At the heart was

Figure 5.10   Map of Roman Empire

Peter Hermes Furian/Shutterstock.com

Rome, surrounded by the numerous conquered lands, the Roman provinces. The provinces were seen as foreign territories under permanent Roman rule and were controlled by local governors appointed by the emperor. There were many cultural and social differences across the vast territories of the empire. The main difference being Rome decided foreign policy and the provinces supplied Rome with resources. But there was a mutually dependent nature to their relationship. Roman provinces need Roman rule for protection from external invasion and internal threats. The provinces were instrumental in disseminating Roman culture, language, and beliefs throughout the empire.

The empire flourished thanks to technological innovations. Among the most useful was *opus caementicium*, or hydraulic concrete, which was capable of setting in wet (underwater) or dry conditions[29]. It was structurally sound and could withstand earthquakes. The older this cement becomes, the stronger it grows. There are examples of marine concrete from Roman days still in use today. The dome of the Pantheon in Rome lasted 2,000 years with no weakness nor signs of decay stands as a terrestrial example of cement. Sadly, this form of concrete was lost for ~1,200 years after the fall of the Roman Empire. In addition to concrete, the Romans experimented with and refined glass making[30]. They made windowpanes, which allowed for windows to be placed in buildings in cold climates. They made goblets, cups, medicine bottles, and funeral masks from glass. Roman architectural innovation brought stacked arches, arcades and walls, and siphons to improve public works and buildings. It was during the Imperial period that the first bound books appeared and would go on to replace scrolls as the preferred means for organizing and managing texts. These technologies were shared across the empire, with the secrets of their manufacture being passed on from maser artisan to apprentice.

In 1 CE, the Roman empire experienced the loss of an essential and prolifically used herb, *silphium*. Silphium was a seasoning as well as a medicine[31]. It was a commodity traded from the Roman province of Cyrene. It was so vital to Cyrenian economy that most of their currency bore an image of the plant or the plant's seed pod. Interesting fact, many scholars today contend that the seed pod of silphium was the original heart emoji[32]. Silphium was used in medicine for a wide variety of ailments, including cough, sore throat, fever, indigestion, general aches, transient pains, warts, contraception, and headaches[33]. Silphium was used as a condiment, similar to salt and pepper today, it could be found in a powdered form on the tables of many Roman aristocrats. Silphium was so popular that it was still being listed as an ingredient in cookbooks and medical texts well into the third century CE even though it was long since extinct.

Medicine during the Roman empire saw a growing reliance on physicians. It is interesting to note that in Rome, anyone could refer to themselves as "doctor"[18]. There was no formal training nor system for accrediting a degree as we think of the title today. Physicians typically began their careers as surgeons in the Roman army and would apprentice themselves to more experienced surgeons to learn their trade. There were female physicians, and they were typically used to serve the healthcare needs of other women. The training of female physicians is not very clear in the historical records, and it seems that they functioned much like a midwife or doula. Healthcare services were free to all citizens and was not often provided to Roman slaves unless the slaves in question were gladiators.

Surgery was the area within medicine where Romans excelled, particularly in relation to *anesthetics*. Anesthetics are substances that reduce the sensation of pain, which can be local or general in their effect. The Romans had a highly developed military surgical system, their knowledge on deadening pain was excellent among the civilizations of the ancient world. The main substances used included opium poppies, henbane seeds, and mandrake[20]. Opium derived from poppies was used to deaden the nerve endings and helped to limit movement. Henbane was used to induce sleep. And mandrake was used to deaden pain, while slowing the heart rate which helped to control bleeding. Even though the Romans had improved knowledge on anesthetics, the best tactic a military surgeon could employ was to finish the operation as quickly as possible[34]. There was no time for finesse as the anesthetics were difficult to attain and maintain true sedation. The faster the procedure could be completed the better for the patient. The first complete Roman surgical tool kit was found in the ruins of Pompeii and included 40 instruments from the home a physician. Among the instruments were double-ended scalpels for more efficient surgery, again, a key feature during a time when anesthetics were weak. Other refined surgical techniques included operations to remove cranial pressure, an operation that included removing parts of the skull and using a metal plate to replace the missing bone. Surgeons in the public arena pioneered *cosmetic surgery*, deliberate modifications with the intent to modify or alter the human body or parts thereof. Some of the elite women of Roman society elected to modify the shape of their eyelids via surgery to make the eyes rounder and thus making the women appear more alluring[35].

Roman surgeons had developed the *spongia somnifera*, the "sleeping sponge" to deliver preparations of mandragora, opium, and henbane extracts that were evaporated by a sea sponge which was held in place over the patient's nose and mouth[18]. This was used for general anesthesia to varying results. Mandragora, the Latin name for mandrake, was used as an analgesic and central nervous system sedative. Mandragora is not used in modern medicine due to its toxic effects. Mandragora contains the active alkaloids scopolamine and atropine. Both alkaloids have been well documented as poisonous substances with the effects including blurred vision, dilated pupils, dizziness, headache, and rapid heart rate. Mandragora was mixed with extracts of opium and henbane by Roman physicians as a means of sedation for minor surgical procedures. The potency and toxicity of the mandragora, opium, and henbane extracts varied considerably and was dependent upon the mode of extraction. With no attempt at purification and limited understanding of precise dosing the use of these extracts in the spongia somnifera came with an elevated risk of causing death from respiratory and circulatory depression.

Roman surgery was utilized in the first attempt at *sexual reassignment surgery* of an adult. Emperor Nero had a complicated love life; he was married to both men and women[9]. He murdered two of his wives, one of them Poppaea who was pregnant he personally strangled in a fit of rage. After Poppaea's death, Nero's grief was said to be inconsolable, and he began looking for a woman who resembled her. In Greece, during an orgy, he met a male slave, Sporus, who resembled his beloved Poppaea. Nero ordered that Sporus was to undergo reassignment, which consisted of having Sporus castrated and dressed in women's clothing. Nero from this point forward addressed Sporus as "diva" (lady in Latin) and married his newly made bride.

Among the aristocracy of Imperial Rome, poisoning was a real and constant threat. Many people lived in fear of being poisoned, including family and close allies of the emperor. A list of some of the more prominent poisonings among the Roman elite can be found in Table 5.2. Not only did people search for potential antidotes, but they were also focused on methods to detect poisons. The *calix*, a very popular Roman drinking vessels consisted of a bowl fixed to a pedestal or stand, were among the most common ways that poison would be delivered. The poisoner would add poison to the wine in an individual's calix. This method would not draw too much attention and would allow a more

Table 5.2 Notable Imperial Age Poisoners

Augustus
(63 BCE–14 CE)
Toward the end of his reign, his wife Livia was believed to have poisoned all of the male sons, nephews, grandchildren, and adopted children of Augustus to give her grandson, Tiberius, the throne; rumored to have poisoned Augustus

Lucius Nonius Asprenas
Consul of Rome (36 CE) was reported to have poisoned ~30 dinner guests all of whom were his political opponents.
No statue of Lucius available, hence a group shot of classical figures.

Caligula
(12 CE–41 CE)
Used poisons to kill gladiators, chariot drivers, and their horses to manipulate sport events for his benefit.

Nero
(37 CE–68 CE)
Considered to have poisoned his stepbrother, Britannicus; the governor of Asia, Silanus; his aunt, Domitia (mysteriously he gained all of her riches); prefect of the praetorian guard, Burrus; ~40 known freemen. Contemplated poisoning the whole Senate for withholding money from him (~425 members).

Source: T. D. Church, compiled with notes from Pliny the Elder[31]

directed application of the poison. Among the wealthy, ***electrum***, an alloy of gold and silver, was a preferred metal for the manufacture of calix. It was believed that the electrum would reveal the presence of poison. When wine was poured into an electrum calix a chemical reaction would occur if an alkaloid-based poison was present. This reaction would cause iridescent colors to ripple across the surface of the wine accompanied by a cascading crackling sound. Pliny the Elder, remarked about the poison detection of electrum stating that rainbows would shimmer on the surface and the meniscus of the wine sparkled and hissed as if on fire[31].

If a Roman was to use poison, they would have had a rather broad selection to choose from. Many poisons were derived from plants such as henbane, thorn apple, deadly nightshade, aconite, hemlock, and cyanide extracted from almonds[19]. They would also utilize mineral poisons and among the most favored were lead, mercury, copper, arsenic, and antimony. The choice of poison was dependent upon the person delivering the poison and often would contain two or more poisons to improve effectiveness or add lethality. Different admixtures were used to produce a range of effects including the amount and duration of pain a victim would experience.

Another method the Romans used for detecting poison was through the use of *glossopetra*, "tongue stones." Glossopetra are fossilized megalodon teeth, which were removed from limestone deposits. To test for poison, the Romans would drip the alleged poisoned wine or liquid onto the glossopetra, upon contact with the wine or liquid the tongue stones would begin to "sweat" or change colors[19]. Glossopetra were seen as a remedy for poison, and often the ground powder from a glossopetra would be recommended with the belief that the powder deactivated the poison. There might be some truth to the use of glossopetra as an antidote through *chelation*. Chelation is a chemical process in which calcium carbonate extracted from the glossopetra from limestone sediments would act to mop up poison molecules, especially arsenic.

A highly sought out antidote was Galen's *theriaka*, sometimes described as an herbal jam or an electuary with ~60 different ingredients. Galen's theriaka was seen as a virtual *panacea*, "cure all" for diseases and poisons alike. Galen of Pergamon (129–219 CE) was among the greatest physicians of the ancient world. Hippocrates had laid down the foundation of Greek medicine while Galen developed its theory and practice into a coherent system. Galen considered the study of philosophy to be essential to a physician's training. He thought that philosophy would enable the physician to be able to discern between truth and illusions. He believed in probing an issue or problem beyond mere surface appearances, which was an essential technique in his form of diagnosis. Galen had developed a standardized method for diagnosis, symptomology, and medical record keeping unlike anything previously utilized. He helped with the formation of new scientific and philosophical fields, chiefly pharmacology, neurology, pathology, and philosophical logic. He is perhaps best known for his use of *comparative physiology*[18]. Dissection of humans was not ethically nor socially acceptable during Galen's lifetime, which limited knowledge about the human body[36]. Galen pioneered the dissection of monkeys, pigs, and other mammals to make correlations to human anatomy. Through this method, Galen clarified the anatomy of the trachea and demonstrated that the larynx was necessary to generate vocalizations. Another discovery made by Galen was that arteries contained blood, not air as was the contemporary belief. Galen knew that the heart pumped blood and was remarkably close to describing the circulatory system in detail but did not complete his work. It is estimated that Galen authored ~400 books, however only 80 survive to date. Galen developed an approach to patient care, which we refer to as *Galenic psychotherapy*, which presented a revolution in patient to physician relationships[37–39]. This method of psychotherapy defined ways to approach and treat psychological problems. Galen provided detailed instructions on how to build rapport, get patients to reveal their deepest passions and secrets, and outlined how to provide them with appropriate care.

The Roman imperial model was not destined to survive. In 286 CE, Rome was divided in an attempt to stabilize the empire and by 395 CE Rome officially became the Western Empire and Eastern Empire. This division brought with it profound cultural, political, and social changes. The Western Empire spoke Latin and followed catholic traditions while the Eastern Empire spoke Greek and followed Greek Orthodox traditions. By 476 CE the unthinkable happened, Rome, the Eternal City, was conquered by foreign invaders and the city was pillaged and her grandeur decimated. This marked the start of the decline of Roman influence in Europe and ushered in the Dark Ages.

5.3 Descent into the Darkest of Ages

Rome at the end of the empire was marred by rampant civil wars as people clamored for power. Diseases, including the plague of Justinian, ravaged the empire[40]. There were a series of military, financial, and political deficiencies that allowed cracks to form in the Roman boarders that were once impregnable. These issues led to the loss of land to invading groups of Goths, Visigoths, Vandals, Huns, and others. The Roman empire in our modern imagination was first and foremost a military state whose political unity was enforced by violence. In actuality, it was the combined and elaborately linked civilizations of the Mediterranean basin and beyond. It included manufacture, trade, and artisans tied together economically. There was widespread literacy, written law, and the foundation of an international language for science, medicine, and literature. In his seminal work, *The Decline and Fall of the Roman Empire*, Gibbon stated that the story of the ruin of Rome was simple and obvious, and instead of inquiring **why** the empire was destroyed, we should instead be surprised that it had lasted as long as it did[41]. The once victorious legions acquired several vices and over time were filled with conscripted men, slaves, and mercenaries who could be bought for the right amount of coin. The emperors became obsessed with power and accumulation of wealth to the point of destruction. The people began to lose land, privilege, and hope. Foreign invaders chipped away at what were once strong and impenetrable borders. The old religion and religious tolerance gave way to Christianity and demanded for the destruction of all things pagan.

Between 500 and 1200 CE, Europe was in the period of time called the Dark Ages[42]. This is a period in which records were not consistent and in some places no history was recorded. There was no centralized government or infrastructure, instead there were small regional rulers. There was a lot of movement of displaced peoples as the empire began to shatter and fragment. The only institutions who consistently preserved any of the ancient knowledge were monasteries. Some monasteries maintained plumbing knowledge, but only for use within the monastery. Latin was still used, but only used for religious learning. Manuscripts were lost, written over, or often destroyed as vestiges of paganism. There was a growing fear of the pagans and the occult and Christianity held little tolerance for the old ways. The use of medicine was seen as pagan, and surgery was seen as sacrilegious. Alcohol and recreational drugs were viewed as vices of the depraved pagans. Alcohol was only to be consumed in relation to the sacraments of Catholicism.

The prior social order instituted by Rome broke down and with it came the loss of specialized knowledge. Architecture and art required patrons to pay for their works. Literary culture and writing declined and in many areas of Europe the literacy rate was nonexistent. The material basics of urban life degraded as roads, aqueducts, and public buildings were unmaintained with the knowledge of how to do so diminishing with each successive generation. Metallurgy and some masonry were maintained but only in areas where socioeconomic conditions were favorable to support these skilled laborers. Skilled craftsmen did not always pass on their craft and many of Rome's greatest innovations were lost and forgotten. Public education was no longer guaranteed. Wealthy individuals might learn to read, but it was not considered necessary to do so. Writing and reading were reserved for clergy. The production of paper and bound books became lost arts, which resulted in many of the ancient works having their ink scrapped off and written over with religious texts glorifying Christianity while demonizing the Roman pantheon.

The Eastern Roman Empire would become the Byzantine Empire and represented a continuation of the Roman Empire. Byzantium was ruled from Constantinople and survived the fragmentation and decline of the Western Roman Empire from 500 CE to Byzantium's conquest by the Ottoman Empire in 1453 CE. Many of the political and cultural artifacts of the Roman world were maintained and preserved, although they underwent changes influenced by the peoples of Asia Minor. The Byzantine Empire was the shining light during Europe's darkest of ages.

REFERENCES

1. Patterson, J. (2020). Military organization and social change in the later Roman Republic. In J. Rich & G. Shipley (Eds.), *War and society in the Roman world* (pp. 92–112). Routledge.

2. Armstrong, J., & Fronda, M. P. (2019). *Romans at war: Soldiers, citizens, and society in the Roman Republic* (p. 374). Routledge.

3. Patterson, J.R. (1992). The city of Rome: From Republic to Empire. *The Journal of Roman Studies, 82*, 186–215.

4. Lomas, K., & Cornell, T. (2005). Introduction: Patronage and benefaction in ancient Italy. In T. Cornell & K. Lomas (Eds.). *'Bread and Circuses': Euergetism and municipal patronage in Roman Italy* (pp. 13–23). Routledge.

5. Orlin, E.M. (2021). *A social and cultural history of Republican Rome* (p. 304). John Wiley & Sons.

6. Strabo. (1917 [17 CE]) Geographica, I: Libri I, II. In H. L. Jones & J. R. S. Sterrett (Eds.), *Loeb Classical Library* (Vol. 1, p. 575). Harvard University Press.

7. Slater, W. J. (1991). *Dining in a classical context* (p. 217). University of Michigan Press.

8. León, V. (2009). *Working IX to V: Orgy Planners, Funeral Clowns, and Other Prized Professions of the Ancient World* (p. 336). Walkerand Company.

9. Seutonius, G. T. (2007 [117 CE]). In R. Graves (Ed.), *The Twelve Caesars*. Penguin.

10. Whitmore, A. (2018). *Phallic magic: a cross cultural approach to Roman phallic small finds*. In A. Parker & S. McKie (Eds.), *Material approaches to Roman magic: Occult objects and supernatural substances* (pp. 17–31). Oxbow Books.

11. Moser, C. (2006). Naked power: The phallus as an apotropaic symbol in the images and texts of Roman Italy. In *Undergraduate Humanities Forum 2005-6: Word & Image*. University of Pennsylvania.

12. Levin-Richardson, S. (2019). *The brothel of Pompeii: Sex, class, and gender at the margins of Roman society* (p. 243). Cambridge University Press.

13. Stephenson, J. (2016). Dining as spectacle in late Roman houses. *Bulletin – Institute of Classical Studies, 59*(1), 54–71.

14. Brunet, S. (2004). Female and dwarf gladiators. *Mouseion: Journal of the Classical Association of Canada, 4*(2), 145–170.

15. Murray, S. (2003). Female gladiators of the ancient Roman world. *Journal of Combative Sport, 7*(3), 1–16.

16. Karabatos, I., Tsagkaris, C., & Kalachanis, K. (2021). All roads lead to Rome: Aspects of public health in ancient Rome. *Le Infezioni in Medicina, 29*(3), 488–491.

17. Fagan, G.G. (2001). The genesis of the Roman Public Bath: Recent approaches and future directions. *American Journal of Archaeology, 105*(3), 403–426.

18. Maya, S.P. (2022). On medicine, physicians, and healers in Ancient Rome. *Hypothekai, 6*, 40–77.

19. Cilliers, L., & Retief, F. (2019). Poisons, poisoners, and poisoning in ancient Rome. In P. Wexler (Ed.), *Toxicology in antiquity* (2nd ed., pp. 231–242). Academic Press.

20. Cesarik, M., et al. (2016). Roman military medicine and Croatian archaeological perspectives. *Collegium Antropologicum, 40*(3), 171–176.

21. Ryan, G. (2021). *Naked statues, fat gladiators, and war elephants: Frequently asked questions about the ancient Greeks and Romans.* (p. 280). Prometheus. 22.Cilliers, L., & Retief, F. (2019). Lead poisoning and the downfall of Rome: Reality or myth? In P. Wexler (Ed.), *Toxicology in antiquity* (2nd ed., pp. 221–229). Academic Press.

23. Stewart, S. (2019). "Gleaming and deadly white": Toxic cosmetics in the Roman World. In P. Wexler (Ed.), *Toxicology in antiquity* (2nd ed., pp. 301–311). Academic Press.

24. Olson, K. (2009). Cosmetics in Roman antiquity: Substance, remedy, poison. *The Classical World, 102*(3), 291–310.

25. Olson, K. (2014). Masculinity, appearance, and sexuality: Dandies in Roman antiquity. *Journal of the History of Sexuality, 23*(2), 182–205.

26. Johnston, C. E. (2014). Beware of that cup!: The role of food-tasters in ancient society. In *Classical Studies* (p. 134). University of Otago.

27. Höbenreich, E., & Rizzelli, G. (2019). Poisoning in ancient Rome: Images and rules. In P. Wexler (Ed.), *Toxicology in antiquity* (pp. 289–300). Elsevier.

28. Ogle, M. B. (1910). Laurel in ancient religion and folk-lore. *The American Journal of Philology, 31*(3), 287–311.

29. Deming, D. (2020). The aqueducts and water supply of ancient Rome. *Ground Water, 58*(1), 152–161.

30. John, P.O., et al. (2019). *Greek and Roman technology: A sourcebook of translated Greek and Roman texts* (2nd ed., p. 772). Routledge Sourcebooks for the Ancient World.

31. Pliny, G. S. (1967 [45 CE]). In H. Rackham (Ed.), *Natural history in ten volumes: Volume I. Praefatio, Libri I, II* (Vol. I, p. 378). Harvard University Press.

32. Parejko, K. (2003). Pliny the elder's silphium: First recorded species extinction. *Conservation Biology, 17*(3), 925–927.

33. Amigues, S. (2004). Le silphium-État de la question. *Journal des Savants, 2*(1), 191–226.

34. Westphalen, N. (2020)., Roman warfare, ships and medicine. *Journal of Military and Veterans Health, 28*(3), 11–22.

35. Blanco-Dávila, F. (2000). Beauty and the body: The origins of cosmetics. *Plastic and Reconstructive Surgery, 105*(3), 1196–1204.

36. Malomo, A., Idowu, O., & Osuagwu, F. (2006). Lessons from history: Human anatomy, from the origin to the renaissance. *International Journal of Morphology, 24*(1), 99–104.

37. Kaufman, D. (2017). Galen on reason and appetite: A study of the de moribus. *Apeiron (Clayton), 50*(3), 367–392.

38. Xenophontos, S. (2014). Psychotherapy and moralising rhetoric in Galen's newly discovered avoiding distress *(Peri Alypias). Medical History, 58*(4), 585–603.

39. Robinson, A. (2013). Galen: Life lessons from gladiatorial contests. *The Lancet* (British edition), *382*(9904), 1548–1548.

40. Toner, J. (2018). *Roman disasters* (p. 216). Polity Press.

41. Gibbon, E., Bury, J. B., & Piranesi, G. B. (1946). *The decline and fall of the Roman Empire*. Heritage Press.

42. Hekster, O., de Kleijn, G., & Slootjes, D. (2013). Crises and the Roman Empire*: In Proceedings of the Seventh Workshop of the International Network Impact of Empire (Nijmegen, June 20–24, 2006)*. Impact of Empire (Vol. 7). BRILL.

Chapter 6

Voyages of Discovery: The Silk Road

Our focus in this chapter will be trained on the movement of people, ideas, goods, diseases, and drugs through trade and expansion along the longest terrestrial trade route from history. The commercial and mercantile networks established along this route moved goods between civilizations in unprecedented ways. Smuggling of goods became normalized as taxes and prohibitions became established. In conjunction, there was an expansion of religious and political powers as nations attempted to control trade and exploit both peoples and resources. Trade routes between empires over land circulated monies and differentially made some extremely wealthy while exploiting others. Bribery, smuggling, and marauding took hold. The Voyages of Discovery make this time in human history sound much more romantic than the truth, which was the exploitation of peoples to allow wealth to be accumulated by a few. Thanks to germs, improved military technology, and improved transportation, parts of the world became subjugated much more readily than others. Goods, merchants, and trade were setting the stage for globalization.

6.1 Silk Road Exchanges

The Silk Road was an important overland and costal trade network [1, 2]. It connected well over 5,000 miles (8,047 km) of trade routes between China and the Mediterranean coasts of North Africa and Anatolia. In the early part of its use, the Silk Road carried goods and ideas between the Roman empire and the Chinese empire and was active between 118 BCE and 1450 CE. The Romans sent wool, gold, and silver for trade with the Chinese sending silk and jade. The Silk Road's path originated in Xi'an, followed the Great Wall of China to the northwest, bypassed the Takla Makan desert, climbed the Pamirs Mountains, crossed the plans of Afghanistan, and continued through Persia onto a destination in Cairo or Constantinople. Merchandise would then be loaded onto ships and sailed around the Mediterranean Sea to be offloaded in distant markets. There were very few ancient peoples who traveled the entirety of the Silk Road. Goods were handled in a staggered progression, moving from city to city through merchants and traders to its destination. Empires rose and fell, and the commodities of choice changed with the times. When Rome broke apart, the Byzantines began sending horses, alfalfa, wine grapes, and magic potions and poisons. China sent back to Constantinople new fruits such as peaches and apricots, which were mistakenly called Persian or Armenian plums[3]. In addition, the traders carried with them cinnamon, ginger, and other spices that could not be grown in the

West[4]. Spices were important because they had numerous utilities from food preservation to flavoring to pharmaceutical reasons. Throughout the long history of the Silk Road, the traders who moved goods across the vast distances encompassed the Bactrians, Sogdians, Syrians, Jews, Arabs, Iranians, Turkmens, Chines, Indians, Somalis, Greeks, Romans, Georgians, and Armenians (see Figure 6.1). Alongside goods, the Silk Road promoted cultural exchange, wherein the exchange of philosophies, technologies, cultural trade, transmitted diseases, and religion occurred with regularity.

Figure 6.1 Route of the Silk Road

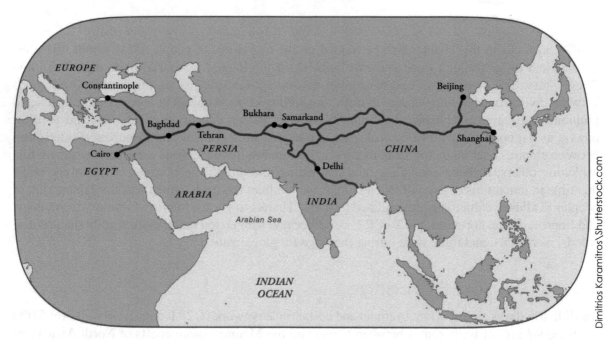

The Silk Road was home to many religions with the dominant religions being Buddhism, Islam, Judaism, Sikhism, Hinduism, and Christianity[5]. Buddhism began in India and followed the trade route to spread eastward into Southeast Asia, China, and Japan. Islam moved eastward along the trade route from Arabia into India. Judaism advanced north and westward along the trade route from Israel into Africa and Europe. Sikhism flourished in Punjab and Pakistan. Hinduism encompassed India, Afghanistan, and parts of Southeast Asia and Indonesia. Christianity spread from Europe into Turkey and established monasteries along the trade route.

Tolerance of drugs and wine differed among the religions of the Silk Road. Christianity, Islam, and Judaism all viewed any form of inebriation as being sinful, except for wine within Christian Europe. Buddhism viewed any intoxicant, which consisted of anything that distracts from the path of enlightenment (not solely drugs or alcohol), as a diversion from the path to nirvana. A maxim held by Mahayana Buddhism stated "anything ingested, inhaled, or injected into the system without reverence for life becomes an intoxicant"[6]. In Hinduism, the use of intoxicants was not banned, per se.

Substances like alcohol and cannabis should be used with restraint and knowledge of potential side effects. Wine, beer, and cannabis have all had a long tradition of being consumed during festivals like Holi and Deepavali. *Dharma*, one of four key components of the aims of life within Hinduism, provides some insight into how Hindus viewed inebriation. Dharma does not have a simple English translation but most closely relates to concepts like duty, rights, conduct, virtue, and ethics. Dharma would require that we attempt to understand each individual and their circumstances, it is a choice to consume intoxicants and if the consumer knows the danger, they should be left to their decision to use or not use. Confucianism, which is more of a philosophy of ethics than a formal religion, views human beings as being improvable, teachable, and perfectible through self-cultivation and communal and personal actions. Use of intoxicants were not prohibited under this philosophy, but consumption in excess would have been seen as an improvable or teachable moment.

Zoroastrianism represents one of the oldest practiced religions in the world. It traces its roots back to the fifth century BCE in the Persian empire[7] and was replaced after Alexander the Great's conquest of Persepolis with the Hellenistic Pantheon. It made a resurgence between 250 BCE and 230 CE along parts of the Silk Road where it received renewed interest[8]. Zoroastrianism held a belief in a single god, had a moral code of good and evil, and believed in the unfolding of the final events of mankind. Zoroastrianism considered drinking wine to be a sacred duty and viewed drug use as a mechanism to attain an altered state of consciousness, a divine state of communion with god. Zoroastrianism was practiced side by side with the other major religions found along the Silk Road peacefully for a time. However, an inscription from Cappadocia made in the third century CE, boasts of the persecutions of Christians, Jews, and Buddhists carried out by a Zoroastrian High Priest[9]. This was the catalyst the other religions needed to force Zoroastrianism to the fringes of the Silk Road and began a smear campaign wherein Zoroastrianism was not representing divinity or enlightenment, instead it preached heretical ideology. This politicization of religion was the undoing of the coexisting harmony of all the religions and greatly affected the culture of the Silk Road, leading to many skirmishes on the basis of religion and religious doctrine.

The religious skirmishes and the threat of goods being stolen by bandits or marauders led to unique military technologies being invented to help keep the peace and the movement of goods (Figure 6.2). There were new chariot designs that accommodated a driver and a mounted bowman, which allowed for a near constant barrage of arrows from a mobile platform. Stirrups became a staple of the military forces and represented perhaps one of the most ingenious inventions. Stirrups allowed the rider to be in a standing position on horseback and increased the range of arrows, allowing the rider to fire over the head of their mount. Bows also underwent a revolution from simple hunting bows to composite recurve bows. This added to the speed and power of the arrows lobbed. Ultimately, in the 1300s CE gunpowder and guns would replace bows

Figure 6.2 Ancient Fresco of the Silk Road, Military on Horseback

youm118\Shutterstock.com

as the weapons of choice[10]. There was an explosion of lances and pikes, with several deadly variations that oscillated in size and length as time progressed. Lances and pikes were employed to chase down bandits and marauders who were on foot or horseback.

Rest stops, or caravanserais, became more frequent along the Silk Road. Many of them started as areas where caravans could stop for rest and refreshment. The small watering holes grew into *trading cities* which housed the militaries, brothels, and a wide range of service-related industries to facilitate the movement of goods along the route to their destinations. These trading cities saw the rise of the first embassies as customs and beliefs from a wide range of people came into contact and diplomatic influences began to rise[3]. Three of the key functionary roles embassies deployed were envoys, ambassadors, and missionaries. An *ambassador* was an accredited diplomat sent as an official representative on behalf of their home nation or king to function as the voice of the sovereign in foreign lands. Some ambassadors had the ability, if necessary, to enact war if the situation required. The main roles of the ambassador were to secure favorable trade, advance their sovereign's wishes, and see to the fair treatment of their countrymen. An *envoy* functioned as a messenger or representative, ranking below an ambassador, and typically sent on specific diplomatic or trade missions. Envoys did not have the ability to enact wars, engage in trade agreements, or to formally provide agreements to treaties. *Missionaries* were sent on religious missions, typically to promote religious undertakings or provide charity in foreign lands while also spreading their religious doctrine.

Figure 6.3 Ancient Arabian Pharmacopoeia and Tools

The Silk Road saw some unique advancements in drugs and drug consumption. There are a number of existing pharmacopoeias, written texts on mixing and manufacturing medicines, which were traded from Egypt, Arabia, Greece, India, Sumer, and China. These books contained medicinal recipes and listed experiments undertaken with substances and herbs as related to human health and well-being. These ground-breaking treatises even reached conclusions related to surgical intervention, like wound closure, wound care, and removal of tumors. Some contained information on poisons, antidotes, and detailed toxicology (Figure 6.3). Some of the works went as far as removing the gods, demons, spirits, and miasmas from their texts as they no longer held power in this nubile world of science and medical discovery. There was a rise in the use of *solanaceous plants* and *hallucinogenic plants*. Solanaceous plants are members of the nightshade family and includes potatoes, tomatoes, peppers, eggplants, and belladonna[11, 12]. Solanaceous plants produce some powerful narcotics and several anodynes (pain reliving). Hallucinogenic plants affect the brain and can alter the mental and emotional states of humans who ingest them, examples would be opium poppy, cannabis sativa, cannabis indica, kola nut, and betel nut. Evidence of an increase in the transport of these plants can be seen in both export and import records kept between the merchants. In addition, archaeologists have found a variety of drug related *paraphernalia* in excavations from the trading cities[13]. Paraphernalia refers to the equipment, apparatus, or furnishing used in or that is necessary for a particular activity, drug consumption in our case, to be performed. Things archaeologists have uncovered include pipes, preparation trays and implements, storage jars and mixing cups, braziers, and fumigators. These artifacts range from the mundane to the extremely ornate, highlighting the importance of some of these devices for the consumption of drugs.

As tariffs, duties, and the value of goods varied, so too did the amount of smuggling and the kinds of goods smuggled. Items with low tariffs or duties would not have been worth smuggling. Unlike today where there is an extensive list of contraband, smuggling of goods in the ancient world was less about forbidden goods and more about avoiding import and export duties. Silk from China, gemstones from India, and rare incense from Arabia would most likely have been smuggled if a higher profit for the merchant could be obtained by not paying duties[14]. Taxes to move goods from one part of the Roman empire to another averaged 1/40th of the goods value either in kind or in coin. Taxes on goods coming into the empire from outside faced duties between 1/4th and 1/3rd of the goods value either in kind or in coin[13]. Alcohol and hallucinogenic drugs may have been smuggled to avoid scrutiny by zealous religious leaders who saw these goods as being antithetical to the mission of their religious beliefs.

Drug consumption was not on the minds of the **alchemists** of the Silk Road when they invented distilling[15, 16]. Alchemy was an extraordinarily complex quasi-mystical predecessor to modern chemical engineering. Alchemy was preoccupied with attempting to understand the base nature of substances and their constituents. Through a variety of methods alchemists attempted to unlock the inner secrets of substances in an attempt to gain insight into the cosmos, the elements of nature, and life itself. In order to reduce substances to their base components, alchemists needed a way to distill the components from one another. **Distilling** is a process by which alcohol is separated from water using evaporation and condensation, and without alchemists distilled spirits and liqueurs would not exist in the world. Unlike wine or beer, which use fermentation, spirits require the second stage of distillation. Distilled alcohol, however, took over 900 years of refining before it gained the popularity it has today. A brief history of distilling alcohol is detailed in Table 6.1.

Table 6.1 Brief History of Distilled Alcohol

Date	Detail
700 CE	Abu Musa Jabir ibn Hayyan, Arabian alchemist, credited with designing the **alembic pot still**
110 CE	First documented use of distilled alcohol, used in an Italian medical school but not consumed for recreation. First mention of Irish Whiskey and German Brandy—both were considered medicinal at the time and not consumed widely.
1347 CE	Wine alcohol was often utilized as a treatment for the Bubonic Plague.
1347–1351 CE	Wine alcohol use for the treatment of the Plague stretched from England to India.
1618 CE	**Aqua Vitae** (water of life), first mention of recreational drinking of alcohol appears in Italy.
1650 CE	Importation of rum into New England from the West Indies begins in earnest. Rum became exceptionally popular among the poor and lower classes because of its extremely low price.

Source: T.D. Church

Figure 6.4   Alembic Pot Still

EduardoPolo\Shutterstock.com

The invention of the alembic pot still, which consisted of two vessels connected via a tube, allowed for the distillation of chemicals (Figure 6.4). The basic concept of distilling has always been somewhat simple, to make a harder alcohol from a lower alcohol base. But why do we need the added steps involved with distilling liquor? Why not continue fermentation to produce a higher alcohol by volume percentage? And here in lies the problem… It is all related to the yeast which governs the Science of Alcohol. Yeast eats up the sugars (in the process of making beer or wine) and expels delightful waste products by farting out CO_2 and secreting alcohol. The problem lies in the fact that the more alcohol and CO_2 produced, the less sugar there is for the yeast to feed upon. And at a certain point, typically between 14% and 18% alcohol by volume, the alcohol levels become too toxic for the yeast to remain viable. To create hard liquor, we need to move beyond the yeast. This requires the physical separation of water and alcohol using the evaporation and condensation methods of distilling. The yield of distilled liquor is around 40% alcohol by volume.

The Silk Road brought together disparate cultures and customs in the endeavor of monetary gain and trade. The trade in illegal goods and highly tariffed goods led to a burgeoning smuggling economy. This economy set down smuggling routes to bring exotic and illegal goods to customers in highly regulated markets. The money to be made from the Silk Road brought about several seedy practices from piracy and marauding to smuggling and theft, all in the name of trade. The routes and practices laid down over the centuries remain intact today, though the products being smuggled are far more potent and deadly than the solanaceous and hallucinogenic plants from history.

6.2 Byzantine, Ottoman, and Arabian Contributions

The area of the Eastern Roman Empire from Constantinople to Alexandria and onto Persepolis changed hands from the Byzantine Empire to the Arabian Caliphates and finally onto the Ottoman Empire (Figure 6.5). The area of control grew and contracted, yet each subsequent empire had maintained control of the two main ports of the Western Silk Road in Constantinople and Alexandria. Several inventions from these empires have impacted drug consumption, medicine, and food cultures for generations.

It was in this area of the Silk Road where the knowledge and preservation of Egyptian, Greek, and Roman medical texts was curated. Many of the texts were lost or destroyed when the Western Roman Empire fell. A large number of the texts from the Byzantine Empire were translated into Arabic and were expanded with new knowledges and discoveries. The advancements included new and enhanced surgery techniques and instruments, addition of new plants as compounds for medicines, and incorporation of a body systems review for standardized diagnosis[17].

An Arabian and Turkish architectural design element was the *divan* where low cushioned couches were positioned along the outer wall of a room and became synonymous with a salon-styled

Figure 6.5 Height of the Arabian Caliphate Empire

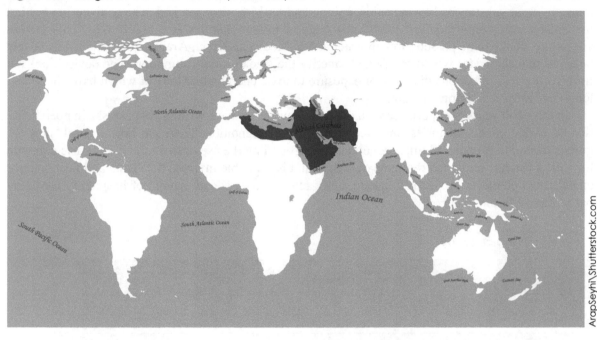

ArapSeyhi\Shutterstock.com

smoking culture[18]. This was before the trade in tobacco from the Americas was introduced, and the items being smoked often consisted of opium, cannabis, and/or hashish. In the days before a more

conservative form of Islam became the norm there existed casinos where gambling and sometimes prostitution were readily available. These establishments offered wine, beer, hashish, and opium for the enjoyment of their patrons. **Hashish** is a resin or concentrate made from cannabis, produced by collecting the most potent materials from the cannabis plant[19]. The sap producing elements of the plant are pressed to release the sap and "crystals" resulting in a sticky resin. Upon curing and drying, the resin is a much denser and more potent material than leaf cannabis.

An amazing invention allowed the hashish to be smoked. The device is known by many names, **shisha**, **hookah**, **nargile**, or **qalyan**[20]. Shisha was introduced by Abu'l-Fath Gilani ~1560 CE and it spread throughout the Persian Empire and into India, Turkey, and northern Africa. Tobacco was not

Figure 6.6 Shisha Anatomy

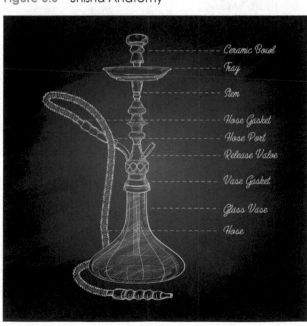

Ceramic Bowl
Tray

Stem

Hose Gasket
Hose Port
Release Valve

Vase Gasket

Glass Vase

Hose

Netkoff\Shutterstock.com

available in Europe or India until 1640 CE and did not gain in popularity until 1690 CE. Prior to tobacco, other substances like cannabis, opium, and hashish were smoked. The engineering behind the Shisha water pipe required some knowledge of hydrodynamics (see Figure 6.6). This system allows the smoke to be passed through water and in Medieval Persia, Arabia, and India it was falsely believed that the water would purify and sanctify the smoke for consumption. The device does not limit pathogens, infectious diseases, or exposure to toxic chemicals. Many of which have short- and long-term effects on human health.

In the ~460 years of experience with shisha, many people have written about shisha in poetry, fiction, state documents, histories, and even technical documentation. There has been several "how to" guides related to proper and improper etiquette surrounding the use of shisha[21]. The basic etiquette for shisha use has remained the same over time and is available in Table 6.2. Time and fashion have embellished elements of shisha etiquette, but it remains as a social symbol of hospitality for many parts of the Middle East.

Table 6.2 Shisha Etiquette

1. If possible, only smoke shisha in good company. Smoking on your own is not prohibited, but shisha was originally used in social settings and was a symbol of hospitality.

2. Shisha should be poisitioned on the floor. Putting the waterpipe on the ground is how it is traditionally used. It is very rare to find shisha on a table in Arabia or Egypt.

3. Keep the conversation calm. Talking loudly and gesturing hectically will disturb everyone's rest and can spoil the comfortable atmosphere, potentially leading to disaster if the shisha gets broken.

4. The hose should never be passed onto the next smoker in the round, instead it should be placed on the table or hung to the waterpipe. The next individual can take the hose when they want, and should not feel pressured to smoke.

NOTE: The above etiquette should not be interpreted to promote shisha smoking. Keep in mind that smoking of any kind has serious health related concerns, including cancer, heart disease, and other comorbidities that will seriously impact quality of life.

Source: T.D. Church

The **Order of Hashshashin**, a Persian mystery cult of assassins, were a medieval group of skilled assassins who were experts in the profession of killing important people[22, 23]. This group of individuals were highly influential in the medieval Islamic world for ~135 years. Eventually the Order would be caught off guard and their influence was removed by the Mongols in 1257 CE.

Hashshashin is an Arabic word for "hashish users" or "hashish eaters" and contemporary writers, like Marco Polo, proclaimed that the assassins carried out their deadly business while under the influence of hashish[24]. This is problematic as *hashish* use exhibits some short-term effects that would make being an effective assassin difficult. The short-term effects of hashish use include problems with memory and learning; distorted perception (sights, sounds, time, and touch); difficulty in thinking and problem solving; loss of coordination; and increased heart rate with an increase in the potential for anxiety and panic attacks[22]. Now, I do not know about you, but if I were to hire an assassin to carry out a very high-profile assassination, I would want someone who could remember the plan, had clear senses, could think on their feet if the situation went south, and definitely was not prone to having a panic attack when action was necessitated. The Order of Hashashin has had a resurrection in modern video games under the gaming franchise Assassin's Creed, who utilize the historical and mythological identities of the Order to create a multimillion-dollar enterprise.

A world-wide multibillion-dollar modern enterprise was nearly outlawed in 1500 CE when dervishes in Mecca consumed an excessive amount of coffee and caused a public spectacle [25]. The dervishes were dancing and causing a lot of disruption in the grand bazaar, they allegedly knocked over merchandise, scared away customers, and caused a small riot to erupt in their wake. The dervishes were incarcerated while a council of theologians, lawyers, and nobles deliberated on the virtues and vices of coffee. This council found the dervishes guilty, and the drinkers were poised to be sentenced to public execution. Thankfully, the Sultan—an avid drinker of coffee—overheard the deliberations and revoked their decision. The Sultan organized a brand new council, who came to the conclusion that drinking coffee was an approved activity as the consumer could "read sacred texts without getting tired"[25].

The discovery of coffee is a bit controversial and shrouded in mystery with two prevalent and comparable stories vying to be the origin story (Figure 6.7). The first story places the discovery in ~900 CE in Yemen, the other story appears in 1671 CE from Ethiopia. The latter is the most popular version of the legend, and it goes something like this[26]… Kaldi, an Abyssinian goat herder from Kaffa, was out herding his goats near a monastery in the highlands. He came upon a very jubilant sight wherein his goats were bleating loudly, jumping around, and practically dancing on their hind legs. He was concerned and

Figure 6.7 Coffee

RachenArt\Shutterstock.com

began investigating and found the source of their excitement—small shrubs with red berries. Kaldi tried some of the coffee cherries and felt energized himself. He filled his pockets and his bag with as many berries as he could and rushed home to his wife. Kaldi's wife advised that he go to the monastery to share the "heaven sent" cherries with the monks. The monks looked at the cherries with distain, with one claiming they must be the "devil's work." The monk threw the cherries on the fire, and according to legend, the aroma of the roasting beans made the monks curious about the taste of the cherries. The cherries were scooped out of the fire, crushed to put out the glowing embers, and covered with hot water to preserve the berries. The monks throughout the monastery had smelled the brewed coffee and came to find out what the aroma was. The head monk proclaiming that the beverage would help in spiritual practice as it was enlightening and energizing.

There are multiple legends related to the discovery of coffee in Arabia, but the oldest story comes from Yemen. The Yemenis version of the tale is similar to the Ethiopian version, which is paraphrased and condensed herein[26]… Mullah Schladelich, sometimes he is titled as Sheik and sometimes not depending on the version of the story, was a "true" believer of Islam but would be overtaken by sleep any time he attempted to read the Koran. He tried reading in the morning, in the evening, in public, all alone, and in every conceivable way but he still would succumb to sleep. He decided to try and read the Koran near some caves, thinking the fresh air would help. He stumbled upon a bush with red berries and in his weariness consumed some of the cherries. He took as many cherries as he could carry and ran to the nearest monastery. He became devoted to Islam because the coffee cherries helped him focus and remain awake. He proceeded to plant and grow the bushes around the monastery. The berries became highly valued by the monks because the drink they produced helped keep them awake and attentive during their prayers and supplications.

Alchemists were working towards unlocking the secrets of the universe through distillation, and apothecaries were busy crafting medicines, poisons, and *electuary*. Electuary are paste-like, thick combinations of honey, syrup, or sugars mixed with a wide variety of plant, mineral, and animal materials to be consumed orally as medicine. Not to be outdone by the alchemists, the apothecaries of this period developed and relied heavily on the ***gem electuary***. The gem electuary was a unique cordial, crafted with the intent to improve the health of the consumer. The admixture varied depending upon the apothecary and the coin purse of their client, but featured items like ground white pearls; blue and yellow sapphire dust; ground emeralds, garnets, red coral, amber; gold, silver, ivory filings; chamomile (daisies); saffron, cardamom; cinnamon; frankincense; honey; and rose sugar in a heady dilution of sweet wine[27]. This concoction equated to an expensive and potentially toxic honey paste. It may have helped with transient heartburn, but most likely helped to put a steady stream of heavy metals into the blood of the consumers. The inundation of the heavy metals would have hastened the consumers death and accelerated their descent into madness, blindness, and/or immobility. Electuaries were intended to fortify the brain and restore the heart, the liver, and the uterus. Apothecaries would often prescribe the general electuaries to help improve melancholy, sadness, shyness, and solitude. Gem electuaries were prescribed to treat all the thing a general electuary would treat but was used to treat a broader set of symptoms like soothing heart tremors and alleviate syncope (or fainting)[28].

Pearls typically get classified as gemstones; however, they are not minerals per se. They are similar to dental tartar and are produced by marine bivalve mollusks. It is the response of the mollusk to an intrusive grain of sand, which the mollusk coats in a calcium matrix to make the offending material less irritating. Pearls have been used in medicine since ancient times. The pearls would have been pulverized into a powder and then dissolved into liquids or used in topical applications for a wide range of disorders. Pearls were used to treat poisonings, lung tuberculosis, increase strength and wellbeing, used to alleviate morbid conditions, balancing of the humors, soothing the liver, reducing irritability, and relieving menstrual cramps[29]. Pearls are composed of 82–87% calcium carbonate. **Calcium carbonate** is a primary ingredient in modern antacids. Calcium carbonate helps to regulate cell permeability, maintains acid-base balance, is involved in nerve transmission and muscle relaxation, and is required for Krebs cycle functioning and maintenance.

The greatest contribution from the Byzantine to Ottoman Empires was the preservation of Roman and Greek science, medicine, and mathematics. One of the greatest scholars was Ibn Sina (Latin name "Avicenna") 980–1037 CE, who has been named the patron of Arabic medicine[30]. Avicenna was a polymath who authored ~240 books in subjects ranging from theology to science to medicine. He is credited with translating several Greek and Roman medical texts into Arabic, as such he is responsible for keeping much of the ancient knowledge from being lost during the Dark Ages. He contributed to medicine through the development and cataloging of ~750 simple and compound drugs. He even compounded a mild opium-based remedy into pill form, which he imprinted with **mash Allah** or "gift of Allah." In Western Medicine, we credit Avicenna with being the father of evidence-based medicine and the double-blind clinical trial.

After the fall of the Western Roman Empire, the Byzantine Empire remained a stalwart bastion of medical knowledge. The Ottoman and Arabian Empires saw the preservation of knowledge, the expansion of innovative technologies, and the development of refined practices. The use of hashish by assassins, development of unique paraphernalia for smoking, the expansion of coffee, and the use of gemstones as treatment were exceptional additions to history.

6.3 Indian Contributions

India was an ancient land, much older than many of the cities and towns that began to dot the Silk Road landscape (Figure 6.8). An artery for trade established in India was called the Great Royal Road and connected the cities of Allahabad, Delhi, and Taxila with the Silk Road. In the late antiquity of the Silk Road, India would play a prominent role in the maritime trade extension that linked India with Africa, Arabia, and Southeast Asia. The name India is derived from the Indus River with the name Bharata being used to denote the country in historical and political documents. India was the birthplace of four of the great world religions—Hinduism, Jainism, Buddhism, and Sikhism. India was a land of mystery and a place of profound knowledge in mathematics, science, architecture, and medicine.

Ayurvedic medicine represents one of the oldest and consistently practiced forms of complete healthcare, originating in India over 3,000 years ago. In Sanskrit, Ayurveda (आयुर्वेद) translates to "science" or "wisdom" of life. This medical practice is based on the premise that an individual's health and wellness depend upon a very delicate balance between the mind, body, and spirit[31]. As a medical practice, Ayurveda is intended to promote good health, not to fight disease. The treatments can be targeted toward specific health problems when the need arises, but the goal is to prevent ill health from developing.

Ayurveda views the human body as being composed of five basic elements—space, air, fire, water, and earth (Figure 6.9). These elements combine to form three life energies or forces, referred

Figure 6.8 India at the Height of the Mogul Empire

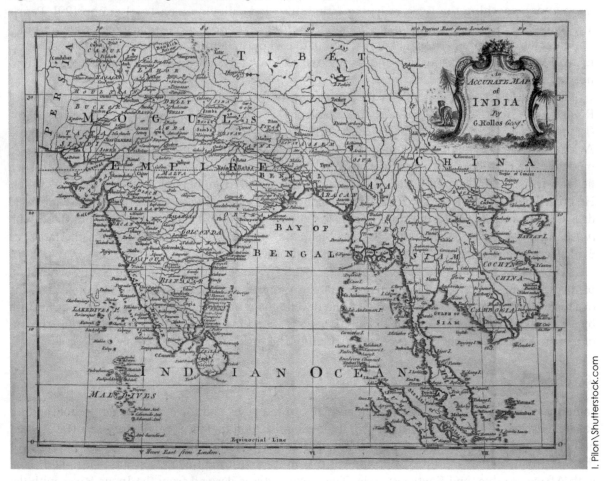

I. Pilon\Shutterstock.com

Figure 6.9 Ayurvedic Medicine Text from Kerala, India

AjayTvm\Shutterstock.com

to as *doshas*. The doshas are associated with elements, responsible for key bodily principles, and if imbalanced can result in manifested consequences for the individual (see Table 6.3). Everyone has a unique composition of doshas, with one of the three doshas being more dominant than the other[32]. Each dosha is responsible for controlling different bodily functions. The doshas can be regulated, improved, or halted using blood purification, massage, physical movement (yoga), medical oils, herbs, and enemas or laxatives.

Table 6.3 Doshas of Ayurvedic Medicine

Dosha	Elements	Principle	Example Consequences
Vata	Air and Space	Principle of movement representing lightness and flexibility. Responsible for all activity in the body—breathing, circulation, and nerve impulses.	Excess of Vata produces anxiety, tension, and high blood pressure.
Pitta	Fire and Water	Principle of transformation representing energy and courage. Regulates the metabolic processes and energy production.	Excess of Pitta leads to inflammation and irritability.
Kapha	Earth and Water	Principle of stability representing peace and serenity. Synchronizes the immune system and fortifies the mind and spirit.	Excess of Kapha causes idleness and weight gain.

Source: T. D. Church (table); information[33]

Over time, Ayurvedic medicine oscillated from generalist to specialist practices and as a result has developed eight component practices. A number of healing mechanism were available to the healer that consisted of medications, meal plans, and meditation. Medications were divided into preventive and healing treatments. Preventive medication was used to promote well-being and extend the life span of an individual. It consisted of making everyday regimens to keep the body in balance. These regimens focused on everything from eating routine and exercise to massage, meditation, and maintaining positive social connections. Healing medication was deployed to mend a disease and was accomplished using internal or external measures. Internal measures utilized detoxification and improved wellness through palliative care. External measures utilized medicinal oils, steam baths, and organic pastes like henna. Ayurvedic prescription of medication followed the methods developed by the eight practices to assist and target specific maladies (Table 6.4).

Pharmacology in Ayurvedic medicine was quite advanced. In order for a medication to be codified and used in practice, it needed to meet four principles[33]. The first principle stated that any substance of natural or synthetic origin is potential medicine. The second principle indicated that any substance to be used as medicine must be thoroughly studied with reference to its nomenclature, identity, properties, application, and safety. The third principle realized that there is a high risk of harm in the use of a substance that has not been adequately understood. And the fourth and final principle cautioned that well-understood substances should not be abused or misused.

The second principle aligns closely with drug development practices of the modern era, in particular the details of the second principle sound like the elements of an FDA application for an Investigational New Drug (IND). From an Ayurvedic perspective, there were four areas that needed to be documented and well-studied to meet the second principle (Table 6.5). This principle required that new medications must be safe and effective, the key tenants of modern drug development[31].

Table 6.4 Eight Components of Ayurvedic Medicine

Ayurvedic Specialty	Description
Kayacikitsa	General medicine, medicine of the body
Kaumara-bhrtya	Pediatrics, medicine of children and infants
Salyatantra	Surgical techniques, extraction of foreign objects from the body
Salakyatantra	Ears, eyes, nose, and mouth (ENT), treatments to assist in hearing, seeing, and breathing
Bhutavidya	Pacification of possessing spirits; treatment for the minds of people who are affected by possession or mental imbalance
Agadatantra	Toxicology, removal of poisons and the science of studying poisons
Rasayanatantra	Use of tonics to increase the lifespan, improve intellect, and restore strength
Vajikaranatantra	Sexual health, aphrodisiacs and treatments for increasing the volume and viability of semen and enhancing sexual pleasure

Source: T. D. Church (table); information[34]

Table 6.5 Elements of the 2nd Principle of Ayurvedic Pharmacologic Drug Development

Element to be Studied	Details
Nomenclature (Namajnana)	• Codification of names • Cross-linking and enumeration of all associated names • Classification of nomenclature • Descriptive analysis of all known names
Identification (Rupajnana)	• Botanical features • Differential properties of the plant parts • Related species • Potential substitutes
Properties (Gunajnana)	• Physico-chemical properties • Pharmacology • Target • Risk-benefit analysis of medication • Interaction with other herbs, known antagonism, known synergy • Adverse effects and cross-medication effects
Applications (Yuktijnana)	• Classification • Disease target • Formulation • Pharmaceutical processing • Dose form • Mode of administration

Source: T. D. Church (table); information[34]

Drug safety refers to a drug having minimal to no adverse effects cause by administration of the medication(s) and that there is a lack of side effects when the medication is continued. *Drug efficacy* represents the ability of the drug to produce the desired effect in the body, for example, aspirin reduces inflammation and headache. Ayurveda put emphasis on identifying and understanding unwholesome interactions between drugs, individual constitution, and food interactions as part of prescribing practice. It would take the Western World nearly 1,500 years to develop a similar model to investigate the safety and efficacy of medications.

Ayurvedic treatments were derived from plants and used some or all parts of the plant for different applications. The most common parts used were roots, leaves, fruits, barks, and seeds. Fermentation was incorporated early into the development of Ayurvedic treatments[35]. These alcoholic beverages used as medicine were classified by the raw material and fermentation process used; consisting of sugar-based, cereal-based, cereal-based with herbs, fermented with vinegar, and tonic wines[36]. Opium was used in several preparations, but was prominently prescribed for diarrhea and dysentery, increasing sexual ability, enhancing muscular ability, and for affecting the brain either as pain relief or to help achieve a restful sleep.

Anatomical knowledge grew under Ayurvedic practitioners, and by ~800 BCE a prominent surgeon Susruta had written a comprehensive collection of surgical practices titled *Susrutasamhita*[37]. Among the surgical texts in this compendium, it is the earliest known works on plastic surgery. Susruta was the first to describe *rhinoplasty*, the surgical improvements performed to alter the appearance of the nose. In ancient times in India, the nose was a sign of dignity and respect. One of the most severe punishments exacted on war prisoners, criminals, and those who participate in infidelity was the amputation of the nose. It would forever mark the individual as being criminal and would permanently disfigure them. Susruta recognized that an extra flap of skin called the pedicle in the forehead could be removed and used to form a new nose[38]. This surgical technique provided Susruta with wealth and fame and his writings contain a level of technical skill in surgery that would not be seen in Western Medicine until the mid-1900s CE.

One of India's best-known cosmetics is *henna*, a dye prepared from the henna tree (*Lawsonia inermis*). The henna tree can be found in hot arid climates like Pakistan and Northern India, with the higher the temperature the darker the pigments within the dye (Figure 6.10). Ayurvedic medicine utilized henna as a topical treatment for stomach pains, menstrual cramps, insect repellant, burns (including sunburns), open wounds, fevers, foot disease and fungus, and the prevention of hair loss[39, 40]. Henna was a very popular trade commodity and had cosmetic uses found in Ancient Rome, Ancient Egypt, Northern Africa, Arabian Peninsula, and throughout South Asia. *Mehndi* is an ancient form of body art utilizing henna to draw temporary tattoos on the hands and legs. The variations and designs

Figure 6.10 Mehndi Designs in Henna

Cora Unk Photo\Shutterstock.com

Figure 6.11 Lord Shiva

Dmitry Rukhlenko\Shutterstock.com

represent the geometry of mandala art and is often associated with Indian religious festivals and weddings. Henna is often applied to the hands and feet of brides prior to and during Hindu weddings and is prominent at festivals such as Karva Chauth, Vat Purnima, Deepavali, Bhai Dooj, and Durga Pooja to name a few (Figure 6.11).

Another herb used in Hindu rituals like Deepavali and Kumbha Mela is Cannabis Indica, specifically in the form of ***Bhang***. Bhang is a cannabis beverage common in Punjab and Pakistan and can be found being served in some countryside restaurants. The general recipe for Bhang can be found in Figure 6.12. The use of Bhang in India goes back thousands of years, with the earliest record of Bhang dating to ~2000 BCE. Bhang has been long associated with Lord Shiva, with one of his many titles being Lord of Bhang[41]. Vedic texts describe Bhang as being a beneficial herb that "releases anxiety" among those who consume the beverage. Siddhartha Gautama (Buddha) was said to have lived on a daily ration of one Bhang seed and nothing else during his six years of asceticism wherein he practiced self-discipline and meditation to achieve enlightenment[42].

Among the sacred elixirs of the ***Devas***, gods of India, existed ***amrita*** and ***soma***. Amrita can be understood as "immortality" and is often referred to in ancient Vedic texts as "nectar." There are numerous references to amrita as the drink of the devas[43, 44]. Soma means "pressed" and refers to the pressing of fruit to make fermented juice, yet in the Vedic texts Soma has been conceptualized as an elixir. The consumption of soma not only healed all illness but was believed to confer great wealth and luck to the consumer[45]. Neither the plants nor recipes for either of these elixirs have been found, and they are widely regarded to be myth or folklore. However, several independent texts from early Indian history recount how these substances were utilized by both mortals and devas alike.

Figure 6.12 General Recipe to Make Bhang

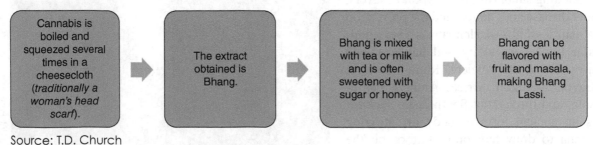

| Cannabis is boiled and squeezed several times in a cheesecloth (*traditionally a woman's head scarf*). | The extract obtained is Bhang. | Bhang is mixed with tea or milk and is often sweetened with sugar or honey. | Bhang can be flavored with fruit and masala, making Bhang Lassi. |

Source: T.D. Church

In addition to religious ideologies that transferred out of India, it has been shown that Ayurveda was widely shared and formed the basis of Chinese and Japanese medical practices. Cannabis as a ritual and sacred rite were exchanged along with the cultural uses of henna. India helped influence medicinal and surgical practices of future generations. Ideology, religion, and cultural artifacts intertwined with a holistic medical practice were all exported along the Silk Road.

6.4 Chinese Contributions

The Silk Road was a formalized trade route, established during the Han dynasty (~130 BCE) starting in Beijing and extending west to the Mediterranean Sea. Among the most valuable assets exchanged along the Silk Road were the exchanges of art, religion, philosophy, technology, language, science, architecture, and medicine. These assets were carried alongside commercial goods the merchants traded from country to country.

Traditional Chinese Medicine (TCM) is the traditional medical practices of China and has flourished with ~2,500 years of practice. The core components of TCM are believed to have been brought to China alongside Buddhist monks traveling from India. TCM includes various forms of herbal medicine, acupuncture, massage (tui na), exercise (qi gong and tai chi), and dietary therapy[46]. Chief among the tenets of TCM is the belief that the body's vital energy (ch'I or qi) radiates through channels (meridians) that have branches connected to bodily organs and as a result influence bodily function. The doctrines of TCM have become heavily influenced by Daoist philosophical texts like the Yellow Emperor's Inner Cannon (Huangdi Neijing) [47]. The Neijing (內功) is a culmination of Daoist philosophy and theory related to lifestyle and living well with the intent of prolonging life. Daoism (alternatively known as Taoism) is responsible for the fundamental philosophies of Chinese astrology, Chinese alchemy, several martial arts (Wushu, Kung Fu, and Tai Chi to name a few), and Feng Shui. Through Chinese alchemy, there are ~13,000 medicinal herbs and minerals employed for over 100,000 medical recipes used in TCM (Figure 6.13). Another text that has influenced TCM is the ***Nan Ching*** (*难经*) or *Canon on Eighty-One Difficult Issues* which outlined how human bodies were seen to be linked in an endless circulation of qi[48]. The Nan Jing underwent some significant changes throughout Chinese history, Table 6.6 highlights a few of the unique additions by dynastic period. One crucial aspect to TCM is the incorporation of systematic correspondence in diagnosing disease. ***Systemic correspondence*** refers to the belief that each internal organ has its own channel for qi as well as correspondence to various aspects of the human body that make it an integrated whole[49]. These aspects include emotions, mental processes, spiritual aspects, physical activity, and the external environment.

Figure 6.13 Ancient Chinese Medical Text

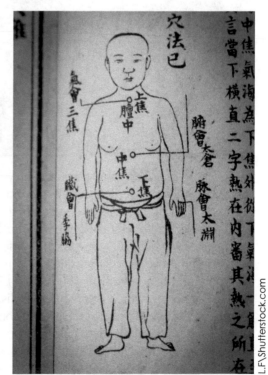

Table 6.6 Nan Jing Changes by Dynasty

Dynasty	Influence to Nan Jing
Han Dynasty (202 BCE–220 CE)	Exorcisms as well as drug therapy joined acupuncture in being founded on systematic correspondence.
Six Dynasties Period (220–589 CE)	Buddhist influences and use of herbal medicines for health; medicine of systematic correspondence becomes formalized.
Sui Dynasty (581–618 CE)	Acupuncture with refined clinical details was incorporated.
Tang Dynasty (618–907 CE)	Daoism influences were incorporated; alchemy and the search for immortality led to many herbs and minerals being added into TCM.

Source: T. D. Church (table); information[50]

Figure 6.14 TCM Drug Powders

berry21477\Shutterstock.com

Daoism is deeply woven into TCM and has been since the earliest beginnings of Chinese culture. The earliest known healers were the Wu in China[51]. The Wu are believed to have practiced shamanism and their healers were predominantly women. The methods they employed in healing involved exorcism and trance-like states entered through hallucinogenic drugs. These trances were used to formulate healing ceremonies and rituals. The physical healing methods of the Wu evolved into acupuncture, acupressure, and moxibustion. Formal Daoist healing practitioners and philosophers formed a school ~400 BCE and incorporated the practices of the Wu from thousands of years of practice into their teachings[50]. Daoist medicine was intimately focused on nature and the natural cycles of life. This natural emphasis emphasized harmony with the seasons and the cyclic flow of qi[50].

Daoist practitioners had a profound influence on the incorporation of exercise and Chinese drug therapies into TCM. *Qi Gong (氣功)* or "life energy cultivation" is a holistic system of coordinated body postures and movements, controlled breathing, and meditation that became central to longevity, spirituality, and martial arts training (Figure 6.14). The most influential Daoist addition to TCM has its roots in *Chinese alchemy*, which was focused on discovery of the "elixir of life" and led to a robust herbal pharmacopeia[52]. The search for the drug to confer good health, great wealth, and immortality led Chinese alchemists to create of a vast array of elixirs, compounds, pills, potions, and teas. Chinese alchemy built a repository of knowledge related to plants, animals, and mineral products. Experimentation with these products gave the early Daoist practitioners of TCM insights into longevity and human health.

The ***Elixir of Life*** was a mythical potion believed to hold the ability to grant the drinker eternal life and/or eternal youth. Later Daoist beliefs would add to the fable by stating the elixir of life had the ability to cure all diseases. Many of the early emperors of China sought the elixir, to date no tangible product has been discovered[53]. Around the year 220 BCE, during the Qin Dynasty, Qin Shi Huang sent his alchemist Xu Fu along with 500 young men and 500 young women out across the eastern seas to seek the elixir, but they never returned. Legend holds that they instead found the island of Japan and began the Japanese population. Shi Huang Di sent out 3,000 young men and women from the Mount of the Immortals in all directions of the compass, sadly none returned with the elixir. Among the imperial court there was a long running traditional practice of ingesting precious substances like jade, cinnabar, hematite, gold, and silver. The belief was that consuming these long-lasting metals and minerals would confer some of their longevity onto the individual who consumed them. Sadly, this practice most likely quickened the death of the imperial court and courtesans.

Chinese involvement along the Silk Road brought great wealth to merchants during the Han Dynasty, where Chinese silk, porcelain, jade, and silver were traded for exotic goods from the West. Along with goods, China gained medical knowledge and adapted Ayurvedic ideas and merged them with Daoist philosophies to create the world's second oldest medical practice. Chinese alchemy gave rise to several real-world medications while in the pursuit of the elixir of life. Folklore holds that while searching for this mythical font of youth, wayward Chinese landed on the island of Japan and began a new nation. Through the incorporation of Daoism with the shamanic rituals of the Wu peoples, China developed specialized knowledge relate to qi that gave rise to martial arts, breathing practices, meditation, and acupuncture.

6.5 Japanese Contributions

Traditional Chinese medicine (TCM) was imported to Japan by Buddhist monks ~650 CE. Acupuncture, acupressure, and moxibustion were among the techniques the Japanese incorporated. By ~700 CE, a unique Japanese medical system emerged, kampo igaku (漢方医学) informally referred to as kampo[54]. Kampo incorporated TCM techniques but relied more on herbal medicines and developed into its own unique traditional practice (Figure 6.15). Anma and shiatsu physical manipulation and biokinesiology techniques were incorporated. Sekkotsu, or Judo musculoskeletal therapy, was an essential skill to help with "bone setting" thanks to the intensity of Japanese martial arts[55]. External wound management was equally important in the practice of kampo. Chief among the medicines of ancient Japan were menthol and sake. Menthol, or Japanese mint, has long been used as a mild stimulant, a germ-killer, and pain reliver. Menthol is applied directly to the skin to soothe away muscle pain, nerve pain, itchiness, insect bites, and allergic reactions. Sake, traditional rice wine, has been used for a variety of medicinal preparations, prominently it was used for pain relief and as a mild anesthetic.

Sake is made by fermenting rice that has been threshed or beaten to remove the outer bran coating. Sake fermentation dates back nearly 2,500 years and coincides with the start of rice cultivation. Sake is the national beverage of Japan and as such has developed its own specialized rituals for serving[56]. Before being served, sake must be warmed in a small porcelain bottle called tokkuri (Figure 6.16). It is then poured into a small porcelain cup called sakazuki[57]. Good etiquette requires that sake should only be sipped and never gulped down. In ancient Japan, during the feudal period, sake was produced

Figure 6.15 Feudal Map of Japan

Tomonobu, Ishikawa, died 1716. World Digital Library.

Source: Library of Congress

Figure 6.16 Tokkuri and Sakazuki

Erdaprasetyo\Shutterstock.com

primarily by the imperial court and by large temples and shrines[58]. Sake has always been the drink of the Shinto kami (gods) and was consumed at religious festivals in their honor. The kami would be offered sake from supplicants who visited their shrines and temples. Shoguns and feudal lords were known to give sake to their retainers and samurai in recognition of their special services and for their merit on the battlefield.

The unique aspects of Japanese traditional medicine, Kampo, and its long history of martial arts led to unique uses of plant medicines. The main religions of Japan, Shinto and Buddhism, helped to solidify a unique relationship with rice wine as being both sacred and medicinal. These traditions flourished until the modern era.

6.6 Closing of the Silk Road

The Silk Road endured through geopolitical clashes and disruptions, through religious freedom and zealotism, and through plague and famine. However, as the Ottoman Empire gained power in

1453 CE, trade between East and West was severed. The Mongol Empire dissolved, and Eastern portion of the Silk Road became economically and culturally separated from one another. The Black Death (1346–1353 CE) a century prior had weakened many of the trading cities along the Silk Road and left portions of the route open for exploitation by marauders and thieves. European nations who were dependent upon spices, silks, and other exotic goods from Asia were forced to seek out other means for obtaining their goods. Changes in ship design, better equipment for navigation, and the spread of gunpowder culminated in the rapid development of large, ocean ready ships. European nations began funding ship voyages in the hopes of finding vast wealth and lands ready for colonization.

The Silk Road had opened routes for trade, diplomacy, and smuggling. The technologies and innovations needed to maintain the road helped advance the fields of philosophy, science, military, and medicine. Spirituality and religion were exchanged along the Silk Road, and in many of the religions, intoxication began to be seen in an extremely negative connotation. The Silk Road ushered in a more globally connected set of civilizations, which allowed for the exchange of goods, ideas, disease, and drugs to move between Asia and Europe. Ultimately setting the stage for military expansion and colonial exploitation.

REFERENCES

1. Hancock, J. F. (2021). *Spices, scents and silk: Catalysts of world trade* (p. 338). CAB International.
2. Frankopan, P. (2015). *The silk roads : A new history of the world* (p. 636). Bloomsbury.
3. Galli, M. (2017) Beyond frontiers: Ancient Rome and the Eurasian trade networks. *Journal of Eurasian Studies, 8*(1), 3–9.
4. Pollard, E. A. (2013). Indian spices and Roman "magic" in Imperial and Late Antique Indomediterranea. *Journal of World History, 24*(1), 1–23.
5. Liu, X. (2011). A silk road legacy: The spread of Buddhism and Islam. *Journal of World History,* 22(1), 55–81.
6. McGovern, W. M. (1919). *Notes on Mahayana Buddhism. The Monist, 29*(3), 381–403.
7. Herodotus, (1996 [440 BCE]). *The histories* (p. 771). Penguin Classics.
8. Stausberg, M. (2012). From power to powerlessness: Zoroastrianism in Iranian history. In A. N. Longva & A. S. Roald (Eds.), *Religious minorities in the Middle East: Domination, self-empowerment, accommodation.* (pp. 171–193). Brill.
9. Sangari, E., & Karbasi, A. (2017). An approach to history from the viewpoint of philosophy of history of Zoroastrianism. *Historical Perspective & Historiography, 27*(20), 55–77.
10. Diamond, J. M. (1999). *Guns, germs, and steel: The fates of human societies.* W.W. Norton & Co.
11. Touwaide, A. (2019). Harmful botanicals. In P. Wexler (Ed.), *Toxicology in antiquity* (2nd ed., pp. 387–399). Academic Press.
12. Rosso, A. M. (2016). Alexandria, an emporium in the Silk Road, and the traffic of unusual medicines. *Societas Internationalis Historiae Medicinae, 22*(2), 26–52.
13. Hartnett, A., & Dawdy, S. L. (2013). The archaeology of illegal and illicit economies. *Annual Review of Anthropology, 42*(1), 37–51.

14. Pedani, M. P. (2008). Ottoman merchants in the adriatic. Trade and smuggling. *Acta Histriae*, *16*(1–2), 155–172.
15. Nummedal, T. E. (2011). Words and works in the history of alchemy. *Isis, 102*(2), 330–337.
16. Moran, B. T. (2005). *Distilling knowledge alchemy, chemistry, and the scientific revolution. New histories of science, technology, and medicine.* Harvard University Press. 224.
17. Stephan, T. (2017). Writing the past: Ancient Egypt through the lens of Medieval Islamic thought. In *Arabic humanities, Islamic thought* (pp. 256–270). Brill.
18. Pfeifer, H. (2022). *Empire of salons: Conquest and community in early modern Ottoman lands* (p. 320). Princeton University Press..
19. Todd, A. (1946). Hashish. *Experientia, 2*(2), 55–60.
20. Gilman, S. L., & *Zhou*, X. (2004). *Smoke: A global history of smoking* (p. 408). Reaktion Books.
21. Chaouachi, K. (2017). Le narguilé: Une tradition ancienne émergeant soudainement dans la modernité. In C. Ferland (Ed.), *Tabac & Fumées: Regards multidisciplinaires et indisciplinés sur l'histoire du tabagisme* (XVe–XXe siècle, pp. 167–191)). Les Presses De L'Universite Laval.
22. Mandel, J. (1966). Hashish, assassins, and the love of God. *Issues Criminology, 2,* 149.
23. Gilmer, J. (2015). Blood & sand. *Medieval warfare, 5*(3), 44–49.
24. Polo, M. (1921 [1274 CE]). *The travels of Marco Polo: the venetian.* JM Dent.
25. Yılmaz, B., Acar-Tek, N., & Sözlü, S. (2017). Turkish cultural heritage: A cup of coffee. *Journal of Ethnic Foods, 4*(4), 213–220.
26. Pendell, D. (2002). Goatherds, smugglers, and revolutionaries: A history of coffee. *Whole Earth, 2002*(108), 7–9.
27. Plouvier, L. (1993). *L'electuaire, un medicament plusieurs fois millenaire. Scientiarum Historia: Tijdschrift voor de Geschiedenis van de Wetenschappen en de Geneeskunde, 19*(1), 97–112.
28. O'Connell, M. (2020). Silk road pharmacy: Debating theriac and defining the natural world. In J. D. Lerner & Y. Shi, *Silk roads: From local realities to global narratives* (pp. 81–96). Oxbow Books.
29. Barroso, M. D. S. (2019). Pearl, an ancient antidote of eastern origin. In P. Wexler (Ed.), Toxicology in antiquity (2nd ed., pp. 401–410). Academic Press.
30. Karimullah, K. I. (2017). Avicenna and Galen, philosophy and medicine: Contextualising discussions of medical experience in medieval Islamic physicians and philosophers. *Oriens, 45*(1-2), 105–149.
31. Sharma, G. (1997). Ethnomedicinal flora: Ayurvedic system of medicine. *Journal of the Tennessee Academy of Science, 72*(3-4), 53–55.
32. Hankey, A. (2010). Establishing the scientific validity of Tridosha part 1: Doshas, Subdoshas and Dosha Prakritis. *Ancient Science of Life, 29*(3), 6–18.
33. Varier, M. R. (2020). *A brief history of ayurveda* (p. 204). Oxford University Press.
34. Pandey, M. M., Rastogi, S., & Rawat, A. K. (2013). Indian traditional ayurvedic system of medicine and nutritional supplementation. *Evidence-Based Complementary and Alternative Medicine, 2013*(376327), 12.

35. Nikolova, P., et al. (2018). Wine as a medicine in ancient times. *Scripta Scientifica Pharmaceutica, 5*(2), 14–21.

36. McHugh, J. (2020). Sīdhu (Śīdhu): The Sugar Cane "Wine" of Ancient and Early Medieval India. *History of Science in South Asia, 8*, 36–56.

37. Susruta, (1911 [800 BCE]). In K. L. Bhishagratna (Ed.), *Susrutasamhita: An English translation based on original Sanskrit text* (Vol. 2). Bharat Mihir Press.

38. Loukas, M., et al. (2010). Anatomy in ancient India: A focus on the Susruta Samhita. *Journal of Anatomy, 217*(6), 646–650.

39. Kahnamoeia, M. B., et al. (2019). Study of henna in Persian medicine and new studies. *Journal of Islamic and Iranian Traditional Medicine, 10*(1), 9.

40. Rehmat, S., et al. (2020). Henna. In M. A. Hanif, et al. (Eds.), *Medicinal plants of South Asia* (pp. 355–368). Elsevier.

41. Godlaski, T. M. (2012). Shiva, lord of bhang. *Substance Use & Misuse, 47*(10), 1067–1072.

42. Aldrich, M. R. (1977). Tantric cannabis use in India. *Journal of Psychedelic Drugs, 9*(3), 227–233.

43. Asthana, S., & Bansal, S. L. (2016). *Role of ayurvedic medicinal plants in ancient India. International Journal of Advanced Science and Research, 1*(8), 4–7.

44. Padhy, S., & Dash, S. K. (2004). The soma drinker of ancient India: An ethno-botanical retrospection. *Journal of Human Ecology, 15*(1), 19–26.

45. Torri, D. (2022). Soma and drug history in Ancient Asia. In P. Gootenberg (Ed.), *The Oxford handbook of global drug history* (pp. 95–112). Oxford University Press.

46. Cheung, F. (2011). TCM: Made in China. *Nature, 480*(7378), S82–S83.

47. Unschuld P. U. (Ed.) (2003 [400 BCE]). *Huangdi Neijing* (Huang Di Nei Jing Su Wen). University of California Press.

48. Unschuld P. U. (Ed.) (1986 [100 BCE]). *Nan-ching the classic of difficult issues* (p. 700). University of California Press.

49. Winkler, C. (2018). Healing by Qi – Sustainable self-regulation. *Journal of Acupuncture and Meridian Studies, 11*(4), 180–180.

50. Kohn, L. (2013). The Daoist body of qi. In G. Samuel & J. Johnston (Eds.), *Religion and the subtle body in Asia and the West* (pp. 30–46). Routledge.

51. Lin, F.-S. (2009). The image and status of Shamans in ancient China. In J. Lagerwey & M. Kalinowski (Eds.), *Early Chinese religion, Part One: Shang through Han* (1250 BC–220 AD) (pp. 397–458). Brill.

52. Meng, S. (2021). Chinese Alchemy. In *The origins of sciences in China: History of science and technology in China* (Vol. 1, pp. 535–589).

53. Pregadio, F. (2022). Time in Chinese alchemy. In D. Yang, V. Lo, & M. Stanely-Baker (Eds.), *Routledge handbook of Chinese medicine* (pp. 427–443). Routledge.

54. Kuchta, K. (2019). Traditional Japanese kampo medicine–History of ideas and practice; Part 1: From ancient shamanic practice to the medical academies of Edo. *Traditional & Kampo Medicine, 6*(2), 49–56.

55. Nimura, Y., Higaki, E., & Yokoyama, Y. (2021). Arts and sciences of Kuatsu: A review of the historical and medical researches. *The Arts and Sciences of Judo*, *1*(1), 102–109.

56. Joya, M. (2006). Food, 'sake' and tobacco. In M. Joya (Ed.), *Japan and things Japanese* (pp. 243–305). Routledge.

57. Grapard, A. G. (2021). Japanese food offerings. *Japanese Journal of Religious Studies*, *48*(1), 165–185.

58. Andreeva, A. (2010). Medieval Shinto: New discoveries and perspectives. *Religion Compass*, *4*(11), 679–693.

Chapter 7

Voyages of Discovery: Piracy and Maritime Empires

The fallout from the closure of the Silk Road led to a rapid expansion of exploration and colonization by sea. By 1340 CE, European exploration had expanded beyond the Mediterranean with Portugal discovering the Canary Islands, followed by the archipelagos of the Azores and Madeira. In 1492 CE, Christopher Columbus made a startling discovery when completely by accident he found North America. Vasco da Gama, a Portuguese explorer, established the first sea route to India in 1498 CE, which brought Portugal and India into a very close trade arrangement that substantially benefited the Portuguese. In 1519 CE, Ferdinand Magellan took a Spanish fleet and navigated from the Atlantic to Asia, discovering an interoceanic passage and favorable trade route for the Spanish Crown. The first person to circumnavigate the world in a single expedition was Sir Francis Drake in 1590 CE sailing for England. This was a *transoceanic* era wherein voyages by ship began to connect the Eastern and Western Hemispheres. There were abundant technological innovations in the areas of navigation, cartography, astrology, ship construction, and meteorology all driven to make transoceanic connections possible. *Global trade* helped to establish and increase trans-regional and global trade networks, which helped move goods. The fledgling global trade network facilitated the spread of religion and other cultural elements such as language and laws, as well as the migration of large numbers of people. *Germs* carried to the Americas by the Europeans ravaged the indigenous peoples. Infections from sexually transmitted diseases, specifically syphilis, traveled from the Americas and ravaged Europe, Africa, and Asia. *Global exchanges* in vast quantities of crops and animals began to alter agricultural patterns, diets, and whole populations around the planet. This was the period that gave rise to one of the most atrocious practices in human history, the *African Slave* Trade. It tore families apart, destroyed cultures, and dehumanized everyone involved.

The *Voyages of Discovery* (~1500–1850 CE) was a period of large-scale transoceanic trade that witnessed the global movement of peoples, materials, and ideas. It was a period of *maritime empires* where the political power of nations became powered by ships and sailors, wind and sail. It fueled a rapid change in scale, technologies, politics, and public reliance on seafaring. There was rapid development of overseas colonies, trading posts, and military strongholds. *Plantations* were large land holdings of wealthy investors, mostly worked by enslaved people who had been trafficked across the oceans. These plantations drew their wealth from cash crops such as sugarcane, opium, silk, indigo, and tobacco, and they dominated the Caribbean and South America. The homes of wealthy individuals in Europe featured a novel piece of furniture, the *curio cabinet* or cabinets of curiosities, where the baubles and trinkets from foreign travels and colonized peoples could be proudly displayed for the amusement of dinner guests. This period focused on the ***three ocean worlds*** consisting of the Atlantic, Indian, and Pacific Oceans where wealth could be accumulated. These three oceans had unique geographies, weather systems, ocean currents, and histories that became tied together as nation after nation in Europe vied for supremacy over the seas.

It did not matter how far a mariner ventured into the distant seas; they remained dependent upon the supporting land infrastructures. ***Seaports*** were towns similar to frontier outposts featuring all manner of ware to refit, refurbish, and relax a sea weary ship and crew. They featured rough drinking establishments and brothels where sailors relaxed, drank, and gambled between voyages. There were also numerous trade and craft shops involved in outfitting voyages and selling of the goods the ships returned with to port. During the early part of the voyages of discovery, most social and economic activities took place at the local level, seaports represented the opposite. They were places that marked the movement of goods and people over long distances. Larger seaports took on an air of ***cosmopolitanism*** as they contained people from a variety of different countries. The cosmopolitan seaports supported significant numbers of foreign nationals, which reflected the seaports ties to places across maritime frontiers. The transplants included benefactors who managed the commercial interests of overseas merchants and sailors, sailors on temporary shore leave, tradesmen, and craftsmen.

Colonial interests featured plantations; those large-scale estates built for farming of specialized cash crops. The Caribbean became a hot bed for ***sugar plantations***, which were highly valued by British, French, Portuguese, and Spanish colonists from the sixteenth to eighteenth centuries CE (Figure 7.1). Sugar grew well in the soil and climate of the Caribbean. Sugar created a unique economy that impacted labor, profits, and local ecology. Sugar displaced many indigenous peoples and led to many of the conflicts between colonizers and natives. Sugar cane processing gave rise to several related commodities such as rum, molasses, and falernum. ***Falernum*** is a sweet syrup used to make many "tropical drinks" with the traditional recipe containing almond, ginger, line, vanilla, cloves, and allspice. Most plantations were operated with slave or indentured labor, which meant that the people making the profits did none of the demanding work.

Figure 7.1   Sugar Cane

Izf\.Shutterstock.com

7.1   Privateers and Pirates

Maritime empires covered large expanses of ocean. Most sovereign nations did not have the ability nor capacity to protect civilian and merchant ships while engaged in wars with other sovereign nations. This opened a place for the ***privateer***, a person or ship who would engage in maritime warfare under a commission of war. A ***Letter of Marque***, or a commission of war, empowered the person or ship to carry on all forms of hostility permissible at sea through war for the country or sovereign who issued the marque[1]. It enabled the bearer of the letter of marque to attack foreign vessels during wartime and sanctioned the taking of ships and their associated cargo as prizes or spoils of war. Captured ships were subject to condemnation and sale under prize law, with the proceeds divided between the privateer sponsors, shipowners, captains, and crew. A percentage of the total share usually went to the issuer of the commission of the Letter of Marque. Robbery under arms was a common occurrence in seaborne commerce, and as a result merchant ships were armed and outfitted to defend their cargo. During war, naval resources became auxiliary to the operations on land, so privateering was a way of subsidizing national power by mobilizing otherwise independently armed ships and sailors.

There were whole fortunes to be made and lost at sea as goods traveled the globe. Privateers could help keep the peace, but the lure of wealth and the bounty of trade vessels sometimes led people to a more illicit profession, piracy. A *pirate* was an individual who committed warlike acts at sea without the authorization of any nation[2, 3]. They were notorious for robbery and kidnapping, criminal violence by ship, stealing of cargo and other valuable items, dealing in stolen goods, and smuggling illegal wares. Often those illegal wares consisted of contraband and prohibited drugs such as opium and cocoa.

Ann Bonny (1697–1721 CE), nicknamed "Lady of the Seas," was an Irish pirate operating in the Caribbean (Figure 7.2)[4]. She was described by her contemporaries as a "good catch" with hair that was as fiery as her temper. She was reportedly able to drink any man under the table and relished in drinking games where she could show her prowess. She was known to be ruthless with her enemies and very fair to civilians. When the Governor of Jamaica captured her, she "plead for her belly," knowing that she would not be hung or killed for piracy as long as the Governor and Magistrate believed her to be pregnant. She was granted mercy by the court, but we are uncertain about what happened to Ann. There is no record of her having been executed and speculation around her final days is murky at best.

Mary Read (1685–-1721 CE) was an English pirate and contemporary with Ann Bonny (Figure 7.3)[4]. She was, as situation required, known as "Mark Read," as she would occasionally impersonate her deceased brother. She dressed as a boy at an incredibly early age. Initially

Figure 7.2   Ann Bonny, Lady of the Seas

German Vizulis\Shutterstock.com

Figure 7.3   Mary Read

German Vizulis\Shutterstock.com

Figure 7.4 Blackbeard

she did so at the urging of her mother to receive her brother's inheritance money. As a teen she dressed like a young man and joined the British navy. While serving the royal navy, pirates boarded and took the ship she served on. Many of the officers fought to the death, while Mary willingly joined the pirates. Shortly thereafter, she was offered the King's pardon, and took a commission to privateer. At the age of 18, she rallied the crew of her privateer schooner to mutiny, and she took control of the ship. She was captain of that ship until her capture by the Governor of Jamaica alongside Ann Bonny one year before her death.

Blackbeard (1680–1718 CE), Edward Teach, was an English pirate who operated in the Caribbean and the Eastern Coast of the British North American colonies (Figure 7.4)[3]. He was notorious for his reliance on a sloop when many of his contemporary pirates preferred the larger and bulkier galleon. He preferred the sloop with its sleek profile and quick maneuverability. He chose to outfit his sloop with over 40 cannons, making his vessel fast and formidable. Before boarding an enemy's vessel, Blackbeard would light cannon fuses made from hemp and tuck them under the brim of his hat. The effect was the stuff of nightmares, a tall and burly man with thick smoke circling his head as he held his sword aloft screaming bloody murder. He was ferocious in battle and reportedly had accumulated and lost at minimum eight grand treasures. When he was shot during his last battle aboard his ship, he supposedly clung to the mast as his ship was scuttled and sank off the coast of Bermuda.

Figure 7.5 The Jolly Roger

Calico Jack (1682–1720 CE), John Rackham, was an English pirate operating in the Bahamas and Cuba[3]. He earned his nickname from the calico, a coarse weave of cotton fabric, that he wore. He is credited with the invention of the *Jolly Roger*, the iconic skull and cross bone flag (Figure 7.5). He promoted the use of the Jolly Roger as a standard among pirates far and wide. When Bonny and Read had lost their ship, he took them on as crew until they were able to recapture their vessel. He was especially fond of hit and run raids on merchant ships, in particular rum running sloops. He was an avid drinker of rum and smoker of cannabis, some reports going as far as to state they were the two things that motivated him most in life.

Henri Caesar (unknown—1718 CE), or Black Caesar, by most accounts an African tribal war chieftain, who was briefly a slave in Haiti[5]. He was a West African pirate, who was known for raiding merchant and slave trading vessels between Africa and the Caribbean. The ladies claimed him to be "huge in size," whereas his crew said he had "immense strength and keen intelligence." Caesar's Rock on the north shore of Key Largo is where he made his port of call and base of operation. He was enticed by food, rum, musical instruments, silk scarves, jewels, and pocket watches. He was known to have a minimum of four pocket watches on his person at any given time. Black Caesar was ruthless with slavers and would often have the captains and officers flayed alive. He would then hang their skin like flags from the mast of the ship to show the price others would pay if they continued in the slave trade. Toward the end of his career, he joined Blackbeard's crew and was serving alongside when Blackbeard died. Legend holds that it took nearly 200 men armed with swords and guns to capture him. From British accounts the fighting raged on for 6 hours. The Governor of Virginia recorded in the legal register that the scourge of Atlantic waters died before he could be taken to the gallows.

Ching Shih (1775–1844 CE), better known as Madame Ching, was a pirate from the middle of the Qing Dynasty in China (Figure 7.6)[6]. In Cantonese, her name, Zhen Shi, would become synonymous with "zombie." Madame Ching commanded over 300 Junk ships, which were manned by between 20,000 and 40,000 pirates. She raided ships of the British, Portuguese, and Dutch empires for tobacco, opium, rum, and sugarcane. She tolerated no violence to women, and if any of her pirates raped a woman, the punishment was severe and quick. She would have the offending rapist castrated on the main deck of the ship in front of everyone. She once commented, "women who seek to be equal with men lack ambition"[4]. She turned her eyes on Qing ships as well, attacking them for silks, jewels, and metal. Madame Ching holds a very rare distinction in pirate history, and she is among a small handful of pirates who successfully retired. At the age of 35, she purchased an island and opened a casino and brothel that she managed until the age of 69.

Figure 7.6 Madame Ching

German Vizulis\Shutterstock.com

Life at sea was rife with hardships. Food was bad and often inadequate, crews were underpaid, and the further you got from land, the worse it would get. To compensate sailors and help keep their mind off their wretched existence, most were provided with a daily allowance of beer and wine. Unfortunately, wine turned to vinegar quickly in tropical climates and beer would often spoil before they were halfway across the Atlantic. The byproducts of sugar making were poised to become big business for the sugarcane plantations in the tropics.

Caribbean islands were colonized by British, Portuguese, Spanish, and Dutch agricultural interests between the sixteenth and seventeenth centuries CE. They funded naval vessels to sail with the plantation merchant ships for protection. Sailors, however, on the gunnery ships did not like babysitting. They yearned to capture pirates or enemy ships for profit. Rum was to become the solution to keeping the sailors' content. The first of the rum products, **kill devil**, was a spin-off from the sugar-refining process, skimming, and molasses processing. This spin-off was a cloudy thick liquid and was distilled into a raw white spirit. By 1650 CE, a pint of rum had been unofficially adopted as part of a sailor's daily ration[7, 8]. In 1687 CE, the Royal Navy guaranteed the supply of spirits for their sailors. This was done in part to appease the governors of the Caribbean colonies who had a surplus of rum. Making rum part of the crew's daily allotment helped reduce the amount of surplus rum. The problem, however, was that rum was 140 proof alcohol, significantly stronger than beer and wine. The higher proof tended to cause a lot of disorder among the crews. To keep the peace, **grog** a diluted rum drink of two parts water, one part rum, sugar, and lime juice became standard on many naval vessels in the Caribbean.

Sugarcane became the most important crop in the Caribbean. Other cash crops such as coffee, indigo, and rice were grown as well, but it was sugarcane that drove the economy of the Caribbean colonies. A unique economic relationship among labor, profits, and ecological consequences would forever change the Caribbean[8]. Grand imperial powers enslaved African peoples to cultivate sugar through slave labor. These imperial powers exploited the bodies of the slaves and eroded the nutrients from the natural environment through aggressive agricultural practices. Conflicts among the imperial powers of England, Spain, France, Portugal, and the Dutch for territorial gain and increased wealth were rampant. Indigenous peoples were either eradicated or enslaved to make way for more plantations. The European focus on sugarcane production devastated whole areas of the Caribbean. As soon as rum was discovered, a new threat emerged, that of alcoholism. Rum was cheaper per liter than wine or beer and as a result became the favored drink of colonists, pirates, privateers, and sailors.

7.2 Norwegian Colonial Interests, 872–1397 CE

The Old Kingdom of Norway (872–1397 CE) was a loose confederation of chiefdoms unified into a single nation of seafarers. The Kingdom encompassed parts of Sweden, Norway, the Shetland and Orkney Islands, Faroe Islands, Iceland, Greenland, New Brunswick, and Newfoundland (Figure 7.7). Vikings represented the seafaring Scandinavian pirates who raided, traded, pillaged, and settled throughout the vast kingdom of Norway[9]. In their iconic longships, the Vikings proved to be expert sailors and navigators of oceans and rivers (Figure 7.8). Vikings had a reputation for being a blood thirsty and violent peoples that excelled at all manner of evil and sinful acts. **Berserkers** were fierce Viking warriors in the tenth and eleventh centuries CE and were believed to be capable of doing things that normal humans could not, including feeling no pain from wounds obtained on the battlefield[10]. They fought with ferocity, and their stamina did not abate over time. The Vikings would consume **psilocybin tea** before battle[11]. The hallucinogenic tea combined with chanting and banging of sword to shield amid other rituals would work the Vikings into a battle rage, a frenzied malestrom.

Eric the Red left Iceland ~980 CE and established the first continuous settlement in Greenland[12]. Greenland, however, was not an ideal place to make a colony. It may have looked reminiscent of Norway and Iceland, but the environment was vastly different. Farming was difficult and native

Figure 7.7 Norwegian Colonial Holdings

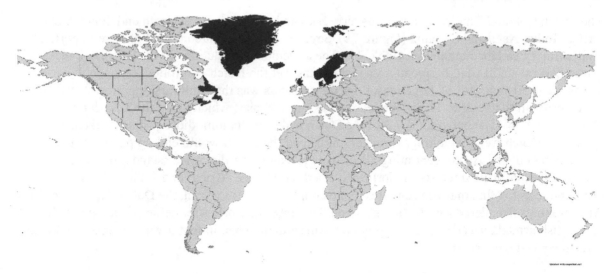

Source: T. D. Church (rendered with https://www.mapchart.net/world.html)

populations were not friendly. Within 20 years of settling the colony, the forests were depleted, which forced the Vikings to rely on trading ships from Europe twice a year for the majority of their supplies. As the trading ships from Europe only came twice a year, the Greenland Vikings had plenty of time between the merchant visits to invent and develop goods to make certain the merchants would return. Perhaps one of the greatest skills the Greenland Vikings possessed was the art of salesmanship. They could enhance the prestige of any given trade item to the point it became legendary, worth far more than its intrinsic value. Greenland was the sole source of

Figure 7.8 Replica of a Norse Longship

maradon 333\Shutterstock.com

alicorn horn, and it was to become a good that the Vikings sold with gusto. Alicorn was in fact the long tusk of a male Narwhal whale. Alicorn by the time it reached mainland Europe, it had been renamed to "unicorn" and was said to have magical healing properties[13]. A cup carved from the unicorn horn would protect anyone who drank from it, as the magic of the horn was said to neutralize any poison placed into its magically imbued cup[14]. In addition, grinding unicorn horn and consuming it in wine or mead was supposedly the cure for melancholia, depression, and male infertility[15].

7.3 Dutch Colonial Interests, 1581–1795 CE

The Dutch Colonial Empire had overseas territories and trading posts in North and South Americas, Africa, India, Asia, and Oceania (Figure 7.9). Several spices the Dutch traded in were important for their culinary and medicinal uses (Table 7.1). The agricultural production of the Dutch colonies comprised several small islands spread over vast oceans, yet the Dutch controlled a monopoly on many spices for ~150 years[16]. A large reason for their success was their military superiority, which was uncontested in the Pacific. There were economic forces at play, which aided the long duration of the Dutch monopoly. The potential rivals of the Dutch had found commodities just as marketable as the spices the Dutch were exploiting. However, in the end the Dutch would end up paying a steep price for their monopoly. By concentrating all of their resources on the Spice Islands in the pacific, the Dutch neglected their interests in North and South Americas, Africa, and India. Ultimately losing those interests to other maritime empires. For example, Peter Stuyvesant, the Dutch Governor of New Amsterdam, surrendered Manhattan Island on September 8, 1664, after being bluffed into believing an English armada was descending upon Fort Amsterdam, when in fact it was a single warship and three unarmed barges[17].

Figure 7.9   Dutch Colonial Holdings

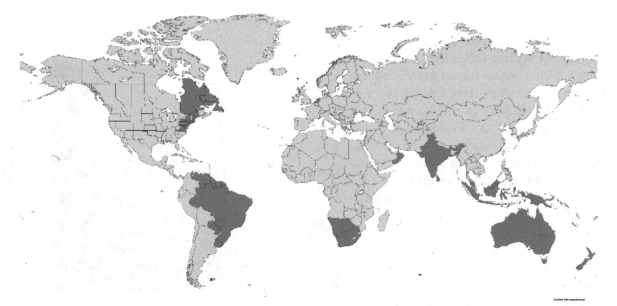

Source: T. D. Church (rendered with https://www.mapchart.net/world.html)

Table 7.1 Spices Traded by the Dutch Colonial Interests

Nutmeg

Antimircobial and antibacterial

Ginger

Used as an anti-rheumatic, diuretic, and aphrodisiac

Cinnamon

Toothache, bad breath, promotes overall health and well being, improves cognitive function, aids in digestion, effective for nausea, vomitting, diarrhea, and gas

Cardamom

Analgesic, asthma and broncia problems, bad breath, antibacterial, anemia, and blood pressure regulation

Tumeric

Antioxidant, anti-inflammatory, boosts brain-derived neurotrophiuc factor, improves brain function, lowers risk of brain disease, lowers risk of heart disease

Cumin

Beneficial for digestion, lowers cholesterol, effective for diabetes, boosts immune system function, aids in fighting osteoporosis

Saffron

Boosts immunity, increases circulation, cardioprotective, effective for diabetes, relieves anxiety, improves bonew strength, imporves nerve function, analgesic qualities, and anti-inflammator

Figure 7.10   Betel Nut

thanasus\Shutterstock.com

A unique herbal drug that the Dutch encountered in Java was the betel nut or the areca palm nut (Figure 7.10). The habit of chewing betel was wholeheartedly adopted by the local Dutch, who went as far as to commission ornate and beautifully crafted boxes to hold the nut, the betel leaf, and other accompaniments for consuming the drug. The local Dutch realized how important betel was to the indigenous populations and utilized betel in their diplomatic repertoire as a sign of hospitality with indigenous elite and chieftains. Betel nut has psychoactive properties and functions as a central nervous system stimulant, similar to caffeine and tobacco[18]. Chewing of the betel stains the mouth, lips, and stool a vibrant reddish yellow color. Severe effects of betel include vomiting, diarrhea, gum disease, excess saliva, chest pain, abnormal heart beats, low blood pressure, shortness of breath and rapid breathing, heart attack, coma, and death[19]. Unlike coffee and tobacco that were traded widely by Dutch competitors, betel remained relatively obscure and unknown outside of Southeast Asia. This is probably due in part to the excess saliva produced that needs to be spit out frequently and the staining of the lips, teeth, and gums, all of which would have gone against European decorum. The Dutch reported that betel could be used to expel gas, kill intestinal worms, remove phlegm, subdue unpleasant body odors, beautify the mouth, induce purification, and kindle the passions.

7.4   Portuguese Colonial Interests, 1415–1822 CE

The Portuguese excelled in exploration, navigation, and shipbuilding. Portugal sailed to, explored, and colonized South America, Africa, and Asia (Figure 7.11). The Portuguese created their colonies to trade for spices, gold, agricultural products, and other resources; to create more markets for Portuguese goods; to spread Catholicism; and to "civilize" the barbarous natives in distant and uncivilized lands[20]. The colonies brought great wealth to Portugal. Portuguese views on alcohol and drugs kept their exploitation of indigenous herbs and plant drugs in check, and they tended to have very harsh views toward excessive drinking and drug consumption. Intoxication of any kind was viewed as a sinful act. While the Portuguese recognized the positive nature of moderate consumption of drugs and alcohol, they had serious concerns over the negative effects of drunkenness. Drunkenness was viewed as self-indulgence, threatening to spiritual salvation, and harmful to societal wellbeing. The Portuguese Empire had tremendous effect on the colonies through exploitative practices that stripped the colonies of their natural resources and forced the populations to purchase inflated Portuguese products. The colonies suffered from high poverty and were forced to comply to a very rigid catholic doctrine that held little tolerance for indigenous practices[21]. The culinary and medical spices the Portuguese used for monetary gain are in Table 7.2.

Figure 7.11 Portuguese Colonial Holdings

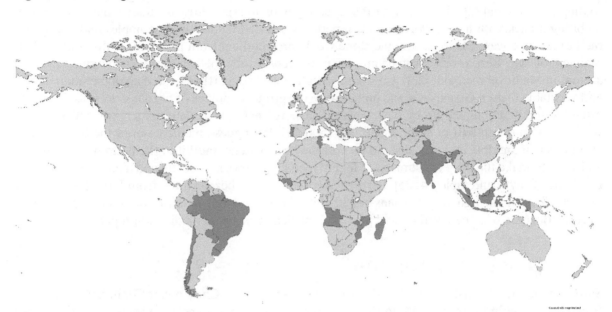

Source: T.D. Church (rendered with https://www.mapchart.net/world.html)

Table 7.2 Portuguese Medicinal Herbs

Jackfruit

Anti-asthmatic, anti-inflammatory, antimicrobial, antibiotic, laxative, aphrodisiac, and the bark is a mild sedative

Pepper

Used as a tonic, medicinal skin oil and to stimulate the appetite

Snake Root

Anthelmintic, carminative, diuretic, expectorant, treatment for chronic chest complaints, asthma, coughs, and pain

Tamarind

Digestive, laxative, and antipyretic

Butea

Used to treat wounds and injuries

Iberian Poppy

Used as a remedy for toothaches, headaches, anxiety, and insomnia

Source: T.D. Church

Vasco da Gama arrived in Kolkata, India in 1498 CE and established a Portuguese settlement and trading post in Goa[22]. He is the first Portuguese person to reportedly use the bezoar stone, which he brought back with him to Portugal. He reportedly seduced the Portuguese nobles and kings with the bezoar who were led to believe the stone would protect them from poisoning, falling ill, and all manners of evil. Bezoar or Goa stone are one of the most exotic medical products obtained from an animal in Medieval medicine[23]. A bezoar is a tightly packed, partly digested agglomeration of hair and vegetable matter. Goats, cats, and horses were the primary sources of bezoar stones, as they were often hacked and coughed up by these animals. The remnant particulate matter was collected and worked into a rough ball or stone shape. By 1500 CE, Portuguese medicine used the bezoar stone as a universal antidote and would shave bits off the bezoar stone, mull it in the bottom of a cup, and add wine to make the drug consumable. Modern medicine views it as costly and a completely useless medicine of myth and fable[24, 25]. Portuguese control of the bezoar trade from India followed suit in 1500 CE, and Portuguese physicians quickly introduced the medicinal uses of Oriental bezoar into Europe. Bezoars were believed to hold powerful magical apotropaic medicinal properties.

7.5   Spanish Colonial Interests, 1492–1976 CE

Sailing under the Spanish Crown in 1492, the Genovese mariner, Christopher Columbus, sailed west from Spain seeking a trade route to the spice islands of the West Indies (Figure 7.12). Columbus encountered North America populated by people he erroneously called "Indians." This discovery began the westward expansion of the Spanish with the mission to bring gold, precious minerals and gems, and silver back to fill the coffers of the Spanish Crown. The Spanish Crown had invested

Figure 7.12   Spanish Colonial Holdings

Source: T.D. Church (rendered with https://www.mapchart.net/world.html)

Table 7.3 Medicines from Spanish Colonial Holdings

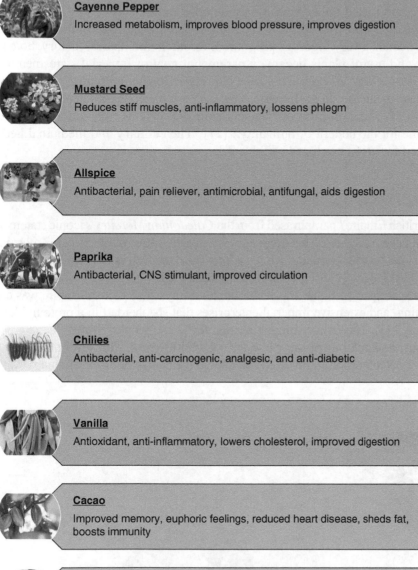

Cayenne Pepper
Increased metabolism, improves blood pressure, improves digestion

Mustard Seed
Reduces stiff muscles, anti-inflammatory, lossens phlegm

Allspice
Antibacterial, pain reliever, antimicrobial, antifungal, aids digestion

Paprika
Antibacterial, CNS stimulant, improved circulation

Chilies
Antibacterial, anti-carcinogenic, analgesic, and anti-diabetic

Vanilla
Antioxidant, anti-inflammatory, lowers cholesterol, improved digestion

Cacao
Improved memory, euphoric feelings, reduced heart disease, sheds fat, boosts immunity

Coca
Anesthetic, analgesic to alleviate pain from headaches, rheumathism, wounds, and sores; relieves hunger and fatigue; causes sedation; treatment for asthma; stimulant for concentration and cognitive function

Source: T.D. Church

considerable resources into securing these valuable commodities. The investments included research into new mining technologies; metal purification techniques; ship navigation; and cartography, and improved naval weaponry[26]. Silver and gold dominated the political, economic, and scientific histories of the Spanish Empire and fueled the expansion of men of letters (*letrados*) who were graduates of universities (*licenciados*). Spain realized that in addition to seeking out wealth through metal and mineral resources, they needed a very vigorous program of research into natural history, botany, and herbal medicines. New and useful plants became a paramount goal of imperial statesmen and scientists alike. Realizing that the New World did not have cities overflowing with gold, the Spanish Crown invested in science and medicine. In an Imperial Decree from the sixteenth century CE, the Crown offered their approval of "…the promise of financial gain, and heightening national prestige through science and medicine for the benefit of humanity…[27]" The culinary and medicinal herbs the Spanish Empire cultivated for profit are listed in Table 7.3.

7.6   British Colonial Interests, 1417–1997 CE

"The Sun never sets on the British Empire" paraphrased from the *Caledonian Mercury's* iconic statement of "on her dominions the Sun never sets; before his evening rays leave the spires of Quebec, his morning beams have shone three hours on Port Jackson, and while sinking from the waters of Lake Superior, his eye opens upon the Mouth of the Ganges"[28]. This epithet means that the British Empire was at one time so vast that there was always some part of it that was under the Sun's rays. The British Empire was one of the most massive, continuing, and extensive imperial enterprises that shepherded in a profound level of global connectivity (Figure 7.13). The British Empire shaped the lives, peoples, travels, economies, technologies, politics, fashions, and cultures of the globe for nearly 400 years. This level of influence had both positive and negative outcomes for all involved and altered the course of history in many ways.

Figure 7.13   British Colonial Holdings

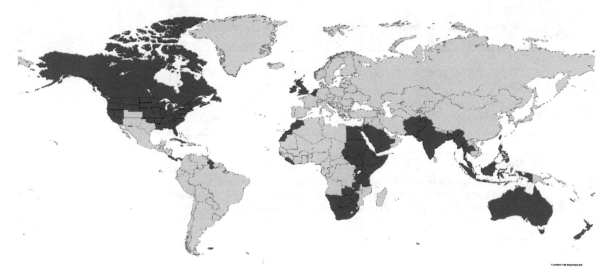

Source: T.D. Church (rendered with https://www.mapchart.net/world.html)

Much like the Spanish, the British Empire recognized the potential of herbs from the New World for culinary and medicinal uses. Botany, the branch of biology focused on the study of plants (their structure, properties, and biochemical processes), was a formalized discipline of study in British universities. Botany as a field of study was expanded under the British Empire to include plant classification and the study of plant diseases and interactions with humans and their environment[29]. British herbalists began researching plants for pure research purposes, which resulted in detailed and rich descriptions with accompanying drawings of plant life from British expeditions worldwide. In pharmacy, these are known as herbarium, collections of preserved plant specimens and associated medical information used for scientific research. In England, between the sixteenth and seventeenth centuries CE, there was a notable increase in plant-based medicines, including folk and ancient remedies. Table 7.4 lists a few of the culinary and medicinal herbs and minerals from the British Empire.

Table 7.4 British Colonial Medicines

Cloves
Digestive aid, procudes phlegm, expectorant, cough suppresor, relieves gas and bloating, antihistamine

Arsenic
Mixed with vingegar and chalk and eaten by women to improve complexion, face powder, toxicity not realized until 1858 CE

Opium
Pain reliver, cough suppresor

Paregoric
Camphorated opium tincture, used for diarrhea, decreased metabolism; made from powdered opium, anise oil, camphor, glycerin, and alcohol

Linctus
Cough drops, cough suppresor; made with opium and pholcodine salt

Gin
Spirt, originally distilled for medicaton; juniper is a diuretic, cleanses fevers and tropical diseases of the colonies

Source: T.D. Church

Apothecaries and chemists in the British Empire employed three types of liquid medications in the form of tonics, potions, and elixirs. *Tonics* were liquid concoctions of different medicinal substances intended to restore health or invigorate. *Potions* were drinks that could contain medicine or poison and were imbued with magical or supernatural powers. *Elixirs* were typically clear and often sweet-flavored liquids used for medicinal purposes. Elixirs were taken orally and intended to cure illness and prolong life. The exotic spices, plants, and minerals that flowed into the Empire provided an abundance of new medicines and poisons that apothecaries and chemists began using in earnest[30].

In the early part of the British colonial expansion, information was bound up in myth, speculation, and ignorance. Large investments were put at risk due to ocean storms and hostile encounters with enemies and natives. There were issues with recognizing weather patterns, topography not yet mapped, and unreliable and under studied oceanic currents. To remedy this problem, accurate maritime knowledge related to a variety of items was needed. Accurate knowledge required not only geographic and oceanic exploration but needed forays along other frontiers of knowledge in the areas of science, metallurgy, botany, zoology, pharmacology, linguistics, and ethnography to name a few[31].

Knowledge became the key to British colonial expansion and led to naval exploration standards to ensure successful colonization ventures; including the standard for crew compliments, the standard for recording natural information, and the standard for recording ethnographic and political information[31]. With these standards, the British navy and colonial services became nearly impossible to stop and allowed for British global dominance. In addition to a ship's officers, the crew for long voyages were recommended to include jewelers, apothecaries, physicians, geographers/cartographers, painters, lapidaries, and alchemists. Jewelers and lapidaries were there to evaluate and document precious stones encountered during the voyage. Apothecaries and alchemists were to examine and document local drugs and poisons. Physicians were there to tend to the health of the crew. Geographers and cartographers were there to evaluate the topography of the lands they encountered and make accurate maps of land and sea. Painters were there to capture images of the landscapes, peoples, and wonders encountered.

British maritime exploration required the recording of natural information, which meant the cataloging of information related to freshwater, islands, beasts, bees, geology, metallurgy, and flora[32]. The cataloging needed to include the nature of freshwater, springs, rivers, and lakes with their diversities in color and taste. If there were islands, what was their composition? How big were the islands, what commodities did they contain, and did they have natural harbors? A detailed description of the fauna and their differences in kind or color with or from European beasts. A description of all the earths encountered with details related to their assorted colors, tastes, fertility, or bareness. The metals and minerals needed to be documented including where they could be found and their abundance. And finally, the flora including details of the trees, fruits, gums, herbs, seed, and any plants favorable to the apothecaries or alchemists.

The last bit of information to be recorded concerned the ethnographic and political details of any natives encountered[32]. Observations related to the manner of planting, fertilizing, and harvesting done by the natives. The statuses and social ranks of native groups. The foods they prepared from local flora and fauna. The greatness and quantity of the leader's holdings, people, and forces. An accounting of the manner in which the natives armed and ordered themselves in war and in protection of their holdings. An understanding of any alliances or rivalries among the native groups encountered was required to be included. With this information, it was possible to disrupt local politics and allow for a smoother colonization process if an area was determined to be of importance to the holdings of the British Crown.

7.7 French Colonial Interests, 1450–1750 CE

The French maritime empire may have been the least influential in terms of navy of the previously discussed empires (Spain, Portugal, Dutch, English, and Norwegian) as their fleet was not as strong nor numerous (Figure 7.14)[33]. What they lacked at sea, they made up for on land and grew to become the most important power in mainland Europe. In the Americas, the French colonial enterprises compromised a swath of untamed land from New Orleans in Louisiana stretching north to Canada. The French were motivated to colonize North America to secure the lucrative Great Lakes and Mississippi River valley fur trade as beaver fur was in high demand in European markets[34]. The European source of beaver fur from Russia was dwindling due to overhunting. The French fur trade saw the building of numerous trading posts where the French interacted directly with Native Americans. Ancient rivalries and feuds between the French and English persisted and carried over from Europe into North America and escalated into the Seven Years' War (or French and Indian War in the Americas) of 1756–1763 CE. Native American tribes were forever altered by this war as the French encouraged the scalping of British soldiers[35]. The Natives were compensated for every scalp they brought to French outposts, and this egregious act was not soon forgotten as the British sought revenge. The French utilized the waterways of North America like Highways with New Orleans and Quebec becoming major international trading hubs. From their other colonial holdings, the French traded in several culinary and medicinal spices; the most important ones they traded in European markets can be found in Table 7.5.

Figure 7.14   French Colonial Holdings

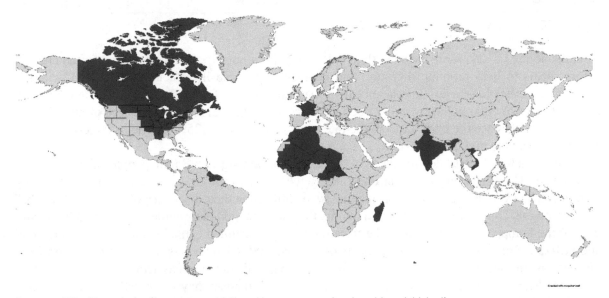

Source: T.D. Church (software used https://www.mapchart.net/world.html)

Among the medicinal plant goods, the French colonial empire brought into the world for trade, the kola nut has become one of the most important. Kola nut remains a key ingredient in modern soft drinks, Coca-Cola and Pepsi-Cola for example. Kola nut is the origin of the Western word "cola." In Nigerian mythology, the kola nut tree is believed to have been the first primordial tree on the Earth. Among the Hausa, Yoruba, Igbo, and Fulani, the kola nut is considered to be a symbol of hospitality and kindness[36]. The kola nut is a caffeine-rich nut, native to tropical Africa. As a stimulant, it

Table 7.5 French Colonial Medicines

Acacia Senegal

"Gum Arabic": treated bleeding, bronchitis, diarrhea, gonorrhea, leprosy, typhoid fever, and upper respiratory tract infections

Desert Wormwood

Treated diabetes, bronchitis. diarrhea, hypertension, and neuralgias

Rooibos

Tea; bronchodilator. antispasmodic, lowers blood pressure, antioxidant

Madagascar Periwinkle

Bitter tonic, galactagogue, emetic; treated rheumatism, skin disorders, and venereal diseases

Khat

Amphetamine-like stimulant; causes excitement, loss of appetite, euphoria, and increased libido; highly addictive

Liquorice

Used for jaundice, expectorant, settled upset stomach; used to make liquor

Source: T.D. Church

contains about 1.5–2% more caffeine than coffee[37]. Kola nuts are tasteless and are often chewed before meals to help promote digestion and counteract possible ill effects from tainted drinking water. Two of the oldest uses for kola nuts are as natural remedies for chest colds and weight loss[36]. Kola nut helps to enlarge lung alveolar ducts and sacs and helps improve the strength of lung tissues. Kola nut can increase the body's metabolic rate by as much as 118–125% and helps the body to burn calories effectively and quicker.

The French colonists documented an African tribe among the Bantu people of Nigeria, the Bashilange. The Bashilange were at one time fierce warriors, prone to violence, and territorially aggressive. They underwent a kind of spiritual awakening upon their discovery of cannabis, "riamba" in their tongue. During this spiritual awakening, the tribe changed their name to Ben-Riamba, meaning "of the hemp" or "from hemp." The tribe reportedly consumed cannabis daily as a social ritual and utilized cannabis for a wide array of medical needs[38]. Riamba was used to relieve pain from injuries, as an antiseptic, to treat tetanus, hydrophobia, delirium tremens from alcoholism, infantile convulsions, neuralgia, nervous disorders, cholera, rheumatism, hay fever, asthma, and skin diseases[39]. Perhaps the most unique use of cannabis, though, was to assist with protracted and painful labor during childbirth. Women who were having difficulty during labor would be offered cannabis to smoke to ease the pain and relax the muscles. The French colonial forces in Nigeria attempted to ban and outlaw cannabis but were not remarkably successful. Riamba smoking culture found its way aboard slave vessels bound for America with some historians theorizing that cannabis in the New World quickly spread thanks to stow-away seeds brought with Bashilange peoples[40].

While the French colonial empire may not have had the strongest naval fleet, it did provide the world's economy with some unique culinary and medicinal herbs. The colonial politics of the French were often questionable, at best, and they had a reputation for not being very kind to the natives in any of their extraterritorial holdings. One of the reasons the French colonial empire began to unravel was the foreign policy of *mission civilisatrice* or "Civilizing Mission"[41]. The French attempted to spread language, religion, and culture through all her colonial enterprises under the ideology that the French had a duty to civilize the barbaric peoples of their empire. This meant that Native and colonial born French were treated more like subjects than citizens. When Enlightenment ideologies spurred France to overthrow the monarchy in revolution, the French were forced to focus internally on building a new democracy. Several of her prior colonial holdings were lost as France could no longer exert control over them while fighting to keep the nascent Republic together.

7.8 Colonial Legacies

The creation of transoceanic trade routes and the subsequent expansion of European dominance gave momentum to the Age of Imperialism. This was an artifact of the voyages of discovery wherein colonial powers from Europe set out to colonize most of the territory on the planet. The demand for trade, commodities, spices, medicines, sugar, and slaves forever altered the world. The indigenous nations in the colonized lands saw the decimation of whole cultural groups as diseases from the Old World ravaged the newly colonized lands. Those indigenous peoples who remained faced forced conversions of religion and forced assimilations into Europeanized cultures. Imported agricultural practices, poor ecological understanding, and a reliance on slave labor created both environmental and social problems that escalated to the point of near collapse. Natural resources were stripped away from the colonies to be absorbed into the commercial enterprise of the European maritime empires.

REFERENCES

1. Rodger, N. A. M. (2014). The law and language of private naval warfare. *Mariner's Mirror*, **100**(1), 5–16.
2. Yo, Ho, Ho, and a bottle of rum! ... A brief history of piracy, *New African*, 2013(526): 22–23.
3. Konstam, A. (2007). *Scourge of the seas: Buccaneers, pirates and privateers* (p. 240). Oxford, UK: Osprey.
4. Yolen, J. (2010). *Sea queens: Women pirates around the world* (p. 112). Watertown, MA: Charlesbridge.
5. Bialuschewski, A. (2008). Black people under the black flag: Piracy and the slave trade on the west coast of Africa, 1718–1723. *Slavery & Abolition*, **29**(4), 461–475.
6. Toler, P. D. (2019). *Women warriors: An unexpected history*. Boston, MA: Beacon Press.
7. Kelley, S. M. (2018). American rum, African consumers, and the transatlantic slave trade. *African Economic History*, **46**(2), 1–29.
8. Goodall, J. L. H. (2016) Tippling houses, rum shops and taverns: How alcohol fuelled informal commercial networks and knowledge exchange in the West Indies. *Journal for Maritime Research*, **18**(2), 97–121.

9. Kolberg, A. S. (2018). Did Vikings really go berserk? An interdisciplinary critical analysis of berserks. *The Journal of Military History*, **82**(3), 899–908.

10. Speidel, M. P. (2002). Berserks: A history of Indo-European "mad warriors." *Journal of World History*, **13**(2), 253–290.

11. Ruck, C. A. P. (2016) Mushroom sacraments in the cults of early Europe. *NeuroQuantology*, **14**(1), 68–93.

12. Diamond, J. (2011). Collapse: How societies choose to fail or succeed. New York, NY: Penguin.

13. Tristan, B. (2020). The pharmaceutical uses of alicorn. *Medical Post*, **56**(6), 46.

14. Fischer, L.-P. & Cossu Ferra Fischer, V. (2011). The unicorn and the unicorn horn among apothecaries and physicians. *Histoire des Sciences M*édicales, **45**(3), 265–274.

15. Dąsal, M., Smakosz, A., Kurzyna, W., & Rudko, M. (2021). "Unicorn horn" drugs in the medical and pharmaceutical culture of Europe. *Farmacja Polska*, **77**(2), 84–94.

16. Bosma, U. (2014). The economic historiography of the Dutch colonial empire. *TSEG-The Low Countries Journal of Social and Economic History*, **11**(2), 153–174.

17. Schoolcraft, H. L. (1907). The capture of New Amsterdam. *The English Historical Review*, **22**(88), 674–693.

18. Goodman, J., Sherratt, A., & Lovejoy, P. E. (2014). Consuming habits: Drugs in history and anthropology. In *Global and historical perspectives on how cultures define drugs* (2nd ed., p. 304). London: Routledge.

19. Chu, N.-S. (2001). Effects of betel chewing on the central and autonomic nervous systems. *Journal of Biomedical Science*, **8**(3), 229–236.

20. Walker, T. D. (2013). The medicines trade in the Portuguese Atlantic world: Acquisition and dissemination of healing knowledge from Brazil (c. 1580–1800). *Social History of Medicine*, **26**(3), 403–431.

21. Chambouleyron, R. & Arenz, K. H. (2021). Amazonian Atlantic: Cacao, colonial expansion and indigenous labour in the Portuguese Amazon region (seventeenth and eighteenth centuries). *Journal of Latin American Studies*, **53**(2), 221–244.

22. Abreu, L. (2020). Health care and the spread of medical knowledge in the Portuguese empire, particularly the Estado da Índia (sixteenth to eighteenth centuries). *Medical History*, **64**(4), 449–466.

23. Xavier, A. B. (2018). The Casa da Índia and the emergence of a science of administration in the Portuguese Empire. *Journal of Early Modern History*, **22**(5), 327–347.

24. do Sameiro Barroso, M. (2014). The bezoar stone: A princely antidote, the Tàvora Sequeira Pinto Collection–Oporto. *AMHA-Acta Medico-Historica Adriatica*, **12**(1), 77–98.

25. Barroso, M. D. S. (2013). Bezoar stones, magic, science and art. *Geological Society, London, Special Publications*, **375**(1), 193–207.

26. Bleichmar, D., De Vos, P., Huffine, K., Sheehan, K. (Eds.) (2009). *Science in the Spanish and Portuguese Empires, 1500–1800* (1st ed, ed., p. 456). Stanford, CA: Stanford University Press.

27. De Vos, P. (2003). An herbal El Dorado: The quest for botanical wealth in the Spanish Empire. *Endeavour*, **27**(3), 117–21.

28. (1821). The British Empire. In *Caledonian Mercury*. Thomas Allen & Co: Scotland, UK.

29. Brockway, L. H. (1979). Science and colonial expansion: The role of the British Royal Botanic Gardens. *American Ethnologist*, **6**(3), 449–465.

30. Simmons, A. (2019). Trade, knowledge and networks: The activities of the Society of Apothecaries and its members in London, c.1670–c.1800. *The British Journal for the History of Science*, **52**(2), 273–296.

31. Irving, S. (2015). *Natural science and the origins of the British empire*. London, UK: Routledge.

32. Caputo, S. (2020). Exploration and mortification: Fragile infrastructures, imperial narratives, and the self-sufficiency of British naval "discovery" vessels, 1760–1815. *History of Science*, **Epub Ahead of Print (*https://pubmed-ncbi-nlm-nih-gov.libproxy1.usc.edu/33153328/* - [Accessed 10 Jul 2022]): pp. 1–20.

33. Ruggiu, F.-J. (2016). Colonies, monarchy, empire and the French ancien régime. In R. Aldrich & C. McCreery (Ed.). *Crowns and colonies: European monarchies and overseas empires* (pp. 194–210). Manchester University Press: Manchester, UK.

34. Slater, S. (2014). Fur traders, voyageurs, and coureurs des bois: Economic masculinities in French Canadian fur trade society, 1635–1754. *Masculinities: A Journal of Identity and Culture*, **2014**(1), 92–119.

35. Abler, T. S. (1992). Scalping, torture, cannibalism and rape: An ethnohistorical analysis of conflicting cultural values in war. *Anthropologica*, **34**(1), 3–20.

36. Manière, L. (2010). Les cultes de la kola dans l'Afrique coloniale: Trajectoires et appropriations d'un phénomène religieux | kola cults in colonial Africa: Trajectory and the appropriation of a religious phenomenon. *Autrepart*, **56**(4), 193–211.

37. Simmonds, P. (1890). The kola nut of Africa. *American Journal of Pharmacy (1835–1907)*, **62**(12), 595.

38. Duvall, C. S. (2019). *The African roots of marijuana*. Durham, NC: Duke University Press.

39. Ambler, C., *Drugs in Africa from the Slave Trade to Colonialism*, in *The Oxford Handbook of Global Drug History*, P. Gootenberg, Editor. 2022, Oxford University Press: Oxford, UK. p. 192.

40. Abel, E. L. (1980). The African dagga cultures. In E. L. Abel (Ed.). *Marihuana* (pp. 136–147). Springer: London, UK.

41. Parsons, C. M. (2018). *A not-so-New World: Empire and environment in French colonial North America* (p. 264). Philadelphia, PA: University of Pennsylvania Press.

Chapter 8

Voyages of Discovery: The New World

The voyages of discovery had been undertaken to find safe and fast passage from Europe to Asia and India. In October 1492, the Americas were discovered as a Spanish fleet sailing east found the Bahamas, Cuba, Haiti, and Puerto Rico before sailing back to Spain. However, the captain in charge of that fateful journey, Christopher Columbus, believed wholeheartedly that the expedition had reached Asia. In 1493, Pietro Martire d'Anghiera (Peter Martyr translated to English), an Italian historian in the service of the Spanish Crown, described the lands Columbus discovered as being *Novi Orbis* (New Globe)[1]. Pope Alexander VI issued four papal bulls (known collectively as the Bulls of Dominion), wherein it was determined how Spain and Portugal would colonize and divide the spoils of this new world. In May 1493, the world outside of Europe was divided along a north–south meridian 100 leagues west of Cape Verde Island in the mid-Atlantic. Sanctioned by the Pope, Spain was effectively granted all the land discovered by Columbus. The mad dash for territory in the New World began as England, France, the Netherlands, Spain, and Portugal launched exploration and colonization efforts. The European countries had been embroiled in wars and skirmishes with one another for centuries and those ancient conflicts would persist. The colonization efforts of the European nations drove out the natives and in some parts of the Americas, whole tribes and groups were decimated by war, disease, or forced assimilation.

In Central and South America in the sixteenth century CE, the Spanish arrived en force conquistadors and catholic priests to tame the savage lands and subdue the Aztec, Maya, and Inca. They established forts, garrisons, and churches throughout the Caribbean and Central America. The military might of Spain appeared unstoppable and quickly their navy secured trade routes that spurred rapid economic growth. The trade and goods from the New World elevated Spain to the wealthiest nation in the world. A title it would hold for nearly 100 years.

Figure 8.1 Christopher Columbus; Barcelona, Spain

kavalenkau\Shutterstock.com

Spain viewed the New World as a treasure trove after the exotic reports from the first Voyage of Christopher Columbus filtered through the Spanish Court. Columbus brought back gold, silver, and a cornucopia of mysterious plants. After subsequent visits, the Spanish Crown began to view the voyages and the New World as a burden. They thought of the New World as sinful, riddled with sickness, disease, and depravity. The Spanish had found the most favorable sea route to the Americas, with the help of the Trade Winds. Thanks to the Trade Winds, the Spanish could traverse the Atlantic in between 3 and 4 weeks. The Spanish had invested a lot of time and money in charting this route. The ever-ambitious empire wanted to get their hands on gold, either from the New World or through taxation of their Old World. The Spanish Crown passed a law, known as the ***Gold Rescue***, which allowed Spanish merchants and colonizers to travel to America to establish "trade" with the natives, but they were required to pay 20% of their earnings to the crown, in some cases it was paid on "potential earnings" in advance[2]. This so-called "trade" typically resulted in the conquistadors subjugating, exploiting, and enslaving the indigenous people. The Portuguese, English, French, and Dutch wanted to know the secret of the Spanish route and how to quickly travel the Atlantic, knowledge the Spanish kept fiercely to themselves.

The end of the sixteenth century CE saw the might of the Spanish armada diminish as it was resolutely defeated by the English who ended Spanish rule of the Atlantic. Quickly, the British and many other nations in Europe began to chip away at the once grand Spanish colonial empire, adding new territories to their own growing colonial enterprises. The New World was stolen from the native populations and carved up to serve European economic and political needs. Many unique spices, medicines, and poisons were to be found and many more were lost to history as they were deemed to be too potent or too satanic to be permitted to exist. Beginning with the conquistadors, who were drunk with power from the Spanish Inquisitions, the eradication of native knowledge and traditional practices became common place.

The most valuable treasures from the New World were natural resources in the form of botanicals and animal furs. Explorers from Europe came in search of precious metals, spices, and jewels; these intrepid entrepreneurs became very disappointed. Stories of El Dorado, the city of gold, in Central and South America claimed many lives as expeditions ventured deep into jungles and forests, the majority were never seen again. The diversity of the flora was astounding. Local knowledge from the native tribes related to plants, remedies, and natural cures was exceptional. Native Americans lived intimately with their environment, while the explorers only wished to tame that environment. Among the favored botanicals were hallucinogens, stimulants, and depressants—all these botanicals were infinitely stronger and greater in variety than anything found in Europe.

8.1 Natives of Central and South America

The first explorers from Spain were tolerant of the native peoples they encountered. They did not work to supplant local shamans or tribal leaders. They were not attempting to impose Christianity or strict Catholic doctrine. They were attempting to learn from the Native Americans. Spanish druggists and doctors in the first decade of the 1500s CE came to learn from the indigenous herbalists. As more reports of the New World full of titillating stories and legends related to native cultural practices found their way into the Spanish Court and the halls of the Vatican, that earlier tolerance swiftly changed. Both the Spanish King and the Pope agreed that the natives needed to be saved from their lives of sin and debauchery. The Vatican issued an edict that made any lands discovered and consecrated to the church would be owned by the country who had brought gods light to the heathens.

Hernán Cortés (1485 CE–1547 CE) and Francisco Pizarro González (1478 CE–1541 CE) were conquistadors sent by the Spanish Crown with the ambition and determination to obtain land, wealth, and glory for king and country. Cortés would see to the downfall of the Aztec empire, and Pizarro the Incan empire. Both were very shrewd men and would be responsible for the devastation of two of the most vibrant native cultures in Central and South America. Through reports returning to the Spanish Crown, disseminated to the Vatican, and eventually being recounted throughout the royal courts of Europe, a grim and exceptionally ethnocentric view of the natives of the Americas was being developed. The Spanish reacted to reports of the drugs of the Natives as being perverse as they thought they were being utilized to see demons, to commune with the devil, and to divine the future. Further, their dependence on these substances made the natives mindless and lethargic. Equally as bad, the Spanish found the depravity of the Natives to have no bounds as they relished in their nakedness. The Spanish were appalled by the unbridled sexuality of the natives and feared the new sexual disease of syphilis. The Spanish were extremely concerned by the idol worship of serpents, animals, and demonic figures the natives reveled in. The Spanish were horrified by the native practice of human sacrifices that filled the natives with wanton bloodlust. In a scathing account from Francisco López de Gómara, Chaplain and secretary to Hernán Cortés, the views of the Spanish toward the natives, the Aztec in particular, were recounted:

> The Spaniards gave beasts of burden to relieve the natives of drudgery… meat to eat which they lacked before. The Spaniards showed them the use of iron and oil lamps to improve their ways of living… They taught them Latin and other subjects which are worth a lot more than all the silver taken from them… it was to their benefit to be conquered, and even more, to become Christians[3].

Figure 8.2 Map of the Aztec Empire

Figure 8.3 Quetzalcotal Pyramid; Tula Hidalgo, Mexico

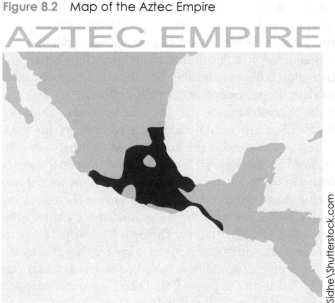

Sidhe\Shutterstock.com

Arturo Verea\Shutterstock.com

8.1.1 Aztec

Prophecies can be misunderstood, misinterpreted, misused, and are often self-fulfilling. The Spanish conquest of the Aztec presents such an example of this problem. Toltec legends speak of the god, Quetzalcoatl, who in human form appeared as a white-skinned, red bearded priest-king who came from the East to build an enlightened kingdom among the native Mexica peoples. After teaching the Mexica how to farm, build, write, and prepare for war, Quetzalcoatl departed by canoe to the West. Quetzalcoatl promised to return; indicating that as the appointed day of his second coming approached, heavenly omens would Foretell of his return. The Aztec adopted the Toltec myth and embellished the tale with Aztec elements. The Aztec version indicated that Quetazcoatl's return would begin the unfolding of Aztec culture. The Aztec were very excited, as they believed their world was about to enter an abrupt and violent end to be renewed into a more glorious kingdom. In 1519, a comet with three heads emitting sparks flew eastward for 40 nights, heralding Hernán Cortés invasion of Tenochtitlán one week later[4]. The comet was the sign the Aztec were awaiting to usher in the end of their grand civilization.

Cortés had truly little military experience, but he was a highly effective leader. By 1519, Cortés had won a few victories and began claiming lands for the Spanish Crown along the coast of the Yucatán Peninsula. With 600 soldiers, 15 horsemen, 15 cannons, and hundreds of Tlaxcalan native carriers and warriors, he marched toward Tenochtitlán, the Aztec capital city[5]. In a series of letters from Cortés to king Charles V, Tenochtitlán was described as an island city in the center of a salt lake, Lake Texcoco, and was laid out in series of grids and concentric circles with a central plaza serving as the ritual and economic hub of the city[6]. The city was crisscrossed with canals, ringed with *chinampas*. Chinampas were floating gardens used for food production, recreation for the royal court, pharmacological libraries, living botanical archives, and medicinal clinics where shaman diagnosed and prepared medicines from growing plants[7]. The Spanish conquistadors were in awe of the advanced hydraulic system that allowed the Aztec to channel fresh water for human consumption, wastewater channels to remove waste, and a preservation system to prevent the salty water of the lake from flooding the city. The city boasted palaces, temples, workshops, and residences glinting and glimmering in the sun light thanks to the white base paint. Most structures were built of adobe walls and thatch roofs. The white painted adobe was adorned by colorful frescos and paintings bathed the city awash with vibrant colors. There were five main causeways leading into the city across the lake, with each causeway wide enough to accommodate 10 men on horseback riding abreast.

The Aztec were initially enamored with the Spanish because they brought with them unknown technology like bells, muskets, and wheels. The Spanish would trade their technology for gold, tobacco, and cacao. Very quickly sentiments changed as the Spanish began more aggressive colonization efforts. Based on experience, the Aztec word for the Spanish became *Cóyotl*. Cóyotl translates to coyote and for the Aztec was a term associated with "trickster" in Aztec folklore, an animal that raids and steals by night. *Cóyoltlahtolli* was the Aztec word for the Spanish language, translating to "coyote tongue." The Spanish began forcing Catholicism onto the Aztec, and those natives who refused to convert to Christianity were abducted and sold into slavery. The Spanish learned early on that the Aztec lacked immunity to certain diseases that, while inconvenient, were manageable by the Spanish. Spanish soldiers who had smallpox, for example, would have their bed sheets and blankets given as "gifts" to the Aztec who were quickly felled by the disease[8]. There is a misconception that the Aztecs suffered from *equinophobia*, the fear of horses. It was believed that as there were no horses in the New World, the Aztecs must have been overcome with fear upon witnessing horses in battle. Seeing a mounted conquistador atop a horse was probably the stuff of nightmares, because of the height, the head of the rider and the head of the horse, and the speed as the horse and rider hurled toward their mark. The fear did not last long as the beasts could be brought down. The Spanish plate armor, helmets, and guns did put the Aztec at a disadvantage in an open theatre of battle. The Aztec had the advantage as they knew their lands and were skilled in hit and run tactics, where they seemed to appear and disappear from the forests before the conquistadors could even form firing lines, let alone prepare their muskets. Further, the Aztec were masters over a number of hallucinogens, and they had knowledge of poisonous frog. The poison from the frogs was employed through their blow darts which they had developed skills in hunting primates. They used hallucinogens and poisons to tip their arrows and the obsidian blades of their deadly *macuahuitl* before engaging the Spanish.

A prominent god among the Aztec and Maya was *Xochipilli*, the prince of flowers. He was the god of flowers, maize, love (romantic and carnal), games, beauty, song, and dance. His statue and paintings were typically adorned with the sacred "five flowers," all of which were highly psychoactive. Xochipilli was typically carved or painted with wide pupils and clenching his teeth. This was an artistic testament to the entheogenic effects of the psychoactive substances associated with the Prince of Flowers, which tended to produce feelings of ecstasy, dilated pupils, and led to jaw tension or bruxism[9].

Figure 8.4 Xochipilli, The Prince of Flowers

Leon Rafael\Shutterstock.com

Two drugs were seen as especially heinous to the Spanish, *ololiuhqui* and *picietl*. Ololiuhqui is the Aztec word for peyote, a cactus with the active compound of lysergic acid amide (LSA). Picietl was the Aztec word for a very potent species of tobacco, *Nicotiana rustica*. By 1629, Spanish tolerance for tobacco and peyote had reached its tolerable limits and Inquisitor Ruiz de Alarcín was sent to eradicate all traces of the hedonistic practices of the natives[10]. He began by rounding up all the Aztec shamans and confiscating all their herbal plants, burning of any plant materials and seeds, and destruction of live plants. Elaborate court cases wherein the shamans were compelled to confess to witchcraft, sorcery, and sodomy. Their confessions were elicited through torture and starvation. This led to additional convictions of people the shamans had implicated as consumers of tobacco and peyote. Religious, recreational, and therapeutic uses of psychoactive flora used by the Aztec and Maya were nearly forgotten until well into the twentieth century CE[11].

Pagan rituals, superstitions, and satanic hedonism were the only reasons for the use of psychoactive plants from the perspective of Spanish Inquisitors in the conquered lands of Central and South America. The widespread use of entheogens in healing rituals was considered necessary by Aztec and Maya shaman. These hallucinogenic drugs enabled the shaman to diagnose the spiritual and physical ills of the people. *Teonanácatl*, "god's flesh," were hallucinogenic mushrooms more potent than psilocybin. Teonanácatl was preferred by the shaman for its intensity as they believed it helped them diagnose and treat more efficiently[12]. Morning Glory seeds from the purple and white flowering plants were psychoactive and sedative. Peyote was more difficult to control and even harder to maintain the high required for shamanistic rituals.

Figure 8.5 Aztec Figure
Wearing Jaguar Pelt

ppart\Shutterstock.com

A ritual plant that was held in high regard by the Aztec were the ***chi'lli***. Chī'lli or hot chili peppers from the genus *Capsicum* were native to the Americas. Chili peppers were cultivated as a dietary condiment for ~6,000 years[13]. Chili peppers were being utilized as a pain reliever for ~4,500 years[14]. Aztec doctors utilized chili pepper oil to treat painful conditions like toothaches, canker sores, and insect bites for example. Maya healers were known to utilize chili pepper oil during childbirth to help alleviate the pain of labor. The knowledge of chili pepper as well as the full breadth of the botanical herbs used by the Aztec would have been shared and passed on through oral transmission from master shaman to apprentice.

Among the ritual activities and repertoires of Aztec shaman existed the embodiment of were-jaguars and protection against nahual. Were-jaguars are similar to our concept of were-wolves; they were the representation of a half-human and half-jaguar rain deity of the Olmec that was adopted by the Aztec[15]. Were-jaguars were guardians of Xibalba (underworld), and they were symbolic guardians responsible for the movement of the soul into the afterlife being escorted by attendant were-jaguars. Nahual were shapeshifting humans who had the ability to take the form of any animal[16]. In Aztec superstition, one became a nahual by entering a pact with one of the Lords of Xibalba. The terms of the pact required the person to provide something special in order to obtain the gift of transformation. This gift was usually the price of a soul, yours or from someone whom the Lords of Xibalba desired to own. Many of the were-jaguar and nahual statues and ceramic vessels contain residue from hallucinogenic plants identified by modern researchers using mass spectrometry analysis. Archaeologists believe that shaman used these containers to hold their prepared hallucinogenic beverages[11]. The shaman would consume hallucinogens and transform into a jaguar by the wearing the pelt of a recently killed jaguar and culminating in a hallucinogen-fueled ritual trance.

8.1.2 Maya

The ancient Mayan civilization, recognizable today for its pyramids like the Temple of Kulkukan at Chichen Itza, was a highly sophisticated society that made significant discoveries and advances in many fields from astronomy to hydraulic engineering. The Mayan Empire was centered between the Tropic of Cancer and the Equator in modern-day Guatemala, Belize, and Mexico. The first encounter the Spanish had with the Maya was not the best in terms of diplomacy. In 1511 CE, a Spanish caravel wrecked in the Caribbean with only a handful of survivors making it to land on the coast of the Yucatán[17]. The shipwreck survivors were captured by a Maya chieftain, who set out to sacrifice the captives. Two of the Spanish men managed to escape and recounted the events of their captivity. The Spanish mobilized and began a series of successive campaigns against the Maya. Between 1512 CE until the fall of the last independent Mayan city in 1697 CE, the Spanish and Maya engaged in conflict. The Spanish levied huge taxes of gold, slaves, and assimilation from the Maya they conquered with each battle taxing more out of the Maya. For their obstinance, the Maya paid dearly. Much of Mayan culture and nearly all of their writings were lost during the Spanish conquests. The amount of information lost is incalculable. A fraction of the Mayan medical practices and knowledge of botanical herbs managed to survive by being passed orally from generation to generation.

Mayan medicine revolved around six key principles[18]. The first was the belief in *ch'ulel* or "life force" which connected all things. The second affirmed that body and soul were connected. The third principle stated that just as plants, humans have a natural and seasonal cycle. The fourth idea was a very grounded philosophy in which no component of the healing process is more important than another. The fifth was to understand the status of the blood, which was accomplished through bloodletting (sacrifices) and testing of the pulses (palpation). And the final principle related to hot and cold as key aspects to balancing health in the body. Plants in Mayan belief choose healers and a special relationship developed between the two. This relationship allowed the healer to instinctively know what plants to use and how best to employ them[19]. A good healer would speak with the plants, and by some accounts the plants would speak back if the healer was powerful.

One of the most important aspects of Maya healing practices was the belief that all components of healing were important. The components consisted of the patient, the healer, their spirits, the plants, prayer, and music, all were equal and necessary for successful treatment[9]. Mayan medicine was holistic and took into consideration every aspect of health. It considered the physical aspects of the patient, the spiritual, and even things we might consider outside the influence of medicine, such as nature. Balance of ch'ulel bound all things together—you, me, mountains, animals, rivers, birds, houses, etc.

Cacao (kakaw to the Maya), or chocolate, is a stimulant. Cacao is derived from the fermented beans of the cacao tree

Figure 8.6   Map of Mayan Empire

MAYA EMPIRE

Sidhe\Shutterstock.com

Figure 8.7   Mayan Codex Featuring Cacao Drinking

JC Gonram\Shutterstock.com

Figure 8.8   Cacao Drinking Goblet

WH_Pics\Shutterstock.com

(*Theobroma cacao*), an evergreen tree from the tropics. The main alkaloids in cacao are caffeine and the xanthine alkaloid theobromine. Cacao was made into a drink and consumed by the Maya elites at celebrations and during social occasions. The Mayan form of cacao was served warm, it was a bitter brew mixed with cinnamon and chilies. It was used as a medicine with the belief it aided healing by strengthening the constitution of the patient[20]. It was seen as a potent male aphrodisiac and could help with those suffering from a lowered libido[21]. It was even used to paint the bodies of high ranking or special captives prior to their sacrifice. Painted sacrifices nourished the Mayan gods with blood and cacao. In the *Popol Vuh*, the Mayan creation myth, cacao was a key ingredient used by the gods to create human life[22]. Cacao was given to the first human civilization by the plumed serpent god Kulkukan delivered from the "Mountain of Sustenance." The cacao tree was viewed as a sacred symbol as it represented the tree of life, similar to the Norse "World Tree," and was believed to connect the natural world with the spiritual world, the present with the past. Mayan kings and members of the Maya elite were the only ones who consumed cacao and a number of ceremonial gold goblets, spoons, and other utensils to consume cacao point to the importance the Maya placed on it[23]. Cacao appears throughout Mayan art and was often carried by the gods, used to depict the hearts of the gods, and even featured prominently as a food the gods would share with one another.

Acan and *IxChel* are a prominent motif in Mayan art and are frequently pictured exchanging cacao[24]. IxChel was the ethereal Mayan goddess of the moon, rainbows, and medicine. IxChel invented weaving and taught the first female Maya the skill. She was partly made of a waterfall and is responsible for rain. IxChel invented watercolors and taught the Maya how to paint. She was responsible for teaching the first medicine women and then men how to speak with, harvest, and prepare medicinal plants. *Acan* was the Mayan god of wine and intoxicating beverages, in particular fermented maize. Acan was very boisterous, delighting in all forms of intoxication and merry making. He enjoyed making a fool of himself while under the influence. His name translates to "groaning," and by all accounts he did a lot of groaning the morning after a long night of partying.

Drinking alcohol—or fermented maize beers—was a central practice of Maya rituals and held a very prominent role due to its psychoactive qualities[25]. Maize was preferred for fermentation and recent archaeologic evidence indicates a variety of maize drinks were made by mixing in different ingredients, such as fruits and chili peppers. Some of the fermented beverages consumed by the Maya included pulque, balché, tepache, and tejuino[26]. *Pulque* or *octli* is an alcoholic beverage made from fermented maize and juice from the maguey. It is still enjoyed in parts of Central Mexico to date. *Balché* was a fermented maize and honey wine. *Tepache* was a mildly alcoholic beverage of fermented maize and pineapple. *Tejuino* was a beverage traditional to Jalisco and was a maize-based beer derived from fermented masa. Alcohol bound the Maya together socially by helping to build and solidify ties between royalty and elites who would drink in rituals together, cementing and reinforcing the hierarchical order. These fermented maize drinks served a spiritual role as well, wherein several of the Mayan deities required intoxication to be able to communicate with and obtain assistance. The use of alcoholic enemas was one way to help speed up the intoxication process[27]. Specially created pottery, hollowed out gourds, and even long bones were implements that would be inserted into the rectum and the Maya would use this device to pour alcohol directly into the intestines of the supplicant. The Spanish, upon witnessing these alcoholic enemas, were equally dumbfounded and appalled. An anonymous account from a Spanish conquistador stated, "…the men are great sodomites, cowards, and, bored with drinking wine with their mouths, lie down and extending their legs, have the wine poured into their anus through a tube until the body is full"[28].

8.1.3 Inca

The rulers of the *Tawantinsuyu*, "Four Regions" would become known as the Inca. Between 1438 CE and 1533 CE, the Inca controlled a vast portion of the Andean Mountains through the modern nations of Peru, Ecuador, Bolivia, Argentina, and Chile. A portion of the Urubamba River connected the highlands of Peru with peoples of the Amazon basin. The Spanish conquest of the Incan Empire was initiated in 1532 CE by Francisco Pizarro and lasted until the fall of Vilcabamba under the campaign led by Martin Hurtado de Arbito in 1572 CE. The first fray in the rule of the Inca came in the early 1520s CE when smallpox, influenza, typhus, and measles

Figure 8.9 Map of Incan Empire

Sidhe\Shutterstock.com

were transmitted south from Central America[8]. It is estimated European-introduced diseases had decimated around 1/3 of the Incan Empire prior to the two cultures having formal contact. In 1532 CE, Pizarro, his elite guard, and a Spanish Dominican friar (who would go on to become Bishop of Cuzco), Vincente de Valverde, met with the Incan emperor, Atahualpa, and his retinue in the Incan city of Cajamarca[29]. The Inca offered the Spanish golden goblets filled with ceremonial *chicha* as a sign of hospitality and cordiality, but the Spanish rejected the beverage and gravely insulted the Inca in doing so[30]. de Valverde read a proclamation from King Charles I of Spain, requiring the Inca accept Spanish rule and convert immediately to Catholicism. Atahualpa, not fully appreciating the royal decree of Spain, disregarded the message and asked the Spanish to leave his presence. The Spanish used this moment to attack the unarmed Inca, captured Atahualpa, and forced the remaining Inca elites in attendance to acquiesce with the demands of the proclamation. Atahualpa offered the Spanish enough gold to fill the room he was imprisoned in and twice that amount of silver for his freedom. The Inca fulfilled this ransom; however, Pizarro double-crossed the Inca and refused to

Figure 8.10 Chicha

SL-Photography\Shutterstock.com

release Atahualpa. The Spanish held Atahualpa until his execution in the autumn of 1533. This did not mark the end of the Inca, much to the chagrin of the Spanish. The Inca regrouped and for forty years engaged the Spanish in bloody skirmishes and battles.

Chicha is a fermented beverage that is made with maize and can include manioc root, cassava, or fruits for flavoring. Chicha was a beverage revered by the Inca. Chicha was consumed at feasts and during festivals, where social connections could be solidified. The production and consumption of chicha required social organization to make the brew. Large batches of well-made chicha could raise the social status of a tribe or group through royal acknowledgment[31]. Chicha was used as rite of passage, especially for the sons of the Inca elite. Young men would get their adult names in ceremonies where chicha was consumed. *Aclla,* or "chosen women," were a group of women who were taken from their families at an early age to become dedicated to Incan religion. These women were trained in the arts of weaving, cooking, and chicha-brewing. These women initiated the chicha process, they were responsible for chewing and masticating the maize into a mushy paste, they would spit into fermentation vessels, and their combined efforts would be fermented. In a gruesome practice, Incan rulers would have the heads of defeated enemies turned into drinking vessels, usually by cutting a hole in the top of the skull, removing the brain, and cleaning out the brain case. The emptied skull would then be filled with chicha. Chicha would then be shared by everyone who took part in the victory. Chicha was integral to Incan culture and featured prominently in Incan life[32].

Much of Incan life was undertaken at higher altitude, which is taxing on the human body. The air pressure is lower at higher altitudes, which reduces the available oxygen one breathes in. Breathing becomes faster in an attempt to regulate the lowered oxygen levels in the blood. Muscles in the body become compromised due to lack of oxygen. Dehydration occurs quickly and with greater frequency. Metabolism is increased as all of the body systems are working in overdrive attempting to compensate for the lack of oxygen. Thankfully, the Inca had help in regulating the body at altitude. They attributed that help to *Khuno,* Incan "snow god" and the god of drugs. Khuno was a high-altitude weather god who created the coca plant and introduced the plant to humans. After chewing the leaves, humans were not concerned about the altitude, cold, or lack of air[33]. On the winter solstice, Inca nobility would provide offerings of gold and coca leaves at shrines dedicated to Khuno. *Coca* is potent central nervous system stimulant obtained from the leaves of the *Erythroxylaceae coca* plant. Coca is best known in the modern world for its psychoactive alkaloid, cocaine.

Visionary hallucinogenic and stimulating drugs permeated North, Central, and South Americas. The abundance of stimulants in the New World was astounding to the Europeans, who had only a few varieties of mildly stimulating drugs. In 1530 CE, Pizarro witnessed the Incan use of coca[34]. There was liberal use of coca by the Inca elites, and it was seen as an Imperial privilege. A sizable portion of the tithing and public works the Inca exacted on their people were tributed to the preparation of coca breads. These breads were consumed in copious quantities by the nobles and were prohibited for all other classes to consume. Pizarro made note of this inequality and used it to his advantage; at the time of the Spanish Conquest, he imposed a democratization of coca consumption by providing coca bread for all Inca. It took some coaxing, as coca bread had been sacrosanct for generations. There was a small, yet resourceful group of Spanish merchants who made vast fortunes from the manufacture of coca bread that was now consumed by all classes of Inca. Coca would eventually lead to conflicts between the Spanish and Inca[35]. The inquisitors saw coca as the product that created an idolatrous populace in need of salvation. Incan, and some Spanish, landlords saw the coca bread as a highly beneficial tool as it made workers on the plantations/haciendas work harder and for longer hours. The disputes were tacitly resolved, but only after a hefty tax was imposed and paid to the clergy.

In the high altitudes of the Andes, freezing temperatures are pretty much guaranteed at night. The freezing temperatures allowed the Inca to create ***chuño***, freeze-dried potatoes[36]. The Inca harnessed the cold Andean climate to their advantage by bringing potatoes into the frigid environment and letting them freeze beneath a cloth overnight. In the morning, the Inca would walk on the cloths to squeeze any residual moisture from the potatoes. Chuño provided the Inca with three particularly important uses[37]. First, it was lightweight, which allowed Inca soldiers to carry copious quantities on them when they went on campaigns with relatively little effort. Second, like freeze-dried foods of today, it was extremely durable and could keep without refrigeration for many years. And third, freeze-drying of the potatoes eliminated the bitter or acidic from many species of potatoes have when eaten raw, making them more palatable without the need for boiling or roasting the potatoes. Chuño proved to be an excellent backup food source in case of drought, natural disaster, invasion, or any other type of crop failure.

The Inca had no formal written language like we are accustomed to seeing. They had no logographs, no pictographs, no discernable alphabet, nor phonetically drawn or written systems. Instead, they relied on the use of ***khipus***, which were intricate devices of twisted, tied, braided, and knotted cords used for record keeping. Khipus were once thought to be simple mnemonic devices, like a rosary or set of mala beads[38]. Mnemonic devices like mala are used to count prayers or mantras. It requires knowledge of the prayers and how the beads are used in order to make sense of the string of beads. Thinking of khipus as a mnemonic device put us at a disadvantage as we had no way of interpreting what the strings and knots were intended to symbolize. Archaeologists have recently theorized that they represent a three-dimensional writing system[39]. Strings of color, different fibers, and twist/know direction have allowed researchers to identify 95 unique signs[39]. These unique signs are enough to constitute a ***logosyllabic writing system***, a system of

Figure 8.11 Inca Khipus

makinajp \ Shutterstock.com

recording with signs for full words and phonetic sounds[40]. Khipus consisted of a top cord to which pendants are attached. Pendants may have groups of knows and subsidiary pendants. Some Imperial Incan khipus contained as many as 1,500 pendants branched over six levels of subsidiaries. The more khipus archaeologists decode, the richer the tapestry of Incan history and culture becomes.

In the beginning of the sixteenth century CE, Christian missionaries from Spain and Portugal first encountered *Ayahuasca*. Ayahuasca is an etheoegenic brewed concoction made out of the *Banisteriopsis caapi* vine and other psychoactive botanical ingredients[41]. The brew is used as a traditional spiritual medicine in ceremonies among the indigenous peoples of the Amazon basin to this day, and has led to a number of "new age" ecotourism events where people go on retreats for self-actualization and wellness[42]. Ayahuasca is a bad rendition of the spelling with Quechua Incan languages where the name is closer to Ayawaska or, even more appropriately, Yagé. In Quechua, Aya can mean "spirit, soul, corpse, or dead body," Waska means "rope or woody vine," and combine the word can be translated as the "rope of the soul" or the "spirit rope of the soul" The Christian missionaries called it "the work of the devil." Indigenous people like the Urarina of Peru called saw it as a treasured sacrament of their religious practices. Those who take ayahuasca will experience symptoms of vomiting and diarrhea, followed by feelings of euphoria, strong visual and auditory hallucinations, mind-altering psychedelic effects, and in some cases extreme fear and paranoia.

Figure 8.12 Banisteriopsis caapi

Eskymaks\Shutterstock.com

Another favored psychoactive from the southern part of the Incan Empire was yerba maté or maté from the holy family (Ilex paraguariensis). Maté is a stimulant tea, equivalent to the caffeine in coffee. Spanish missionaries and conquistadors associated the beverage that consumed so many with idolatry. It was believed to be the elixir of sorcerers, who would drink the beverage and according to conquistadors and clerics, use it to "listen to false oracles from the father of lies, Satan"[43]. In reports to the Vatican, this beverage of the natives was seen as a highly offensive drug. Cardinal Borromeo ordered the Bishops and Jesuit Superior in the New World to put an end to the use of something so potentially "damaging to the health of souls and bodies"[43]. By 1620

Figure 8.13 Yerba Maté

andia\Shutterstock.com

CE, even while prohibited, maté consumption reached epic proportions. The city of Asunción, Paraguay, consumed between 350,000 and 375,000 pounds of maté in that year alone. There were only 500 residents, which equates to 750 pounds of maté per person[44].

Guaraná, *Paullinia cupana*, is a climbing plant found natively in the Amazon. It is a stimulant with a caffeine concentration twice the amount of maté, coffee, or cola by volume. Quechua used the plant to treat minor pain, migraines,

Figure 8.14   Guaraná

guentermanaus\Shutterstock.com

neuralgia, and dyspepsia. Guaraná targets the central nervous system as a stimulant and has been found to boost metabolism by triggering the body to burn calories. Due to its location deep in the jungle, it did not get as much negative attention from Spanish clergy or conquistadors[45]. Guaraná was seen as an aphrodisiac by the Inca and used for a wide range of male sexual health issues. Today, guaraná is a key ingredient of soft drinks and energy drinks, representing Brazil's top export.

8.2   Great Tribes of North America

Amerindian is an anthropological term used to describe the vast cultural and language practices of the North American Native American Tribes[46]. The early explorers from France, England, and Spain came to see the native inhabitants as pagans and attempted to initially convert and then subjugate the natives, including the banning of the use of native languages. Native American languages, however, do not belong to a single Amerindian family, but are clustered into 25–30 smaller linguistic groupings. Typically, all Native American languages are discussed together due to the small number of natives remaining who speaking most of these languages and how little is known about the many vibrant cultures that have been lost due to colonialization. Currently, there are around 25 million native speakers of the more than 800 surviving languages. Most of these speakers live in Central and South America where language use is vigorous, despite the myriad of attempts to stamp it down by the colonizers. In Canada and the United States, only about 500,000 native speakers of an Amerindian tongue remain and each year that number declines[47].

Cultivation of medicinal plants among North American tribal groups shared a common theme, conservation. The medicine men and women would harvest every third plant they found; this protected these sacred plants from overharvesting and made sure a new crop would repopulate year after year[48]. Many of the tribes held the beliefs that the ancestors first started using the plants and herbs for healing after observing animals seeking out and eating specific plants when they were sick. Many of the Native North Americans held a spiritual view of life, and to be healthy, a person had to have a sense of purpose and follow a righteous, harmonious, and balanced path in life[49]. They believe some illnesses were life lessons the person needed to encounter to learn from, and therefore healers should not interfere.

Figure 8.15   Native American Linguistic Groups

Source: Lionel Pincus and Princess Firyal Map Division, The New York Public Library. "Linguistic stocks of American Indians north of Mexico." New York Public Library Digital Collections. Accessed September 14, 2022. https://digitalcollections.nypl.org/items/510d47d9-7d9f-a3d9-e040-e00a18064a99

Among the varied medical beliefs of the North American Natives, the best-preserved details come to us from the Northeastern Woodlands and the Great Plains. In particular, the Haudenosaunee ("People of the Longhouse"), named erroneously during colonization by the French as Iroquois. The English referred to them as the Five Nations, consisting of the Seneca, Cayuga, Onondaga, Oneida, and Mohawk (listed geographically from west to east), extending from Quebec in the North to Kentucky in the South[50]. Among the Haudenosaunee, both men and women filled the role of healer with a tradition of women being among the most skilled. They excelled in the use of plants to treat illnesses, wound care, mending of broken bones, and minor surgeries. Like many of the tribes from the First Nation, they saw illness as having both a natural and spiritual component. The spiritual aspects required songs, spells, dances, ceremonies, and superstition to be employed alongside practical medicine in order to be effective. Three healing professions developed among the Haudenosaunee. There was the need of a healer who performed the practical medicine, a fortune-teller who divined the source of the illness and how to cure it, and the magician who would perform the spiritual rites and battle with evil spirits[51].

Early colonists who encountered the Haudenosaunee often referred to them using the Mohawk name, *Adirondack* or "tree eaters," even better defined as the "tree bark eaters." They got this moniker due to the highly unique relationship trees played among the Haudenosaunee. Trees provided everything they required: food, medicine, shelter, canoes, fuel, and tools. The Haudenosaunee taught some of their skills to the early colonists and showed them how to use maple, spruce, birch, willow, balsam fir, and sassafras to name a few[52]. **Willow Bark Tea** was a potent brew made from the bark of the willow tree or "toothache tree" as it was known to the Haudenosaunee. Willow bark tea was effective in reducing fevers, relieving headaches, and soothing arthritic pains. Willow bark is high in concentration of salicylic acid, which is the active ingredient in aspirin. **Sassafras Tea** was used to treat urinary tract infections, insect bites and bee stings, and reduced swelling in the nose and throat. **Birch Tea** was used to purify the blood, relieved rheumatism, expelled of intestinal worms, and aided in treating eczema. **Maple Syrup** was collected during the early spring, shortly after the first thaw. The syrup would have been collected by tapping the maple trees. The collected sap was boiled to make syrup and used for the preparation of a variety of foods in the spring. A portion of the sap would be fermented to produce a mildly alcoholic beverage that was used both medicinal and recreational. Trees were sacred among the Haudenosaunee because of all they provided to the *Ongweh'onweh* the "real human beings."

Many of the Tribes of North America held great reverence for "Two Spirit" or Berdache peoples. Berdache represent a gender variant. Berdache people within Native Tribes had both male and female spirits; today we would call these individuals transgendered. Berdache were incredibly important and held ceremonial roles within many tribes, especially among the Great Plains and Southwestern Tribes. They were held in such high esteem because they were considered to have immensely powerful spiritual connections to the earth and the spirit world[53]. Berdache had access to male activities like war, hunting, and access to male-only areas and rituals, like sweat lodge ceremonies. Berdache simultaneously had access to female activities like cooking, healing, and fortune telling. They were often raised from an early age to be Shaman among their tribes. Since colonization, there have been ~130 documented Berdache[54]. We'Wha was an accomplished and prominent Zuni Berdache who died in the late nineteenth century CE, see Figure 8.16. We'Wha was a highly revered member of their tribe and acted as an ambassador to several

Figure 8.16 We'Wha, Zuni Berdache

Source: archives.gov

religious and other exploratory parties traveling through the Southwestern parts of the United States. We'Wha was accomplished in pottery and textile arts. They helped to preserve the language, history, customs, and traditions of the Zuni people by working with the United States Bureau of Ethnology. We'Wha was described as "the most intelligent person in the pueblo" by the anthropologists sent to document the Zuni[55]. Thanks to the efforts of We'Wha much of the Zuni traditional culture has been preserved and recorded for future generations to be able to understand who the Zuni were.

Among the Lakota and many of the other North American tribes, Hanblecheyapi or the vision quest (literal translation from Lakota "crying for a vision") were used as rites of passage[56]. Vision quests were undertaken in the early teen years of life, mostly by males. Vision quests required that the initiate or seeker prepare for the ordeal by following a time of fasting, obtaining guidance from their tribal medicine man or woman, and consuming natural entheogens. The hallucinogenic effects of the entheogen were utilized to help unlock or interpret the vision. A vision quest was a journey that the seeker makes alone, wherein they enter the wilderness to obtain personal and spiritual wisdom or guidance from their ancestral spirits. The seeker was tasked with finding a place they felt special and were to construct a 10 foot circle of stones or sticks around them. They were to leave all trappings of daily life outside of the circle, typically entering naked. The seeker was only permitted to take water with them into the circle. Some vision quests would last 2 to 5 days within the circle, where the seeker was required to do serious introspection. The seeker was instructed to focus their heart, mind, and soul on the

Figure 8.17 Native American Medicine Bag

guidance they were seeking. Vision quests were ordeals that challenged the seeker's faith, physical endurance, and required deep focus and fortitude to keep to their commitment. In some tribes, upon completion of the vision quest, the seeker would obtain their adult name usually granted to them by their spirit animal who would manifest while in the hallucinogenic trance. Most would take a feather, piece of fur, or a small stone from the area of the quest and place the item in their medicine bag to ensure a portion of the vision will always be with the individual.

S and S Imaging\Shutterstock.com

The Navajo peoples of the Southwestern United States recount old legends of *Yee Naaldooshii* ("he that walks like an animal") from their tribal history. The Yee Naaldooshii or *skinwalker* is perhaps one of the more complex and terrifying legends of the North American Natives, for certain it is steeped in mystery and evil intent[57]. In Navajo legend, skinwalkers were medicine men, magicians, or witches who had attained the highest level of priesthood and held sacred knowledge. They had, however, chosen to use their power for evil by taking the form of an animal to inflict pain and suffering on others. Skinwalkers had the power to read the minds of others; with eye contact could possess and control someone else's body; caused illness, death, and pestilence; destroyed property; desecrated graves and sacred places; fallowed crops; and would lure people from their homes to be killed or converted depending upon the pleasure of the skinwalker. The process by which one became a skinwalker required the evilest of deeds, killing of a close family member. Skinwalkers were humans who have attained immense supernatural power, including the ability to transform into (or wear the skin of) animals and even other humans. The Navajo, to this day, consider the wearing of the pelt of any animal to be taboo, and as a result they are one of the only Native American groups who wore spun fiber cloth. The skinwalker were said to make use of a special powder for defensive and offensive needs. *Corpse powder* was a deadly dust supposedly made from a mixture of dried and powdered human remains, peyote, and other solanaceous plant materials imbued with dark magics[57]. Skinwalkers would blow handfuls of the powder in the faces of their victims, causing sickness and eventually death. The corpse powder was said to turn the tongue black, and it would swell to epic proportions. After the tongue swelled, the individual would begin to asphyxiate, with convulsions, paralysis, and death following.

Among all the sacred plants of the North American Native Tribes, *tobacco* was the most utilized and the most revered. It was drunk, eaten, and smoked. Tobacco was used in religious ceremonies, rites of passage, and for daily/recreational use. Tobacco is a solanaceous plant that contains the highly addictive stimulant alkaloid nicotine, as well as the hallucinogenic alkaloid harmala[58, 59]. There were at least 15 distinct types of tobacco grown in North America alone. Tobacco was used as a medicine to promote physical, spiritual, emotional, and social wellness. Spiritually, tobacco was used as an offering to the Great Spirit or the ancestors, other people, places, or beings. Tobacco would be used when gifting as a sign of respect and hospitality. When tobacco was scarce within one group, other Native Peoples would refer to their tribe as "being poor." Native American travelers always carried tobacco with them, and when encountering a foreign individual would hold up both hands one containing an axe the other a pipe[60]. The choices

Figure 8.18   Pawnee Boy, circa 1940

FPG/Staff/Archive Photos/Getty Images

Source: https://www.gettyimages.com/detail/news-photo/young-native-american-boy-smokes-the-pipe-of-peace-using-news-

Figure 8.19 Tobacco Curing After Harvest

jeep2499\Shutterstock.com

from this gesture were war or peace and required the foreign individual to decide the course of action. If they choose the pipe, the two would sit and smoke together to show their respect and intentions for peace. Tobacco smoking was a rite of passage and beginning around the age of 7 or 8 boys (in some Tribes girls as well) would begin smoking with their village elders. As of the twenty-first century CE, Native Americans and Amish are the only groups of people who can grow tobacco in the United States without a license.

Tobacco cultivation is a very labor intensive and arduous process. The plant rapidly depletes the most fertile soil, requiring fertilizers, composting, and alternating of fallow and cultivation periods. Wild tobacco does not grow as large or prolifically if left to its own devices. Cultivated tobacco requires constant attention, and tobacco farming for profit places the cultivators under very precarious conditions until the harvest and sale of their tobacco. Colonial tobacco farmers tended to be small family groups and they had little time to grow other food stuffs for themselves or their livestock. Native tobacco farmers pooled their labor with some of the tribe working in tobacco fields, others tending to the fields where the three-sisters (maize, beans, and squash) grew, and still others dedicating time to fishing, hunting, and gathering. At the height of the colonial period, Virginia netted 77 million pounds (35 million kilos) of tobacco for smoking and chewing that was sent to England[10].

In 1492 CE, when Christopher Columbus visited the Caribbean, he encountered Native Caribbeans who smoked tobacco, a practice they had picked up from the mainland natives, most likely the Seminoles from Florida. Rodrigo de Jerez and Luis de la Torre were the first documented Europeans to smoke tobacco. They would end up being questioned and found guilty of heresy by an inquisitor due to their smoking habit. As the court documents stated, "only Satan can confer upon human beings the power to exhale smoke through the mouth"[61]. Ancient Europeans used fumigation to produce smoke for substances like poppies and cannabis, but it did not produce the same exhalant. Tobacco smoke was thick and unlike anything many Europeans had ever witnessed. Tobacco spread from Europe to Africa and eventually into Asia. By 1611 CE, the Spanish Crown had begun the taxation of tobacco exported from Santo Domingo and Cuba, placing the commerce of tobacco squarely under the control of the state monopoly. In 1612 CE, the colonies of Virginia, Carolina, and Maryland were given astronomical quotas of 250,000 pounds (113,398 kilos) of tobacco from each colony to be cultivated and shipped to England under the British mercantile system. **British mercantilism** was the system wherein England acquired the natural resources and raw materials from her colonies, had craftsmen and tradesmen within England who turned the raw materials into finished products, and then sold the products—most of the time back to the very colonies that produced them—for a substantial profit. King James I of England condemned the use of tobacco in 1613 CE, as he found "the smoke from which evokes the horror of an insufferable hell, full of tar"[59]. The King's disgust of tobacco did not stop him from levying a tax on its import that began to make the Crown quite wealthy. Between 1622 CE and 1639 CE, the quota skyrocketed to 1,500,000 pounds (680,389 kilos) of tobacco from each of the colonies.

Tobacco was not greeted with fanfare everywhere it went in the world. England and Spain held tight control over the importation of tobacco into Europe, Africa, and Asia. There were varied reactions in the seventeenth century CE to tobacco ranging from the gruesome to the grotesque[61, 62]. Tsar Michael Fedorovich despised tobacco smoking and ordered that anyone caught smoking should be tortured until they revealed who had supplied them with the tobacco. Both the smoker and the distributor would then have their noses cut off. Sultan Murad IV was said to have taken immense pleasure in sneaking up on the men in his court and army and catching them smoking, even on the battlefield amid war, and punishing those he caught smoking. The punishment dolled out by the Sultan could be beheading, dismemberment, or mutilation of the offender's feet and hands. The punishment was tied more directly to the Sultan's mood at the time of discovery. Ming Emperor Chongzhen instituted the punishment of the death sentence for the trafficking or consuming of tobacco. Pope Urban VII reviled tobacco smoking and would excommunicate anyone "who allows himself such repugnant abuse in sites adjoining the dioceses, and their dependencies"[59]. Use of tobacco was prohibited in Bavaria, Saxony, Zurich, Transylvania, St. Gall, and Sweden. The Persian Shah believed in moderation, but individuals who "abused" tobacco by smoking repeatedly within the same day should be put to death. German-controlled Lunenburg had instituted governance that sent anyone who chewed, nasally ingested, or smoked tobacco to the gallows to be hung.

By the start of the eighteenth century CE, most of the countries had diminished their tobacco penalties, abandoned torture, and stopped the mutilation of their tobacco-consuming subjects. Those nations who had been vehemently against tobacco smoking had shifted their acceptance and became more tolerant as they witnessed the amount of money to be made from the tobacco trade. In the seventeenth century CE, England and Spain instituted a tobacco tax that proved to be quite lucrative and led to other European countries adopting similar taxation strategies—1644 CE Portugal, 1670 CE Austria, and 1674 CE France as a few examples. These new taxation strategies allowed governments to begin selling "legalization rights" or "tobacco sales stamps" to companies selling tobacco products at an exorbitant price. In order to see increases in their profits, the European sovereigns began reducing the harsher penalties and punishments related to tobacco. In some instances, there were new edicts put out proclaiming the benefits and joys of tobacco smoking. Prior distain for the habit of smoking gave way to surface-level acceptance, which had the desired effect and increased consumer demand.

Figure 8.20   'Awa

joanna wnuk\Shutterstock.com

In 1778, the first documented European to visit the Hawai'ian archipelago was James Cook. Cook's visit to Hawai'i was to be the first of many exploitive voyages made to the islands by Europeans and North Americans. The Hawai'ian islands were settled between 1000 CE and 1200 CE by successive waves of Polynesian wayfinders and colony ship voyages. The archeological record shows an increase in **canoe plants** in the mid-1100s CE. Canoe plants were the plants cultivated by the ancient Polynesians and transplanted from one island to another throughout the Pacific Islands. These consisted of 'Awa (kava kava), 'Awapuhi kuahiwi (ginger), Kalo (taro), Ko (sugar cane), Kou kukui (candlenut), Mai'a (banana), 'Uala (sweet potato), 'Ulu (breadfruit), and 16 other non-native Hawai'ian plants that the Polynesians used for food, medicine, or utility[63]. *'Awa*, kava or kava kava, is a member of the pepper family, *Piper methysticum*. 'Awa has been used as an intoxicating drink and medicine by the Hawai'ians for hundreds of years. It has been used as a sedative, used in sacred prayer, hula and haka preparation, appreciated for the hedonic effects, and believed to be a conduit to open communication between the consumer, nature, and the gods. 'Awa provides a range of effects extending from euphoria to sedation and relaxation[64]. As a medicine 'Awa has been used by native Hawai'ians as a traditional medicine to treat general debility, weary muscles, chills, colds, headaches, asthma, diabetes, and urinary tract infections.

8.3 Legacies of Discovery

The global expansion of the Maritime Empires brought with it fundamental and long-lasting changes felt around the world. It saw the exploitation of vast numbers of peoples for the gain of a few. It witnessed great demographic shifts as whole tribes were decimated by disease and violence. It saw forced migration of peoples ripped from their homelands and families to be forced into labor in strange new worlds with completely different flora and fauna. It saw the rapid depletion of the natural resources of one continent to fulfill the avarice of another. The Americas were among the legacies of the Voyages of Discovery. Many areas within North and South America were eventually able to shake the yoke of colonial indentures. However, the newly formed and fledged nations set about on their own manifest destinies and pushed the remaining indigenous peoples to the fringes, while continuing to profit from slave labor. The forced assimilation of Native Americans alongside their forced movement to reserved lands (often far from the lands of their ancestors) saw the loss of much tribal knowledge and history.

The botanical herbs and drugs from the New World have been revered, despised, and desired for hundreds of years. Europeans had no idea how potent and highly effective the plants from the new world would become. Many of the most addictive drugs—alcohol, tobacco, cocaine—all originated or were refined in the New World. Imagine what medicines and drugs remain in the wilderness of North and South America, lost to human knowledge due to the practices of the colonizers early on in the "discovery" of the New World. The loss of traditional lives and their intimate ecological knowledge ranks among the most heinous crimes our ancestors committed.

REFERENCES

1. d'Anghiera, P. M. (2019 [1211 CE]). In F. A. MacNutt (Ed.), *De Orbe Novo, The Eight Decades of Peter Martyr D'Anghera* (p. 432). G. P. Putnam's Sons.
2. Thomas, H. (2005). *Rivers of Gold: The Rise of the Spanish Empire, from Columbus to Magellan* (p. 696). Random House Incorporated.

3. de Gómara, F. L. (2018 [1552 CE]). In N. Griffin (Ed.), *Historia General de las Indias*. Penguin.

4. Joseph, R., & Wickramasinghe, C. (2010). *Comets and contagion: evolution and diseases from space. Journal of Cosmology, 7*, 1750–1770.

5. Álvarez, S. (2016). *Cortés, Tenochtitlan y la otra mar: geografías y cartografías de la Conquista. Historia y grafía, 47*, 49–90.

6. Cortés, H. (2001 [1525 CE]). In A. Pagden (Ed.), *Cartas de Relacíon: Letters from Mexico* (p. 640). Yale University Press.

7. Calnek, E. E. (1972). Settlement pattern and chinampa agriculture at Tenochtitlan. *American Antiquity, 37*(1), 104–115.

8. Patterson, K. B., & Runge, T. (2002). Smallpox and the native American. *The American Journal of the Medical Wciences, 323*(4), 216–222.

9. McBride, M. (2019). Allopathic shamanism: Indigenous American cultures, psychopharmacy, and the prince of flowers. In J. A. Loughmiller-Cardinal & K. Eppich (Eds.), *Breath & smoke: Tobacco use among the Maya* (pp. 93–125). University of New Mexico Press.

10. Breen, B. (2019). *The age of intoxication: Origins of the global drug trade* (p. 288). University of Pennsylvania Press.

11. Carod-Artal, F. J. (2015). Hallucinogenic drugs in pre-Columbian Mesoamerican cultures. *Neurología (English Edition), 30*(1), 42–49.

12. Elferink, J. G. R. (1999). Teotlaqualli: The psychoactive food of the Aztec gods. *Journal of Psychoactive Drugs, 31*(4), 435–440.

13. Madala, N., & Nutakki, M. K. (2020). Hot pepper-history-health and dietary benefits & production. *International Journal of Current Microbiology and Applied Sciences, 9*(4), 2532–2538.

14. Tucker, A. O., & Janick, J. (2019). Aztec botany, agriculture, trade, and medicine. In A. O. Tucker & J. |Janick (Eds.), *Flora of the Voynich Codex: An exploration of Aztec plants* (pp. 13–24). Springer.

15. Etingoff, K. (2015). *Howling at the Moon: Vampires & werewolves in the New World* (p. 64). Simon and Schuster.

16. Corona, A. R. Z. (2021). *Hidden in Darkness: The Nahual Glyph*, in https://tlacuilolli .com/2021/07/20/hidden-indarkness-the-nahual-glyph/.

17. Graham, E., Simmons, S. E., & White, C. D. (2013). The Spanish conquest and the Maya collapse: How 'religious' is change? *World Archaeology, 45*(1), 161–185.

18. Balick, M. J., De Gezelle, J. M., & Arvigo, R. (2008). Feeling the pulse in Maya medicine: An endangered traditional tool for diagnosis, therapy, and tracking patients' progress. *Explore, 4*(2), 113–119.

19. Borchardt, J. K. (2004). Medicine of the Maya Ameridians. *Drug News & Perspectives, 17*(5), 347.

20. T L Dillinger, T. L., Barriga, P., Escárcega, S., Jimenez, M., Salazar Lowe, D., & Grivetti, L. E. (2000). Food of the Gods: Cure for humanity? A cultural history of the medicinal and ritual use of chocolate. *The Journal of Nutrition, 130*(8), 2057S–2072S.

21. Montagna, M. T., Diella, G., Triggiano, F., Caponio, G. R., De Giglio, O., Caggiano, G., Di Ciaula, A., & Portincasa, P. (2019). Chocolate, "food of the gods": History, science, and human health. *International Journal of Environmental Research and Public Health, 16*(24), 4960–4981.

22. Tedlock, D. (1996). *Popol Vuh: The Definitive Edition of The Mayan Book of The Dawn of Life and The Glories of Gods and Kings.* Simon & Schuster.

23. Hurst, W.J., et al., (2002). Cacao usage by the earliest Maya civilization. *Nature,. 418*(6895), 289–290.

24. Murphy, J., & Staff, B. E. P. (2014). *Gods and Goddesses of the Inca, Maya, and Aztec Civilizations* (1st ed.). *Gods and Goddesses of Mythology.* Rosen Publishing Group.

25. Chen, R., et al. (2022). Fermented maize beverages as ritual offerings: Investigating elite drinking during Classic Maya period at Copan, Honduras. *Journal of Anthropological Archaeology,. 65*, 101373.

26. Pérez-Armendáriz, B., & Cardoso-Ugarte, G. A. (2020). Traditional fermented beverages in Mexico: Biotechnological, nutritional, and functional approaches. *Food Research International,. 136*, 1–11.

27. De Smet, P. A., & Loughmiller-Cardinal, J. (2022). *4P-9a: Drink/enema rituals in ancient Maya art.* 2022: https://www.academia.edu/download/65296942/4P_9a_Maya_drinks_enemas_Text_def_2020.pdf - [Accessed August 16, 2022]. pp. 1–67.

28. Henderson, L. (2008). Blood, water, vomit, and wine: Pulque in Maya and Aztec belief. In J. Palka (Ed.), *Mesoamerican voices* (pp. 53–76). Chicago Maya Society.

29. Covey, R. A. (2020). *Inca Apocalypse: The Spanish Conquest and the Transformation of the Andean World* (p. 533). Oxford University Press.

30. Diamond, J. (2011). *Collapse: How societies choose to fail or succeed.* Penguin.

31. Giovannetti, M. A. (2021). Chicha and food for the Inka feasts: their materiality in state production contexts in southern Tawantinsuyu. *Journal of Anthropological Archaeology, 62*, 1–17.

32. Gagnon, C. M., & Juengst, S. L. (2018). The drink embodied: theorizing an integrated bioarchaeological approach to the investigation of chicha de maiz consumption. *Bioarchaeology International, 2*(3), 206–216.

33. Biondich, A. S., & Joslin, J. D. (2015). Coca: High Altitude Remedy of the Ancient Incas. *Wilderness & Environmental Medicine, 26*(4), 567–571.

34. Garofalo, L. J. (2006). Conjuring with coca and the Inca: The Andeanization of Lima's Afro-Peruvian ritual specialists, 1580–1690. *The Americas, 63*(1), 53–80.

35. Gade, D. W. (1979). Inca and colonial settlement, coca cultivation and endemic disease in the tropical forest. *Journal of Historical Geography, 5*(3), 263–279.

36. Osorio, A. (2022). Why Chuño Matters: Rethinking the History of Technology in Latin America. *Technology and Culture, 63*(3), 808–829.

37. de Haan, S., et al. (2012). Effect of production environment, genotype and process on the mineral content of native bitter potato cultivars converted into white chuño. *Journal of the Science of Food and Agriculture, 92*(10), 2098–2105.

38. Hyland, S. (2017). Writing with twisted cords: The inscriptive capacity of Andean Khipus. *Current Anthropology, 58*(3), 412–419.

39. Urton, G. (1998). From knots to narratives: Reconstructing the art of historical record keeping in the Andes from Spanish transcriptions of Inka Khipus. *Ethnohistory, 45*(3), 409–438.

40. Urton, G. (2017). Writing the history of an ancient civilization without writing: Reading the Inka Khipus as primary sources. *Journal of Anthropological Research, 73*(1), 1–21.

41. Elferink, J. G. R. (2016). Ethnobotany of the Incas. In H. Selin (Ed.), *Encyclopaedia of the history of science, technology, and medicine in non-western cultures* (pp. 1808–1817). Springer.

42. Fotiou, E. (2020). Shamanic tourism in the Peruvian lowlands: Critical and ethical considerations. *The Journal of Latin American and Caribbean Anthropology, 25*(3), 374–396.

43. Folch, C. (2010). Stimulating consumption: Yerba mate myths, markets, and meanings from conquest to present. *Comparative Studies in Society and History, 52*(1), 6–36.

44. Jamieson, R. W. (2001). The essence of commodification: Caffeine dependencies in the early modern world. *Journal of Social History, 35*(2), 269–294.

45. Smith, N., & Atroch, A. L. (2010). Guaraná's journey from regional tonic to aphrodisiac and global energy drink. *Evidence-based Complementary and Alternative Medicine, 7*(3), 279–282.

46. Mithun, M. (1990). Studies of North American Indian languages. *Annual Review of Anthropology, 19*(1), 309–330.

47. Jacob, M.M. et al., (2019). "We Need to Make Action NOW, to Help Keep the Language Alive": Navigating Tensions of Engaging Indigenous Educational Values in University Education. *American Journal of Community Psychology, 64*(1–2), 126–136.

48. Kilpatrick, J. F., & Kilpatrick, A. G. (1970). Notebook of a Cherokee shaman. *Smithsonian Contributions to Anthropology, 2*(6), 43.

49. Vogel, V. J. (2013). *American Indian medicine. The civilization of the American Indian* (Vol. 95, p. 622). University of Oklahoma Press.

50. Tucker, T. P. (1999). *Haudenosaunee: Portraits of the firekeepers, the Onondaga Nation* (p. 132). Syracuse University Press.

51. Josef, N. (2020). Medicine masks of the Iroquois people as revealed by the False Faces Society. *Studia Etnologiczne i Antropologiczne, 20*, 1–20.

52. Francis, A. T. (2019). Haudenosaunee forest stewardship. In *Natural Resources* (p. 200). Cornell University.

53. Smithers, G. D. (2014). Cherokee "Two spirits": Gender, ritual, and spirituality in the Native South. *Early American Studies, 12*(3), 626–651.

54. Thayer, J. S. (1980). The Berdache of the Northern Plains: A socioreligious perspective. *Journal of Anthropological Research, 36*(3), 287–293.

55. Roscoe, W. (1988). We'wha and Klah the American Indian Berdache as artist and priest. *American Indian Quarterly, 12*(2), 127–150.

56. Evans, K. L. (2016). Shamanic vision quest: Native American ritual, depth psychology, and renaissance natural magic. *NeuroQuantology, 14*(2), 309–337.

57. Lenhardt, C. (2016). Wendigos, eye killers, skinwalkers: The myth of the American Indian Vampire and American Indian "Vampire" myths. *Text Matters: A Journal of Literature, Theory and Culture, 1*(6), 195–212.

58. Cohen, K. S. (2018). *Honoring the medicine: The essential guide to Native American healing* (p. 448). Ballantine Books.

59. Gilman, S. L. & Xun, Z. (2004). *Smoke: A global history of smoking* (p. 408). Reaktion Books.

60. Burns, E. (2006). *The smoke of the gods: A social history of tobacco* (p. 270). Temple University Press.

61. Meyer, K., & Parssinen, T. (2002). *Webs of smoke: Smugglers, warlords, spies, and the history of the international drug trade* (p. 304). Rowman & Littlefield Publishers.

62. Gately, I. (2007). *Tobacco: A cultural history of how an exotic plant seduced civilization* (p. 416). Grove Press.

63. Abbott, I. A., & Shimazu, C. (1985). The geographic origin of the plants most commonly used for medicine by Hawaiians. *Journal of Ethnopharmacology, 14*(2–3), 213–222.

64. Singh, Y. N. (1992). Kava: An overview. *Journal of Ethnopharmacology, 37*(1), 13–45.

Chapter 9

Voyages of Discovery: The Opium Wars

Secured access to Chinese markets was paramount for European merchants between the twelfth and eighteenth centuries CE. British trade initiatives focused on securing tea and silk access led to many of the colonial decisions made in the seventeenth and eighteenth centuries CE that would bring irreversible changes to China. The Portuguese and Dutch had established cursory trading relations with the Chinese in the twelfth and thirteenth centuries CE, but it did not bloom into the grand trade network either nation had hoped. The Chinese did not have much need or want for European products, they found them to be inferior and unnecessary. The Chinese wanted gold or silver for tea, silks, and spices. In addition, the Chinese were attempting to curtail a burgeoning albeit illegal, opium trade, which had begun to devastate the Chinese people and opened cracks in the long-standing Chinese economic wall. Between internal social unrest and external financial pressures, the first and second Opium Wars bloomed. These wars would forever change China and India as the British Empire used opium to gain increased political access while extorting more wealth from the Asian markets.

9.1   Opium, Europe's Pagan Way

Religious unity of centuries prior began to degrade as the Catholic church lost it is long-held control over the monarchies and fiefdoms of Europe. The Protestant Reformation of the sixteenth century CE had brought Protestantism into sharp contrast with Roman Catholic doctrine and was spearheaded by progressive clergy like Martin Luther and John Calvin. The long tradition of patrilocal authority that endorsed monarchies was eroded by new philosophical ideologies of Rationalism followed by the Enlightenment that focused on representative democratic rule by the people. Europe in the seventeenth and eighteenth centuries CE was undergoing changes in political and economic power. The seventeenth and eighteenth centuries CE brought to the center of inquiry the philosophical belief in *Rationalism*, which looked to reason as being the primary source and test or validation of knowledge[1]. Scientific knowledge as discussed by René Descartes[2], Immanuel Kant[3], and David Hume[4] was believed to be valid as true only if it was arrived at through intellectual inquiry, direct observation, and deductive reasoning. Further, scientific knowledge was no longer ruled by sensory or emotional imperatives as the sole rationale of understanding. Later on in the eighteenth century CE, philosophical beliefs shifted toward *Enlightenment* and utilized a broad range of ideas centered on the belief that human happiness alongside the pursuit of knowledge and reason were the legitimate sources of scientific authority[5]. Scientific authority used observation, experimentation, and sensory experience to evaluate and interpret the world. The Enlightenment as discussed by Voltaire[6], Jean-Jacques Rousseau[7], and John Locke[8] promoted revolutionary ideals like liberty, progress, tolerance, fraternity, constitutional government, and the separation of church and state.

The shift in philosophical and political thought had implications for drugs. Instead of being considered pagan and evil, drugs reemerged as a novel source of study and utility. Drugs were starting to be protected and utilized by doctors, pharmacists, and chemists who were beginning to harness their true potential. Drugs and medicines had always been an important means of communication across cultures and were often shared. The increase in mobilization of energies and the movement of resources by the West led to a progressive control of local plants, animals, and minerals as potential sources for drugs. Chief among the pagan drugs that had been viewed with suspicion for centuries was opium. By the end of the Renaissance, it had been elevated to a scientific and cultural commodity of interest and wonder.

Laudanum, an opium-derived drug invented by the Renaissance polymath, Paracelsus, was still widely popular in the seventeenth and eighteenth centuries CE. Laudanum was available as a tincture of opium, which contained between 10 and 14% powdered opium by weight[9]. Diluted in wine or alcohol, laudanum was distinguished by the telltale reddish-brown color of the mixed tincture. Laudanum was bitter tasting, and it was common practice to add a spoonful of sugar or honey or dilute the laudanum in tea. The main uses for laudanum were as an analgesic and for cough suppression, especially in adults with tuberculosis or in children who were teething. Because of the taste, laudanum had some competitors like Vinum Opii. ***Vinum Opii*** was a tonic consumed to relieve pain. It was a combination of opium, cinnamon, cloves, and sweet sherry wine, which gave it a very agreeable smell and a sweet taste. The opium content was lower in Vinum Opii, between 7 and 9% by weight. Due to the lower opium content, Vinum Opii tended to cause less cases of nausea and vomiting than a tincture of pure opium or Laudanum.

Laudanum was the name given to the drug by Paracelsus. Between the sixteenth and eighteenth centuries, the recipe would adapt and vary depending upon location and by the amount of coin an individual had to spend on the concoction. Some of the more expensive varieties were composed with gold foil and crushed pearls added to the original base of alcohol and opium. Scholars are not completely sure where the name is derived from, and Paracelsus left few clues as to the origin of the name. In Latin, *laudare* means to praise. In Persian, *ladan* refers to a resin obtained from gum trees. Latin and Persian were both languages that Paracelsus could read and write with ease, but the origin of the name Laudanum was never shared with anyone. By the middle of the seventeenth century CE, the

Figure 9.1 Laudanum

Naturally. Photography/Shutterstock.com

recipe for Laudanum had become simplified and standardized, consisting of alcohol and opium[9]. By the nineteenth century CE, Laudanum was widely available in Europe and the United States. The drug could be purchased from pubs, grocers, barbers, tobacconists, pharmacists, and even some confectioners. Laudanum was seen as a miracle drug and was used for a wide range of ailments, including "women's troubles"/hysteria, tuberculosis cough, gout, arthritis, rheumatism, cholera, diarrhea, and melancholia to name a few. By some estimates, laudanum represented up to 30% of sales for some chemists, pharmacists, and apothecaries.[10]

Opium was used by the aristocracy of Europe and made widely popular by poets, writers, and artists. The Royal House of Sweden, the Royal House of Denmark, Peter the Great, Catherine the Great, Fredrick II of Prussia, Maria Theresa of Austria, Louis XV, and Louis XVI were all very fond of opium[11-13]. An influential physician in the 1700s captured the sentiment toward opium in a now infamous *Treatise on opium, founded on practical observations*, wherein George Young stated: "it makes for pleasant dreams, frees you from fear, hunger and pain, and provides the regular consumer with punctuality, tranquility of spirit, presence of the soul"[13]. Literary notables like Johann Wolfgang von Goethe, Samuel Taylor Coleridge, Mary Shelley, Lord Byron, William Wordsworth, John Keats, and Walter Scott were inspired by and wrote about what Goethe called, "an enchanting narcotic juice"[14]. It might appear, at least at the surface level, that by the nineteenth century CE there was a lot more acceptance of opium. Opium could be found in antitussive elixirs, lozenges to calm the nerves, teas for insomnia, and even Laudanum for colic, toothaches, and asthma. While opium was a known psychoactive and could affect the body in diverse ways, the widespread and ubiquitous use of opium was being done in what the people of the times would have called the "pagan way." The ***pagan way*** was the acknowledgment that opium would have impact on one's central nervous system and would produce a range of effects, yet opium was mostly consumed to aid in the reduction of stress, easing of distress, and promoting of general well-being[15]. This was equated to the "pagan way" because it seemed similar to the ways the Victorian era poets, historians, and artists interpreted the ways the Romans and Greeks approached plant-based medicine. In the imagination of the Victorians, opium was self-medicated to help ease the social condition. Social scandal was not generated by the overconsumption of opium during the Victorian era, instead chronic alcoholism was seen as being more socially unacceptable.

Scandal was most definitely inculcated among consumption patterns of alcohol. There was for the first time since the ancient Greeks, a discussion and concern around patterns of consumption of alcohol. ***Compulsive consumption*** was an extremely specific type of behavior, which was seen as inappropriate, typically excessive, and most certainly disruptive to the lives of the alcoholic[16]. The disruption tended to extend to the families of the alcoholic, especially if they were part of the Ton, part of high society. The good and bad deeds of the alcoholic were seen as extensions of how the broader family functioned, acted, and behaved. Compulsive consumption led to unique solutions for people to deal with the incorrigible actions brought out by alcohol. There was a belief that if anyone was disorderly in their consumption, they needed to consume more and in larger quantities if they were to reorder their behavior[17]. And like any other not so acceptable habit, if someone did consume in copious quantities, they should conceal themselves from public view and scrutiny as much as possible. It was acceptable to be a drunk behind closed doors, but once the door opened to the public, you needed to behave and act according to your societal station. Your best way of handling this type of situation was to act as though you were stone cold sober. It was the Victorian mantra of keeping up appearances at all costs.

9.2 Smuggling and the Sand Road

Between the fourteenth and seventeenth centuries CE, the Italian cities of Genoa and Venice served as the distribution hubs for goods, drugs, and spices entering Europe from Asian merchants. The northern portion of the Silk Road trade routes had been compromised beginning in the mid-fifteenth century CE and goods were not flowing through consistently with the frequency they once had. The northern route had fallen victim to the ruin of the Mongol Empire in Northern India, subsequent waves of plagues, increased banditry, and an ever-increasingly open hostility toward Christians and Europeans in general[18, 19]. This left the southern portion of the Silk Road as the only viable over-land trade route for the exotic and highly prized commodities from Asian markets. The southern route passed through Baghdad and onto Egypt where it would be loaded onto ships in Alexandria. The goods would board Genoese and Venetian merchant ships and be transported throughout Europe. This arrangement was of immense benefit to the Genoese and Venetian merchant guilds until alternative shipping routes had been established.

An unlikely business venture was proposed toward the end of the 1400s CE. Italian financers and Portuguese navigators entered into a collaboration. The financers would pay for and outfit a trade expedition led by Vasco da Gama, who successfully charted the course around the Cape of Good Hope to Calcutta in 1497 CE[20]. This single trip would revolutionize trade networks between Europe and the markets of India and China. Muslim control over the ports in Egypt was increasing and had begun to manifest into shipping delays on several goods with many being destroyed. Thanks to da Gama's expedition, the stranglehold of Genoa and Venice was relaxed. The charted route da Gama navigated allowed European merchants to

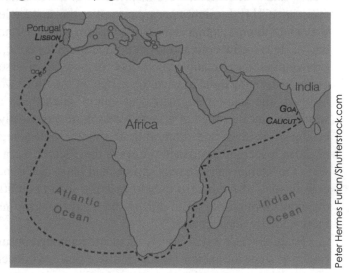

Figure 9.2   Voyage of Vasco da Gama, 1497–1499

circumvent the Genoese and Venetian monopolies and seek out their own goods. A ship could carry far more cargo than camels or horses and the trip was much shorter.

In an effort to limit potential hazards from taking ships around Africa, the Portuguese established ports in the Sudan and Ethiopia and in Morocco and Egypt. Caravans would travel the Sahara between the Portuguese ports to transport gold and silver and eventually Iberian opium. It has been estimated that 1 ton of gold was smuggled and up to 10 tons of Iberian opium per year across the Sahara[12, 21]. Portugal had foreseen the possibility of transporting Iberian opium into China for profit as they were the first to note that Chinese opium was not as potent. Chinese opium was far inferior to the opium produced in Spain (Iberian) and Egypt. The problem they faced was the imbalance in trade, China was not particularly interested in any wares or goods produced by Europe. Due to religious restrictions, opium was difficult to move freely. In Spain, it was difficult to export opium due to restrictions related to the inquisition and in Egypt, it was difficult due to Muslim control. Both Catholicism and Islam were very much against the use of opium, equating its use with sin. This left Portugal with the problem of getting Iberian opium out of Spain and into China. The other large problem Portugal faced was the inability to secure the waters around Africa, which made it difficult to move goods in the Atlantic. The **Sand Road**, or the smuggling route between Morocco, Egypt, and the Sudan or Ethiopia across the Sahara, was the solution. The Portuguese were the first of the European nations to begin exploiting the Chinese market through the smuggling of opium[22]. The Dutch and the English took note of the success of the Portuguese.

9.3 Celestial Empire of China

Classically, China viewed itself not as a nation-state, nor an empire with clearly identified boarders and subjects. Instead, China saw itself as the center of the only known civilization in the world[23]. It was the embodiment of the celestial heavens on Earth. China viewed all other kingdoms, tribes, and peoples as being equally or less civilized depending upon how close they were to China culturally and politically. Chinese cultural and political influence reached from the core provinces, through even more remote southern, northern, and western provinces, to garrisoned territories populated chiefly by ethnically non-Chinese peoples. Beyond those borders, China envisioned its relations with most other states as consisting of a tributary system, wherein distant kings and chiefs were seen as less civilized and should act as loyal subordinates to the Chinese Emperor. To the Imperial court in Beijing, distant peoples defined their places in the world by their relationships with and tributes paid to the emperor. Relations were to be maintained through the receipt of tribute by the Imperial court. Gold, silver, and jade were the preferred forms of tribute. The more tribute a distant land provided, the more amenable the court would be. It was this tributary system that allowed China to maintain trade and diplomatic relations with many other countries.

When Europeans first encountered the Chinese, China had extraordinarily little interest in trading with Europeans. The Chinese found the Europeans to be no better than barbarians who lacked any refinement. Between 1500 and 1600 CE, Europeans were only permitted to do business in the port of Canton and could only trade with ministers appointed directly by the Imperial court[24]. Despite multiple pleas and entreaties from British, Portuguese, Spanish, and Dutch merchants and diplomats, China refused to open other ports to foreigners. The Chinese viewed European goods as far inferior to their own and did not buy many goods from the merchants in Canton. There were only a handful of embassies and Christian missionaries were not permitted to travel to the interior of China. The Chinese strictly controlled Europe's access to Chinese markets and made certain there were as few points of contact as possible.

Opium use in China between sixteenth and nineteenth centuries CE oscillated from endemic to pandemic proportions as consumption grew from what appeared to be isolated to more widespread use. The concepts of endemic, epidemic, and pandemic borrowed from public health and epidemiology function as a way of framing the perceived threat of opium use within China. The word *endemic* comes from the Greek *endemos*, meaning in or among the people. Adding the prefix *epi-* meaning upon gives us the word epidemic, or "upon the people." Adding *pan-* as in pandemic means "all people." **Endemic** refers to a characteristic, in our case opium use, which is seen in a subset of the population, environment, or region[25]. Opium is present, but it is being used in relatively low frequency.

Epidemic is something that affects a disproportionately substantial number of people within a population, community, or region at the same time[26]. Epidemics are characterized by very widespread sudden growth of something harmful. Seemingly, overnight opium use skyrocketed and spread from Canton to other surrounding towns and cities. *Pandemic* is what happens when an epidemic becomes very widespread and affects whole regions, nations, continents, or the entire world[27]. Opium use in China during the nineteenth century CE could be found in nearly every province leading up to the Opium Wars.

As early as 1516 CE, the Portuguese and other European merchants noted that Chinese consumption of opium was much higher than compared to Mediterranean use. This was most likely due to the percent of active morphine found in opium during this time. On average, the Iberian poppy contained 16% morphine by volume, the Indian poppy contained 8% morphine, and the Chinese poppy had a scant 6% morphine. Gram for gram the Iberian poppy was twice as potent as the Indian poppy and two-thirds more potent than the Chinese poppy. The Portuguese had figured out that the Iberian poppy was the commodity that would grant them access to the once isolated Chinese markets. The Iberian poppy would open China's tight control over goods and stood to give the Portuguese a commodity they could bargain with to their benefit. The change of fortunes had been set into motion and was about to get a huge boost from civil unrest in Ming China[28].

The Ming dynasty ruled over China for 276 years (1368–1644 CE) and was the last imperial dynasty in China to be ruled by ethnic Han Chinese[24]. The Han ruled between eras of Mongol and Manchu dominance. Ming China was a colossal force, wielding immense cultural, economic, and political power that extended into East Asia and the Turks to the west, Vietnam and Myanmar to the south[23]. Under Ming rule, the Chinese civil service system was perfected and became both highly stratified and highly competitive. All the top officials entered into the bureaucracy by passing a standardized government examination. Ming architects were responsible for the construction of the Forbidden City and the Temple of Heaven. Ming architects and engineers made Beijing the capital of the empire and the center of the Celestial Empire.

Figure 9.3 Temple of Heaven

zhuda/Shutterstock.com

The end of the Ming dynasty was the culmination of a number political and natural catastrophes that allowed the ethnic Manchus of northern China to take control. There were a series of rebellions that had severely weakened the Ming internally. Those parts of China not in open rebellion faced a cycle of catastrophic floods along the Yellow River, which was followed by widespread famine. The Chinese people were convinced that the Ming had lost the Mandate of Heaven and were no longer the rightful rulers of the Celestial Empire. The Ming dynasty ended when the emperor Chongzhen hung himself from a tree in the rear gardens of the Forbidden City. The Qing dynasty began in 1644 CE. The Manchu princes of the Qing dynasty did little to quell the discontent of the general public in China. The

Qing court let piracy run rampant on the Yellow and Yangtze Rivers and in the harbors along the Chinese coast. Secret societies and cults began to flourish. Rural provinces who were denied food and assistance began flaring into open rebellion. The culmination was a brutal Civil War that erupted between North and South China. Jesuit and Protestant missionaries from Europe helped to fan the flames of discontent and disgust. These missionaries incited the Chinese people by pointing out that the "real blame for the strife lay with the greed and cruelty of the Manchu regime…"[24]. The Qing Civil war is considered to be one of the bloodiest wars in human history; the number of deaths can be seen in Table 9.1 shown in relation to the U.S. Civil War and the French Revolution to provide some context.

Table 9.1 Deaths from Civil War in China, United States, and France

Name of War	Number of Deaths
Qing Civil War	50,000,000
United States Civil War	620,000
French Revolution	1,000,000

The Qing dynasty was fairly relaxed about opium for nearly 100 years; however, the implementation of two laws in 1729 CE would function as the catalyst for increased armed conflict between the Europeans and Chinese that would escalate into war a century later with the British. Emperor Yun-Chung issued a law that (1) prohibited opium trade with Europeans and (2) provided the sentence of strangulation for opium smugglers and proprietors of opium smoking dens[24]. The edict prohibiting opium trade with Europeans was intended to stop exchange of tea, spices, and silk for opium. The imperial reserves were being depleted of precious metals and exotic spices and Yun-Chung believed it was due to an increase in usage of opium provided by the foreign traders. The pro-

hibition did not impact cultivation and production of Chinese opium; it was intended to keep the European opium from depleting the treasury. The edict calling for the strangulation of opium smugglers and owners of smoking dens was put into place to curtail illegal importation of opium, which at the time was largely being carried out by the Portuguese[11]. In 1729 CE, an estimated 1.5 tons of opium was smuggled into China via Portuguese smugglers. In 1793 CE, Emperor Cha-Ching prohibited the importation of foreign opium and the cultivation of domestic opium. This one event provided the Portuguese smugglers with a huge advantage. With

Figure 9.4   Illustration of Opium Smokers in China

Marzolino/Shutterstock.com

the domestic opium no longer available, the demand for Iberian opium product skyrocketed. The rationale for the sweeping prohibition provided by the imperial court was that the drug, once used by "peasants and persons of dubious reputation" had now infiltrated into the homes of members of good families, students, officials, and the imperial court. By 1820 CE, over 750 tons of Iberian opium was being smuggled into China by the British. This caused a revision to the edict, which now applied the death penalty to both dealers and consumers who were caught with Iberian opium. In 1840 CE, opium smuggling had surpassed 2,000 tons of Iberian opium being smuggled by the British[12].

Long before the maritime smuggling of opium, all classes in China had some knowledge of opium. The use of opium was so widely known that it was featured as an ingredient in baked goods, which was a practice unique to Chinese culture. In addition, there are Byzantine records of an expedition to the imperial court of China in 700 CE, wherein the Byzantine delegation brought several liters of Galen's theriaka as a gift for the Emperor[29]. From 700 CE onward, the preparation and use of opium was part of the official Chinese pharmacopeia. For as much as the imperial court attempted to make opium use appear to be a product of contemporary design, China had a long standing history and unique cultural practices associated with opium.

9.4 Opium Smuggling and War

Naval battles between the Dutch, Portuguese, and British fleets over opium smuggling, spice trades, and access to Chinese markets escalated from occasional skirmishes to the brink of all-out war. These encounters saw the countries involved slowly chipping away at the other fleets and defenses. In the beginning of the 1800s, the British East India Company emerged victorious and took the lion's share of access to the Chinese market and profit from opium smuggling. The East India Company had invested in building large plantations in Bengal and Punjab, India, where the Iberian poppy had been transplanted and was being cultivated in large volume. The proximity of India allowed for faster delivery to Canton by ocean and overland routes. The British Prime Minister, Viscount Palmerston, used his influence between 1830 and 1865 CE to shape British foreign policy[30]. He was allegedly receiving royalties for his unwavering support of the East India Company. He lobbied for company interests in parliamentary debates and smoothed over foreign relations faux pas when the East India Company got itself embroiled in international misconduct.

The Honorable *East India Company* was a private mercantile company that engaged in a long

Figure 9.5 Seal of the East India Company

Oleg Iatsun/Shutterstock.com

series of wars and diplomatic gerrymandering to gain control of much of India and Asia by the nineteenth century CE[31]. The company was originally chartered by Queen Elizabeth I on December 31, 1600 CE. The Queen had formed the East India Company to conduct trade in the Indian Ocean, initially with Mughal India and the East Indies for the purposes of securing spices, indigo, cotton, and other luxury goods for the crown. Eventually, the East India Company expanded to encompass Qing China. The company continued to grow exponentially and accounted for over half of the world's trade by 1833 CE, controlling many of the basic commodities of the world like cotton, silk, indigo dye, salt, spices, saltpeter, tea, and opium[32].

By 1803 CE, at the pinnacle of its influence, the East India Company had a private army of around 260,000 men. By all estimates was twice the size of the standing British army at the time. The East India Company had taken large plots of land in India thanks in part to its private army, exercising military power over the Bengali and Punjabi peoples and assuming administrative functions for these colonial holdings. The East India Company instituted a monopoly system on opium farming and cultivation, and built large plantations focused on cultivating the Iberian poppy. Only British-sanctioned plantations were permitted to grow opium under colonial law in India and the East India Company ensured that all other opium production, especially native Indian poppy production was prohibited and fiercely regulated. The East India Company could not be compromised by carrying opium on company ships into China, however. They had a company image to uphold after all… The East India Company resorted to the commission of privateers and smugglers who were well paid from the Company's inexhaustible payroll to smuggle on average of 900 tons of opium per year from Bengal and Punjab each, with a combined total of ~1,800 tons[32].

China went from advantage to deficit in terms of trade with the British. In the beginning part of the eighteenth century CE, Britain had a huge trade deficit with Qing China. The British were paying high taxes on luxury goods in demand from British citizens like tea and silk. By the middle part of the eighteenth century CE, Britain had balanced the trade deficit with Qing China due in large part to the Indian Opium plantations beginning to produce and smuggle opium. By 1838 CE, the East India Company had gained the upper hand and was poised to exploit its growing trade advantage over Qing China. The British were making huge profits as the Chinese were losing goods and silver in unprecedented volumes.

On June 3, 1838 CE, Emperor Tao-Kuang summoned all his ministers and advisors to the Forbidden City to discuss the growing trade imbalance between China and the British. The emperor was concerned about the depletion of the imperial vaults of precious metals, silks, and spices. Those summoned fractioned into two polarized opinions that had the court nearly split. The two options were (1) legalize opium, return cultivation to the Chinese people, and implement taxes; and (2) maintain the current policy of trade with the British. Neither of the two options were very palatable to the Emperor. Before the two opinions could reach a resolution, Viceroy Lin Zexu interdicted 1,400 tons (2,800,000 pounds or 1,270,059 kilograms) of opium in Canton and ordered all the seized opium to be summarily dumped into the Bay. These actions set into motion the First Opium War, with the British parliament declaring war, stating the actions in Canton were an "intolerable attempt to interfere with free trade"[33]. Queen Victoria, who had just turned 19 years old and was only 1 year into her reign as sovereign, reacted to the event by declaring war on China in 1839 CE[34]. In her address to parliament, she stated:

"Events have happened in China which have occasioned an interruption of the commercial intercourse of my subjects with that country. I have given, and shall continue to give, the most serious attention to a matter so deeply affecting the interests of my subjects and the dignity of my crown" – Queen Victoria[35], emphasis added.

Figure 9.6 Queen Victoria, 5 years Post-Coronation

The British government and the British East India Company dispatched a military force to China. The combined British naval forced used superior naval and gunnery might to trample Chinese encampments, forts, and meager ships[30]. Each skirmish added to the accumulated devastation taken by the Chinese forces and barely scathed the British fleet. The Chinese had attempted to form a flotilla and blockade the British ships from entering the Pearl River. The Chinese ships were no match for the British barque and schooners and their advanced cannons and were quickly routed. By 1842, the Qing dynasty had admitted defeat and was forced to sign the *Treaty of Nanking*.

The Treaty of Nanking, signed August 29, 1842 CE and effected June 26, 1843 CE, was a peace treaty agreed upon by the United Kingdom and the Qing dynasty of China[36]. This was a highly unequal treaty as China had many concessions and Britain had no obligations in return. The treaty was demoralizing and exploitative. The terms of the treaty are outlined in Table 9.2. Opium was not discussed in the official documents between Britain and China[11]. Opium would remain prohibited by an expressed request of the British, although distribution would not be hindered nor

Figure 9.7 Opium War 1839–1842 British forces attack Chinese Forts on Chuenpee Island

halted by Chinese authorities. The Treaty of Nanking had granted an obscene level of indemnity and extraterritoriality to Britain through the opening of five treaty ports for trade and cession of Hong Kong Island to British control. In addition, the First Opium War came with a huge loss of prestige for China. The war eroded much of the Chinese claim to regional power, with many of the East Asian neighbors taking note of Qing China's weakness.

Table 9.2 Treaty of Nanking, 1843 CE

Terms of the Treaty
• £21 million pounds sterling[1] to be paid by the Chinese in installments over 3 years
• Relinquishing of Hong Kong and Amoy to British control
• Opening of five additional ports for commerce: Shanghai, Canton, Ningbo, Fuzhou, and Xiamen
• British-fixed tariffs for good sold within these ports
• Freedom of merchants to trade with whomever they choose

In the wake of the First Opium War, the Qing imperial court was exceptionally slow to meet the terms of the Treaty of Nanking. The French and the United States pressured the Qing court to extend similar concessions in 1844 CE in terms of trade allowances. The British were not satisfied with the terms of the Treaty and set out to rework the treaty to provide additional privileges in the favor of British interests. To add insult to injury, the

Figure 9.8   Opium War between Britain and China 1839–1842 Attack on First Bar Battery

Everett Collection/Shutterstock.com

British pushed for additional concessions from the Chinese in 1854 CE, with the top concessions being: (1) opening of all ports in China to foreign trade; (2) universal 0% tariff rate on all British imports; (3) legitimization of British opium trade; and 4) freedom of travel by the British throughout China. All of this came to a head, when in 1856 CE, the *HMS Arrow*, a light wooden screw despatch gunnery vessel in service to the British Navy, was boarded by Chinese officials in Hong Kong[37]. The *Arrow* was a known smuggling ship and had been registered as operating out of Hong Kong (a new British crown colony). The Chinese officials who had boarded the ship arrested the 12-man crew under the suspicion of piracy and smuggling. Captain Thomas Kennedy was in the midst of negotiating with the Viceroy of Canton who was refusing to pay the agreed upon price for the 5 million kilos of opium the *Arrow* was carrying. Captain Kennedy watched in horror as his ship was boarded, his crew arrested, and the cargo seized. The icing on the disaster cake was witnessing the British flag being forcefully down from the gaff of his ship and trampled upon by the Chinese Officials. Captain Kennedy demanded the release of his ship, return of the cargo, payment for the shipment in full, the return of his men, and a formal apology for the alleged insult to the British flag[36]. His argument was that under the extraterritoriality clause of the Treaty of Nanking, the Chinese had no authority to do the heinous acts committed aboard the *Arrow*. The Chinese

---

[1] With inflation, this would equal £1,862,926,766 as of 2021.

were within their rights to board the ship, as its Hong Kong registration had expired. The Viceroy refused to issue an apology for the flag and released all but three of the crew members, who were sent to the gallows as pirates. The British destroyed four Chinese forts on the coast and went about sinking over two dozen Qing junks. China did not have any military forces to spare to protect its sovereignty against the British onslaught because it was amid a political uprising and was trying to quell the Taiping Rebellion. The Taiping Rebellion had Beijing currently embroiled in civil unrest and Chinese forces were woefully stretched thin.

Remarkably close to the events of the HMS Arrow, a French Catholic missionary, Auguste Chapdelaine, was arrested in Guangxi[38]. The missionary was charged with preaching Christianity outside of the confines of the treaty port cities and for cavorting with known Taiping rebellion leaders[39]. Father Chapdelaine was sentenced to public execution; however, his captors beat him to death before his sentence could be carried out. The French government would use this incident as an excuse to join with the British in the Second Opium War. France, Russia, and the United States all sent envoys to the British Governor in Hong Kong to offer military support. However, Russia would not end up sending any military aid; instead, they amassed their own army along China's northern border. Diplomatic efforts were quickly renewed between China and the United States, and with an offer of additional and exclusive trading

Figure 9.9 Battle of Palikao Second Opium War

Marzolino/Shutterstock.com

Figure 9.10 Eight Mile Bridge in Baliqiao Second Opium War

Marzolino/Shutterstock.com

Figure 9.11 Da Nang Bombing by French Fleet, 1858

Marzolino/Shutterstock.com

rights, the United States signed an agreement for neutrality in the Second Opium War. This agreement did not last long, as the Chinese garrison at Canton shelled and sank a U.S. Navy steamer. The Chinese had confused the United States ship with a French vessel. To be fair, England, United States, and France

Figure 9.12 British and French Fleets Attack Chinese Forces, Hai River:

did share flags emblazoned with similar colors – red, white, and blue. The confusion was a justified faux pas, even if not accepted. The U.S. Navy retaliated and razed all forts near and around Canton, dissolving the short-lived agreement between Qing China and the United States. The combined forces of British and French fleets began attacking the Chinese coast, opening the Second Opium War in 1856 CE.

In June 1858 CE, hostilities between the Qing, French, British, and American forces ended with the signing of the ***Treaty of Tientsin***. The Chinese considered this treaty to be another unequal set of demands, as the Chinese had many stipulations to fulfill. France, England, and the United States had no obligations under the terms of the treaty. The terms of the treaty are outlined in Table 9.3. Under this new treaty, the importation of opium would remain nominally forbidden and similar to the Treaty of Nanking, China would not halt nor hinder the movement of opium.

Table 9.3 Terms of the Treaty of Tientsin

Terms of the Treaty
• Opening of 11 additional ports to foreign trade, including Kowloon, Tientsin, Peking, Newchwang, Taiwan, Hankou, and Nanjing
• Shanghai ceded to the French
• Foreign residents permitted throughout China
• Right of foreign vessels to navigate freely on the Yangtze River
• Total freedom of movement for foreigners for the purposes of travel, trade, or missionary activities
• Religious liberty to all Christians to practice freely in China
• China to pay an indemnity of 6 million taels of silver (2 taels to France, 2 taels to Britain, and 2 taels for merchant compensation)
• Official Chinese documents were banned from referring to British and French officials and citizenry by the character 夷 (Yi), "Barbarian"

Let us not forget about the Russians, who in 1858 CE had begun stationing armed forces along their southern border with China. The presence of this force, along with the Taiping Rebellion and armed conflicts with the British, French, and American forces left China wary and reluctant to engage in yet another conflict. Before a war could be ignited, the Qing and the Russians agreed upon and signed the *Treaty of Aigun* in May 1858 CE[40]. The terms of the treaty were straightforward. Russia was to gain the left bank of the Amur River, which pushed the northern border of China south from the Stanovoy mountains. In 1860 CE, Count Ignatyev of Russia (1842–1917 CE) negotiated the *Treaty of Peking*, when he convinced the Chinese that Russia was their friendly neighbor and would assist in the protection of China from outside aggression. China agreed to the new treaty with the hopes of building an alliance with Russia that would help protect the Qing from further foreign invasions from Europeans. Under this new treaty, Russia gained additional land and control over a non-freezing port on the Pacific Ocean. China yielded Haishenwai to Russia, who renamed the city to its current name of Vladivostok. Vladivostok would become Russia's southeastern most city and one of its most prosperous port cities.

The Opium Wars were significant as they eroded and diminished Manchu rule while opening China to foreign influence. The control exerted by Western countries turned China into a quasi-feudal quasi-colonial state. The Opium Wars divided China into *spheres of influence* for the next ~125 years[36]. Spheres of influence is a military term that refers to an area within a country over which another country claims exclusive and sovereign rights. The degree of control exerted by the foreign power is dependent upon the military force involved and the diplomatic interactions between the two countries. Among the Chinese people, the Opium Wars represented a very disgraceful defeat, but the Chinese would use this shame to strengthen China to keep such events from ever happening again[41]. The Chinese began to study the social, political, and economic systems of the West and began implementing aspects that would serve to make China strong again. In a century and a half, China would again rise to a position of global power, wherein the countries that had once exploited China would become economically indebted to her.

9.5 Chinese Resolutions and Solutions to Opium

The Empress Dowager Tseu-Hi was regent of China 1861–1873 CE and 1875–1906 CE. She was the regent until her son, Chih, turned 17 in 1873 CE and then again in 1875 CE when he died mysteriously from venereal disease. Some have speculated that the Empress Dowager had knowingly supplied her son with concubines and prostitutes known to have syphilis. The Empress Dowager was a known opium addict and was very resentful of Western interference in Chinese affairs. In 1863 CE, she dealt a significant blow to East India Company profits when she legalized the importation and consumption of opium in China. To make the wound sting a little more, she imposed a 5% royalty on the importation of foreign opium and a 5% royalty on sales of foreign opium[42]. During his short two-year reign 1873–1875 CE, Emperor Chih continued to erode the East India Company's profit margins. He enacted a renewal of opium cultivation in southwest China. In addition,

Figure 9.13 Tomb of the Empress Dowager, Zunhua, Hebei, China

beibaoke/Shutterstock.com

the Emperor began a public education campaign to inform his people about the dangers of opium[42]. This was a first of its kind in preventative educational and public health campaign. Another innovative development of Emperor Chih was the establishment of the world's first detoxification centers for those wanting to quit their opium addiction. This was to become the very first ***drug rehabilitation*** program and it was initiated in China. These centers were funded by the government and were established to educate the people about the dangers of opium, to assist addicts in detoxifying, and to teach those working toward an opium free life a trade or skill. It was revolutionary in a world where addiction was seen as a weakness of the individual's virtue or spirit. Instead of blaming the victim, Qing China was focused on helping those under the stranglehold of opium's addictive nature to overcome the drug. Further their program recognized that reintegration into society would not work if the individual did not have a skill or trade.

By 1895 CE, China was producing ~85% of its internal demand for opium and was poised to begin supplying all of Asia with opium within a few short years. It was only at this point that the British Parliament concluded that large-scale traffic in opium was a "morally indefensible enterprise"[32]. The majority of this Parliament had members who in 1838 CE had recommended that Britain go to war with the Chinese for the "preservation of such an important source of income"[37]. The Parliament of 1895 CE voted unanimously to sanction Chinese sales of opium in other parts of Asia and the world and set out to sanction and embargo Chinese vessels carrying opium. If Britain could not control the opium market, they would make certain no one else would be able to either.

The British used opium in two separate countries as a form of socio-political control. In China, opium was used to provide a trade advantage for the British. In India, opium was used as a political tool to help subdue the masses while garnering workers at a substantially reduced rate[43]. The Chinese pulled themselves out of their opium need to become self-sufficient and effectively reduced the number of people addicted to opium. The Indians fell deeper into the throws of British Imperialism and were subjected to many more vices—alcohol and opium to name a few[44]. Table 9.4 outlines the effects of British opium in both India and China.

Table 9.4 Effects of British Imposed Opium Use

Chinese Attitude Toward Opium	Indian Attitude Toward Opium

• Punishment for use, sales, and distribution for much of the Qing dynasty was death
• 0.5% of the total population were addicted to opium
  • Entering the twentieth century CE there were progressively lower rates of opium consumption due to government programs
  • An estimated 0.25% represented actual addicts in the early part of the twentieth century CE
• Opium use was tied to civic and familial dishonor
	• No official laws against use, sales, or distribution of opium until the twentieth century CE
	• Opium use was seen to be similar to alcohol consumption in India
	• Higher overall rates of consumption, 5–8% of the total population was addicted to opium
	• Opium use was tied to personal honor

By 1906 CE, it was estimated that the dramatic social and political changes surrounding opium had little effect on consumption patterns or generation of new users[45]. Instead, the Chinese changes in opium tolerance and rehabilitation support saw rates of addiction as low as 0.5% of the total population with a subsequent reduction to 0.25% of the population. In 1906 CE, there were an estimated 27,000,000 Chinese people living in Qing China. At 0.5%, the number of Chinese opium addicts in 1906 CE would have been around 140,000. At 0.25%, the number of Chinese opium addicts in 1906 CE would have been ~67,000. The 0.5% figure is 60 times higher than the number of people in the United States who were prescribed Valium in 2019 CE at an estimated 8,400,000 people. By 2020 CE, there were an estimated 58 opioid prescriptions written for every 100 Americans, representing nearly 18,900,000 prescriptions written[46]. While the British at the close of the nineteenth century CE believed the Chinese selling opium in Southeast Asia was the most immoral and reprehensible action a nation could undertake, no one was prepared for the devastation prescription opioids would cause in the United States a century later.

REFERENCES

1. Bennett, J., (2018) A history of "Rationalism" in Victorian Britain. *Modern Intellectual History*, *15*(1), 63–91.
2. Descartes, R. (2012). La géométrie. In D. E. Smith & M. L. Latham (Eds.), *Discours de la methodé* (p. 272). Dover Publications Inc.
3. Kant, I. (2004 [1797 CE]). In M. Friedman (Ed.), *Die Metaphysik der Sitten* (p. 119). Cambridge University Press.
4. Hume, D. (2003 [1739 CE]). *A treatise of human nature: Being an attempt to introduce the experimental method of reasoning into moral subjects* (p. 455). Dover Publications, Inc.
5. Stachoň, M. (2021). Enlightenment and social progress – Back to the enlightenment. *Studia z Historii Filozofii*, *12*(4), 43–63.
6. Voltaire. (2005 [1759 CE]). *Candide, ou l'Optimisme*. Simon & Schuster.
7. Rousseau, J.-J. (2010 [1762]). *Du contrat social, ou, Principes du droit politique*. Ernest Flammarion.
8. Locke, J. (1995 [1692 CE]). *An essay concerning human understanding*. Prometheus Books.
9. Smale, R. *Addiction and creativity: from laudanum to recreational drugs. Journal of Psychiatric and Mental |Health Nursing*, *8*(5), 459–463.
10. Levitt, R. (2013). Unsafe Medicine: Laudanum in the 19th Century. *Wellcome History*, 51,, 24–25.
11. Laamann, L. P. (2016). *Drugs and empire*. In J. M. MacKenzie et al. (Eds.), *The Encyclopedia of Empire* (p. 2816). Wiley-Blackwell.
12. Booth, M. (2013). *Opium: A history*. St. Martin's Griffin.
13. Young, G. (1753). *A treatise on opium, founded upon practical observations*. A. Millar.
14. Goethe, J. W. (2014 [1808 CE]). In M. Greenberg (Ed.), *Faust: A tragedy*. Yale University Press.
15. Schirmann, F. (2013). *Badness, madness and the brain – the late 19th-century controversy on immoral persons and their malfunctioning brains. History of the Human Sciences*, *26*(2), 33–50.

16. Rimke, H., &Hunt, A. (2002). *From sinners to degenerates: the medicalization of morality in the 19th century. History of the Human Sciences, 15*(1), 59–88.

17. Bynum, W. F. (1984). *Alcoholism and degeneration in 19th century European medicine and psychiatry. Addiction, 79*(4), 59–70.

18. Frankopan, P. (2015). *The silk roads: A new history of the world* (p. 636). Bloomsbury.

19. O'Rourke, K. H., de la Escosura, L. P., & Daudin, G. *Trade and empire.* In S. Broadberry & K. H. O'Rourke (Eds.), *The Cambridge economic history of modern Europe* (pp. 96–120). Cambridge University Press.

20. Da Gama, V. (2009 [1499 CE]). In G. J. Ames (Ed.). *Em nome de Deus: The journal of the first voyage of Vasco da Gama to India, 1497–1499* (Vol. 4, p. 182). Brill.

21. Boyajian, J. C. (2008). *Portuguese trade in Asia under the Habsburgs, 1580–1640.* The Johns Hopkins University Press.

22. Breen, B. (2019). *The age of intoxication: Origins of the global drug trade* (p. 288). University of Pennsylvania Press.

23. Faust, D. R. (2016). *The rise and fall of the Ming Dynasty* |(The Rise and Fall of Empires Ser.). Rosen Publishing Group.

24. Michael, F. (1986). *The Last of the Imperial Order: The Manchu or Ch'ing Dynasty* (pp. 159–174). Routledge

25. Ignaszewski, M.J., *The epidemiology of drug abuse.* The Journal of Clinical Pharmacology, *61*, S10–S17.

26. Courtwright, D. T. (2012). Addiction and the science of history. *Addiction, 107*(3), 486–492.

27. Berridge, V., & Mars, S. (2004). *History of addictions. Journal of Epidemiology & Community Health, 58*(9), 747–750.

28. Peterson, B. B. (Ed.) (2000). *Part VI: The Ming and Qing Dynasties and the Coming of the Opium Wars (pp. 1–12).* Routledge.

29. Hancock, J. F. *Spices, scents and silk: Catalysts of world trade* (p. 338). CAB International.

30. Sharman, J. C. (2019). Power and profit at sea: The rise of the West in the making of the international system. *International Security, 43*(4), 163–196.

31. Roukis, G. S. (2004). The British East India Company 1600–1858. *The Journal of Management Development, 23*(10), 938–948.

32. Miller, J., & Stanczak, G. (2009). Redeeming, ruling, and reaping: British Missionary Societies, the East India Company, and the India-to-China Opium Trade. *Journal for the Scientific Study of Religion, 48*(2), 332–352.

33. Hanes, W. T., & Sanello, F. *The opium wars: the addiction of one empire and the corruption of another.* Sourcebooks, Inc.

34. Melancon, G. (1999). Honour in Opium? The British Declaration of War on China, 1839–1840. *The International History Review, 21*(4), 855–874.

35. Victoria, Q. (2014 [1907 CE]). In A. C. Benson & R. Brett (Eds.), *The Letters of Queen Victoria* (Vol. 2). Cambridge University Press.

36. Zhong, W. (2010). The roles of tea and opium in early economic globalization: A perspective on China's crisis in the 19th century. *Frontiers of History in China*, *5*(1), 86–105.

37. Cobbing, A. (2018) *A Victorian Embarrassment: Consular Jurisdiction and the Evils of Extra-territoriality.* International history review, *40*(2), 273–291.

38. Fay, P.W. (1970). The French Catholic Mission in China during the Opium War. *Modern Asian Studies*, *4*(2), 115–128.

39. Vann, M. G. (2010). Of pirates, postcards, and public beheadings: The pedagogic execution in French Colonial Indochina. *Historical Reflections*, *36*(2), 39–58.

40. Yu, B. (2015). China-Russia relations: Tales of Two Parades, Two Drills, and Two Summits. *Comparative Connections*, *17*(2), 147–161.

41. Waley, A. (2013 [1958 CE]). *The opium war through Chinese eyes*. Routledge.

42. Macauley, M. A. (2009). Small Time Crooks: Opium, Migrants, and the War on Drugs in China, 1819–1860. *Late Imperial China*, *30*(1), 1–47.

43. Windle, J. (2012). Insights for contemporary drug policy: A historical account of opium control in India and Pakistan. *Asian Journal of Criminology*, *7*(1), 55–74.

44. Richards, J. F. (1981). The Indian empire and peasant production of opium in the nineteenth century. *Modern Asian Studies*, *15*(1), 59–82.

45. Feige, C., & Miron, J. A. The opium wars, opium legalization and opium consumption in China. *Applied Economics Letters*, *15*(12), 911–913.

46. Jalali, M. S., et al. (2020). The opioid crisis: a contextual, social-ecological framework. *Health Research Policy and Systems*, *18*(1), 1–9.

Chapter 10

The Great Equalizer

Poison has always been a part of human civilization. It is laden with curiosity and genius, scientific discoveries, and empirical knowledge interwoven with intrigues, crimes, politics, personal tragedies or successes, wars, and natural disasters. Our knowledge of toxic substances has grown in tandem with our knowledge of medicines[1]. *Poison* can be defined as any substance natural or manmade capable of causing illness or death when introduced or absorbed by a living being. Poisons can be simple or complex in their chemical structures. Poisons cover a broad range of chemicals, including pesticides, herbicides, industrial solvents, house-hold chemicals, prescription drugs, illicit drugs, venom, plant extracts, and microbial excretions, to name a few. Some chemicals become poisons when used inappropriately or in great quantity. Just as medicines can become deadly when used inappropriately or in sufficient quantity. Poisons are characterized by biologists as harmful substances absorbed by the body, the skin, the lungs, or the digestive tract. *Venoms* are organic poisons that are injected by a bite, sting, or spray. *Toxins* are used to classify all organic poisons that are produced by living things and are created by a function of nature. Toxins are produced by bacteria, fungi, plants, insects, amphibians, marine fish and plants, animals, and reptiles such as snakes and lizards. Toxins can activate a harmful chemical reaction, alter a metabolic enzyme or reaction, promote or demote concentrations of chemicals within the body, and disrupt normal chemical or electrical responses throughout the body. The use of poisons is at least as old as human civilization (10,000 BCE) but most assuredly stretches further back into human pre-history. Poisons have been used for many purposes across the vast span of human existence as weapons, anti-venoms, and even medicines. Poisons have given rise to toxicology. *Toxicology* is a formalized branch of science intimately concerned with the nature, effects, and detection of poisons. Toxicology draws from related fields such as biochemistry, histology, pharmacology, pathology, anatomy, and physiology to understand and classify poisons and their symptomology. The study and classification of toxic substances became a systematic field of inquiry in the late nineteenth century CE.

Poison was known by our earliest ancestors and used by both ancient tribes and early civilizations. It was most likely used for hunting and war. As a tool for hunting, poison would quicken and ensure the death of prey. As a tool for war, poison would make an enemy sick, paralyzed, or hasten their death. Poisons became more advanced and ancient cultures began forging weapons designed specifically for the delivery of poisons. We know that ancient peoples used conventional weapons such as axes, clubs, spears, and eventually swords (Figure 10.1). There was a refinement

Figure 10.1   Example of Indigenous Poison Darts in the Amazon

Ammit Jack/Shutterstock.com

to armaments as humans continuously sought to find more subtle and destructive means to cause death[2]. Poison was the means to achieve this goal. Archaeologists have found spear shafts and tips with specialized grooves that would have been used for storing or holding poisons like tubocurarine[3, 4]. *Tubocurarine* is a toxic alkaloid found in the bark of a climbing vine found in Columbia, Venezuela, and Brazil from the Chondrodendron tomentosum vine, and is known for its use in poison darts and arrows by indigenous peoples[5]. Tubocurarine is a powerful paralytic that causes a decrease in muscle activity of the voluntary muscle groups. The use and existence of toxic substances would have been highly prized, and knowledge was held as secret by higher-ranked members of a tribe or clan. Toxins would have been emblems of great power as they could appear to take away life through magic or other worldly powers. Toxins would have added to the mystique of medicine men, witches, sorcerers, and witch doctors making them more foreboding[2, 6].

The danger with any substance, poisons included, lies in the dosage. Some extremely dangerous substances are relatively harmless in small doses, but anything can become toxic if enough is ingested or absorbed. The act of poisoning in ancient times was often used as a subtle and mysterious means of killing. Poison was often reserved for higher-ranking members of tribes. The sudden and often violent deaths from poisonings led to the association in some cultures with poisons being akin to dark magic, spirits, and otherworldly creatures, demons, or gods[7]. The varied ways in which tribes, nations, and civilizations throughout history have plotted with poison against enemies and allies alike are inestimable. Poison was impossible to detect by early healers and physicians. If poison was suspected, it was difficult to determine which poison was used. The problem with accurate diagnosis spilled over into the creation of accurate antidotes, which were not exactly useful even when the poison was known. As bountiful as the poisons were in antiquity, the volume of individuals who trafficked in them was even more copious[1]. There were very few regulations and even less restrictions on dangerous plants, animals, and minerals throughout our distant past. Exotic substances from far and wide could easily be obtained assuming one had enough coin and was willing to pay.

For much of our history, we derived poisons from natural sources, from plants, animals, and mineral sources[8]. *Animal poisons* included cantharadine (blister beetles), toads, frogs, and salamanders. Poisonous insects, snakes, spiders, and scorpions were used depending on location and availability. *Mineral poisons* were drawn from minerals such as lead, mercury, copper, arsenic, and antimony. Artisans and craftspeople who worked with lead, silver, or gold would occasionally be subjected to fumes from the smelting processes of these metals and in some cases would die because of their craft. *Vegetable poisons* were among the best-known poisons and frequently used to profound effect. Some of the deadliest plants like belladonna, henbane, datura, rhododendron, mandrake, monkshood, hemlock, hellebore, and opium were widely known and deftly applied as poisons. Professional poisoners were known to test the potency of their mixtures, which usually contained multiple toxins, on animals, slaves, and convicts. Mass poisoning did occur in rare instances and would occur more frequently during stressful periods like during wars or disease epidemics. Poison in human history has been seen as the great equalizer. It can be administered by anyone, and it has the potential to affect everyone. It does not require brute strength or keen intellect to be delivered. It crosses boundaries of age, sex, gender, race, and ethnicity to harm and kill without prejudice.

10.1 The Poisonous Houses of the Renaissance

"Lasciate ogne speranza, voi ch'intrate[1]" – Dante Alighieri[9]

The Italian Renaissance peaked during the *Quattrocento* (fifteenth) and *Cinquecento* (sixteenth) centuries CE. Italy had attempted to maintain as much of the culture of Rome as it could but much of the ancient world had fallen to ruin. This period of time is best known for its resurgence of and rekindled interest in art, architecture, sculpture, literature, music, philosophy, science, and exploration[10]. Throughout the Renaissance, Italy was embroiled in war. Northern Italy and Upper Central Italy were divided into several warring city-states led by noble houses. Dominant cities included Milan, Firenze (Florence), Pisa, Siena, Genova (Genoa), Ferrara, Mantova (Mantua), Verona, and Venezia (Venice). A series of domestic disputes, foreign invasions, and feudal states competing for power in Italy was the make-up of the Italian Wars (1494–1559 CE). These wars drove diplomacy and intrigue, often employed in conjunction, to new and unique levels of utility. One of the many arts cultivated during this turbulent period was the black art of poisoning.

During the Renaissance, wine and food were the most preferred means of delivering poison to a target. Poison jewelry were very fashionable and were available as rings, necklaces, and amulets with hidden compartments to conceal poison[11].

Poison jewelry was all the rage among courtiers, assassins, and even clergy (Figure 10.2). Not all poison jewelry contained poisons, some carried antidotes and cure-alls and some were used to smuggle secret notes. During the Italian Renaissance, poison became a popular form of killing. The increase in poison was stimulated by their increased availability. Between the 1500s and 1700s CE it was quite easy to acquire poisons from apothecaries, physicians, herbalists, trades people, alchemists, and sorcerers. Artisans and artists were an additional source for poisons as things like wood varnishes, gold leaf materials,

Figure 10.2 Example of a Poison Ring

Art_Pictures/Shutterstock.com

---

[1] "Abandon all hope, ye who enter here"; Dante calls out the quote written above the gates of Dis in the second layer of hell in the book Inferno: La Divina Commedia.

and some pigments for paint were made from highly toxic minerals[12, 13]. Some examples of materials used by artisans included white lead, lead antimonite yellow, cinnabar, and green arsenic to name a few. *Apothecaries* sold various medicinal wares, were open to the public, and substances traditionally used for curative purposes were employed for sinister and diabolic means[14].

The Italian Renaissance was a hotbed of political, economic, and social intrigue. No families epitomized this better than the noble Houses of Borgia and de'Medici. Jealousy, intrigue, and homicide surrounded these families. The Borgia and de'Medici are believed to have dispatched those who thwarted their political, economic, or social plans with arsenic or cantarella or similar poisons delivered through the food they provided to their guests and enemies. Murder by poison required administering a poison in repeated or large doses, depending upon the poison selected and the urgency behind the murder. Women and teenagers could conveniently perform the delivery of poison as they were trusted with the preparation of food, serving of wine, or administration of medicines[15]. Renaissance women of nobility had plenty of reasons to commit murder due to lack of economic opportunity, limited property rights, and difficulty in escaping the marriage bond (often arranged by their father without their consent).

Figure 10.3 Engraving of Pope Alexander VI

Morphart Creation/Shutterstock.com

Rodrigo Lanzol Borgia (1431–1503 CE) was appointed Cardinal by Pope Callixtus in 1455 CE and became Pope Alexander VI (Figure 10.3) in 1492 CE[16]. Pope Alexander VI was the richest man in the College of Cardinals, a known nepotist, and highly immoral. He practiced simony, the buying and selling of ecclesiastical privileges and indulgences. Simony was considered highly sacrilegious as it consisted of buying spiritual favors in return for temporal money. It is the selling of divine grace by a human being who has no ownership over the divine. In addition, Pope Alexander VI practiced *lechery*, which was excessive or offensive sexually activities or lustfulness[17]. The Vatican during Pope Alexander VI hosted lavish sex parties where prostitutes were known to attend. Pope Alexander VI encouraged bishops and cardinals to increase their wealth through their privileges from the church. He would then invite the rich cardinals and bishops to sumptuous meals at the Borgia residence. The *regalo dei Borgia*[2] a codename for their favored poison la cantarella would be given to the wealthy clergy. Under the current catholic laws, ownership of the property of cardinals and bishops would revert to the church on their death, which meant that all their accumulated wealth went directly to Pope Alexander VI. These tricks allowed the Borgia to become one of the wealthiest and most powerful Houses in Italy. The Borgia dynasty finally broke as by divine justice, Pope Alexander VI had mistakenly drunk poisoned wine intended for a guest at one of his many banquets[18].

Lucrezia Borgia (1480–1519 CE), Duchess-Consort of Ferrara, Modena, and Reggio, was a Spanish-Italian noblewoman of the illustrious House of Borgia (Borja in Spanish). Think murder by poison during the Renaissance, and Lucrezia Borgia comes quickly to mind (Figure 10.4). Willful,

---

[2] Italian for "gift of the Borgia".

beautiful, socially keen, sexually promiscuous, and by historical reputation ruthless, Lucrezia was said to rival her brother Cesare and her father, Pope Alexander VI, in jealousy, intrigue, and homicide. She was known to dispatch those who thwarted her political and economic ambitions with a dash of white arsenic in their drinks. Exceedingly rare during the Italian Renaissance, she reigned as the Governor of Spoleto, a position usually reserved for cardinals. Her father was a cunning and ruthless politician who personally arranged Lucrezia's three marriages with the strategy of a master chess player. Each of Lucrezia's marriages advanced the Borgia's political positioning (see Table 10.1).

Figure 10.4 Lucrezia Borgia

Source: Lucrezia Borgia, Duchess of Ferrara, Dosso Dossi (Italian, 1489–1542), https://artvee.com/dl/lucreziaborgia-duchess-of-ferrara/

Table 10.1 Husbands of Lucrezia Borgia

Arranged Husbands of Lucrezia Borgia
Giovanni Sforza (1466–1510 CE), Lord of Pesaro and Gradara, Count of Catignola
Alfonso d'Aragona (1481–1500 CE), Duke of Bisceglie and Prince of Salerno
Alfonso d'Este (1476–1534 CE), Duke of Ferrara, Modena, and Reggio

Lucrezia was highly educated and was reportedly able to speak fluent Spanish, Catalan, Italian, and French. In addition, she could read Latin and Greek. She was described as having a natural beauty and a grace that made her to appear to "walk on air" [19]. There was a darker side to Lucrezia as there were several allegations of incest with her brother Cesare Borgia, claims of poisonings of rival families, and murder of secret lovers. The writers and sources of the time disagree and contradict one another with great frequency regarding Lucrezia's culpability with some of the alleged poisonings. We may never know the full truth about Lucrezia, but she is from one of the most influential and dubious Houses of Renaissance Italy.

Arsenic is a grey-appearing metalloid (Figure 10.5) and exists in its metallic state in three forms: yellow, black, and grey with grey being the predominate type[20]. Arsenic poisoning manifests in two distinct ways through short- and long-term poisoning. Short-term poisoning occurs over a brief exposure period with symptoms of vomiting, abdominal pain, encephalopathy, and watery diarrhea that contains blood. Long-term poisoning occurs over an extended exposure period with symptoms of thickening of the skin, darker color skin tone, abdominal pain, diarrhea, heart disease, neuropathy, convulsions, and tumor growth. The end result of arsenic poisoning is coma and death. The organs of the body typically affected by arsenic are

Figure 10.5 Grey Arsenic Metallic Crystals

MarcelClemens/Shutterstock.com

the lungs, skin, kidneys, and liver. The symptoms of arsenic poisoning resemble cholera, which was a common occurrence in the cities of Renaissance Italy, as a result arsenic poisoning often went undetected[21]. Arsenic carries the moniker of "inheritance powder" because impatient heirs were known or suspected to use arsenic to accelerate the receipt of their inheritances[20].

Pedro "Perotto" Calderón (????–1498 CE) was a Spanish man born of the lower nobility and served as Chamberlain to Pope Alexander VI. Among the ladies in waiting of the House of Borgia he was often referred to as *dell'ingombrante*[3][22]. Perotto is believed to be the father of an illegitimate son of Lucrezia Borgia known by the moniker *Infans Romanus*. Lucrezia's son, Giovanni Borgia, was issued a papal bull (public decree) that recognized him as the adopted son of Pope Alexander VI, earning him the nickname "Infant of Rome." The body of Pedro and one of Lucrezia's handmaidens, Pantasilea, were found floating in the Tiber River on Valentine's Day in 1498 CE. Sources writing during this time indicate the deaths were due to La Cantarella, most likely administered by Cesare[22].

The ideal poison should be reliable, effective, deceptive, and slow acting but strong enough to kill the intended victim. The Borgias specialized in disposing of cardinals, bishops, nobles, and rivals by using several kinds of poisons, such as arsenic, strychnine, cantharidin, and aconite. They would have incorporated these poisons into drinks, clothes, gloves, book pages, flowers, and "medicines"[15]. The latter being the most insidious, as the Borgia would claim to be assisting you in your time of need, but their medicines tended to hasten one's death, not keep it at bay. ***La Cantarella*** was a deadly concoction created and used by the Borgia to fatal ends. The recipe was a family secret, however, scholars believe it was a variation of arsenic mixed with phosphorous and other compounds with the full composition remaining unknown to date[23]. From fragmented accounts, it appears that cantarella was a complex mixture consisting of arsenic combined with the alkaloids of putrefaction secreted by the corpses of dead animals in the late stages of decay[1]. The Italian historian and physician, Paolo Giovo (1483–1552 CE) had indicated that cantarella was an off-white powder with a pleasant taste which resembled sugar[24]. Cantarella was almost always mixed in liqueur or fortified wines and served in small amounts. Further, Giovio alluded to the fact that the efficacy of the poison was proved in several murders[22]. Cantarella was described as functioning with time-clock precision and depending on the desires of the poisoner, it could kill in a day, a month, or even a year. Victims were recorded as presenting with a variety of symptoms including confusion, vomiting, abdominal pain, and diarrhea all of which could mimic several diseases of the time[23]. La Cantarella was a mysterious name to give the poison… in Italian it means "little songbird," in Latin it means "small cup," in Greek it means "drinking cup," and in Spanish it means "sing it." We may never know why the Borgia called it la cantarella, but it was feared by many of the Italian nobility.

Cesare Borgia (1475–1507 CE), Duke of Valentinois, was a Spanish-Italian nobleman, politician, and ex-cardinal of the House of Borgia[22]. Cesare served as *Condottiero*[4] for King Louis XII of France. Cesare was the first person in history to resign a cardinalate, which he did in 1498 CE. His fight for political power served as a major inspiration for *Il Principe* by Niccolò Machiavelli[25]. Cesare had carved out a state for himself in Central Italy but was unable to hold the state together and according to Machiavelli it was due to illness not a lack of foresight or determination of will. Cesare was the last

---

[3] Italian for bulky, cumbersome, unwieldy, or troublesome.
[4] Italian formal title for the captain of a mercenary or hired group of professional soldiers.

Italian benefactor of Leonardo da Vinci, whom he employed as a military architect and engineer[26]. After his work with Cesare, da Vinci was unsuccessful in finding further patronage in Italy. Cesare was known to wear luxurious and gaudy garments bedazzled with many valuable metals and gems. He wore a leather mask over half his face, due to disfigurement caused by advanced stages of syphilis in the later part of his life. Machiavelli described him as secretive and taciturn, loquacious and boastful, having an inexhaustible energy, and an unrelenting genius in military and diplomatic affairs[27].

Caterina Sforza (1463–1509 CE), Countess of Forlì and Dowager Lady of Imola, was an Italian noblewoman[28]. She was the illegitimate daughter of Galeazzo Maria Sforza, Duke of Milan. Caterina was married three times, the first two were arranged marriages for political gain and the last one was by choice and for love (see Table 10.2). Caterina was devoted to practicing alchemy and had many rare occult books, and it was believed that she had a good working knowledge of poisons[29]. She had even written her own alchemical set of recipes for beauty[30]. Caterina loved hunting and was a skilled archer, often being able to outshoot many of her noblemen. She had a passion for dancing and loved to host lavish balls. Caterina resisted Cesare Borgia, who had attempted to take her lands by conquest. She was captured and forced to face his fury and imprisonment in Rome for 3 months. In the final months of her life, Caterina confessed to a monk in Forlì about her time in captivity, she stated *"se io potessi scrivere tutto, farei stupire il mondo*[5]*"*[31].

Table 10.2 Marriages of Caterina Sforza

Husbands of Caterina Sforza
Girolamo Riaro (1443–1488 CE), Count of Forlì and Imola
Giacomo Feo (1471–1495 CE), Count of Forlì
Giovanni de'Medici il Popolano (1467–1498 CE)

The House of Medici was founded by an Italian family in the Republic of Firenze, Tuscany, who made their fortune through banking. They owned and controlled the largest and one of the most prosperous banks in Europe, which allowed them to gain political power and prestige. The de'Medici became the Vatican's bankers. In Firenze exist the Medici Granducal Archives, where in generations of de'Medici journals, writings, and accumulated knowledge are preserved[32]. Among the texts there exists knowledge on poisons, drugs, alchemy, magical recipes, and antidotes from notable members of the family such as Cosimo Pater Patriae de'Medici, Caterina Sforza, Grand Duke Cosimo I and his sons, and Catherine de'Medici. The Grand Dukes of the de'Medici tested poisons and potential antidotes on death-row convicts and recorded the outcomes with morose detail of the play-by-play from exposure to death[33]. Records from the city councils of Frienze contained detailed testimony of poisoning "contracts" arranged by de'Medici family members. These records boldly named victims and amounts paid for their confirmed deaths, complete with dates and when tractions were completed, and the number of payments made.

Giovanni di Pierfrancesco de'Medici (1467–1498 CE) was born as an Italian nobleman of the House of Medici of Firenze[34]. He was stripped of formal titles in his childhood and became *il*

---

[5] Italian translation: "if I could write everything that happened, I would shock the world."

Popolano[6]. Giovanni was the son of Pierfrancesco di Lorenzo de'Medici, a member of a secondary branch of the House of Medici. After his father's death, which was attributed to poisoning, Giovanni was sent to live with his cousin Lorenzo il Magnifico de'Medici. Lorenzo kept all of Giovanni's inheritance and spent it frivolously, instead of being a responsible administrator of Giovanni's trust. Giovanni was exiled from Firenze in 1494 CE. One year before his death, Giovanni married Caterina Sforza, Lady of Forlì and Imola. His heir and son, Giovanni dale Bande Nere de'Medici became Duchy of Mantua. Sources writing at the time of his death provide mixed accounts, some indicate he died of natural causes, while other believed he was poisoned by his own cousins[27].

Figure 10.6   Catherine de'Medici, Engraved Illustration

Morphart Creation/Shutterstock.com

Catherine de'Medici (1519–1589 CE) was the Black Queen of France[35]. She earned the moniker Black Queen due to her known affiliation with the Italian necromancer Cosimo Ruggeri and French diviner Nostradamus (Figure 10.6). These affiliations made people at the French royal court see her as a practitioner of the Dark Arts. Adding to the mystique were the number of bodies that seemed to amass in her wake. Catherine was thought of as a sorceress, because of her knowledge and the access she had to very skilled scientists. It is difficult to get a full understanding or appreciation of who Catherine was, because so many of her contemporaries went to great lengths to paint her as being powerful or wicked or both. Before being married to the King of France, she was trained in Italy as a de'Medici, which meant she learned the subtle art of making poisons or potions to murder people who stood in her way. Her 50 years in the French royal court did require that she maintain power, often by using poison or the fear of it, to keep her rivals at bay. Catherine was surrounded by her *escadron volant*[7], who were a cadre of beautiful women who were fiercely loyal to their queen and were known to do whatever was necessary to help Catherine maintain power in court. A cunning example exists in how Catherine manipulated the women in the French court to adopt the custom of perfuming their leather gloves[36]. These perfumed gloves, or "sweet gloves," were scented with herbs, spices, woods, and flowers, featuring jasmine, violet, iris, and orange blossom. She then used the perfume against those in her retinue that spoke ill of her or who needed to be removed by providing them with her own poisoned perfumes. The unsuspecting ladies would apply the poisonous perfumes to their gloves and as they sweat, the poison would be absorbed into their skin much more efficiently.

Isabella di Aragona (1470–1524 CE), Princess of Naples, Duchess Consort of Milan; *suo jure*[8] Duchess of Bari, Princess of Rossano and Lady of Ostuni, was an Italinan noblewoman whose life

---

[6] Italian translates to "the commoner."
[7] French translated to "flying squadron."
[8] Latin translated to "in one's own right," used to denote a noble title that was owned instead of gained through marriage.

was characterized by political crises caused by the Italian Civil Wars[37]. She found herself often torn between her native Kingdom of Naples and her marital home of the Duchy of Milan. She was married to Gian Galeazzo Sforza, which was a difficult marriage and she had little support from the people in Milan. Her husband preferred the company of young men and only fulfilled his husbandly duties on four known occasions to father his four children[38]. Her husband was killed during the war under dubious causes and the House of Sforza lost many of its holdings. Louis XII of France absconded with her son in a scathing letter stating he took the young man "to France to marry his daughter." In reality Isabella's son was taken to a monastery, and she never saw him again. Isabella petitioned Emperor Maximilian to liberate her son from France, but her plea fell on deaf ears. As a result, Isabella developed a hatred for the French and did everything she could to remove all French presence from her beloved Italy. Reflecting on the tragedies she had endured, she began signing official documents as *Isabella, unica nella*[9] *disgrazia [39]*. Her daughter Bona was shipped off for marriage to become the Queen of Poland. Isabella died from mercury poisoning, which she was using to treat the advanced stages of syphilis. It has never been proven, but Historians believe she was the inspiration behind da Vinci's Mona Lisa[26].

Niccolò di Bernardo dei Machiavelli (1469–1527 CE), Secretary of the Second Chancery of the Republic of Firenze was an Italian diplomat, politician, historian, philosopher, and humanist[26]. He has been considered to be the father of modern political philosophy and political science (Figure 10.7). He is descended from the old Marquesses of Tuscany, architects of the Florentine *Gonfalonieres*[10]. Machiavelli lived during a very tumultuous era in Italy wherein Popes waged wars against Italian city-states. France, Spain, and the Holy Roman Empire all battled for reginal influence and control of the Papal seat. He served as a diplomat and military adviser of the de'Medici family. This work as a diplomat brought Machiavelli into contact with Cesare Borgia, Lucrezia Borgia, Caterina Sforza, and other prominent members of Italian nobility as he served in an official capacity for the House of de' Medici. Due to his interactions with the Borgia and de'Medici, Machiavelli had a healthy fear of poisoning. He feared poisoning more than any other form of death and was known to bring his own food and wine to banquets[16, 40].

Leonardo di ser Piero da Vinci (1452–1519 CE), was an Italian polymath[41]. Being born out of wedlock, his legal name contained *di ser Piero* indicating his father was of the nobility but did not claim him as a legitimate heir (Figure 10.8). Leonardo was an artist, sculptor, scientist, engineer, architect, and anatomist. He was the true definition of a "Renaissance man" or "universal genius." Today, he is best known for his artistic works, including the Mona Lisa, the Last Supper,

Figure 10.7 Machiavelli's Statue at Uffizi Gallery

James.Pintar/Shutterstock.com

---

[9] Italian, translation: "Isabella, unique in misfortune."
[10] Italian formal title, translated to "standard bearer." Was one of the highest levels of civic magistrates that could be bestowed.

Figure 10.8 da Vinci's Statue in Firenze, Italy

and the Vitruvian Man. Preserved and available for review in digital format his notebooks contained detailed drawings and notes on science and invention, anatomy, cartography, paining, paleontology, mathematics, architecture, machines, and engineering[42]. He conceptualized flying machines hydrodynamic power, optics, a type of armored fighting vehicle, concentrated solar power, an adding machine/computer, and the double hull[42]. He was commissioned by the Houses of the Borgia, de'Medici, Sforza, and Aragona for both art and devices of war[26].

A peculiar poison that became popular in the Renaissance was ***antimony***. Antimony is a lustrous grey metalloid found in nature as the sulfide mineral stibnite. Antimony has been used since ancient times as a powder for both medicine and cosmetics. As a cosmetic, antimony is best known as a key ingredient in making kohl, the eyeliner made famous by the Egyptians and later Persian empires. Certain compounds of antimony are highly toxic, in particular the forms of ***antimony trioxide*** and ***antimony potassium tartrate*** are exceptionally deadly[1]. When heated, antimony reacts with oxygen to produce antimony trioxide. Cups made from pure antimony were used to store wine for 24 hours, with the resulting solution becoming antimony potassium tartrate. Antimony potassium tartrate was initially used as a powerful emetic, however, during the Renaissance it was found to be more toxic than it was therapeutic[43]. Exposure would cause respiratory irritation, pneumoconiosis, antimony spots on the skin, acrid metallic taste, gastrointestinal distress, cardiac arrhythmias, profuse sweating, and excessive vomiting. The symptoms of poisoning from antimony potassium tartrate would begin manifesting about 30–45 minutes after ingestion. Effects varied based on the amount consumed and the period of exposure. If an individual survived an antimony poisoning, they would suffer from hair loss and develop a scaly skin rash known as lichen planus. Severe antimony poisoning closely resembled arsenic poisoning, which in turn mimicked the symptoms of cholera.

Poison during the Italian Renaissance was feared just as equally as it was revered, and it was utilized for political gain. It was exploited by Popes, nobility, and commoners with deadly and tragic success. Women employed it to escape marriages, gain land, and wealth. Men used it to remove political rivals, build wealth, and to wage war. It was given to prisoners to test the strength of new poisons or gain information on potential antidotes. Poison was easy to find and depending upon your social standing even more difficult to avoid. Among the ever-changing political backdrop of the Italian Renaissance, poison rose to become the great equalizer of men.

10.2 Political, Social, and Medical Uses of Poison

Historically, poisons have been used as political tools to maintain order, succession of monarchs, and preserve secrets. Poisons were used in times of war to help gain an advantage or protect key assets from falling to the enemy. In rare instances poisons were utilized as medicines, a few proving to be successful. Even with knowledge of the damage poisons could unleash, we have used them for cosmetic purposes; entrusting them to some of our most delicate body parts. The fear and unease surrounding poisons elevated them to the supernatural and we have, at times, associated poisons with witchcraft. In some locations we have both knowingly and unknowingly poisoned our own environment and ultimately our communities.

Despite the negative effects conferred by poison, which were abundant between the tenth and fourteenth centuries CE, the Persian Empire had found a few cures to exist among poisons. The general public of the time, however, viewed all medicine as poison and most were very distrusting of medicines. Iranian born Persian physician, philosopher, and scholar Muhammad ibn Zakaríya al-Razi had pioneered a unique use of poison for treatment[44]. Better known in the Western world by his Latinized name, Rhazes. His discovery was related to mercury chloride, which was known to apothecaries and alchemists as ***corrosive sublimate***. Corrosive sublimate was used to create an ointment used to cure what Rhazes described as "the itch," which today we know as scabies. Scabies is an infestation caused by a mite, Sarcoptes scabiei. The mites burrow under the skin to lay their eggs in the upper layer of the skin. There is an intensely painful rash caused by the mites as they burrow and the rash spreads as their eggs hatch. Corrosive sublimate was an effective treatment because of mercury's ability to penetrate the skin. The poisonous nature of mercury effectively killed the eggs and mature mites. As the mites and their eggs died the itch dissipated.

Poisoning during the Reformation period of England (1509–1688 CE) was regarded as one of the most cowardly and unsporting methods of murder. Poisoning was seen as exclusively a wife's weapon because it was her main duty to provision the house, and she alone oversaw cooking. This gave women ample opportunity to poison their husbands. During Tudor and Stuart England, the heart of the Reformation, poisoning of a husband or employer was seen as a kind of petty treason by common law. Sir John Coke (1563–1644 CE) a member of parliament in the British House of Commons had detailed the hideousness of poisoning: "…of all murders poisoning is ye worst and most horrible: 1. Because it is secret; 2. Because it is not to be prevented; 3. Because it is most against nature and therefore most heinous; 4. It is also a cowardly thing"[11]. When women did poison their husbands, they were often accused of witchcraft. There is a famous case involving Mary Bell[11], who was brought to court for the alleged poisoning of her husband in 1657 CE. The difficulty with poisoning of the time was that they were "invisible" crimes. Poisoning was seen as a very vicious way to murder someone, as poison allows for no self-defense, no way for the victim to understand what is happening to them, and was frequently done in secret usually over an extended period of time. In addition to poisoning, Mary Bell was charged with witchcraft with the charge claiming she had mixed potions and used evil charms against her husband. ***Witchcraft*** by definition is the use of sorcery or dark magic wherein the practitioner is in direct communication with the devil or a familiar. Poisoning because of its deception and secrecy was often linked to witchcraft. As it would occur at many points in human history, witchcraft was a claim made by powerful men intent on charging powerless women with a falsified crime. Frequently this claim led to the torture of women as the male authorities attempted to obtain a confession. Many women underwent deadly tests to prove they were not witches, like the swimming test or the search for witches marks on their bodies. There was a lot of hullabaloo surrounding Mary Bell's alleged treasonous behavior, the cold-blooded way she had used poison, her malice and wickedness were shown as signs of her consort with the devil. Her trial was a sham, and the prosecutors blurred the lines between witchcraft, murder, and treason to paint a ghastly picture of Mary Bell before her jurors.

---

[11] Date of birth and date of death not recorded.

Figure 10.9 Salem Witch Trials

WITCHCRAFT AT SALEM VILLAGE.

Everett Collection/Shutterstock.com

Colonial history of the United States had a very famous set of witch hunts that occurred in the sleepy little hamlet of Salem Village in the Massachusetts Bay Colony between 1692 and 1693 CE. The witch hunts were the combined efforts to identify witches, rather than a coordinated pursuit of known witches. These events most likely put all of the women of Salem Village on edge, as any behavior that was not congruent with Puritanical behavior would have potentially marked her for investigation. A series of accusations led to investigations and ultimately persecutions of 19 witches[45]. The convicted witches went to the gallows for crimes that we believe today were to have been the result of ergotism from contaminated rye. Two young girls, Betty Parris and Abigail Williams, both had severe convulsions and displayed odd and strange behavior in the early summer of 1692 CE[46]. The village doctor, William Griggs, after much deliberation and reluctance diagnosed the girls as bewitched[46]. Shortly after the diagnosis, other members of the Salem Village began having similar symptoms (Figure 10.9). The townsfolk voted to search for and persecute all witches within Salem. Many of the reported symptoms related to the bewitching of Salem Village can be explained by the symptoms of ergot-induced poisoning. Because medical and scientific knowledge was sparse, the fungus on the rye was probably chalked up to sunburn or lack of water making the rye look a little different. No one would have really given it much consideration as the rye was needed to make flour for bread. After eating contaminated rye bread, the ergotism would have caused the muscles to twitch and spasm, severe convulsions would have followed, delusions and hallucinations would have been produced as the lysergic acid in the ergot was metabolized. Doctor Griggs who was a deeply religious and devoted man was most likely unaware of ergotism and would have looked for other explanations of the odd behavior of the young girls, coming to the conclusion that the events witnessed were emblematic of witchcraft.

Humans have been known to poison themselves for beauty. During the Renaissance we used belladonna to dilate the pupils of women to make them appear more seductive. In the Roman Era, the Middle Ages, and the seventeenth century CE women used lead-based powders and creams to make their skin appear fairer. And in the modern era, we use Botox (botulinum toxin) to remove wrinkles on the face, help with underarm sweating, and, more recently, as a way to enhance ones testicular assets[47]. Cosmetics have had a long history of using poisonous materials all in the name of beauty. In the 1800s CE, a Victorian practice to keep one's face looking youthful required that women coat their face with opium before going to bed. Upon waking, to complete the youthful look, the woman was instructed to briskly wash her face with ammonia. If you had sparse eyebrows or if your eyelashes were not voluminous, mercury applied nightly was used. The Sears & Roebuck company in the United States carried a product called Dr. Campbell's Arsenic Complexion Soap, which one could scrub their way to a lighter complexion[48]. White lead powders, vermillion lipstick (red mercury sulfide), and red lead rouge were still in use well into the 1960s CE.

Figure 10.10   Pewter on Display Henry Whitfield House

LEE SNIDER PHOTO IMAGES/Shutterstock.com

In the United States, during the colonial period (1607–1776 CE), lead exposure was an unpleasant fact of everyday life. *Lead poisoning* has long lasting toxic effects[49, 50]. It can enter the body after dissolving in water, milk, wine, vinegar, or acidic food that had been served from or stored in leaden containers (Figure 10.10). It can be inhaled as a dust or absorbed through the skin. The circulatory system deposits lead in internal organs, where it remains for weeks. Lead damages the brain and nervous system, kidneys, and intestines. In the bone, lead accumulates and can last for decades.

Most who are exposed to lead get the *dry gripes* an extreme abdominal pain caused by lead poisoning. In Colonial America, all but the very poorest of the colonists ate and drank from lead-glazed earthenware and used drinking cups and eating utensils made from pewter (an alloy of tin and lead). The wealthy Colonial Americans not only dined on pewter but also displayed it lavishly in their homes. Also, anyone who shouldered a musket during the American Revolutionary War (1775–1783 CE) touched lead while loading or casting musket balls and shot.

Supposedly the creation of a seventeenth century Sicilian woman named Giulia Tofana (1651 CE), *Aqua Tofana* was colorless, tasteless, and odorless, and was believed to have been a composite mixture of, arsenic, blister beetle venom, pennywort, and snapdragon[51]. It could purportedly kill with deadly precision. The doses of Aqua Tofana could be calculated to kill immediately, in a week, a month, or years later, for the poisoner who wanted the plausibility of a natural death or to ensure they had a believable alibi[52]. Some accounts indicate that victims gradually lost their hair and teeth and would shrivel up as if all the water had been drawn out of their body until they finally died in agony. Others indicated there were no serious symptoms at all, that the victims simply fell into lethargy from which they would never recover. The poison was typically administered via food, but it could be applied to the cheek if the victim were likely to kiss it[53]. Giulia bottled her deadly liquid in innocuous-looking cosmetic vials. Since most of her customers were women looking to do away with their husbands, the cosmetic bottles would have been indistinguishable from the other nostrums and treatments found in a lady's vanity. Pope Clement XIV (1705–1774 CE) was rumored to have been a victim of Aqua Tofana, as was Wolfgang Amadeus Mozart[54]. In 1829 CE, 38 years after his death, his widow Constanze told Mozart enthusiasts Vincent and Mary Novello that on his deathbed Mozart had declared "I am sure that I have been poisoned. I cannot rid myself of this idea ... Someone has given me Aqua Tofana and calculated the precise time of my death"[55]. Giulia did meet justice when a soldier identified her attempting to flee Rome wearing a nun's habit. Under torture, she confessed to poisoning over 500 men all through the use and sale of her poison between the years of 1633 and 1651 CE. In one version of the capture of Giulia, she and her daughter were executed for murder in Campo de' Fiori in Rome in 1651 CE[51]. Additionally, three of her assistants and ~30 lower-class women who were customers of Giulia were summarily executed. Customers of Giulia who were from the upper class had a vastly different outcome. Some were imprisoned and some even escaped punishment altogether by asserting they had no knowledge that "cosmetics" were capable of being poisons. In other retellings, Giulia and her daughter were brutally beaten to death by an angry mob who had chased them through the streets of Rome... One thing is certain, Giulia eventually faced justice for her work as a poisoner.

In the mid-1600 to early 1700s CE in France, a unique phrase came into being that tried to make light of the string of poisonings that were occurring among the upper classes. ***Poudre de succession***, "succession" or "inheritance powder," was the phrase that would become synonymous with arsenic. Thanks to a string of wives and children of well-to-do husbands and fathers who had mysteriously and unexpectedly died, the French adopted the moniker as a way indicate the utility of the poison. The disposal of troublesome heirs via poisons was supposedly initiated by Marie-Madeleine-Marguerite d'Aubray, Marquise de Brinvilliers (1630–1676 CE)[56, 57]. The Marquise had killed her father in 1666 CE and then set in motion the murder of her brothers Antoine and François D'Aubray in 1670 CE[58]. This gained her through inheritance the family fortune and titles. In 1672 CE, the Marquise's lover, Captain Godin de Sainte-Croix, died mysteriously. Among his possessions, he left a red leather box full of poisons and all of Marquise de Brinvillier's letters, which accounted in grand detail all the treacherous and despicable activities she had perpetrated. The Marquise fled for her life, but eventually was found by a gendarme and brought to Paris, where she was beheaded, and, for good measure, her body burned. Her legacy, however, was the phrase *poudre de succession* which remains to describe the rationale used to gain the inheritance of her male family members via poison[59].

In 1873, a grisly account of murder and fraud took center stage in the British newspapers as accounts of Mary Ann Cotton (1832–1873 CE), referred to as "The Black Widow," was tried and convicted of poisoning her stepson, Charles Edward Cotton, with arsenic[60]. She is believed to have been a serial killer, who killed 11 of her 13 children and 3 of her 4 husbands, all of whom she had been named as sole benefactor on their insurance policies. This was the first-time science had been utilized in a court case as the physician who attended Charles had kept blood and urine samples. Utilizing the relatively new method for detecting the presence of arsenic in tissue samples, the jury was provided with irrefutable proof of the poison used. Mary was sent to the gallows on 24 March 1873 CE, and reports indicate that she did not die on the gallows quickly. The rope was set too short, and her neck did not break immediately, instead she died by strangulation[60]. She did not confess to the other numerous murders that surrounded her, but her demeanor on the day of her execution seemed to indicate she was responsible.

Figure 10.11   Grigori Rasputin

Grigori Rasputin (1869–1916 CE) proved to be a very difficult man to kill (Figure 10.11). On 30 December 1916, a group of nobles summoned him to the home of Prince Felix Yusupov and set into motion their attempt to end the life of the powerful holy man[61]. They began by poisoning him with cyanide laced tea and cakes with no change in his demeanor. His assassins then gave him three glasses of wine, which had been laced with cyanide. While he appeared to get drunk from the wine, the cyanide did not seem to be having any effect on him. Nearly six hours after he had arrived and been given a series of massive doses of cyanide via the food he consumed; Rasputin had no symptoms normally associated with cyanide poisoning. *Cyanide* is a fast-acting poisoning, with symptoms normally appearing within a few minutes of exposure[62]. The early symptoms include headaches, dizziness, irregular heartbeat, shortness of breath, and vomiting. This is typically followed by seizures, slowing heartrate, lowered blood pressure, loss of consciousness, and cardiac arrest. If an individual is able to survive cyanide poisoning, there will be long-term neurological problems that persist. After the sixth hour with no outward signs or symptoms of cyanide poisoning, Prince Yusupov drew a revolver from his inside coat pocket, leveled it at Rasputin, and reportedly looked Rasputin in the eyes while he said, "say a prayer"[61]. The Prince shot Rasputin point-blank in the chest. The group left him for dead. A few minutes later, Rasputin allegedly jumped up and began attacking his assailants. Rasputin chased his killers into the courtyard, but his attackers began bludgeoning him and shot him repeatedly. Rasputin still did not die nearly 10 hours after the initial dose of cyanide. In a last-ditch effort, the killers wrapped him tightly so his arms and legs could not move, and tossed him into the freezing river, where hypothermia caused him to finally die[63]. This ordeal solidified his nickname as the "Mad Monk."

Alan Turing (1912–1954 CE) was a British mathematician, logician, and cryptanalyst made famous for his role in deciphering Nazi coded messages during World War II (WWII). He is considered to be the father of modern computer science, thanks to his revolutionary work in creating *Turing machines*[64]. Turing machines were mathematical models of computing wherein a machine used symbols on a readable metal tape that referenced a stored table of rules and was capable of initiating and solving computer algorithms (Figure 10.12)[65]. In 1952, Turing was accused of and prosecuted for homosexual acts[66]. To avoid prison, Turing elected to undergo treatment that

Figure 10.12 Alan Turing, Manchester, England

Dutchmen Photography/Shutterstock.com

would chemically castrate him through the use of *Diethylstilbestrol (DES)*, a nonsteroidal estrogen. A month before he would have turned 42 years old, Turning was found in his home dead. His autopsy lists his cause of death as suicide by cyanide poisoning, however the medical examiner noted that the evidence was more consistent with accidental poisoning than deliberate or intentional poisoning. Mysteriously, there was a half-eaten apple found beside his body. The apple was never tested for cyanide, but it was speculated the poison was consumed by Turing via the apple. Friends of Turing had speculated it was the cause of his death, as he loved re-enacting the scene from Walt Disney's *Snow White and the Seven Dwarfs* (1937 CE) where the Evil Queen imbued apples in her poisonous brew intended to make snow white sleep forever. More likely, however, it was accidental poisoning via inhalation of cyanide fumes from Turing's home laboratory where he utilized potassium cyanide to electroplate gold onto metals. In 2013, Queen Elizabeth II pardoned Alan Turing for the crime of homosexuality and apologized for the awful treatment Turing had endured[67]. By 2017, the Alan Turing Law became the informal name of a United Kingdom law that pardoned men who were historically convicted of homosexual acts.

Figure 10.13 Lois Gibbs and Her Children, Missy and Michael, Love Canal Protest 16 Oct 1978

Source: https://nyheritage. contentdm.oclc.org/digi-tal/collection/p16694coll1/ id/1370/rec/503

In the Fall of 1978 CE, a quaint residential community would be forever changed as it was discovered the homes of nearly 230 families had been built on top of an abandoned chemical dumpsite in Love Canal, New York[68]. The events that transpired in the suburb of Niagara Falls, New York, led to one of the most egregious environmental catastrophes in American history (Figure 10.13). In the 1890s CE, an enterprising man, William T. Love (1873–1959 CE), set about excavating a canal along the banks of the Niagara River. This canal was envisioned to connect Lake Erie to Lake Ontario and would allow for shipping and recreational boats to travel between the two Great Lakes. This canal would, in addition, harness diverted water to be used to generate an inexhaustible supply of energy. The abundance of locally generated energy would in turn bring in new industries. Workers would commute to modern factories, shop in modern malls, and have a rich and diverse community emanating from a planned urban development, tentatively named Model City. The plan hinged on the need for local electricity. By 1893 CE, Tesla and Westinghouse had unveiled new generators and transformers that could amp up electricity to high voltages and transport it across long distances, making the need for local generation of electricity obsolete. This put an end to Model City, but left "Love's Canal" project, by this point a 3,000 foot long by 100 foot wide gash in the ground to languish and fade into obscurity. By the mid-point of World War II, the Hooker Electrochemical company had acquired the land and began using it as a dump, eventually disposing of over 20,000 tons of toxic waste[69]. Later this toxic waste would be shown to contain over 82 known carcinogens like benzene and dioxin[69]. In 1953 CE, the canal and its toxic waste were covered with dirt, and sold to the local school board for $1 with the acknowledgement that it was filled with chemical waste[70]. An elementary school, a park, and residential homes were built on the land anyway. In the late 1970s CE with three subsequent years of unusually heavy snows followed by uncharacteristically large amounts of late spring and early summer rain, residents began complaining of a sickening smell[71]. The Environmental Protection Agency (EPA) sent inspectors out to Love Canal. The reports filed by the inspectors cited the discovery of rusting barrels of waste that had pushed their way to the surface, potholes that oozed deep black waste, and basements filled with an oozing muck with an odor that penetrated the sinuses[72]. The neighborhood was evacuated, a national emergency declared, and a full investigation was launched by the EPA and Centers for Disease Control (CDC). Early estimates for the families living along Love Canal came with a dismal prediction of 1 in 10 chance of developing cancer solely from breathing in the polluted air. Of the 36 residents who provided blood for testing nearly 70% had chromosomal damage[73]. The birth defect rate for children born to parents who had lived near the canal was higher than entire state of New York. Between 1979 and 1996 CE, 725 former residents of Love Canal had died[74]. The homes, school, and public areas of Love Canal were leeching poisons into the environment that had profound and deadly consequences for the unsuspecting residents.

In modern times, poisoning has become a favored way to get rid of political rivals or to silence defected ex-government officials. When poisoning occurs for political reasons, it is usually highly publicized and spreads fear among other potential dissidents and defectors. In 2004 CE, Viktor Yushchenko (1954 CE), the third President of Ukraine (Figure 10.14), while amid his election campaign survived a botched assassination attempt after ingesting dioxin (TCCD)[75]. The attempt had left Yushchenko with visible facial scaring. In 2006, Alexander Litvinenko (1962–2006 CE), former Russian Federal Security Service (FSB) and ex-KGB, was assassinated with the use of Polonium 210-induced acute radiation syndrome in his home in England[76]. In 2018, Sergei Skripal (1951 CE) was enjoying dinner with his daughter Yulia who was visiting him at his new home in England[77]. Sergei and Yulia were poisoned with a Russian developed Novichok nerve agent, after long stays in Salisbury Hospital both were released. In 2020, Alexey Navalny (1976 CE), a lawyer, anti-corruption activist, and Russian opposition leader was hospitalized after being poisoned

Figure 10.14 Viktor Yushchenko, Displaying Signs of TCCD Poisoning

360b/Shutterstock.com

with a Novichok nerve agent, he was medically evacuated to Germany for treatment[78]. He returned to Russian in January 2021 where he was arrested and jailed under claims of treason against the Russian state. Amnesty International listed Navalny as a prisoner of conscience in May 2021. ***Prisoner of conscience*** refers to anyone who has been wrongly detained and imprisoned because of their race, sexual orientation, religion, or political views. This term is also utilized for those have been who imprisoned for the nonviolent expression of their conscientiously held beliefs.

Novichok nerve agents are a group of closely related molecules designed between 1971 and 1993 CE with the expressed purpose of death[79]. These are extremely toxic organophosphorus compounds that impact the human central nervous system with varying degrees of affect. Novichok translates to "newcomer" in Russian and was used as the designation of new chemical entities developed through state chemical research grants issued by the former Soviet Union and continued by the Russian Federation. Most Novichok agents are delivered either as an inhalant gas or a liquid. The most potent of these agents begin to show symptoms within 30 seconds of dispersal. The initial symptoms can manifest as muscle spasms, seizures, excessive production of saliva, and tears. Due to the lethality of Novichok agents, only a small amount is needed to kill an individual, which makes it easy to transport and distribute.

Poisons have had many uses in human history ranging from medical and cosmetic treatments to political retaliation to environmental devastation. One of the psychological factors associated with poison is that it is deadly and nearly undetectable without technology, which can cause fear and paranoia. Even scarier to contemplate, without knowing what an individual has been poisoned with it may be difficult to identify an antidote in time to save them. From history we have seen poisons that are fast acting and near instantaneous in delivering death, while others take time to bring on death. In the not so distant past, environmental disasters caused by industrial waste poisoned whole neighborhoods and caused the deaths and birth defects of hundreds of people.

10.3 Toxicology Ends the Mystique

Toxicology is a very broad scientific field of study, which incorporates biology, chemistry, pharmacology, and medicine in its endeavor to study the dangerous and adverse effects of chemicals, toxins, and toxicants on humans[80]. Toxicology in practice allows for the diagnosis and treatment of toxicity. *Toxicologists* are experts at identifying, understanding, and treating poisons and poisonings. Among the factors toxicologists consider when investigating a potential poisoning include dosage, route of exposure, duration (acute versus chronic) of exposure, age, sex, behavior, and environment. Today, toxicologists test for poisons using *in vivo* (whole animal/individual), *in vitro* (isolated cells or tissue samples), or *in silico* (computer simulation) to identify, understand, and detect potential toxins. Toxicology as a discipline of science has several branches, including medical toxicology, clinical toxicology, forensic toxicology, computational toxicology, and occupational toxicology. Perhaps the best-known branch of study is forensic toxicology, thanks in part to television shows like *Quincy, M.E.*; *Crime Scene Investigation – Miami*; *Crime Scene Investigation – New York*; and *Body of Proof*. *Forensic toxicology* combines pharmacology, clinical chemistry, anatomy, and physiology to assist in the medical and legal investigations related to deaths, poisonings, drug use, and industrial exposure to toxic agents[81]. Forensic toxicologists do not focus on the potential verdict or legal outcome of their investigations, but rather their concerns center around obtaining and interpreting results to assist in understanding the causes of death of victims.

Figure 10.15 Engraved Illustration of Paracelsus

Morphart Creation/Shutterstock.com

Philippus Aureolus Theophrastus Bombastus von Hohenheim (1493–1541 CE), or Paracelsus for short (Figure 10.15), was a Swiss polymath and was skilled as a mystic, psychic, physician, alchemist, philosopher, theologian, botanist, and astrologer[82]. He is considered to be the "Father of Toxicology" for emphasizing the value of observation in combination with conventional learning. Drawing on his love for chemistry and biology Paracelsus pioneered the practice of toxicology. Within his Third Defence, he stated "only the dose makes the poison"[83]. Paracelsus would use this statement to defend his use of inorganic and toxic substances when practicing medicine. Many of his contemporaries were critical of Paracelsus's penchant for substances that were believed to be too toxic to be used for therapeutic benefit. Paracelsus believed diseases were located in specific organs and he extended that belief to include toxicity. In short, he believed there were specific sites in the body where chemicals exerted their greatest effect[43]. Paracelsus believed in the need to standardize dosages in pharmacology. He was the first to study mercury for therapeutic potential and he is credited with inventing laudanum. Paracelsus believed that physicians needed to study and understand physical sciences if they wished to be good at their craft. He was the first to note the connection between environmental toxins and disease, the therapeutic use of diet, and the discovery that illness often has an emotional or psychological component that needs treatment as well as the physical ailments.

James Marsh (1794–1846 CE) was a Scottish chemist who invented the *Marsh Test* as a sensitive method to detect arsenic in 1836 CE[84]. The Marsh Test would become the standard for ~100 years. Prior to the Marsh Test, arsenic was untraceable in the body, which made arsenic a very convenient weapon. Marsh was inspired to develop the test, which was highly sensitive for the time, being able to detect as little as one-fiftieth of a milligram. He invented this test after being called to prove arsenic had been used in an 1832 CE poisoning. The case involved a man who had allegedly poisoned his own grandfather. Marsh used hydrogen sulfide to generate arsenic gas in tissue sample and was unable to prove beyond a shadow of a doubt that the deceased was in fact poisoned by arsenic. Marsh was able to detect arsenic in the sample as a yellow precipitate was formed, but it did not keep very well and by the time it was presented to the jury, it had deteriorated. The convicted man was released, and the charges were dropped. Marsh used the inaccuracy of the test to spur him into action and he developed the Marsh Test[85]. This method utilized sulfuric acid and arsenic-free zinc to interact with a tissue sample that contained arsenic. The reaction produced an arsine gas, which had the faint smell of garlic. When the gas was ignited and decomposed to pure metallic arsenic, when transferred to a cold surface, produced a silvery-black residue.

Mathieu Joseph Bonaventure Orfila (1787–1853 CE) was a Spanish chemist and the founder of toxicology education and he is frequently heralded as the "father of toxicology"[86]. In 1840 CE, Marie-Fortunée Lafarge (1816–1852 CE), a French woman, was convicted of murdering her husband with arsenic[87]. Lafarge had access to arsenic and arsenic had been found in her husband's food. Yet no arsenic could be found in the corpse. Orfila was asked by the court to test samples from the exhumed corpse of Lafarge's husband as well as food known to have been consumed by Monsieur Lafarge. Orfila insisted that the local chemists who had found no arsenic in the body (via three different attempts) witness his experiments[88]. Orfila used the same test materials and chemical reagents that the local chemists had used in their tests and performed the Marsh Test in an anteroom of the courthouse. After obtaining the results, Orfila entered the courtroom, supposedly followed by the local chemists all of whom had their heads bowed low. Orfila declared that arsenic was indeed present in every sample tested. He indicated that the arsenic found was to the exclusion of any extraneous sources. The courtroom was stunned as Orfila explained the misleading results obtained by the local chemists with the Marsh Test. It was not the test that gave the false results, instead it was the chemists who had performed the test incorrectly.

Jean Servais Stas (1813–1891 CE) was a Belgian chemist, famous as the co-discoverer of the atomic weight of carbon. Stas was internationally known for his skill in accurately determining the atomic weights of many elements through the work he did to obtain the weight of carbon. Stas was so skilled that he was able to detect alkaloid poisons in bodily fluids and tissues of corpses years after their deaths. He had provided conclusive evidence that Belgian Count Hippolyte Visart de Bocarmé (1818–1851 CE) was responsible for killing his brother-in-law through the use of nicotine poisoning by performing chemical reactions on tissues from the deceased. The work performed by Stas set the stage for chemical detection of organic toxins from a number of different specimens, including bodily fluids, hair, and tissue.

The 1900s CE in the United States witnessed the recognition of forensic toxicology as a valuable asset to the legal system. The nation's first medical examiner's office and toxicology laboratory was established in New York in 1918 CE, led by Charles Norris (1867–1935 CE) and Alexander Gettler (1883–1968 CE)[89]. Charles was New York's first appointed medical examiner (1918–1935 CE) and was responsible for pioneering forensic toxicology in America. Two cases gave Norris his notoriety and proved the necessity for government funding of toxicology. The first was in 1924, when Norris was asked to investigate the "looney gas building," an industrial plant where tetraethyllead (TEL) was compounded[90]. TEL is a fuel additive, which added led to gasoline providing a substantial gain in engine compression for automobiles. The problem was that a number of workers exposed to TEL had become insane with several then dying shortly after the insanity appeared. It was Norris who had found that the company, Standard Oil, was exposing employees to TEL without providing adequate ventilation or other protective measures. The second case was in 1926 when a man was caught carrying parts of a woman's body toward the Brooklyn waterfront, intent on disposing the parts into the East River[91]. The rest of the woman's body was found dismembered in the man's apartment. The man in question claimed that the woman had fallen asleep after drinking whiskey in his apartment and after he woke up, he had found her dead. In his panic, he had decided to carve her up to make disposal easier. Norris concluded that the woman had died of carbon monoxide poisoning and was not killed by the man directly. It was a faulty stove in the man's apartment that had caused the woman's death. The man was acquitted of murder and was instead charged with illegally dismembering a corpse.

Alexander Oscar Gettler (1883–1968 CE) was a forensic chemist and toxicologist in the New York medical examiners office between 1918 and 1959 CE[89]. Charles Norris hired Gettler with the understanding that Gettler would be willing to conduct any chemical testing required in criminal investigations that were brought to the medical examiner's office. Gettler created many new tests to isolate poisons[92]. He would begin by poisoning raw liver and attempting to isolate ever-smaller amounts of poison from the tissue[93]. These tests would often yield crystal formation, melting and boiling point analysis, color reactions, and titration reactions[94]. Gettler was the first to use spectrometry in criminal investigations, using the methodology to solve the murder of four children via thallium[95]. Gettler would go on to teach at New York University Graduate School where he had established the nation's first toxicology course in 1935 CE.

Frances Glessner Lee (1878–1962 CE) was a pathologist at Harvard Medical School and Chief Medical Examiner in Boston and among the first forensic scientists educated in the United States (Figure 10.16)[96]. She was very influential in the development of forensics. She had created the Nutshell Studies of Unexplained Death in 1945 CE, a series of 20 true crime scene dioramas, which

Figure 10.16 Glessner, Nutshell Studies, Parsonage Parlor

Edwin Remsberg/Alamy Stock Photo

Source: https://www.si.edu/nutshell-studies

she painstakingly created in minute detail in dollhouse scale. These dioramas were used for training homicide investigators. She created these dioramas to help investigators to "convict the guilty, clear the innocent, and find the truth in a nutshell"[97]. Of the 20 dioramas, 18 are still in use for teaching purposes by the Maryland Chief Medical Examiner's office. Glessner Lee helped to establish the Department of Legal Medicine at Harvard University and was the first female police captain in the United States. She is known as being the "mother of forensic science."

In terms of forensic studies in toxicology, isolation and analysis of samples should start as soon as possible after death. Death by poison can occur in a variety of ways. Poisons require specialized tests and forensic laboratories are typically altered to the possible use or involvement of poisons in advance to allow time to get the tests prepared and ready for evaluation. There are three stages in most toxicologic evaluations that includes (1) extraction of the sample, (2) separation of the compounds or drugs within the sample, and (3) identification with precise methods to clearly identify the compounds or drugs of interest[81]. *Extraction* is a method used to separate *immiscible compounds* (those that do not easily mix) based on their solubilities. Extraction allows testable materials to be removed from the others. It helps to make samples homogenous prior to undergoing chemical testing. *Separation* of compounds or drugs under chromatographic detection provides definitive proof of the structure of the substances within a given sample. *Identification* is the final stage in analysis and relies on the use of spectroscopic, immunoreaction, nuclear magnetic resonance, mass spectrometry, and molecular biologic methods to determine what the compounds or drugs obtained from a toxicological sample are. If a toxin is detected, confirmatory and often quantitative testing will be performed. Quantitative testing helps to determine how much of a compound or drug was involved in the death[98]. A positive identification of a toxin is achieved when two (or more) independent analyses are performed. Ideally more than one methodology for identification will have been used. Table 10.3 details the types of specimens typically collected for specific causes of death.

Thanks to the work of enterprising individuals, toxicology as a field of study helped to remove the mystique that surrounded the great equalizer of peoples, poison. Toxicology became the science of poisons. As a field of inquiry, toxicology deals with (1) the properties of poisons, (2) methods of detection and quantitative determination of poisons in body tissues and fluids, (3) the lethal or fatal

Table 10.3 Specimens Typically Collected by Cause of Death

Cause of Death	Typical Specimens Collected
Suicides, motor vehicle crashes, and industrial accidents	Blood, urine, vitreous humor, liver
Homicides and/or suspicious deaths	Blood, urine, vitreous humor, gastric contents, bile, liver, hair
Drug-related	Blood, urine, vitreous humor, gastric contents, bile, liver, hair
Volatile substance abuse	Blood, urine, vitreous humor, lung fluid or tied-off lung, liver
Heavy metal poisoning and/or exposure to other poisons	Blood, urine, vitreous humor, liver, hair, kidney

doses of various poisons, (4) the action of poisons on living tissues, and (5) the proper antidotes—if they exist—to be used to counteract poisoning[92]. The work of chemists, pathologists, physicians, and pharmacists we now understand that there is no substance known that acts to harm under all circumstances and in all doses. As Paracelsus would remind us all, it is not necessarily the potency of the drug, but the dose that kills.

REFERENCES

1. Nepovimova, E. & Kuca, K. (2019). The history of poisoning: From ancient times until modern ERA. *Archives of Toxicology*, *93*(1), 11–24.
2. Borgia, V. (2019). The prehistory of poison arrows. In *Toxicology in antiquity* (pp. 1–10). Elsevier.
3. Osborn, A. J. (2016). Paleoindians, proboscideans, and phytotoxins: Exploring the feasibility of poison hunting during the last glacial-interglacial transition. *Journal of Ethnobiology*, *36*(4), 908–929.
4. Bisset, N. G. (1989). Arrow and dart poisons. *Journal of Ethnopharmacology*, *25*(1), 1–41.
5. Huang, Y., & Bu, Q. (2022). Adverse effects of phytochemicals. In *Nutritional toxicology* (pp. 355–384). Springer. .
6. Jones, D. E. (2021). On plant poisons. In D. E. Jones (Ed.), *Poison Arrows: North American Indian Hunting and Warfare* (pp. 1–6), University of Texas Press.
7. Graf, F. (2007). Untimely death, witchcraft, and divine vengeance. A Reasoned Epigraphical Catalog. *Zeitschrift für Papyrologie und Epigraphik*, 139–150.
8. Sohail, H. A., et al. (2020). Venoms, poisons and toxins: Evolution and impact of amazing molecules. *Journal of Venom Research*, *10*, 1–6.
9. Alighieri, D. (2002 [c. 1308]). *Inferno: La Divina Commedia* (p. 736). Anchor Books.
10. Caferro, W. P. (2008). Warfare and economy in Renaissance Italy, 1350–1450. *Journal of Interdisciplinary History*, *39*(2), 167–209.
11. Herman, E. (2018). *The Royal Art of Poison: Filthy palaces, fatal cosmetics, deadly medicine, and murder most foul*. St. Martin's Press.
12. Burgio, L. (2021). Pigments, dyes and inks: Their analysis on manuscripts, scrolls and papyri. *Archaeological and Anthropological Sciences*, *13*(11), 1–16.
13. Mozzato, A. (2013). The pigment trade in Venice and the Mediterranean in the second half of the fifteenth century. *Renaissance Studies in Honor of Joseph Connors*, *2*, 171–179.
14. Gentilcore, D. (2003). Introduction to the world of the Italian Apothecary: Apothecaries," Charlatans" and the Medical Marketplace in Italy, 1400–1750. *Pharmacy in History*, *45*(3), 91–94.
15. Retief, F., & Cilliers, L. (2000). Poisoning during the Renaissance: The Medicis and the Borgias. *The South African Society for Medieval and Renaissance Studies*, *1017*(3455), 1–11.
16. Hibbert, C. (2008). *The Borgias and their enemies: 1431–1519* (p. 328). Harcourt, Inc.
17. Marchandisse, A. (2011). Le pape qui fait scandale, Les Borgias. Au-delà des scandales. *Historia*, (Spécial 2), 16–77.

18. Westphal, E. R. (2019). The forgetting of God and the victory of Dyonisus: Tension and proximity between the sacred and the secular in postmodernity. In E. R. Westphal (Ed.), *Secularization, cultural heritage and the spirituality of the secular state* (pp. 83–101). Brill Schöningh.

19. Bradford, S. (2005). *Lucrezia Borgia: Life, Love, and Death in Renaissance Italy* (p. 448). Penguin. 448.

20. Hempel, S. (2013). *The Inheritor's Powder: A Tale of Arsenic, Murder, and the New Forensic Science.* New York, NY: WW Norton & Company. 278.

21. Mari, F., et al. (2006). The mysterious death of Francesco I de'Medici and Bianca Cappello: An arsenic murder? BMJ, *333*(7582), 1299–1301.

22. Meyer, G. J. (2013). *The Borgias: The Hidden History* (p. 512). Bantam Books.

23. Karamanou, M., et al. (2018). Toxicology in the Borgias period: The mystery of Cantarella poison. *Toxicology Research and Application, 2*, 1–3.

24. Giovio, P. (2016 [1552 CE]). *Dialogo dell'imprese militari et amorose, di monsignor Giouio vescouo di Nocera: Con un ragionamento di messer Lodouico Domenichi, nel medesimo soggetto; Con la tauola* (p. 214). Wentworth Press. 214.

25. Machiavelli, N. (2020 [1513 CE]). *Il principe* (p. 92). Ali Ribelli Edizioni.

26. Strathern, P. (2009). *The artist, the philosopher, and the warrior: The intersecting lives of Da Vinci, Machiavelli, and Borgia and the world they shaped* (p. 480). Bantam Books.

27. Machiavelli, N. (1921 [1532 CE]). In P. Ravasio (Ed.), *Istorie fiorentine* (p. 469). Paravia.

28. Lev, E. (2011). *The Tigress of Forlì: Renaissance Italy's Most Courageous and Notorious Countess, Caterina Riario Sforza De'Medici* (p. 316). Houghton Mifflin Harcourt.

29. Fernández González, T. (2022). Caterina Sforza: La condottiera alchimista. In D. Cerrato (Ed.), *Nuevos itinerarios e investigaciones en la literatura y cultura italiana* (pp. 171–178).Librería Dykinson.

30. Sforza, C. (2009 [1500 C]). In G. Coulson (Ed.), *Experimenti de la excellentissima ma Signora Caterina da Forli* (p. 30). CreateSpace Independent Publishing Platform.

31. Sforza, C. (2009 [1499 CE]). In E. Caruso (Ed.), *Ricette d'amore e di bellezza di Caterina Sforza, signora di Imola e di Forlì.* Il Ponte Vecchio.

32. Assonitis, A. (2020). *The Medici Archive* (p. 524). The Routledge Companion to Digital Humanities and Art History. Routledge.

33. Rankin, A. (2021). *The poison trials: Wonder drugs, experiment, and the battle for authority in renaissance science* (p. 312). University of Chicago Press.

34. Guidi, R. L. (2017). L'insolito Memoriale di fra'Antonio da Vercelli per Lorenzo de'Medici. *Albertiana, XX*(1), 167–199.

35. Sutherland, N. M. (1978). Catherine de Medici: The legend of the wicked Italian queen. *The Sixteenth Century Journal,* , 45–56.

36. McIlvenna, U. (2013). 'A stable of whores'? The 'Flying Squadron'of Catherine de Medici. In J. Duindam (Ed.), *The Politics of Female Households: Ladies-in-Waiting across Early Modern Europe* (pp. 179–208).Brill

37. Del Popolo, M. (2021). Gli spazi di corte della signoria di Isabella di Castiglia in Sicilia (1470–1504). *Studia Historica. Historia Medieval, 39*(2), 51–78.

38. Pavoncello, N. (1980). Gli ebrei di origine spagnola a Roma. *Studi Romani, 28*(2), 214–220.

39. Croce, B. (1939). Due letterine familiari di principesse italiane del Quattrocento. *Humanisme et Renaissance,. 6*(3), 294–303.

40. Fichte, J. G. (2016). On Machiavelli, as an author, and passages from his writings. *Philosophy Today, 60*(3), 761–788.

41. di Napoli, A. (2020). Il Leonardo dei Borgia e dei Medici. Splendore e declino dell'artista-scienziato. *L'Idomeneo, 2019*(28), 9–24.

42. da Vinci, L. (2012 [1819 CE]). *The notebooks of Leonardo da Vinci* (Vol. 1, p. 396). Dover Publications Inc.

43. Gantenbein, U. (2017). Poison and its dose: Paracelsus on toxicology. In P. Wexler (Ed.), *Toxicology in the Middle Ages and Renaissance: A Volumen in History of Toxicology and Environmental Health* (pp. 1–10). Elsevier.

44. Bachour, N. (2015). Healing with mercury: The uses of mercury in Arabic medical literature. *Asiatische Studien-Études Asiatiques, 69*(4), 831–866.

45. Haarmann, T., et al. (2009). Ergot: From witchcraft to biotechnology. *Molecular Plant Pathology, 10*(4), 563–577.

46. Purdy, S. (2007). Conjuring history: The many interpretations of the Salem witchcraft trials. *Rivier Academic Journal, 3*(1), 1–18.

47. Carlson, J. (2016). Hollywood's smooth new move: Scrotox. *The Hollywood Reporter, 422*(33), 36.

48. Bentley, R., & Chasteen, T. G. (2002). Arsenic curiosa and humanity. *The Chemical Educator, 7*(2), 51–60.

49. Zebroski, B. (2015). Colonial and Early American Pharmacy. In Zebroski (Ed.), *A brief history of pharmacy* (pp. 122–136). Routledge.

50. McCord, C. P. (1953). Lead and lead poisoning in Early America-the Pewter Era. *Industrial Medicine and Surgery, 22*(12), 573–577.

51. Dash, M. (2017). Aqua Tofana. In P. Wexler (Ed.), *Toxicology in the Middle Ages and Renaissance* (pp. 63–69). Elsevier.

52. Farndon, J. (2016). *Wie würden Sie jemanden so vergiften, dass die Polizei Ihnen nicht auf die Schliche kommt?* In J. Farndon (Ed.), *Können Thermostate denken? Absurde Fragen, die Sie ins Grübeln bringen* (pp. 13–18). Springer.

53. Feci, S. (2020). *Trame di donne all'indomani della peste romana del 1656: La vicenda dell'acqua tofana.* MEFIRM: Mélanges de l'École française de Rome : Italie et Méditerranée modernes et contemporaines, *132*(1), 59–71.

54. Cumston, C. G. (1923). A note on the poisoners of the Sixteenth and Seventeenth centuries. *Annals of Medical History, 5*(4), 402–408.

55. Jacobs, H. C. (2005). Mozart empoisonné! Extraits de la presse parisienne sur la propagation d'une rumeur au milieu des années 1820. *Revue de Musicologie*, *91*, 455–468.

56. Pirot, E. (1883). *La marquise de Brinvilliers: Récit de ses derniers moments (manuscrit du P. Pirot, son confesseur) Notes et documents sur sa vie et son procès* (Vol. 1, p. 310). Alphonse Lemerre.

57. Dumas, A. (1856). *La Marquise de Brinvilliers: La Comtesse de Saint-Géran, Jeanne de Naples* (p. 313). Libraire Theatrale. 313.

58. Carroll, E. (2012). Potions, poisons and "inheritance powders": How chemical discourses entangled 17th century France in the Brinvilliers rrial and the poison affair. *Voces Novae*, *4*(2), 3–20.

59. Anger, J.-P., & Goullé, J.-P. (2015). Les femmes, le poison et... l'histoire. *Toxicologie Analytique et Clinique*, *27*(2), S12.

60. Wilson, D., & Yardley, E. (2013). The psychopathy of a Victorian serial killer: Integrating micro and macro levels of analysis. *Journal of Criminal Psychology*, *3*(1), 19–30.

61. William Le, Q. (2021). The true story of Rasputin's end. *Russia, China and Eurasia*, *37*(4), 463–469.

62. Dolly, S. (2017). The autopsy of Russia's Holy Devil. *Forensic Magazine*, *13 Dec 2017.*

63. Kendrick, J. M. L. (2004). Russia's imperial blood: Was Rasputin not the healer of legend? *American Journal of Hematology*, *77*(1), 92–102.

64. Bowen, J. P. (2016). Alan Turing: Founder of computer science. in *School on Engineering Trustworthy Software Systems*. Springer.

65. Turing, A. M. (1936). On computable numbers, with an application to the Entscheidungsproblem. *Journal of Mathematics*, *58*(345–363), 230–265.

66. Vincenzi, M. (2013). Alan Turing and the poisoned apple. In M. Emmer (Ed.), *Imagine Math 2: Between Culture and Mathematics* (pp. 255–262).Springer.

67. Doan, L. (2017). Queer history queer memory: The case of Alan Turing. *GLQ: A Journal of Lesbian and Gay Studies*, *23*(1), 113–136.

68. Beck, E. C. (1979). The love canal tragedy. *EPA Journal*, *5*, 17.

69. Phillips, A. S., Hung, Y.-T., & Bosela, P. A. (2007). Love canal tragedy. *Journal of Performance of Constructed Facilities*, *21*(4), 313–319.

70. Brown, M. H. (1979). Love Canal and the poisoning of America. *Atlantic Monthly*, *244*(6), 33–47.

71. Thomson, J. (2016). Toxic residents: Health and citizenship at Love Canal. *Journal of Social History*, *50*(1), 204–223.

72. Borman, S. A. (1983). Environmental monitoring at love canal. *Analytical Chemistry*, *55*(9), 943A–948A.

73. Picciano, D. (1980). Love canal chromosome study. *Science*, *209*(4458), 754–756.

74. Gensburg, L. J., et al. (2009). Mortality among former Love Canal residents. *Environmental Health Perspectives*, *117*(2), 209–216.

75. Sorg, O., et al. (2009). 2, 3, 7, 8-tetrachlorodibenzo-p-dioxin (TCDD) poisoning in Victor Yushchenko: Identification and measurement of TCDD metabolites. The Lancet, *374*(9696), 1179–1185.

76. Harrison, J. et al. (2017). The polonium-210 poisoning of mr alexander litvinenko. *Journal of Radiological Protection, 37*(1), 266.

77. Talukder, M. I. A. (2021). Sergei Skripal: A study of the covert operation to assassinate the Russian double agent. *OPUS International Journal of Society Researches, 17*(38), 5525–5544.

78. Treisman, D. (2022). Putin unbound: How repression at home presaged belligerence abroad. *Foreign Affairs, 101*(3), 40–53.

79. Steindl, D., et al. (2021). Novichok nerve agent poisoning. *The Lancet, 397*(10270), 249–252.

80. Hartung, T. (2009). Toxicology for the twenty-first century. *Nature, 460*(7252), 208–212.

81. Lappas, N. T., & Lappas, C. M. (2021). *Forensic toxicology: Principles and concepts* (2nd ed., p. 544). Academic Press.

82. Weeks, A. (2013). Paracelsus and the Idea of the Renaissance. In H. Koopman & F. Baron (Eds.), *Die Wiederkehr der Renaissance im 19. und 20. Jahrhundert–The Revival of the Renaissance in the Nineteenth and Twentieth Centuries* (pp. 89–113). Brill mentis.

83. Paracelsus, (2015 [1538 CE]). In P. N. Wheeler (Eds.), Four works (p. 210). CreateSpace Independent Publishing Platform.

84. Afshari, R. (2016). The chronicle of arsenic poisoning in the 19th century. *Asia Pacific Journal of Medical Toxicology, 5*(2), 36–41.

85. James, O. and M. Lodge, (2003). The limitations of 'policy transfer' and 'lesson drawing' for public policy research. *Political Studies Review, 1*(2), 179–193.

86. Farrell, M. (1994). Pioneer forensic toxicologists: Marsh, Orfila and their predecessors. *Crimnologist, 18*(1), 33–36.

87. Bertomeu-Sánchez, J. R. (2017). The truth about the Lafarge affair: Poisons in salons, academies, and courtrooms during the nineteenth century. In H. Klippel, B. Wahrig, & A. Zechner (Eds.) *Poison and poisoning in science, fiction and cinema: Precarious identities* (pp. 37–56).Springer.

88. Orfila, M. J. B. (1817). *A general system of toxicology: Or, a treatise on poisons, drawn from the mineral, vegetable, and animal kingdoms, considered as to their relations with physiology, pathology, and medical jurisprudence* (p. 250). McCarey & Son.

89. Blum, D. (2011). *The poisoner's handbook: Murder and the birth of forensic medicine in jazz age New York* (p. 336). Penguin.

90. Norris, C., & Gettler, A. O. (1925). Poisoning by tetra-ethyl lead: Postmortem and chemical findings. *Journal of the American Medical Association, 85*(11), 818–820.

91. Vance, B. M. (1938). The work of a medical examiner's office: A description of how it is accomplished in New York city. *American Journal of Medical Jurisprudence, 1*(2), 95–100.

92. Gettler, A. O. (1934). Toxicology in the medicolegal necropsy. *American Journal of Clinical Pathology, 4*(1), 50–65.

93. Gettler, A. O., & Weiss, L. (1943). thallium poisoning: I. The detection of thallium in biologic material. *American Journal of Clinical Pathology*, *13*(6), 322–326.

94. Gettler, A. O., & Weiss, L. (1943). Thallium poisoning: II. The quantitative determination of thallium in biologic material. *American Journal of Clinical Pathology*, *13*(7), 368–377.

95. Gettler, A. O., & Weiss, L. (1943). Thallium poisoning. III. Clinical toxicology of thallium. *American Journal of Clinical Pathology*, *13*(8), 422–429.

96. Lee, F. G. (1951). Legal medicine at Harvard University. *Journal of Criminal Law, Criminology and Police Science*, *42*, 674–678.

97. Bouchard, G. (2019). Murder in miniature. *Performance Research*, *24*(5), 93–100.

98. Wilks, M. F. (2020). Bringing chemistry to medicine–The contribution of Paracelsus to modern toxicology: Chemical education. *Chimia*, *74*(6), 507–508.

Chapter 11

Nineteenth Century

The 19th century CE is full of paradoxes and polarizations. The century begins with pseudoscience and culminates in scientific revolution. It is a period of extreme naivety and burgeoning knowledge[1]. It was a time of profound change for some and great hardships for others. Today we live in a world surrounded by drugs. We have drugs for our pain, drugs for our diseases, drugs for our allergies to the outside world, drugs for sexual pleasure, and even drugs for our mental wellbeing. Our drugs have been rationally designed and our drugs have been clinically tested. We have factories and sterile facilities where our drugs are synthesized or purified from natural sources. Our drugs can be fermented, and our drug are engineered. In general, our drugs actually do what they are intended to do… and for the most part, they are effective and safe when used as prescribed. This amazing world of pharmaceuticals and our belief in the power of our drugs was not always a view held by our ancestors.

It has only been ~200 years since we began using synthesized drugs that we mass produced in factories (Figure 11.1). It was during the ***Industrial Revolution*** that many of our modern drugs began to appear in earnest. The Industrial Revolution marked a huge leap in human history, where we witnessed the process of change as people transitioned from an agrarian and handicraft economy to one dominated by industry and machine manufacturing[2]. By the late eighteenth century CE and lasting until the early twentieth century CE, the industrial revolution would alter the world in unprecedented ways. There was a huge movement of people to industrial and urban centers. Until the nineteenth century CE, most manufacturing was done in people's homes, using hand tools and basic machines. Industrialization marked a drastic shift to powered, specialty machinery where manufacturing was done in large

Figure 11.1 Factory on a river in Pennsylvania. 1857 watercolorby James Fuller Queen

Everett Collection/Shutterstock.com

factories that facilitated mass production. The iron and textile industries, along with the development of the steam engine, were the driving forces behind the industrial revolution. Industrialization brought about an increased volume and variety of manufactured goods and improved standard of living for some, it resulted in grim employment and abysmal living conditions for the poor and working classes. Wages for low-skilled factory workers were low and working conditions were dangerous and monotonous on the best of days. Being low-skilled or unskilled meant that workers had extraordinarily little job security and were easily replaced. There were no child labor laws, and children were an integral part of the labor force with many working long hours and due to their smaller frames and height were often used for highly dangerous tasks, like cleaning inside the machinery. Urban sprawl brought on by the considerable number of people migrating to cities for employment meant that housing was inadequate, overcrowded, polluted, unsanitary, and was the perfect place for disease to run unabated.

11.1 Early Nineteenth Century Medical Beliefs

In the early part of the nineteenth century CE, disease transmission was not fully understood nor appreciated. Disease was seen as a combination of inherited susceptibility and individual intemperance. In cases where neither of those options were useful in determining where a disease originated from, people turned to climate and locations, which were deemed to be pleasant and productive or riddled with noxious exhalations. *Inherited susceptibility* were the predispositions of health that were inherited from your parents[3]. If you father had gout, you would get gout. If your mother had tinnitus, you would get tinnitus. *Individual intemperance* was a fancy way of indicating that one's lifestyle, often viewed as a lack of self-control, led people to an immoderate rate of consumption. *Noxious exhalations* were miasmas, environmental causes of "bad air" that when mingled with melancholy left people feeling portentous and dark[4]. There was no real concern about water or air-borne infections, as these were not seen as transmission vectors for disease.

Bad air was something that permeated the urban centers and its symptomology relied on things such as temperature and passions. Most diseases could be remedied with the right type of air and control over one's emotions[4]. Smallpox, scarlet fever, or measles expressed similar general symptomology including "diseased parents," exposure to cold night air, sedentary habits, anger, wet feet, and abrupt changes of temperature. Fevers were caused by injury, bad air, violent emotions, irregular bowels, and extremes of heat and cold. Cholera was seen to be the result of rancid or putrid food, brought on by "cold fruits" such as cucumbers and melons, and fueled by passionate fear or rage. Treatments relied heavily on a "change of air" together with emetic and laxative purgation and bleeding by cup or leech to clear "impurities" from the body. In the early nineteenth century CE, there were an extremely limited range of useful medicines and people desperate for a cure would often turn to the power of prayer when medicines seemed to fail.

By the 1800s CE, bloodletting had been divided into four therapeutic applications, which consisted of venesection, arteriotomy, cupping, and leeching[5]. *Venesection* was the deliberate incision of a vein for the removal of blood, which was often taken from the median cubital vein. The median cubital vein is located on the arm, opposite the elbow. *Arteriotomy* was an incision of an artery for the removal of blood, with either the ulnar or radial artery being used. *Cupping* was an incredibly unique process that involved localized bloodletting through a technique known as scarification (scraping of the skin) followed by cupping. Cupping involved placing a dome shaped glass over the scarified skin and extracting the air in the cup by suction or prior heating, which would pull blood from the scar into the cup. *Leeching* required the application of the medicinal leech (Figure 11.2), *Hirudo medicinalis*, applied to the skin to remove blood[6]. At each feeding a medicinal leech can ingest about 5 to 10 mL (1 to 2 teaspoons, respec-

Figure 11.2   Medicinal Leeches, Nineteeth Century CE

AlessandraRC/Shutterstock.com

tively) of blood, constituting nearly 10 times its own body weight. Bloodletting, by whatever means necessary, was believed to accomplish the goal of relieving the body of "congested" or "bad blood" and inflammation. Any health problem could be bled away, or so the prevailing thought of the day beheld. Venereal diseases, brain inflammation, epilepsy, hysteria, organ disease, cancer, and tuberculosis were prime candidates for bloodletting.

There was a great risk of being bled to death and it did occur, especially in instance where the bloodletter was inexperienced. A famous case of someone being bled to death is that of President George Washington (1732–1799 CE)[7]. Washington awoke on the morning of 14 December 1799 CE and complained that he could not breathe. A messenger was sent out immediately to fetch the doctor but as the time passed, Washington became increasingly distraught and anxious. He feared the physician would not arrive in time. Washington called for the overseer of his slaves to perform the act and bleed him. From numerous accounts, the cut was deep, and the reports indicate the President lost between ½ and ¾ pint of blood before the wound closed. The physician arrived and over the next 8 hours, Washington was bled four additional times. By evening, America's first president was dead. The official cause of death being listed as croup, an upper respiratory infection. Six weeks after his death, a separate physician indicated that Washington most likely was killed from the excess of blood he had lost.

There were real concerns about death in the 1800s CE with two of the biggest fears being that of the body snatchers and being buried alive. As an anatomist in the United States and in the United Kingdom, it was at times difficult to get cadavers[8]. There were no mechanisms like we have today where the body could be donated to science after death. A lucrative trade in human bodies began to take root near universities and training hospitals. The *body snatchers* or *resurrectionists* were known to deliver freshly obtained corpses, usually through dubious means, to students, surgeons, and teachers for dissections. These individuals were seen as extremely offensive, repugnant, and very unpopular. Many would prowl around graveyards and keep tabs on recent graves and then under the cloak of night would descend to dig up the newly inurned corpses. These individuals were rejected by every class of society from the elites to the lowest criminal classes. It became so bad that cities had to protect the rights of the deceased by passing laws like the Anatomy Act of 1831 in Boston, Massachusetts, as a way to "more effectually to protect the sepulchers of the dead, and to legalize the study of anatomy in certain cases"[9]. This was followed closely by the Anatomy Act of 1832 in

England, which required bodies to be gifted to specific hospitals or universities prior to the persons death if they wished to assist the study of science[10].

The fear of being buried alive, ***taphophobia***, was rampant in the United States during the nineteenth century CE[11]. Burial practices did not feature embalming in all cases, and there were reports—urban myths probably—that people were mistaken as dead and buried only to awaken in pitch black, 6 feet underground. Inventions like the ***safety coffin*** were a series of inspired creations with the intent of aiding someone who was buried alive[12]. These safety coffins had a number of features that would allow the prematurely buried to escape, breathe while underground, and even signal to those above ground for help. ***Grave bells*** were among the simplest of ways to let people know you were buried alive[13]. A string leading from inside the coffin up to bells that were near the gravestone was relatively inexpensive and could be used in emergencies to signal that someone was alive. A common phrase "saved by the bell" gets its origins from the use of grave bells to literally save one's life. Many of the fears of being buried alive peaked during the cholera epidemics of the nineteenth century CE, when people weakened by the disease would appear dead when they were in fact asleep.

The pharmacopeias of the early nineteenth century CE were built out of trial and error, inherited lore, and/or mystical theories. It is said that medicines were concocted with a mixture of empiricism and prayer. ***Empiricism*** is a philosophical belief that all knowledge is derived from our sense-experience interactions. Within medical practice, empiricism is a methodology founded on experience without the aid of science or theory, it relies solely on direct observation and experimentation. Many of the medicines of the first half of the nineteenth century were made with water- or alcohol-based extracts of freshly ground or dried herbs, animal bone, animal fat, and a variety of minerals. Medicines were employed through one of five general vehicles consisting of tinctures, poultices, soups, teas, and liniments[14]. ***Tinctures*** were small vials of medicine ~2 oz (4 tablespoons) and were slight infusions of at least two if not more medicinal elements. ***Poultices*** were soft, moist masses of cloth, bread, meal, or herbs applied hot as a medicament externally to the body and were kept there until they cooled. ***Soups***, same concept as soup today, were liquid mixture of various herbal medicines served hot. ***Teas***, again similar concept as tea today, were decoctions or infusions made by pouring boiling water on medicinal herbs. ***Liniment*** was a medicated topical preparation, usually in the form of a cream or lotion, applied directly to the skin.

Morbidity in the nineteenth century CE by gender revealed that males were dying in large part from occupational injuries and exposure to toxic substances (alcohol and opium included), while females experienced higher rates of death due to childbirth and violence. The violence that women faced was often in the form of domestic violence and the penalties for domestic abuse were nowhere near as comprehensive as today. Many women lived in fear of their husbands. Two of the diseases that were adding to the morbidity were consumption and cholera. ***Consumption***, or as we know it today tuberculosis, was a disease that seemed to consume the individual from the inside out, with the victim's weight dropping dramatically as the disease progressed[15]. Consumption led to extreme coughing fits that would bring up greenish or yellow sputum. Over the course of a few hours, the sputum begins to contain more and more blood. Tuberculosis is a highly contagious infection caused by a bacterium that attacks the lungs and if left untreated can impact the bone, brain, and central nervous system. ***Cholera*** is a water-borne infection of the small intestine that produces copious amounts of watery diarrhea[16]. The diarrhea lasts for several days and occurs alongside vomiting and muscle cramping. These conditions quickly escalate to dehydration, electrolyte imbalance, and death. The external manifestation results in sunken eyes, cold skin, decrease in skin elasticity, and a bluish tint to the face and neck all of which mimics the appearance of corpses. The mortality rate for untreated cholera is between 60% and 70%.

Two highly unique disease tied to environment and industrialization were pea-soupers and Phossy Jaw. *Pea-Soupers* were thick chemically laden fogs and hazes usually containing high concentrations of sulphur[17]. Pea-Soupers were found in cities like London, Paris, and New York where a thick yellowish, greenish, or blackish fog would blanket the city with air pollution. The pollution contained soot particulates and poisonous sulphur dioxide from the numerous coal furnaces and ever-expanding industrial sprawl. *Phossy Jaw* was a work-related condition among young women working in match factories[18]. Women were preferred for the task of match making as their slender fingers could do the delicate work of gluing the phosphorous onto the match heads. Their close proximity to phosphorous every day caused them to develop an incurable necrosis in the jaw and long bones as phosphorus leeched the calcium from the bone.

In the United States a very unique and completely American disease began permeating the minds of the people, neurasthenia. *Neurasthenia*, sometimes referred to as nervous exhaustion, has been described as a poorly defined constellation of symptoms including lassitude, loss of will, emotionally drained, high irritability, and fatigue from the most mundane tasks[19]. Neurasthenia appeared to disproportionately affect those who performed cerebral work, like physicians, lawyers, engineers, inventors, etc. It also became a general catch-all term for conditions that would later be classified as "stress." Reported findings of those suffering from neurasthenia included a loss of interest in mental labor, heart disturbances, and periods of emotional outburst[20]. Treatments included cold water cures, diets, exercise, arsenic, and other home remedies (Figure 11.3). By the later part of the 1800s CE, Americans were drinking over 30 gallons of mineral water from ~500 natural springs around the country annually. *Mineral water* was believed to help soothe the effects brought on by neurasthenia, because the minerals that naturally occurred in spring water were curative and presented a much better choice for drinking than city water. Many of the physicians of the 1800s CE recommended that their patients drink between 3 and 5 glasses of mineral water per day as a preventative measure between the "inactive phase" of their neurasthenia[20].

Figure 11.3 Antique Waterbottles

Zoran Milosavljevic/Shutterstock.com

Popular in the United States during the nineteenth century CE were emetics. *Emetics* are a group of agents that produce nausea and vomiting, primarily used as emergency measures for poisoning or to remove toxins from the body. Emetics cause gastric irritation, stimulate the central nervous system chemoreceptors, or use both methods to induce vomiting[21]. Emetics in the Americas came in a wide arrange of forms, typically from mineral or herbal sources. The emetics that were most prominent included salt, beer and crushed garlic, blue vitriol, ipecacuanha, and apomorphine. *Salt water* was an easy home remedy, and the drinking of heavily salted water was one way to quickly "loosen the belly" and make the consumer vomit. Excessive consumption of salt water can lead to diarrhea, electrolyte imbalance, distortion, and dehydration if not careful. An old folk emetic was the combination of stale *beer and crushed garlic*, which was believed to be effective at ridding the body of snake venom after being bitten by a poisonous snake[22]. Snake venom does not usually collect in the stomach, so drinking such a vile concoction on top of the snake bite was adding insult to injury. *Blue vitriol*, better known as copper sulfate, was recommended for hemlock poisoning and opium overdose[23]. Blue vitriol is highly poisonous, it causes lysis of red blood cells, breakdown of muscle tissues, and kidneys failure. *Ipeacuanha*, or Ipecac for short, was a thick syrup made from the dried roots of the ipecacuanha plant[24]. Ipecac is not used in medicines today. It was used as an expectorant at low doses and as a fast-acting emetic at higher doses[25]. Ipecac was a vital component of every household medicine cabinet in the nineteenth century CE as it was used to treat poisonings of all kinds. It did not stop or lower the absorption rate of toxins that had been consumed and only caused vomiting 50% of the time it was taken. *Apomorphine* is a potent hallucinogenic drug made from the bulbs and roots of water lilies[26]. Apomorphine was synthesized in the early 1800s CE and was a successful emetic as it ensured vomiting rates of ~95%. Apomorphine is an extremely potent, non-selective dopamine agonist, acting on both the D1 and D2 receptors in the brain. It was used to horrible effect in early attempts at gay conversion therapy. Apomorphine was used to induce severe nausea and the hallucinatory effects coupled with the drugs known capacity to make consumers susceptible to suggestion was used in ineffective attempts to recondition gay men[27]. This form of torture would continue well into the beginning of the twenty-first century CE.

11.2 Quackery and Pseudo-Science

When we hear the word prohibition in the United States, most of us instinctively think of the early part of the 1900s CE when alcohol was prohibited for 13 long years with cannabis becoming outlawed shortly thereafter. However, these instances of drug prohibition are not the first and not the last restrictions to be placed on substances in our history... In the War of the Second Coalition (1798–1801 CE), Napoleon Bonaparte (1769–1821 CE) won Egypt after his successful campaign at the Battle of the Pyramids (Figure 11.4). Napoleon found vast proportions of the Egyptian lower class were consuming hashish on a regular basis[28]. Reports indicate that Napoleon was appalled by their blatant use of hashish. To be fair alcohol was banned

Figure 11.4 Napoleon Looking Upon a Mummy in Egypt

Morphart Creation/Shutterstock.com

by Muslim law in Egypt, which in turn led to the use of hashish by the people as a means of relaxation and enjoyment. It did not take long for Napoleon's soldiers to begin consuming hashish in their downtime as a means to relax. The accounts indicated that Napoleon was livid when his commanders reported his army's new recreational activity, and in 1801 CE it resulted in the creation of the world's first *cannabis prohibition law*. Napoleon was reported to have told his war council that "habitual smokers and drinkers of this plant lose their reason and suffer from violent delirium in which they are liable to commit excesses of all kinds"[29]. Cafes or restaurants serving hashish were forcibly closed and ordered to be walled up and their proprietors imprisoned in work camps for a minimum of three months. These new restrictions led to the Egyptian people rioting against the prohibition. Four months after the prohibition was put into place, the combined English and Ottoman-Turk armies brought the prohibition to an end when they defeated Napoleon's army and captured Egypt. Napoleon's soldiers took the hookah and hashish back to France and by 1805 CE, it is estimated that hashish was available for purchase in ~70 shops in Paris alone.

After routing Napoleon from Egypt in 1801 CE, the United Kingdom took control of the country. Many of the artifacts found by the French at the end of their occupation of Egypt were seized and taken for display in the British Museum. The Rosetta Stone was among the spoils of war that found its way to the Museum where it resides to this day. Egypt under British rule witnessed a flood of unique artifacts into London fueling the *Egyptomania* craze[30]. Historians, archaeologists, wealthy citizens, members of the middle classes, and soldiers flocked to the country to explore its treasures and enjoy exotic vacations. This period has come to be known as the Rape of the Nile. The wealthy tourists were eager to bring home souvenirs, including whole mummies which could be purchased from street vendors in Cairo for only a few pounds sterling. Historical and archaeological sites were vandalized and much of Egyptian history was lost, destroyed, and removed in the mad dash to quell British Egyptomania.

Egyptomania took a very gruesome turn between 1830 and 1840 CE in London as *Mummy Unwrapping Parties* became all the rage and were the centerpiece for very fashionable social events for the upper classes[30]. Invitations to these parties were very much sought after, as they were considered to be the most exotic affairs for the social season[31]. Mummies would be laid on top of a table in the parlor to be unwrapped after dinner. Invited guests would be treated to a rich and sumptuous meal full of wines and liquors. After eating, the guest would adjourn to the parlor and the ghastly process of unwrapping the mummy would begin. Any trinkets found during the unwrapping process would be given as mementos to the invited guests. Copious amounts of liquor and wine would have continued to be doled out during the unwrapping. Some of the parties would be accompanied by their own string quartet, who provided background music throughout the torrid events of the evening. One side effect of these mummy unwrapping parties was the unique and pungent odor many of the mummies were reported to have had[30]. Some guests would vomit from the stench, others would leave, and many a young woman was reported to have passed out overcome by the odor. Dubious accounts of the mummies being used as medicine, aphrodisiacs, and even drugs. "Mummy" was an excipient listed in the British pharmacopeia[32]. The linen wrappings taken from the mummies were added to tinctures, poultices, and concoctions to confer longevity or improve sexual health[33]. Mummy wrappings were so abundant in London during this time that some street food vendors would wrap food in the discarded linens as they were cheaper to purchase than newspaper. Bits of mummy flesh were ingested directly or added as a compounding ingredient to liquid and solid medicines. Should the mummy prove to be male—after all the linen wrappings had been removed—their shame would only increase as the penis and testicles were thought to aid in impotence, confer fertility, and improve sexual vigor.

Phlogisticated nitrous air was a gas first synthesized by English chemist and natural philosopher, Joseph Priestley (1733–1804 CE) in 1772 CE and would go on to become known as nitrous oxide[34, 35]. *Phlogisticated* refers to a process to exhaust oxygen within a sealed tube by burning a combustible material (charcoal or phosphorus), with the remaining gas produced in the process being composed chiefly of nitrogen. Nitrous oxide (NO_2) is a potent dissociative inhalant capable of causing analgesia, depersonalization, derealization, dizziness, euphoria, and flanging (sound distortions)[36]. It has been known to cause slight hallucinations and has a mild aphrodisiac effect. Most individuals who are exposed to the gas appear stuporous, dreamy, sedated, and many "get the giggles" where they erupt in bouts of laughter for no apparent reason. NO_2 did not become an anesthetic, nor was it used in medicine for nearly 100 years after it was originally discovered. In the United States, NO_2 was employed by traveling carnivals and circuses as a means of soliciting more patrons[37]. Samuel Colt, inventor of the Colt 45 revolver, was a traveling lecturer in these carnivals who made use of nitrous oxide inhalation on audience volunteers. It was through the use of nitrous oxide while providing hands-on demonstrations of his prototype revolver that Colt was able to garner enough money to finance and produce his first five-shot revolver (Figure 11.5). Laughing gas was provided during intermissions at operas and theater performances in London to help the audience have enhanced experiences. Among the British and American upper classes, "laughing gas parties" were all the rage. These parties of the wealthy helped to make the euphoria inducing properties of NO_2 common place and normal in the mid to late 1800s CE[38].

Figure 11.5 Example of the Five-Shot Revolver

Lucus Hunt/Shutterstock.com

The early part of the nineteenth century CE was full of quackery and an expansion of pseudosciences which dominated medicine and pharmaceutical sciences. *Quackery* is the promotion of fraudulent, ignorant, and usually dangerous medical or drug practices[1]. Quackery requires the skill of a quack or charlatan. *Quack* refers to the person or persons who pretends, professionally or publicly or both, to have skills, knowledge, qualifications, or credentials they do not possess. Quacks in the nineteenth century CE were known to use impure or bad blood as a vague yet frequently cited cause of many of the illnesses people experienced. Quacks are sometimes referred to as charlatans or snake oil salesmen. *Charlatans* are professional swindlers, often employing confidence tricks or other forms of deception to gain money, fame, or other advantages. *Pseudoscience* represents a form of fake or only partly true science represented as being a full-fledged and legitimate science[39]. Pseudoscience relies on statements, beliefs, or practices that claim to be rooted in science and fact but were derived in the absence of evidence gathered and were not constrained by any credible scientific methodology. Pseudoscience is often characterized by contradictory, exaggerated, or unfalsifiable claims. There is a reliance on the practitioner of pseudoscience on confirmation bias rather than rigorous attempts to prove or refute their hypothesis through reproducible methodology. *Confirmation bias* only seeks out information that will support and confirm the claim being made while ignoring and actively discrediting information that does not support said claim. Confirmation bias relies on stereotypes to help support the claims, often inciting strong emotional reactions (positive and negative) to information in support of their claim. Pseudoscience has a lack of transparency or openness to evaluation by other experts. Theories generated through pseudoscience tend to exist in a world absent of systematic processes and practices.

Two of the most prominent pseudosciences during the nineteenth century CE were phrenology and physiognomy (Figure 11.7). Phrenology was a highly popular practice, in fashion, and regarded as scientific fact. Phrenology claimed to be able to identify temperamental characteristics such as aggression and passionate traits such as lust (or amativeness) simply by feeling the lumps and bumps on an individual's skull. The central tenant of phrenology was based on the idea that the brain was the organ of the mind, and as such certain regions or areas acted as modules or regulators for specific emotional, moral, and primal impulses. *Phrenology* was the process of determining an individual's psychological and emotional attributes by observing and palpating (feeling) the individual's skull[40]. Diagnosis required the phrenologists to run their fingertips and palms over the skulls of their patients to feel for enlargements, indentations, fissures, and bulges. As the century progressed, additional ways of evaluating the skull were incorporated like using a tape measure or craniometer to get measurements of specific features of an individual's skull (Figure 10.8). *Craniometer* was a special caliper developed to allow for fine measurements of the skull in greater detail. Similar to phrenology was *physiognomy*. Physiognomy was the art of evaluating moral and emotional character from observation of one's facial characteristics[41]. It was claimed that not only could one determine moral character from the assessment of facial features and expressions, physiognomy was also used to discern ethnic origin. Where phrenology attempted to determine mental and emotional abilities, physiognomy was intent on correlating a person's outward appearance to their personality and demeanor. Both were discredited and shown to be cornerstones of a pervasive scientific racism and a part of the eugenics movements of the

Figure 11.6 Craniometer, External Spring Caliper

Gabriel Dominella/Shutterstock.com

Figure 11.7 Phrenology Map on Porcelain Head

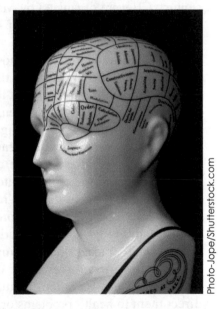

Photo-Jope/Shutterstock.com

nineteenth and twentieth centuries[42]. The pseudosciences of phrenology and physiognomy attempted to prove a baseless hypothesis about the inferiority of non-white races.

When the living did not have the answers for the problems in one's life, there was always the opportunity to use psychic energy to communicate with the dearly departed. Areas of the occult gained prominence in the nineteenth century CE, with the séance becoming an important aspect of life. *Séance* was the practice of communing with the spirits of the dead and required the use and agency of a medium in order to pierce the veil between the living world and the world of the dead[43]. The medium was claimed to have psychic abilities and would communicate for the spirits of the dead. Séance is a French word, meaning "seat," "session," or "sitting together." It became used to describe a meeting of people, gathered to receive messages from ghosts or to listen to a spirit medium have discourses with or relay messages between the living and spirits who may be present (Figure 11.8). Some of the most famous séances conducted during the nineteenth century CE were organized by Mary Todd Lincoln (1818–1882 CE), wife of President Abraham Lincoln (1809–1865 CE)[44]. Mary was distraught after the loss of her son and organized a séance in the White House attended by the President and other prominent Senators, Congressmen, and prominent members of society[45].

Figure 11.8 Illustration of the Lincoln Family

Everett Collection/Shutterstock.com

Thanks in part to a growing interest in Spiritualism, England in the nineteenth century CE witnessed the rise of healing séance and psychic surgeries. *Spiritualism*, was a social movement in which people believed in the continuity of one's consciousness after their death and that there was the potential to communicate and interact with the departed's spirit[46]. Spiritualism brought with it unique tools of its quasi-religious trade, including Tarot Cards, Ouija boards, crystal balls, and psychic shops. *Healing séances* were performed by psychics and mediums who used "unseen hands" and through their connection with the spirit world they would gain "wisdom of higher, multidimensional" sciences[39]. During these healing séances the psychics and mediums would be able to perform *spiritual operations* on the attendees who may or may not have even known they had an illness. These operations required the psychic or medium to converse with the spirits who would direct them to health problems or issues within the aura or spirit of an attendee. If the health problem was serious enough, the psychic or medium may need to perform *psychic surgery[47]*. Psychic surgery was the greatest illusion of the séance arsenal as it was mock surgery performed with the bare hand of the psychic or medium to convince the "patient" that their disease had been rendered harmless. Sometimes, the psychic or medium would have fake blood packets or bits of animal livers concealed and at the right time would drop the tissue or pop the blood packet to add to their performance. The bits of animal livers would be tossed by a hidden accomplice at the right moment to add to the effect.

When we think of sofa styles today, we have a lot of variety to choose from (Figure 11.9). There are love seats, sectionals, or settees. A couch, made necessary, thanks in part to the corset, was the *fainting couch* in the early part of the 1800s CE[48]. Fainting couches were essentially a daybed with a curvy wooden frame and back with one end being raised. Every household of respect had fainting couches in the common rooms. Due to tight corsets and extremely heavy clothing, it was common for women to periodically faint from lack of oxygen[49]. The fainting couch and through the use of smelling salts women

Figure 11.9   Example of a Fainting Couch

Michael C. Gray/Shutterstock.com

could recover while the dinner party or cocktail hour progressed, often times happening with them laid out on the couch recovering[50]. *Smelling salts* are chemical compounds that function as a stimulant, primarily used to arouse someone to consciousness. The active compound is ammonium carbonate, a colorless-to-milky-white crystalline solid. When mixed with water it creates an *aromatic spirit of ammonia*. Smelling salts work because the human body aggressively reacts to ammonia gas. When sniffed, the gas irritates the nostril membranes and lungs, which causes a sharp inhalation reflex, pulling in more oxygen. Smelling salts raise an individual's blood pressure, heart rate, and oxygen levels, helping brain activity and reactivating the sympathetic nervous system. It is similar to jump starting an engine and relies on our fight or flight processes to get us away from the ammonia.

There was a mysterious illness afflicting women beginning in the middle of the nineteenth century CE, it was hysteria. *Hysteria* was a condition of exaggerated or uncontrollable emotion expressing itself as excitement or irritability in excess[51]. Popular medical thought at the time believed that hysteria manifested itself in women with a broad constellation of symptoms, including anxiety, shortness of breath, fainting, insomnia, irritability, nervousness, and sexually forward behavior. It was primarily a women's husband who would make the initial diagnosis and then have it confirmed by a physician[3]. Really the diagnosis was given mostly to women who dared to disobey their Victorian husbands. There were a few cures to free the woman from her hysteria one involved opium and the other required the women to achieve "hysterical paroxysm." *Hysterical paroxysm* was a very misogynistic way of ridding the woman of her hysteria, as it required that she achieve an orgasm provided by her husband.

While men were not subjected to hysterics, they did have their own sexual woes to contend with during the nineteenth century CE. *Masturbation* was widely believed to be not only morally wrong but also very harmful to the health of males[52]. A psychiatrist and soon to be physician-in-chief at Hôpital Salpêtrière in Paris, Jean-Etienne Dominique Esquirol (1772–1840 CE) had made masturbation a classifiable and concerning mental disorder, and had stated that masturbation was "recognized in all countries as a cause of insanity"[53, 54]. Self-pollution, self-abuse, or onanism were the terms used to describe masturbation and it was thought to be morally destructive and physically harmful if left unabated. Benjamin Rush (1746–1813 CE), a signer of the Declaration of Independence and skilled surgeon, argued that "self-abuse is the root of all evil and leads to excessive drinking and other forms of self-wastage. Avoid engaging in this disgusting habit"[55]. Today, it is a scientific fact that masturbation is a common and normal sexual activity. In the nineteenth century CE, a vast array of physical and mental disorders was believed to be caused by masturbation. Men, it seems, were predisposed to base needs, and had to combat habitual urges that threatened to deplete their vital energies through fornication, masturbation, and nocturnal emissions[56]. Men were counselled by their families, clergy, physicians, and friends to avoid sexual interactions of all kinds unless there was the intent of procreation.

Food was seen as a way to get young men and adolescent boys to not fixate on their penises nor fall victim to the self-abuse of masturbation. Two men who thought that through good nutrition, a strict diet, and exercise self-abuse could be curbed were Sylvester Graham (1794–1851 CE) and Dr. John Harvey Kellogg (1852–1943 CE). Sylvester Graham was the inventor of the Graham Cracker and Dr. Kellogg was the inventor of granula, which would become corn flakes, and the founder of the Kellogg's food company. Graham was not a big fan of sex, in fact, as a puritanical minister he preached that the carnal desires felt by man were the root cause of headaches, epilepsy, and insanity[57]. In 1829 CE in an attempt to keep his congregation from falling into the wild throws of passion, he invented a bland cracker, which in his mind was the perfect replacement for masturbation and tempering sexual urges[58]. This cracker would go on to become the graham *cracker*, the staple in America's favorite campfire confection s'mores. Dr. Kellogg was a physician and Seventh-Day Adventist who founded a sanatorium in Battle Creek, Michigan where he promoted his healthy way of living (Figure 11.10). *Granula*, the original name for Kellogg's Corn Flakes, was invented by Dr. Kellogg as part of his healthy living practice. This practice consisted of healthy eating and weight management. He recommended plenty of exercise, no excessive calories, vegetarianism, and abstinence from alcohol and tobacco. Masturbation, in Kellogg's opinion, was the unhealthiest thing one could participate in as it

Figure 11.10 America's Favorite Campfire Confection—S'Mores

Olga Miltsova/Shutterstock.com

degraded one's body, mind, and soul[59]. Circumcision of male babies was a practice that Kellogg endorsed, claiming that it would help the baby avoid self-harm in his teens and adulthood[60, 61]. Dr. Kellogg was so influential that for ~100 years circumcision at birth became standard practice in delivery wards across the United States. Diet was the second way Kellogg envisioned to help halt masturbatory habits. All spices, pickles, and sugar were, to Kellogg, the root of vice and if consumed would lead people to masturbation, smoking, drinking, and all manner of deviance and vice[62]. These erroneous and often times damaging beliefs about masturbation led to a lot of misinformation to enter into public belief. Many of those beliefs about male sexuality would go unchallenged until the sexual revolution of the 1960s CE.

11.3   Snake Oils, Cure-Alls, and Addiction

Science and chemistry in the beginning of the nineteenth century CE was in its infancy but was attempting to make revolutionary advances in pharmacology. There was an ongoing quest for the perfect drug, a *panakeiai* or panacea. The miracle cure or wonder drug that would cure every and anything. Several substances made during this time claimed to be successively more modern, improved, or enhanced versions of ancient remedies. Approximately 70,000 concoctions of rare and special ingredients were available, some stocked on shelves in the early pharmacies of the United States and Europe and others sold by gypsies and traveling "doctors." Many of these ill-fated wonder drugs contained psychoactive drugs like opium. *Quicksilver*, or mercury, was a favorite ingredient and was used to fatal ends (Figure 11.11). Any drug or concoction could be widely advertised in publications, on posters, and in billboards even if they held no medical benefit or hope for cure. There was no regulation nor control over the marketing of products in the 1800s CE. You could claim your product cured cancer, even if it had been proven to cause cancer and no one would bat an eye about the false claims made by your ad. If you could pay the advertising fee, you were free to promote your product.

Figure 11.11   Mercury

megaflopp/Shutterstock.com

Mercury in the beginning of the nineteenth century CE was considered to be a wonder drug. It was employed to treat every and anything that ailed people. Scrapped your knee? Rub some mercury on it. Have problems with regularity? Forget fiber, get some mercury into your diet. Headache? Massage mercury into the temples. If quicksilver was not leaking from at least one orifice, you were considered to be extremely unhealthy. Mercury was and remains highly toxic and a small amount is sufficient to lead to mercury poisoning. Symptoms of mercury poisoning include chest pains, heart and lung problems, coughing, tremors, violent muscle spasms, psychotic reactions, delirium, hallucinations, suicidal tendencies, restless spleen syndrome, testicular torsion, and anal leakage[63].

Snake oil has come to define any substance that holds no valid medicinal use, and is sold as a remedy for any and all diseases even those that were made-up or invented to sell the product[1]. These were fraudulent medicines that had absolutely no snake extracts in their formula. These types of fake medicines were known as "snake oil" in the United States, "viper oil" in Europe, and "water snake oil" in China. The exact formula of these concoctions varied among the producers, but many contained mineral oil, fatty oil (either from beef or pig fat), crushed red pepper, turpentine, camphor, juniper, and trace amounts of opium. Snake oil was often sold from a traveling "doctor" who had flimsy and dubious credentials to their name. They would come into a town and with great fanfare and boisterous marketing techniques would sell their fake medicines to the unsuspecting[64]. Snake oil salesmen would have used pseudo-scientific claims and confidence gambits to provide evidence of how the specific medicine worked. Snake oil charlatans would often employ an accomplice, who would be casually positioned in the crowd. This accomplice is known as a shill, a patsy, or a plant. The shill would attest to the healing value of the product and often would buy the first bottle to help encourage sales. Some would even proceed to take the medicine in front of the crowd and proclaim they could feel its healing effects. Mysteriously, the "doctor" and shill would leave town before their customers realized they had been cheated[22].

A wide variety of drugs were marketed and sold in retail locations and via mail order with no oversight or protections for consumers. These drugs were marketed to cure disease, improve appearance, restore vitality, and invigorate the constitution all without any scientific data to support the claims. Two examples are Boschee's German Syrup and Hamlin's Wizard Oil. ***Boschee's German Syrup*** was sold to help treat conditions of consumption, pneumonia, hemorrhages, asthma, severe coughs, croup, and other throat and lung diseases. Sample bottles were available for 10 cents with full size bottles costing 75 cents[65]. After returning from fighting for the Union Army in the U.S. Civil War, Col. Green bought the rights to his father's medicinal syrup which contained laudanum, alcohol, and extract of August Flower. He began marketing the concoction as Boschee's German Syrup (Figure 11.12). Laudanum in the United States during the nineteenth century CE was a combination of opium, morphine, codeine, and cocaine, which made for a much more potent drug than its European cousin. Boschee's German Syrup was a highly addictive product and made Col. Green a millionaire in the first year of sales[66]. Boschee's claimed to be created in Germany, but was manufactured in Pasadena, California.

Hamlin's Wizard Oil was created by two traveling magicians, John Austen Hamlin and Lysander Hamlin, who were part of a carnival that featured a medical show (Figure 11.13). These medical shows gleefully mimicked other vaudeville like shows and featured musical comedy, minstrels, magic tricks, burlesque, dog and pony circuses, pantomime, menageries, bands, pie-eating contests, and even early motion pictures[67]. The Hamlin brothers were excellent performers and knew how to make profits appear. They claimed that their Wizard Oil could cure neuralgia, toothaches, diphtheria, rheumatism, and cancer. The main ingredients of Wizard Oil

Figure 11.12 Boschee's German Syrup

Source: https://digital.library.ucla.edu/catalog/
ark:/21198/zz0002hj14

Figure 11.13 Hamlin's Wizard Oil

Source: https://www.loc.gov/pictures/
item/2002719119/

were ammonia and chloroform, which probably caused more harm than good. Wizard Oil had advertisements in farmer's almanacs, newspapers, and magazine periodicals[68]. Hamlin's Wizard Oil was even useful for curing a slew of farm and domestic animal diseases. Hamlin's Wizard Oil was sold to farmers who could use the concoction for their families pain and the pain of their livestock.

Smoking opium became a common practice during the 1800s CE. Opium had been used as a medicine for centuries, but the Chinese method of smoking opium took root in Europe and the United States, and swiftly became widespread. Opium smoking spread initially with Chines immigrants and spawned a number of notorious opium dens in Chinatowns throughout Europe and the Americas. Bohemian communities in Europe, especially the neighborhoods of Montparnasse and Montmartre in Paris became Opium Capitals. These Opium Capitals controlled the majority of opium distribution throughout Europe from the early nineteenth century CE to 1918 CE. *Bohemians* can be best described as writers or artists who have very informal and highly unconventional social habits[69]. Bohemians typically lived very communally and would share their space with others, often times squatting in abandoned buildings[70]. Bohemians were the Victorian Era version of a urban gypsy and were often described as vagabonds and wanderers.

Wormwood, *Atremisia absinthium*, is an herb that is highly prized for its distinct aroma, herbaceous flavor, and pharmacological effects. Wormwood is native to Europe, but has been transplanted to Asia, Africa, South America, and the United States. It has long been considered a hallucinogen and potent poison and, as such, it was banned in the United States between 1912 and 2007 CE[71]. Wormwood is a component used to make alcoholic beverages. *Vermouth* is a wine-based beverage that has been flavored with extracts of wormwood. *Absinthe* is perhaps the most well-known alcoholic beverages to feature wormwood. Absinthe is a rich emerald-green alcoholic drink that is prepared from the essential oil of wormwood paired with anise and fennel (Figure 11.14). Absinthe was popularized among famous artists and writers from the nineteenth and twentieth centuries CE, including Toulouse-Lautrec, Degas, Manet, van Gough, Picasso, Hemingway, and Oscar Wilde[72]. The main alkaloid in wormwood is *thujone*. Distilling wormwood in alcohol increases the thujone concentrations making the alcohol much more potent[73]. Thujone has been shown excite the central nervous system, can lead to seizures, paralysis, and death at high concentrations[74].

Figure 11.14 Absinthe

Victor Moussa/Shutterstock.com

The social, economic, and political imbalances between countries throughout the 1800s CE were instrumental in how the commodity chain functioned. The use and sales of drugs through different economic channels helped to shape beliefs about drugs and how drug markets functioned. The popular concept of the word "drug" took on two meanings by the mid-point of the 1800s CE. *Drug* was used to refer to medicine, and drug was used as a way to express vice and addiction with the addition of criminality, danger, and illegality. Scientifically, there was growing interest in *intoxication* which was the Victorian eras notion of addiction[38]. Intoxication was the idea that external compounds interacted with internal substances that caused an imbalance in how the body reacted or responded. Some of the compounds we take in are necessary and others like poisons are deleterious and still others like drugs could be beneficial or detrimental. Drugs were beginning to be thought of as having a chemical process and it was through the activation of that process which led to intoxication. In addition, this was the start of ***pharmacologicalism***, which was a largely arbitrary, somewhat socially clueless, and highly profitable division of drugs into the categories of "good drugs" and "bad drugs"[75]. Good drugs represented those drugs that people spent money on to assist with health, today we would consider prescription drugs to be "good drugs." Bad drugs represented those drugs that society shunned and attempted to suppress, today we would consider recreational drugs taken for enjoyment and not medication to be "bad drugs." The problem with pharmacologicalism is that the boundary between good and bad drug shifts with context, fad, and whimsy. What is a good drug today may end up being a bad drug tomorrow. In reality, there is no such thing as a good drug or bad drug, there are just drugs. What makes them good or bad is the use and intent behind the use, which is socio-politically motivated in most cases.

Excessive use of drugs and alcohol had been incorporated into a constellation of ruinous behaviors of which Victorian society sought to discourage and suppress. Those ruinous behaviors were known as ***vices***, habits which weakened one's moral character[76]. Some of the most concerning behaviors were gambling, prostitution, drinking, drug use, and sexual deviance. During the latter part of the 1800s CE, people who were unable to control their vices were thought of as having ***compulsive behaviors***, which made them unable to stop doing the wrong, harmful, or unnecessary actions inherent in their vice. This was the same era in human history that saw drug and behavioral addictions as being rooted in the vices of the individual. When it pertained to drugs, their vice highlighted their chemical dependency which was influenced by their compulsive behaviors which fueled addiction.

11.4   Social Progress and Scientific Innovation of the Late Nineteenth Century

"It was the best of times, it was the worst of times, it was the age of wisdom, it was the age of foolishness, it was the epoch of belief, it was the epoch of incredulity…" Charles Dickens[77].

In the above quote, Dickens summarizes the feel of the latter half of the nineteenth century CE quite well. There was a running epithet in the Late Industrial Revolution, related to the notion of "progress." Notably, the progress that most notably gets discussed is related to social, economic, and scientific advancements. Progress is a very loaded term, as it implies a change from a primitive form to a more complex or "civilized" form. It makes us think of human society as evolving in a linear manner with clear demarcations and points of growth experienced by everyone. We are lulled into believing that progress is a good thing, helping to tame nature and bring the uncivilized into modernity. We are led into thinking that progress means more opportunity for everyone. Progress is seen as a good and necessary force in how societies improve… But is it truly? The human quest for progress had led us to the brink of environmental collapse, has pitted ethnic groups against one another, has seen poverty rise, and led to vast differences between nations. However, many scholars still use progress as a badge of honor to show how societies have changed over time.

The Industrial Revolution was a time of change, tensions, and competition that saw scientific, economic, and social progress[78, 79]. ***Scientific progress*** was the idea that humans increase their ability to solve problems and make advancements through the application of science and technology.

The measure of scientific progress is in how the scientific community of a nation begins to collectively learn and increase their knowledge through the accumulation of written and shared scientific wisdom. *Economic progress* relied on a sophistication of trade, innovation, monetary, and manufacturing systems that improve commerce. The goal is the generation of wealth for more of the populous. Economic progress is measured by an increase in profits and the expansion of markets. More products that are made in less time for less money allow for the increase in profits. New transportation methods, like the use of the steam engine for shipping vessels at sea and locomotives on land, helped to improve global trade which expanded the markets for goods. *Social progress* was concerned with the processes in which societies overall become better and more sophisticated. It looks at political stability as a central marker of success. Social progress should provide for an acceptable standard of living for all. Similarly, there should be equal access to the law and equal treatment under the law for all citizens. A shared set of social norms and values would create a sense of unity and identity that is reflected back in the behavior, art, literature, and cultural ephemera of the citizens. Key aspects of social progress include the disappearance of slavery; a rise in literacy rates; lessening of inequalities based on sexuality, gender, race, and ethnicity; reformation of capital punishment; and declines in poverty. All the upheaval caused by the Industrial Revolution and the mad dash to identify progress had some serious and negative effects in people's lives. Insomnia, neuroses, and exhaustion became increasingly prevalent as the century came to a close. It was not progress, but it was an era marked by colonialism, social class rigidity, over pricing of goods, and overcrowding of urban centers.

The latter part of the 1800s CE witnessed an increase in turmoil and social unrest. Religion was facing different crises of faith as the catholic church had to deal with evolution, fracturing with the church and a rise in the converts to Protestant beliefs. Family dynamics were changing as people moved from extended family dwellings in the countryside to single family units in the city. Economics were changing and many people were now relying on the ever-expanding factory systems, which paid daily, and may or may not retain employees for the long term. Some people were seeking a return to the good old days, others fell into disarray as they navigated the modern world, and still others were in a liminal space. *Liminal* is a term borrowed from sociology and anthropology to indicate how someone can occupy a position at, or on both sides of an issue, they are in between two transitional states[80]. Think of a window, one side is in the house the other is outside, the space between is liminal. These liminal individuals of the 1800s CE were unable to adapt to the past and wholly unprepared for the future. Swept up in the midst of the rapid changes and seemingly unstoppable technological advances, people were looking for some respite. *Escapism* became a normalized part of life as people were happy to accept drugs with the capacity to alter their state of mind and influence their perception of pleasure and time. The drugs helped ease away tensions and provided a refuge from the difficulties the people were experiencing.

By the middle of the 1800s CE, drugs had begun to change. No longer was it necessary to carry bulky and large volumes of plant stuffs around with you to treat diseases and illnesses. Not only would it have been necessary to carry a wide variety of plants, it would have also required a large amount of plant materials to be useful to treat different diseases. All of that changed with the discovery of *pure compounds*, which removed the uncertainty inherent in the unequal potency of natural plants[81]. Pure compounds represent the chemical structures that can be synthetically manufactured, and their chemical structure remains constant for much longer. Pure compounds meant it was possible to attain exact dosing every time the medication was used. Pure compounds helped to improve the margin of safety for consumers because the dose and potency remained constant. Physicians medicine bags could now carry the equivalent of several acres worth of plant stuffs and offer a wider range of drug options thanks to pure compounds. By the end of the 1800s CE, drugs had moved out of the realm of magic, ceremony, and rites into science.

There were some revolutionary people in the latter half of the 1800s, who worked to advance science, medicine, and pharmacology. These individuals included Florence Nightingale (Figure 11.15), Sigmund Freud, Jacques-Joseph Moreau de Tours, Henri René Albert Guy de Maupassant, Alexander Wood, Louis Pasteur, and Marie and Pierre Curie. Florence Nightingale (1820–1910 CE) was the manager of nurses at the Scutari barracks hospital in Constantinople (modern day Istanbul) during the Crimean War (1853–1856 CE), where she was instrumental in organizing and tending to the wounded soldiers[82]. She helped pioneer a triage system that helped to identify worst to best outcome in an emergency/trauma setting. She was responsible for giving nursing a highly favorable reputation and after the war she established the professional foundation for nursing with the establishment of her nursing school at St. Thomas' Hospital in London. Nightingale adapted her previous knowledge and skills from providing care in a disaster setting and tailored it to everyday care within a hospital. She was known to be quite liberal with providing opium or morphine to alleviate the pain and suffering of her patients.

Sigmund Freud (1856–1939 CE) was an Austrian neurologist and creator of the psychoanalytic method for clinically evaluating and treating mental disorders and neuropathologies (Figure 11.16) [83]. ***Psychoanalysis*** was the clinical method Freud invented for treating psychopathologies that involved direct dialogue between a patient and trained psychoanalyst. Freud initiated the world's first global clinical research trial which featured self-report surveys, extensive literature reviews, and culminated in the generation of the many and potential uses for cocaine as a therapeutic agent[84]. This study was the first full scale global drug trial sponsored by a pharmaceutical company, Parke-Davis. Park-Davis had allegedly paid Freud in cocaine in addition to a modest monetary stipend. Additionally, Park-Davis paid for Freud to endorse their cocaine product as being superior to their competitor's product, Merck being the competition. Coincidentally, Merck had obtained Freud's endorsement of their product as well. We do not know the terms of his endorsement offer from Merck, suffice it to say he was making quite a bit of money from cocaine. Freud was rarely seen consuming alcohol but was a heavy user of cocaine from age 29 to 41. Freud had become the world's authority on cocaine, with reports indicating that he believed that cocaine was an extremely useful medicine[85]. Freud originally believed that the drug could be taken without any

Figure 11.15   Florence Nightingale

Everett Collection/Shutterstock.com

Figure 11.16   Sigmund Freud

Everett Collection/Shutterstock.com

consequences. He tested his assumptions on himself as a subject and ultimately developed an addiction. At age 42, he withdrew from the drug, ceased advocating for its use publicly, and refrained from further discussion of the drug. It is an odd case because upon quitting the drug Freud never turned the psychoanalytic lens inward to consider his own self addiction. Much later in life when asked about his cocaine use, Freud had said "I was making frequent use of cocaine. I had been the first to recommend the use of cocaine in 1885, and this recommendation has brought serious reproaches down on me"[83, 85]. In terms of substance abuse among other individuals, Freud would have used a developmental perspective to understand addiction. From this standpoint, Freud would have concluded that many individuals who abuse alcohol and drugs have developed strong unconscious dependency needs because of a frustrated quest for parental love and approval in childhood.

Jacques-Joseph Moreau de Tours (1804–1884 CE), better known by his nickname "Moreau de Tours," was a French physician turned psychiatrist and the founding member of "Les Club des Hashischins" in Paris[86]. Moreau de Tours was the first physician to do systematic research on the effects of cannabis, specifically on its central nervous system effects. He catalogued, analyzed, and recorded his observations in great detail. Moreau de Tours believed that cannabis provided a unique means to understand the human mind and should therefore be the subject of scientific investigation[87]. He established *Les Club des Hashischins* as an enclave of Bohemians (writers and artists) with illustrious members like Gautier, Baudelaire, Delacroix, Nerval, Verlaine, Rimbaud, Hugo, and Balzac. Moreau de Tours recorded the results of the "sessions" and published them in a series on utopias or artificial paradises created through recorded discussions under the influence of cannabis[88].

Henri René Albert Guy de Maupassant (1850–1893 CE), best known as Guy de Maupassant, was a French writer and the master of the short story format[89]. His stories are representative of the naturalist school of thought and many of his works depicted human lives and destinies intertwined with social forces of disillusionment and pessimism[90]. Guy de Maupassant was famous as being among a list of 46 Parisian literary and artistic notables who endorsed a letter sent to the mayor and city leaders of Paris to vehemently decry the construction of the Eiffel Tower. They believed it would be a blight on the beauty of the Parisian landscape and would detract rather than attract potential tourists, scholars, and students. Guy de Maupassant became the most notorious ether addict of the late 1800s CE. Guy de Maupassant's ether use towards the end of his life caused him to develop a fear of the public, an obsession for solitude, a growing preoccupation with self-preservation, and a deep fear of death coupled with paranoia of persecution[91].

By the 1840s CE, there was an increasing interest in a more direct and controlled application of drugs. In 1844, Dr. Francis Rynd (1801–1861 CE) an Irish physician had invented the hollow needle and the metal cylinder of the syringe[92]. He is credited with giving the first successful injection of a drug directly into the blood stream of a human. In 1851 CE, *Dr. Alexander Wood* (1817–1884 CE) a Scottish physician improved on the metal syringe and created the all-glass syringe[92]. The glass syringe was far superior to its metal predecessor as it allowed the user to estimate dosages based on the levels of liquid observed through the glass. In addition, the glass syringe allowed air bubbles to be detected and removed prior to administration (Figure 11.17). There are reports that Rebecca Massey (1820–1895 CE), Dr. Wood's wife, was the first documented intravenous morphine

Figure 11.17 Glass Hypodermic Syringe

fifelio/Shutterstock.com

addict and thanks to her husband's invention had died of an overdose. However, those reports are a bit unfounded as Rebecca outlived her husband by 9 years, albeit the causes of her death are not well known. Dr. Wood is credited with the popularization and acceptance of injection as a medical technique and his work led to the widespread use and acceptance of the *hypodermic needle[93, 94]*.

Louis Pasteur (1822–1895 CE) was a French chemist and microbiologist (Figure 11.18) who discovered the principles of vaccination, fermentation, and pasteurization[95]. His work helped to lay the foundations for modern concepts of hygiene and public health. Perhaps his most important clinical work was laying down the foundations of the germ theory of disease based on the identification of micro-bacterial organisms between 1860 and 1864 CE. He is known to the public for his work with milk and wine, wherein he invented the techniques to stop bacterial contamination, the process which bears his name, pasteurization[96].

Marie Salomea Skłodowska–Curie (1867–1934 CE) and *Pierre Curie* (1859–1906 CE) were physicists and chemists, whom after marrying (Figure 11.19), worked and pioneered research into the radioactivity of polonium and radium[97, 98]. The Curies were awarded a Nobel Prize in Physics in 1903 for their theory of radioactivity. *Radioactivity* was a term created by Marie Curie and was used to describe the ionizing radiation that gets emitted as nuclei within atoms degrade spontaneously and gradually. In 1911 Marie Curie won the Nobel Prize for Chemistry for the discovery of polonium and radium and the techniques she invented for the isolation of the radioactive isotopes. *Radium* was famously discovered and isolated by Marie and Pierre Curie who gave their health and in Marie's case, her life, for their work with the radioactive element[99]. Radium was embraced by the medical community of the late 1800s/beginning 1900s CE for its

Figure 11.18   Louis Pasteur

Everett Collection/Shutterstock.com

Figure 11.19   Pierre and Marie Curie

Everett Collection/Shutterstock.com

remarkable ability to destroy cancerous cells in the body. There was a catch, however, radium will affect any cell it encounters, cancerous or not. While it was good at killing cancer, it also destroyed surrounding noncancerous cells.

In addition to the science, treatments, and practice paradigms discussed above. The first of many diagnostic devices were created and used for the first time in the nineteenth century CE. Table 11.1 details some of the most important medical devices created and first utilized during the 1800s CE. Table 11.1 does not represent a comprehensive list as there were many more devices used for medicine that are both gruesome and deadly, many of which have thankfully fallen out of favor.

Table 11.1 Brief List of Important Medical Devices of the Nineteenth Century

Year	Device
1816*	Stethoscope
1840*	Kymograph
1850*	Binocular Microscope
1851*	Ophthalmoscope
1851	Glass-tube Hypodermic Needle
1895*	X-Ray

Source: T. D. Church * – will be discussed in further detail below.

Stethoscope (1816 CE) was invented to aid in the diagnosis of respiratory and cardiac disorders[100]. The stethoscope would become an iconic symbol of the medical profession. *Kymograph* (1840 CE) was an analog device created to graphically measure blood pressure and muscular contractions[101]. *Binocular microscope* (1850 CE) was an improvement to the instrument used to see objects too small to be seen with the naked eye, the improvement was to allow observations using both eyes[102]. *Ophthalmoscope* (1851 CE) was created to allow physicians to inspect the retina and other parts of the eye and ear[103]. *X-Ray* (1895 CE) provided a way to look inside the human body without cutting it open and could clearly identify bone structures, which initiated the field of medical imaging[104].

11.5 Pure Compounds and Mass Production of Drugs

With the discovery of pure compounds and an expanding ability to chemically synthesize drugs the nineteenth century CE saw a rapid expansion of pharmaceuticals and addition of new drug classes. Science had unlocked the active components of the drugs that were the most active in humans, the alkaloids. *Alkaloids* are nitrogenous organic compounds of plant origin, which have pronounced physiological actions on humans. Alkaloids are formations of carbon (C), hydrogen (H), and nitrogen (N). Alkaloids were a part of the larger discovery and cataloging of *nuclear elements*, the constituents of organic and mineral matter. The catalog of nuclear elements is today referred to as the *periodic table*. These discoveries helped to catapult the creation of pure compounds in the synthesis and manufacture of drugs. By no means did these scientific discoveries make medicine any less "magical" but it did help to unmoor drugs from their ancient tethers of myth, legend, and magic. Table 11.2 highlights a selected list of drugs created from pure compounds.

From Table 11.2 the drugs denoted with an asterisk (*) will be discussed in a little more detail. For this section, the drugs will not be presented in the chronological order as listed in Table 11.2, but rather will be discussed by drug class. The first of the drug classes will be the drugs derived from opium. *Morphine* is an alkaloid of opium and has the ability to calm or suppress pain[105]. Morphine is stronger than opium and was first synthesized in 1806 CE. Morphine was used in battlefield medicine to astounding effect. The screaming and lamenting from field surgery tents became impossibly silent and it was often difficult to locate where the ward was in many encampments because there were no cries of pain to guide you. Morphine revolutionized the field of surgery as it proved to be a great pain reliever and sedative. It was employed near the end of the American Civil War

Table 11.2 Selected List of Pure Compound Discoveries of the Nineteenth Century CE

Year of Discovery	Pure Compound
1806	Morphine*
1832	Codeine
1832	Chloral hydrate*
1833	Atropine
1841	Caffeine
1844	Amyl Nitrite, Butyl Nitrite*
1848	Paraldehyde*
1853	Acetylsalicylic (Aspirin)
1855	Cocaine*
1863	Barbiturates*
1877	Paracetamol
1880	Mescaline*
1883	Heroin*
1887	Amphetamine
1893	Methamphetamine
1902	Vernol/Barbital*

(1861–1865 CE) and in the Franco-Prussian War of 1870 CE[106, 107]. In 1877 CE, a study conducted by a German physician reported the first historical cases of morphine addiction, claiming that the drug was wholly responsible for the scourge of morphine addiction[108]. Subsequent studies made the point to place the onus of addiction on the weakness of the character of the addict and went on to claim that chemical dependency to morphine is not possible[109]. *Chemical dependency* was the idea that an individual could become dependent upon a chemical due to the compulsively repeated alteration of brain chemistry from a chemical substance to elicit feelings of relief, well-being, or euphoria. By 1880 CE, there were a growing number of morphine addicts. It is believed that ~25% of the first identified morphine addicts were women, many of whom had been prescribed morphine as a cure for their hysteria. In addition, ~65% of all morphine addicts were believed to be therapists, health personnel, or relatives thereof as these individuals had easy access to morphine.

Heroin was a product created by the Bayer Company and was initially sold in a double package with aspirin (Figure 11.20). Heroin was synthesized in 1883 CE but did not gain in popularity until 1898 CE. By 1898 CE, Heroin inundated pharmacies. An avalanche of marketing

Figure 11.20   Heroin, Bayer Co

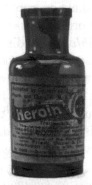

Source: DEA.gov https:// museum.dea.gov/ museumcollection/ collectionspotlight/ artifact/heroin-bottle

materials, including brochures accompanied the commercial release of Heroin. The brochures avoided any mention of the addictive qualities of the drug. Instead, the brochures focused on other "truths" of the product. Heroin was shown to have the opposite effect to that of morphine as it increased activity. Heroin was said to be able to calm all fears. Small doses of heroin stopped coughing of all types, including the coughing fits brought on by tuberculosis. Perhaps the most intriguing of the claims the brochures made was that morphine addicts treated with heroin immediately lost all interest in morphine. Conveniently, the brochure did not mention that the morphine addicts would go on to crave heroin. Heroin does produce the same anesthetic effect as morphine, but it does so at a much lower dose. Heroin does have a euphoric effect when the drug initially onsets and for a brief window of 15–30 minutes the drug functions as a gentle stimulant before the sedative effects manifest.

Morphine and heroin were venerated by Western missionaries in China and were seen as the best way to counteract opium addiction. Because of the intervention of these missionaries, morphine and heroin were given the colloquial name of "Christ's opium." Our ability to treat opium addiction has not progressed over the past 125 years, and today in 2022 the plan to treat heroin addiction is with yet another opium derivative (Figure 11.21). Methadone is an opioid derivative, and it produces similar feelings to other opioids while helping to minimize or reduce the withdrawal feelings a heavy her-

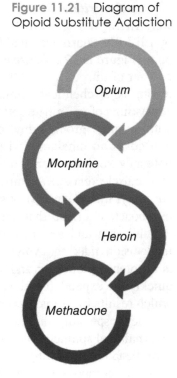

Figure 11.21 Diagram of Opioid Substitute Addiction

Source: T. D. Church

oin user experiences upon quitting the drug. In medicine, this is referred to as replacement therapy. Replacement therapy is a harm reduction technique in which one drug is substituted for another drug, hopefully one that is less harmful. Clinically, this would be done to make a serious difference in the health and wellbeing of a patient. Replacement therapy can be thought of as *substitute addiction*, wherein one addiction is swapped out for another, and as we have seen with opioids this can become an endless cycle of addiction passing from generation to generation with slight improvement.

Toward the middle of the 1800s CE, two new classes of drugs emerged. *Hypnotic* or Soporific drugs, commonly referred to as "sleeping pills," represent a class of psychoactive drugs whose primary function is to induce sleep and are often used in the treatment of insomnia[81]. Hypnotics can be used for surgical anesthesia as well. The second class of drugs represented the barbiturates. *Barbiturate* is a drug that functions as a CNS depressant[110]. Barbiturates provide a wide spectrum of effects that range from mild sedation to complete anesthesia. Two of the most popular hypnotics were chloral hydrate and paraldehyde. *Chloral hydrate* was synthesized in 1832 CE and was used to reduce anxiety and facilitated sleep before surgery[111]. *Paraldehyde* was synthesized in 1848 CE and was used to reduce anxiety, as a treatment for acute alcoholic dementia, and as a sedative[112]. The philosopher, Fredrich Nietzsche (1844–1900 CE), was reportedly addicted to chloral in addition to cannabis, opium, and cocaine during his lifetime[113].

Figure 11.22 Amyl Nitrite Capsules

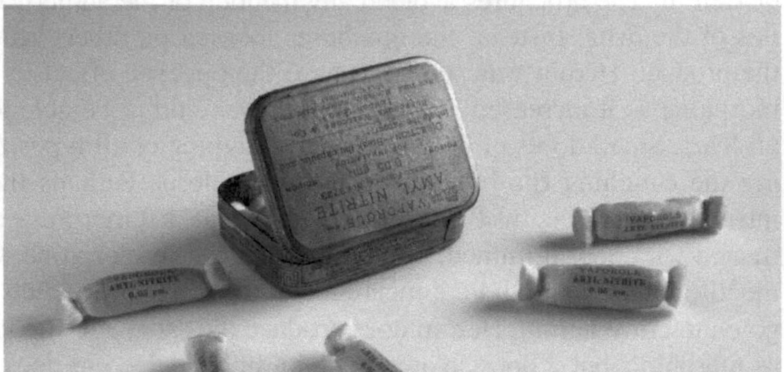

Credit: A675774, Small tin, contains amyl nitrite ampoules made by Burroughs Wellcome and Co. of London, English 1910. White background, some capsules spilled in front of case. Science Museum, London. Attribution 4.0 International (CC BY 4.0)

Amyl nitrite and ***butyl nitrite*** were first synthesized in 1844 CE by Eli Lilly Pharmaceutical Company (Figure 11.22). ***Nitrite*** is a salt or ester of nitrous acid[114]. Amyl nitrite is a chemical compound consisting of a nitrite attached with an amyl group. Amyl nitrite is used as an inhalant, and it is a potent vasodilator, and involuntary muscle relaxer. As an inhalant, amyl nitrite has a very strong psychoactive effect that features disinhibition and loss of restraint in decision making. Amyl nitrite is a potent vasodilator and works quickly to expand blood vessels, which results in a rapid lowering of blood pressure. Amyl nitrite signals for relaxation of involuntary muscles, especially the blood vessel walls. In addition, amyl nitrite relaxes both the internal and external anal sphincter muscles. The physical effects of amyl nitrite include a decrease in blood pressure, headache, flushing of the face, increased heart rate, dizziness, and flanging. Butyl nitrite is a chemical compound consisting of a nitrite attached with an alkyl group instead of an amyl group. Amyl and butyl nitrites function similarly to one another. During the 1800s CE, nitrites were used medically to treat heart diseases, specifically angina[115]. ***Angina*** is the medical term for chest pain or pressure and is a condition that typically appears when one does not have enough blood flow to the muscles of the heart. Abuse of amyl nitrite can cause injury to the red blood cells, which ultimately interferes with the cells ability to transport oxygen to vital tissues. Three other serious injuries can occur from overuse of amyl nitrite. The first is ***hypoventilation***, which occurs when ventilation is not adequate enough to exchange gases in the lungs. The second is ***hypotension*** also known as low blood pressure, which occurs more frequently in the arteries of the systemic circulatory system. And the last, and potentially most peculiar, of the serious events is ***synesthesia***. Synesthesia is a perceptual phenomenon in which the stimulation of one sensory or cognitive pathway leads to automatic, involuntary experiences in a secondary or cognitive pathway in the brain[116].

Cocaine was synthesized in 1855 CE, and received a lot of fanfare thanks to a grandiose publicity campaign with advertisements claiming cocaine to be "nourishment for the nerves" and "a harmless way to treat sadness"[38]. The stimulant and hunger-suppressant properties of coca had been known for centuries, however with the isolation of the cocaine alkaloid an unknown euphoric property of the drug became apparent. Cocaine in the 1800s CE was typically administered in liquid form and towards the end of the century was injected using the hypodermic needle. Effects from the drug begin within seconds (hypodermic needle) to minutes (ingested) and the effects last between 5 and 95 minutes. Cocaine targets the reward pathway in the brain by inhibiting the reuptake of serotonin, norepinephrine, and dopamine, which makes it highly addictive[38]. Table 11.3 highlights the psychological and physical effects produced by cocaine. The use of cocaine was split among three different opinions toward the end of the nineteenth century CE. There was a group of people who believed cocaine was an extremely dangerous and easily abused drug. Another group saw it as a therapeutic wonder, a panacea that could rarely be abused. And a group who thought it was useful for specific treatments for specific types of people. It was seen equally as being a wonder drug for a variety of ailments, as well as a poison intent on destroying human morality and dignity.

Table 11.3   General Effects of Cocaine

Psychological Effects	Physical Effects
• Loss of contact with reality • Intense feelings of happiness or agitation • Euphoria • Increased energy and activity	• Fast heart rate • High blood pressure • Increase body temperature • Sweating • Large dilated pupils • Localized numbing

Source: T.D. Church

The Native American Church, originally established in Oklahoma in the latter part of the 1800s CE, was a monotheistic religion focused on the Great Spirit. Within this religion, many of the traditions of the Native Americans in the United States and the First Nation in Canada have been preserved. Among the traditions is the view of peyote as a sacrament of the religion and it is used to commune with the Great Spirit. Peyote had long been used in Native American rituals and its hallucinogenic effects were both feared and revered. Louis Lewin (1850–1929 CE) was a German pharmacologist and toxicologists, who would help pioneer ethnobotany. Lewin received his first sample of peyote cactus in 1887 CE[117]. Lewin created a drug classification system for psychoactive drugs that was in use for nearly 75 years before it was revised and incorporated into a larger classification schema (Figure 11.23), Table 11.4 is Lewin's classification[118]. Lewin was the first to describe the chemical processes of peyote and he is credited with the discovery of the mescaline alkaloid, which is responsible for the psychoactivity of the cactus[119]. **Mescaline** was first identified in 1888 CE and first synthesized in 1919 CE. Mescaline is known for its hallucinogenic effects, which are comparable to LSD and psilocybin, but with some unique characteristics. Mescaline produces alterations in thinking, distorts the sense of time and self-awareness, and produces vivid closed- and open-eyed visualizations. **Kaleidoscopic experience** was the terminology Lewin had used to describe the vibrant and intense colors, which manifested more clearly with eyes closed or with eyes open in low lighting. The prominence of color is distinctive and would appear with a brilliance and intensity not witnessed with other hallucinogens. The visualizations appeared in recurring visual patterns and included stripes, checkerboards, angular spikes, multicolor dots, and simple fractal designs that would become complex as the drug high took effect. In describing mescaline,

Figure 11.23   Kaleidoscope Pattern

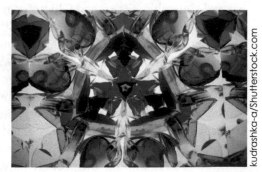

kudrashka-a/Shutterstock.com

Aldous Huxley (1894–1963 CE) stated, "the amorphous shapes one can see are like looking at animated stained glass illuminated from light coming through the eyelids"[120].

Table 11.4 Lewin's Psychoactive Drug Classification[118]

Drug Classification	Definition
Inebriantia	Inebriants, produce feelings of drunkenness. Examples: Alcohol or ether
Excitantia	Stimulants; produce feelings of alertness, concentration, and focus. Examples: Cocaine or amphetamine
Euphorica	Euphoriants; produce feelings of pleasure, excitement, wellbeing, and happiness. Examples: Heroin
Hypnotica	Tranquilizers; produce calm feelings used to treat anxiety, fear, and tension. Examples: Chloral hydrate
Phantastica	Hallucinogens, specifically Entheogens; produce alterations in perception, mood, consciousness; cognition; and behavior. Examples: Peyote or ayahuasca

Barbital, marketed under the brand name *Veronal,* was first synthesized by German chemists Emil Fischer (1852–1919 CE) and Joseph von Mering (1849–1908 CE) in 1902 CE. Veronal was the very first commercially available barbiturate and was dispensed initially for "insomnia induced by nervous excitability"[110]. Veronal would be used as a hypnotic and sleeping aid and at higher doses would exhibit heavy sedative effects. The main intent of the drug was to initiate, sustain, or lengthen sleep. Veronal would prove to be very dose-dependent with effects raining from anxiolysis to complete loss of consciousness. *Anxiolytic* is the drug classification for antipanic or antianxiety agents that help to reduce fear and anxiety[81]. Both Fischer and Mering would end up overdosing on their own discovery. With prolonged use of Veronal, tolerance to the drug will build up. This tolerance to the drug required larger and larger doses to attain the desired effect. The discovery of the tolerance problem would prove to be deadly for both men.

Other drugs that were not synthesized in this century but were of interest in medicine were Hashish and Cannabis, Ether, and Chloroform. *Hashish* and *cannabis* were ancient drugs and were used in the 1860s CE in Germany as an anesthetic. Between 1800 and 1900 CE hashish was at the peak of its medicinal use, with hashish compounds being commonplace in European and American medicine. Evidence of the misuse of hashish was relatively non-existent, however it faced near widespread opposition in Asia and Africa. Toward the end of the nineteenth century CE, *cannabis* was waning in favor among physicians. It was a coarse produce, whose active ingredients were not fully understood. Cannabis had a lack of purified extract and as a result was seen as being too primitive for clinical application. Public perception varied, but many saw cannabis and hashish as Fredrick Nietzsche—a self-reported user—viewed it as very beneficial. Nietzsche was certain that cannabis allowed one to come close to attaining "the prodigious velocity of mental processes"[113].

Chloroform was synthesized in 1831 CE by Samuel Guthrie (1782–1848 CE) in the United States and independently a few months later by Eugène Soubeiran (1797–1859 CE) in France and Justus von Lieberg (1803–1873 CE) from Germany[121]. Chloroform is a sweet-smelling, colorless liquid used as an industrial solvent as well as for general anesthesia[122]. Chloroform is created through the action of chlorine bleach (calcium hypochlorite) upon acetone (propanone) or ethanol to create a haloform reaction. Today chloroform is often used in TV shows and movies when someone is going to be kidnapped. The assailant will use a chloroform-soaked rag, sneak-up behind their target, and place the cloth over the mouth and nose of their victim to cause unconsciousness. While it does cause general anesthesia, it is not long lasting.

Ether is an organic compound (Et2), is highly flammable, and is colorless as a liquid. It has been around since the thirteenth century CE as it was discovered in 1275 CE and synthesized in 1540 CE. In 1846 CE, ether found a new and unique role to fulfill thanks in part to William T.G. Morton (1819–1868 CE)[123]. Morton was a dentist and pioneered a way to use ether as a sedative and analgesic. On 16 October 1846 CE a crowd of doctors, students, and members of the general public filled the surgical amphitheater of Massachusetts General Hospital. They were there to witness as Morton instructed a patient to inhale the fumes from an ether-soaked sponge. After the patient was sufficiently sedated, a surgeon skillfully removed a tumor from the patient's neck. When the patient awoke from his ether-induced slumber, the surgeon asked how he felt, to which the patient replied, "feels as if my neck's been scratched"[123]. There was no pain felt during the surgery, which was miraculous for the time! Up until this point in history, surgery was brutal and the faster it could be performed the better. Fully conscious patients would often bite down on leather straps or bits of wood while the surgeons would do their work. Ether made surgery a comfortable experience for patients, while affording surgeons time while working on anesthetized patients. This new discovery allowed for more and more complex and beneficial surgical techniques to be pioneered.

Both ether and chloroform had many practical uses in the nineteenth century CE, serving as analgesics, sedatives, industrial solvents, and recreational uses. *Analgesics* are drugs that function as muscle relaxants and pain relievers. *Sedatives* are drugs that assist in achieving a calming, sleep-inducing effect on the body. By 1850 CE, ether was a major component in many prescriptions used by druggists and chemists. By 1860 CE, ether was seen as a "plague upon mankind"[124]. Ether quickly became the scourge of the poor as it was often cheaper to purchase than beer. Ether also contributed to the decadence of high society where it was inhaled rather than ingested[125].

Figure 11.24 Example of Late 1800s CE Soda Fountain

Brian Logan Photography/ Shutterstock.com

11.6 Soda and Cigarettes, Rise of the American Pharmacy

In the 1800s CE, local drugstores evolved into the central hub of activity and entertainment in many American towns and neighborhoods (Figure 11.24). American Pharmacists were integral to providing beverages that were part pharmacology, part refreshment, and part entertainment. By 1850s CE people were going to their local drugstore to "procure a fountain drink to cure or aid some physical malady"[126]. Many customers would travel to their local soda fountains early in the morning to get a refreshing and "healthy" beverage to start their day off right. Sodas were sold as "bracers" or "pick-me-up's" and these specialty tonics provided physical and mental stimulation that only a pharmacists soda fountain could provide. Some of the syrups being mixed with the soda water contained caffeine or other addictive substances.

All drugs were basically over the counter and pharmacists in the nineteenth century CE would make concoctions of drugs like cocaine and caffeine (for headache relief) and mix them into soda beverages to make them more palatable. The use of soda, however, started to get some negative attention and press as some people began to see the carbonated elixirs as habit-forming. Among the concoctions available, nervines started to garner the lion's share of attention. *Nervines* were nerve tonics, specifically they were medicines that were intended to act therapeutically on the nerves with the expressed hope that they would cause sedation that would calm the nerves[127]. Strong drug syrups were added to soda water by pharmacist who manufactured the tonic drinks. Many of these syrups contained strychnine, cannabis, morphine, opium, heroin, and/or cocaine in various combinations.

In 1876 CE, Philadelphia pharmacist Charles Elmer Hires (1851–1937 CE) developed and sold Root Beer[128]. *Root Beer* is made from the root bark of the sassafras tree or from the sarsaparilla vine. The consumption of root beer in the Americas pre-dates colonial times, where Native American tribes in the Northeast were known to create beverages and medicinal remedies from sassafras roots. Hires Root Beer was sold as a powder that could be reconstituted into a syrup and then added to soda water by pharmacists. It was originally sold as a drink to "purify the blood and make cheeks rosy" and marketed as "the greatest health-giving beverage in the world"[129].

In 1885 CE, pharmacist Charles Alderton (1857–1941 CE) created *Dr. Pepper* while working at Morrison's Old Corner Drug Store in Waco, TX[130]. The patrons at Morrison's soda fountain learned about Alderton's new drink and began ordering a "Waco," the now iconic name had not quite caught on. The syrup used to make Dr. Pepper contained 23 different ingredients, which were a closely guarded trade secret. Dr. Pepper was originally marketed as an energy drink and "brain tonic" that was sold with some exaggerated claims. One famous advertisement claimed that Dr. Pepper, "aids in digestion, and restores vim, vigor, and vitality"[127].

By the middle of the nineteenth century CE, there were well over 100 carbonated beverages that contained coca extract or pure cocaine as an ingredient (Figure 11.25). In 1885 CE, John S. Pemberton (1831–1888 CE) a druggist in Atlanta, GA registered and commercialized *Coca-Cola*[131]. Coca-Cola was initially a frothy alcoholic drink that contained cocaine. Pemberton had been wounded by a saber during the American Civil War and was looking for something to help alleviate his ongoing pain. He had developed a morphine addiction and had begun experimenting with various pain killers and tonics to help overcome his addiction. Coca-Cola was the result of his efforts. In 1886 CE, Atlanta became a "dry" city as it prohibited the sales and distribution of alcohol. As a result, Pemberton was forced to eliminate the alcohol and in place added the now iconic kola nuts for their caffeine and citrus extracts for their refreshing flavor.

Figure 11.25 Coca-Cola Bottles

ferdyboy/Shutterstock.com

Coca-Cola was marketed as the "supreme remedy" and "calming drink." Pemberton sold the rights to Coca-Cola shortly before his death to another druggist, Asa Griggs Chandler (1851–1929 CE). In 1888 CE, Chandler had purchased the recipe for $240.00,[1] and began packaging and selling Coke in replaceable barrels with a refrigerated pour spout[132].

Figure 11.26   7up Sign

Hi-Point/Shutterstock.com

Bib-label lithiated lemon-lime soda does not sound very appealing and was thankfully renamed to *7up* (Figure 11.26). Charles Leiper Grigg (1868–1940 CE) created 7up in the late part of the nineteenth century CE[129]. Grigg opened Howdy Corporation in St. Louis, Missouri, and began testing a variety of citrus based sodas. Lemon-lime won over grapefruit-lime in a series of blind taste tests and Grigg quickly began marketing his new tonic across the United States[133]. Grigg believed that 7up was the cure for alcoholic hangovers, and one of 7up's original marketing slogans boldly proclaimed, "it takes the ouch of the grouch"[134]. The original recipe for 7up contained *lithium citrate*, a known mood stabilizing drug. Lithium citrate is a powdered form of a soft, silvery-white metal used for mood stabilization in the treatment of manic states and bipolar disorder[135]. As a medication, lithium citrate has several common side effects including constipation, diarrhea, nausea, tremors, and skin rash to name a few. Lithium citrate was a component of the 7up recipe until it was removed in 1948 CE.

Around 1820 CE, *hand-rolled cigarettes* were the predominate combustible form for consuming tobacco[136]. Hand-rolling is the process of rolling tobacco leaves in fine paper. It can take an expert roller between 2 and 4 minutes to produce a cigarette, which limited the habit of smoking. In 1830s CE, the French provided the world that would become the iconic name for the paper wrapped combustible tobacco sticks, "cigarette"[137]. It would take a decade for the name to become adopted by English speakers worldwide. In the Southern states of the United States, there was a failed attempt to promote the spelling as cigaret, as the French feminine form "ette" was unsettling to the fragile masculinity of Southern Gentlemen[138]. Needless to say, cigaret did not catch on nor stick as the official spelling. In 1865 CE, Washington Duke (1820–1905 CE), an American tobacco industrialist from Durham, North Caroline, began to pre-roll cigarettes and sell them in bundles of 10 for a profit. People enjoyed the convenience of having the cigarettes already rolled. It led to an increase in smoking and an increase in people sharing cigarettes with one another. In 1881 CE, James Bonsack (1859–1924 CE) was granted the patent for his latest invention, the cigarette rolling machine[139]. The machine Bonsack invented could automatically roll cigarettes and was capable of producing thousands a day.

Most cigarettes made by mechanical process contain "reconstituted tobacco" commonly referred to as "sheet." Sheet contains the recycled tobacco stems, stalks, scraps, collected dust, and floor

---

[1] This would be equivalent to $7,500.00 in 2022.

sweeping (sometimes containing rat feces) that have become bound together with chemical additives and fillers. James Bonsack rented his first two cigarette rolling machines to the American Tobacco Company (ATC) owned by James Buchanan Duke (1856–1925 CE) in 1884 CE[140]. Part of the deal between Bonsack and Duke provided for a dedicated mechanic, which resulted in fewer breakdowns of the rented machines. This allowed Duke to outpace his competitors and gave ATC a lucrative competitive advantage. ATC went from making about 40,000 hand-rolled cigarettes daily to ~4 million mechanically produced in a day. The mechanical production of cigarettes promoted a noticeable increase in smoking. Prerolled cigarettes were available for those who did not know how to or did not want to roll their own tobacco. Cigarettes became available in quantities that were sold by the pack, with ATC setting the standard of 20 cigarettes per pack. Cigarettes were available for sale everywhere American consumers shopped, even in drug stores and pharmacies[141]. Sadly, many American chain pharmacies and drug stores sell the cancer producing cigarettes to this day.

11.7   Addiction Gains Prominence

What we think about addiction very much depends on who we believe is addicted, and this is a holdover from the Victorian Era. We still make unreasonable judgements about who an addict is or might be. Addiction as a concept became more widespread toward the end of the nineteenth century CE, thanks in part to the Industrial Revolution. The nineteenth century CE saw an unprecedented expansion in production and exportation of cheap spirits, like ether and chloroform. The latter part of the 1800s CE saw improved isolation of and increased use of psychoactive alkaloids (morphine, heroin, and cocaine, for example). Alongside the increase in available drugs there was a rise in non-medical use of these products. There were new ways of consuming drugs with the invention of the hypodermic needle, inhalants, and smoking cigarettes. And the world, determined to capitalize on the progress of the industrial revolution, saw global migrations of people in unprecedented numbers. Many of these global migrations were forced as economic conditions pushed people to their limits. As people moved, they brought their favorite vices with them... Chinese laborers introduced smoking opium to their new homes on distant shores during this globalization movement where people followed the labor demand. The nineteenth century CE put into motion several crucial components in the addiction process, explicitly the variables of exposure, price, and mode of administration. The 1800s CE set into motion a number of our modern drug problems and it was all done in the name of scientific and economic progress.

REFERENCES

1. Kang, L., & Pedersen, N. (2017). *Quackery: A brief history of the worst ways to cure everything* (p. 352). Workman Publishing.
2. Stearns, P. N. (2020). *The industrial revolution in world history* (5th ed., p. 304). Routledge.
3. Scull, A. (2015). *Madhouses, mad-doctors, and madmen: The social history of psychiatry in the Victorian era* (p. 400). University of Pennsylvania Press. 400.
4. Halliday, S. (2001). Death and miasma in Victorian London: an obstinate belief. *British Medical Journal, 323*(7327), 1469–1471.

5. Greenstone, G. (2010). The history of bloodletting. *BC Medical Journal, 52*(1), 12–14.

6. O'Dempsey, T. (2012). Leeches—the good, the bad and the wiggly. *Paediatrics and International Child Health, 32*(sup 2), 16–20.

7. Cheatham, M. L. (2008). The death of George Washington: An end to the controversy? *The American Surgeon, 74*(8), 770–774.

8. Keith, N. M., & T.E. Keys, T. E. (1957). The anatomy acts of 1831 and 1832; a solution of a medical social problem. *A.M.A. Archives of Internal Medicine, 99*(5), 678–94.

9. Senate, (1831). *An act more effectually to protect the sepulchres of the dead, and to legalize the study of anatomy in certain cases*, in *No. 21*, M.H.O. Representatives, Editor. House of Representatives. p. 4.

10. Kingdom, P. U. (1832). An Act for regulating Schools of Anatomy. In H. O Lords (Ed.), *2 & 3 Will. IV c.75*. Parliament of the United Kingdom.

11. Cascella, M. (2016). Taphophobia and 'life preserving coffins' in the nineteenth century. *History of Psychiatry, 27*(3), 345–349.

12. Wójcicka, N. (2011). The living dead: The uncanny and nineteenth-century moral panic over premature burial. *Styles of Communication, 2*(1), 176–186.

13. Wade, J. (2016). *The Ingenious Victorians: Weird and Wonderful Ideas from the Age of Innovation* (p. 288). Pen and Sword.

14. Youngson, A. J. (2018). *The scientific revolution in Victorian medicine* (2nd ed., p. 240). Routledge.

15. Zaragoza, J. M. (2012). The most brutal word: Definitions of incurable disease in the 19th Century French medicine. *Asclepio, 64*(2), 491–515.

16. Alter, G., & Oris, M. (2005). Childhood conditions, migration, and mortality: Migrants and natives in 19th century cities. *Social Biology, 52*(3–4), 178–191.

17. Corton, C. L. (2015). *London fog: The biography*. The Belknap Press of Harvard University Press.

18. Bartrip, P. W. (2002). *The Poorest of the Poor and the Lowest of the Low': Lucifer Matches and 'Phossy Jaw*. In P. W. Batrip (Ed.), *The Home Office and the Dangerous Trades: Regulating Occupational Disease in Victorian and Edwardian Britain* (pp. 171–231). The Wellcome Trust Centre for the History of Medicine.

19. Beard, G. (1869). Neurasthenia, or nervous exhaustion. *The Boston Medical and Surgical Journal, 3*(13), 217–221.

20. Smith, D. R. (1907). The treatment of certain phases of neurasthenia. *California State Journal of Medicine, 5*(6), 146–148.

21. Shally-Jensen, M. (2019). *Purgatives and emetics*. In M. Shally-Jensen (Ed.), *Alternative Healing in American History: An Encyclopedia from Acupuncture to Yoga* (p. 410). Greenwood.

22. Mehlman, M. J. (2005). Quackery. *American Journal of Law & Medicine, 31*(2–3), 349–363.

23. Wang, S. C., & Borison, H. L. (1951). Copper sulphate emesis: A study of afferent pathways from the gastrointestinal tract. *American Journal of Physiology-Legacy Content, 164*(2), 520–526.

24. Lee, M. R. (2008). Ipecacuanha: The South American vomiting root. *The Journal of the Royal College of Physicians of Edinburgh, 38*(4), 355–360.

25. Rangan, C. (2012). *Diuretics, ipecac, and laxatives.* In D. G. Barceloux (Ed.), *Medical toxicology of drug abuse: Synthesized chemicals and psychoactive plants* (pp. 200–232). John Wiley & Sons, Inc..

26. White, W. (2009). Addiction medicine in America: It's birth and early history (1750–1935) with a modern postscript. In R. Ries, S. Miller, & R. Saitz (Eds.), *Principles of addiction medicine* (pp. 327–334). Lippincott Williams & Wilkins.

27. Taba, P., Lees, A., and Stern, G. (2013). Erich Harnack (1852–1915) and a short history of apomorphine. *European Neurology*, *69*(6), 321–324.

28. Guba, D. A. (2020). *Taming Cannabis: Drugs and Empire in Nineteenth-Century France.* Intoxicating Histories Book 1 (Vol. 1, p. 302). .

29. Kozma, L. (2011). Cannabis Prohibition in Egypt, 1880–1939: From Local Ban to League of Nations Diplomacy. *Middle Eastern Studies*, *47*(3), 443–460.

30. Baber, T. T. (2016) Ancient corpses as curiosities: Mummymania in the age of early travel. *Journal of Ancient Egyptian Interconnections*, *8*(1), 60–93.

31. Moshenska, G. (2014). Unrolling Egyptian mummies in nineteenth-century Britain. *The British Journal for the History of Science*, *47*(3), 451–477.

32. Dawson, W.R. (1927). Mummy as a Drug. *Proceedings of the Royal Society of Medicine*, *21*(1), 34–39.

33. Rogers, B. (2015). Unwrapping the past: Egyptian mummies on show. In J. Kember, J. Plunkett, and J. Sullivan (Eds.), *Popular exhibitions, science and showmanship, 1840–1910* (pp. 215–234). Routledge.

34. Priestley, J. (1890). On the phlogiftication of spirit of nitre. In J. Priestley (Ed.), *Experiments and observations on different kinds of air, and other branches of natural philosophy, connected with the subject* (Vol. III). T. Pearson.

35. Priestley, J. (1789). XI. Experiments on the phlogistication of spirit of nitre. *Philosophical Transactions of the Royal Society of London*, (79), 139–150.

36. De Vasconcellos, K. (2010). Nitrous oxide who will have the last laugh? Part 1. *Southern African Journal of Anaesthesia and Analgesia 16*(24), , 1-44.

37. Yang, Q. H., & Alston, T. A. (2019). Phineas T. Barnum, Gardner Q. Colton, and Painless Parker were kindred Princes of Humbug. *Journal of Anesthesia History*, *5*(1), 13–21.

38. Jay, M. (2014). *High society: The central role of mind-altering drugs in history, science, and culture* (p. 192). Simon and Schuster.

39. Wrobel, A. (2014). *Pseudo-science and society in 19th-Century America* (p. 256). University Press of Kentucky.

40. Twine, R. (2002). Physiognomy, phrenology and the temporality of the body. *Body & Society*, *8*(1), 67–88.

41. Hassin, R., & Trope, Y. Facing faces: Studies on the cognitive aspects of physiognomy. *Journal of Personality and Social Psychology*, *78*(5), 837–852.

42. Hilts, V. L. (1982). Obeying the laws of hereditary descent: phrenological views on inheritance and eugenics. *Journal of the History of the Behavioral Sciences*, *18*(1), 62–77.

43. Holloway, J. (2006). Enchanted spaces: The séance, affect, and geographies of religion. *Annals of the Association of American Geographers*, 96(1), 182–187.

44. Lause, M. A. (2016). *Free spirits: Spiritualism, republicanism, and radicalism in the Civil War era* (p. 248). University of Illinois Press.

45. Horowitz, M. (2009). *Occult America: White House séances, Ouija circles, Masons, and the secret mystic history of our nation* (p. 304). Bantam.

46. McCorristine, S. (2021). Spiritualism, mesmerism and the occult, 1800–1920. Volume 2, Mesmerism and hypnotism (1st ed.), In McCorristine (Ed.), *Mesmerism and hypnotism*. Routledge.

47. Pimentel, M. G., Alberto, K. C., & Moreira-Almeida, A. (2016). Investigations of psychic/spiritual phenomena in the nineteenth century: somnambulism and spiritualism, 1811–1860. *História, Ciências, Saúde—Manguinhos*, *23*(4), 1113–1131.

48. Marcellus, J. (2008). Nervous women and noble savages: The romanticized "other" in nineteenth-century US patent medicine advertising. *Journal of Popular Culture*, *41*(5), 784–808.

49. Schwarz, G. S. (1979). Society, physicians, and the corset. *Bulletin of the New York Academy of Medicine*, *55*(6), 551–590.

50. Fee, E., et al. (2002). The effects of the corset. *American Journal of Public Health*, *92*(7), 1085–1085.

51. Smith-Rosenberg, C. (1972). The hysterical woman: Sex roles and role conflict in 19th-century America. *Social Research*, *39*(4), 652–678.

52. Carol, A. (2002). Doctors and the stigmatization of masturbation (end of the 18th century-start of the 19th century). *Revue d'histoire Moderne et Eontemporaine 49*(1), 156–172.

53. Esquirol, E., & Esquirol, J. É. D. (1838). *Die Geisteskrankheiten in Beziehung zur Medizin und Staatsarzneikunde* (Vol. 1). Verlag der Voss'schen Buchhandlung.

54. Esquirol, J. É. D. (1805). *Des passions considérées comme causes, symptômes, et moyens curatifs de l'aliénation mentale, thèse, etc.* l'Ecole de Medecine.

55. Rush, B. (1812). *Medical inquiries and observations, upon the diseases of the mind*. Kimber & Richardson.

56. Twisselmann, B. (2002). *A mind of its own: A cultural history of the penis* (p. 368). Free Press.

57. Graham, S. (1838). *A lecture to young men on chastity: Intended also for the serious consideration of parents and guardians*. George W. Light.

58. Davis, J. C. (2017). *From head shops to whole foods: The rise and fall of activist entrepreneurs*. Columbia University Press.

59. Kellogg, J. H. (1886). *Man, the masterpiece: Or plain truths plainly told about boyhood, youth and manhood*. Condit & Nelson.

60. Loignon, A. E. (2019). Cornflakes, god, and circumcision: John Harvey Kellogg and Transatlantic Health Reform. In *Philosophy* (p. 257). University of Texas.

61. Darby, R. (2003). The masturbation taboo and the rise of routine male circumcision: A review of the historiography. *Journal of Social History, 36*(3), 737–757.

62. Rossner, S. (2006). John Harvey Kellogg (1852–1943): 'Masturbation results in general debility, unnatural pale eyes and forehead acne'. *Obesity Reviews, 7*(2), 227–228.

63. Norn, S. et al. (2008). Mercury—a major agent in the history of medicine and alchemy. *Dansk Medicinhistorisk Arbog, 36*, 21–40.

64. Anderson, A. (2015). *Snake oil, hustlers and hambones: the American medicine show* (p. 200). McFarland & Company, Inc. 200.

65. *Boschee's German Syrup, Marin Journal*, 1877: San Rafael, CA.

66. Jordan, S. A. (2005). William Saunders, pioneer in ethical herbal products: Pharmacist was famous for marquis wheat, but earned reputation as manufacturer of herbal extracts. *Canadian Pharmacists Journal / Revue des Pharmaciens du Canada, 138*(2), 41–44.

67. McNamara, B. (1971). The Indian medicine show. *Educational Theatre Journal, 23*(4), 431–445.

68. Donohue, J. (2006). A history of drug advertising: the evolving roles of consumers and consumer protection. *The Milbank Quarterly, 84*(4), 659–699.

69. Lloyd, R. (2017). The New Bohemia as urban institution. *City & Community, 16*(4), 359–363.

70. Moss, G., Wildfeuer, R., & McIntosh, K. Classic Bohemia: Paris and Greenwich Village. In G. Moss, R. Wildfeuer, & K. McIntosh (Eds.), *Contemporary Bohemia: A Case Study of an Artistic Community in Philadelphia* (pp. 15–26). Springer.

71. Terrill, W. C. (2022). *Dudes, decadence, and degeneracy: Criminalisation of Absinthe in the United States* (pp. 1–17). Cultural and Social History, *Ahead of Print:*(https://doi.org/10.1080/147 80038.2022.2109977).

72. Lanier, D. (2004). *Absinthe – The cocaine of the Nineteenth Century: A history of the hallucinogenic drug and its effect on artists and writers in Europe and the United States* (p. 195). McFarland and Company, Inc..

73. Lachenmeier, D. W., et al. (2006). Thujone—cause of absinthism? *Forensic Science International, 158*(1), 1–8.

74. Patočka, J., & Plucar, B. (2003). Pharmacology and toxicology of absinthe. *Journal of Applied Biomedicine, 1*(4), 199–205.

75. Courtwright, D. T. (2012). Addiction and the science of history. *Addiction, 107*(3), 486–492.

76. Huggins, M. (2015). *Vice and the Victorians*. Bloomsbury Publishing Plc.

77. Dickens, C. (2007 [1859 CE]). In R. Maxwell (Ed.), *A tale of two cities* (p. 448). Penguin Books.

78. Salmi, H. (2013). *19th Century Europe: A cultural history* (p. 200). John Wiley & Sons. 200.

79. Raadschelders, J. C. (1997). The progress of civil society: A 19th-century American history of governments. *Administration & Society, 29*(4), 471–489.

80. Turner, V. (1977). *The Ritual Process*. Cornell University Press.

81. Jones, A.W. (2011). Early drug discovery and the rise of pharmaceutical chemistry. Drug testing and analysis, *3*(6), 337–344.

82. Dossey, B. M. (2010). Florence Nightingale: A 19th-century mystic. *Journal of Holistic Nursing*, *28*(1), 10–35.

83. Gundlach, H. (2004). Sigmund Freud und die Lauterkeit. *Berichte zur Wissenschaftsgeschichte*, *27*(3), 175–185.

84. Cole, J. R. (1998). Freud's dream of the botanical monograph and cocaine the wonder drug. *Dreaming, 8*(3), 187–204.

85. Freud, S. (1885). *Über Coca* (p. 26). Verlag Von Moritz Perles Publisher.

86. Moreau de Tours, J.-J. (1845). *Du hachisch et de l'aliénation mentale: études psychologiques* (p. 431). Fortin, Masson. 431.

87. Ledermann, F. (1988). Pharmacie, médicaments et psychiatrie vers 1850: Le cas de Jacques-Joseph Moreau de Tours. *Revue d'histoire de la pharmacie, 76*(276), 67–76.

88. Renner, C. (2012). *À propos de Moreau de Tours et du haschisch. Histoire des Sciences Médicales, 46*(4), 367–372.

89. Bartlett, H. (1936). *Guy de Maupassant, sa vie, son oeuvre, et la critique américaine*, in *Litterature Francaise* (p. 78). McGill University. .

90. Maupassant, G. D. (1983 [1889 CE]). *Fort comme la mort. Oeuvres completes* (p. 212). Feedbooks.

91. Drouin, E., & Péréon, Y. (2019). *Maupassant's folie, from unpublished letters. L'encephale*, *45*(5), 454–455.

92. Norn, S., Kruse, P. R., & Kruse, E. (2006). On the history of injection. *Dansk medicinhistorisk arbog, 34*, 104–113.

93. Wood, A. (1858). Narcotic injection in neuralgia. *British Medical Journal, 1*(88), 755.

94. Wood, A. (1855). New method of treating neuralgia by the direct application of opiates to the painful points. *Edinburgh Medical and Surgical Journal, 82*(203), 265–281.

95. This, H. (2022). Louis Pasteur: de la physico-chimie à la biologie. Comptes Rendus. *Chimie*, *25*(G1), 237–251.

96. Pasteur, L. (1876). In F. Faulkner & D. C. Robb. Études sur la bière, ses maladies, causes qui les provoquent, procédé pour la rendre inaltérable: Avec une théorie nouvelle de la fermentation (p. 418). Gauthier-Villars.

97. Karyakin, O. (2021). Maria Sklodowska-Curie, Pierre Curie. *Cancer Urology, 17*(2), 195–199.

98. Curie, M. (1923). In C. Kellogg & V. Kellogg (Eds.), *Pierre Curie* (p. 232).. Macmillan.

99. Mould, R. (1999). Marie and Pierre Curie and radium: history, mystery, and discovery. *Medical Physics, 26*(9), 1766–1772.

100. Fayssoil, A. M. D. (2009). René Laennec (1781–1826) and the Invention of the Stethoscope. *The American Journal of Cardiology, 104*(5), 743–744.

101. van Bronswijk, P., & Cohen, A. F. (2008). The first recordings of pharmacological effects. *British Journal of Clinical Pharmacology, 66*(5), 588–593.

102. Louw, D. F, Sutherland, G. R., & Schulder, M. (2003). From microscopic to astronomic, the legacy of Carl Zeiss. *Neurosurgery, 52*(3), 668–674.

103. Pearce, J. M. S. (2009). The Ophthalmoscope: Helmholtz's Augenspiegel. *European Neurology*, *61*(4), 244–249.

104. Mould, R. F. (1995). The early history of X-ray diagnosis with emphasis on the contributions of physics 1895–1915. *Physics in Medicine & Biology*, *40*(11), 1741–1787.

105. Wicks, C, Hudlicky, T., & Rinner, U. (2021). Morphine alkaloids: History, biology, and synthesis. In H.-J. Knölker (Ed.), *The alkaloids: Chemistry and biology* (pp. 145–342). Elsevier.

106. Lewy, J. (2014). The army disease: Drug addiction and the civil war. *War in History*, *21*(1), 102–119.

107. Veit, R. (1996). "A Ray of Sunshine in the Sickroom": Archaeological insights into late 19th-and early 20th-century medicine and anesthesia. *Northeast Historical Archaeology*, *25*(1), 33–50.

108. Levinstein, E. (1877). *Die Morphiumsucht*. Verlag Von August Hirschwald Publisher. 164.

109. Kane, H. H. (1881). *Drugs that enslave: the opium, morphine, chloral and hashisch habits* (p. 216). , Blakiston.

110. Dundee, J. W., & McIlroy, P. D. A. (1982). The history of the barbiturates. *Anaesthesia*, *37*(7), 726–734.

111. Snelders, S, Kaplan, C. & Pieters, T. (2006) On cannabis, chloral hydrate, and career cycles of psychotropic drugs in medicine. *Bulletin of the History of Medicine*, *80*(1), 95–114.

112. Ban, T. A. (2006). The role of serendipity in drug discovery. *Dialogues in Clinical Neuroscience*, *8*(3), 335–344.

113. Ciaccio, J. (2018). Between intoxication and narcosis: Nietzsche's pharmacology of modernity. *Modernism/Modernity (Baltimore, MD)*, *25*(1), 115–133.

114. Berlin, R. (1987). Historical aspects of nitrate therapy. *Drugs*, *33*(4), 1–4.

115. Brunton, T. L. (1867). On the use of nitrite of amyl in angina pectoris. *The Lancet*, *90*(2291), 97–98.

116. Newell, G. R., & Spitz, M. R. (1988). Nitrite inhalants: Historical. In H. W. Haverkos & J. A. Dougherty, Editors. *Health hazards of nitrite inhalants* (pp. 1–14). National Institute on Drug Abuse.

117. Macht, D. I. (1931). Louis Lewin, pharmacologist, toxicologist, medical historian. *Annals of Medical History*, *3*(2), 179–194.

118. Lewin, L. (1924). *Phantastica: Über die berauschenden, betäubenden und erregenden Genußmittel*. Verlag von Georg Stilke.

119. Lewin, L. (1888). Ueber Anhalonium Lewinii. *Archiv für experimentelle Pathologie und Pharmakologie*, *24*(6), 401–411.

120. Huxley, A. (2010 [1954 CE]). *The doors of perception: And heaven and hell*. Random House.

121. Montgomery, J., & Robertson, A. (2012). Vapours, gargles, darts and bougies: Victorian ENT treatments. *Journal of Laryngology and Otology*, *126*(11), 1159–1163.

122. Pawling, J. R. (1948). Dr. Samuel Guthrie, Discoverer of Chloroform. *Anesthesia & Analgesia*, *27*(1), 17–18.

123. Morton, W. T. G. (1850). Comparative value of sulphuric ether and chloroform. *The Boston Medical and Surgical Journal, 43*(6), 109–119.

124. Schneider, A., & Helmstädter, A. (2015). The evil of the unknown-risk-benefit evaluation of new synthetic drugs in the 19th century. *Die Pharmazie-An International Journal of Pharmaceutical Sciences, 70*(1), 60–63.

125. Crocq, M.-A. (2022). Historical and cultural aspects of man's relationship with addictive drugs. *Dialogues in Clinical Neuroscience, 9*(4), 355–361.

126. Funderburg, A.C. (2002). *Sundae best: A history of soda fountains* (p. 232). Popular Press.

127. Levin, J. (2021). *Soda and fizzy drinks: A global history* (p. 184). Reaktion Books.

128. Falvo, K. R. (2021). Charles E. Hires and the drink that wowed a nation: the life and times of a Philadelphia entrepreneur. *Pennsylvania History: A Journal of Mid-Atlantic Studies, 88*(1), 134–137.

129. Bly, E. (2007). *Just what the doctor ordered: A medical history of soft drinks.* in *16th Annual History of Medicine Days, March 30th and 31st,* 2007. Health Sciences Centre.

130. Sanders, P. (2001). Texas History 101: Folks have favored the taste of Dr Pepper for a long time. In *Texas Monthly.* Texas Monthly, a Division of Emmis Publishing.

131. Harris, N. (1995). The world of Coca-Cola. *The Journal of American History, 82*(1), 154–158.

132. Elmore, B. J. (2013). Citizen Coke: An environmental and political history of the Coca-Cola Company. *Enterprise & Society, 14*(4), 717–731.

133. Hausch, B. J., Lorjaroenphon, Y., & Cadwallader, K. R. (2015). Flavor chemistry of lemon-lime carbonated beverages. *Journal of Agricultural and Food Chemistry, 63*(1), 112–119.

134. El-Mallakh, R. S., & Roberts, R. J. (2007). Lithiated lemon-lime sodas. *American Journal of Psychiatry, 164*(11), 1661–1662.

135. Cousins, D. A., et al. (2020). Lithium: past, present, and future. *The Lancet Psychiatry, 7*(3), 222–224.

136. Hanafin, J., & Clancy, L. History of tobacco production and use. In R. Loddenkemper & M. Kreuter (Eds.), *The tobacco epidemic* (pp.1–18). Karger Publishers.

137. Gately, I. (2007). *Tobacco: A cultural history of how an exotic plant seduced civilization* (p. 416). Grove Press.

138. Schmitz, D. (2018). *Only flossy, high-society dudes would smoke'em: gender and cigarette advertising in the nineteenth century.* In C. Stabile (Ed.), *Turning the century: Essays in media and cultural studies* (pp. 100–121). Routledge.

139. Gilman, S. L. & Xun, Z. (2004). *Smoke: A global history of smoking* (p. 408). Reaktion Books.

140. Porter, P.G. (1969). Origins of the American Tobacco Company. *Business History Review, 43*(1), 59–76.

141. Enstad, N. (2018). *Cigarettes, Inc: An intimate history of corporate imperialism* (p. 336). University of Chicago Press.

Chapter 12

Twentieth Century Music and Media

Music and mass media became increasingly important in American society during the 1900s. Music and media connected our households in new ways and began to shape human impressions of the world and their place within that world. When drugs are involved, music and media can become enhanced, propelled, and used as cultural markers to identify belonging or deviance (two sides of the same coin). This chapter will explore how music and mass media have shaped our beliefs of drugs and equally important how the twentieth century helped to further define the *pharmacologicalism* of the nineteenth century. Within the twentieth century, the notion of "good" vs "bad" drug extends from drug onto drug users and quickly became countercultural or subcultural markers, often, associated with characteristic substances of abuse. Sometimes, these associations were loosely made by media or politicians and assigned varying levels of deviance, fear, and mistrust onto those targeted.

Music has the amazing capacity to alter our moods, enhance our memories, and heighten both our capacity for love and heartache. Music is one of the few universal languages. It brings us together and has the power to move us physically and emotionally. Musicians have used drugs to enhance their creativity and listeners have used drugs to heighten their pleasure in experiencing the music. Throughout human history there has been a rich representation of drugs and alcohol in music, and while some modern research has shown higher levels of drug use in specific genres of music, the relationship has always been complex. Drug representations may provide a normalizing effect for some listeners, but drugs and music are powerful mechanisms to strengthen social bonds and build a sense of community. In the musical history of the United States, between 1940 and 2000, some music genres have become synonymous with specific drugs, Figure 12.1. To quote the iconic Sonny Bono and Cher, "the beat goes on…"[1] and decade after decade the associated drug via music genre becomes correlated with counterculture groups, especially in the later half of the twentieth century. It is important to keep in mind that we should not assume causality and exaggerate the links between musical genres and assorted forms of drug use. Information about musical and drug preferences is useful, however, in targeting and building interventions following harm reduction initiatives effective for deployment at music festivals and venues.

Figure 12.1   Counterculture, Drugs, and Music 1940–2000

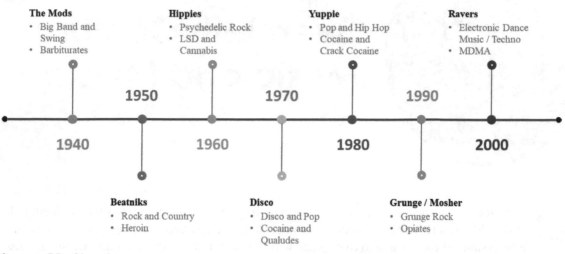

Source: T.D. Church

Media tends to sensationalize the best and the worst of historical events. Media related to drugs—both licit and illicit—tends to focus our attention through four methods: (1) setting the agenda and defining public interest; (2) framing issues through a highly subjective filter; (3) indirectly shaping individual and community attitudes toward risk; and (4) fueling cultural and political discourse. When youth, drugs, and counterculture combine, the media—at least the media of the past 50 years—focuses our attention on the worst or most radical issues. This often leads consumers of the news to conclude that all youth who listen to rap also smoke pot (as an oversimplified example). The role of the media takes on a different feel when it is provided government support and funding. Media has the power to do some extraordinary things with those funds, a few examples are highlighted in Table 12.1. More so than any other decade, the 1980s served as a fitting example of how a perfect storm of drugs, funding, and lack of data combined to form an onslaught of misinformation that fueled a moral panic.

Table 12.1   Media Type by Government Support, 1950–1990

Funded Media Type	Decade
Public Service Announcements (PSAs) • Duck and Cover [2] • Narcotics: Pit of Despair [3] • Zombie Door [4]	1950–1970
Anti-drug Campaigns • Partnership for a drug-free America • Afterschool specials	1980–1990

Source: T.D. Church

Throughout this chapter, we will discuss counterculture and subculture to denote the individuals who take part in drug use within an associated decade. For our purposes, ***counterculture*** defines a group within a culture with its own distinctive characteristics in opposition to the dominant culture. ***Subculture*** describes groups within a culture that have their own distinctive characteristics that distinguish them from the larger culture. Subculture values and norms stay compatible with the dominant culture. Both define belonging in group that exists outside of the mainstream or popular culture. One of them—counterculture—tends to carry heavier baggage and is seen as being defiantly outside and against the norm.

Are there telltale signs to signify who belongs to a counterculture or subculture? The simple response is… Sometimes. Some of the signifiers express themselves in the fashion, music, and slang all used to show ingroup membership. Counterculture tends to be more against the grain and gets expressed in very visual ways. Subculture tends to closely mimic its parent culture and expresses itself in more subtle ways. Members in both counterculture and subculture are marked as "outsiders," "others," "different," or "not normal" by the majority. This othering delineates the members of the counterculture and subculture as having beliefs and ideologies that stand in opposition to the established social order. Music can act as a strong way to identify for individuals in fringe groups. Media can either help or harm fringe groups, depending upon how those groups are portrayed.

12.1   1960s: Hippies and Hallucinogens

The hippies were an important part of American society, even if their ideas and lifestyle forever solidified them as part of the counterculture of the 1960s[5]. When you hear the word hippie, what comes to mind? Drugs, long hair, bright colors, and naked people dancing in the rain? While the hippies did tend to embody all these characteristics, they inspired several sociocultural aspects of peace and tolerance, which had long-lasting effects. Many individuals who self-identified as hippies were artists and musicians and would often write music or create art expressing their beliefs, emotions, hopes, and concerns. When hippies came together, impromptu music concerts often ensued. They would drink, smoke, sing, dance, make love, and revel in all things quintessential to being hippies. The hippie movement culminated in 1969 through "An Aquarian Exposition" of rock and roll, music, and art, more commonly known for the geographic location where the music festival took place, Woodstock, New York. Today, we think of the Woodstock Music and Art Fair as the height of the hippie experience where years of drug and musical experimentation and changing societal practices converged and blossomed in the summer of love. By the mid-1960s, rock and roll had become synonymous with the youth movement, which in turn was linked with the civil rights, antiwar, antipoverty, women, gay and lesbian, and countercultural movements of the period.

In general, the ***Hippies*** represented a youth movement from the United States during the 1960s which had its beginnings in the Haight-Ashbury area of San Francisco, CA. By the mid-1960s, hippies had become a counterculture that went on to influence other countries around the world as well as subsequent generations of drug users. In general, hippies sought to free themselves from the rigid societal restrictions of capitalism, suburban life, and corporate culture. Hippies were seen as free spirits who choose their own way and were dedicated to finding new meaning in life and interactions with others. Table 12.2 highlights some of the key differences between hippies and mainstream society. Hippies were out to promote a message of peace and love and were vocal about their opposition to America's involvement in the Vietnam War. The Hippie movement was a catalyst for the Civil Rights Movement, the Sexual Revolution, and Women's Liberation Movement. Some hippies believed our society was moving too far away from nature, and that to be nude was our natural state. Some hippies went out into public nude to show their support and belief in a return to a more natural lifestyle. As can be assumed these types of public displays were a shock to the more conservatist and prudish post-Victorian sensibilities of the U.S. middle and upper classes. Musical shows, sit-ins, rallies, and street fairs were a few nonviolent ways the hippies shared their views on the world around them.

Table 12.2   Differences Between Hippies and Mainstream

Social/Cultural Category	Hippies	Mainstream
Appearance	Long hair, beards, bright and loose-fit clothing	Short hair (men)/Medium hair (women), no beards, monochromatic and tailored clothing
Art and Music	Bright, psychedelic influenced, expressive, lively, hand made	Big band, conservative dress, manufactured
Love and Sex	Open, experimental without guilt or jealousy, often spontaneous and in group settings, open about nudity	Closed, traditional, monogamous, nudity was frowned upon outside of the bedroom
Travel	Very little baggage, often done by van or station wagon that served as homes, no planning or care for the destination	Lots of baggage, plane and destination, hotels, and reservations, well planned out
Drugs	Credited with making LSD mainstream, known for smoking copious amounts of cannabis, alcohol—beer and wine	Alcohol—cocktails, cigarettes, and prescription drugs only

Source: T.D. Church

Among the accounts from former hippies, there is one critical central theme that became synonymous with their identity, cannabis smoking. Hippies began experimenting with cannabis and had positive experiences, many would go on to say that their cannabis use opened their mind and showed them the hypocrisies of capitalism and the government. The U.S. government had lied about how bad cannabis was, and yet the hippies who partook found a broader sense of community and love than what they experienced in mainstream society. Cannabis smoking became their symbol of resistance. Their cannabis smoking led them to critically evaluate civilization, and many realized the need to replace the evils of pollution, consumerism, capitalism, communism, politics, commerce, and religion with a new vision of brotherhood bound together with a shared destiny and a renewed appreciation for nature. The music of the hippies recorded the joy and love of the antiwar movement, the rejection of the military industrial complex, and the fake patriotism that was killing people and destroying the Earth. Their focus on harmony, nature, and peace became a spiritual movement which has been euphemistically called the Cannabis Revolution. This was represented through the youth of every race, ethnicity, religion, and sexuality coming together and communing around cannabis smoking. Their revolution against mainstream society became a global phenomenon. As their spiritual journey culminated in the later part of the 1960s, hippies began to—as Timothy Leary would champion—"turn on, tune in, and drop out" using LSD to enhance their connection to one another [6].

Lysergic Acid Diethylamide (LSD), colloquially "acid," is a potent hallucinogen. The effects typically include altered thoughts, feelings, distortions of time, and awareness of one's surroundings. Acid and the resulting "trip" or "psychedelic experience" became a staple of the 1960s counterculture. In an effort to curtail use of LSD among youth, a popularly promoted and highly dubious belief was the idea that LSD would "break chromosomes." This concern was further advanced with some very shoddy research conducted in the mid-1960s concerning pregnancy and LSD usage[7]. While women who used LSD during pregnancy have given birth to children with birth defects, the rate is not higher than what is seen in the general population. To further complicate matters, most of the women in the research study reported using other drugs during pregnancy as well, so it would be difficult to single out LSD as "the cause." This misconception boiled down to the fact that for hundreds of years in the United States, ergot was used as an effective, if not risky, mechanism of abortion. One unique attribute of LSD is that it does not appear to be addictive per se, yet regular users do experience tolerance that requires the users to take increasing dosages to attain their high.

The synthetization of LSD has been credited to Albert Hofmann, who in 1938 extracted the chemical from the ergot fungus. We have encountered ergot before in this book, think back to the Ancient Greeks (Chapter 4)—they utilized ergot as a very deadly poison that resulted in *ergotism*. To jog your memory, ergotism causes painful seizures and spasms, diarrhea, paresthesia (pins and needles), itching, convulsive symptoms, mania or psychosis, headaches, and vomiting. Hofmann was able to remove the poisonous attributes of ergot and isolated the pure compound of LSD. The hallucinogenic properties were discovered in 1943 when some LSD was accidently absorbed through the skin by Hofmann. By the time the hallucinogenic effects began to manifest, Hofmann was on his bicycle riding home from the lab. At home, he indicated that he saw fantastic images, colors, shapes, and light and dropped down in a state of pleasant stupor [8]. With his curiosity peaked, Hofmann decided to begin controlled experiments. On April 19, 1943, what would become "Bicycle Day," he took a dose of 250 micrograms. This time Hofmann indicated that he felt dizzy, confused, and paralyzed and the visions he saw were decidedly frightening. His assistant accompanied him as he cycled home while having a not-so-great psychedelic experience, a "bad trip"[9].

So how does LSD work? Chemically it is quite beautiful—it falls into a group of serotonergic psychedelics, but it is atypical as it is significantly dopaminergic. *Serotonergic* means related to or working on serotonin. *Dopaminergic* means related to or working on dopamine. In the brain, LSD binds to the D2 receptor, which initiates the psychoactive effects of the chemical in humans. Through the cross-activation of serotonin and dopamine, LSD prolongs those psychoactive effects. Average effects of LSD last between 6 and 12 hours depending on dosage, tolerance, body weight, and age.

In the United States, the average dose of LSD is between 40 and 500 micrograms, an amount that is equal to one-tenth the mass of a grain of sand. Interestingly, threshold effects can be felt with as little as 25 micrograms.

LSD follows a similar pattern of clinical effect among users. After ingestion, 0–30 minutes, users begin to experience dizziness, nausea, weakness, muscle twitches, and anxiety. This initial period can cause people to believe the acid they were sold is not working, because they are not experiencing any intense drug effects. Between 30 and 60 minutes, blurred vision, increased contrasts, visual patterns, feelings of unreality, lack of coordination, and tremulous speech will start occurring to the user. The 1–4 hours mark witnesses increased visual effects, wavelike motions, impaired distance perception, euphoria, and a feeling of time passing slowly. Effects begin to wane 4–7 hours. Finally, 7–12 hours should see a return to "normal" as the drug effects taper off for the user. Most users will enter the late effect stage 12–18 hours and experience headache, fatigue, and a deeply contemplative state. This contemplative state gives some users a period of intense self-reflection, with a considerable number finding renewed creativity, personal growth, and sense of well-being. This period of intense self-reflection is known formally as ego dissolution or ego death, which allows some to have a strong feeling of unity with their surroundings and produce a mystical experience.

The experience that most LSD users are seeking is the ***hallucination***, broad sensory experiences that are unreal but experienced or understood by the user to be real. There are several hallucinations the human brain can manifest under the influence of LSD. Table 12.3 outlines the six major hallucinogenic events one could experience. Most individuals hope for strong visual hallucinations, believing the strength of the visualizations to be a direct correlation to the strength and potency of the drug. Sadly, for those seeking the kaleidoscopic experience, this is a misconception. A majority of individuals using LSD will experience two or more of the hallucination types simultaneously.

Table 12.3 Common Types of Hallucinations

Auditory Hallucination (or Paracusia)	Incorporate hallucinations with the sense of hearing
Somatic Hallucination	Involve hallucinations experienced with the sensation and perception of a physical experience occurring with the body
Tactile Hallucination	Hallucinations encompassing the sense of touch
Kinesthetic Hallucination	Consist of hallucinations with the sense of bodily movement
Visual Hallucination	Contain hallucinations related to the sense of sight, kaleidoscopic vision, and enhancement of colors and patterns
Lilliputian Hallucination	This term derives its names form Jonathan Swifts *Gulliver's Travels* and involves Gulliver's experience with the Lilliputian peoples... This form of hallucinations changes the size of ordinary things in our mind making them appear smaller than they normally are or further away than they actually might be

Source: T.D. Church

Not all hallucination experiences are created equal, however. Some psychedelic substances provide pseudohallucinations, illusions, sensory experiences, or sensory distortions and not full-on hallucinations. *Pseudohallucinations* are sensory experiences that are unreal but experienced and understood by the individual as being unreal. Pseudohallucinations provide *sensory experiences* by providing changes in visual, auditory, olfactory, gustatory, and tactile sensations. While these changes impact how one experiences the world around them, there is still the knowledge that what they are experiencing is not real. *Illusions* represent sensory distortions of normal reality wherein the sensation is present but is incorrectly perceived and/or misinterpreted by the user. Illusions typically are defined in terms of optical, auditory, tactile, or temporal illusions. Illusions provide *sensory distortions* through changes in the intensity, quality, or spatial form of normal sense perceptions.

The hippies were by their nature very curious, and they used drugs to explore altered states of consciousness. Hippies of the 1960s viewed LSD and its use as a form of *enlightenment*. While experiencing LSD, a user will often experience a profound enlightenment about themselves, the world, or both. An individual in this state of enlightenment is keenly aware of the action or state of attaining or having attained deep—albeit—spiritual knowledge or insight, in particular the awareness which frees the individual from subjective self-identity. Many of the Hippies who used LSD held the belief that psychedelic drugs, music, and art would allow one to transcend the external world, discover the truths of existence, and promote harmony. Timothy Leary, Richard Alpert, and Alan Watts—all university professors—were popular in the 1960s for relating their firsthand experiences resulting from the use of psychedelics and detailing how the drug would enlighten the mind and expand one's creative and connective energies[10].

12.2   1970s: Disco and the Decadence of Cocaine

It would be difficult to discuss the 1970s without talking about *disco*. While President Richard Nixon had initiated the first war on drugs in 1972, the rate of cocaine and other illicit drug usage was on the rise. If disco had not become the dominate youth subculture, it is likely that cocaine would not have become such a ubiquitous fixture of the 1970s. Disco is a music genre and subculture that emerged in the early 1970s and lasted until 1983[11]. It emerged from the nightclub scene in urban United States. It influenced music, fashion, lyrics, and other cultural ephemera all hyper-focused on having a fun time on the dance floor of a discotheque to the loud sounds of records spun by a disc jockey (DJ) enhanced by a light show and narcotics.

From its origins, disco music permeated with and celebrated cultural difference. At the beginning of the 1970s, many of disco's recognizable DJs were Latinos or African Americans, and quite a few of them were African American women. The audiences for this first wave of disco were (predominantly) urban straight and gay African Americans, straight and gay Latinos, and white gay men dancing in African American and gay night clubs in major urban centers like New York, Los Angeles, and Chicago. Disco became an amalgamation of music from venues popular with African Americans, Latino Americans, Italian Americans, LGBT Americans (mostly African American and white gay men), and occasionally influenced by the psychedelic rock popularized in Philadelphia and New York. Disco is typified by "four-on-the-floor" beats, syncopated basslines, string sections, horns, electronic piano, synthesizers, and rhythm guitars. Disco fashion consisted of expensive, extravagant, and increasingly sexier fashions.

If the dance floor is the heart of the disco scene, the DJ represented its pulse. The DJ, a turntablist who was adept at mixing music for the dance floor, was responsible for leading dancers to the dance floor using bass and treble mixed to move one's feet. A good DJ could feel the mood of the dance floor and would skillfully select records according to the energy they felt. An amazing DJ could predict and react to the audience in a symbiotic way to find common musical ground, taking dancers from low to high and back again. The DJ and dancers working in harmony to produce the electric feel of pure embodied experience.

Disco DJs would employ the art of remixing of existing songs, using reel-to-reel tape machines and multiple turntables. They would add in percussion breaks, new sections of melody, and incorporate unique sounds (like car horns, sounds of traffic, trains speeding by, etc.). DJs needed to excel in the art and science of *beatmatching*—playing two tracks at the same tempo (speed the song is playing) and phase (mixing the bets from both tracks playing in-time with one another)—allowing for seamless movement across a musical journey. The equipment in the early days of disco was not very sophisticated, sometimes held together with duct tape and bazooka gum, but it did not curb the inventive ways a good DJ could manipulate sound and reach into our souls.

Disco brought together dance, fashion, music, and a thriving club drug subculture. ***Club drug subculture*** is best characterized as the use of drugs that would enhance a user's experience of dancing to the loud, bass-heavy music, and flashing neon lights. There was a shift in the way American's thought about drugs in the 1970s. In particular, the public use and displays of famous celebrities consuming drugs in exclusive disco clubs led to the glamorization of some of these substances. Andy Warhol, Liza Minnelli, Elizabeth Taylor, Debbie Harry, Grace Jones, Michael Jackson, Calvin Klein, Elton John, Rick James, Freddie Mercury, Cher, David Bowie, Salvador Dalí, and Jackie Kennedy Onassis were all regulars and often indulged[12]. Many people began to equate the drugs being used in the disco scene as "soft drugs." ***Soft drugs*** were erroneously believed by the naïve public to be nonaddictive and less damaging to the health than "hard drugs" (i.e., heroin). Because celebrities—many listed above—were consuming cocaine, it became seen as a soft drug. Celebrities would not do anything that was addictive or harmful, right? This was the misconception; soft drugs were thought to have fewer psychoactive and fewer adverse side effects than street drugs. The most popular and common disco "soft drugs" are listed in Table 12.4.

Table 12.4   The Names of the Disco "Soft Drugs"

Drug	Disco Name
Cocaine	Blow
Amyl or Butyl Nitrite	Poppers
Quaaludes	Disco Biscuits
Lysergic Acid Diethylamide (LSD)	Acid
Amphetamines	Speed

Source: T.D. Church

The massive quantities of drugs consumed in discos produced the next cultural phenomenon indicative of the disco era—promiscuous sex. The 1970s were the high-water mark of American's open acceptance of sexual expression of all kinds. The pornography business was booming, DJs were providing music for both the disco and—in Los Angeles at least—the theme music for the growing adult film industry[13]. As the 1970s progressed, there was an increasing rate of promiscuity and public sex. *Promiscuity* is the practice of having sex frequently with different partners, often being indiscriminate in the choice of sexual partners. *Public sex* is defined as performing sex acts in a public venue with one or more persons. The dance floor of the disco was the central arena of seduction with sex taking place in bathroom stalls, exit stairwells, and other semi-secluded spaces. Promiscuity and public sex became a staple of the disco era and represented a broader trend toward exploring a freer and sexually adventurous expression in the 1970s. Attitudes toward same-sex attraction were trending toward more open expression and inclusion, but this sexually forward freedom would not last beyond 1982.

Cocaine was the drug that would become associated with disco. Ian Schrager, cofounder of Studio 54, remembered Steve Rubell (cofounder of Studio 54) remarking that "disco goes with cocaine like peanut butter still goes with jelly"[14]. Most disco clubs by the mid-to-late 1970s in major cities of the United States did little to hide the rampant drug use, sexuality, and decadence synonymous with the disco scene. The waiters ran around shirtless in short booty shorts and waitresses often wore skimpy bikinis, even in the dead of winter in Northeast cities. The décor of many of the disco clubs featured blatant symbolism of sex and the club drug scene—many of them focusing on cocaine.

Cocaine is a powerfully addictive stimulant made from the leaves of the coca plant; we have traced its use in this book from the Age of Discover thru the Industrial Revolution. It is a versatile drug and is commonly snorted, inhaled as smoke, or dissolved in water and injected into a vein. The psychological effects of cocaine range from loss of contact with reality, intense feelings of happiness, through extreme agitation. The physical effects include fast heart rate, sweating, and enlarged pupils. Severity and duration of the psychological and physical effects vary based on amount, frequency of use, age, gender, and purity of drug.

In the age of disco, *insufflation* (colloquially referred to as "snorting," "sniffing," or "blowin") was the most common method of ingesting powdered cocaine. Upon insufflating, cocaine coats and is absorbed through the mucous membranes lining the nasal passages. This results in the euphoric effects being felt in the brain within 5 minutes. Insufflation, when used in moderation, is a noninvasive and virtually painless way for drug delivery. The mucosa within the nasal passage allows for quick absorption of drugs—regardless of whether it is in liquid, powdered, or aerosol formulation. Insufflation is a preferred method to consume a variety of illegal substances and can lead to significant, permanent damage to the nose, sinus cavities, and pharyngeal complex. Insufflation bypasses the liver and stomach in the first-pass metabolism, preventing drug degradation that occurs during the digestive process. Ergo, cocaine insufflation allows the drug to be easily absorbed into the bloodstream.

As an individual insufflates cocaine, the drug travels from the mucosa into the vasculature of the pulmonary system. Basically, traveling from the nose to the heart into the lungs to be converted into oxygen-enriched blood. The enriched blood with cocaine then travels back through the heart and onto other organs. When it hits the brain, typically 3–5 minutes post insufflation, the cocaine binds to the dopamine transporters and prevents the brain from removing excess dopamine from the brain's synapse and receptor system. This blocking continues until dopamine accumulates and produces short-term positive effects (euphoria, empowerment, and elevated energy) from having an overabundance of dopamine in the brain. Some of the cocaine will clump in the nasal passage and become coated with mucous. Following the natural process of foreign material in the nose, the mucous-coated cocaine will descend from the pharyngeal system, into the esophagus, and into the stomach for processing. As the cocaine dissolves in the stomach acid and moves to the intestines, a small amount of drug gets processed by the liver and put into the blood eventually hitting the brain around 30 minutes post-metabolism.

Insufflation in the 1970s took on a ritualized set of practices. Powdered cocaine was typically poured onto a flat, solid surface and then is divided out into bumps, lines, or rails prior to insufflation by use of a straw (plastic beverage straw, tightly rolled paper / money, etc.). The amount of cocaine in a line varies widely from person to person and occasion to occasion; Table 12.5 details the "average" amounts of cocaine. Some individuals may be heavy handed in cutting out the lines, other may be anemic in the amount provided.

Table 12.5   Cocaine Dosing by Line Type

Line Type	Size	Average Dosage
Bump	Smallest amount individuals do	~35 mg per dose
Line	Typical amount individuals do	~60 mg per dose
Rail	Largest amount individuals do	~140–160 mg per dose

Source: T.D. Church

Bumps were the favored amount in the disco scene because they could be easily done while on the dance floor from one of disco's more unique artifacts, a "coke spoon," or an intentionally grown long fingernail. A vast array of specialized jewelry purpose built with cocaine insufflation in mind became very fashionable among disco-goers, such as a sliver cross, which tapers into the classic coke spoon shape at the distal end. Lines and rails were typically done away from the dance floor, in the bathrooms on the back of sinks, toilets, or urinals or other flat surface. Lines and rails required the use of a straw to be able to complete the insufflation.

Amyl or Butyl Nitrite, colloquially called "poppers," was introduced in Chapter 8 during the nineteenth century. As a drug, poppers fall under the category of *inhalant*. This class of drugs typically produce a mild to moderate psychoactive effect, disinhibition, and loss of restraint in decision-making. Poppers are potent *vasodilators* which rapidly expand blood vessels, resulting in the lowering of blood pressure. They also signal the relaxation pathway for involuntary muscles, particularly within the blood vessel walls and internal and external anal sphincters. Poppers produce physical effects that include decrease in blood pressure, headache, flushing of the face, increased heart rate, and dizziness.

By the mid-point of the 1970s, poppers had gained the status of "club drugs" in heterosexual disco scenes and attained a cult-like devotion within the homosexual disco scene. Poppers would often be paired with stimulant drugs such as cocaine and amphetamines. The euphoric state produced by the nitrites becomes intensified and prolonged when mixed with stimulant use. The combination increases libido and lowers inhibitions. The vasodilator relaxes smooth muscles, like the sphincter, which facilitates prolonged anal intercourse.

Methaqualone, better known by the brand name Quaalude, is a barbiturate-like synthetic drug with anxiolytic, sedative, and hypnotic qualities [15]. Clinically, Quaaludes were used in the early 1970s in the treatment of insomnia and also prescribed for muscle relaxation. Between 1971 and 1973, Quaaludes increasingly became popular as a club drug among disco goers. People reported that Quaaludes gave users a feeling of suspended motor coordination with reported sensations of one's arms and legs being turned into Jell-O. *Motor coordination* in this context relates to the combination of body movements created with *kinematic* (spatial direction) and *kinetic* (force) parameters that result in actions (walking, running, dancing, etc.). By the late 1970s, Quaaludes had become a common date rape drug.

In 1972, Quaaludes represented one of the most frequently prescribed sedatives in the United States. Prescribed doses of Quaaludes tend to promote relaxation, sleepiness, and sometimes a feeling of euphoria. Pharmacologically, methaqualone causes a drop in blood pressure and slows the pulse. It was discovered by happenstance by some disco club attendees that the euphoric effects of Quaaludes could be magnified if taken with alcohol, and it became an exceedingly popular fixture in the early disco scene. By 1973, methaqualone had been placed as a Schedule II narcotic by the DEA, making it difficult to prescribe and illegal to have without a prescription. Nine years later, in 1982, methaqualone was withdrawn from the market by the FDA removing it from U.S. medical practice. Quaaludes became rare on the streets in the United States, but skyrocketed to one of the top drugs confiscated through interdiction efforts at the borders with Canada and Mexico. By 1984, the DEA had made methaqualone a Schedule I drug, indicating it had no medical utility and posed a high likelihood of misuse.

LSD, following the footsteps of the Hippie generation, became a regular attendee of many disco clubs. Instead of being used for personal enlightenment and self-awareness as popularized in the 1960s, LSD in the 1970s was solely being used for entertainment purposes. *Entertainment* here represents the act of providing one with an enjoyable experience, often accompanied by music and lights. An agreeable occupation for the mind, a diversion, an amusement, and with LSD the heightening of a performance. Instead of spiritual awakening or self-discovery, LSD was now being employed to boost consumer-based experiences related to music, dance, and performance venues. The sense of culture formed by 1970s' LSD enthusiasts was a bond shared together centered around a commercial musical venue and capitalist exchange.

Amphetamines are central nervous system stimulants which affect chemicals in the brain that contribute to hyperactivity and impulse control. Clinically, amphetamines are utilized to treat ADHD and improve cognitive focus. Recreationally, amphetamines are used as aphrodisiacs and euphoriants. The effects of *euphoria*, increased desire for sex, coupled with the increased wakefulness made amphetamines perfect for the sexually charged dance floors of the disco scene. Euphoria refers to an affective psychological state characterized by feelings of intense pleasure happiness, contentment, and excitement. Chemically induced euphoria can be highly addictive due to the reward response they induce in the brain. Amphetamines induce a state of euphoria and are highly addictive. Amphetamines could be obtained in pill form with a prescription until the mid-1970s, when they became a Schedule II controlled substance.

Toward the later half of 1974, *methamphetamine*, a more potent cousin of amphetamine, hit the disco scene like a freight train. Methamphetamine was easy to produce in small labs, usually right in the kitchens of addict's homes from commonly available chemicals. This form of drug manufacture gave methamphetamine one of its iconic street names, "stove top." It was a cheaper alternative to cocaine, stronger than legally obtained amphetamine, and would rise to epidemic proportions among gay men and rural communities throughout the United States.

By 1979, an extraordinarily strong anti-disco sentiment began developing in the United States. Disco was being criticized as being mindless, consumerist, overproduced, and escapist. There was a large burnout from the hedonistic and overindulgent lifestyle led by disco-goers. Changes in the political and economic climates of the United States began trending toward a repressive conservativism that starkly contrasted the liberal experimentalism of the 1970s. Promiscuous sex and rampant drug use came to a quick halt as HIV/AIDS emerged in 1981. HIV/AIDS instilled a fear of intimacy as people did not fully understand how the disease was contracted. Along with the AIDS epidemic, the country developed a renewed homophobia, which was spurred on by the fear of the "gay disease" sweeping the nation. Conservative groups and the zeal of fundamentalist religious beliefs rallied against the debauchery and hedonism of drug use, wild music, and rampant sexuality. Some went as far to claim HIV/AIDS to be the vengeance of god in reaction to the excess of disco. Disco did not go out with a bang, it died with a mournful whimper and by 1983 became synonymous with polyester, leisure suits, greasy sex-crazed men, and the suspiciously alluring sounds of ABBA and the Bee Gees. Disco tried to keep party going until it just could not boogie no more. The big disco sounds went silent and were being replaced as early as 1981 by pop, rock, and hip-hop.

12.3   1980s: The Drug Panic

Throughout the twentieth century, drug use went through cycles of intense public scrutiny and concern to relative indifference. Different generations have scapegoated different substances, mainly through the use of cultural or social sanctions. A turning point was reached in 1985, when public concern erupted due to increasing use of cocaine and crack-cocaine. The level of concern spread and generated a drug panic, and the speed with which this panic spread was so unexpected. The 1960s was a period of sociopolitical change as cannabis and psychedelics became popular. This led into the 1970s and marked a high-water point in both the use and public acceptance and tolerance of illegal drug consumption. The 1980s saw a change from the open and accepting attitudes of the previous two decades to a conservative set of values related to drugs. This view of drugs in the 1980s extended to the drug users who were seen as criminal, problematic, and in need of incarceration or, if circumstance favored, rehabilitation.

The rising change in public perception of drugs in the 1980s was called by media outlets at the time a *Drug Panic*. A *panic*, from a social science perspective, represents a sudden sensation of fear, which is so strong it dominates or prevents reason and logical thought. Panic in this context replaces logic with overwhelming feelings of anxiety, looming fear, and frantic agitation. Panics may occur singularly in individuals or manifest suddenly in large groups as mass panic. A drug panic can be understood as a widespread feeling within the public that something is terribly wrong with their society because of the illegal activities of drug addicts and abusers. As with other forms of panics, the drug panic saw the emergence of a singular element—in this case, crack-cocaine within urban neighborhoods as a threat to societal values and interests.

Public attention and concern shifted from the carefree drug-consuming 1970s to an oppressive fear of drug abuse in the 1980s. It was as though the United States had reached carrying capacity in its relationship with drugs. **_Carrying capacity_** is a term borrowed from ecology and refers to the number of individuals who can be supported within an environment without degrading the natural, cultural, and social resources available. In other words, how many people can be supported without reducing the ability to maintain the desired quality of life over the long term. In terms of public policy, only so many issues can rank near the top as a major concern to public health and safety, and there can only be one number one. Drug abuse held the number one position in the American public opinion polls for nearly 5 years, Figure 12.2 [16, 17].

Figure 12.2   Public Opinion Polls Naming Drug Abuse as a Major Issue

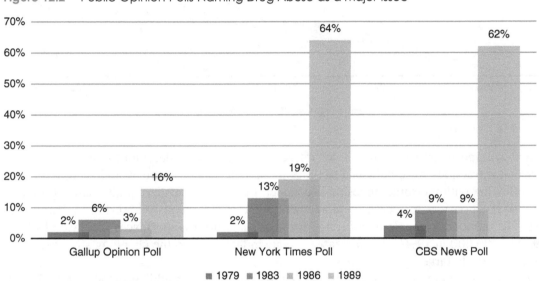

Source: Gallup Opinion Poll, New York Times Poll, and CBS News Poll

Another concrete measure of how certain conditions or phenomena are perceived as burning issues at a given point in time is to look at the focus being given through the media. Looking at the number of articles published on these burning issue topics in magazines and newspapers gives an indication of public opinion, or at least of public focus. Performing a search in EBSCO host or Google Scholar for newspaper and magazine articles published with keywords related to "drug abuse," "drugs and adolescents," "drugs and athletics," "drugs and work," "drugs and famous people," and "drug education" shows a remarkably interesting trend, Figure 12.3.

In addition to the growing focus from the media, there were legal and legislative changes related to drug use, distribution, and manufacture that were beginning to solidify. In New York City, in 1986, Mayor Ed Koch was pushing to have the death penalty extended to any drug dealer convicted of possessing at least a kilogram (2.2 pounds) of either cocaine or heroin. New York Governor Mario Cuomo in the same year called for a life sentence for anyone convicted of selling three vials of crack, the equivalent of $50 as sold on the street. These political rumblings set the stage for many of the zero tolerance policies implemented in the later part of the 1980s. **_Zero tolerance policies_** refer to policies

Figure 12.3 Newspapers and Magazine Articles Featuring Drug Key Words

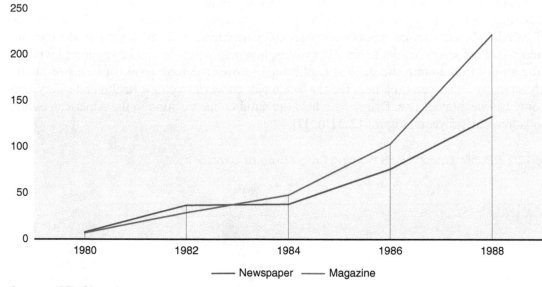

Source: T.D. Church

intended to impose strict punishment for infractions of a stated rule, with the intention of showing others that infractions were punished to the extreme and hopefully this would serve to deter others from following with the same undesirable conduct. Instead of considering alternative programs, the knee jerk reaction was to increase enforcement while simultaneously lowering the parameters for arrest. The number of people incarcerated for nonviolent drug law offences increased from 50,000 in 1980 to 400,000 in 1996. This increase was due in large part to the changing structures that were disproportionately targeting minorities.

Drug testing emerged as a mechanism to identify potential drug addicts in the middle of the 1980s. By 1987, it is estimated less than 25% of Fortune 500 corporations in the United States required drug testing of their employees. One year later, in 1988, this number rose to 60%. The change in frequency of companies' drug testing coincided with President Regan's issuance of Executive Order (EO) 12564, which instituted mandatory drug testing for all Federal employees. The penalty for failing the drug test under EO 12564 construed the individual as having possession of a controlled substance and resulted in mandatory revocation of employment, benefits, and pensions. EO 12564 provided for imprisonment for some Federal employees who failed their drug test. The Armed Services instituted new drug testing regulations in 1986 following the EO. Officers who tested positive for drug use faced automatic dismissal for the first offense and revocation of all benefits and pensions. Enlisted service members would receive compulsory treatment for their first offense and automatic dismissal for any subsequent infractions. The proportion of individuals who tested positive through drug testing dropped from just under 30% in 1980 to 3% in 1986. **Drug tests** are the technical analysis of biological specimen (urine, hair, blood, breath, sweat, and/or saliva) to determine the presence or absence of specified parent drugs or their metabolites. As can be imagined, drug tests exist in several methods with varying degrees of accuracy, sensitivity, and detection. Applications of drug testing are summarized in Table 12.6.

Table 12.6 Applications for Drug Testing

Application	Rationale
Athletics/Professional Sports	Detection of the presence of performance-enhancing substances
Employment	Screening for drugs prohibited by law
Parole/Probation	Screening for drugs prohibited by law
Law Enforcement	Screening of drugs prohibited by law Presence and concentration of alcohol (ethanol) in blood

Source: T.D. Church

To have a valid detection method for the presence of drug, the test must have accuracy, sensitivity, and reliable detection. *Accuracy* refers to the ability to measure the true amount or concentration of a substance within a sample. *Sensitivity* represents the ability of a test to correctly identify the individuals who are using a substance. The more sensitive a test, the fewer *false-negative* results it should produce. The less sensitive a test, the more *false-positive* results are produced. *False-negative* is the inability to identify the presence of a drug even though it is present within the individual; or the ability to identify the presence of a drug even though it is not present within the individual. *False-positive* describes a test result with incorrectly indicates the presence of a drug when it was never there. Finally, the *detection* signifies the length of time a substance or the resulting chemical changes (metabolites) remain identifiable. Together these three elements can be thought of as a bullseye, with the intent of achieving the mark or homing in on the target (positive proof of drugs). Detection times of drugs vary by biological sample used for detection, Table 12.7. False positives can be detected from drugs people need to take for other conditions or diseases, Table 12.8.

Drug detection tests can be divided into common and uncommon drug screens. Common drug screens will test for THC (cannabis), opiates (heroin, opium, morphine, and codeine), PCP (Phencyclidine), amphetamines, and cocaine. Uncommon drug screens require specialized labs to be performed and include screens designed to test for barbiturates, benzodiazepines, methadone, LSD, Steroids, MDMA (ecstasy), and opioids (oxycodone, hydrocodone). There is a famous quote from anonymous, Federal drug testing facilitator, who in the later part of the 1980s stated, "drug tests are made to be beaten, and most likely the addict or alcoholic knows just how to do that" [18].

Arguments on the problems with drug testing were quick to be raised, beginning in the late 1980s and continuing until today. At the heart of the arguments are ethical concerns related to flawed technologies, invasion of privacy, and inappropriate focus. It is important to keep in mind that the law is not always ethical, and ethics are not always lawful. In terms of flawed technology, the arguments raised indicate that the real-world performance of testing is much lower than is often thought to be of merit. Many of the tests are probably adequate for rehabilitation and treatment situations, possibly adequate for pre-employment situations, but definitely not adequate for dismissing employees. The invasion of privacy. Due to the ease and simple ways of invalidating a drug test, the only true way to ensure the test is to monitor the individual. This means that the specimen must be observed leaving

Table 12.7   Average Drug Detection Times

Drug	Class	Street Name	Urine Detection Time	Blood Detection Time
Amphetamine	Stimulant	Speed	Up to 2 days	Up to 12 hours
Benzodiazepines	Depressants/ sedatives/hypnotics	Bennies	Therapeutic dose: 3 days chronic use: 4–6 weeks or longer	Up to 48 hours
Cocaine	Stimulant	Coke, crack, rock cocaine	Up to 4 days	Up to 48 hours
Codeine	Analgesic/Opiate	N/A	2 days	Up to 12 hours
Ethyl alcohol, ethanol	Depressants/ sedatives/hypnotics	Alcohol, liquor, beer, wine, booze, hooch	2 to 12 hours	Up to 12 hours
Heroin	Analgesic/Opiate	Smack, tar, chasing the tiger/dragon	2 days	Up to 12 hours
Marijuana, Cannabinoids	Hallucinogen	Pot, dope, weed, hash, hemp	Single use: 2 to 7 days Prolonged, chronic use: 1 to 2 months or longer	Up to 336 hours
Methamphet-amine	Stimulant	Speed, ice, crystal, crank	Up to 2 days	Up to 37 hours
MDMA	Stimulant	Ecstasy, XTC, ADAM, lover's speed	Up to 2 days	Up to 48 hours
Morphine	Analgesic/Opiate	N/A	2 days	Up to 12 hours

Table 12.8 False-Positive from Prescription and OTC Drugs

Drug (Prescription or OTC)	Used to Treat	False Positive
Dextromorphan	Cough, Cold	Opiates, PCP
Diphenhydramine (Benadryl)	Antihistamine, allergy medication	Opiates, Methadone, PCP
Metformin (Glucophage)	Diabetes	Amphetamine ,Methamphetamine
Pseudoephedrine (Sudafed)	Sinus, nasal congestion	Amphetamine, Methamphetamine
Methylphenidate (Ritalin)	ADHD	Amphetamine, Methamphetamine, LSD
Dopxylamine (Unisom)	OTC sleep aid	Methadone, PCP
Tramadol (Ultram)	Pain	Opiates, PCP
Phentermine (Adipex-P)	Weight loss	Amphetamine
NSAIDs (Ibuprofen, naproxen)	OTC nonsteroidal anti-inflammatory meds	Barbiturates, THC, PCP, Benzodiazepines
Antidepressants (numerous—Zoloft, Seroquel)	SNRI, SSRI, depression, neuropathy, anxiety	Methadone, Opiates, Benzodiazepines, Amphetamine, Methamphetamine, LSD
Proton Pump Inhibitors (PPIs, omeprazole)	Gastroesophageal Reflux Disease and Heartburn	THC

the body. If you have a lot of warning bells and red flags appearing in your mind, that is a good thing. There have been many legal objections raised in the courts about drug testing since the 1980s and are focused on legal requirements of prior notice, consent, due process, and cause. And finally, there are some who believe that drug testing has the wrong focus. Instead of attempting to catch the alcoholic or drug abuser, the focus of management should be concerned with work performance decline instead. Effective management practices portend an infinitely better approach to managing workplace substance abuse concerns.

Unbeknownst to the American public, we were poised to enter a nationwide crusade against drugs. Between June and September 1986, at every possible opportunity, President Ronald Reagan made a call for a "nationwide crusade against drugs, a sustained, relentless effort to rid America of this scourge" [19]. President Reagan began proposing legislation that would cost taxpayers $2 billion to fight the drug problem. Within this legislation, $56 million was earmarked for drug testing of federal employees. In September 1986, the House of Representatives approved the legislation with some modifications, including increased funds for drug enforcement, stiffer federal sentences, increased spending for education and treatment programs, harsher penalties against drug-producing countries who did not cooperate in U.S.-sponsored eradication programs. The final bill was approved by the Senate in October 1986 with a cost of $1.7 billion and featured a new provision that the death penalty was to be utilized for convicted drug kingpins. The Anti-Drug Abuse Act was signed into law by Ronald Reagan in October 1986.

The earmarked "education and treatment programs" took on some unique qualities between 1986 and 1989. Features that today are considered ***anti-drug propaganda***. The quintessential slogan of this era was issued by the First Lady's office when Nancy Reagan said, "Just Say No." ***Anti-drug propaganda*** was a media campaign spread by government and media outlets who provided information, ideas, or rumors deliberately spread widely to influence public opinions and to preserve the "self-interest of the nation." During the later part of the 1980s, the government used posters, media ads, TV shows, and animation to scare kids and teenagers into saying no to drugs.

"Just Say No" was an attempt to discourage children from engaging in illegal recreational drug use by having them simply say "no" to peer pressure. This slogan, however, was too simplistic and reduced drug awareness to a hyper-focused and not very useful catch phrase. Even worse, it did not provide any skills for kids being peer pressured beyond saying "no" and did not give advice on how to get away from peer pressure. Further, "Just Say No" added to the stigma about people who used drugs and labeled them as "bad." The stigma extended toward people who were addicted to drugs being labeled as making a cognizant amoral choice to use drugs. They did not have the fortitude or the willpower to just simply say "no" and that equated them to being weak, inferior, bad, and evil. In some instances, it equated them to being un-American and even criminal.

Figure 12.5   Just Say No

Public Service Announcements (PSAs) became big business and a multitude of media campaigns fought to secure the lucrative federal funds from the Anti-Drug Act. One of the more aggressive of the anti-narcotic campaign brands was Partnership for a Drug-Free America (PDFA), and in 1987 launched the "This is your brain" PSA and associated poster campaign. TV Guide would go on to name the commercial as one of the top one hundred television advertisements of all time. The slogan quickly became a parody and in the late 1980s to 1990s, "this is your brain on [*insert noun here*]..." became a catchphrase. Pamphlets, books, newsletters, and videotapes were offered for sale to concerned parents, teachers, and youth organizers who wanted to put a stop to drug use. These publications warned of glassy-eyed zombies high on cannabis, teens sprinkling cocaine on popcorn at parties, junkies nodding out on every street corner, and crack addicts invading every neighborhood.

The drug of concern in the 1980s was ***crack***, a potent crystalline form of cocaine. It skyrocketed to prominence in urban areas of the United States in 1985. Crack is a free-base form of cocaine. ***Freebasing*** is the act of heating crack and inhaling the resulting smoke. Crack has a melting point of 98C and is volatile at temperatures above 90C, providing an active drug for smoking. Direct flame to the drug will burn it too fast and not release any of the free base smoke. Crack is produced through a debasing process where sodium bicarbonate (baking soda), cocaine, and water are mixed slowly together and heated. When the water has completely evaporated the resulting rock-like lump is crack. Crack before 1985 was very obscure, which

Figure 12.6   Crack Cocaine

Kevin L Chesson/Shutterstock.com

made the suddenness of its widespread use and the degree to which it caught on in some neighborhoods a newsworthy story. There was the impression that a major drug crisis had erupted virtually overnight.

With the passage of the Anti-Drug Abuse Act of 1986, a disproportionate system of enforcement was established in how crack and cocaine were treated within the criminal justice system. Crack came with a five-year mandatory minimum prison sentence for possession of five grams (1/3 of a tablespoon). The average sentence length for individuals convicted with possession of crack was 115 months (~9.5 years). Cocaine had a five-year mandatory minimum prison sentence for possession of 500 grams (~1 pounds). The average sentence length for individuals convicted with possession of cocaine was 87 months (~7.25 years). When asked about the disparity of the two penalties for the same drug, Representative Dan Lungren (coauthor of the Anti-Drug Abuse Act) stated, "we didn't really have an evidentiary basis for the sentencing guidelines" [20]. Upon enactment of the new legislation, minority youth experienced harsh crack-related sentences.

In June 1986, a media storm shook the nation with the death of two young and exceptionally talented athletes from crack cocaine only 8 days apart from one another. Len Bias died June 19, 1986; he was 23 at the time of death. Len was the University of Maryland, first-team All-American basketball forward. The Boston Celtics had selected Len as their second overall pick in the 1986 NBA draft on June 17, 1986. Len died from cardiac arrhythmia induced by a crack cocaine overdose. It was his first-time trying crack, which had been brought to a celebratory party by friends of a friend. Len's death was felt to be especially devastating, because of the proximity of Maryland's campus to the nation's capital. Don Rogers died June 27, 1986; he was 24 at the time of death. Don was the UCLA co-player of the game in 1983 Rose Bowl for the Bruins and in 1984 had tied a Rose Bowl record gaining two interceptions. The Cleveland Browns selected Don as their eighteenth pick in the 1984 NFL draft. Don died from a heart attack caused by crack cocaine. It was his first-time trying crack, and like Len's death, he held a celebratory party, and the drugs were brought to the party by people Don did not know personally. The deaths of these two young men were felt especially deeply across the country. Sports figures and celebrities tend to be glorified in the United States, and the death of someone famous is not only a catastrophe, the source of death for the celebrity is often viewed as being more common and representative in the general public than it truly is.

There was real violence being caused by crack cocaine in the 1980s, and unfortunately that violence was being focused on specific locations and among specific peoples. Black communities between 1984 and 1989 were facing several social injustices, far more than any other community in America. Data available from the Center for Disease Control (CDC) indicates that the homicide rate for black males aged 14 to 17 more than doubled and for black males aged 18 to 24 nearly tripled [21]. During the same time period (1984–1989), black communities experienced a 20–100% increase in fetal death rates, low birth-weight babies, weapons arrests, and the number of children placed into foster care. The reasons for these huge disparities have been traced by some to the crack epidemic, which would have long-run consequences for crime and family upheaval. Crack was cheaper than cocaine, and drug dealers disproportionately targeted urban areas of decay and minority housing areas as places to set up shop. Although more white people would come to use crack, there were more people of color who carried the weight of being drug offenders. By 1989, offenders were comprised of 83% Black, 10% Hispanic, 5.8% White, and 1.2% Other Races [22]. Crack was used by a wide range of peoples from varied races, genders, and socioeconomic statuses, but people of color were hit the hardest through law enforcement and unfair judicial practices.

Black communities did not initiate crack use and distribution; it was pushed into black communities by social and economic forces outside the control of the community members. Thanks to systemic violence and structural violence, crack became entrenched in many urban inner-city neighborhoods. *Systemic violence* refers to the harm people suffer from the social structure and the institutions that sustain and reproduce those harms. This type of violence represents institutional practices or procedures that negatively affect groups or individuals in psychological, mental, cultural, economic, spiritual, or physical ways. *Structural violence* concerns systematic ways in which social structures harm or otherwise disadvantage individuals. Structural violence is subtle, often invisible, especially to those who have never experienced it before. Sadly, this type of violence has no specific group or individual who can (or will) be held responsible for initiating the cycle of violence. Crack in the inner-city of American cities exploited the economic inequalities of the neighborhoods (lack of jobs), social inequalities (lower rates of public education/access to education), and for many young males appeared as a fast and effortless way to make a lot of money. Because of structural violence, crack dealers did not pause to consider the consequences that would further social disintegration within the very communities where they lived.

The crack dealers were not solely to blame for perpetuating structural violence; crack bingers and addicts had an equal role to play. Together the dealers and addicts invented a very unique consumer marketplace. On one hand, the crack dealers were exhibiting economic and entrepreneurial greed and crack addicts through desperation and addiction would find the money to support their habit. A new economic paradigm took root, ***street capitalism***, as an economic pattern where individuals bet their lives on the rewards of selling "rock," crack; where people gave themselves over to the crack pipe; and the often-merciless authorities indiscriminately incarcerated those caught in the clutches of the crack underworld [23]. While crack addicts and customers had no formal protections against dishonest or mean-spirited dealers, they did have acumen to take their business elsewhere. The consumers, who often, were frequent purchasers in a big and incredibly competitive market. They would pool their information on who sold weak crack, who short-changed the customers, and who treated the customers the best.

Crack addiction is a profoundly serious condition. Symptomology of a frequent crack user includes dry mouth and nose, bad breath, frequent lip licking, irritability and argumentative, erratic and violent behavior, inability to remain still, excessive sweating, and dilated pupils. Colloquially, we refer to individuals who are extremely addicted to crack as ***crack fiends***. Habitual crack users become adapted to an anxious and paranoid way of life, often fearing that someone is trying to do them harm or steal their meager horde of dollar bills. Crack users quickly build up a tolerance to the drug and as a result require ever-increasing amounts of drug to bring the user to a sense of normality. Heavy users often cannot function physically, emotionally, or mentally without crack. Maladaptive behaviors such as lying, cheating, stealing, missing work, financial problems, and legal issues all become profoundly serious effects intent on destroying the addict's life and threaten the same for everyone associated with the addict. Crack fiends will do whatever it takes to secure their next high; resorting to stealing, prostitution, or robbery to secure their next hit.

Crack can affect a woman and her unborn fetus in many ways. During the early months of pregnancy, crack may increase the risk of miscarriage. Crack may cause the unborn fetus to have a stroke, permanent brain damage, or heart attack. ***Crack Babies*** who are born to mothers who use crack are frequently delivered prematurely, have low birth weights, smaller head circumferences, and are shorter in length than other babies. Late effects in the children born addicted to crack include behavior problems, deficits in cognitive performance, lower information processing, and inability to sustain attention to tasks. A relative few, who had higher rates of exposure to crack in the womb, presented with language and memory problems. The number and frequency of crack babies were grossly exaggerated, and the numbers of babies addicted to crack were elevated in public reports delivered via the nightly news. There were, sadly, babies born addicted and a number of which were true "crack babies," but the number reported in 1987 and 1988 made it seem that every child born was a crack addict.

The National Institute on Drug Abuse (NIDA) is a federal scientific research institute under the NIH. The Department of Health and Human Services tasks NIDA with addressing the most fundamental and essential questions related to drug use, including tracking emerging drug use trends. Their research attempts to understand how drugs work in the brain and body, developing and testing new drug treatment and prevention approaches, and dissemination of findings. In looking at data collected in 1985 and 1988, we see a polarization of drug use, which has divided usage and taken it to some unique extremes, Table 12.9 [24]. On one hand, the episodic or even the regular but less than weekly cocaine user was becoming less common. On the other hand, the weekly or more and the daily or daily user was becoming more common. This is problematic, because it is heavy drug users who typically cause most of the social problems associated with drug abuse—that is, crime, prostitution, theft, etc.

Table 12.9 NIDA—National Household Survey Data 1985 and 1988

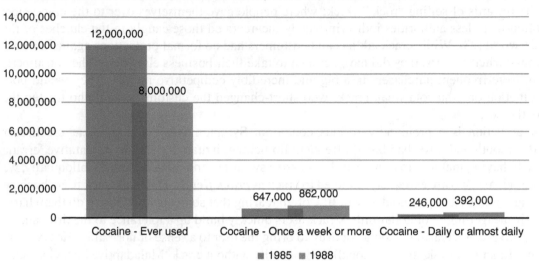

Source: NIDA National Household Survey

The Drug Abuse Warning Network (DAWN) represents data compiled from the incidence of drug-misuse from emergency room reports and fatal drug overdoses file by medical examiner's reports. It is a national database and points toward unique trends. Data for 1979 and 1989 related to heroin and cocaine emergency room data is shown in Table 12.10 [25]. Even though fewer people are using illegal drugs overall, more Americans in 1989 were using heroin heavily and more were taking cocaine with grave consequences. There were two factors contributing to the increase in emergency room visits relate to cocaine and heroin. The first factor, route of administration, the proportion of individuals who smoked (as opposed to snorted) cocaine increased in the reported percentage of

Table 12.10 DAWN—Decade of ER Visit Data, Heroin and Cocaine

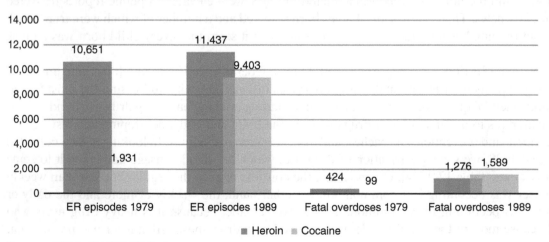

Source: NIDA, DAWN ER Data

emergency room visits from 6% in 1984 to ~33% in 1988. The second factor, drug mixing or ***speedballing***, the use of cocaine and heroin together in combination. Speedballing creates a ***synergistic effect***, wherein the effect of heroin and cocaine taken together is greater than the sum of their separate effect at the same dose.

In a data report generated through the CDC's, WISQARS™ searchable database[1], it is possible to generate a report that provides data on the leading causes of death, 1986 to 1988, Table 12.11 [26]. The last column, "All Ages," in the list shows the average causes of death within the United States. Read over the table and look for crack cocaine or illegal drug overdose. If you cannot find that data, it is ok… The number of illegal drug deaths between 1986 and 1989 total is 7,479. Far fewer deaths than the number 10 cause in the table. To put this into perspective, the number of prescription drug deaths between 1986 and 1989 total is 32,965. More people died from prescription drug than illegal drug overdoses during this period. This is not what we were led to believe by the media outlets at the time that made it appear that crack cocaine was impacting every neighborhood and harming every family in the United States.

Table 12.11   WISQARS: Leading Causes of Death, 1986–1989, All Races, Both Sexes

10 Leading Causes of Death, United States
1986 - 1989, All Races, Both Sexes

Rank	<1	1-4	5-9	10-14	15-24	25-34	35-44	45-54	55-64	65+	All Ages
1	Congenital Anomalies 32,389	Unintentional Injury and Adv. Effects 11,487	Unintentional Injury and Adv. Effects 8,217	Unintentional Injury and Adv. Effects 8,512	Unintentional Injury and Adv. Effects 73,915	Unintentional Injury and Adv. Effects 66,830	Malignant Neoplasms 61,248	Malignant Neoplasms 153,944	Malignant Neoplasms 390,996	Heart Disease 2,469,460	Heart Disease 3,024,866
2	SIDS 21,618	Congenital Anomalies 3,644	Malignant Neoplasms 2,470	Malignant Neoplasms 2,084	Homicide & Legal Int. 22,832	Homicide & Legal Int. 27,577	Heart Disease 48,489	Heart Disease 128,370	Heart Disease 353,194	Malignant Neoplasms 1,284,776	Malignant Neoplasms 1,927,503
3	Short Gestation 13,798	Malignant Neoplasms 2,165	Congenital Anomalies 1,070	Homicide & Legal Int. 1,120	Suicide 19,843	Suicide 26,641	Unintentional Injury and Adv. Effects 44,563	Unintentional Injury and Adv. Effects 28,995	Cerebro-vascular 45,005	Cerebro-vascular 516,546	Cerebro-vascular 595,546
4	Respiratory Distress Syndrome 13,498	Homicide & Legal Int. 1,490	Homicide & Legal Int. 635	Suicide 973	Malignant Neoplasms 7,799	Malignant Neoplasms 21,500	Suicide 20,681	Liver Disease 18,751	Chronic Low. Respiratory Disease 42,340	Chronic Low. Respiratory Disease 265,679	Unintentional Injury and Adv. Effects 382,425
5	Maternal Complications 5,699	Heart Disease 1,321	Heart Disease 569	Congenital Anomalies 810	Heart Disease 4,186	HIV 18,821	HIV 19,541	Cerebro-vascular 18,533	Unintentional Injury and Adv. Effects 30,768	Pneumonia & Influenza 257,081	Chronic Low. Respiratory Disease 322,136
6	Unintentional Injury and Adv. Effects 3,791	Pneumonia & Influenza 812	Pneumonia & Influenza 258	Heart Disease 684	Congenital Anomalies 1,958	Heart Disease 14,380	Homicide & Legal Int. 15,358	Suicide 14,617	Liver Disease 27,977	Diabetes 119,978	Pneumonia & Influenza 293,249
7	Placenta Cord Membranes 3,566	Perinatal Period 516	Benign Neoplasms 193	Chronic Low. Respiratory Disease 306	HIV 1,640	Liver Disease 4,360	Liver Disease 13,776	Diabetes 9,702	Diabetes 24,745	Unintentional Injury and Adv. Effects 104,800	Diabetes 162,917
8	Perinatal Infections 3,550	Meningitis 511	Chronic Low. Respiratory Disease 135	Pneumonia & Influenza 232	Pneumonia & Influenza 1,081	Cerebro-vascular 3,809	Cerebro-vascular 9,538	Chronic Low. Respiratory Disease 8,922	Pneumonia & Influenza 16,027	Athero-sclerosis 82,395	Suicide 122,339
9	Intrauterine Hypoxia 3,276	Septicemia 363	Anemias 132	Cerebro-vascular 181	Cerebro-vascular 1,005	Pneumonia & Influenza 3,221	Diabetes 5,204	HIV 7,475	Suicide 14,180	Nephritis 72,061	Liver Disease 105,463
10	Pneumonia & Influenza 2,614	HIV 330	Cerebro-vascular 120	Benign Neoplasms 166	Chronic Low. Respiratory Disease 754	Diabetes 2,595	Pneumonia & Influenza 5,140	Homicide & Legal Int. 7,310	Nephritis 8,071	Septicemia 62,993	Homicide & Legal Int. 87,775

Source: CDC.gov

---

[1] https://wisqars.cdc.gov/fatal-leading

Was there a drug panic in the 1980s? Yes and no... The increase in concern related to crack cocaine was accompanied by an increase in measurable harm. In public health, **measurable harm** represents an ability to identify and measure physical, psychological, and/or societal harms related to drug abuse. The measurable harm in the 1980s was cause in part by an increase in heavy, chronic drug use of two drugs—heroin and crack cocaine. Sadly, media and government officials did not make a sober or systematic assessment of the facts. The concern over drugs in the late 1980s was a panic. But only existed because of arguments and facts that were overblown and not presented appropriately to the American public. Drug use had become the number one problem in the United States—as measured by public opinion. The panic that was promoted by the media led to some serious repercussions, many of which we are still facing today. These repercussions were related to law enforcement crackdowns, a growing crisis mentality due to the crackdowns, media coverage and overblown statistics, and media campaigns with misleading advice. All these elements together produced a sense of public concern that grew between 1986 and 1989. And then the concern and panic faded as drug addiction was replaced by increasing national debt, the Cold War, poverty, and the environment. Drug addiction would remain a public concern but has not been the sole concern facing the nation since 1989.

12.4 | 1990s: The Burgeoning Opioid Epidemic

Medical media, in particular pharmaceutical media used in the 1990s, was not intended for public consumption, instead it was driven by a few influential companies and geared toward prescribing physicians. This was the rise of an unregulated area of healthcare that would kick off one of the worst drug epidemics plaguing the modern era. Pharmaceutical companies rely on Medical Science Liaisons (MSLs) and sales representatives to help get information about new drugs available to the market disseminated to medical staff in hospitals and private practice. **Medical Science Liaisons** are intended to act as conduits of information related to new research developments, clinical trial activities, and therapeutic approaches. They are employed by pharmaceutical, biotechnology, medical device, and managed care companies. MSLs are responsible for direct field communication with prescribing or primary treating health-care providers about medical and science information related to their employers' medical product portfolios. Pharmaceutical sales representatives work in tandem with MSLs, and they are salespeople employed by pharmaceutical companies to persuade doctors to prescribe their companies drugs to patients. Drug companies in the United States spend ~$5 billion annually sending representatives to doctors, to provide product information, answer questions on product use, and deliver product samples. The activities of MSLs and Sales Reps were not regulated and had little oversight until 2002 when these interactions became governed according to limits established by the Code on Interactions with Health Care Professionals, created by the trade group representing companies within the pharmaceutical industry, Pharmaceutical Research and Manufacturers of America (PhRMA). In the 1990s, there was no clearly defined set of guidelines related to the ethical interactions between health-care professionals and the pharmaceutical company representatives.

The unregulated interactions of MSLs and Sales Representatives set the stage for the opioid crisis that began in the 1990s and has escalated through today. The **Opioid Epidemic** refers to the growing number of deaths and hospitalizations from opioids, including both prescription and illicit drugs. In recent years, death rates from these drugs have increased rapidly to over 40,000 a year, or 115 a day, across the United States. Drug overdose is now the leading cause of accidental death in the United States, due in large part to the Opioid Epidemic [27]. Much of this crisis began as a result of an article published in *Scientific American* in 1990 by Ronald Melzack in which he questioned why opioids were reserved for cancer pain and had been entirely neglected in chronic pain states [27]. There were some maligned data and unsubstantiated reports used by Melzack when he made the false claim and equated all forms of pain to be the same. The complete disregard of the complex biopsychosocial phenomena inherent in chronic pain, and blatant disregard of professional and academic protest, allowed opioids to grow into the primary therapeutic choice for non-cancer pain treatment in theUnited States. The American Pain Society (APS) launched an extremely influential media awareness campaign in 1995 intent on positioning "pain as the fifth vital sign." The hope of APS was to invigorate research to lead to a standardized evaluation and treatment plan for pain symptoms. This had the untended effect of opening the flood gates for research to target pain and set the stage for opioids to dominate the pharmaceutical markets of theUnited States.

Opioids are a classification of drugs derived from, or synthesized to mimic, opium. Morphine, the most abundant natural opioid found in opium, was used for centuries to relieve pain as we have seen throughout history within this book. As medicine advanced, scientists found ways to replicate the effects of morphine to make it stronger or weaker depending on the need. There tends to be some confusion regarding the differences between opioids and opiates, people tend to use the terms interchangeably, which can be both inaccurate and unsuitable. *Opioid* is a broad term used to describe any type of substance, either natural or man-made (synthetic) that binds to opioid receptors in the brain, Table 12.12. An *opiate* refers to natural substances that can be extracted from the flowering poppy plant. All opiates are opioids, but not all opioids are opiates. Both opioids and opiates can be highly addictive and are frequently misused.

Table 12.12 Types of Opioids

Type	Example
Natural opioids	Codeine, morphine, heroin
Synthetic opioids	Fentanyl, methadone
Semisynthetic opioids	Hydrocodone, oxycodone

Source: T.D. Church

In the 1990s, pharmaceutical companies began to develop increasingly potent formulations of opioids for pain and through their MSLs and Sales Representatives, they began to push synthetic and semisynthetic opioids to physicians. The companies used their MSLs to deliver false information that these drugs were either less addictive or nonaddictive in comparison to morphine. The MSLs led physicians to believe these new opioids had no dangerous or serious side effects. Physicians were given incentives to prescribe these drugs and were prescribing for any indication of pain, as they were presented with data indicating no repercussions to patients taking them. This growth in the prescription opioid business was directly propelled by the dispensation of opioids. This trend has persisted until today with more prescriptions for opioids being written annually than any other medication, contributing to the state of the epidemic we now find ourselves embroiled within.

OxyContin (oxycodone) is an opioid used for treatment of moderate to severe pain, developed by Purdue Pharmaceuticals (Purdue Pharma) and was made available for retail prescription sales in 1995. When OxyContin hit the market, it was flaunted as being a "miracle drug." Individuals who were suffering with chronic or debilitating pain, this pill was intended to give some respite and provide them with an opportunity to heal. What made OxyContin unique was the introduction of an extended time-released formulation, which allowed users to take one pill every 12 hours. Purdue Pharma presented information and data in such a way that it led to rampant addiction, overprescribing, and a huge public

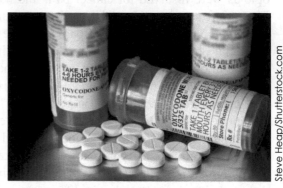

Figure 12.7   OxyContin (oxycodone)

Steve Heap/Shutterstock.com

health crisis. Purdue knowingly downplayed risks associated with OxyContin while simultaneously engaging in aggressive marketing campaigns, highlighting the benefits of their new formulation. On the manufacturing end, Purdue Pharma, owned by the Sackler Family, allegedly generated false data and made unsubstantiated and bold claims in OxyContin's marketing strategies. The company and the shareholders made billions of dollars from this single medication's sales. The Opioid Epidemic that began in the late-1990s and 2000s and persists till today can be linked to OxyContin's unfathomable volume in prescriptions for pain management.

The misleading of the public and the misdirection of the medical community about the truly addictive nature of OxyContin was where Purdue Pharma—as advised by their publicity consulting firm—were eventually found in 2005 to have actively engaged in fraud [28]. McKinsey & Company was the consulting firm that aided Purdue Pharma in their marketing plan and advised for an aggressive promotion of OxyContin. The pharmaceutical executives and employees of Purdue Pharma were not the only culprits in the misappropriation of OxyContin. The company had developed extremely close ties with hospitals and insurance companies, which added to the problem and allowed for the egregious misrepresentations to persist across the board. In addition, a substantial proportion of prescribing physicians were given highly lucrative perks for overprescribing OxyContin and downplaying the medication's highly addictive properties. Some of the rewards for the highest prescribing physicians and hospital employees included all-inclusive luxury vacations to Hawai'i, Tahiti, the Caribbean, and Mediterranean. Hundreds of prescribing physicians received six-figure payments, with thousands more paid well over $25,000 to endorse the benefits of OxyContin [29]. When revenue reached a plateau, McKinsey & Co. would push for a marketing strategy that endorsed a renewed focus on high-dose pills, which are among the most dangerous and highly addictive.

The time-release mechanism of OxyContin was supposed to make this opioid less susceptible to misuse and reduce the risk of addiction. This would be proven not to be the case, and it quickly became clear that users circumvented the extended-release gelatin coating by crushing the OxyContin and extracting the Oxycodone. They could swallow the Oxycodone directly or as was becoming increasingly popular, dissolve the drug in water and then inject it for a quicker high. Many of those who become addicted to opioids do so after initially receiving a prescription for pain. The highly addictive nature of these painkillers makes it easy for the human brain to crave more of them. Opioids work by attaching to proteins in the brain, spinal cord, and gastrointestinal tract called opioid receptors. When opioids attach to opioid receptors, they set about blocking transmission of pain messages to the brain. The result is a feeling of little to no pain. Many synthetic opioids induce a euphoric feeling to form in a user's body. Individuals who abuse opioids report feelings of pleasure, warmth, contentedness, and drowsiness, as well as a sense of tranquility.

While opioids are amazingly effective in treating pain, tolerance to the drug develops, which requires users to consume increasingly higher doses to achieve the same effect. It is only after their prescription ends that many users realize they have become dependent on the effects of opioids to function normally. At that point, they are forced to either get clean and endure the pain that comes with the withdrawal symptoms of opioids or look for another means of getting their high. Symptoms of opioid withdrawal can include anxiety, muscle aches, irritability, insomnia, runny nose, nausea, vomiting, and abdominal cramping. These symptoms are often accompanied with an increase in the individual's pain and is often why some individuals turn to illicit drugs. Because prescription opioids are so expensive, users may resort to heroin or other illicit substances instead. It is often cheaper, more potent, and easier to locate than the legally sourced prescriptions that users were taking before. It has been estimated that ~80% of people using heroin began their addiction with a prescription to another opioid [30]. Whereas first-time opioid addicts who initiate with heroin, represent ~20% of individuals develop opioid addiction.

The Opioid Epidemic is an equal opportunity offender. It affects people in all demographics and from all levels of society, including teens, seniors, veterans, and the LGBTQ community. Even those who do not use or abuse opioids can feel the effects of the epidemic if opioid abuse is common in their area or if their loved ones have addiction issues. The economic burden of opioid abuse and the emotional burden put on families of an addicted individual have been devastating. The latest wave of the Opioid Epidemic, which hit mid-2013, saw a shift in momentum toward synthetic opiates, namely fentanyl. Fentanyl is ~50 times more potent than heroin and ~80–100 times stronger than morphine. The problem with fentanyl is a rising tide of illicitly manufactured fentanyl (IMF), which gets distributed through illegal drug markets. IMF has become a popular additive to other drugs because of its extreme potency, which makes other drugs cheaper, more powerful, more addictive, and more deadly [31]. IMF-laced drugs are extremely dangerous, and many people may be unaware that their illegally purchased drugs have been cut with fentanyl. This lack of awareness has proven to be deadly and has led to an astronomical number of overdoses in recent years.

12.5   2000s: Raves and EDM, Synthetic Music, and Synthetic Drugs

Electronic Dance Music (EDM), sometimes referred to as dance music, club music, or house, represents a broad range of percussive electronic and sampled music made largely for nightclubs, raves, and festivals. EDM is produced by a DJ who creates a set, or seamless selection of tracks mixed by segueing from one sampling of music to another. Typically, these are highly percussive, featuring a lot of drum and bass overlays presented in a syncopated 16th note style. Most EDM music is energetic and fast paced. In the late 1980s and early 1990s, following the emergence of raves, EDM achieved widespread popularity in Europe. Acceptance of EDM was not universal in theUnited States, even though electro and Chicago House were quite popular. Mainstream media and the record industry of the 1990s was openly hostile toward EDM [32]. Raves had led governments in the United States at the state and city level to enact laws and policies against large music parties due to the perception of EDM with drug culture. Between 2000 and 2010, EDM had attained global popularity and slowly was gaining acceptance in theUnited States. The American music industry was working hard to rebrand the underground American rave culture in the public eye. As a result, EDM became a large umbrella term for multiple music genres, including house, techno, trance, drum and bass, dubstep, and their associated subgenres.

The rave scene in the United States really came to prominence in the later part of the twentieth century. *Raves* were organized dance parties held at nightclubs, outdoor festivals, warehouses, and featured performances from several DJs over the course of hours to days. Some of the classic features common in early U.S. raves are listed in Figure 12.4. Sometimes, raves were not a welcome occurrence in cities and law enforcement would clamp down on venues often times barring parties from even happening. To circumvent this, in the early rave scene there would often be what can be referred to as *squat parties*, held in unauthorized, secret venues. Often these would be hosted in unoccupied homes, abandoned warehouses, unused aircraft hangers, or other similar areas. There would, at times, be elaborate "clues" for party attendees to follow to get to the party location. Squat parties would either steal electricity or bring in their own generators for power. Law enforcement raids and anti-rave laws presented a huge challenge to the rave scene, all due to its association with illegal drugs.

Figure 12.4   Classic Features of Raves

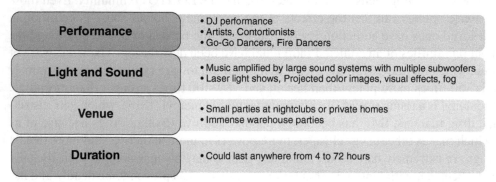

Performance	• DJ performance • Artists, Contortionists • Go-Go Dancers, Fire Dancers
Light and Sound	• Music amplified by large sound systems with multiple subwoofers • Laser light shows, Projected color images, visual effects, fog
Venue	• Small parties at nightclubs or private homes • Immense warehouse parties
Duration	• Could last anywhere from 4 to 72 hours

Source: T.D. Church

Raves featured loud music, drugs, and dancing. It took on a unique and "textbook free" form of dancing, whereby the movements were intentionally not predefined, and the dance was performed random sets of movements. Over time, distinct "rave"-like dance moves did appear but were not ubiquitous. *Raving* as a dance form required that dancers take inspiration from the music, their current mood, and observation of other people dancing around them. Unique to the U.S. rave scene were the incorporation of two key hip-hop elements, street dance and battles. *Street dance* is a technical style of dance that evolved alongside EDM and rave culture [33]. Street dance is catch-all for a variety of urban dance forms such as breaking, popping, locking, and house. Street dance in the United States is a form of vernacular dance that is highly improvisational and social in nature, encouraging interaction and connection with spectators and other dancers. ***Dance Battles*** are a form of street dance wherein a single dancer or a crew will engage in freestyle dance competitions where in the "competitors" attempt to outdo one another for the applause and cheering of the crowd. While freestyle raving has built a highly stylized and complex set of moves over the years, these moves are adaptable to any dancer and change to fit the music and context. All raving techniques require the dancer to use their body as an extension of the music, to loosen up, and let the music flow through their bodies to create a unique form of movement [34]. Many ravers claim to be able to feel the music better while under the influence of MDMA, ketamine, and/or other hallucinogenic drugs [35].

Overall, the U.S. rave scene tended to have a shared interest in nonviolence and a renewed fondness of psychedelia and drug experimentation. Rave culture in the United States incorporated disco culture's same love of dance music, drug exploration, sexual promiscuity, and hedonism. In this context, ***hedonism*** refers to the pursuit of pleasure and, more specifically, sensual indulgence. Where disco had thrived in the mainstream, rave culture made a conscious effort to stay underground. A key factor motivating raves to remain underground had to do with curfew and the standard 2 a.m. closing time of clubs in most U.S. cities. It was a desire to keep the party going past legal hours of operation that created the underground direction.

Club drugs vary a great deal by area, availability, time, and even the event itself. In addition to methamphetamine and LSD (club drugs discussed previously), the new drugs that were poised to become synonymous with raves are listed in Table 12.13. People attending raves were seeking out substances that would enhance their sensory experiences at these events. Club drugs at the height of the rave scene (~1995–2005) were used for somewhat different reasons than other recreational drugs. Rave drugs were utilized to engender a sense of empathy and social communion among those using them. Rave drugs were taken to broaden one's experience while promoting feelings of oneness, belonging, and love. Rave drugs were relatively cheap as opposed to disco era drugs and easily accessible.

Table 12.13   New Club Drugs for the Rave Era

Drug	Street Name
MDMA	Ecstasy, molly, adam
Gamma-hydroxybutyrate	GHB
Ketamine	Special K

Source: T.D. Church

Pure MDMA (3,4-methylenedioxy-methamphetamine) is a synthetic drug available in a crystalline powder that users swallow or snort. Pressed pills containing MDMA are known as ecstasy. MDMA exerts its effects by stimulating the central nervous system. Increasing levels of the neurotransmitters serotonin, dopamine, oxytocin, and norepinephrine flood the brain. These chemicals are related to mood, energy levels, heart rate, blood pressure, bodily and tactile sensations and—in some individuals—sexual arousal. MDMA is chemically similar to both stimulants and hallucinogens, producing feelings of increased energy, pleasure, emotional warmth, and distorted sensory and temporal perception. MDMA produces a very euphoric high and takes 30 to 45 minutes after ingestion to manifest effects. Depending upon purity of the drug, these effects last 4–6 hours. MDMA is classified as an *empathogen*; this is a class of psychoactive drugs that produce experiences of emotional communion, oneness, relatedness, and emotional openness (empathy or sympathy). In the United States, MDMA is predominately used by males aged 18–25. The use of

Figure 12.8 Ecstasy Pressed Pills

Couperfield/Shutterstock.com

MDMA typically begins at 21 years of age. Sexual orientation appears to influence MDMA usage rates, with gay and bisexual men and women being twice as likely as their heterosexual counterparts to use MDMA [36].

Widespread drug use is viewed by some as a normal part of gay culture and a staple of the gay nightlife scene in the United States. This normalized drug use is a highly researched area in preventive health and epidemiology. There are a wide variety of reasons for the higher rates of drug use among gay males. To be clear, the choice to use drugs is highly individual regardless of sexual orientation and generalizing it to a population has the propensity to reinforce negative stereotypes. Based on the epidemiology data, there appears to be four distinct reasons that drug use remains high among gay men. The first, repressed feelings and distress. Society has only recently become accepting and understanding of gay lifestyles, relationships, and individuals. LGBT people encounter repression daily and unlike their straight counterparts, LGBT people must continuously undergo the "coming out" process. At every new employment, meeting of new friends, or even joining social groups or sporting activities, LGBT people must consciously determine the most appropriate time to "come out" [37]. This continuous "outing" can trigger fears of rejection, hate, loneliness, and loss just as it did the first time. It can be a highly traumatic event for some. The second reason relates to the environment. Historically, the only places that LGBT individuals could interact freely and somewhat safely with other LGBT individuals has been at a bar, club, or private establishment that caters to gay individuals. Many of these facilities fuel drug and alcohol use, often normalizing it as part of the LGBT experience. The third reason relates to heightened expectations around sexual activity. There is a tendency for gay male culture to glamorize youth, sex, and sexual prowess. With drug use, this can sometimes only be achieved by mixing drugs such as MDMA and Viagra to achieve the sexualized ideal of gay masculinity. And the final reason has been tied to higher rates of depression. Often, LGBT individuals will mask their depression through drug use. Depression is often fueled by feelings of low self-esteem, anxiety, and even guilt surrounding those who have confusion around their sexual orientation.

MDMA is responsible for *interactional experiences*, wherein users report an emphasis on feelings of well-being, interpersonal closeness, and sensuality that is not necessarily accompanied by sexual feeling or desire. MDMA has mixed results with regards to its effects on sexual desire. Users will either have inhibited sexual responses or enabled a prosexual set of responses. In general, MDMA is a bonding drug and promotes affectionate physical contact—hugging, touching, or cuddling. The majority of users do not express a desire for sex or in initiating sex while high. MDMA is known to increase arousal in males, yet it is largely sympathetic, as the effects are more closely associated with emotional connection. An erection does not always equate to a need for sexual response, sometimes it is the result of close emotional connection. *Sextasy* is the name used to refer to the combination of ecstasy and Viagra (sildenafil). Sextasy is used for its stimulating effect (MDMA) and its ability to enhance sexual ability, aka erection (Viagra). Both drugs dilate blood vessels and a rapid increase in blood flow puts the individual at a higher risk for heart attack and stroke, regardless of age.

The phrase "EDM" first appeared in the United States in 1985, the same year the DEA made MDMA a Schedule I drug. MDMA and EDM have coevolved as the catalyst for a subculture uniquely suited to each other. MDMA provides a heightened sensory perception, "increased enjoyment of music and repetitive action" [38]. EDM features repetitive, bass heavy music conducive for the MDMA experience. MDMA entices people to dance, DJ Lady Miss Kier of Dee-Lite (Groove is in the Heart)[39] once commented, "perhaps more than any other genre, EDM shows are less about watching the performer than moving to them." At the heart of rave culture and EDM is a unique philosophy, PLUR, an acronym for *Peace, Love, Unity, Respect (PLUR)*. It has become a unique code of conduct among party goers in which people take care of one another during raves/EDM events to keep people safe and alive.

Safety has become a concern, especially when the illicit sale of MDMA makes it prone to being cut. *Cut* in this context refers to the adulterating of drugs. Drug dealers will cut their product by adding less expensive illicit and potentially toxic substances to increase the amount of their product. This can effectively double or triple their product for sale. People purchase MDMA pills, crystal, and powder from an illegal market, with little certainty as to what these contain. Given that illegal drugs are not subject to strict production standards, nor rigorous quality control, consumers become exposed to the risks of poisoning or accidental overdose because of contamination, adulteration, and unknown strength and purity. MDMA is often cut with other substance such as ephedrine, ketamine, caffeine, cocaine, methamphetamine, and fentanyl. The DEA has reported that ~15% of MDMA seized in New York over the past 4 years contained any MDMA. When MDMA was present, it was often mixed with other drugs and ~1% was pure MDMA [40].

Another prominent rave drug is *Gamma-Hydroxybutyric Acid (GHB)*, which is a potent central nervous system depressant often abused for its ability to produce euphoria and reduce anxiety. GHB is a potent sedative and amnestic drug. GHB is a naturally occurring metabolite of the inhibitory neurotransmitter gamma-aminobutyric acid (GABA) found in the brain. The natural metabolite is present in vastly lower concentrations. When taken recreationally, GHB floods the brain eliciting both positive and negative effects. The positive effects include euphoria, increased sex drive, and a sense of tranquility. The negative effects involve excessive sweating, loss of consciousness, nausea, hallucinations, amnesia, and coma. GHB was originally available as a nutritional supplement as it was believed to have anabolic effects and was used by bodybuilders for muscle building and fat reduction. In 1900, the FDA issued an advisory warning declaring GHB use unsafe and illegal except under physician supervision. By 2000, GHB was placed in Schedule I by the DEA due to its growing popularity as a date rape drug.

Roughly 95% of GHB is metabolized in the liver, and its half-life ranges from 30 to 60 minutes. Only 5% of the parent drug is excreted via the kidneys. Detection of GHB in the urine may be difficult after 24 hours due to the short half-life. A tiny bit of GHB goes a long way, with not much difference (often as little as a 1 milliliter/¼ teaspoon) between the dose that will get one high and one that renders them unconscious. Overdosing with GHB is easy to do and comes on with little to no warning [41].

GHB has become one of the chemsex drugs popular among gay males, aged 18–35. *Chemsex* refers to gay or bisexual men using drugs to facilitate sex with other men; sometimes referred to *pnp* or *party-and-play*, especially in the United States. Chemsex represents a subculture of recreational drug users that has emerged within the EDM scene who engage in high-risk sexual activities under the influence of potent illegal drugs. The *circuit party* subculture is another mega dance event, catering to gay men. Circuit parties came to resemble raves but are highly publicized and professionally produced. While open to anyone, these parties are social events for gay men. These events are often described as a celebration of gay life and gay sexuality, an expression of freedom, and testament to the strength of the gay community. There is often a fair amount of promiscuous sex and drug use at these events. GHB is known to increase libido and reduce inhibitions. GHB makes it difficult for males to ejaculate, which means sex lasts an extended period of time (2–4 hours). With lowered inhibitions, unsafe sex is more likely. HIV, syphilis, herpes, and gonorrhea are potential outcomes of participating in chemsex. Multiple partners in one sexual encounter is not uncommon. GHB is often combined with other club drugs to boost the effects of the other chemicals, the predominate drugs being methamphetamine and MDMA.

Ketamine induces trance-like states while providing general pain relief, sedation, and memory loss with psychological reactions as the medication wears off, including hallucinations. Ketamine is used clinically for starting and maintaining anesthesia. Recreationally, ketamine is used at subanesthetic doses to produce a dissociative state, characterized by depersonalization and derealization. *Subanesthetic* is the administration of an anesthetic drug under the recommended dose from a pharmacologic point of view. *Depersonalization* is a sense of detachment from one's physical body. *Derealization* is a sense of detachment from the external world. Some

Figure 12.9 Ketamine

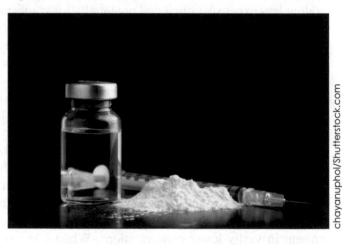

chayanuphol/Shutterstock.com

individuals who consume sufficiently high doses of ketamine may enter a *K-Hole*, a state of extreme dissociation with visual and auditory hallucinations. Users describe the sensation of the K-Hole as watching yourself fall into a well or open pit. Ketamine is odorless and tasteless, and it can induce confusion and mild amnesia, implicating it as a date rape drug.

In the beginning of the 1970s, ketamine was released in new formulations available in capsules, which contain ketamine in powdered or crystalized forms. The formulations were quickly taken from therapeutic use to illicit use. By the 1980s, ketamine was a recreational drug that had grown in popularity among club kids and was often used to cut MDMA/ecstasy. Ketamine is a cheap excipient and as it is odorless and tasteless made for a good filler in MDMA pressed pills. Use, purchase, and sale of ketamine at parties, dance clubs, and raves have grown exponentially since then, solidifying ketamine as one of the "club drugs" of the EDM age.

Raves were underground events, well known for their drug usage, music, dancing, and immortalized by the prolific use of glow sticks. A burgeoning consumer focused EDM festival party scene has surpassed the secretive and underground feel of rave culture. The commercial nature of EDM has morphed rave culture into a money-making behemoth with millions of people around the globe participating in a culture of hedonism and music. The commodification of rave culture is a looming reminder of how far EDM has taken the music beyond its humble underground beginnings. EDM festivals cost upward of $150–$500 for tickets, some venues feature $10,000 special VIP packages. There is corporate sponsorship with advertisements prominently displayed and DJs pulling in $100,000 or more a night to play sets in Las Vegas nightclubs or the desert of California. There exists an entire segment of tourism geared toward EDM festivals and unique destinations like Ibiza, Phuket, Patagonia, and Tahiti. The sense of community, belonging, and compassion engendered by raves has been replaced by image, glamour, and extravert spending. The capitalist switch in EDM has led to devastating effects, as can be seen in the way the venue promoters reacted during the tragic events behind the Astroworld deaths in 2020[42]. Instead of stopping the music to make critical announcements and to get medical personnel activated the party raged on, causing eight deaths and hundreds of injuries as partygoers rushed the stage where Rapper Travis Scott was performing. EDM parties have also been shown to have environmentally damaging effects. In 2019, the Glastonbury Festival in England witnessed environmentally damaging levels of illicit substances in the Whitelake River. The river runs through Glastonbury and was near the venue site, and due to public urination on and near the site of the party venue, excessive levels of MDMA and cocaine were found in the river water. MDMA was 104 times greater downstream than upstream and cocaine was 40 times higher downstream[43]. It was potent enough to harm aquatic wildlife. The impact of large EDM events is not always anticipated and can have profound effects. Raves went from an underground experience to a mainstream nightlife industry and EDM has become one of the world's most popular music genres and lucrative money producing ventures for many companies [32].

REFERENCES

1. Sonny and Cher, (1967) *The Beat Goes On.* In *In case you're in love.*
2. Rizzo, A. (1952). *Duck and Cover* (9 min). Federal Civil Defense Administration.
3. Marshall, M. (1967). *Narcotics: Pit of Despair* (29 min). United States.
4. Babbitt, A. (1970). *Zombie Door* (31 min). Hanna-Barbera.
5. Bousalis, R. R. (2020). The counterculture generation: Idolized, appropriated, and misunderstood. *The Councilor: A Journal of the Social Studies, 82*(2), 1–26.
6. Leary, T. (1966). *Turn On, Tune In, Drop Out,* in *Turn On, Tune In, Drop Out.* Mercury Records.
7. Ford, S. D. (1969). *LSD and the law: A framework for policy making. Minnesota Law Review, 54,* 775–804.
8. Hofmann, A. (1979). *How LSD originated.* Journal of psychedelic drugs, *11*(1–2), 53–60.

9. Schultes, R. E., & Hofmann, A. (1979). *Plants of the gods: Origins of hallucinogenic use* (p. 192). McGraw-Hill.

10. Watts, A. (2013). *The joyous cosmology: Adventures in the chemistry of consciousness* (2nd ed.). New World Library.

11. Shapiro, P. (2015). *Turn the beat around: The secret history of disco* (p. 384). Farrar, Straus and Giroux.

12. Haden-Guest, A. (2015). *The Last Party: Studio 54, Disco, and the Culture of the Night.* Open Road Media.

13. Paasonen, S., & Saarenmaa, L. (2007). The golden age of porn: Nostalgia and history in cinema. In S. Paasonen, K. Nikunen, & L. Saarenmaa (Eds.), *Pornification: Sex and sexuality in media culture* (pp. 23–32). Berg.

14. Schrager, I. (2017). *Studio 54.* Rizzoli.

15. Owen, F. (2003). *Clubland: The fabulous rise and murderous fall of club culture* (p. 320). St. Martin's Press.

16. Gallup. (2021). *Illegal Drugs: In Depth Topics A to Z.* 2021 [21 Nov 2021].

17. Times. (2021). *Site Map of Public Opinions.* 2021 [21 Nov 2021].

18. Cowan, T. R. (1987). Drugs and the workplace: To drug test or not to test? *Public Personnel Management, 16*(4), 313–322.

19. Goode, E., & Ben-Yehuda, N. (1994). The American drug panic of the 1980s. In E. Goode & N. Ben-Yehuda (Eds.), *Moral panics: The social construction of deviance* (pp. 327–348). Blackwell Publishing.

20. Goodman, J., Sherratt, A., & Lovejoy, P. E. (2014). Consuming habits: Drugs in history and anthropology *Global and historical perspectives on how cultures define drugs* (2 ed., p. 304). Routledge.

21. NCHS, (2017). *Compressed Mortality File, 1979–1988 (machine readable data file and documentation, CD-ROM Series 20, No. 2V) as compiled from data provided by the 57 vital statistics jurisdictions through the Vital Statistics Cooperative Program,* N.C.F.H. Statistics, Editor. Hyattsville, Maryland.

22. DOJ, (1990). *Bureau of Justice Statistics Data Report, 1989* (p. 103). U.D.O. Justice, Editor. Office of Justice Programs.

23. Levitt, S. D., & Dubner, S. J. (2009). *Freakonomics: A rogue economist explores the hidden side of everything by* (3rd ed.). Harper Collins Publisher.

24. DHHS, NIH, & NIDA. (2011). *National Household Survey on Drug Abuse, 1987–1988.* Interuniversity Consortium for Political and Social Research.

25. DAWN. (2014). *National estimates of drug-related emergency department visits, 1979–1989 - all visits,* in *data tables.* Drug Abuse Warning Network.

26. CDC. (2021). *10 Leading causes of death, United States: 1986–1989, all races, both sexes* (p. 1). WISQARS: National Vital Statistics System.

27. WilsonPoe, A. R., & Morón, J. A. (2018). *The dynamic interaction between pain and opioid misuse. British Journal of Pharmacology, 175*(14), 2770–2777.

28. Kaczmarek, E. (2021). *Promoting diseases to promote drugs: The role of the pharmaceutical industry in fostering good and bad medicalization. British Journal of Clinical Pharmacology,* 2021. Ahead of Print(https://bpspubs.onlinelibrary.wiley.com/doi/abs/10.1111/bcp.14835), 1–6.

29. Alonso, J. S. (2021). Purdue pharma deceptive research misconduct: The importance of the use of independent, transparent, current research. *Voices in Bioethics, 7,* 1–6.

30. Jalali, M. S., et al. (2020). The opioid crisis: A contextual, social-ecological framework. *Health Research Policy and Systems, 18*(1), 1–9.

31. Dai, Z., et al. (2019). *Fentanyl and fentanyl-analog involvement in drug-related deaths. Drug and Alcohol Dependence, 196*(1 March 2019), 1–8.

32. Conner, C. T., & Katz, N. (2020). *Electronic dance music: From spectacular subculture to culture industry. YoUnG, 28*(5), 445–464.

33. Markula, P. (2020). *Dance, movement and leisure cultures. Leisure Studies, 39*(4), 465–-478.

34. Collin, M. (2018). *Rave on: Global adventures in electronic dance music.* Serpent's Tail.

35. Anderson, T. (2009). *Rave culture: The alteration and decline of a Philadelphia music scene.* Temple University Press.

36. Kerr, D. L., & Oglesby, W. H. (2017). LGBT populations and substance abuse research: An overview. In J. VanGeest, T. Johnson, & S. A. Alemango (Eds.), *Research methods in the study of substance abuse* (pp. 341–355). Springer.

37. Orne, J. (2011). 'You will always have to "out" yourself': Reconsidering coming out through strategic outness. *Sexualities, 14*(6), 681–703.

38. Moore, K., Wells, H., & Feilding, A. (2019). *Roadmaps to regulation: MDMA* (p. 158). Beckley Foundaiton Press.

39. Deee-Lite. (1990). Groove is in the Heart. In *World Clique.* Elektra.

40. Parrilla, M., et al. (2021). Portable electrochemical detection of illicit drugs in smuggled samples: towards more secure borders. In *Proceedings of the CSAC2021: 1st International Electronic Conference on Chemical Sensors and Analytical Chemistry.* MDPI.

41. Williams, J. F., & Lundahl, L. H. (2019). Focus on adolescent use of club drugs and "other" substances. *Pediatric Clinics, 66*(6), 1121–1134.

42. Patel, V., & Kasakove, S. (2021). *What to Know About the Houston Astroworld Tragedy,* in *New York Times.* [Retrieved on 22 Nov 2021]: https://www.nytimes.com/article/astroworld-festival-what-to-know.html.

43. Snapes, L. (2021). *Glastonbury: Drug traces from on-site urination could harm rare eels,* in *The Guardian.* Guardian News & Media Limited. https://www.theguardian.com/music/2021/sep/28/glastonbury-drug-traces-from-on-site-urination-could-harm-rare-eels.

Chapter 13

Drug Control in the Modern Era

Over the past 100 years, drugs, both licit and illicit, have come under increasing levels of control through ethical beliefs, law enforcement, and regulatory mechanisms geared toward the safe and efficacious use of medical products. Drugs are available for purchase as prescription, over the counter, or illegal. The system for determining if a drug is legal has been flawed from its inception and persists today. There have been historical prejudices associated with who is using a drug and how to control their use. In addition, drugs have become imbued with ethical and moral values, which adds value judgements onto the users of "bad" drugs, causing them to often be vilified. In general, the U.S. drug control policy has been built out of a punitive logic of deterrence, which assumes targeting the drug supply through hardline law enforcement will prevent drug use by making drugs scarcer, more expensive, and riskier to buy [1].

Drug control policy in the United States has been based on a deceptively simple theory of deterrence wherein the application of the force of law against the supply of illegal drugs (predominately focused on cocaine, cannabis, and heroin) will decrease drug consumption [2]. By following this logic, law enforcement pressure is applied at every juncture in the drug trafficking supply chain. This means that law enforcement is responsible for eradicating the production and processing of drugs abroad as well as interdicting drugs at the border to affect domestic distribution and sales. The application of treatment, prevention, research, and education all play second or third chair in the grand punitive orchestra that is U.S. law enforcement.

One of the primary strategies and line of defense is to intercept all international shipments of drugs at key points of entry into the United States. This is a task traditionally assigned to law enforcement agencies, but in the post-cold war world, the military is becoming increasingly tasked with drug interdiction duties. The last line of defense against the drug supply is at home, where local law enforcement efforts are designed to disrupt domestic drug distribution and sales. This is accomplished by raising the likelihood of arrest, prosecution, and administration of rigid punishment for both dealers and users [3].

Drug enforcement activities are undertaken through the Department of Justice (DOJ) via the Drug Enforcement Administration (DEA), and Federal Bureau of Investigation (FBI). Overview of legal drugs and control of marketed products is under the purview of the U.S. Department of Health and Human Services (HHS) via the Food and Drug Administration (FDA). Research and prevention activities are controlled by HHS via the National Institute for Health (NIH) under the auspices of the National Institute on Alcohol Abuse and Alcoholism (NIAAA) and the National Institute on Drug Addiction (NIDA). The organization tasked with prevention, education, and treatment is Substance Abuse and Mental Health Service Administration (SAMHSA). SAMHSA has two dedicated branches, the Center for Substance Abuse Treatment (CSAT), which is responsible for the development of treatment plans and research related to addictive substances, and the Center for Substance Abuse Prevention (CSAP), which focuses on the development and implementation of comprehensive prevention systems. The relationships of these Federal organizations are displayed in Figure 13.1.

Figure 13.1 US Federal Offices

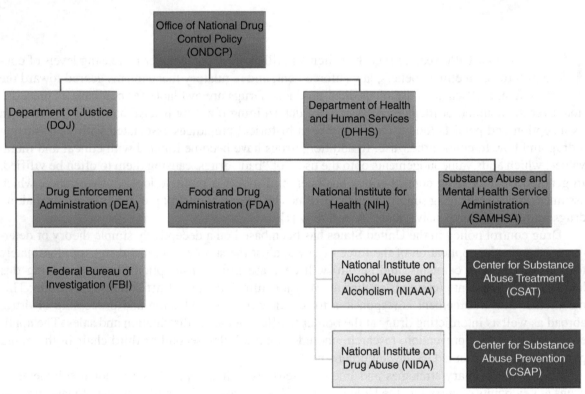

Source: T.D. Church

13.1 Ethical Concerns

Ethics, sometimes thought of as "moral philosophy," is the systematizing, defending, and recommending of concepts and action behind right and wrong. *Conduct* refers to the way a person behaves, especially on a particular occasion or in a particular context. Ethical conduct is often viewed as conduct that is good for individuals or society. Ethics establish obligations and duties that people owe to others and society. *Ethics* seeks to answer questions of human morality by defining concepts such as good and evil; right and wrong; virtue and vice; or justice and crime.

Morality can be best understood as the differentiation of intentions, decisions, and actions between those that are designated as right or wrong or proper and improper. Morality is governed by *codes of conduct*, the sets of rules outlining our social norms, religious rules, and responsibilities of, and proper practices for, individuals. Morality has two opposing attributes immorality and amorality. *Immorality* is the active opposition to morality and represents the violation of moral laws, societal norms, and standards. *Amorality* is an unawareness of, indifference toward, or disbelief in any particular set of moral standards or principles. Amorality is a belief that nothing is morally right or morally wrong, and content that morality does not exist. Morality refers to the set of standards that enable people to live cooperatively in groups. It is what societies determine to be "right" and "acceptable." Sometimes, acting in a moral manner means individuals must sacrifice their own short-term interests to benefit society. There are some who would define morality as personal belief and ethics as the standards of community.

In medicine and pharmacy, we need to use morality and ethics as they relate to medical policy and practice. *Bioethics* refers to the study of ethical issues emerging from advances in biology and medicine [4]. Bioethics includes the study of values relating to primary medical care and other branches of medicine. It looks at broad human questions ranging from debates over the boundaries of life (ergo: abortion and euthanasia); surrogacy; organ donation; and medical care refusal for religious or cultural reasons to name a few. The scope of bioethics is extremely broad and can keep pace with theoretical applications of medicine and biotechnology; some examples include cloning, gene therapy, life extension, human genetic engineering, and even astroethics. *Astroethics* will be needed if Elon Musk gets his way and we begin colonizing other planets and moons in our solar system, it refers to ethics related to life in space [5, 6].

Medical ethics represents the study of moral values and judgements as they apply to medical practice. This form of ethics tends to be narrowly applied to professional concerns, whereas bioethics has a broad theoretical approach making it applicable to all biomedical sciences. Medical ethics seeks to inform health-care professionals and enable them to make moral decisions related to difficult clinical decisions. It accomplishes this by providing a set of values the medical professionals can refer to in instances where confusion or conflict arises. Medical ethics allow doctors, care providers, and families to work together toward the same common goals and develop treatment plans to best fit the situation in which they are needed.

Medical ethics relies on five principle elements, the easiest way to recall the principles is with the mnemonic of ABCDE – Autonomy, Beneficence, Confidentiality, Do no harm (non-maleficence), and Equity [4]. *Autonomy* refers to self-determination or the ability to make decisions about oneself. The decision process must be free from both controlling interferences by others and personal limitations preventing making a meaningful choice or decision (such as inadequate understanding, lack of information, or faulty reasoning). *Beneficence* is a moral obligation to act for the benefit of others. Beneficence utilizes obligations to confer benefits, to prevent and remove harms, and to weigh and balance the possible goods against the costs and possible harms of an action. *Confidentiality* requires that the information a patient reveals to a health-care provider is private and has limits on how and when it can be disclosed to a third party. It comes with the premise that the provider must obtain permission from the patient to make such a disclosure. *Non-maleficence* or *do no harm* entails the obligation not to inflict harm intentionally. It is the first statement in the Hippocratic Oath. Non-maleficence is useful in dealing with difficult issues surrounding the terminally ill and critically injured. *Equity* or *justice* requires giving others what is due to them. It encompasses a group of norms related to distribution of benefits, risks, and costs. Justice may be distributive, criminal / punitive, or reificatory. *Distributive justice*, in a medical context, requires patients with similar cases to be treated in an equivalent manner, and for there to be overarching equality of access to finite health resources. *Punitive justice* seeks to punish any action that violates justice. *Reificatory justice* is concerned with righting injustice or setting unjust situations right.

Figure 13.2   Historical Timeline of Key Ethical Issues

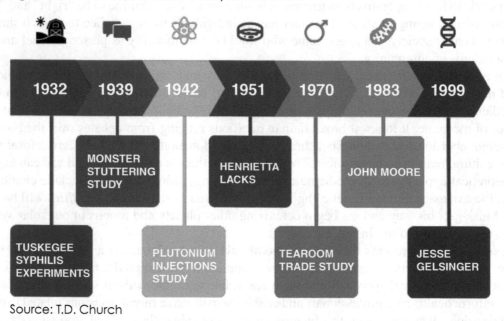

Source: T.D. Church

From the list above (Figure 13.2), we will discuss three of the cases, Tuskegee Syphilis Experiments, Monster Stuttering Study, and Henrietta Lacks. The other cases, not discussed, have each in their own way influenced various aspects of medical ethics in the United States. If ethical cases of malpractice are of interest, check out the cases not discussed from the listing above for more information. Worldwide, the cases listed above are just a small number of ethical and legal cases that have occurred over the past 100 years; many of which were devastating to individuals and scaring to the medical profession. The sad truth is that with ethics, while they can function to avoid or circumvent potential issues in medical practice, we tend to employ them as a reactionary approach to help curb an ongoing or prior injustice.

13.1.1   Ethics – Three Historical Examples

The *Tuskegee study of untreated syphilis* was a medical study that took place in 1932 CE and ended 40 years later in 1972 CE. It was originally slated to run for 3 months only. The Tuskegee study has been referred to as the longest nontherapeutic experiment on human beings in medical history [7]. The study was conducted in Tuskegee, Alabama, with over 600 African American men. Some of the participants were given active syphilis and "observed to determine the natural progression of the disease" [7]. There have been several ethical concerns raised from the Tuskegee syphilis experiment with the top three being lack of informed consent / improper consent, withholding of proper treatment, and unbalanced participant pool.

Figure 13.3 Tuskegee Study

The U.S. Public Health Service in partnership with Tuskegee University began the syphilis study in 1932 CE. The purpose of the study was to observe the natural history of untreated syphilis; however, the nature and purpose of the study was withheld from the participants. In total 600 participants were enrolled. All the study participants were men, poor, African American, and sharecroppers. The study participants were divided into disease and control groups. The disease group had 399 individuals with latent syphilis. The control group had 201 noninfected individuals. As an incentive to get people to enroll in the study, the men were promised free medical care.

The "free medical care" was dubious at best. The latent group were given placebos, ineffective methods of treatment, and diagnostic procedures masked as treatment. The latent group were never informed of their diagnosis. Many of these men were young and unmarried, and by extension they risked infecting others not involved with the study. Further, as the sexual partners were not a part of the enrolled study participants, they were not followed by the research team nor provided any medical care. By 1947 CE, fifteen years after the study began, an effective treatment of penicillin was available to treat syphilis, and this treatment was withheld from the latent group and not made available to their sexual partners.

Syphilis is a highly contagious sexually transmitted infection and if left untreated can lead to fatal health problems. Syphilis is caused by the bacterium *Treponema pallidum,* (Figure 13.4). The signs and symptoms of syphilis vary depending upon which of the four stages is presenting. Stage 1, the primary stage, appears as a single chancre, a firm, painless, and non-itchy skin ulceration. Stage 2, the secondary stage, exhibits a diffuse rash, usually on the palms of the hands and / or the soles of the feet with some individuals expressing sores in their mouths. Stage 3, latent

Figure 13.4 Syphilis

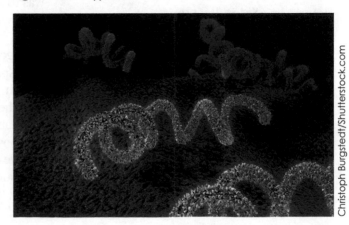

stage, syphilis can remain inactive (dormant) in the body for years before activating again with few or no symptoms. Stage 4, the tertiary stage, there are gummas (soft noncancerous growths) that appear in the liver, brain, testes, and heart. The last stage can lead to blindness, deafness, mental illness mimicking schizophrenia, heart disease, bone deterioration, collapse of the central nervous system, and death.

It is worth noting that in 1927 CE, Alabama had passed a law that required the reporting and treatment of venereal diseases, syphilis included. The U.S. Public Health Service blatantly ignored the state law, choosing to disregard the impact of untreated syphilis on the subjects and their sexual partners. To further complicate the issue, accurate records were not kept by study staff and the true number of individuals who died from syphilis acquired from this study is not known. The erroneous beliefs of medical staff of the time surrounding the nature of African Americans sexual behavior clouded the study. These elements placed the health of an entire community in jeopardy and left a highly communicable disease untreated. This study laid the foundations for African Americans' growing and continued distrust of the medical system, especially public health programs. It produced an unneeded fear of medical procedures, including vaccinations and set the stage for mistrust of the health-care profession for generations. In the 1970s CE, a class action suit was filed by the survivors of the Tuskegee experiments. No new laws were enacted from this lawsuit. Further, neither Tuskegee University nor the government claimed any responsibility for injury during the experiment. Each survivor received a settlement of ~$40,000 (the equivalent of $287,000 in 2021 dollars).

The *Monster Study*, as it was nicknamed by peers and colleagues of the lead principal investigator (PI), Wendell Johnson, horrified that the experiments were being done on orphan children to confirm a rather flimsy hypothesis [8]. This study was so badly received among peers that the results were never published in a peer-review journal. The sole record that remains is from the PI's graduate student, Mary Tudor, her dissertation is the only official record of the details of this questionable experiment. The Monster Study was a stuttering experiment performed on 22 orphan children. The study was conducted through the University of Iowa in 1939 CE under the direction of Johnson and Tudor. This study featured a randomized design and sorted the children into two groups. Group 1 had 11 children who received positive speech therapy and praise for their fluency. Group 2 had 11 children who received negative speech therapy and were belittled for speech imperfections, even if they had none at the start of the study. The experiment ran from January to June of 1939. The hypothesis was to see if stuttering could be induced in healthy children. If it could, then the hypothesis continued that it would be possible to remove stuttering in an analogous manner. Half of the students were told their speech was fine, the other half were told their speech was as bad as people said, if not worse.

The children met Tudor individually for 45 minutes per week. Group 1, positive cohort, were told positive and reassuring things like: "you will be able to speak better than you are now," "pay no attention to what others say about your ability to speak, they do not recognize your stuttering is only a phase," "you speak so well, others will want to hear

Figure 13.5   Kid Stuttering

Roman Yanushevsky/Shutterstock.com

what you have to say," and "you should always speak in public because you do it so well." Group 2, negative cohort, were told negative and disciplinary things like: "you have the symptoms of a child who is beginning to stutter," "you must stop yourself immediately," "use your will power," "do anything you can to keep from stuttering," and "do not ever speak unless you can do it right." As can be surmised, the positive cohort showed marked improvement and began excelling with their schoolwork. They were highly social and had a newfound courage. The negative cohort showed dramatic declines in socialization, their schoolwork suffered, and many refused to speak in public. Two of the children in the negative cohort developed nervous ticks that accompanied their stuttering.

None of the participants in the study were told the intent of the research. All the orphans believed they were going to receive speech therapy (for problems that none of them exhibited prior to the study). Tudor did appear to have some remorse for her actions, and one year after the experiment she returned to the orphanage to voluntarily provide follow-up care. It was too late; however, the damage was already done. The children who were in the negative cohort of the experiment suffered negative psychological effects, with most of them retaining life-long speech problems. Dr. Zebrowski, assistant professor of speech pathology and audiology at the University of Iowa, stated "the results from this experiment are the largest collection of scientific information on the phenomenon of stuttering. This work was the first to discuss the importance of the stutterer's thoughts, attitudes, beliefs, and feelings and continues to influence views on stuttering greatly" [9].

Henrietta Lacks was an African American woman, whose cervical cancer cells became the source of the ubiquitous HeLa cell line used worldwide in a wide variety of research. *HeLa* is an immortal cell line; it was the first immortal cell line and represents the oldest and most prolifically used human cell line in research. On January 29, 1951 CE, Henrietta went to John Hopkins University Hospital because she felt a "knot" in her womb and was experiencing vaginal bleeding. She had been pregnant before, but this was completely different. John Hopkins University Hospital was one of only a few hospitals that would treat African Americans in the 1950s CE. Upon examination, a large and malignant tumor was found on Henrietta's cervix. In addition, the "knot" did prove to be a pregnancy. After giving birth, Henrietta suffered a severe hemorrhage. Howard Jones, MD, Henrietta's physician, took a biopsy of the cervical mass for laboratory testing. It was determined that she had a malignant epidermoid carcinoma of the cervix. In 1970, some of the tumor tissue was retested and the diagnosis was reclassified to adenocarcinoma. Following standard treatment in the 1950s CE, radium tubes were inserted on either side of the tumor as an inpatient procedure to irradiate the tumor. This was the best therapy for the time and after the tubes were removed, Henrietta was discharged with instructions to return for X-rays and follow-up. Two additional cervical samples were taken without Henrietta's permission or knowledge in the weeks to follow. One of the samples was healthy tissue and the other was cancerous. George Gey, physician and cancer researcher at Hopkins, was provided with the tissue. The cells from the cancerous sample eventually became known as the HeLa immortal cell line. Gey was astounded because in his lab, Henrietta's cells doubled every 20-24 hours, whereas samples collected from other patients would die a few hours after harvesting. On October 4, 1951 CE, at age 31, Henrietta succumbed to her cancer and died in Hopkins Hospital, the cancer had metastasized throughout her entire body. Yet, her legacy and unknown contribution to science lived on.

HeLa cells have gone on to do amazing things, albeit no informed consent was obtained for the source cells nor was Henrietta nor her family ever compensated for her contribution. It is estimated that scientists have grown ~20 tons of HeLa cells and there are ~11,000 patents involving the HeLa

Figure 13.6 HeLa Cells

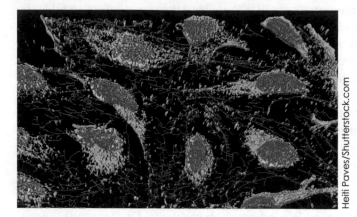

Heiti Paves/Shutterstock.com

cells [10]. There has been a vast array of accomplishments HeLa cells have made in scientific research and medicine over the past 70 years. A few of those accomplishments include the development of virology as field of study, vaccines, antiviral therapies, Polio vaccine, genetic medicine, cloning, amniocentesis for genetic disease testing, cryogenics, in vitro fertilization, stem cell isolation, genetic hybridization, development of Herceptin, blood type identification, HPV vaccine, identification of HIV, telomerase inhibitor medication, tuberculosis vaccine, nanotech, and a variety of ethical and scientific standards being developed. These are only a few of the advances that science has made working with HeLa cells. Cells that Henrietta Lacks never gave her consent to be used for research.

The cases mentioned above did add to the growing ethical concerns related to medical research in the United States and helped to influence the *Belmont Report*. The Belmont Report was written by the National Commission for the Protection of Human Subjects of Biomedical and Behavioral Research. The Commission was enacted to meet the mandate of the National Research Act of 1974 and was charged with identifying the basic ethical principles to inform the conduct of biomedical and behavioral research involving human subjects. A part of the commission's charge was to develop guidelines to assure that such research would be conducted in accordance with those principles. Informed by monthly working group sessions that spanned four years and an intensive four-day deliberation session in 1976 CE, the Commission published the completed Belmont Report in 1978. It defined the basic ethical principles of *respect for persons (autonomy)*, *beneficence*, and *justice*. These three principles would be enforced and monitored by *Institutional Review Boards (IRBs)* and would act as the ethical polestar to guide the decisions the IRBs would make regarding human research in the United States [11].

Under the Belmont Report, *respect for persons* requires that 1) all individuals are treated as autonomous agents, and 2) individuals who are of diminished autonomy must be protected. Autonomous agents have the ability to deliberate about personal choices and act upon those deliberations. Diminished autonomy refers to individual with an illness, mental disability, cognitive deficits, or immaturity that would prevent them from being fully autonomous agents. Respect for persons provides four conditions that need to be met: 1) voluntary consent, 2) informed consent, 3) protection of privacy and confidentiality, and 4) right to withdraw without penalty from a study.

Beneficence, as defined by the Belmont Report, requires the examination of the risks and benefits of the study. The study should do no harm toward the participants. The benefits of participating in the study must be maximized while harm is minimized. Any risk that is present must be justified by the benefits of participating in the study and should not add additional burden or harm onto the participants.

Justice, under the auspices of the Belmont Report, requires that the benefits and risks of research be evenly distributed across all members of society. This means that the disadvantaged must not bear the risks of research, while the advantaged reap all the benefits. Sadly, this inequal distribution of risks has happened far too often throughout human history. The principle of justice seeks to end that imbalance and provide equal distribution of risks, harms, and benefits to all peoples

The three fundamental ethical principles of the Belmont Report are the guiding principles employed by *Institutional Review Boards (IRBs)* when considering a human subject research proposal for approval. An IRB is a committee that applies research ethics by reviewing the methods proposed for research to make sure they are ethical. IRBs are formally designated to approve (or reject), monitor, and review biomedical and behavioral research involving humans. IRBs are required to have a quorum at a minimum of 5 members – at least 1 member representing the scientific community, 1 member who is "nonscientific," and 1 member who is a member of the community (ergo: not affiliated with the institution or university). IRBs have several duties, including, but not limited to [12]:

- Ensuring the risks to subjects are minimized
- Procedures within the research design are consistent and represent sound science
- Where appropriate, using procedures already being performed in the subject for diagnostic or treatment purposes
- Ensuring the risks to subjects are reasonable in relation to any anticipated benefits
- Selection of subjects is equitable
- Informed consent will be obtained from all participants
- Informed consent will be appropriately administered and documented
- Research plan makes adequate provision for the monitoring of data to ensure safety of participants
- Provisions to protect the privacy of participants and maintain the confidentiality of data

With these duties in mind, IRBs review and have the authority to approve, require modifications (to fulfill approval), or disapprove all research activities under their review.

13.1.2 Ethics – Three Modern Examples

This section will review some modern ethical concerns. Ethics are not law and sometimes the law is not ethical. In addition, bear in mind that ethical solutions may not have a "right" or "correct" answer. Ethics attempts to get to the best solution to fit the circumstances of a specific set of conditions, which may vary from case to case. The three modern ethical questions will include 1) syringe exchange programs, 2) euthanasia vs lethal injection, and 3) cannabis as medicine for children. Try to keep your mind free from prejudice and preconceived notions you may have surrounding these issues. After the presentation of each of the three cases, there will be a pro and con discussion using the principle elements of medical ethics ABCDE.

The timeline in Figure 13.7 sets the stage for the key events in the history of syringe exchange in the United States between 1973 CE and 1992 CE. Syringe exchange programs are community-based initiatives that allow intravenous (IV) drug users to exchange used syringes for clean, sterile ones. This functions as a public health effort to stem the spread of HIV/AIDS, hepatitis B, and other blood-borne pathogens. Syringe exchange programs focus on harm reduction. Harm reduction is a set of ideas and interventions in public health that seek to reduce the harms associated with both drug use and ineffective drug policies. In the syringe exchange model, harm reduction provides a way to introduce HIV education, testing, and condom distribution alongside IV needle exchange and bleaching kits. Harm reduction is based on the concept of acknowledging the dignity and humanity of people who use drugs and bring them into communities of care with the goal to minimize negative consequences and promote optimal health and social inclusion.

Figure 13.7 Syringe Exchange Historical Events

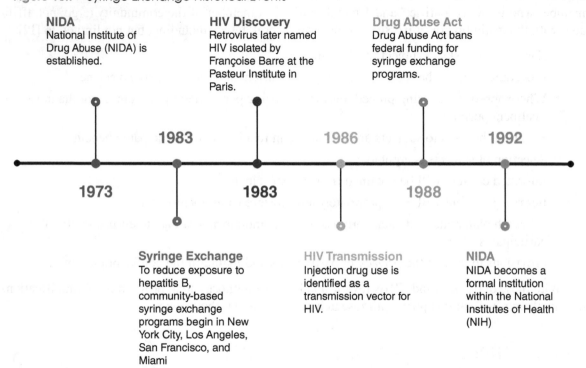

NIDA
National Institute of Drug Abuse (NIDA) is established.

HIV Discovery
Retrovirus later named HIV isolated by Françoise Barre at the Pasteur Institute in Paris.

Drug Abuse Act
Drug Abuse Act bans federal funding for syringe exchange programs.

1983
1986
1992

1973
1983
1988

Syringe Exchange
To reduce exposure to hepatitis B, community-based syringe exchange programs begin in New York City, Los Angeles, San Francisco, and Miami

HIV Transmission
Injection drug use is identified as a transmission vector for HIV.

NIDA
NIDA becomes a formal institution within the National Institutes of Health (NIH)

Source: T.D. Church

Syringe exchange programs in the United States operated between the first and second war on drugs (Figure 13.8), both of which made it difficult to fulfill the mission due to federal restrictions and withdrawal of funding. The first war on drugs provided federal funding for drug use prevention and treatment as part of its strategy for alternative drug control mechanisms. At the onset of the NIDA in 1973 CE, there was a lot of support for piloting a series of syringe exchange programs in major urban centers within the United States. By 1983 CE, the first funded programs began in the United States. The second war on drugs would forever change the landscape, however, with the passage of the Anti-Drug Abuse Act (referred to as the Drug Abuse Act). The key features included anti-drug enforcement and penalties enhancement; interdiction and national drug interdiction improvement; demand reduction, treatment, and rehabilitation; and anti-drug act funding.

Figure 13.8   War on Drugs

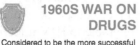

1960S WAR ON DRUGS

Considered to be the more successful of the two Wars on Drugs. Did provide funding for drug use prevention and treatment. Education campaigns were based out of fact and treatment programs were well funded.

1980s

• Initiated by Ronald Reagan
• Increased punitive criminal justice sanctions
• Reduction of alternative drug control mechanisms (ergo: drug use prevention, drug treatment, harm reduction)
• Increases in arrests of mid and low-level drug dealers and users

1960s

• Initiated by Richard Nixon
• International efforts at drug crop reduction
• Interdiction at the borders
• Apprehension of major drug traffickers
• Funding of alternative drug control mechanisms (ergo: drug use prevention, drug treatment)

1980S WAR ON DRUGS

Considered the least successful of the two Wars on Drugs. This is the one most readily remembered by the public. Targeted communities and individuals with very harsh penalties for drug possession. Education campaigns were based out of fear and erroneous data and treatment programs lost funding.

Source: T.D. Church

Considering syringe exchange programs, the Drug Abuse Act of 1988 included a clause that no federal funds would be used for support of needle exchanges, unless the surgeon general could certify two things: 1) needle exchange needed to be shown to decrease the spread of HIV infection; and 2) needle exchange needed to be shown to decrease drug abuse. A herculean task, as neither the decrease of HIV nor the decrease of drug abuse requirements could be shown to be a direct benefit from needle exchange programs. In effect, the Drug Abuse Act made the requirement to maintain funding impossible to meet. Overnight, harm reduction became unspeakable in federal policy and unfundable through federal granting mechanisms. "Intervention," "risk reduction," and "harm reduction" became dirty words in the realm of federally funded programming related to addiction. Instead, the focus shifted to the identification of and treatment geared toward *risk groups*. This shift to a risk-group-based paradigm began to categorize populations based on behavior, led to a biased view of individualized harm, and created a one-size-fits-all set of prevention tactics aimed at IV drug users. Harm reduction was forced to move to grassroots mobilization with public health research, outreach, and education becoming increasingly funded through private organizations and donors. This created situations where some things were funded some of the time, but not all things were available all the time.

Figure 13.9   IV Drug Addiction

Di Studio/Shutterstock.com

The Center for Disease Control and Prevention (CDC) has estimated that IV drug users inject themselves ~1,000 times per year [13]. This increases their risk of contracting HIV by an order of 1,000 to 1 (average risk is ~25,701 to 1). According to data obtained by SAMHSA, as of 2020, America has an estimated 2,500,000+ IV drug users, of which 650,000 are HIV+ [14]. IV drug users accounted for 15% of all new HIV infections. Women and minorities are increasingly vulnerable to HIV infection via IV drug use, see Table 8.1. The most vulnerable population are newborn and nursing children of IV drug users, which represent ½ of all HIV infections among children (~9,400 children under 13 living with HIV). As this data shows, there are many IV drug users and not having dedicated syringe exchange programs increases the vulnerabilities and exposures these individuals experience on a regular basis.

Table 13.1 IV Drug Use by Race, Ethnicity, and Gender

Racial/Ethnic Group	Males	Females
Caucasian	10%	40%
African American	29%	32%
Latino	28%	33%
Asian / Pacific Islander	9%	16%
American Indian / Alaska Native	17%	39%

Source: CDC[13]

Needle exchange programs accomplish at least two ethical objectives: 1) they protect injection drug users from co-occurring infections and 2) by extension they protect the drug users' sexual partners, needle-sharers (and their sexual partners and needle-sharers), and children born to injection drug users. It does not diminish the autonomy of the drug user and by extension promotes dignity in the treatment of these individuals through harm reduction tactics with or without syringe exchange programs. IV drug users who are addicted will continue to use. The utility of a syringe exchange program is in providing access to needles, health education, and a direct opportunity for outreach. Needle-exchange programs have been estimated to help prevent HIV infection at a cost of between $4,000 and $12,000 per injecting drug user annually. It costs an annual average of $190,000 to treat an injecting drug user for HIV in the United States [15]. Hospitalizations cost over $700 million each year for substance-use-related infections. Needle-exchange programs have been shown to reduce these costs in cities where they operate and help link people to treatment to cease drug use. With these considerations in mind, the ethical question to be answered here becomes, should needle-exchange programs be given allocated funds from the government to provide services?

Our next topic involves the ending of human life. In the examples, we will discuss one case that presents death as a choice (euthanasia) and the other denotes death as the fulfillment of a legal sentence (lethal injection). *Euthanasia* is a deliberate intervention undertaken with the express intention of ending a life to relieve intractable suffering or pain. *Lethal injection* is the practice of killing an individual using a lethal dose of drugs administered intravenously related to their egregious criminal activity. Although similar there are differences between lethal injection and euthanasia: one is a choice, and the other is compulsory.

There are subtle differences between euthanasia and physician-assisted suicide, yet these terms are often used interchangeably. *Euthanasia* involves a physician administering drugs to a patient in a clinical setting, typically at their request, to bring about their death to end suffering. *Physician-assisted suicide* is where a physician provides a patient with a prescription, which they can use to procure the necessary drugs to bring about their own death at a time and place of their choosing. Euthanasia gets further classified as being either voluntary or involuntary. *Voluntary euthanasia* is conducted with the express consent of the patient. At the time of writing this chapter, voluntary euthanasia is currently only legal in the states of Oregon and Washington. Both states have an incredibly detailed procedures where the patient's autonomy is tested at several junctures to determine their choice is truly and freely their own. *Involuntary euthanasia* is undertaken without consent of the patient. Here another person makes the decision typically because the patient is unable to make the decision on their own (ergo: coma, diminished capacity, and so on). To further complicate things, euthanasia is further defined two procedural classifications, passive and active euthanasia. *Passive euthanasia* is where life-sustaining treatments like mechanical ventilation is deliberately withheld. *Active euthanasia* is where someone uses lethal substances or forces to terminate a patient's life, whether by the patient's or somebody else's choosing.

Euthanasia, as might be expected, is a hotly debated topic and tends to polarize individuals into either pro-euthanasia or con-euthanasia stances [16]. The major arguments for both sides have been summarized in Figure 13.12. In terms of ethical arguments, the con-euthanasia side would claim that doctors must uphold non-maleficence and "do no harm." The con side of the argument would believe

Figure 13.10   Summary of Major Pro and Con Euthanasia Arguments

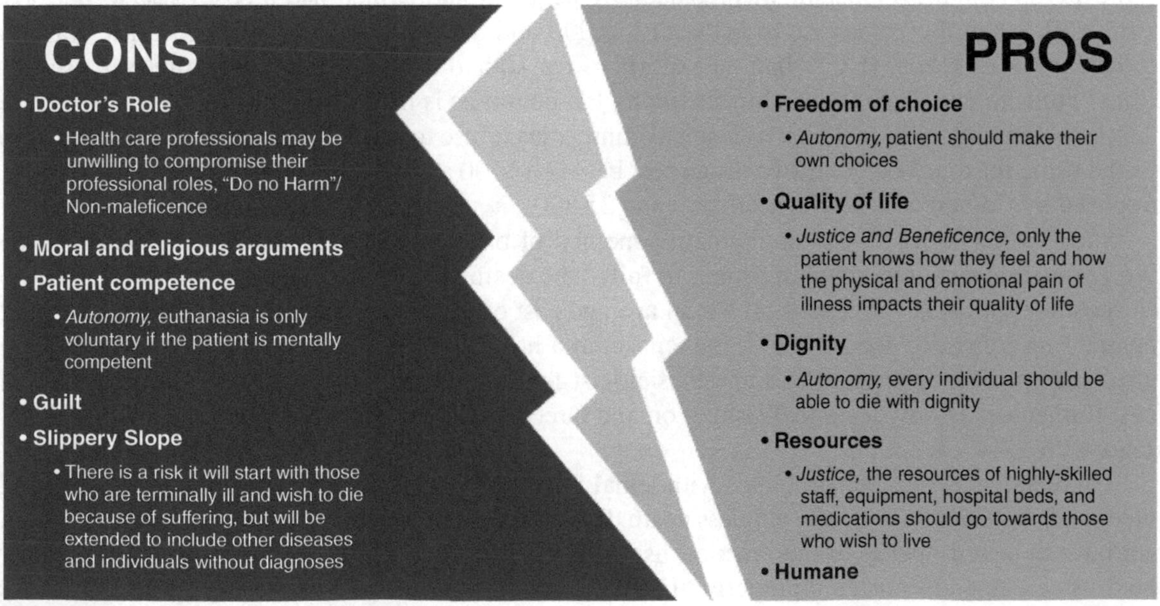

Source: T.D. Church

that autonomy was only upheld if the patient was competent and able to make rational decisions. The pro-euthanasia argument would pivot around autonomy as the patient exercising their freedom of choice and their right to die with dignity. The pro side of the argument would rely on justice to say that everyone is entitled to a good quality of life with no suffering. Justice would be employed to make the claim that the resources of highly skilled staff, equipment, hospital beds, and medications should be diverted toward those who wish to live, rather than those who are seeking to terminate their lives.

Whereas euthanasia is seen mostly as a medical procedure, lethal injection is reserved for the punishment of capital crimes [17]. Lethal injection is believed to be a more humane and less expensive method of execution. Firing squad, hanging, and electrocution have all become seen as being overly painful and traumatic for the prisoner and those observing the death penalty being carried out. Lethal injection relies on *Carson's cocktail* to be effective and deliver death, which we believe to be efficient and pain free. The problem with lethal injection, we are unable to get any good customer experience data firsthand as the result is permanent. Carson's cocktail is a three-drug method devised by a pathologist from Oklahoma as an alternative to the gruesome and sometimes not effective electric chair. Carson's cocktail involves first anaesthetizing the individual, followed by the administration of a paralytic agent, and finally stopping the heart from beating [18]. Whether being used for euthanasia or lethal injection, the following three drugs are recommended as the most humane method and should be used in succession. From its introduction in the 1970s, the three drugs that made up Carson's cocktail have been 1) *sodium thiopental* to induce unconsciousness; 2) *pancuronium bromide (Pavulon)* to cause muscle paralysis and respiratory arrest; and 3) *potassium chloride* to stop the heart.

Cost varies for lethal injection and is based on medication type and availability as well as the protocol used; some states only require one or two of the drugs recommended in Carson's cocktail (Figure 13.11). There is a vast difference in costs and availability for these drugs. For example, early in the 1990s sodium thiopental was replaced by pentobarbital, which had a cost of $500 per dose until 2012, when the price rose to between $15,000 and $25,000 [19]. The price increase was due to the European Union (EU)'s ban on exports to the United States because the drug was used for capital punishment. Capital punishment among EU countries is illegal and seen as a highly barbaric practice. Many international pharmaceutical companies refuse to export the drug to the United States for the same reason. The other two drugs cost between $500 and $800. Brining the humane cocktail proposed by Carson cost between $15,500 and 25,800.

States which elect to use an alternative method of one or two drugs instead of Carson's three, like Texas, can carry out lethal injections to fulfill the death penalty sentence at a cost of around $86. The cost for euthanasia in a hospital has an average cost of $950 for the drugs, plus the body removal fee and / or cremation fees of $700. Euthanasia in a hospital will cost around $1,650, not including hospital room fees, physician and anesthesiologist fees, psychology or social work fees, or nursing fees. Euthanasia is only legal in Washington and Oregon, whereas lethal injection is legal in all U.S. states with a few exceptions.

There are some serious problems with lethal injection. One fallacy that many hold is that lethal injection is believed to deliver a painless death. Physicians and pharmacologists have been very vocal and have objected openly to the practice, as lethal injection may in fact inflict excruciating pain if the drugs are not administered properly. "I can feel my body burning," Michael Wilson is reported as

Figure 13.11   Lethal Injection Protocol Variations by State

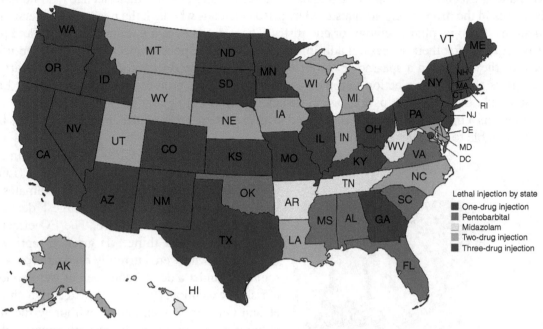

Source: T.D. Church

stating 20 seconds after his execution began in Oklahoma on January 9, 2014 [20]. In a similar case from Arizona, Joseph Rudolph Wood began gasping for air about 13 minutes after being injected, "Wood's jaw dropped, his chest expanded, and he let out a gasp. The gasps repeated every five to twelve seconds. They went on and on, hundreds of times" [21]. A final appalling case of an execu-

tion lasting 26 minutes, the longest of any in Ohio to date occurred when Dennis McGuire was injected, it is reported that he "appeared unconscious but gasped repeatedly as he lay on a gurney, his stomach rising and falling and his mouth opening and shutting" [21]. Justice Antonin Scalia wrote in 1994 CE about a case involving the murder of a young girl, "how enviable a quiet death by lethal injection …" in discussing the sentencing of the girl's murderer [22].

Why is lethal injection so excruciating? The selection of the drugs does not always adhere to the recommended three-drug cocktail. The procedure is

Figure 13.12   Capital Punishment via Lethal Injection

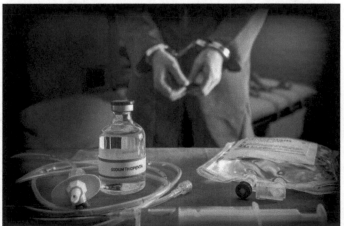

typically done in the absence of medically trained personnel. Medical professionals often refuse to participate in executions, citing that it stands in direct violation of non-maleficence ("do no harm"). This results in the drugs being administered by prison officials who lack the necessary understanding of anatomy, biology, pharmacology, or chemistry. These drugs have a unique complexity and precision is required for their successful administration. Often the people injected are not even unconscious, or they linger in a spasmodic state for minutes until the drugs stop the lungs or heart. The challenge is that lethal injection becomes a procedure with a protocol for administration. Lethal injection embodies a greater psychological distancing from killing another human being, due to its appearance as a medical procedure as opposed to an execution – this renders lethal injection as being "more palatable to the general public" [23].

Figure 13.13   California Governor Gavin Newsome

Matt Gush/Shutterstock.com

On March 13, 2019 CE, Governor Gavin Newsome implemented an Executive Order (EO) in California, granting a reprieve for 737 inmates who were waiting execution on the largest death row list in the Western hemisphere. The EO effectively accomplished three things: 1) granted reprieves to the inmates who were currently on death row – they remained under a death sentence but were no longer at risk of execution; 2) closed the execution chamber at San Quentin prison; and 3) withdrew the state's lethal injection protocol, the formally approved procedure for carrying out executions. With no protocol in place, any attempt at performing a lethal injection would be a criminal offense. At the time it was

seen as a highly symbolic move because legal challenges to lethal injection have many times stalled in California – 2006 CE, 2012 CE, and 2016 CE are examples where voters rejected initiatives to abolish the death penalty. As of August 26, 2021 CE, the California State Supreme Court effectively weakened efforts to overhaul California's death penalty when the Supreme Court unanimously ruled that current state law provided little legal support for lethal injection and effectively struck down capital punishment in the state in its entirety [24].

The last ethical case we will explore is related to medical cannabis, more specifically, medical cannabis in pediatric populations. There is a growing body of research related to the potential benefits of cannabis in the treatment of chronic and persistent diseases affecting pediatric populations, Figure 13.14.[1]

Prior to being prohibited in 1937 CE, there were more than 20 prescription medicines containing cannabis which were available from local pharmacies. These 20 prescriptions were used to treat over 100 separate illness until 1942 CE when it became illegal to use. Many of the illnesses treated with these prescriptions were in pediatric populations, with the majority of these not having a secondary line of therapy, extending up until the present. In 1996 CE, California – the state that was the first to prohibit cannabis in 1937 CE – enacted the ***Medical Cannabis Regulation and***

[1] *Disclaimer:* not all the indications listed in Figure 13.14 have been rigorously tested nor peer reviewed. More research is desperately needed to make sense of the findings and in some cases confirmatory reports are warranted for some of the more astounding claims.

Figure 13.14 Pediatric Uses for Cannabis

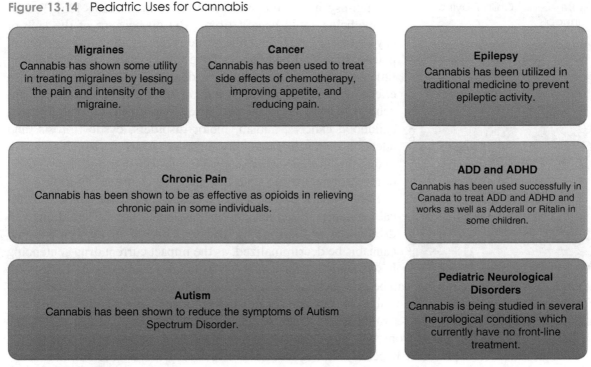

Migraines
Cannabis has shown some utility in treating migraines by lessing the pain and intensity of the migraine.

Cancer
Cannabis has been used to treat side effects of chemotherapy, improving appetite, and reducing pain.

Epilepsy
Cannabis has been utilized in traditional medicine to prevent epileptic activity.

Chronic Pain
Cannabis has been shown to be as effective as opioids in relieving chronic pain in some individuals.

ADD and ADHD
Cannabis has been used successfully in Canada to treat ADD and ADHD and works as well as Adderall or Ritalin in some children.

Autism
Cannabis has been shown to reduce the symptoms of Autism Spectrum Disorder.

Pediatric Neurological Disorders
Cannabis is being studied in several neurological conditions which currently have no front-line treatment.

Source: T.D. Church

Safety Act (MCRSA). MCRSA allowed the legal basis for qualified patients to possess or cultivate medical cannabis; patients' primary caregivers to possess or cultivate medical cannabis; and – most importantly – licensed physicians, osteopaths, and surgeons were able to recommend cannabis as a medical treatment for a specific set of ailments. The conditions covered by MCRSA were cancer, anorexia, AIDS / HIV, chronic pain, spasticity, glaucoma, arthritis, and migraine. It paved the way for ***compassionate use***, a treatment option that allows for the use of an unauthorized medicine. Under very controlled conditions, drugs in development can be made available to groups of patients who have a disease with no satisfactory authorized therapies. Compassionate use treatments are only permissible if the medicine is expected to help patients with life-threatening, long-lasting, or seriously debilitating illnesses that are not successfully managed with currently approved drugs.

Figure 13.15 Cannabis and Kids

Compassionate use was claimed for a few pediatric cases related to cancer, epilepsy, and chronic pain. But it was highly controversial due to the nature of cannabis being psychoactive and the age of the pediatric patients. Beginning around 2016, though, research had begun to provide exciting developments regarding the medical uses of ***cannabidiol (CBD)***,

Figure 13.16 Child Playing in Cannabis

Morphart Creation/Shutterstock.com

the non-psychoactive cannabinoid found in cannabis [25]. Pediatric medicine could benefit from CBD oil because of the lack of any associated "high" feeling while receiving the full spectrum of potential medical benefits conferred by cannabis. Extraordinarily little research has been done to date to examine the long-term effects of cannabis use on childhood development. Currently, cannabis is being used in the pediatric environment to treat epilepsy, childhood cancers, autism, motor disorders, cystic fibrosis, and attention deficit hyperactivity disorder (ADHD) [26]. It is worth noting that in states where cannabis has been approved for medical or recreational use, no state has approved its use for children.

The American Academy of Pediatrics (AAP) opposes medical cannabis, including the compassionate use for children with debilitating or life-limiting diseases. AAP does recommend that cannabis be decriminalized, as the impact current drug sentencing has related to cannabis tends to break families apart [27]. AAP adamantly states that cannabis can be extremely harmful to adolescent health and development [28]. Further research is needed to determine efficacy and correct dosing for cannabinoid oils for children; and it needs to undergo the same scrutiny as any other medication prior to approval. Table 13.2 below outlines the ethical arguments from AAP alongside supporters of cannabis in pediatric medicine.

As the above examples have hopefully shown, medical ethics deals with some remarkably interesting cases. This section was only a brief introduction to some of those topics. At its heart, medical ethics involves examining a specific problem, usually a clinical case, and using values, facts, and logic to determine the best course of action to fit a specific set of circumstances to achieve a

Table 13.2 Pro and Con Arguments for Pediatric Cannabis Use

AAP Arguments Against Cannabis	Supporters Arguments for Cannabis
• Impairs memory acquisition	• Can alleviate pain and discomfort
• Impairs concentration	• Is often the only available medication
• Interferes with learning, linked to lower odds of completing high school/obtaining a college degree	• Non-psychoactive components of cannabis do not have the same psychological issues
• Alterations in motor control coordination, and judgement tied to long time use	• Consumable components of cannabis are safer than some prescription drugs currently available
• Linked to psychological problems	
• Poor lung health	
• Higher likelihood of developing drug dependency in adulthood	

Source: T.D. Church

thoughtful outcome. Keep in mind that ethics does not seek to be THE correct course of action, instead it seeks to be the most appropriate course of action based upon the available facts as the situation unfolds. In some instances, appropriate ethics may not be legal and, as is often the case, laws are not always ethical.

13.2 Legal Control

Justice is blind, or at least we hope it is blind and using factual information to attend a verdict. A historical look at the laws that made drugs illegal in the United States tells us a different story. Social class and ethnic prejudices permeate the legal control of illegal substances. In some instances, there were real concerns related to health and safety, but many of the early legislation of nonmedical drug use was driven by class, race, and ethnic concerns. Prohibition of alcohol was in part a response to the drinking practices of European immigrants (the new lower class), who were displacing jobs along the East Coast. The alcohol temperance movement became closely affiliated with the antinarcotics movement and carried with it tendencies that were anti-Catholic, anti-Irish, anti-Italian, anti-Polish, and anti-Semitic. In an effort to obtain more federal power, Southern members of congress corrupted the legal system by exploiting racist myths such as "cocainized" ex-slaves, who were only concerned with raping white women. Cocaine became illegal after it was associated with the sexual activities of African American males following the Reconstruction period of the Antebellum South. Opium was first restricted in California in 1875 CE, when it became synonymous with Chinese immigrant workers. Cannabis was legal until the 1930s CE, when it became associated with the lethargic activities associated with Mexican immigrant workers in the South. LSD, legal in the 1950s CE, became illegal in 1967 CE when it became associated with the hippie counterculture. Exaggerated claims of drugs causing violence have surfaced in public and political discourse time and time again with the focus alternating between cannabis, heroin, LSD, crack cocaine, and most recently, methamphetamines.

Throughout the 1900s CE, there numerous acts, policies, and laws put into legislation related to the control of illegal substances. Figure 13.17 presents a rough timeline of the major legislative elements that have shaped our modern legal control of substances, with the dashed black lines representing some of the most influential. We will not be reviewing each of these pieces of legislation, as this is not a direct review of the mechanisms of legislation. Instead, this section will present the main elements that have informed our modern law enforcement related to controlled substances. Although vast portions of American society were addicted to cocaine, heroin, morphine, and opium in the early twentieth century CE, there was curiously little crime recorded with these addictions. It was the Harrison Act, which has been shown to be predominately a revenue and registration measure, which led to near total prohibition of the use of heroin, cocaine, and opium that was the catalyst for crime and violence to become associated with drug distribution. With all legal sources no longer able to sell these now illicit medicinal products, those addicted had to turn to criminal entrepreneurs who were able to sell drugs illegally for a substantial profit.

America commenced the control of illegal substances domestically first. Then the focus shifted to abroad, where military force and violence was unleashed upon peasant farmers who grew opium, coca, and cannabis to support their families. These actions led to poor diplomatic relations and whole foreign populations wary of U.S. military presence in their countries. Domestically, police operations and imprisonment were expanded and mostly directed against drug users, most of whom had never

Figure 13.17 Acts, Amendments, and Propositions Legislating Substances in the US

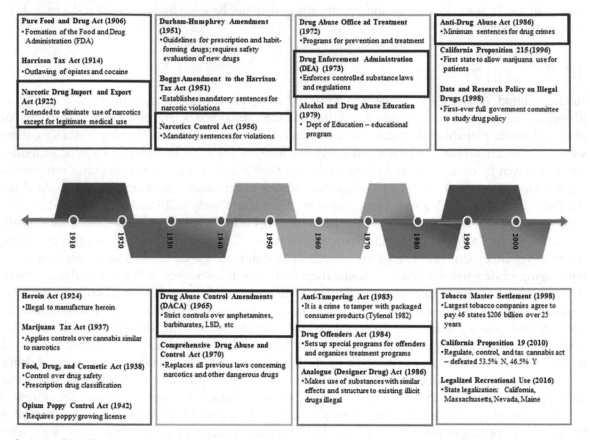

Source: T.D. Church

committed any violent crimes. Both acts of drug control have disproportionately targeted the poorest and the lowest level participants in the narcotics economy. These dual sides of the U.S. drug policy have failed to reduce either the overall quantities of drugs manufactured and smuggled or the number of seriously addicted drug abusers in the United States.

In a press conference on June 17, 1971 CE, President Richard Nixon declared drug abuse as "public enemy number one." He concluded his speech by saying, "in order to fight and defeat this enemy it is necessary to wage a new, all-out offensive" [29, 30]. With this speech, Nixon laid the foundation for the first war on drugs, which would culminate in a speech delivered to congress. In his speech to congress, Nixon stated, "right now, the federal government is fighting the war on drug abuse under a distinct handicap, for its efforts are those of a loosely confederated alliance facing a resourceful, elusive, worldwide enemy" [31]. In practice, Nixon's programs and legislation emphasized treatment and rehabilitation for drug addicts, with a unique focus on rehabilitating heroin addicts with methadone. Nixon was vying for rehabilitation because he believed lower crime rates would bolster his reelection bid. Tragically, however, his incendiary rhetoric expanded a climate of hostility toward those with drug problems. Current policies perpetuate Nixon's military language while deemphasizing treatment. Nixon's speech to congress where he opened the war on drugs invigorated the need for a federal and centralized control and administration over the agencies, state laws, and law enforcement activities in the United States. On July 1, 1973 CE, the *DEA* was enacted. The purpose behind the creation of the DEA was to enforce the controlled substances laws and regulations of the United States. *Controlled substances* encompass illegal or prescription drugs that are restricted and controlled, meaning that the manufacturing of the drug or substance as well as its ownership, delivery, use, and disposal are restricted by the government. The DEA was empowered to bring to the criminal and civil justice system of the United States, or any competent jurisdiction, organizations, and their principal members involved in the growing, manufacture, or distribution of controlled substances appearing, in or destined for, illicit traffic in the United States [31]. The DEA had the authority to recommend and support non-enforcement programs aimed at reducing the availability of illicit controlled substances. With the federal authorization of the DEA, there was now a centralized group dedicated to consolidating and coordinating the government's drug control activities.

The DEA of 2022 CE is slightly more refined in its mission statement and is responsible for enforcing the provisions of the controlled substances and chemical diversion and trafficking laws and regulations of the United States [1]. In addition, the enhanced version of the DEA conducts operations on a worldwide basis to interdict drugs from crossing the border into the United States. The DEA disrupts and dismantles illegal drug organizations by arresting their members, confiscating their drugs, and seizing their assets. The DEA creates, manages, and supports enforcement-related programs, domestically and internationally, aimed at reducing the availability of and demand for illicit controlled substances. The DEA is responsible for the classification of illicit drugs into the infamous schedule. Drug, substances, and certain chemicals used to make drugs are classified into five distinct schedules depending upon the drug's acceptable medical use and the drug's abuse or dependency potential, Figure 13.18[2]. Classified drugs are often referred to as controlled substances, and they range from street drugs such as methamphetamine to prescription medications like Xanax that must be obtained with a physician's order from a pharmacist. All controlled substances have a common thread – they tend to be dangerous because they can be habit-forming.

On October 27, 1970 CE, President Nixon signed the Controlled Substances Act, which listed what would from that point forward be considered controlled substances [32]. The Act outlined differing "levels of danger" for controlled substances and grouped them into the five distinct schedules. The Act established significant legal recourse for making, distribution, or diverting any of those controlled substances outside of the new legal framework. Some controlled substances were made outright illegal (Schedule I). The remaining substances are legal (Schedule II–V) but only appropriate for use under the direction of a medical provider with a legitimate prescription fulfilled by a pharmacist. Thus, creating the rule of thumb, it is always illegal to possess any controlled substance without a prescription.

The Controlled Substances Act puts drugs into the schedule based on its medical value and potential for abuse. Drugs get initiated into the schedule through a DEA process wherein the DEA evaluates the drug's value to medical treatments and relative potential for abuse to decide where the drug lands on the scale. Congress did not define abuse within the Controlled Substances Act, but for

---

[2] *Note:* this list is intended as a general reference list and is not a comprehensive listing of all controlled substances.

Figure 13.18   Classification of Illicit Drugs

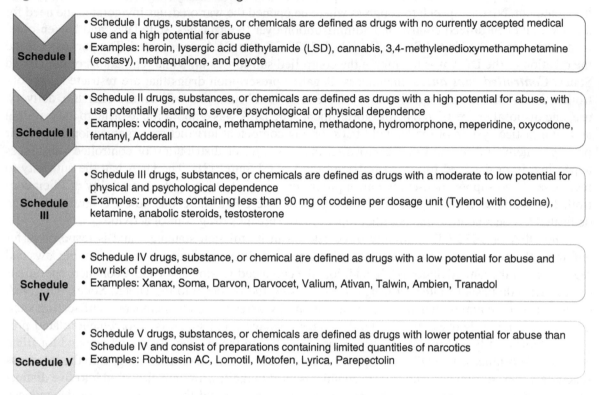

Schedule I
- Schedule I drugs, substances, or chemicals are defined as drugs with no currently accepted medical use and a high potential for abuse
- Examples: heroin, lysergic acid diethylamide (LSD), cannabis, 3,4-methylenedioxymethamphetamine (ecstasy), methaqualone, and peyote

Schedule II
- Schedule II drugs, substances, or chemicals are defined as drugs with a high potential for abuse, with use potentially leading to severe psychological or physical dependence
- Examples: vicodin, cocaine, methamphetamine, methadone, hydromorphone, meperidine, oxycodone, fentanyl, Adderall

Schedule III
- Schedule III drugs, substances, or chemicals are defined as drugs with a moderate to low potential for physical and psychological dependence
- Examples: products containing less than 90 mg of codeine per dosage unit (Tylenol with codeine), ketamine, anabolic steroids, testosterone

Schedule IV
- Schedule IV drugs, substance, or chemical are defined as drugs with a low potential for abuse and low risk of dependence
- Examples: Xanax, Soma, Darvon, Darvocet, Valium, Ativan, Talwin, Ambien, Tranadol

Schedule V
- Schedule V drugs, substances, or chemicals are defined as drugs with lower potential for abuse than Schedule IV and consist of preparations containing limited quantities of narcotics
- Examples: Robitussin AC, Lomotil, Motofen, Lyrica, Parepectolin

Source: T.D. Church

federal agencies responsible for classifying drugs, *abuse* is when individuals take a substance recreationally and develop personal health hazards or pose risks to society. ***Medical value*** is determined through large-scale clinical trials to prove therapeutic utility and follows the requirements set out by the FDA for any drug entering the market.

If a drug has been mis-scheduled, needs scheduled, or potentially needs removed from scheduling, the process is similar. Congress could pass a law that changes or restricts a drug's schedule. Congress has left scheduling to federal agencies like the DEA. There have been a few exceptions and typically involve major public health concerns. An example occurred in 2000 when Congress passed the Hillory J. Farias and Samantha Reid Date-Rape Prevention Act, which added gamma hydroxybutyric acid (GHB), a date-rape drug, to Schedule I [33].

The typical way a drug gets scheduled, re-scheduled, or removed can also be initiated by the U.S. attorney general initiating a review process that looks at the available evidence to potentially schedule or change the schedule of a drug. As can be imagined, there are multiple steps within this type of review [34]:

1. The DEA, U.S. Department of Health and Human Services (HHS), or public petition initiates the review

2. The DEA requests HHS to review the medical and scientific evidence to assess a drug's schedule

3. HHS utilizes the FDA to evaluate the drug and its schedule through an analysis across eight factors (see below)

   a. Upon completion of the FDA analysis, the FDA sends its recommendation back to HHS

4. HHS recommends a schedule based on the scientific evidence complied in the FDA's recommendation

5. The DEA conducts its own independent review in tandem to the FDA's review of the drug and with the determination from HHS, sets the final schedule

The factors used in the FDA evaluation of a drug to classify it for scheduling include [34]:

1. Actual or relative potential for abuse

2. Scientific evidence for a drug's pharmacologic effect

3. State of current scientific evidence for a drug's medical use

4. History and current patterns of abuse

5. Scope, duration, and significance of abuse

6. Risk to the public health

7. Psychological or physical dependence liability of the drug

8. Is the substance an immediate precursor of a substance already controlled

A drug's schedule sets the foundation for the federal regulation of a controlled substance. Schedule I drugs face the strictest regulations. Schedule I are illegal except for limited and well-controlled research, and Schedule II have limited utility for medical purposes with the DEA's approval. Criminal law in the United States, while guided by the scheduling system, does consider other factors when sentencing. A drug's schedule functions as an important policy guide. A stricter schedule allows the DEA to limit access more stringently to a drug and its supply, with the intent on making access to illegal drugs more difficult.

In 2019 CE, the FBI estimated a total of 1,558,862 arrests for drug law violations in the United States [35]. Nationwide, law enforcement made an estimated 10,085,207 arrests in 2019 CE. U.S. jails and prisons are filled – many to capacity – with people charged with crimes related to drugs. To give some perspective, the second and third highest number of arrests in 2019 CE were for property crimes (1,074,367) and violent crimes (495,871). Legal repercussions for people caught engaging in illegal activities involving controlled substances face a variety of consequences including time in jail or federal prison, heavy fines, community service, probation, house arrest, and criminal records that affect one's ability to get or maintain a job, receive approval for college loans and home loans, vote, own a gun, or join the military.

The penalties for drug-related charges are determined by several factors: substance, amount of substance, activity the individual was engaged in, were they in a restricted area (i.e. () school zone), and prior encounters with law enforcement. Individuals committing serious crimes with substantial amounts of dangerous drugs are more likely to receive harsher penalties. Schedule I–V drug possession charges vary by state [36]. Individual first-time offenders caught selling some Schedule I

Figure 13.19 Drug Free Zone Notification

Sue Smith/Shutterstock.com

drugs can face 5–40 years in prison, and up to $2 million in fines. Penalties are based on the amount of the substance that is discovered and which drug from the Schedule I list the individual has in their possession – heroin, LSD, ecstasy, and peyote carry the heaviest sentencing. Frequently, individual first-time offenders caught selling Schedule II drugs can face a maximum of 20 years in prison and a fine of up to $1 million. In most cases, individual first-time offenders caught selling Schedule III drugs can face up to 10 years in prison and up to $500,000 in fines. Schedule IV offenders caught selling face a maximum of 5 years in prison and up to $250,000 in fines. Schedule V offenders face no more than 1 year in prison and no more than $100,00 in fines. For each of the penalties listed above, it is of note that the maximum penalties can be doubled for distributing to minors or distributing in a drug-free zone. Additionally, if the crime involves a state, national, or international border, the offense constitutes a federal charge with harsher penalties, including life in prison. If there is an excessive quantity of drug, it can result in the death sentence being applied punishment.

In the United States, the sentencing guidelines for illegal drugs incorporate the actions of use, possession, manufacture, and distribution into setting the penalty. *Use of drugs* entails using an illegal controlled substance not prescribed by a licensed physician or medical practitioner. Illegal use of drugs in the legal system means use, possession, or distribution of drugs prohibited by the Controlled Substances Act of 1970[37]. *Possession* of an illegal substance is defined as knowing of the drug's presence and having physical control of the drug. This is further defined as actual possession and constructive possession. *Actual possession* is when the illegal substance is physically on an individual's person. You can think of it like this, if you are wearing a watch you have actual possession of your watch. *Constructive possession* is defined as an individual being in possession of an illegal substance even when it is not on their physical person, and it is also possible for more than one person to be in possession of

Figure 13.20 Clandestine Lab

Darwin Brandis/Shutterstock.com

the illegal substance. Possession is not the same as ownership [38]. The owner of an object may not always be in possession of an object. For example, an owner of an electronic tablet could lend it to someone else to review class notes. The person reviewing the class notes would then possess the electronic tablet. However, the owner does not give up ownership implied by lending the tablet to their classmate.

Manufacture refers to the act of being involved in any step of the illegal drug production process. A more technical definition of manufacture is the production of an illegal substance by means of chemical synthesis or natural extraction [39]. Drug manufacturing requires the manufacturer had possession of a drug, or the chemicals necessary to manufacture a drug and that the individual had an intent to manufacture. Drug manufacturing requires more than simple drug possession. The action of manufacturing has come to encompass a wide range of activities related to the varied processes of drug production. The clearest example of drug manufacturing is a clandestine in-house lab where illegal substances are being produced. It also extends to anyone involved in selling necessary precursor chemicals, specialized drug production equipment, and other operational support structures for the manufacture of illegal substances.

Drug distribution is the sale, transfer, exchange, import, or export of illegal drugs. There is a difference between drug trafficking and drug distribution. Drug trafficking involves the weight of the drugs, while drug distribution involves the movement of the drugs. It is worth noting that one does not need to be caught in the act of selling or distributing drugs. Simply having a large amount of cash and large quantity of controlled substances constitutes drug distribution. Drug distribution encapsulates a variety of different illegal activities, including but not limited to:

- Shipping drugs via mail
- Transporting drugs via car, boat, plane, or other mode of transportation
- Selling drugs to another individual or group of individuals
- Giving drugs to another individual or group of individuals
- Advertising the sale of drugs
- Coordinating the transport or sale of drugs

There are a few variations to the theme of distribution within U.S. law enforcement. **Actual distribution** refers to the physical transfer of a controlled substance to another individual. **Constructive distribution** is the intent to sell or distribute illegal substances through one's actions or the quantity of drugs in their possession. For example, if there is evidence of a large quantity of drugs, baggies of assorted sizes, and a scale which would infer that the individual was preparing their drugs to be "packaged to sell" rather than for personal use. The intent to distribute can thus be inferred without any evidence of actual distribution. **Attempted distribution** describes the situation wherein an individual attempts to transfer a controlled substance to someone else but is prevented from doing so.

Drug trafficking or the **illegal drug trade** represents the global black market dedicated to the cultivation, manufacture, distribution, and sale of drugs subjected to drug prohibition laws. Throughout the world, most jurisdictions prohibit trade – except under license – of many types of substances. Consumption of illegal drugs is widespread globally and remains exceedingly difficult for local authorities to impede their popularity. Large-scale drug trafficking remains one of the few capital crimes in the United States and can result in a death sentence prescribed at the federal level. The United States, despite all efforts, is still the world's largest importer of illegal drugs [40].

Although narcotics are illegal in the United States, they are seen by many different segments of the population as a recreational activity. Illegal drugs have become worldwide commodities and unfortunately, the illegal drug market is the fastest growing industry in the world, and some would argue the most profitable [41, 42]. Economically speaking, illicit drugs could be considered a commodity with strong demand, resulting in their sales at a higher price. There are several factors related to this high price that include potential legal ramifications; potential for violence from other dealers and buyers; importation and transportation costs; and processing and storage fees. It might not be too surprising to discover that when it comes to drug pricing for illegal substances, most of the cost is set by risk. The risk of being harmed, killed, or in prison, and as a result drug dealers want to be appropriately compensated for taking the risk associated with dealing. The chart below shows the breakdown of cost components for drugs – in this example cocaine –being sold at retail, Table 13.3. The percentages of the overall cost by risk are a little dated, being developed for 1990, but does give some perspective toward how costs breakdown over risks for dealers in drug trafficking.

Table 13.3 Percentage of Cost Components for Cocaine Sold as Retail

	PERCENTAGE
Wholesale price of drug	1
Importing of drug	12
Retail labor	13
Higher-level labor	~3
Drug and asset seizures	8-11
Money laundering fees	2-4
Packaging, processing, and inventory costs	~2
Compensation for risk of prison	24
Compensation for physical risk	33
Total	**100**

Source: Caulkins[43]

Another economic issue related to drug trafficking is related to economic losses for drug dealing neighborhoods. Between 1980 and 1990 CE, drug-related homicide was at a high record. In some U.S. cities, the average was ~425 homicides per year. The increase in drug violence became increasingly tied to ethnic minorities due to media portrayal and aggressive profiling. Even though the rate of violence varied tremendously among American cities, urban centers and ethnic enclaves were disproportionately targeted for police enforcement. For example, between 1985 and 1995 CE Miami had three times the national homicide average [44]. This crime rate was correlated with African American, Cuban, Colombian, and Puerto Rician neighborhoods by the local media. The DEA showed the crime rate was correlated with regions with low employment and was not entirely dependent on ethnicity. The public, however, believed their local media and some once vibrant ethnic neighborhoods lost commerce as people stopped going there for shopping, dining, and / or entertainment. Ethnic neighborhoods have a higher chance of becoming labeled as "bad" or "drug heavy" areas, which has negative repercussions for those neighborhoods. These repercussions trace across lines of economics, politics, and stigmatization. It is in these environments where substance abuse, criminal involvement, suicide, and murder begin to take hold and in effect become a self-fulfilling prophecy of neighborhood degradation.

Drug distribution networks represent the coordinated efforts to manufacture, transport, and sell drugs. These can be small groups of 1–3 individuals up to large organizations of 1,000 individuals. Open-air markets represent the lowest level of the drug distribution network and typically feature dealers who are often selling to finance their own use [45]. The characteristics of an open-air drug market are often dependent on the type of drug being sold – most commonly, heroin, crack, cocaine, and cannabis. Those drugs that can be sold in small, pre-packaged amounts. Open-air drug markets are often located in inner city or urban areas, and share the following common features:

Figure 13.21   Street for Open-Air Drugs in Philadelphia

Sandra Ciccarelli/Shutterstock.com

1. Located in economically depressed neighborhoods
2. Dealers sell from static sites, so customers know where to find them
3. Typically located near a transportation hub where there is a level of legitimate activity
4. Markets with a reputation for selling drugs can grow large, the concentration of activity in a small area will be hard to disguise

The war on drugs has not achieved victory on any of the stated goals of reducing either the quantity of drugs or the level of drug consumption in the United States. A fact that is underscored by addicts and casual drug consumers spending ~$150 billion a year on cannabis, cocaine, heroin, and methamphetamine [46]. Drug trafficking and drug enforcement have become extraordinarily lucrative industries, providing both licit and illicit incomes to criminal syndicates, corporations, politicians, and law enforcement agencies domestically and abroad. Federal spending on antidrug programs and enforcement reached its all-time high in 2021, with a reported $40.5 billion being spent. The requested funding for 2022 CE is higher at $45 billion [1]. There is an estimated $25 billion in state and local funds being spent on imprisonment, law enforcement, and prosecution for drug-related charges. Over 1.5 million people are currently imprisoned for drug-related charges, with a cost exceeding $10 billion annually, and the demand for more prison cells for drug offenders accounts for half the cost of new prison construction [47].

The current drug policy of the United States is deepening our diplomatic burden while doing little to remedy the drug problems domestically. There is a growing disparity along racial lines where African Americans are stopped and searched for drugs more frequently than Caucasians, upon entering the country, while driving or simply walking down the street. This persecution and profiling under the guise of combatting drugs means that people of color are disproportionately imprisoned, families dislocated, and employment or educational prospects decimated. The United States is in desperate need of redefining both its burgeoning drug problem and its failing drug policy. In effect, the drug policy has generated a downward spiral of failed and costly attempts to cut foreign supply while ignoring the very real problems of domestic abuse. Drug production abroad is not the source of the U.S. domestic drug crisis; it is responding to the demand related to the internal drug problems. Drug policy must be removed from the realm of criminal justice and placed squarely in the palm of social justice. By mislabeling drugs as a national security threat, the United States has diverted attention and needed funding from serious sociopolitical health problems to a high-tech militarized set of campaigns directed at our borders and on foreign soil. A social justice approach to the drug problem would mean that the surgeon general, rather than the attorney general or four-star military general, would be responsible for correcting the nation's antidrug programs. Moving the drug problem from criminal justice to public health will allow for a focus on rehabilitation instead of incarceration.

13.3 Regulatory Mechanisms

In this section, we will shift gears from illegal substances and focus on the regulation of medical products in the United States. The *FDA* is responsible for protecting and promoting public health, which is accomplished through the control and supervision of food safety, tobacco products, dietary supplements, prescription and over-the-counter pharmaceutical (medications), vaccines, biopharmaceuticals, blood transfusions, medical devices, electromagnetic radiation emitting devices, cosmetics, animal foods and feed, and veterinary products[3]. FDA is a federal agency of the HHS. FDA was empowered by the U.S. Congress to enforce the federal food, drug, and cosmetic act, which serves as the primary focus for the agency.

At the start of the twentieth century CE, there were no federal regulations to protect the American public from dangerous drugs [48]. The early pharmaceutical market was filled with products like Boschee's German Syrup and Hamlin's Wizard Oil. These products were far from harmless and if not handled appropriately could be quite harmful. The makers of these concoctions knew that their remedies were useless, yet they continued to pick the pockets of Americans hopeful for longevity, a cure for their cold, or a miracle for their cancer. They played on those fears and in return provided, at best, an opioid addiction or, at worst, death from toxic poisoning. Today, the medical product review process in the United States has become the recognized gold standard. Medical products must undergo a rigorous evaluation that proves their safety, quality, and effectiveness before they can be put into the market and sold to consumers. *Medical products* are defined as devices, products, articles, methods, systems, or merchandise, which are primarily utilized by a) health-care professionals for the diagnosis, treatment, or prevention of disease or injuries; or b) caregivers under the direction and supervision of medical professionals in the treatment or prevention of disease or injuries.

The FDA lists 53 milestone events between 1848 CE and 2006 CE, which have shaped the mission and goals of the FDA [49]. While the list provided by FDA provides a historical frame of reference, for our purposes, this list will be truncated to the top eight events relevant to controlled substance regulation, Figure 13.24[4]. Our journey begins on June 30, 1906 CE, when President

---

[3] Per the "About" section of the FDA's website – http://www.fda.gov
[4] *Note*: The selected FDA milestones were chosen because of their relevance to the topic of this book, drugs of abuse. The FDA has had a much broader and richer history of regulatory events not represented in this snapshot. For a full listing of the major events in FDA history, follow the reference in this footnote [44].

Roosevelt signed the Food and Drugs Act, alternatively known as the Wiley Act into effect. Politically, Harvey Wiley was a progressive and in favor of laws that made better the human living conditions and sought to expose, often in gruesome detail, the hazards of industrialization and the modern marketplace. The grotesque conditions surrounding the meat-packing industry had been vividly recounted in Upton Sinclair's book The Jungle and became the triggering force behind a comprehensive food and drug law. This Act prohibited interstate commerce in adulterated or misbranded drugs and foods and made it illegal to transport unlawful food and drugs across state lines. The foundation of the law rested on the regulation of the product labeling. Drugs needed to be defined with the standards of strength, quality, and purity via the U.S. Pharmacopoeia and the National Formulary. They could not be sold in any condition unless the specific variations from the standards were plainly stated on the products label. The U.S. Pharmacopoeia is a compendium of drug information, published annually by the US Pharmacopeia Convention (USP)[50]. The National Formulary is an official compendium of formulas for the compounding and testing of medication. It was formerly issued by the American Pharmaceutical Association but is now published by USP Pharmacopeial Convention and provides standards and specifications used to evaluate source, chemistry, physical properties, tests for identification and purity, dosage range, and class of use. The Act stipulated that the food or drug label could not be false or misleading about any ingredients, and further, the presence and amount of 11 identified dangerous ingredients, including alcohol, morphine, heroin, and cocaine, had to be clearly listed.

Democratic Congressman Francis Barton Harrison of New York harnessed the growing alarm over drug addiction in 1914 CE to motivate the US Congress to pass its first major national antinarcotics law. The Harrison Narcotics Tax Act sought to control the production, sale, and use of opium (and its derivatives), cocaine, and cannabis. Cannabis would get left out of the final bill due to pressure from the medical field who indicated that it was not habit-forming. Enforcement of the Act began in 1915, which saw a diminished supply of opium by mid-1915[51, 52]. The use of the term ***narcotic***, which is derived from Ancient Greek *narko*, "to make numb," was chosen to be in title of the Act as it referenced not just opiates but also cocaine. Unfortunately, this set a precedent of frequent legislative and judicial misnaming of various (usually illegal) substances as "narcotics." In popular media, law enforcement agencies and among the public the term narcotics is today used very broadly, frequently pejoratively, to refer to a wide range of illicit substances. Narcotics, as a result, has come to represent any illegally used drug. It functions as a useful shorthand for referring to a controlled substance in a context where its legal status outweighs its physiological effects. Unappreciated at the time of signing the Act into law, it marked the beginning of the criminalization of addiction and the black market for drugs in the United States.

President Franklin Roosevelt signed into law the Food, Drug, and Cosmetic Act (FDCA) on June 25, 1938 CE. The goal was to improve public safety and the major provisions of the Act were to regulate cosmetics and medical devices; require that safety directions be included with medicines; require that new medicines be approved by the FDA; companies needed to prove that any new drug was safe for use; outlawed false therapeutic claims; enhanced food quality and safety standards (ergo: packaging); began control of product advertising; and authorized factory inspections and enforcement [48]. The Act was passed in the wake of a therapeutic disaster that occurred in 1937 CE. Elixir Sulfanilamide, a form of the new sulfa wonder drug for pediatric patients had been marketed by S.E. Massengill Company, a Tennessee drug manufacturer. The main solvent in this untested product was

Figure 13.22 Drug Control Events in FDA Timeline

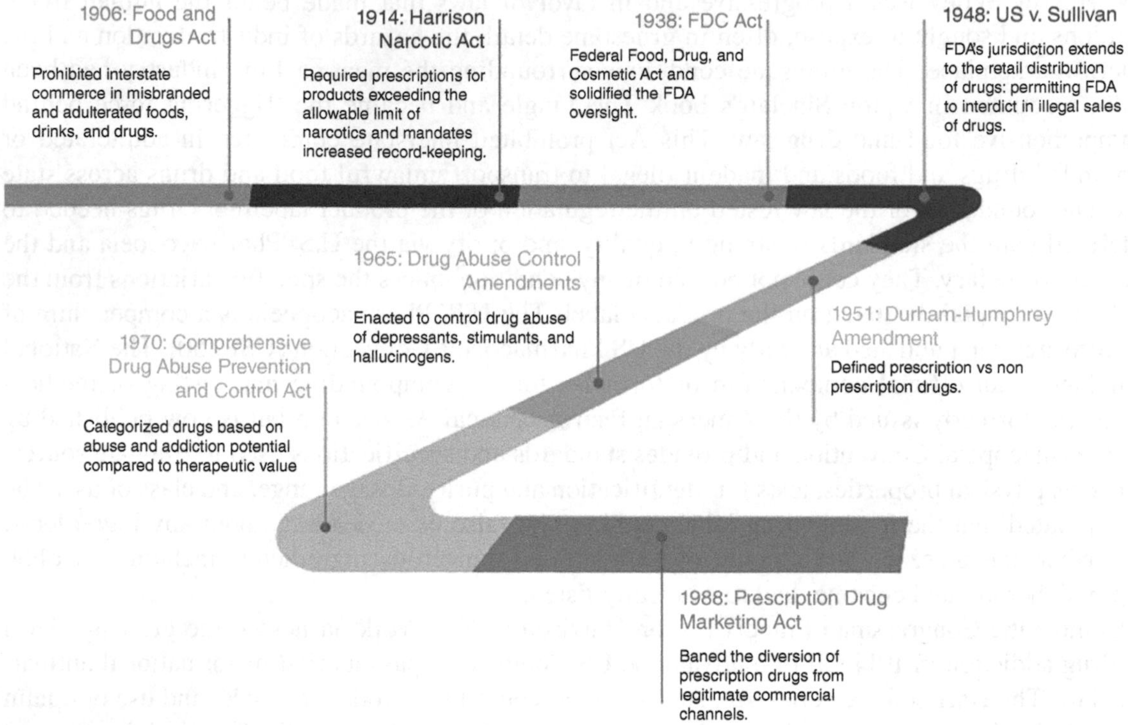

1906: Food and Drugs Act

Prohibited interstate commerce in misbranded and adulterated foods, drinks, and drugs.

1914: Harrison Narcotic Act

Required prescriptions for products exceeding the allowable limit of narcotics and mandates increased record-keeping.

1938: FDC Act

Federal Food, Drug, and Cosmetic Act and solidified the FDA oversight.

1948: US v. Sullivan

FDA's jurisdiction extends to the retail distribution of drugs: permitting FDA to interdict in illegal sales of drugs.

1965: Drug Abuse Control Amendments

Enacted to control drug abuse of depressants, stimulants, and hallucinogens.

1970: Comprehensive Drug Abuse Prevention and Control Act

Categorized drugs based on abuse and addiction potential compared to therapeutic value

1951: Durham-Humphrey Amendment

Defined prescription vs non prescription drugs.

1988: Prescription Drug Marketing Act

Baned the diversion of prescription drugs from legitimate commercial channels.

Source: T.D. Church

a highly toxic chemical analog of antifreeze and resulted in over 100 deaths, the majority of whom were children [53]. The public outcry reshaped the drug provisions of the new law to prevent a similar event from happening again and propelled the Act through congress. The new law recognized that U.S. consumers had a desire to self-medicate and therefore required instructions for safe usage of medications. As a result, from this point forward drugs would be required to bear adequate directions for safe use, which included all known warnings.

In 1948 CE, the Supreme Court ruled in the US versus Sullivan case wherein the court upheld the FDA's authority in the regulation of retail distribution of drugs [54]. This ruling permitted FDA to interdict in pharmacies illegal sales of drugs, most notably the illegal sales of barbiturates and amphetamines. Under the Food, Drug, and Cosmetic Act of 1938, a number of "prohibited acts" relating to drugs were outlined, 21 USC 331[55]. The prohibited acts are the cornerstone of the FDA's statutory regime to "protect the consumer by applying the [FDCA] to articles from the moment of introduction (or delivery for introduction) into interstate commerce all the way to the moment of their delivery to the ultimate consumer" [54]. It is the enacting, either through action or by cause, of one of the prohibited acts that can trigger a federal civil or criminal case under the FDCA. Based on an underlying finding that a drug is adulterated, misbranded, or unapproved for sale. This was determined to have strict liability, which meant there was no requirement under the law for the FDA to prove intent to commit the prohibited acts.

Thirteen years after the FDCA went into effect, it received a major amendment, the Durham-Humphrey Amendment of 1951. This amendment contained a specific requirement related to the labeling of drugs that move in interstate commerce as well as provisions that affect prescription practice. Drugs that cannot be used with relative safety in self-medication must bear the legend "Caution: Federal law prohibits dispensing without prescription" on their labels[56]. This amendment, often referred to as the *Prescription Drug Act*, estab-

Figure 13.23   Writing a Prescription

lished that some drugs simply could not be labeled safe for use and required medical supervision for individualized directions. This amendment provided clear definitions of what constitutes a prescription drug, who is responsible for identifying said drugs, and the conditions under which a prescription could be refilled. *Prescription drugs*, from this point forward, would refer to pharmaceutical drugs that legally required a written medical prescription from a licensed health-care professional.

There were several events that made the 1960s CE memorable in the United States. It was an era molded by events like the Vietnam War, flower children, rock and roll music, the Hippie countercultural movement, the trial of the Chicago Seven, the fight for civil rights, Woodstock, and an increasing use of recreational drugs. There was a growing concern from health-care, political, and legal leaders about the increase in the use of illegal drugs, especially among the youth. But this was being overshadowed by the abuse of what were at the time legal drugs, or better stated, drugs that had not been officially declared illegal (ergo: LSD, amphetamines, and some barbiturates). A few key opinion leaders made the case that traffic in heroin and other narcotics was being eclipsed by these types of drugs. In response to these allegations, Congress passed the Drug Abuse Control Amendments of 1965, and the law was signed into effect by President Lyndon Johnson. The amendments targeted three classes of products to better control or outlaw their use: 1) depressants, specifically barbiturates (addictive tranquilizers); 2) stimulants, specifically amphetamines; and 3) hallucinogens, specifically LSD. The amendments designated certain stimulant, depressant, or hallucinogenic drugs as controlled, requiring licensing for sales and distribution. Hallucinogens were effectively banned, and the sales of amphetamines and barbiturates were severely restricted.

The Comprehensive Drug Abuse Prevention and Control Act of 1970, commonly referred to as the Controlled Substances Act, was signed into law on October 27, 1970 CE by President Richard Nixon. The Act placed all substances that were regulated under existing federal and state law into one of five comprehensive schedules (discussed in Section 8.2). The scheduling is based upon the substance's medical use, potential for abuse, and safety or dependence liability. The Act established a unified legal framework to regulate certain drugs that were determined to pose a risk of abuse and dependence. The Act applies to drugs that are medical or recreational, legally or illicitly distributed, but does not apply to all drugs. Rather, it applies to specific substances and categories of substances that have been designated for control by Congress or through administrative proceedings. The Act also extended to *controlled substance analogues*, which are intended to mimic the effects of controlled substances and chemicals commonly used in the manufacture of controlled substances. The Act has two key legal goals 1) to ensure that patients have access to pharmaceutical controlled substances for authorized medical purpose and 2) to protect public health from the dangers of controlled substances diverted into or produced for the black market[57]. This created two overlapping legal schemes, referred to collectively as the provisions. ***Registration provisions*** required entities working with controlled substances to register with the DEA and take various steps to prevent diversion and misuse of controlled substances. ***Trafficking provisions*** established penalties for the production, distribution, and possession of controlled substances outside the legitimate scope of the registration system.

In 1988, the Prescription Drug Marketing Act (PDMA) went into effect to address growing problems related to three forms of prescription drug diversion, 1) wholesale diversion of prescription drugs domestically; 2) fraudulent re-importation of prescription drugs (alternatively known as false export diversion; and 3) distribution of drug samples by manufacturer representatives. ***Drug diversion*** refers to prescription medicines obtained or utilized illegally. It involves the diversion of drugs from legal and medically necessary uses toward uses that are illegal and typically not medically authorized or necessary. Prior to the enactment of the PDMA, the distribution of prescription drug samples was not regulated. In the findings in support of passage of the law, Congress, noted[58]:

1. American consumers could not purchase prescription drugs with the certainty that the products were safe and effective.

2. The existing system of providing drug samples to physicians through manufacturer's representatives had been abused for decades and resulted in the sale to consumers of misbranded, expired, and adulterated pharmaceuticals.

3. The effect of those conditions created an unacceptable risk that counterfeit, adulterated, misbranded, sub-potent, or expired drugs would be sold to American consumers.

The safety of the public and access to effective medical products have given rise to a growing and highly applicable career choice for many in Science, Technology, Engineering, and Mathematics (STEM) fields. ***Regulatory science***, as defined by the FDA, is the science of developing new tools, standards, and approaches to assess the safety, efficacy, quality, and performance of regulated products [59]. Regulatory science is the examination of the public effects of each technological advancement in the development, manufacture, delivery, and application of medical products. It represents the set of regulations, standards, rules, and other legal issues in relation to the public, including issues such as environmental impact, effects on public health, safety in the workplace and in using equipment, marketing, sales, and distribution of products. It is a growing discipline seeking to integrate technological advances in science, medicine, and engineering with mechanisms to protect people's health while serving the wider public interests. From the FDA's perspective, regulatory responsibilities universally apply to the protecting of public health; supplying accurate, science-informed information; ensuring safety and proper labeling; and regulating the manufacturing, marketing, and distribution of medical products. Protecting the public health is accomplished by ensuring the safety, effectiveness, and security of human and veterinary drugs, medical devices, vaccines, and biological products. Providing the public with accurate, science-informed information ensures safe and appropriate use of medical products, foods, and cosmetics. Ensuring the safety and proper labeling extends across all levels of FDA oversight to keep people healthy. The FDA as a federal agency collaborates with both state and local law enforcement to ensure effective controls are enforced over substances (drugs, tobacco, vaping products, supplements, and so on) deemed to be a danger to individuals and society writ large. Currently the field of regulatory science is facing a talent shortage and is in need of individuals who have an interest in science and medical products [60].

13.4 Addiction Research and Services

In the United States, the *NIH* is an agency dedicated to medical and health research. The NIH-funded research programs have led to longer life expectancy and improved health throughout the United States. Life expectancy in the United States jumped from 47 years in 1900 CE to 78 years in 2009 CE, and disability in people over age 65 has dropped dramatically in the past three decades [61]. NIH has been advancing understanding of health and disease for over a century and is credited with being the world's largest source of biomedical research funding. Thanks to NIH-funding, some of the more recent advances have led to the development of vaccines to protect against an array of life-threatening diseases, including influenza, meningitis, and cervical cancer.

Administratively, NIH falls under the HHS and consists of 27 institutes and centers. NIH's program activities are organized and represented by these institutes and centers, many of which are disease or organ specific in nature – however, through translational and transdisciplinary research mechanisms there is broad integration of the research across programs with the goal of advancing human health and longevity. Among the institutes and centers of the NIH, there are two that deal directly with controlled substance research. The *NIAAA* was established in 1970 CE and conducts research focused on improving the treatment and prevention of alcoholism and alcohol-related problems to reduce the enormous health, social, and economic consequences of this disease. The *NIDA* was established in 1974 CE with the mission to advance science on the causes and consequences of drug use and addiction and to apply that knowledge to improve individual and public health.

The *HHS* is comprised of 11 operating divisions, including eight agencies in the U.S. Public Health Service and three human services agencies. Together, the divisions administer a wide range of health and human services and conduct life-saving research for the United States, with the underlying mission "to protect and serve all Americans." The CDC, NIH, and FDA are three of these agencies. Another important agency under HHS related to drug abuse is the *SAMHSA*. SAMHSA leads public health efforts aimed at advancing the behavioral health of the United States and improving the lives of individuals living with mental health and substance use disorders, and their families. Two of SAMHSA's priority areas are 1) combating the opioid crisis through the expansion of prevention, treatment, and recovery support services; and, 2) advancing prevention, treatment, and recovery support services for substance use [62].

One of the centers under SAMHSA, the *CSAT* exists to promote community-based substance use disorder treatment and recovery support services. Their services are directed toward individual and families in every community. CSAT helps to improve access, reduce barriers, and promote evidence-based treatment strategies. They work to close the gap between available treatment capacity and demand for treatment. They support the adaptation and adoption of best practices by community-based treatment programs and services. CSAT works to improve and strengthen substance abuse treatment organizations and systems.

The other center under SAMHSA, the *CSAP* works with federal, state, public, and private organizations to develop comprehensive prevention systems. CSAP accomplishes this by providing national leadership in the development of policies, programs, and services to prevent the onset of illegal drug use, prescription drug misuse and abuse, alcohol misuse and abuse, and underage alcohol and tobacco use. They promote effective substance abuse prevention practices to enable states, communities, and organizations to apply prevention knowledge effectively. They created the drug-free and crime-free neighborhood campaigns that help to reduce availability and access to controlled substances through increases in criminal sanctions and fines. More recently, they have been successful with building supportive workplaces, schools, and community campaigns. These campaigns are geared toward providing supportive spaces to foster well-being and overall safety for those struggling with addiction.

Research helps to improve the reach, accessibility, and quality of care for substance use prevention, treatment, and recovery services. A new field of academic study, *addiction sciences*, led by scientists with backgrounds in psychology, public health, social work, pharmacology, anthropology, history, communications, and medicine, is focusing on developing, testing, and disseminating scientific advances for families and individuals struggling with addiction. Addiction science is a truly transdisciplinary scientific study of the nature, causes, consequences, prevention, and treatment of addiction-related problems[63]. Addiction science bridges the gap between science, practice, and policy to educate (and be educate by) those impacted by addiction. In general, addiction sciences focus on three broad areas – prevention and education, treatment, and recovery.

13.5 Coordinated Drug Control

It is not always possible to predict all potential misuses of substances, and the procedures used in their control need to be customizable for unique circumstances and settings. This chapter has taken us through several areas related to drug control, from legal and ethical concerns to regulatory oversight and research organizations. Throughout the twentieth century, drug policy has been dominated by a dogmatic view aligned with strict prohibition and the criminalization of drug cultivation, production, trade, possession, and use. The intention behind this adherence to prohibition has been to create a drug-free world. Unfortunately, the *war on drugs* has not only failed, but it has also proven to be unsustainable and, in many ways, undermines efforts to improve access to health, protect the environment, reduce drug related violence, and protect the human rights and dignity of many communities.

Prohibitionist drug policies have a significant impact on treatment, prevention, and harm reduction services for people who use drugs, an example of this can be seen in need exchange programs. The criminalization of drug use and possession of drug paraphernalia creates a significant barrier to providing harm reduction services and functions as a barrier keeping individuals from accessing much needed services. This puts people at risk and increases the chance for blood-borne diseases like HIV and worse, death by overdose to proliferate. Prohibition serves to reinforce social stigma and discrimination against people who use drugs, many of whom can and will be denied health care due to their drug use. Women who use drugs face particularly strong stigma, even more so if they are pregnant, with them being denied prenatal care or provided an adequate substitution therapy. This denial of services for pregnant women who misuse, or abuse substances puts the life of her unborn child in jeopardy. Social stigma related to substances of abuse constrains government spending on narcotic substance abuse treatment services as funds become diverted for enforcement practices.

It is incumbent on all of us to urge for prohibitionist policies related to drug use be reformed and harm reduction approaches need to be adopted. Changing the existing policies will significantly impact efforts to strengthen access to treatment for people who use drugs. This change in thinking will allow us to move drug addiction from a criminally sanctioned activity to a behavioral health issue. It is a sad truth that the *war on drugs* has become quite literal. Law enforcement approaches to counter the drug trade has fueled a vast militaristic response intent upon interdicting drugs. This has in many instances led to an arms race between law enforcement and drug suppliers, one attempting to limit drug access while the other is protecting their investments.

The illegal drug market is highly profitable due to the nature of the business, its own illegality. While it is cheap to grow and produce most illegal drugs, the price dramatically increases when a drug is trafficked out of the country. This price increase is due to the physical, legal, and financial risks involved in the act of trafficking. Proceeds from the drug trade are one of the main sources of income for organized crime who often profit substantially from economic gain in the form of "taxes" on opium, heroin, and cocaine. It will be difficult to target the profitability of drugs, because the high profits remain a big enticement for continued involvement in organized crime. Sadly, the immense profits obtained from drug trafficking allow drug cartels to exert powerful influence over governments, security services, and local communities through corruption, bribery, and intimidation tactics.

Our current use of prohibition as the sole approach to drug policy has not been as effective as anticipated. It is time to engage seriously with the issues surrounding drug policy in the United States. New policies and drug control efforts must work side-by-side with communities, individuals, and organizations to meet common goals. If we do not consider the voices of those who have been stigmatized and marginalized, our efforts toward progress will at best be limited and at worst be rendered untenable. At the present moment, illegal drugs are winning the fight. It is time to change out old tactics and apply new strategies if this war is truly going to won.

REFERENCES

1. Andreas, P. (2021). *US drug control policy*. Institute for Policy Studies.
2. Fisher, C.E. (2022). *The urge: Our history of addiction* (p. 400). Penguin Press.
3. Westrate, D. L. (2019). The role of law enforcement. In R. F. Perl (Ed.), *Drugs and foreign policy* (pp. 79–99). Routledge.
4. Veatch, R. M., & Guidry-Grimes, L. K. (2019). *The basics of bioethics* (4th ed.). Taylor & Francis.
5. Szocik, K., Rappaport, M. B., & Corbally, C. (2021). Genetics, ethics, and mars colonization: a special case of gene editing and population forces in space settlement. In O. A. C. Torres et al. (Eds.), *Astrobiology: Science, ethics, and public policy* (pp. 157–176). Scrivener Publishing.
6. Torres, O. A. C. (2021). Astrobioethics: Epistemological, astrotheological, and interplanetary issues. In O. A. C. Torres et al. (Eds.), *Astrobiology: Science, ethics, and public policy* (pp. 1–15). Scrivener Publishing.
7. Thomas, S. B., & Quinn, S. C. (1991). The Tuskegee Syphilis Study, 1932 to 1972: implications for HIV education and AIDS risk education programs in the black community. *American Journal of Public Health*, *81*(11), 1498–505.
8. Silverman, F. H. (1988). The "monster" study. *Journal of Fluency Disorders*, *13*(3), 225–231.
9. Perkins, K., & Kieffer, B. (2013). *Iowa experiments* (pp. 45–59). Iowa Public Radio.
10. Skloot, R. (2010). *The immortal life of Henrietta Lacks*. Crown.

11. OHRP, (1979). *The Belmont Report: Ethical principles and guidelines for the protection of human subjects research*. Office of Human Research Protections: www.hhs.gov/ohrp/human-subjects/guidance/belmont.html (Accessed December 13, 2021).

12. OHRP, (2013). *IRB Guidebook*, in *Chapter III: Basic IRB Review*, H.a.H. Services, Editor. Office of Human Research Protections http://www.hhs.gov/ohrp/archive/irb/irb_chapter3.htm.

13. CDC, 2018. *Persons Who Inject Drugs (PWID)s*. Center for Disease Control and Prevention, https://www.cdc.gov/pwid/index.html (Accessed Dec 17, 2021).

14. SAMHSA, (2021). *Harm reduction: Health and human services' overdose prevention strategy*. Substance Abuse and Mental Health Services Administration: https://www.samhsa.gov/find-help/harm-reduction (Accessed Dec 17, 2021).

15. CDC, (2019). *Syringe Services Programs (SSPs) FAQs*. Center for Disease Control and Prevention. https://www.cdc.gov/ssp/syringe-services-programs-faq.html (Accessed Dec 17, 2021).

16. Mendz, G. L., & Kissane, D. W. (2020). Agency, autonomy and euthanasia. *The Journal of Law, Medicine & Ethics, 48*(3), 555–564.

17. Hahn, M. P. (2012). Review of palliative sedation and its distinction from euthanasia and lethal injection. *Journal of Pain & Palliative Care Pharmacotherapy, 26*(1), 30–39.

18. Romanelli, F., Whisman, T., & Fink III, J. L. (2008). Issues surrounding lethal injection as a means of capital punishment. *Pharmacotherapy: The Journal of Human Pharmacology and Drug Therapy, 28*(12), 1429–1436.

19. Berger, E. (2020). Courts, culture, and the lethal injection stalemate. William & Mary Law Review, *62*(1), 1–82.

20. CBS, (2014). *Condemned man's last words: "I feel my whole boddy burning"*. CBS News. https://www.cbsnews.com/news/okla-man-says-he-can-feel-body-burning-during-execution/#textMcALESTER2C20Okla20E2809320Almost20two20decades20after20thewords20were2C2022I20feel20my20whole20body20burning22 (Accessed Dec 18, 2021).

21. Galvan, A., & Murphy, S. (2016). Three executions gone wrong: Details of lethal injections in Arizona, Ohio, Oklahoma. In *The Mercury News*. Bay Area News Group.

22. Oransky, I. (2003). Who—and how—to kill are focus of US death penalty cases. *The Lancet, 362*(9392), 1287.

23. Dresser, R. (2014). Drugs and the death penalty. *Hastings Center Report, 44*(1), 9–10.

24. Berry III, W. W. (2021). Cruel and unusual non-capital punishments. *American Criminal Law Review, 58*: p. 1627-1660.

25. Wang, G. S. (2017). Pediatric concerns due to expanded cannabis use: Unintended consequences of legalization. *Journal of Medical Toxicology, 13*(1), 99-105.

26. Doherty, M., et al. (2020). Use of oral cannabis extracts in the pediatric palliative care setting: A retrospective chart review. *Palliative Medicine, 34*(3), 435–437.

27. Hall, W., & Lynskey, M. (2020). Assessing the public health impacts of legalizing recreational cannabis use: the US experience. *World Psychiatry, 19*(2), 179–186.

28. Hines, L., et al. (2018). Medical marijuana for minors may be considered child abuse. *Pediatrics, 142*(4), 1–5.

29. RNF. (2021). *Public enemy number one: A pragmatic approach to America's drug problem.* Richard Nixon Foundation. https://www.nixonfoundation.org/2016/06/26404/ (Accessed Dec 20, 2021).

30. RNF. (2016). *President Nixon Declares Drug Abuse "Public Enemy Number One".* https://youtu.be/y8TGLLQlD9M. 4:37min.

31. Tarricone, J. (2020). *Richard Nixon and the origins of the War on Drugs.* BPR: The Boston Political Review: https://www.bostonpoliticalreview.org/post/richard-nixon-and-the-origins-of-the-war-on-drugs (Accessed Dec 20, 2021).

32. Gabay, M. (2013). The federal controlled substances act: schedules and pharmacy registration. *Hospital Pharmacy*, *48*(6), 473–474.

33. Marinetti, L., & Montgomery, M. (2010). The use of GHB to facilitate sexual assault. *Forensic Science Review*, *22*(1), 41–59.

34. USC. (2022). *21 U.S. Code § 811: Authority and criteria for classification of substances*, in *21 – Food and Drugs*. United States Congress: https://uscode.house.gov/view.xhtml?req=granuleid%3AUSC-prelim-title21-chapter13-subchapterI-partB&edition=prelim (Accessed Mar 8, 2022).

35. FBI. (2019). *Uniform Crime Reporting (UCR) Program*. Federal Bureau of Investigations. https://ucr.fbi.gov/crime-in-the-u.s/2019/crime-in-the-u.s.-2019/topic-pages/persons-arrested (Accessed Dec 21, 2021).

36. USSC. (2017). *Mandatory minimum penalties for dreug offenses in the federal system.* United States Sentencing Commission. https://www.ussc.gov/research/research-reports/mandatory-minimum-penalties-drug-offenses-federal-system (Accessed Dec 21, 2021).

37. USC. (2008). *42 U.S. Code § 12210 – Illegal use of drugs*, in *42 – The Public Health and Welfare*. United States Congress. https://uscode.house.gov/view.xhtml?req=granuleid:USC-prelim-title42-section12210&num=0&edition=prelim (Accessed Dec 22, 2021).

38. Rengert, G. F. (2018). *The geography of illegal drugs.* Routledge.

39. USC. (2021). *21 U.S. Code § 841 – Prohibited acts A* in *21 - Food and Drugs.* United States Congress. https://www.govregs.com/uscode/title21_chapter13_subchapterI_partD_section841 (Accessed Dec 22, 2021).

40. Kilmer, B., et al. (2014). *How big is the u.s. market for illegal drugs?* (pp. 1–4). RAND Corporation.

41. Seddon, T. (2020). Markets, regulation and drug law reform: towards a constitutive approach. *Social & Legal Studies*, *29*(3), 313–333.

42. Moeller, K., & Sandberg, (2019). Putting a price on drugs: An economic sociological study of price formation in illegal drug markets. *Criminology*, *57*(2), 289–313.

43. Caulkins, J. P., &Reuter, P. (1998). What price data tell us about drug markets. *Journal of Drug Issues*, *28*(3), 593–612.

44. Torres, C.E., D'Alessio, S. J., & Stolzenberg, L. (2021). Market dynamics and systemic violence: A longitudinal examination of market penetration, entry deterrence, and excess capacity in the illicit drug market. *Journal of Drug Issues*, *51*(1), 143–158.

45. Barnum, J.D., et al. (2017). Examining the environmental characteristics of drug dealing locations. *Crime & Delinquency*, *63*(13), 1731–1756.

46. Midgette, G., et al. (2019). *What America's users spend on illegal drugs, 2006–2016* (p. 95). RAND Corporation.

47. DOJ. (2019). *Federal Bureau of Prison (BOP) system, FY 2019 budget request for BOP* (p. 4). Department of Justice. https://www.justice.gov/jmd/page/file/1033161/download (Accessed Dec 22, 2021).

48. Woosley, R. L. (2013). One hundred years of drug regulation: where do we go from here? *Annual Review of Pharmacology and Toxicology, 53,* 255–273.

49. FDA. (2007). *Milestones of Drug Regulation in the United States.* Food and Drug Administration. https://www.fda.gov/media/109482/download (Accessed Dec 23, 2021).

50. USP. (2021). *United States Pharmacopoeia.* United States Pharmacopeia. https://www.usp.org/.

51. Lederer, E. (1916). The Harrison Narcotic Act. *The Journal of the American Pharmaceutical Association, 5*(7), 720–723.

52. Terry, C.E. (1915). *The Harrison Anti-Narcotic Act. American Journal of Public Health, 5*(6), 518.

53. Ballentine, C. (1981). Taste of raspberries, taste of death: the 1937 elixir sulfanilamide incident. *FDA Consumer Magazine, 15*(5), 1–4.

54. Black, H.L. (1948). *U.S. Reports: United States v. Sullivan,* in *332 U.S. 689* (pp. 689–707). U.S. Supreme Court, Editor. https://www.loc.gov/item/usrep332689/ (Accessed Dec 28, 2021): [Periodical] Retrieved from the Library of Congress.

55. USC. (1940). *United States Code: Federal Food, Drug, and Cosmetic Act,* in § 331. Prohibited acts (pp. 99–100). https://www.loc.gov/item/uscode1940-005021009/ (Accessed Dec 28, 2021): [Periodical] Retrieved from the Library of Congress.

56. Hamburg, M. A. (2010). Innovation, regulation, and the FDA. *New England Journal of Medicine, 363*(23), 2228–2232.

57. CRS. (2021). *The Controlled Substances Act (CSA): A Legal Overview for the 117th Congress, Updated February 5, 2021.* Congressional Research Service: https://crsreports.congress.gov/product/pdf/R/R45948 (Accessed Dec 28, 2021).

58. USC. (1988). *Prescription Drug Marketing Act.* US Congress: https://uscode.house.gov/statutes/pl/100/293.pdf (Accessed Dec 31, 2021).

59. FDA. (2011). *Advancing Regulatory Science at FDA: A Strategic Plan* (pp. 1–37). U.S.D.o.H.H. Services, Editor. Food and Drug Administration: Washington, DC.

60. Richmond, F. J., & Church, T. D. (2020). Graduate training capacity for regulatory professionals at US universities: Are we facing a talent crisis? *Therapeutic Innovation & Regulatory Science, https://doi.org/10.1007/s43441-020-00111-9 [Accessed Jan 10, 2020],* 1-6.

61. Collins, F. S. (2015). Exceptional opportunities in medical science: A view from the National Institutes of Health. *The Journal of the American Medical Association, 313*(2), 131–132.

62. SAMHSA. (2019). *Strategic Plan FY2019–FY2023* (pp. 1–38). Substance Abuse and Mental Health Services Administration. https://www.samhsa.gov/sites/default/files/samhsa_strategic_plan_fy19-fy23_final-508.pdf (Accessed Dec 31, 2021).

63. IAS. (2021). *What is addiction science?* USC Institute for Addiction Science: https://ias.usc.edu/what-is-addiction-science/ (Accessed Dec 31, 2021).

Chapter 14

Warfare and Terror

" The supreme art of war is to subdue the enemy without fighting," Sun Tzu, *The Art of War[1]*. Humans have held a great penchant for war throughout our short sordid history. We have become adept at striking terror in the hearts and minds of peoples we wish to dominate and control. We have built machines and munitions capable of destroying our world. We have engineered common diseases into deadly and devastating plagues. In the modern era, we have harnessed biological, chemical, and atomic mechanisms to enforce our dominance and expand the boundaries of fear.

Terrorism, as defined by Homeland Security is the "unlawful use of force and violence against persons or property to intimidate or coerce a government, the civilian population, or any segment thereof, in furtherance of political or social objectives" [2]. There is a bit of ambiguity in this definition, however, as the term "terrorism" does not imply what form of weapon is being utilized to perpetrate the act of terrorism. Any device used with the intent to inflict damage or harm to living creatures, structures, or systems is, by definition, a *weapon*. Weapons are used to increase the efficacy and efficiency of a variety of human activities—hunting, crime, law enforcement, self-defense, and warfare. Threats from terrorism are typically broken down into one of four broad categories: (1) traditional weapons; (2) biological agents; (3) chemical agents; and (4) atomic weapons.

Broadly speaking, weapons include anything used to gain a strategic, material, or mental advantage over an adversary or enemy target. While ordinary objects like sticks, stones, cars, or even pencils could be used as weapons, when we talk about *traditional weapons*, we are discussing weapons that are expressly designed like clubs, swords, and guns [3]. Something that has been repurposed, converted, or enhanced to become a weapon of war is referred to as being *weaponized*, such as weaponized virus or weaponized lasers. Modern weapons are more complicated and include things like intercontinental ballistic missiles and biological and chemical weapons.

Conventional weapons are generally defined as weapons in relatively wide use but are not capable of being used for mass destruction. *Weapons of mass destruction* include nuclear, biological, and chemical weapons as these can kill and bring significant harm to many people in a singular event. Conventional weapons would be any armament used in domestic and transnational crimes, conflicts, wars, and frequently are subject to human rights violations. Conventional weapons include small arms and light weapons, plus grenades and sea/land mines. These weapons are deployed primarily for their explosive, kinetic, or incendiary potential.

Throughout history, a wide range of substances, from toxic plants and venomous insects and reptiles to infectious agents and noxious chemicals, have been weaponized across civilizations from all geographic locations. Humans have increasingly become more deadly with the implements we create for war. *Biological weapons* are perhaps among the earliest weapons of terror humans learned to harness. This form of weapons employs viable, living organisms, such as pathogens, venoms, and toxic plants, insects, or animals. *Chemical weapons* take a little bit more sophistication and knowledge to exploit and get to work well. This form of weapons utilizes poisonous gases, dust, or smoke and incendiary materials to burn, blind, choke, or asphyxiate. Chemical weapons in the modern age are predominately synthetic and man-made chemicals that can be mass produced.

Some of our most venerated mythologies and legends reflect the early invention of biological weaponry in ancient cultures and represent the actual practice of biological warfare. Greek mythology provides us with the tales of Hercules, the Achaeans, and Odysseus. Hercules, upon defeating the Lernean Hydra, slit open the corpse and dipped his arrows in the venomous blood, gifting him with a never-ending supply of envenomed arrows. In the Iliad, Homer regales us with tales of the Trojan War, where in the Achaeans used toxic projectiles against the Trojans [4]. The wounds inflicted by these projectiles were described as oozing black blood that never congealed nor healed (indicative of viper venom). In the Telegony, Odysseus is killed by his son Telegonus with a spear that had been tipped with the toxic spine of a stingray [5]. From Roman mythology in the Aeneid, Virgil recounts the use of poisoned spears wielded by the early Romans while defending Rome from invasion [6]. In the Vedic classic, Rigveda, the god Indra uses poisoned arrows and spears to defeat his enemies [7].

Chemical, biological, radiological, or nuclear weapons have been utilized by humans for centuries in warfare. More recent examples of their uses include waging war (World War I, World War II, and the Iran-Iraq War); ethnic conflict (chemical weapon use in Syria); terrorism (release of sarin gas in the Tokyo subway, Post 9-11 anthrax via USPS); and political assassination (former Soviet spies attacked with ricin and polonium-210). At the heart of these forms of warfare are the agents. Biological, chemical, and nuclear weapons employ a variety of agents. Many of the modern agents are solely designed for use as weapons, with very limited alternative utilities. The effects of the agents depend on a host of characteristics including delivery method, immune response, physical protections, and ability to treat. In terms of human casualties, the key features of an agent include its classification and effect from contact/interaction with the agent. Broadly speaking, *agents* represent biologic, chemical, or radiological / nuclear entities used for the purposes of war or terrorism. *Biologic agents* include bacteria, fungi, toxins, or viruses. *Chemical agents* include incapacitating or lethal agents. *Radiologic / nuclear agents* refer to ionizing or nonionizing radiation. There can be a wide variety of physical properties across classes of agents. These properties determine the optimal delivery system, route of exposure, and persistency in the environment. In modern use, the physical properties of an agent determine the best method for delivery (Figure 14.1). Biologic, chemical, and radiologic/nuclear agents cause one or more of four effects from exposure (Table 14.1).

In addition to physical damage, biologic, chemical, and radiologic/nuclear agents can cause a host of psychological effects. The presentation of the psychological effects may be appropriate to a given hazard (acute stress reaction, for example) or they could enhance the response to an incident. The majority, though, tend to cause mental incapacitation ranging from anxiety to psychosis or delirium.

Figure 14.1   Agent Delivery Method

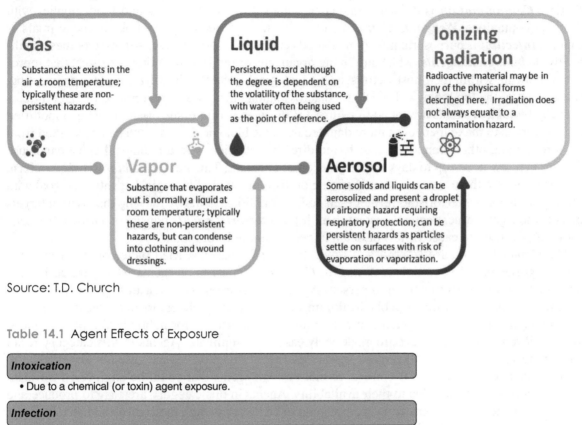

Source: T.D. Church

Table 14.1 Agent Effects of Exposure

Intoxication
• Due to a chemical (or toxin) agent exposure.

Infection
• Due to a live biological agent exposure.

Irradiation
• Due to ionizing radiation agent exposure.

Injuries
• Due to exposure to trauma or physical degradation from any agent.

Source: T.D. Church

The psychological effects can occur any time including real time response during a hazardous event or much later as post-traumatic stress disorder (PTSD). Warfare and terrorism employing biological, chemical, and radiologic/nuclear agents will have profound effects on the victim as well as the soldier tasked with unleashing them.

14.1   Biological Agents

From ancient to modern times, biological agents have been used with increasing lethality in warfare and terrorist acts. Biological weapons have been employed by humans since prehistoric times and have been honed into three distinct categories of armaments—contamination, weaponization, and infection. *Contamination* is the deliberate contamination of water sources and food supplies with poisons or contagions. *Weaponization* is the use of toxins and microbes from plants and animals as weapons. *Infection* is purposeful infection of goods and people with disease. All three of these methods rely on *biological agents*, which are living organisms or replicating entities (viruses) that reproduce or replicate within their host victims; or is a biological entity that is utilized for its venom, sting, or bite. A list of the top biological agents used across human history are highlighted in Table 14.2.

Many biological agents are found in nature, yet the agents used in terrorism have been modified by the terrorists to make them even more dangerous. Some biological agents can be transmitted from person to person, others cannot be transferred directly. Infection with a biological agent can cause infection in a few hours up to days before it becomes apparent. This has led to *bioterrorism*, a form of terrorism where there is an intentional release or dissemination of biological agents. The goal with bioterrorism is for the terrorist to further their social or political goals by making the civilian targets feel as if their government cannot protect them [8]. *Bioterrorist agents* consist of viruses, bacteria, or other germs used to cause illness or death in people, animals, or plants.

The Center for Disease Control and Prevention (CDC) has classified bioterrorism agents into three categories based upon potential hazard. *Category A* consists of agents which are easily disbursed or transmitted from person to person. Agents in this category result in high mortality rates and have the potential for major public health impacts. Category A bioterrorism agents may result in public panic and societal disruption and will require special actions for public health preparedness. *Category B* represent agents that are moderately easy to disseminate. Agents in this category result in moderate mortality and will require specific enhanced diagnostics and disease surveillance to curtail transmission. *Category C* consists of bioterrorism agents that could be engineered for mass dissemination in the future due to their availability. Agents in this category are easy to produce and disseminate. Category C agents carry the potential to be linked to high morbidity and mortality rates and represent massive public health impacts.

It has been estimated that ~80% of bioterrorism agents are zoonotic in origin and can be harnessed as biological weapons. *Zoonotic* refers to infections that can be naturally transmitted between animals and humans, ranging from mild to serious illness and even death. Ebola, HIV, and most strains of influenza are *zoonoses*. Zoonoses (plural form of zoonosis) are diseases spread from animals (typically vertebrates) to a human host. Zoonoses require a minimum interaction across three species, one pathogen and two host species, with people and another animal species acting as the reservoir for the infection.

Zoonotic agents are classified according to the characteristics that define hazard to health and are rated according to infectivity, pathogenicity, transmissibility, and ability to neutralize. *Infectivity* is the aptitude of an agent to penetrate and multiply in the host. *Pathogenicity* refers to the ability of the agent to cause a disease after penetrating the body. *Transmissibility* represents the ability of the agent to be transmitted from an infected individual to a healthy one. And *ability to neutralize* relates to preventive tools used to diagnose the infection and therapeutic means to render the infection innocuous. It is a delicate balance, if the pathogen enters the host and is initially mild in severity, it will go unnoticed because the infected individual is less likely to seek medical attention. When the pathogen is severe causing immediate life-threatening symptomology and potential death, it triggers an aggressive public health response with the intent to suppress and contain the outbreak. From the

Table 14.2 Most Frequently Used Biological Agents Throughout History

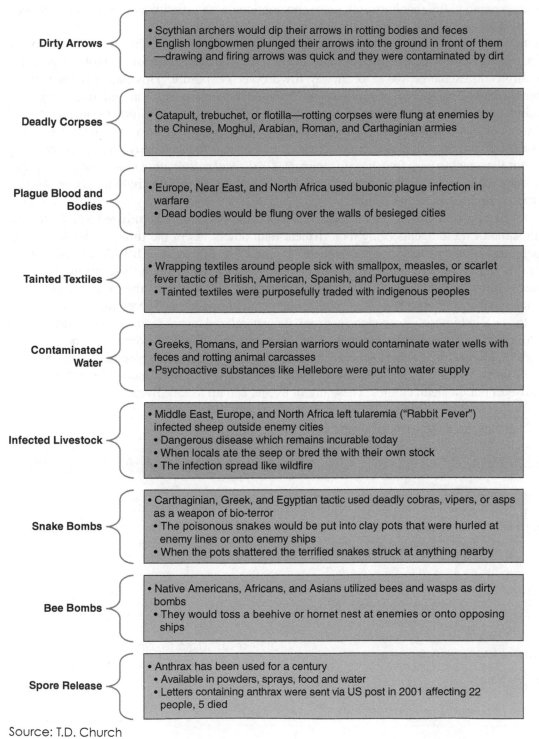

Dirty Arrows
- Scythian archers would dip their arrows in rotting bodies and feces
- English longbowmen plunged their arrows into the ground in front of them —drawing and firing arrows was quick and they were contaminated by dirt

Deadly Corpses
- Catapult, trebuchet, or flotilla—rotting corpses were flung at enemies by the Chinese, Moghul, Arabian, Roman, and Carthaginian armies

Plague Blood and Bodies
- Europe, Near East, and North Africa used bubonic plague infection in warfare
- Dead bodies would be flung over the walls of besieged cities

Tainted Textiles
- Wrapping textiles around people sick with smallpox, measles, or scarlet fever tactic of British, American, Spanish, and Portuguese empires
- Tainted textiles were purposefully traded with indigenous peoples

Contaminated Water
- Greeks, Romans, and Persian warriors would contaminate water wells with feces and rotting animal carcasses
- Psychoactive substances like Hellebore were put into water supply

Infected Livestock
- Middle East, Europe, and North Africa left tularemia ("Rabbit Fever") infected sheep outside enemy cities
- Dangerous disease which remains incurable today
- When locals ate the seep or bred the with their own stock
- The infection spread like wildfire

Snake Bombs
- Carthaginian, Greek, and Egyptian tactic used deadly cobras, vipers, or asps as a weapon of bio-terror
- The poisonous snakes would be put into clay pots that were hurled at enemy lines or onto enemy ships
- When the pots shattered the terrified snakes struck at anything nearby

Bee Bombs
- Native Americans, Africans, and Asians utilized bees and wasps as dirty bombs
- They would toss a beehive or hornet nest at enemies or onto opposing ships

Spore Release
- Anthrax has been used for a century
- Available in powders, sprays, food and water
- Letters containing anthrax were sent via US post in 2001 affecting 22 people, 5 died

Source: T.D. Church

pathogens point of view, it will be maximizing evolutionary fitness if the pathogen is able to enter a host, replicate, spread to another host with ease, and continue with little impediment. The pathogen loses fitness if it is unable to replicate in the host or transmit to a new host [9].

In general, biological agents are transmitted through one or more routes. The transmission routes consist of parenteral, contact exposure, and oral-fecal routes. *Parenteral* transmits biological agents through bodily fluid exchange, blood, or airway (by droplets) exposure. This transmission method requires that the biological agents get emitted by an infected individual, which are inhaled or ingested by surrounding people. *Contact exposure* is the method where agents are transmitted from an infected individual to a surface and the agent then can be transmitted to another host. A door handle, sink faucet, elevator call button, cell phone, or any other myriad objects touched daily act as the conveying mechanism for the agent to pass from host to recipient. *Oral-fecal routes* allows an agent to be spread through objects, foods, or other items contaminated with the feces of infected individuals, or through sexual contact with an infected individual.

In the modern context, any germ, bacteria, or virus could potentially be utilized as a biological agent. With some of these agents being mor virulent than others. As of the time this book is being written, there are ~30 agents deemed "of concern" by the CDC (Table 14.3)[10]. These agents have been given this ranking based on their availability and the ease with which these agents could be disseminated within a population. It is almost impossible to memorize all the details about these potential biological agents and how they would interact within a host. Therefore, it is crucial to understand the risk of bioterrorism and the appropriate generalized response to a terrorist attack until public health officials can provide information on what citizens should be doing. In general, at the first evidence of a bioterrorist attack, get away from large groups of people, cover the mouth and nose with layers of fabric to filter air, and wash your body with soap and water. Upon exiting the shower, it is imperative to put on clean clothes. These minor events add up to save lives.

Table 14.3 Biological Agents of Concern

Biological Agent	Disease Caused by Agent
Bacillus anthracis	Anthrax
Clostridium botulinum toxin	Botulism
Yersinia pestis	Plague
Variola major	Smallpox
Francisella tularensis	Tularemia
Filoviruses (Ebola, Marburg) and Arenaviruses (Lassa, Machupo)	Viral hemorrhagic fevers
Brucella species	Brucellosis
Epsilon toxin of Clostridium perfringens	Food poisoning

Chapter 14 Warfare and Terror **345**

Biological Agent	Disease Caused by Agent
Salmonella	Food poisoning
Burkholderia mallei	Glanders
Burkholderia pseudomallei	Melioidosis
Chlamydia psittaci	Psittacosis
Coxiella burnetii	Q fever
Ricinus communis (castor beans)	Ricin toxin poisoning
Staphylococcal enterotoxin B	Food poisoning
Rickettsia prowazekii	Epidemic Typhus
Influenza Virus	Influenza
Mycobacterium tuberculosis	Multi-drug resistant TB and Extensively drug resistant TB

Source: CDC.gov

An example of bioterrorism occurred after the terrorist attacks on 9/14 in the United States, when anthrax spores were mailed to key offices and high-level targets via the USPS (Figure 14.2). This resulted in 22 people, including 12 mail handlers, becoming exposed to anthrax. Out of which, five people died with the remaining 17 becoming seriously ill [11]. The prime suspect in the politically motivated bioterrorist attack, Bruce Edwards Ivins, committed suicide in 2008. **Anthrax** is an infection caused by the bacterium Bacillus anthracis. Anthrax bacteria is spread either through animal contact or via spores in the air or soil. Upon entering a living creature, anthrax produces powerful exotoxins. Anthrax exotoxins are composed of a cell-binding protein, known as protective antigen (PA), and two enzyme components, called edema factor (EF) and lethal factor (LF). These three protein components act together to impart their physiological effects often to lethal ends [12]. Anthrax-induced death is typically sudden, with dark, non-clotting blood that oozes from body orifices. Anthrax infection can occur from four mechanisms—skin infection, lung, intestinal, and injection.

Figure 14.2   Anthrax

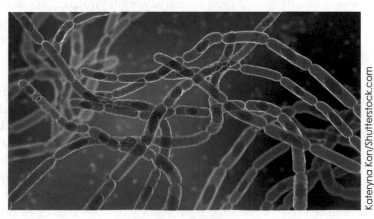

Kateryna Kon/Shutterstock.com

Skin infections represent 95% of all human cases and carries a risk of death ~24%. Intestinal infections have a risk of death between 25% and 75%. Respiratory anthrax of the lungs from the inhalation of anthrax spores presents with a death rate between 50% and 80%. The deadliest form, injectable anthrax, is also the least likely for mass distribution due to route of administration, carries a death rate between 75% and 99%.

Ebola has the potential to be weaponized for use in biological warfare (Figure 14.3), a fact that was made all too apparent in 2015 when North Korea suggested they had the capability to distribute a large amount of Ebola into the United States [13, 14]. Ebola carries a considerable risk of death, killing 25–90% of those infected, with an average kill rate of 65%. The risk of death is most often due to low blood pressure from loss of fluids and typically manifests 6–16 days after the first symptoms appear. ***Ebola Hemorrhagic Fever*** is a viral hemorrhagic fever caused by ebolavirus. Symptoms occur between 2 days

Figure 14.3   Ebola

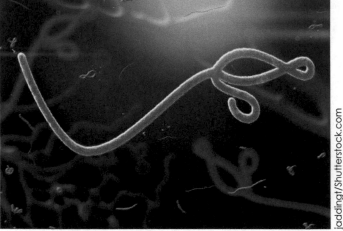

jaddingt/Shutterstock.com

and 3 weeks post exposure to the virus. Symptomology includes fever, sore throat, muscle pain, and severe headaches. The initial symptomology proceeds to vomiting, diarrhea, rash, decreased function of the liver and kidneys. Some people will begin to bleed both internally and externally as their organs exsanguinate.

Biological warfare, aka ***germ warfare***, is the use of biological toxins or infectious agents such as bacteria, viruses, insects, and/or fungi with the intent to kill, harm, or incapacitate humans, livestock, or agriculture as an act of war. This is done through the use and dispersal of biological weapons. In the modern era, biological warfare is focused on three distinct applications. The first is ***anti-personnel*** or the use of biological agents as weapons against humans. In this application, the biological weapon would ideally have a high infectivity, high virulence, no available vaccines, and must have an availability of an effective and efficient delivery system. The second is ***anti-agricultural*** which uses plant diseases to destroy or decimate enemy agricultural and commercial aquacultural resources. This application would bring with it massive disruption of plant-based food sources for both humans and livestock. The final application is ***anti-livestock*** where zoonotic diseases are delivered to disrupt or destroy livestock or to introduce diseases that will spread to the human population through animal contact. Diseases in this application include foot-and-mouth disease, bovine encephalitis, rinderpest, African swine flu, Asian bird flu, and psittacosis in chicken. Biological warfare carries with it a high potential for the loss of life and an underlying psychological component which will erode trust and faith between citizen and government.

In 1975, twenty-two member nations of the United Nations (UN) agreed to prohibit the development, production, and stockpiling of biological and toxin-based weapons. As of November 2021, 183 countries have signed the agreement [15]. The articles of the Biological Weapons Convention state that each nation party to the convention will undertake to never, under any circumstances, to develop, produce, stockpile, or otherwise retain:

1. Microbial or other biological agents, or toxins whatever their origin or method of production, of types and in quantities that have no justification for prophylactic, protective, or other peaceful purposes.
2. Weapons, equipment, or means of delivery designed to use such agents or toxins for hostile purposes or in armed conflict [15].

It is not the biological agents or toxins themselves which have been sanctioned, instead it is the purposes for which the agent could be employed that are prohibited. This allows researchers to continue to work with these biological agents and toxins to hopefully find curative or preventative measures should they be utilized for terror or war.

14.2   Chemical Agents

Chemical agents are—part and parcel—cheap, accessible, and relatively easy to transport. ***Chemical agents*** represent poisonous vapors, aerosols, liquids, or solids that have toxic effects on individuals. These chemicals can be naturally occurring in the environment or synthetically manufactured in a lab. Release of chemicals can be unintentional as in the case of an industrial accident, an example could be a railway tanker full of chlorine that is accidently derailed and releases a cloud of chlorine gas upon impact. Release of chemicals can be intentional as in the case of a terrorist attack, an example would be the 1995 use of sarin gas in the Tokyo subway system.

Chemical warfare involves using the toxic properties of chemical substances as weapons. This includes the offensive use of living organisms in biological warfare as well as the use of nonliving toxic products produced by living organisms (toxins such as botulinum, ricin, and saxitoxin) would be considered chemical warfare (Figure 14.4). When thinking about chemical weapons, it is important to keep in mind that these types of weapons can be divided into two main types of weapons, based on their intended action. ***Lethal agents*** are those chemical capable of causing death. ***Incapacitating agents*** are chemical agents that produce temporary physiological or mental effects, or both, which render an individual incapable of concerted effort in the performance of normal activities. Lethal chemical agents are divided into six categories related to their area of effect (Table 14.4).

Figure 14.4   Tear Gas in Public.

bgrocker/Shutterstock.com

Table 14.4 Lethal Chemical Agent

Blood Agent

- Toxic chemical agents that affect the body by being absorbed into the blood; these are fast-acting, potentially lethal toxins; either cyanide-or arsenic-based.

Blister Agent (Vesicant)

- Chemical compounds that cause severe skin, eye, and mucosal pain and irritation; name for their ability to cause severe chemical burns, resulting in painful water blisters on the bodies of those affected; mustard gas is a classic example.

Nerve Agent (Nerve Gas)

- Class of organic chemicals that disrupts the mechanisms by which nerves transfer messages to organs; poisoning by nerve agent leads to constriction of pupils, profuse salivation, convulsions, and involuntary urination / defecation; death by asphyxiation or cardiac arrest occurs in minutes after exposure; Sarin is perhaps the best known.

Nettle Agent (Urticants)

- Variety of chemical warfare that produce corrosive skin and tissue injury upon contact, resulting in erythema, urticaria, intense itching, and a hive-like rash.

Pulmonary Agent (Choking Agent)

- Agents designed to impede a victim's ability to breathe; operate by causing a build-up of fluids in the lungs, which leads to suffocation; inhalation of these agents cause burning of the throat, coughing, vomiting, headache, pain in chest, and respiratory & circulatory failure; chlorine gas is perhaps the most common.

VomitingAgent

- Chemicals that cause vomiting; prolonged exposure can be lethal.

Source: T.D. Church

Incapacitating chemical agents typically have transient effects that tend to cause temporary physiological or mental effects. A common incapacitating agent is pepper spray used for personal protection. Incapacitating chemical agents are primarily used for defense or riot control. Agents in this category are incapacitating because they may cause temporary loss of vision, produce mucous membrane irritation, diarrhea, or even hyperthermia. The most common forms of incapacitating agents include tear gas, sleeping gas, pepper spray, and mace. There are five ways of attacking with fire. The first is to burn soldiers in their camp; the second is to burn their stores; the third is to burn baggage-trains; the fourth is to burn arsenals and magazines; the fifth is to hurl dropping fire amongst the enemy. Sun Tzu [1].

Some of the earliest surviving reference to chemical warfare appear in the Indian epics *Ramayana* and *Mahabharata*. These epics contain recipes for creating poison weapons, toxic smokes, and chemical weapons. Alexander the Great brought incendiary fire arrows and bombs back with him from his journey to the Indus basin. Arsenical smokes and phosphorous firebombs are referenced in Sun Tzu's *Art of War*, wherein he advises on the use of fire (quote above) and chemical weapons. During the Peloponnesian War, Spartan forces besieged an Athenian city and placed a mixture of wood, pitch, and sulfur under the city walls, when lit, the noxious smoke incapacitated the Athenians. A similar tactic was used during the Roman-Persian wars, where a mixture of bitumen and sulfur crystals were ignited producing sulfur dioxide which killed many of the Roman soldiers. Taino people used gourds filled with ashes and ground hot peppers to create a blinding smoke before they attacked Spanish Conquistadors. Leonardo da Vinci created a powder of sulfide, arsenic, and verdigris that when inhaled by the enemy would cause asphyxiation [16, 17].

Our modern notion of chemical warfare emerged in the mid-nineteenth century. Through the development of modern chemistry and associated industries a variety of new materials were made available through industrial processes—synthetics, surfactants, dyes, pigments, turpentine, resins, carbon, explosives, phosphates, ammonia, acids, titanium dioxide, and hydrogen peroxide, to name a few. One of the first proposals for industrialized chemicals being deployed for warfare was made by Lyon Playfair, British Secretary of the Science and Art Department in the 1850s during the Crimean War. Playfair proposed a cacodyl cyanide artillery shell for use against enemy ships and an end to blockades that were keeping British ships from resupplying ports along the Black Sea. Cacodyl cyanide is extremely toxic and produces symptoms of both cyanide and arsenic poisoning. It is highly explosive and creates a very potent lachrymatory agent (induces tears). After deliberation, the use of cacodyl cyanide was denied use by the British Ordnance Department as being far too dangerous.

Near the end of the American Civil War, John Doughty, a New York schoolteacher proposed the offensive use of chlorine gas artillery shells. The concept was to fill empty artillery shells with ~3 quarts of liquid chlorine. Upon impact these shells would be capable of generating a chlorine gas cloud between 2,000 and 3,000 feet. When liquid chlorine is released, it quickly forms a gas that stays close to the ground and spreads rapidly. The gas is not flammable, but it can react explosively in the presence of other chemicals like turpentine or ammonia. As chlorine gas encounters moist tissues such as the eyes, throat, and lungs, an acid reaction is produced that chemically burns these tissues. It is a potent pulmonary agent and leads to asphyxia. The Chief of Union Ordnance denied use of the chlorine gas artillery shell due to ethical and logistical concerns. Namely blow back from the chlorine gas shell as there was no way to control the direction of the wind, and a sufficient wind gust would make the weapon dangerous for their own troops.

In 1899, world leaders and representatives from 26 governments met for an International Peace Conference to negotiate modern warfare and codes for conducting warfare at The Hague. The conference was among the first formal discussions regarding the laws of war and war crimes. It marked the first formal attempt at international law to curtail the use of technology in manufacturing implements of war. Among the key negotiations was the generation of the Declaration Concerning Expanding Bullets. It was a treaty aimed at prohibiting technical specifications about weapons systems, namely, the construction of bullets. The resulting conference led to the writing of three main treaties and three additional declarations (Table 14.5).

Table 14.5 Treaties and Declarations of the Hague Convention of 1899

	Treaty/Declaration	Signatories
Main Treaties	Convention for the Pacific Settlement of International Disputes	All 26 signatories—Germany, Austria-Hungary, Belgium, China, Denmark, Spain, United States, Mexico, France, United Kingdom, Greece, Italy, Japan, Luxembourg, Montenegro, Netherlands, Persia, Portugal, Romania, Russia, Serbia, Siam, Sweden and Norway, Switzerland, Ottoman Empire, and Bulgaria
	Convention with respect to the Laws and Customs of War on Land	Signatories from all nations above, except China.
Supplemental Declarations	Convention for the Adaptation to Maritime Warfare of the Principles of the Geneva Convention	Signatories from all nations above.
	Declaration concerning the Prohibition of the Discharge of Projectiles and Explosives from Balloons or by Other New Analogous Methods	Signatories from all nations above, except United Kingdom and United States.
	Declaration concerning the Prohibition of the Use of Projectiles with the Sole Object to Spread Asphyxiating Poisonous Gases	Signatories from all nations above, except United States.
	Declaration concerning the Prohibition of the Use of Bullets which can Easily Expand or Change their Form inside the Human Body such as Bullets with a Hard Covering which does not Completely Cover the Core, or containing Indentations	Signatories from all nations above, except United States.

Source: United Nations

In dissenting across all of the supplemental declarations, U.S. Naval Captain Alfred Thayer Mahan, justified for voting against the measures by stating, "the inventiveness of Americans should not be restricted in the development of new weapons"[16]. Internationally, The Hague Declaration of 1899 and subsequent the Hague Convention of 1907 forbade the use of poison or poisoned weapons in warfare.

The Hague Convention appeared to be working, but only 7 years later in 1914, World War I (WWI) erupted. Over the four-year period of WWI, it has been estimated that more than 124,000 cubic tons of chemical agents were produced. Of which ~51,000 tons of pulmonary, lachrymatory, and vesicant agents were deployed by both sides of the conflict. An estimated 1.3 million causalities have been attributed to chemical warfare, with ~260,000 civilian death. In 1939, World War II (WWII) embroiled the world in war. Chemical warfare with aerosolized gases was revolutionized by Nazi Germany, who expanded research and development and in 1937 had invented Tabun gas and in 1939 had refined Sarin gas. Imperial Japan used ~1,000,000 tons of mustard gas in campaigns throughout Southeast Asia. Hydrogen cyanide and carbon monoxide gases were responsible for 90% of the ~6 million Jews killed by Nazi Germany. The lofty ideals espoused in the Hague Declaration and the Hague Conventions were not upheld by the signatories through the course of both World Wars.

One of the most terrifying chemical weapons used on the battlefields of WWII was white phosphorous munitions (Figure 14.5). ***White phosphorus munitions*** are weapons which are self-igniting and can burn upwards of 4,800°F. White phosphorus is a waxy solid, that burns easily and is employed for its unique smoke, illumination, and incendiary attributes. White phosphorus ignites upon encountering oxygen, producing exceptionally high-temperature heat and characteristic opaque white smoke. Munitions with the chemical have been used as incendiary weapons, to lay down smoke screens, or as signal markers for aircraft. White phosphorus munitions cause injuries through two mechanisms—incendiary and inhalation. ***Incendiary*** mechanisms are related to the electromagnetic radiation from the exothermic chemical reaction of phosphorus with oxygen in the air cause extreme thermal reactions, these can lead to immediate Second-, Third-, and Fourth-degree burns. Phosphorous is absorbed into the body through the burned area and can cause liver, heart, and kidney, damage or lead to multiple organ failures. ***Inhalation*** produces a unique set of outcomes. White phosphorous creates thick clouds of phosphorous pentoxide when it meets oxygen in the air. Phosphorous pentoxide is typically harmless, but does cause temporary irritation to the eyes, mucous membranes, and respiratory track. Large concentrations can cause permanent respiratory damage and asphyxiation. White phosphorous munitions were feared by both sides within the conflict.

Figure 14.5 WWII White Phosphorous Bomb

Everett Collection/Shutterstock.com

The Vietnam War (1961–1971) saw the ubiquitous use of Agent Orange by the U.S. forces. ***Agent Orange*** is an herbicide and defoliant chemical containing traces of dioxin (mainly TCDD) and was used tactically during the war (Figure 14.6). Agent Orange's primary use was to defoliate the jungles of Vietnam. The hope of the U.S. Armed Forces was that by exploiting the ability of the chemicals to kill off foliage they could eliminate the Viet Kong's ability to use the jungle to their opportunity. ***TCCD*** (tetrachlorodibenzo-p-dioxin) is the most potent form of dioxin. The fat-soluble nature of TCDD causes it to enter the body easily through physical contact or ingestion. It is classified as a human carcinogen because it attaches to proteins in cells, where it moves to the nucleus and influences gene expression. TCCD causes serious genetic deformities, including—cleft palate, mental disabilities, hernias, extra fingers & toes, deformed limbs, skin disease, and a variety of cancers in the lungs, larynx, and prostate[18]. Estimates indicate nearly 3 million people were infected with TCDD through Agent Orange spraying by the U.S. military during the course of the Vietnam War.

The prior two examples showed chemicals being utilized under the guise of war. Chemical weapons can also be used for terrorism. In 1995, members of Aum Shinrikyo—a Japanese Doomsday Cult obsessed with worldwide apocalypse—detonated several packages of sarin gas in the Tokyo subway system, killing 12 people and injuring over 5,000. *Sarin* is a synthetically engineered chemical nerve agent (Figure 14.7). Of all the nerve agents, sarin is the most toxic and rapidly acting of the known chemical warfare agents. Typically, sarin is a clear, colorless, and tasteless liquid that has no odor in its pure form. It evaporates into a vapor when in contact with oxygen and rapidly diffuses into the environment. Symptoms will appear within a few seconds after exposure to the vapor. Sarin causes its toxic effects by preventing the proper operation of an enzyme that acts as the body's "off switch" for neuromuscular junctions within glands and muscles[19, 20]. This enzyme deactivates the nerve signaling molecule acetylcholine. Without an "off switch," the glands and muscles are constantly being stimulated and induced to flex or fire. People who are exposed to sarin typically experience full body seizures and exhibit pinpoint pupils. Exposed people may become tired from the physical exertion of every muscle contracting repeatedly and are no longer be able to keep breathing. It causes suffocation from respiratory paralysis.

The *Chemical Weapons Convention* was signed into being 1997 with 193 State Parties approving the UN treaty [21]. Under this international convention, any toxic chemical, regardless of its origin, is considered a chemical weapon unless it is used for purposes that are not prohibited. As of 2000, 70 different chemicals have been identified as chemical warfare agents and their use and stockpiling has been banned[21]. Under the convention,

Figure 14.6   Agent Orange Dispersal

Everett Collection/Shutterstock.com

Figure 14.7   Tokyo Sarin Gas

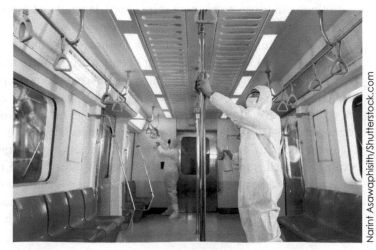

Narint Asawaphisith/Shutterstock.com

chemicals toxic enough to be used as chemical weapons or that may be used to manufacture such chemicals have been divided into three scheduled categories of concern. *Schedule 1* are chemicals with few legitimate uses. These chemicals may only be produced or used for research, medical, pharmaceutical, or protective purposes (ergo: chemical weapons sensors). An example of a Schedule 1 chemical would be nerve agents. *Schedule 2* are chemicals which have no large-scale industrial uses but may have legitimate small-scale uses. Examples of Schedule 2 chemicals would include dimethyl methylphosphonate, a precursor to sarin but also used as a flame retardant. *Schedule 3* chemicals have legitimate large-scale industrial uses. Examples of Schedule 3 chemicals include phosgene and chloropicrin; both have been used as chemical weapons; phosgene is important in manufacturing plastics, and chloropicrin is a fumigant.

14.3   Atomic Agents

"Every thinking person fears nuclear war, and every technological state plans for it. Everyone knows it is madness, and every nation has an excuse" Carl Sagan once stated[22]. The development and use of nuclear weapons had a profound and notable impact on many aspects of American culture, including architectural design, the creation of cocktails, and the rise of lifestyle drugs. The Atomic Age spanned from the late 1940s through the mid-1960s and is characterized by references to nuclear science and reactions to the atomic bomb. It was during this time that the United States underwent a period of mass suburbanization. The construction and design aesthetic featured modern, sleek, and streamlined designs. Many of the homes and public structurers featured interior decorative elements inspired by the Atomic Age. Several themed cocktails became staples of the after work happy hour and home bar. A *Cocktail* is a mixed alcoholic drink, which are mixed either as one type of alcohol with juices—as soft drinks—or as multiple alcoholic drinks with juices, teas, or sodas. Some of the popular drinks from the atomic age included Rocket Man, Apricot Fission, Cognac Zoom, Ray Gun, and the Oppenheimer Martini. The latter was a recipe that was allegedly modified by the scientist when he was finally able to smuggle enough vermouth into the top-secret facilities, where he was working [23].

Tiki bars became the "emotional bomb shelters of the Atomic Age" [24]. *Tiki* represented a ginchy and fun bit of cultural ephemera that filtered into cocktails, stemware, and themed drinks that romanticized tropical cultures, typically Polynesian. Tiki capitalized on escapism as a means to overcome the stress of the cold war and suburban life. Tiki became popular due to the rise of suburban culture and the new middle-class who promoted a growing leisure culture in the United States. Popular tiki inspired cocktails dominated inside and outside the home, including Blue Hawaii, Cobra's Fang, Flying Saucer, Star Fire, Mai Tai, Rum Barrel, Scorpion, Test Pilot, and Zombie (Figure 14.8). Many of these

Figure 14.8 Tiki Cocktails

Brent Hofacker/Shutterstock.com

cocktails featured cocktail umbrellas, fancy swizzle sticks, flowers, and plastic animal toys to complete the tiki aesthetic.

Suburban life for women in the 1950s and 1960s saw the rise in *lifestyle drugs*. Unlike a drug one might take because they needed to cure a condition or to manage an illness, *lifestyle drugs* were drugs taken by choice because it might improve one's life, function, or appearance. Post-WWII there was an astounding development of new medicines—tranquilizers, new amphetamines, and barbiturates. Weight loss products were being sold containing amphetamines and ephedrine [25]. National marketing campaigns of these medicines increased their use and helped to make them somewhat normalized in society. There were social changes afoot in domestic America, in suburban homes the mass use of medicines and drugs became normalized and took hold. Many of the new stimulants, tranquilizers, and sedative medicines were unknowingly overprescribed and grossly misused. Amphetamines and barbiturates were called "mother's little helpers" as many women developed a habit for the stimulation and sedative effects of these medicines.

Amphetamines as a class of drug suppress appetite, increase alertness and stamina, and induce exhilaration. Paradoxically, they calm down people suffering from attention deficit and hyperactivity disorders (ADHD). Methamphetamine was produced under the brand name Methedrine by Burroughs Welcome and was among the earliest formulations of amphetamine. It was marketed as a dietary aid and with other amphetamines were advertised in journals aimed at prescribing doctors of the 1950s and 1960s. Methamphetamine, the drug that is ravaging LGBT communities worldwide, kept housewives slim in the 1950s and 1960s (Figure 14.9). It was originally sold as an injectable liquid and sold in the millions of milliliters. It gave rise to the Bay Area speed shooting scene of the early 1960s. Public demand for methamphetamine quickly led California to ban the drug at the state-level, which encouraged the first illegal meth labs to pop up in California in 1962 and 1963.

Figure 14.9 1950s Housewife

To cut the high housewives were experiencing, Valium became wildly popularized. *Valium (diazepam)* is a benzodiazepine used to treat anxiety, alcohol withdrawal, seizures, muscle spasms, and to provide sedation before medical procedures. Valium became known as "Mother's Little Helpers" because of its alleged ability to "help" or "treat" the pressures of motherhood and other womanly problems [26]. Leo Sternbach began tinkering with benzodiazepines, a relative obscure class of compounds, in the 1950s and 1960s. Over the course of the decade, he tested ~40 different formulations of benzos, but all formulations proved ineffective. In 1956, he added methylamine to one compound and the resulting white powder that was produced made his lab mice sleepy and calm. In 1963, the FDA approved Valium a name Sternbach borrowed from Latin, meaning to be strong and well"." Valium quickly became entrenched in the suburban household and was an afternoon delight of housewives looking to come down from their morning amphetamines.

The Atomic Age carried an underlying fear, the fear of atomic weapons. It was a fear that luckily would not be realized. In 1945, the United States used atomic weapons, and they were most powerful and devastating weapons ever invented. Nearly 200,000 civilians and military personnel died from injuries sustained from the explosions over the Japanese cities of Hiroshima and Nagasaki. *Atomic weapons* are explosive devices deriving their destructive force from nuclear reactions, either fission (fission bomb) or from a combination of fission and fusion reactions (thermonuclear bomb). Both bomb types release massive quantities of energy from relatively small amounts of matter. Both bombs devastate entire cities by blast, fire, and radiation effects. While the bomb attacks heralded the end of WWII they shepherded in the Cold War. The Cold War was a nuclear arms race between the United States and Soviet Union from 1950 to 1995. Each country and their allies continually attempted to out-develop each other in the field of nuclear armaments. This achieved only one goal, *mutually assured destruction*, which was the nuclear option of all-out war where there would no longer be a survivable scenario. It was calculated that the joint technological capabilities had reached a point where a nuclear war would ensure the destruction of the Earth ×100 fold [27].

Thermonuclear detonation typically occurs in the troposphere, where the energy released has the most devastating effect and occurs in four waves. In the map shown in Figure 9.12, the arrow is pointing to the University of Southern California in Los Angeles, where most of this book was written. The darkest circle represents the blast zone where between 40% and 50% of the total energy of the bomb would be disbursed. The blast zone would be a radius of ~2 mile/3.2 kilometer with complete destruction of everything. The thermal radiation zone would receive between 30% and 50% of the total energy of the bomb, the second circle extending out from the center. The thermal radiation zone would extend out to a radius of ~5 miles/8 kilometers and would feature severe to moderate damage. The ionizing radiation zone would represent ~5% of the total energy (slightly more in a neutron bomb) and would encompass the area from the center out to the third circle. The ionizing radiation zone would extend out to a radius of ~9 miles/14.4 kilometers and would witness moderate damage. The final zone, residual radiation *zone*, would extend out from the center to the last circle in the map. The residual radiation zone would contain ~5–10% of the total energy with the mass of the explosion and would continue to radiate the area for up to 50 years post detonation (Figure 14.10). The blast effect of the bomb is created by the coupling of immense amounts of energy, spanning the electromagnetic spectrum, with the surroundings. When an air burst occurs, lethal blast and thermal effects are more rapidly disbursed than lethal radiation effects. Wind, topography, and other features of weather and the environment will determine the area of effect.

One of the more devastating effects of the explosion is the resulting *firestorm*, the incendiary effects that accompany a nuclear explosion. The thermonuclear explosion initiates fires. Some of these fires will be blown out by the shock wave produce as the mushroom cloud rises and rapidly heats the air. Other fires that do not get blown out will attain such an intensity that they create and sustain their own wind systems. If a few of the firestorms combine, the resulting *massive firestorm* will heat the air and cause winds of hurricane strength (category 4) directed inward toward the fire. The heat and subsequent wind vortex work in tandem to super ventilate the firestorm and causes it to grow rapidly, unabated.

Figure 14.10 Representation of Thermonuclear Explosion, Los Angeles

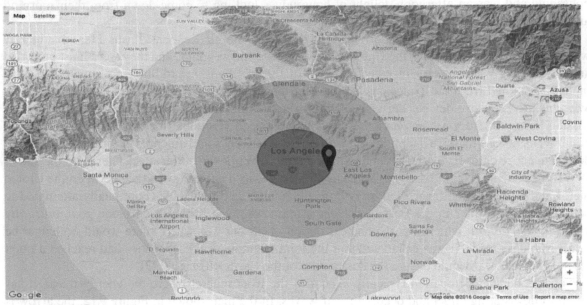

Source: T.D. Church

Against a nuclear attack, little protection can be conferred. In the blast zone there would be no protection due to the explosion and intense firestorm (Figure 14.11). If you can find cover, a minimal degree of protection is conferred within the thermal radiation zone. If you were to be standing upright and uncovered in the residual radiation zone it is highly likely you would receive significant injury or death. A method pioneered by the Civil Defense Administration in the United States during the early 1950s was ***duck and cover***. Duck and Cover was a Public Service Announcement (PSA)[1] made into a film shown in every grade school as a disaster response method for personal protection against the effects of a nuclear bomb. The method would only be effective in the first few crucial seconds-to-minutes after detonation. The PSA taught students upon the first flash of intense heat and light, one should

Figure 14.11 Nuclear Test Explosion, Nevada

Everett Collection/Shutterstock.com

---

[1] https://youtu.be/LWH4tWkZpPU

(Figure 14.12): (1) stop; (2) get under some cover; (3) drop/duck to the ground; and (4) lie face down and cover exposed skin with clothes or hands [28]. As a social countermeasure, duck and cover could potentially save lives. People tend to be naturally curious, and few would resist the urge to run to the windows to look for the source of light. Unbeknownst to the looky-loos, the slower moving blast wave would be rapidly advancing toward them. When the blast wave hit the window, the glass would implode, shredding those who went to look for the source of the flash, as thousands of shards are hurled at velocities of ~200 mph (322 kph).

Health effects from nuclear explosions are due primarily to air blast, thermal radiation, initial radiation, and residual radiation (or fallout) [29]. Nuclear explosions produce air blast effects, which easily rupture eardrums, collapse lungs, and hurl people and debris at high velocity. The intense pulse of thermal radiation burns skin, ignites fires, and melts metal. The initial radiation effects release large amounts of neutron and gamma radiation, which mutates cells, kills organs, and halts normal bodily processes. The residual radiation (or fallout) effects are from soil and water vapor mixed with the highly radioactive fission products and gets thrown up into the air with the mushroom cloud, the debris is carried back by wind, and contaminates a broad area leaking radiation into the environment for up to 50 years. ***Radiation poisoning/radiation sickness*** is an illness and constellation of symptoms resulting from excessive exposure to radiation (Figure 14.13). There are two forms of radiation, nonionizing, and ionizing. ***Nonionizing radiation*** comes in the form of light waves, microwaves, and radar. Nonionizing radiation does not cause tissue damage but can interfere with the electronic functioning of some implantable medical devices like cardiac pacemakers. ***Ionizing radiation*** exhibits immediate effects on human tissue in the form of x-rays, gamma rays, and particle bombardment (neutron beam, electron beam, protons, mesons, etc.). Ionizing radiation is used in industrial

Figure 14.12 Duck and Cover

Source: https://www.gettyimages.com/detail/news-photo/students-at-a-brooklyn-middle-school-have-a-duck-and-cover-news-photo/566420175?adppopup=true

Figure 14.13 Carbon Shadow Hiroshima

Source: https://www.gettyimages.com/detail/news-photo/world-war-ii-human-shadow-on-bank-steps-in-hiroshima-after-news-photo/566461875?adppopup=true

and manufacturing practices, medical testing, medical treatments, weapons, and weapons development. Radiation exposure can occur as a single large exposure (acute) or as a series of small exposures spread over time (chronic).

Radiation sickness is associated with acute exposure and expresses via four characteristic stages in its set of symptomologies (Figures 14.14 and 14.15). The first stage, ***prodromal stage*** manifests with nausea, vomiting, and diarrhea lasting a few minutes to several days. This transitions to the second stage, ***latent stage*** where symptoms appear to be disappearing and the person appears to be recovering. The ***overt stage*** involves problems with the cardiovascular, gastrointestinal, hematopoietic (stem and bone marrow cells), and central nervous system. The last stage, ***recovery or death stage*** will feature either a slow recovery over a period of years, or the poisoning will prove to be too fatal, and the individual will experience a painful death as their body slowly shuts down, system by system.

Damage by radiation is irreversible. Once the cells in the human body are damaged by radiation, they are unable to repair themselves. It is possible to halt the progress of radiation poisoning, and time is a crucial component. As quickly as possible the individual needs to perform the sequence of events depicted in Figure 9.17. The severity of symptoms and illness (acute radiation sickness) depends on the type and amount of radiation, how long an individual was exposed, and which body parts were exposed [30]. It is difficult to determine the amount of radiation exposure from a nuclear event, the best signs related to the severity of exposure are the length of time

Figure 14.14 Radiation Exposure

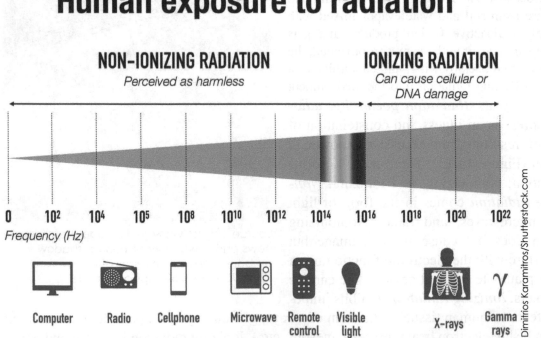

Human exposure to radiation

NON-IONIZING RADIATION
Perceived as harmless

IONIZING RADIATION
Can cause cellular or DNA damage

Frequency (Hz): 0, 10^2, 10^4, 10^5, 10^8, 10^{10}, 10^{12}, 10^{14}, 10^{16}, 10^{18}, 10^{20}, 10^{22}

Computer   Radio   Cellphone   Microwave   Remote control   Visible light   X-rays   Gamma rays

Dimitrios Karamitros/Shutterstock.com

Figure 14.15 Radiation Sickness Treatments

Clothing	Remove and discard all clothing and shoes; eliminates ~90% of external contamination
Shower	Rinse with water and soap to remove residual radiation; lowers the risk of internal contamination from inhalation, ingestion, or open wounds
Thyroid Function	Use ***potassium iodide (KI)*** to block thyroid uptake of radiation
Gastrointestinal	Use ***prussian blue***, given in tablet form, binds to the radioactive elements cesium and thallium in the intestines and prevent them from being absorbed; allows these compounds to move through the digestive system and leave the body as feces
Elimination	***Diethylenetriamine pentaacetic acid (DTPA)*** is a substance that binds to metals; it binds to the radioactive elements plutonium, americium, and curium; these radioactive particles pass out of the body in urine, decreasing residual radiation
Blood Products	Use ***Filgrastim*** or ***Neupogen*** to stimulate the growth of white blood cells
Bone Marrow	Receive a ***bone marrow transplant*** to assist in bone marrow reproduction

Source: T.D. Church

between the exposure and the onset of symptoms, the severity of symptoms, and the severity of changes in white blood cells. Typically, if an induvial vomits less than an hour after exposure, it is a signal that the radiation dose received was exceedingly high and death may be expected. Cardiovascular, intestinal, and other body system exposure will require treatments that target those body systems and symptoms. When multiple systems have been exposed it is important to triage and treat the most critical body system first.

In 2006, there were 20,000 nuclear weapons accounted for within the world. This arsenal represents 10× the amount needed to destroy our global civilization[14]. Many within that arsenal represented strategic nuclear weapons, which were 1000× more powerful than the bombs that destroyed Nagasaki and Hiroshima. ***Strategic nuclear weapons*** refers to nuclear weapons that are designed to be used on targets often in settled territory far from the battlefield as part of a strategic battle plan, such as military bases, military command centers, arms industries, transportation, economic centers, and energy infrastructure, and heavily populated areas such as cities and towns, which often contain such targets. Strategic nuclear weapons were poised for rapid deployment to key targets from halfway around the world and were capable of transit times of 30 minutes or less. By 2017, a substantial proportion of those missiles are unaccounted for after the dissolution of the former Soviet Union [31].

The missing nuclear ordnances pose a real threat and if they fell into the wrong hands could led to a post-nuclear fallout (Figure 14.16). In studying the effects of nuclear war, the RAND corporation calculated that the detonation of less than 50 medium-sized nuclear warheads would have devastating effects globally [32-34]. In the models, humanity would be negatively affected for nearly 75 years.

Figure 14.16   Nuclear Fallout Timeline of Events

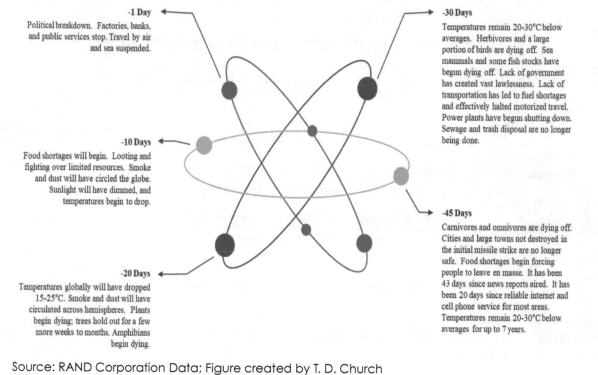

-1 Day
Political breakdown. Factories, banks, and public services stop. Travel by air and sea suspended.

-30 Days
Temperatures remain 20-30°C below averages. Herbivores and a large portion of birds are dying off. Sea mammals and some fish stocks have begun dying off. Lack of government has created vast lawlessness. Lack of transportation has led to fuel shortages and effectively halted motorized travel. Power plants have begun shutting down. Sewage and trash disposal are no longer being done.

-10 Days
Food shortages will begin. Looting and fighting over limited resources. Smoke and dust will have circled the globe. Sunlight will have dimmed, and temperatures begin to drop.

-45 Days
Carnivores and omnivores are dying off. Cities and large towns not destroyed in the initial missile strike are no longer safe. Food shortages begin forcing people to leave en masse. It has been 43 days since news reports aired. It has been 20 days since reliable internet and cell phone service for most areas. Temperatures remain 20-30°C below averages for up to 7 years.

-20 Days
Temperatures globally will have dropped 15-25°C. Smoke and dust will have circulated across hemispheres. Plants begin dying; trees hold out for a few more weeks to months. Amphibians begin dying.

Source: RAND Corporation Data; Figure created by T. D. Church

There would be worldwide famine, deadly frosts, and 35–45% global loss of ozone. The drop in temperature world-wide would reduce the world's growing season by 10–40 days. The temperature drops would also decrease rainfall and accelerate the desertification of marginal areas. The loss of human lives would be in the hundreds of millions or billions. The fallout approximated timeline has been recreated in Figure 9.16 and assumes the same 50 medium-sized nuclear warheads being detonated globally.

Chernobyl exists as a macabre monument of the devastation a nuclear event could unleash. On Saturday, 26 April 1986 a nuclear reactor in the Chernobyl Power Plant, near the city of Pripyat in the north of the Ukrainian Soviet Socialist Republic (SSR). This nuclear reactor malfunction stands as the worst nuclear disaster in human history in terms of the economic and casualty costs. It is one of only two nuclear energy accidents rated at seven, the maximum severity based on the International Nuclear Event Scale. The emergency response coupled with the later decontamination of the environment involved more than 500,000 personnel and cost an estimated 18 billion Soviet rubles (~US$70 billion, adjusted for inflation). In the aftermath of the Chernobyl Disaster, 237 people suffered from acute radiation sickness, with 31 dying within three months after exposure. In the years after, over 4,000 cancer deaths caused by Chernobyl have been reported from individuals who had contact with the contaminated zone. Roughly 5,800 casualties from a host of non-accident causes have been reported from clean-up workers between 1986 and 1995. An exclusion zone of 30 kilometers (19 miles) has been established with water, flora, and fauna continuously monitored for bioaccumulation of radioactivity. Pripyat remains a ghost town and is frozen in 1986 on the date of evacuation. The Chernobyl Disaster gives us an image of the potential fallout of nuclear war (Figure 14.17). To quote Robert McNamara, "the indefinite combination of human fallibility and nuclear weapons will lead to the destruction of nations"[35].

14.4 Preparedness

Preparedness is defined by Homeland Security as "a continuous cycle of planning, organizing, training, equipping, exercising, evaluating, and taking corrective action

Figure 14.17 Pripyat, Ukraine - Amusement Park Chernobyl Disaster

Kochneva Tetyana/Shutterstock.com

in an effort to ensure effective coordination during incident response" [36]. Disaster preparedness requires one to be informed about what kind of disasters might occur where they live, work, or visit. In the United States, a great resource to assist in becoming prepared can be found at ***ready.gov/myplan***. This website is kept current and is searchable by area or topic.

Emergency preparedness begins with you and requires that you be informed, be aware, and be ready (Figure 14.18) [37]. Watch TV, listen to the radio, or check the internet for official news and information about potential threats. In the advent of nuclear explosion, get inside the nearest building to avoid radiation, brick or concrete structures are the best. Stay inside for 24-hours unless local authorities provide other instructions. Biological and chemical agents require you to cover your mouth

Figure 14.18 Have a plan

elenabsl/Shutterstock.com

EMERGENCY PREPAREDNESS

MAKE A PLAN   BUILD A KIT   BE INFORMED

and nose with layers of fabric that can filter the air, but still allow breathing (e.g., two to three layers of cotton, such as a t-shirt, handkerchief, or towel). In a declared biological emergency or developing epidemic avoid crowds. Check government sources like ready.gov for more in-depth information.

As we have become more technologically capable, our ability to destroy has increased exponentially. We have the ability to cause suffering with biological and chemical agents and the ability to eradicate all life on this planet with nuclear ordinances. We hold the future of humankind in our hands, the question is do we have the capacity to protect or destroy that future. If we could only harness the energies we expend toward hate and fear of one another towards loving and respecting one another, imagine how far we could go together...

REFERENCES

1. Tzu, S. (2003 [512 BCE]). *The art of war* (p. 104). Fine Creative Media Inc.
2. FBI. (2021). *Strategic intelligence assessment and data on domestic terrorism* (pp. 1–40). Department of Homeland Security.
3. Diamond, J.M. (1999). *Guns, germs, and steel: The fates of human societies*. W.W. Norton & Co.
4. Homer. (2007). In R. Fagles & R. Merrill (Eds.), *The Iliad* (p. 464). University of Michigan Press.
5. Burgess, J. S. (2014). The death of Odysseus in the Odyssey and the relegony. *Philologia Antiqua: an International Journal of Classics*, 7, 111–122.
6. Virgil. (2009). *The Aeneid*. Simon and Schuster.
7. Anonymous. (2005). In W. Doniger (Ed.), *The Rig Veda* (p. 352). Penguin Classics.
8. Oliveira, M., et al. (2020). *Biowarfare, bioterrorism and biocrime: A historical overview on microbial harmful applications. Forensic Science International, 314* (Available at: https://doi.org/10.1016/j.forsciint.2020.110366 [Accessed Jan 13, 2021]).
9. Recht, J., Schuenemann, V. J., & Sánchez-Villagra, M. R. (2020). Host diversity and origin of zoonoses: The ancient and the new. *Animals*, *10*(9), 1672–1686.
10. Kortepeter, M. G., & Gerald, P. W. (1999). Potential biological weapons threats. *Emerging Infectious Diseases*, 5(4), 523–527.
11. Guillemin, J. (2011). *American anthrax: Fear, crime, and the investigation of the nation's deadliest bioterror attack* (p. 336). Henry Holt and Company.
12. Anderson, P. D., & Bokor, G. (2012). Bioterrorism: pathogens as weapons. *Journal of Pharmacy Practice*, 25(5), 521–529.
13. Conlon, K. (2015). *North Korea threatens to attack U.S. CNN World News*. [Accessed on Sep 9, 2015]: https://www.cnn.com/2015/08/15/world/north-korea-threats/index.html.
14. Cordesman, A. (2018). *Statement before the House Committee on Foreign Affairs Subcommittee on Terrorism, Nonproliferation and Trade Subcommittee on Asia and the Pacific: "More than a nuclear threat: North Korea's Chemical, Biological, and Conventional Weapons"* (pp. 1–32). www.csis.org, Center for Strategic & International Studies.
15. UN. (2021). *Convention on the Prohibition of the Development, Production, and Stockpiling of Bacteriological (Biological) and Toxin Weapons and on Their Destruction.* United Nations, Office for Disarmament Affairs: https://treaties.unoda.org/t/bwc [Accessed Nov 27, 2021].

16. Spiers, E. M. (2020). *Agents of war: A history of chemical and biological weapons* (p. 224). Reaktion Books.
17. Mayor, A. (2019). Chemical and biological warfare in antiquity In P. Wexler (Ed.), *Toxicology in antiquity: A volume in history of toxicology and environmental health* (pp. 243–255). Elsevier.
18. Stellman, J. M., & Stellman, S. D. (2018). *Agent Orange during the Vietnam War: The lingering issue of its civilian and military health impact. American Journal of Public Health, 108*(6), 726–728.
19. Reis, J., & Mizusawa, H. (2019). Environmental challenges for the nervous system and the brain in Japan. *Revue Neurologique, 175*(10), 693–697.
20. Okumura, T., et al. (2005). The Tokyo subway sarin attack—lessons learned. *Toxicology and Applied Pharmacology, 207*(2), 471–476.
21. UN. (1992). *Convention on the Prohibition of the Development, Production, Stockpiling and Use of Chemical Weapons and on their Destruction*, O.f.D. Affairs, Editor. UNODA.
22. Sagan, C. (1980). *Cosmos*. Random House Publishing Company.
23. Brooks, K., Bosker, G., & Darmon, R. (1998). *Atomic cocktails: Mixed drinks for modern times.* Chronicle Books.
24. Kristen, S. (2003). *The Book of Tiki* (p. 288). Taschen.
25. Rasmussen, N. (2008). *On speed: The many lives of amphetamine.* NYU Press.
26. Herzberg, D. (2009). *Happy pills in America: from Miltown to Prozac.* JHU Press.
27. Brook, R., Dodge, M., & Hogg, J. (2020). *Cold war cities: Politics, culture and atomic urbanism, 1945–1965* (p. 332). Routledge.
28. Rizzo, A. (1952). *Duck and cover.* Federal Civil Defense Administration, 9 min.
29. Boyer, P. (1994). *By the bomb's early light: American thought and culture at the dawn of the atomic age* . (p. 464). Univ of North Carolina Press.
30. Donnelly, E. H., et al. (2010). Acute radiation syndrome: Assessment and management. *Southern Medical Journal, 103*(6), 541–546.
31. Zaitseva, L. (2020). 10. Nuclear trafficking in ungoverned spaces and failed states. In A. Clunan & H. A. Trinkunas (Eds). *Ungoverned spaces* (pp. 193–212). Stanford University Press.
32. RAND. (1953). *Worldwide effects of atomic weapons: Project SUNSHINE* (p. 107). RAND Corporation.
33. Brown, W. M. (1969). *Limiting damage from nuclear war* (p. 105). RAND Corporation.
34. Greenfield, S. M., Rapp, R. R, & Walters, P. A. *A Catalog of Fallout Patterns* (p. 88). RAND Corporation.
35. McNamara, R. S. (1992). *The changing nature of global security and its impact on South Asia* (Vol. 18). Washington Council on Non-Proliferation.
36. DHS. (2021). *Plan and prepare for disasters.* Department of Homeland Security: https://www .dhs.gov/plan-and-prepare-disasters [Accessed Nov 26, 2021].
37. Davis, L. M., & Ringel, J. S. (2009). *Public health preparedness for chemical, biological, radiological, and nuclear weapons* (p. 24). Massachusetts Institute of Technology.

Chapter 15

Modern Addiction and Our Path Forward

To say we have only scratched the surface of human drug use would be the simplest and easiest way to end this book. It would tie things up neatly, leave room for further inquiry, and give fuel to many sides in the moral debates surrounding addiction. As we have learned together, ***addiction*** is a chronic disease characterized by drug seeking and use, and addiction is compulsive or difficult to control, despite knowledge of harmful consequences. Our modern understanding of addiction has been forged from our historical experiences with substances. Who is addicted has become equally important as what one is addicted to in our conceptualization of addiction. We will not take the easy way out and will end this book by tracing the modern path we took to reach our concept of addiction and conclude with some thoughts related to the future of addiction.

Alcohol, addiction, and dependency date back to the beginnings of human civilization and most likely extend back further. Since then, we, as a species, have grappled with trying to understand addiction. Should addiction be thought of as a sin or a disease? Should morality or medicine inform our treatment of addiction? Is addiction caused by the substance, the individual's inability to resist, their psychology, response to a traumatic event, or by social and environmental factors? Should substances be strictly regulated or freely available? The attitudes and beliefs about addiction have oscillated wildly between opposing attitudes on these issues. At times, it feels as though the rug gets pulled out from under us as we attempt to forge a cohesive understanding of addiction, leaving us no further along in our understanding than we were 15 years ago.

15.1 Beginnings of a Medical Understanding of Addiction

Our modern understanding of Addiction is tied in part to the work of physicians and psychiatrists who attempted to make sense of addiction. These physicians and psychiatrists include individuals such as Pinel, Rush, von Brühl-Cramer, Kraepelin, Bleuler, Freud, and Jung to name a few. ***Philippe Pinel*** (1745—1826 CE) was a French psychiatrist who proposed one of the first taxonomies of mental disorders in 1806 CE. Pinel attracted the attention of psychiatrists and physicians alike because his taxonomy was based on his extensive observations of psychiatric inpatients. His efforts at developing the taxonomy were intent on developing more humane, nonmedical, and nonviolent treatments for his patients whose mainstream medicine treated worse than animals. From his taxonomy, Pinel was able to develop a nascent nosology. *Taxonomy* is best defined as the practice and science of classification of things or concepts into a coherent list or listing. *Nosology* is a classification scheme used in medicine to classify diseases. In order for a medical condition to be fully classified requires understanding the cause of the condition, which is limited to there being only one cause. In addition to understanding the cause of the condition, nosology requires detailed effects on the body, symptoms produced, and any associated factors used in identifying and describing the condition. Pinel's mental illness nosology detailed the conditions of melancholia, mania, dementia, and idiotism[1]. *Melancholia* was described as a mental condition characterized by a manic-depressive state identified by extreme depression, bodily complaints, and often featured hallucinations and delusions. Pinel believed melancholia was brought on by chronic abuse of alcohol. *Mania* was defined as excitement manifested by mental and physical hyperactivity, disorganization of behavior, and elevation of mood. *Dementia* referred to an unusually progressive condition marked by a constellation of cognitive deficits, including memory impairment, aphasia, and an inability to plan/initiate complex behavior. *Idiotism* was identified as having an extreme degree of mental deficiency, and when expressed, the individual had a mental age of less than three or four years. Pinel was very pragmatic about treatment for disease; he had remarked in 1806 CE that "it is an art of no little importance to administer medicines properly: but, it is an art of much greater and more difficulty acquisition to know when to suspend or altogether to omit them"[2].

Benjamin Rush (1745–1826 CE) was a signer of the Declaration of Independence and has been regarded as the father of American psychiatry[3]. In 1792 CE, Rush campaigned for Pennsylvania Hospital to build a separate mental health ward where patients could be kept and cared for inhumane conditions. In 1821 CE, he published the first American textbook on psychiatry. Rush had pioneered a therapeutic approach to diagnose and treat addiction gradually. Prior to his work, drunkenness was viewed as being sinful and a moral weakness of the individual. His view was that alcoholism was a form of medical disease and proposed that alcoholics should be weaned off their addiction. His beliefs of alcoholism were centered only on strong liquors, as Rush viewed wine and beer to be "salutary thirst-quenchers"[4]. Rush instilled the idea that people with mental illness were people who had an illness, rather than inhuman animals. His work helped to humanize the treatment of the morally ill.

Constantin von Brühl-Cramer[1] was an influential physician in German-speaking countries in the early part of the nineteenth century CE. In 1819 CE, he wrote a treatise on *trunksucht*, German for drunkenness[5]. In this treatise, he coined the term dipsomania. *Dipsomania* referred to the irresistible and constant need people had to drink alcohol, despite strong internal moral struggles against excessive drinking. His views on dipsomania produced a lens through which the abuse of alcohol was witnessed at the expense of all other interests. The dipsomaniac would undergo periods of binge drinking followed by periods of general sobriety. The recurring bouts of binge drinking would sometimes be accompanied by a deep wanderlust in the dipsomaniac or manifest as suicidal impulses.

Emil Kraepelin (1856–1926 CE) has been heralded as the founder of German modern scientific psychiatry. He was instrumental in the fields of psychopharmacology, psychiatric genetics, and in the diagnosis and classification of mental illness. His views on psychiatric etiology stressed the vital role of biological and genetic factors in mental illness and he emphasized the importance of detailed

---

[1] von Brühl-Cramer's date of birth and date of death are difficult to pinpoint with accuracy, and as a result have been left out purposefully.

diagnosis and description of conditions to aid in treatment planning. Kraepelin viewed chronic alcoholism to be a mental disorder[6]. By 1895 CE, Kraepelin stopped consuming all alcohol; this was due to his growing belief that chronic alcoholism provoked cortical brain lesions which were precursors responsible for permanent cognitive decline. Later in his life, Kraepelin wrote with increasing fervor on several social policy issues and became a very ardent and unabashed Social Darwinist. He became a strong and highly influential proponent of eugenics. He focused on alcoholism, crime, degeneration, and hysteria as genetic aberrations or flaws. Kraepelin believed that institutions like the education system and the welfare state broke the process of natural selection and undermined the Germans' biological "struggle for survival"[7].

Eugen Bleuler (1857–1939 CE) was a Swiss psychiatrist and eugenicist, best known for his contributions of mental illness. Many of the modern psychiatric terms for mental illness and diagnoses were developed and described by Bleuler, including schizophrenia, schizoid, autism, depth psychology, and ambivalence[8]. Bleuler was interested in morality, the human mind, how individuals developed and interacted with morals throughout the course of their lives. He explored the connection between his concept of moral idiocy, and its relationship to neurosis and alcoholism. *Moral idiocy* was described by Bleuler as an inability to understand moral principles and values coupled with an inability to act according to them, often without impairment of the individuals reasoning and intellectual faculties of the individual[9]. Bleuler had speculated that acute alcoholic hallucinosis or delirium tremens could be a sign of underlying paranoid schizophrenia manifested in individuals due to their chronic and excessive consumption of alcohol. *Delirium tremens* is a transient condition caused by withdrawal from alcohol after long-term alcohol use where the individual experiences a very rapid onset of uncontrollable shaking/shivering, confusion, nightmares, increased agitation, disorientation, visual and auditory hallucinations, tactile hallucinations, raised body temperature, high blood pressure, and heavy sweating[10]. Delirium tremens typically manifests between day two and three of alcohol withdrawal and can persist for up to three days post-onset. The association between delirium tremens and schizophrenia has been largely disproven by current data[11]. The work of Bleuler and our modern evaluation of the relationship highlight the frequency with which schizophrenia and chronic alcoholism have co-occurred throughout history.

Sigmund Freud (1856–1939 CE) viewed substance abuse from a developmental perspective[12]. He concluded that many individuals who abuse alcohol and drugs do so as a coping mechanism which has developed into a set of strong unconscious dependency needs due to a frustrated quest for nurturance from parents in childhood. Freud believed there existed a deep longing for parental affection and attention that went unfulfilled during early childhood. These unfulfilled needs have pushed some to fill the longing with substances to fill the emotional void or to chemically repress latent feelings of longing. While this may be true for some individuals, it was not the case for everyone. It also did not fully describe or identify relapses during recovery. If the individual received psychotherapy for their sense of emotional distance and need for nurturing, why would there be a need to return to addiction?

Carl Jung (1875–1961 CE) was a Swiss psychiatrist and psychoanalyst who pioneered the analytical method of psychology[13]. Sadly, Jung wrote extraordinarily little about addiction. His main rationale was that he feared he would be misunderstood by the scientific community of his day. Jung's legacy would be his profound influence on one source of help available to people who manifest problems with addiction. He is responsible for influencing William "Bill" Wilson (1895–1971 CE), the main founder of Alcoholics Anonymous (AA)[14]. Wilson thanked Jung for his revolutionary work in the concept of the self, which would go on to function as the main foundation of "fellowship" in the AA model. Fundamentally, Jung understood the psychological function of drugs was not solely the changing of moods (calming, stimulating, exciting, etc.). Jung believed that drugs provided temporary changes to mood and perception as well as permanent modifications to the user's inner world. Chemical substances tend to work at a much deeper level of psychic functioning, and they often blurred the boundaries between the inner (self) and outer (social) world. Jung was preeminent in the field of psychoanalysis at grasping the underlying secret of enduring recovery from addiction. He realized that addiction exists because the substance completed missing parts within the addict. In order to fully overcome addiction, the addict would be required to undergo a radical conversion to something equally satisfying. Jung believed that loneliness, shame, and secrecy—the inherent aspects in the addiction process—functioned to isolate the individual and held profound impact within the recovery process. Socialization, acceptance, and honesty would help individuals avoid addiction. To Jung, "every form of addiction is bad, no matter whether the narcotic be alcohol or morphine or idealism"[15].

If you have concluded from the above list of researchers that the medical conversations surrounding addiction have been historically dominated by middle-aged white men, you would be correct. There needs to be better representation from women and people of color involved in the conversation, which will help us truly build a broader understanding of addiction. An unfortunate consequence of the psychological explanations of addiction to substances, and even behavioral addictions like gambling, sex, or smart phones, they have all been gathered under a common pattern which regards them all as different expressions of a singular underlying psychological syndrome. Beyond psychological explanations for addiction, there are other factors that need to be considered, including biology and genetics; environment and background; and social and cultural factors that can influence how addiction begins, takes hold, and persists. Addiction medicine in the twenty-first century CE has been assisted by the development of a broad diagnostic classification system for addiction, supported by neurobiological research and genetic studies. From a psychological perspective, we have reached a, somewhat, if not daunting, informative hypothesis that the majority of addictions share common properties. These properties manifest in how addiction exerts and reinforces its control. Through social and psychological reinforcement, addiction trains the brain to crave biologically rewarding stimuli which reinforce seeking out similar sensations whether they be food, sex, or drugs.[16].

15.2 Temperance and Prohibition in the United States

Control over addiction has centered on will power for nearly 200 years. Individuals of weak morality and low faith were the most susceptible to the follies of addiction. *Temperance* was a very prominent Victorian Era virtue, embodying the control over excess and was often scaffolding for other virtues like chastity, modesty, humility, self-control, decorum, abstinence, and forgiveness[17]. Temperance involved the restraining of excess to an external impulse like overconsumption of alcohol, sexual desire, extreme vanity, or uncontrolled anger. By the start of the twentieth century CE, the term "temperance" came to be synonymous with a spectrum of beliefs related to alcohol consumption spanning from moderation to absolute abstinence. Between the eighteenth and twentieth centuries CE, the United States underwent three temperance movements. A ***temperance movement*** is a social reform movement initially focused on reducing alcohol consumption. The goals of these movements were to promote drinking with absolute temperance or at a minimum with moderation. The Early Temperance Movement occurred between 1784 and1861 CE. The Second Temperance Movement occurred between 1872 and 1893 CE. And the Third Temperance Movement, the most successful of the temperance movements, began in 1893 CE and lasted until 1933 CE. The Third Temperance Movement was so successful because it aligned its goals with the Women's Christian Temperance Union (WCTU) founded in 1874 CE[18]. The combined efforts from the two movements advocated for temperance and women's rights simultaneously and together saw the enactment of the 19th Amendment to the U.S. Constitution. The 19th Amendment was ratified in 1920 CE and gave women the right to vote.

Three revolutionary and vastly different women were influential in the women's movement. The women were unique in their roles within the broader temperance movement, but all three were steadfast in their advocacy for an alcohol-free America. The women were Carrie Nation, Susan B. Anthony, and Frances E. Willard. ***Carrie Nation*** (1846–1911 CE), also known as Hatchet Granny, was an extremely radical member of the Temperance Movement (Figure 15.1). She opposed alcohol so fervently that she would attack taverns and saloons with a hatchet, claiming a divine ordination to promote temperance and justified her hatcheting open beer kegs and whiskey barrels. She was equally against cannabis and tobacco and was once quoted as saying "I want all hellions to quit puffing that hell fume in god's clean air"[19]. She developed a hatred of alcohol after her first husband died from complications due to his alcoholism. In Kansas, where Nation began her temperance work, she campaigned for the enforcement of a state ban on the sale of liquor. She claimed to have had a revelation in a dream, and was told to go to Kiowa, Kansas. On June 7, 1900 CE, Nation who gathered several rocks, "smashers" as she labeled them, and made her way to Dobson's Saloon. She barged through the front door and announced "men, I have come to save you from a drunk-

Figure 15.1 Carrie Nation, 1900 CE https://www.loc.gov/item/2014685633/

ard's fate"[20]. She then set out to destroy the saloon's stock with her smashers. Before the day was over, she had destroyed two other saloons. She would go on to be arrested more than 35 times for "hatchetations" as she called them, destroying bar fixtures and stock with a hatchet all while singing hymnals or reciting bible verses.

Susan B. Anthony (1820–1906 CE) was an influential social reformer and women's rights activist, playing a prominent role in the temperance movement, women's suffrage movement, and the American Anti-Slavery Society (Figure 15.2)[21]. She was deeply committed to social equality and began a lifelong career of activism at the age of 17 where she had collected over 1,000 signatures for an anti-slavery petition. Anthony was raised in a temperance family, her immediate family totally abstained from alcohol and her wealthy father organized one of the first temperance societies in New York State. By the time she was 24, Anthony had joined the Daughter's Union, an auxiliary branch of the Sons of Temperance. The Daughter's Union was responsible for hosting dinners to raise funds for the Sons of Temperance. During a fundraising dinner, Anthony stood and gave a public speech that created a sensation in the sleepy little mining town of Rochester, NY, and catapulted her into public speaking. In 1852, Anthony was selected to be a Daughter's Union representative at a national meeting of the Sons of Temperance. She stood and attempted to deliver a speech, but she was reminded by some of the men that her place was to listen and learn, she was not invited to speak. Abruptly and quietly she departed the meeting, with the majority of the women in attendance leaving with her. She organized her own meeting and

Figure 15.2 Susan B. Anthony, 1870 CE

Everett Collection/Shutterstock.com

initiated the first national women's temperance society in the United Sates. She went on to obtain 28,000 signatures on a petition to prohibit the sales and distribution of alcohol in New York, and she presented it to the state legislature[22]. There was a wealthy sarsaparilla soda manufacturer in the audience, and he would go on to fund a speaking tour throughout New York State. The speaking tour promoted temperance while extolling the virtues of sarsaparilla. Shortly after, due to opposing views, Anthony would abandon the temperance movement and would spend the remainder of her life devoted exclusively to the women's suffrage movement. In 1872 CE, Anthony entered a barbershop in Rochester, NY, which doubled as a makeshift voter registration office. She insisted that she had as much right as any man to vote. The startled voting officials allowed her to register, after Anthony threatened to sue them. A scant four days later, she cast her vote for Ulysses S. Grant (1822–1885 CE) for president of the United States. She was arrested and charged with voter fraud and illegal voting. Anthony had 7 months until her trial and she used that time to deliver an amazing series of speeches in ~30 nearby towns. Within these speeches, Anthony poignantly stated, "it was we, the people; not we, the white male citizens; nor yet we, the male citizens; but we, the whole people, who formed the Union"[23]. She died at the age of 86 in 1906 CE, 14 years before women would earn the right to vote.

Frances E. Willard (1839–1898 CE) was a teacher, temperance reformer, and suffragist (Figure 15.3)[24]. Willard served as the First Dean of the Women's College at Northwestern University in 1873 CE, a position she held until 1874 CE when she resigned to join the WCTU. By 1879 CE, she had become the President of the WCTU, a position she held until her death in 1898 CE. Willard was instrumental in raising the age of consent in many states as well as advocating for and passing labor reforms for the eight-hour workday. Willard saw temperance and suffrage as being synonymous and argued for legal rights against violent acts against women committed by drunk men, which was a common occurrence in and out of the home in the late nineteenth century CE[25]. Willard contended that it was far too easy for men to get away with their crimes without women's suffrage. Willard believed that "temperance is moderation in the things that are good and total abstinence from the things that are foul"[26]. Though she would not live to see either passed, Willard was instrumental in helping to get the 18th Amendment (Prohibition of alcohol) and the 19th Amendment (Women's right to vote) to the Constitution passed.

Figure 15.3 Frances E. Willard, 1880 CE

Everett Collection/Shutterstock.com

The first American political lobby was the *Anti-Saloon League* (1893–1933 CE), and they lobbied for the national prohibition of alcohol in the United States[27]. *Prohibition* was to become a nationwide constitutional ban on the production, importation, transportation, and sale of alcoholic beverages. The Anti-Saloon League was founded in Progressive Era beliefs and drew heavy support from Protestant ministers and their devout congregations in the South and rural North. With a solid power base and economic support, the League rose to become the most powerful prohibition lobbying group in America. In 1919 CE, the League celebrated its largest gain when the nationwide prohibition was written into the Constitution through the passage of the 18th Amendment. *National Prohibition* was a 13-year period between 1920 CE and 1933 CE during which the sale of alcoholic beverages was expressly prohibited.

The National Prohibition in the United States succeeded, briefly, in markedly reducing arrests for drunkenness, but only in the short term. It did nothing to reduce the social, economic, and medical problems associated with alcoholism, especially among young men. Prohibition did see the rise of organized crime as gangsters cashed in on bootlegging, rum-running, and other illicit activities that set the foundation for the American mafia. *Speakeasies* were illicit establishments that sold alcohol during prohibition[28]. The name is an amalgamation of the words "speak easy," which defined the practice of speaking quietly about these types of establishments in public or private, so as not to alert gossiping neighbors or law enforcement. Speakeasies became the de facto term for a secretive establishment that sold alcohol without a license. The illicit alcohol trade depended upon the smuggling and transportation of alcohol.

Law enforcement had ensured the only remaining source of alcohol was found in industrial alcohol. The industrial alcohol had begun to be diverted by bootleggers. Government officials made the decision to add dangerous compounds to the alcohol, such as methanol. It has been suggested that ~10,000 people died from the poisoned alcohol with an equal amount becoming blinded or suffering from other serious injuries[29]. Bootleggers and rumrunners moved alcohol from Canada, Cuba, and Mexico into the United States. *Rum-running* referred to smuggling of alcohol, typically done via boat. ***Bootlegging*** applied to smuggling over land, wherein liquor bottles would be strapped to a person's leg or body and walked to its destination. Both rum-running and bootlegging were methods employed to counter Prohibition and supply speakeasies with alcohol to make illegal beverages[30]. Gangsters and mobsters like Al Capone (1899–1947 CE), Lucky Luciano (1897–1962 CE), and Bugs Moran (1893–1957 CE) profited from the National Prohibition and helped to keep the alcohol flowing into American cities[31]. Their activities extended into prostitution, extortion, gambling, and theft, but it was Prohibition that made them wealthier than any of their other dubious enterprises.

In 1933 CE, the National Prohibition ended in a thunderous applause, a crescendo, and a sound unlike any other before—JAZZ—swept through the speakeasies of Chicago, New York, and New Orleans. *Jazz* was the sound of swing and blue notes, call and response vocals, polyrhythms, and improvisation[32]. Music halls, big band stages, and jazz clubs thrived in the Prohibition world of 1930–1933 CE and post-Prohibition 1934–1950 CE. Many of these jazz clubs featured excessive drinking of alcohol, use of heroin and cocaine, and the smoking of tobacco and cannabis. The use of illegal substances occurred across racial and gender lines in unprecedented ways. Illegal substances became the great social equalizers, at least in the dance halls, on the stages, and at the clubs where jazz was performed. Outside of these jazz venues, however, life for women and people of color was bleak at best.

With the introduction of the Prescription Drug Act in 1954 CE, access to several narcotic drugs became restricted. This did not seem to halt the desire for or access to these narcotics, however. In the American psyche, drugs would go on to become associated with counterculture and fringe groups. Certain drugs would become tied intrinsically to the music and fashion of specific decades in the 1900s CE[33]. The 1960s CE was the era of psychedelic rock and was associated with psychedelic drugs like LSD, psilocybin, and cannabis. The 1969 CE Woodstock music festival represented the largest festival for its time, culminating in a mix of love, peace, music, and drugs. The crash came in the 1970s CE. The 1970s represented a changing era as rock transitioned to disco to punk. The deaths of Jimi Hendrix who overdosed on sleeping pills followed closely by the deaths of Janis Joplin and Jim Morrison both overdosing on heroin brought the peace and love movement of the prior decade to an end. The 1970s CE witnessed the rise of stimulants and hyper-stimulants in the form of cocaine, methamphetamine, and speed. The 1980s CE brought back rock and pop music and witnessed the birth of hip hop. Drugs in the 1980s CE transitioned from stimulants to empathogens migrating from crack cocaine to cannabis to ecstasy. The 1990s CE began dark and ended in a flurry of color as the music scenes moved from grunge to rave, the drugs changing with the music. Grunge was more about depressants like heroin and sedatives, while rave needed empathogens like ecstasy. These musical eras brought fans to concerts, dance halls, and assorted venues to experience the music together. There is a strong relationship between drug use and music choices, as people utilized drugs to enhance or experience a sense of community and belonging. The danger of these new social bonds was enough to encourage substance misuse which tracked to rising addiction. Some individuals during each of these decades went from casual user to desperate addict depending upon their social circles and availability of substances. Social and cultural forces held a unique influence over the addictive cycle in profound ways.

Temperance Movements and Prohibition combined the prevailing beliefs of the nineteenth century CE and the early twentieth century CE into a view of addiction where biology, social environment, lapses of faith, and vice (or immorality) converged in the perfect storm to create addiction[34]. Taken individually, biology, social environment, lapses of faith, and vice can be manageable. In conjunction, these four elements bring about a host of medical, social, and moral problems that can cascade into chronic abuse and with enough time that abuse becomes addiction.

15.3   Rehabilitation and Education

Addiction is a treatable disorder. It cannot be completely cured, but people can recover from the yoke of addiction. **Recovery** is a process of change wherein an individual actively seeks to improve their health and wellness, live a self-directed life, and strive to reach their full potential while avoiding drugs and drug abuse behaviors. Treatment for addiction is not a cure and it requires work and dedication to remain sober. Addiction can be managed, and many treatments today enable people to counteract addiction's disruptive effects on their brain and on their behavior. The chronic nature of addiction means that some people will return to drug use after they attempt to stop; this is known as **relapse**. Relapse is a part of the process of recovery for some. Relapse rates for drug use are analogous to rates of relapse for other chronic medical illnesses. If treatment is stopped, relapse is likely. For many, addiction looms outside the doors of group or individual therapy and a missed therapy visit becomes an opportunity for addiction to gain a foothold. Relapse is a normal part of recovery with some drugs, and can be extremely dangerous, even deadly. Heroin, for example, can be difficult to quit for some individuals. If someone who has been sober for a few months and relapses, the eminent danger is overdose. The individual may not realize that their tolerance to heroin has diminished, yet they will dose themselves as if they had not stopped and in doing so can easily overdose. An **overdose** can be expressed in several ways but describes the effect when an individual uses enough of a drug to produce uncomfortable feelings, life-threatening symptoms, or death. Overdoses can be intentional, but most are accidental.

Drug withdrawal is one of the key reasons many drug addicts do not seek treatment for their addiction. They fear the pain and agony of the detoxification process. **Withdrawal** refers to a constellation of physical and emotional symptoms, including restlessness or sleeplessness in addition to depression, anxiety, and other mental health conditions that occur when an individual stops using drugs. There are some medications that can help the brain adapt gradually to the absence of the drug, like methadone for heroin addiction. These treatments act slowly and help prevent drug cravings while providing a calming effect across body systems. There are several triggers and stress cues that can occur during the recovery process that can trigger a relapse. **Stress cues** are often linked to the ritual and socialization of drug use, and include things like people, places, things, and moods associated with one's prior contact with drugs and form common triggers for relapse. In addition to the physical withdrawal from drugs, the behavioral components that have been built during addiction need to be addressed if treatment and recovery are to be successful. Table 15.1 highlights the top six current behavioral therapies used in the treatment of addiction.

Table 15.1 Behavioral Therapies to Treat Drug Addiction

Therapy	Description
Behavioral therapies	Umbrella term for therapies that treat mental health disorders through modification of attitudes and behaviors.
Cognitive-behavioral therapies	Seek to help patients recognize, avoid, and cope with situations that trigger drug use.
Contingency management therapies	Utilize positive reinforcement such as providing rewards or privileges for remaining drug free.
Motivational enhancement therapies	Employs strategies to make the most of an individual's readiness to change their behavior and enter treatment.
Family therapies	Help people (young people in particular) with drug use problems, as well as their families and addresses the influences people have on drug use patterns and improves overall family dynamics and function.
Twelve-step facilitation (TSF) therapies	Individual therapy programs delivered in 12 weekly sessions to prepare people to become engaged in lifelong 12-step mutual support programs.

Source: T. D. Church

There are two well-known TSF therapies in the United States, AA and Narcotics Anonymous (NA). *Alcoholics Anonymous* was founded in 1935 CE as a fellowship of recovering alcoholics who support one another as they move toward sobriety. A hallmark of AA is their use of the 12-Steps Toward Recovery as covered in *The Big Book*[35]. There is an emphasis in the 12-Step program on finding a *higher power*, a power greater than alcohol in whom the recovering alcoholic can place their trust as recovery proceeds. This trust is an essential component within the recovery process and will not be successful without it. This makes AA difficult for atheists and those who do not believe in a Judeo-Christian god. AA members claim that there is no other solution to addiction than a spiritual one. This stands in contention to the conflicting understanding that alcoholism represents a disease. AA is solely focused on the relationship of alcohol to the alcoholic and does not lend itself well to other addictive behaviors. This is problematic as many people are not solely addicted to one substance. As the late Carrie Fisher (1956–2016 CE) posited "saying you're an alcoholic and an addict is like saying you're from Los Angeles and from California"[36].

Narcotics Anonymous was founded in 1953 CE and was modeled on the success of the AA program[37]. The 12-Step model used in AA was expanded and developed for people with varied substance abuse issues. NA describes addiction as a *progressive disease* with no known cure[38]. This means addiction is a disease that affects every area of an addict's life: physical, mental, emotional, and spiritual. It is labeled as a progressive degree, because upon becoming addicted to a substance, the disease gets worse if the person remains in active addiction. A truly vicious cycle gains power over the individual and they must consume increasingly more of the drug to attain the same high.

As more substance gets consumed, it increases the need for the drug both physically and psychologically. Within the NA rubric, all drugs are considered equal, including alcohol. NA is a more comprehensive approach to treatment and has had remarkable success.

Figure 15.4   AA 12-Step Program

One	Admission
• Admission that the individual is powerless over alcohol, and that their lives have become unmanageable.	

Two	Recognition
• A Power greater than the individual could restore sanity.	

Three	Submission
• Decision to put the will and life of the individual into the care of god as the individual understand them to be.	

Four	Understanding
• The individual takes a hard look at their life to this point and undertake a moral accounting of their actions.	

Five	Confession
• Confession to god, to the individual, and to others regarding the specific nature of their past misdeeds.	

Six	Readiness
• The individual is entirely ready and prepared to have god remove their defects of character and lapses of morality.	

Seven	Humility
• Acknowledge and ask for assistance from god to remove the individuals' shortcomings.	

Eight	Reparation
• Make a list of all the people the individual harmed and become willing to make things right with those people.	

Nine	Apology
• Apologize and make amends to those who were named in the list, whenever possible, except when doing so would injure or harm the individual or others.	

Ten	Integrity
• The individual takes full responsibility for their actions, continues to take inventory of themselves, and whenever they are wrong to promptly admit it.	

Eleven	Meditation
• Use of prayer and meditation to improve the individual's contact with god as they understand them to be, praying that god will help them stay on a path to recovery.	

Twelve	Awakening
• After completing the prior steps, the individual should have had a spiritual awakening and as a result will vow to carry their message to alcoholics and practice the principles of the program in all their affairs.	

Source: T.D. Church

Drug Abuse Resistance Education (D.A.R.E.) was founded in 1983 CE as a joint initiative of the Los Angeles Police Department (LAPD) and Los Angeles Unified School District (LAUSD)[39]. D.A.R.E. is an educational program that seeks to prevent the use of controlled drugs, gang membership, bullying, and violent behavior among grade, middle, and high school students in the United

States. D.A.R.E. is a drug control strategy and was born out of the 2nd War on Drugs in America. Students who enter the program sign a pledge not to use drugs or join gangs. Local police officers provide in-school and interactive curriculum to deliver the government's beliefs about the "real" dangers of recreational drug use. D.A.R.E. has had a lot of criticism, mostly centered around the effectiveness of its curriculum which does not appear to have much influence over adolescent drug initiation or use[40]. Table 15.2 details the highlights of the D.A.R.E. educational components by grade level.

Table 15.2 D.A.R.E. General Curriculum by Age Group

Grade Level	Curriculum Topics
4th–6th Grades	Tobacco smoking, tobacco advertising, drug abuse, inhalants, alcohol consumption and health, and peer pressure.
7th–8th Grades	*Keepin' it Real*—Over the Counter drugs, prescription drug abuse, methamphetamine, bullying, gangs, and internet safety.
9th–10th Grades	Equal emphasis is placed on helping students to recognize and cope with feelings of anger without causing harm to themselves or others.
11th–12th Grades	Resisting alcohol, drugs, and peer pressure; emphasis is placed on Promise (not driving drunk or riding with a drunk friend) and Graduation Challenge (not driving drunk or riding with a drunk friend).

Source: T. D. Church

The early 1980s CE saw the rise of several educational and outreach programs. There was a rise in the volume of media targeting youth and young adults that grew out of President Ronald Regan's War on Drugs during the 1980s CE and 1990s CE. *Just Say No* was an attempt to discourage children from engaging in illegal recreational drug use by simply saying "no." If you were offered drugs at a party, just say "no." If you were offered drugs while walking down a city street, just say "no." The slogan was created and championed by First Lady Nancy Regan during her husband's presidency. *Just Say No* was too simplistic and reduced drug awareness to a catchphrase. There was no additional information provided on what to do after you say "no." *Just Say No* helped to add to the stigma of drug users as "bad" or "wicked." The stigma extended itself toward people who are addicted to drugs as being labeled as making a conscious and very amoral choice to engage in drug use. *Just Say No* eroded the complexities of addiction down to a singular choice of Yes or No and disregarded the context, situation, and biology of individuals living with addiction.

The large-scale U.S. anti-narcotics campaign led by organizations like ***Partnership for a Drug-Free America (PDFA)*** represented one of the few successful advertising organizations from the 1980s CE who are still in operation. Their mission was to provide drug prevention materials and substance abuse resources for parents, grandparents, kids, and teens. Their goals were to help kids and teens reject substance abuse and promote healthy behaviors. They used propaganda to influence attitudes and behaviors via persuasive and engineered information[41]. *This Is Your Brain* was launched in 1987 CE using three televised ***public service announcements (PSA)*** and a subsequent poster campaign. TV Guide has named the commercial one of the top one hundred television advertisements of all time[42]. The imagery of the commercial equated the human brain to an egg frying in a pan, which attempted to reduce drug use to harm based on the fact that drugs would fry your brain. It was a scare tactic, and again, did not include any of the nuances nor lived experiences of those with addiction. Perhaps, the slogan would have been more powerful if they had found a way to incorporate home fries and toast into their message. The slogan quickly attained pop culture status and became a parody. By the late 1980s CE into the 1990s CE, "this is your brain on [insert noun here]" became a comical catchphrase.

Figure 15.4   Just Say No Campaign Poster

In 2011 CE, as an alternative to the War on Drugs paradigm and in an effort to reduce racial disparities in law enforcement, a new national program was initiated, Law Enforcement Assisted Diversion (LEAD)[43]. LEAD is a new harm-reduction oriented process for handling low-level offenses like drug possession, sales, and prostitution and was developed and launched in Seattle, WA. LEAD represents the collaboration between police, prosecutors, civil rights advocates, public defenders, political leaders, mental health and drug treatment providers, housing providers and other service agencies, business organizations, and neighborhood leaders. Together these individuals have worked to find novel ways to handle the problem of individuals who cycle in and out of the criminal justice and mental health systems under the prior model of arrest, prosecution, and incarceration. In a LEAD program, law enforcement officers have the discretionary authority at the point of contact with an offender to divert these individuals into a community-based, harm-reduction intervention for law violations often driven by unmet behavioral and mental health needs. Instead of the traditional criminal justice system model of booking, detention, prosecution, conviction, and incarceration, individuals get referred to a trauma-informed intensive case-management program. These case-management programs provide a wide array of supportive care services, including transitional and permanent housing, drug treatment, employment training, and mental health care. LEAD holds the promise of being a new model of rehabilitation within law enforcement. In this new model, prosecutors help communities respond to public safety issues originating from unaddressed public health needs like addiction, undertreated mental illness, homelessness, and extreme poverty[44]. LEAD utilizes a public health framework to effect change. LEAD has been adopted by ~35 counties in 21 states with a substantial number of counties in the process of exploring or adopting a LEAD model.

15.4   Diagnosing Addiction

Our ability to adequately identify addiction as a disease has become refined over the past 70 years. With a diagnosis it becomes possible to set a treatment plan and identify one's prognosis. *Diagnosis* refers to the identification of a disease based on the signs and symptoms manifested by the disease.

As with mental health, addiction requires certain criteria to be present in order for a diagnosis. One of the main purposes of diagnosis is to guide treatment planning. A systematic catalog of diagnoses is highly useful as it helps health professionals (psychiatrists, psychologists, social workers, physicians, etc.) identify what has been shown to be effective treatment with a drug or specific therapy. A diagnosis aids in establishing a prognosis for the patient and allows for communication among different professionals involved in the patient's care. ***Prognosis*** is the prospect of recovery as anticipated from the usual course of a disease or specific variables within a case. In addiction treatment, the most effective strategy has been to follow an evidence-based approach. ***Evidence-based approach*** refers to a strategy that is derived from or informed by objective ***evidence*** like research and scientific studies as a ***base*** for determining the best approach or ***practice***. The United States did not have a good method for diagnosing addiction until 1952 CE with the publication of the *Diagnostic and Statistical Manual of Mental Disorders* (DSM-1). Since 1952 CE, there have been eight iterations, culminating in the most current version the DSM-5. The general changes to the DSM can be found in Table 15.3. Specific details related to the diagnosis of intoxication, addiction, and abuse are summarized in Table 15.4.

Table 15.3 DSM 1–5 General Details

Version	Year	Number of Pages	Number of Diagnoses	Details
DSM-I	1952	130	106	• Based largely on the mental disorders developed by the Department of Defense after WWII
DSM-I Special Supplement	1965	130	106	• Alignment with the International Classification of Diseases (ICD)
DSM-II	1968	134	182	• Incorporated principles of psychodynamic and psychoanalytical psychiatry
DSM-III	1980	494	265	• Introduction of multiaxial system for diagnosis • Psychoanalytic language replaced by "criteria sets" with reliably identified symptoms • Homosexuality narrowed to ego-dystonic homosexuality • This was the first time the DSM working group had representation from Women and People of Color
DSM-III-R	1987	567	292	• Ego-dystonic homosexuality removed

Version	Year	Number of Pages	Number of Diagnoses	Details
DSM-IV	1994	866	297	• Nearly half of all entries had the addition of "clinical significance" requirement
DSM-IV-TR	2000	943	297	• Text accompanying disorders was revised, but no significant changes to any diagnostic criteria • This was the first time the DSM working group had representation from patient advocates
DSM-V	2013	947	300	• Multiaxial model replaced by dimension component to diagnostic categories

Source: T.D. Church[45-52]

Table 15.4 DSM 1–5; Diagnosis of Intoxication, Addiction, and Abuse

Version	Criterion
DSM-I	• Acute and chronic alcohol and drug intoxication were labeled brain syndromes • Categorized as **Sociopathic Personality Disorder (SPD)**—which encompassed antisocial reaction, dissocial reaction, sexual deviation, and addiction
DSM-II	• New category *Personality Disorder and Certain Other Non-Psychotic Disorders* • Four subcategories: Personality Disorders, Sexual Deviations, Alcoholism, and Drug Dependence • **Drug Dependence**—diagnoses describe patients who are addicted to or dependent on drugs other than alcohol, tobacco, and ordinary caffeine-containing beverages; required evidence of habitual use or a clear sense of need for the drug
DSM-III	• **Substance Use Disorders**—including substance abuse and substance dependence are detailed in their own categories • **Substance Abuse**—defined by a pattern of pathological use, impairment in social or occupational functioning, and duration of use lasting for at least one month • **Substance Dependence**—considered to be a severe form of use; requires one or more signs of physiological dependence (tolerance or withdrawal)

Continued

Version	Criterion
DSM-III	• Alcoholism and drug addiction are grouped together with other stigmatizing behaviors (ergo: antisocial reactions, sexual deviations, personality disorders, sexual disorders) • *Substances* were defined as substances which generate behavioral changes; these substances with more or less regular use by patients have an effect on the central nervous system • Five classes of substances were identified as generating both abuse and dependence—alcohol, barbiturates, opioids, amphetamines, and cannabis • Diagnoses accompanying the substance use disorders rely on operational criteria; including age at onset, complications, predisposing factors, prevalence, sex ratio, differential diagnosis, and familial pattern
DSM-IV	• Substance Use Disorders replaced by Substance-Related Disorders to reflect a broader purview • This includes disorders related to the taking of a drug of abuse (including alcohol), to the side effects of a medication, and to toxin exposure • Eleven classes of substances were identified: alcohol, amphetamine, caffeine, cannabis, cocaine, hallucinogens, inhalants, phencyclidine, sedatives, hypnotics, and anxiolytics • Two distinct categories of disorders • *Substance use disorders*—included substance abuse and dependence • *Substance-induced disorders*—included substance intoxication, substance withdrawal, substance-induced delirium, substance-induced persisting dementia, substance-induced amnestic disorder, and substance-induced psychotic, mood, anxiety, sexual dysfunction, and sleep disorders • *Dependence*—on a substance is defined as a cluster of three or more symptoms occurring at any time in the same 12-month period • Dependence requires one of two specifiers: with physiological dependence or without physiological dependence, reflecting the presence or absence of tolerance or withdrawal
DSM-V	• Substance-Related and Addictive Disorders—renamed to include addictive disorders • Contains 10 categories of drugs and gambling disorders • Substance-Related and Addictive Disorders are defined broadly by the following criteria: • All drugs that are taken in excess have in common direct activation of the brain reward system, which is involved in the reinforcement of behaviors and the production of memories; • The pharmacological mechanisms by which each class of drugs produces reward are different, but the drugs typically activate the system and produce feelings of pleasure, often referred to as a "HIGH";

Version	Criterion
DSM-V	• Individuals with lower levels of self-control may reflect impairments of brain inhibitory mechanisms, may be particularly disposed to develop substance use disorders • ***Substance Use Disorder***—a cluster of cognitive, behavioral, and physiological symptoms indicating that the individual continues using substances despite significant substance-related problems • ***Substance-induced Disorder***—include substance intoxication, substance withdrawal, and other substance/medication-induced mental disorders; including psychotic disorders, bipolar and related disorders, depressive disorders, anxiety disorders, obsessive-compulsive and related disorders, sleep disorders, sexual dysfunctions, delirium, and neurocognitive disorders

Source: T.D. Church[45, 47, 48, 50-52]

The most recent version of the DSM-5 has made criteria available for substance-related addictive disorders and these criteria assists in the screening for substance and behavioral disorders. Table 15.5 contains the criteria for diagnosis. For each criterion asked of an individual, an affirmative score counts as one point. The points are then totaled, and this score provides the severity index, which has an associated degree related to the individual's substance use disorder. This diagnosis criterion is useful for diagnosing alcohol, caffeine, cannabis, hallucinogen, inhalant, opioid, sedative/hypnotic/anxiolytic, tobacco, and non-substance (gaming, food, sex, etc.)-related disorders quickly in an emergency room setting for example. Further evaluation is needed to assist in the individual's treatment, but the severity index proves useful as a quick and adequate diagnostic tool. It is interesting to note that in the DSM-5, the word "addiction" has been omitted from the official substance use disorder diagnostic terminology. This omission was purposeful as addiction is an uncertain definition and carries potentially negative connotations.

Table 15.5 Criteria for Substance-Related and Addictive Disorders

Criterion	Severity
Use in larger amounts for longer periods of time than intended	Severity is designated according to the number of symptoms endorsed:
Unsuccessful efforts to cut down or quit	0–1: No diagnosis
Excessive time spent using the substance	2–3: Mild Substance Use Disorder
Intense desire/urge for substance (craving)	4–5: Moderate Substance Use Disorder
Failure to fulfill major obligations	6+: Severe Substance Use Disorder
Continued use despite social/interpersonal problems	
Activities/hobbies reduced given use	

Continued

Criterion	Severity
Recurrent use in physically hazardous situations	
Recurrent use despite physical or psychological problem caused by or worsened by use	
Tolerance	
Withdrawal	

Source: DSM-V[52]

Addiction is influenced by many factors, including biologic functions, social factors, psychological issues, and environmental concerns. Biology is not destiny; many factors are incorporated into the drug use and addiction process, not just brain chemistry or social situations. Addiction is unique for each person it touches, but it manifests in predictable patterns. Addiction is a continuous and progressive set of events often working in concert to change behavior. Once established, addiction will dominate the life of the drug user and will push them into an endless cycle of drug seeking and drug consumption. There is hope, there are organizations and treatments that can help. However, recovery will not be successful if the addict does not want to quit.

15.5 Our Path Forward is Open Communication

The story of human addiction is far from over, there is much we do not know nor fully appreciate. We need more people involved in research from all fields of scientific inquiry and clinical care if we are to be equipped to deal with addictions in the future. We need to challenge our existing ideas of who addicts are and what it means to be addicted. Reducing the stigma, changing our views of the criminality of addiction, and expanding our compassion for those who are addicted are all things we need to do. We need to treat those with addiction in ways that are compassionate and maintain the addicted persons' dignity. The past seventy years have shown us that people with a modest amount of chemical knowledge can design ever increasingly addictive substances, often done in makeshift or clandestine labs. There is a growing concern over the influx of fentanyl, which is cheaper and more deadly as an additive found in street drugs in an alarmingly increased rate. A drug nearly as addictive as opioids and alcohol is sugar and because it is considered to be a food, we tend to ignore how devastating it is to health and how very pervasive it truly has become. Cartels have become better at getting drugs across borders and for every individual interdicted in a border check, at least two others have smuggled the product across the border and into circulation. Social media has provided new outlets for advertising of alcohol, tobacco, cannabis, and vaping as Tik Tok phenoms create trends and challenges for others to emulate and post a responding video. We have come to cheer for the main characters in media like Walter White in *Breaking Bad* or Teresa Mendoza in *La Reina del Sur* who are deeply involved in drug supply[53, 54]. In the United States, there are two diseases that every family will be affected by, with at least one close family member suffering through cancer and another struggling with addiction. We need more researchers, we need more supportive care, and we need better methods for managing and caring for those affected by addiction. The path forward seems daunting and difficult, but it is not unmanageable. Open and honest discussion about drugs is a step in the right direction. If we continue to keep drug use and addiction hidden and not discussed, it will only serve to perpetuate the problems we have seen throughout history.

REFERENCES

1. Pinel, P. (1809). *Traité médico-philosophique sur laliénation mentale* (2nd ed., p. 492). J. Ant. Brosson.

2. Pinel, P. (1806). *Un traité sur les aliénés.* Messers Cadell and Davies.

3. Rush, B. (1812). *Medical inquiries and observations, upon the diseases of the mind.* Kimber & Richardson.

4. Rush, B. (1823). *An inquiry into the effects of ardent spirits upon the human body and mind: With an account of the means of preventing, and of the remedies for curing them* (8th ed., p. 36). James Loring.

5. von Brühl-Cramer, C. (1819). *Ueber die trunksucht und eine rationelle heilmethode derselven: Geschrieben zur beherzigung für jedermann* (p. 94). In der Nicolaischen Buchhandlung.

6. Kraepelin, E. (1904). Lecture XI: Alcoholic mental disturbances. In E. Kraepelin (Ed.), *Lectures on clinical psychiatry* (pp. 97–107). William Wood & Co.

7. Kraepelin, E. (1900). Die Pflicht des Staates in der Pflege der Geisteskranken | The duty of the state in the care of the insane. *American Journal of Psychiatry, 57*(2), 235–280.

8. Bleuler, E. (1906). *Affektivität, suggestibilität, paranoia* (p. 144). Verlag nicht ermittelbar.

9. Kendler, K. S. (2020). Eugen Bleuler's views on the genetics of schizophrenia in 1917. *Schizophrenia Bulletin, 46*(4), 758–764.

10. Grover, S., & Ghosh, A. (2018). Delirium tremens: Assessment and management. *Journal of Clinical and Experimental Hepatology, 8*(4), 460–470.

11. Fusillo, T. F. (2022). Mental illness and addiction: Lessons from the county hospital inpatient psychiatric ward. *International Journal of Medical Students, 10*(2), 210–211.

12. Freud, S. (2013). 1. Listening or dispensing? Sigmund Freud on drugs. In J. Clemens (Ed.), *Psychoanalysis is an antiphilosophy* (pp. 17–43). Edinburgh University Press.

13. Jung, C. G. (1960). I. The autonomy of the unconscious mind. In C. G. Jung (Ed.), *Psychology and religion* (pp. 1–39). Yale University Press.

14. McCabe, I. (2018). *Carl Jung and alcoholics anonymous: The twelve steps as a spiritual journey of individuation* (p. 188). Routledge.

15. Jung, C. G. (1959). *Erforscht die Phänomenologie des Selbst* (p. 393). Bollingen Foundation Inc.

16. Crocq, M.-A. (2022). Historical and cultural aspects of man's relationship with addictive drugs. *Dialogues in Clinical Neuroscience, 9*(4), 355–361.

17. Aaron, P., & Musto, D. Temperance and prohibition in America: A historical overview. In M. H. Moore & D. R. Gerstein (Eds.), *Alcohol and public policy: Beyond the shadow of prohibition* (pp. 127–181). National Academy Press.

18. Worth, R. (2008). *Teetotalers and saloon smashers: The temperance movement and prohibition* (p. 128). Enslow Publishing, LLC.

19. Burns, E. (2004). *Spirits of America: A social history of alcohol* (p. 336). Temple University Press.

20. Finan, C. M. (2017). *Drunks: An American history* (p. 344). Beacon Press.

21. Litwin, L. B. (2016). *Susan B. Anthony: Social reformer and feminist* (p. 128). Enslow Publishing, LLC.

22. Stanton, E. C., et al. (1889). *History of woman suffrage*. Susan B. Anthony.

23. Anthony, S. B. (1873, Nov 5, 2022). On women's right to vote. *Lend Me Your Ears: Great Speeches in History* 2022, 694–695.

24. Willard, F. E. (1889). *Glimpses of fifty years: The autobiography of an American woman* (698). Woman's temperance publication Association.

25. Webb, H. (1999). Temperance movements and prohibition. *International Social Science Review, 74*(1/2), 61–69.

26. Willard, F. E. (1883). *Woman and temperance: Or the work and workers of the Woman's Christian Temperance Union* (p. 638). Park Publishing Co.

27. Furbay, H. G. (1903). The Anti-Saloon League. *The North American Review, 177*(562), 434–439.

28. Sismondo, C. (2011). *America walks into a bar: A spirited history of taverns and saloons, speakeasies and grog shops* (p. 336). Oxford University Press.

29. Duke, S. B. (1994). Drug prohibition: An unnatural disaster. *Connecticut Law Review, 27*, 571–612.

30. Blumenthal, K. (2011). *Bootleg: Murder, moonshine, and the lawless years of prohibition* (p. 160). Roaring Brook Press.

31. Beshears, L. (2010). Honorable style in dishonorable times: American gangsters of the 1920s and 1930s. *The Journal of American Culture, 33*(3), 197–206.

32. Lusted, M. A. (2014). *THE ROARING TWENTIES: Discover the Era of Prohibition, Flappers, and Jazz* (p. 128). Nomad Press.

33. Shildrick, T., & MacDonald, R. (2006). In defence of subculture: young people, leisure and social divisions. *Journal of Youth Studies, 9*(2), 125–140.

34. Jay, M. (2010). *High society: The central role of mind-altering drugs in history, science, and culture* (p. 192). Simon and Schuster.

35. Wilson, B. (1939). *Alcoholics anonymous: The big book* (p. 368). Ixia Press.

36. Fisher, C. (2009). *Wishful drinking* (p. 176). Simon and Schuster.

37. NA. (2008). *Narcotics Anonymous* (6th ed.). Narcotics Anonymous World Services.

38. White, W., et al. (2020). *"We Do Recover" Scientific Studies on Narcotics Anonymous*, in *Selected Papers of William L. White*. [Accessed Nov 6, 2022]: https://www.chestnut.org/resources/0ca3d4e1-cd32-4c53-96f1-a0db838d1419/2020-Review-of-Scientific-Studies-on-NA.pdf.

39. Gates, D. F. (1986). LAPD's Project DARE tells youths to resist drugs. *School Safety, 1986*(3), 26–27.

40. Lynam, D. R., et al. (1999). Project DARE (drug abuse resistance education) is not successful, and we need to ask why. *Journal of Consulting and Clinical Psychology, 67*(4), 590–593.

41. Elwood, W. N. (1994). *Rhetoric in the war on drugs: The triumphs and tragedies of public relations* (p. 182). Greenwood Publishing Group.

42. Buchanan, D. R., & Wallack, L. (1998). This is the partnership for a drug-free America: Any questions? *Journal of Drug Issues, 28*(2), 329–356.

43. Collins, S. E., Lonczak, H. S., & Clifasefi, S. L. (2019). Seattle's law enforcement assisted diversion (LEAD): program effects on criminal justice and legal system utilization and costs. *Journal of Experimental Criminology, 15*(2), 201–211.

44. Joudrey, P. J., et al. (2021). Law enforcement assisted diversion: Qualitative evaluation of barriers and facilitators of program implementation. *Journal of Substance Abuse Treatment, 129*, 1–7.
45. APA. (1952). *The diagnostic and statistical manual of mental disorders* (1st ed., p. 103). American Psychiatric Association.
46. APA. (1965). *The diagnostic and statistical manual of mental disorders* (Special Supplement ed., p. 103). American Psychiatric Association.
47. APA. (1968). *The diagnostic and statistical manual of mental disorders* (2nd ed., p. 134). American Psychiatric Association.
48. APA. (1980). *The diagnostic and statistical manual of mental disorders* (3rd ed., p. 494). American Psychiatric Association.
49. APA. (1987). *The diagnostic and statistical manual of mental disorders* (3-R ed., p. 567). American Psychiatric Association.
50. APA. (1994). *The diagnostic and statistical manual of mental disorders* (4th ed., p. 866). American Psychiatric Association.
51. APA. (2000). *The diagnostic and statistical manual of mental disorders* (4-TR ed., p. 943). American Psychiatric Association.
52. APA. (2013). *The diagnostic and statistical manual of mental disorders* (5th ed., p. 947). American Psychiatric Association.
53. Bernstein, M., et al. (2008). *Breaking Bad*. AMC.
54. Ossorio, Á. (2011) *La Reina del Sur*. M. Cruz, et al.